EXPLORING CHILD BEHAVIOR

THIRD EDITION

DONALD B. HELMS
JEFFREY S. TURNER

MITCHELL COLLEGE

BROOKS/COLE PUBLISHING COMPANY
MONTEREY, CALIFORNIA

564 02739

Brooks/Cole Publishing Company
A Division of Wadsworth, Inc.

Printed in the United States of America
10   9   8   7   6   5   4   3   2   1

Library of Congress Cataloging-in-Publication Data
    Helms, Donald B.
    Exploring child behavior.

    Bibliography: p.
    Includes index.
    1. Child psychology.   I. Turner, Jeffrey S.
II. Title.
BF721.H37   1986   155.4   85-22339
ISBN 0-534-05880-9

ISBN 0-534-05880-9

Sponsoring Editor: C. Deborah Laughton
Marketing Representative: Tom Braden
Editorial Assistant: Mary Tudor
Production: Stacey C. Sawyer, Montara, Calif.
Manuscript Editor: Loralee Windsor
Permissions Editor: Mary Kay Hancharick
Text and Cover Design: Nancy Benedict
Cover Illustration: Historical Museum of the City of Vienna
Text Illustration: Mary Burkhardt
Photo Researchers: Judy Mason/Bob Neisworth
Typesetting: Boyer & Brass, San Diego
Printing and Binding: R. R. Donnelly & Sons, Co.

Preface

Writing this revision of *Exploring Child Behavior* was a challenging task. Publication of a third edition usually means that the first and second editions have succeeded with the intended audience of instructors and students in doing what a textbook should do: transmit ideas and information and induce readers to think about what is being conveyed. The challenge was to make this new edition better than its predecessors. We are eager to share both the successful features of the first two editions and the additions and changes that we feel make this third edition superior.

As a scientific discipline, child development encompasses a vast array of figures, statistics, facts, and theories. Our major endeavor in the planning and writing of *Exploring Child Behavior* was to offer relevant child development data and at the same time provide practical applications of the data. This endeavor required an enormous amount of careful deliberation and decision making.

It was difficult to decide which topics to add, expand, condense, or omit. Since 1976, when *Exploring Child Behavior* was first released, a wealth of important new research findings has emerged. The relevance of this research for new students was our criterion for determining whether to include it in this edition.

We continue to offer students a broad, research-based survey of the individual's development from conception through adolescence. We treat the material both topically and chronologically: For each chronological stage, we cover physical and motor development; social and personality development; cognitive, perceptual, and language development; and development of imagination, creativity, and play activities. In this way we are able to offer the instructor both chronological and topical tables of contents.

For example, personality and social learning can be examined as a single topic, by studying Chapters 8, 11, 16, and 20 together, or the topic can be examined within the chronological framework of the text. The text continues to assist student comprehension by covering the material in many relatively short and therefore easily assimilated chapters.

We have tried to make our writing style clear and concise and our examples appropriate to the everyday world of children. For those who deal or will be dealing with youngsters—as parents, nurses, educators, or in some other capacity—we hope that the interpretations and applications given will provide a better overall understanding of the developing child. We offer separate chapters on children's imagination, creativity, and play, the expressive aspects of children's behavior that so many first edition users found useful. "Boxed" material is selectively used throughout the text to highlight applications and research studies. Chapter introductions and summaries help students manage and remember the text material, and annotated suggested reading lists give involved students some advice for further study on their own. And because visual material continues to gain in importance as a teaching tool, we have included a generous illustration program of photographs, tables, and figures.

The content has been updated throughout; however, we want to mention several changes in particular. The first section of the text contains a chapter on research issues and techniques followed by a chapter that offers a thorough overview of the theoretical underpinnings of child development including an overview of a wide range of critically important theories—those of Piaget, Freud, Erikson, Skinner, Bandura, Maslow, and Lorenz. This is followed by a chapter on the psychosocial history of child development, which we hope will give students a better understanding of theories and their practical extensions into various cultures.

In the beginning was the textbook. Today the text is only the start of a well-designed teaching and learning package. Because we were obviously the closest individuals to the text, we prepared the *Instructor's Manual*, The *Instructor's Test Item File*, and the *Student Workbook*.

The *Instructor's Manual* is designed to make teaching from *Exploring Child Behavior* more efficient. For each text chapter, we included in the *Instructor's Manual* a chapter outline, teaching objectives, suggestions for lecture topics, ideas for observation exercises and for classroom activities, discussion questions, and a film guide. The *Instructor's Test Item File* contains more than 1000 multiple-choice test questions to save the instructor time in test preparation.

The *Student Workbook* will help the student organize and remember the text material. For each *Student Workbook* chapter, we have written a chapter outline and synopsis, learning objectives (keyed to the teaching objectives of the *Instructor's Manual*), key concepts (with identification and definition questions), multiple-choice practice test items, true/false questions, short answer questions, and the answers to all questions.

We hope we have created a truly useful textbook package. We also hope that the student will find this third edition of *Exploring Child Behavior* informative, enjoyable, and enlightening and that the result will be greater appreciation and understanding of children's behavior.

Acknowledgments

The writing and preparation of a textbook requires the effort and support of many individuals. Our appreciation is extended to those developmentalists who reviewed the manuscript and contributed to its improvement, coherence, and overall refinement. They are: Ruth Ault, Davidson College; Charles Austad, Bemidji State University; Alice Blackmon, CSU/ Northridge; James Booth, Community College of Philadelphia; Gregory Brown, Central Missouri State University; Mary Anne Christenberry, Augusta College; Lawrence Clark, South East Missouri State University; Richard Fabes, Arizona State University; Nathan Fox, University of Maryland; Allen Gottfried, CSU-Fullerton; E. G. Haugh, St. Mary's College; Dennis Molfere, Southern Illinois University; Sue Schmitt, North Seattle Community College; Claire Smith, North Seattle Community College; Thomas Sommerkamp, Central Missouri State University; Catherine Sophian, Carnegie Mellon University.

We wish to thank all the fine people at Brooks-Cole who have given us such a warm welcome: first our appreciation to our editor, C. Deborah Laughton, for her invaluable assistance in the production of this edition. Our thanks go also to Mary Tudor (editorial assistant), who guided the text through its development, and to Janice Barber who typed so much of the manuscript. Our sincere appreciation is extended to Ms. Loralee Windsor, for her copyediting. Finally, we thank Ms. Stacey Sawyer, who as production manager oversaw the entire production of the book.

For the first edition of this text we extend our deepest gratitude to Baxter Venable, our editor, for his valuable advice, direction, and continuous encouragement in the original development of this project. We also extend special acknowledgment and thanks to Dr. Morton Bloomberg of Western Connecticut State College, whose detailed and insightful review of the entire project led to many valuable additions and modifications.

There are many teachers in the Southeastern Connecticut School Districts whose cooperation enabled us to explore and examine various facets of the school-age child's development. To our students we also owe special acknowledgment, because their interest, enthusiasm, and questioning spirit have stimulated our writing since the very beginning.

Finally, we want to thank our wives and families, whose patience, tolerance, love, and encouragement sustained us through the years that it took to complete this endeavor. Nancy Turner's medical knowledge and experience with children added depth and insight to several sections of the book. To Molly Helms, our amanuensis, we extend our deepest appreciation for the countless hours she devoted to typing, proofreading, and reviewing. Her dedication to the development of this project has been a source of continual inspiration.

April 1985

Donald B. Helms

Jeffrey S. Turner

Contents in Brief

Contents in Detail

Part One
Child Development: An Overview   1

Chapter One
Issues and Techniques   2

Chapter Two
Theories of Child Development   25

Chapter Three
Childhood through the Ages: A Psychosocial History   59

Part Two
Infancy and Toddlerhood 79

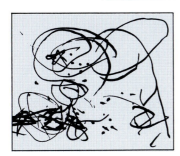

Chapter Six
Physical Growth and Development   138

Chapter Seven
Cognition, Perception, and Psycholinguistics   154

**Chapter Eight
Personality and Social Learning**   **186**

**Chapter Fifteen
Cognition, Perception, and Psycholinguistics   343**

**Part Five
Adolescence**   **433**

Chapter Twenty
Personality and Social Learning

463

Chapter Twenty-One
Problems of Adolescence

495

Part One
Child Development:
An Overview

Chapter One

Issues and Techniques

**It takes a lot of knowledge
to know how little we know.**

Dagobert D. Runes

Introduction

A child is born, and day by day, month by month, from childhood to adolescence to adulthood, the human organism develops in a variety of ways. Both physical and behavioral developments are clear to laypeople, as well as to psychologists. Rapid physical growth—as evidenced by the expression "My, how you've grown!"—and the transformation of the pesky kid next door into a mature young adult are examples of such developments.

The life cycle is full of these developments, and most of us react to them with a mixture of emotions. We look on in delight as our baby takes a first step or speaks a first word and eagerly record both milestones in the "baby book." We marvel at our child's developing abilities to think and socialize with others at an early age. We watch with mixed emotions as our little child climbs into a school bus on the first day of school, and later in life we fight back a tear as we attend our grown child's wedding. Studying developmental psychology will not shield us from these emotions, of course, but it may help us avoid confusion about at least some aspects of human development.

What Is Developmental Psychology?

Developmental psychology is the study of the behavioral changes that occur during the entire life span, from birth to death. Childhood (ages

0–12), adolescence (the teenage years), and adulthood (ages 20 and upward) are the three major subdivisions of developmental psychology. In this text we will concern ourselves with child and adolescent development.

Developmental psychologists investigate such areas as **cognition** (thinking), **psycholinguistics** (development of language), **physiology** (growth), and **socialization.** Specialists in each of these subfields attempt to describe, understand, and explain the changes that occur in children, especially those that are universal. For example, developmental psychologists have determined that most children speak their first word when they are about a year old and begin to walk within a month or two thereafter, regardless of race, ethnicity, or culture. These psychologists also observe and measure behavioral alterations. While some changes are slow and others rapid, most behaviors seem to develop in orderly, predictable ways. Infants creep before they walk, coo before they babble, and think in simple terms before they use advanced logic and reason. Each of these changes usually results in more refined and adaptive behavior that should make the child more competent, efficient, and adaptable to life's many challenges and demands.

Developmental psychology is a rapidly growing field of study that produces immense quantities of research findings every year. In this text, we will examine relevant research, as well as specify and explain the behavioral changes of childhood and adolescence.

Numerous other disciplines are child oriented and also attempt to explore behavioral development. Parents, cultural anthropologists, educators, nurses, pediatricians, and social workers all seek to understand children's behavior. These groups contribute to the vast and growing amount of research in the field of developmental psychology. Despite all this research, developmental psychology is a field abounding with unanswered questions. As research continues, however, we gain more accurate insights into child and adolescent behavior and are able to define developmental psychology's increasing subdivisions and categorize life's major stages in smaller developmental units (see Table 1.1).

Developmental Psychology: Issues and Concerns

Child developmentalists must first act the role of philosopher, asking such questions as: What is the nature of children? Are we born with "bad" or "evil" tendencies (original sin) as some religions teach, or are we born in the image of God (good and godlike) as other theologies state? (We hasten to note that behavior is not intrinsically good or bad, but each culture often determines and interprets behavior along these lines.) If we are not born with good or bad tendencies, is our behavior learned, and if so, how? Do we develop desirable or undesired behavior only after a series of interactions with our environment? Can we change these behaviors? Are we governed by our emotions, our intellect, or a combination of the two?

These questions and countless others have been the concern of philosophers and educators for centuries. Furthermore, as we shall soon see, many of these underlying issues have also produced great controversy within the field of child development.

Heredity and Environment: The Nature–Nurture Controversy

A major question in psychology is the relative importance to human development of genetic and environmental factors. This is known among philosophers as the nature-nurture controversy.

The controversy centers around the question whether one's biological forces (genetic and physiological makeup, including the brain) contribute more to one's development than environmental factors (one's surroundings and experience). This question has plagued scientists for years, with many camps developing in the process. Currently,

Table 1.1 Human Development: A Chronological Approach

Life Stage	Approximate Time Period
Prenatal period	Conception to birth
Infancy	Generally 0–2 years
Toddlerhood	2–3 years of age
Early childhood	Generally 3 or 4 to about age 5
Middle childhood	Either 6–9 or 6–12, depending on the use of the terms *late childhood* or *preadolescence*
Adolescence	Generally the teenage years (13–19) or commencing with the onset of puberty to emancipation from parents or to commitment to work or to the formation of identity (a developmental rather than a chronological phenomenon)*
Young adulthood	20–30 or 20–40
Middle adulthood	30–64 or 40–64 or 65
Later adulthood	62, 65 (the retirement years)

*As the individual matures, chronological age becomes a progressively poorer criterion.

hereditarian psychologists believe that most behavior depends on genetic endowment. The opposite group, the environmentalists, assert
that environment is the major contributor to an individual's behavior.
Others seem to be uncertain on the issue, and still others question the
significance of the entire argument. Since there are few definitive
answers, the argument seems futile. The critical issue is how heredity
and environment interact to affect development.

Most development depends on both biological and environmental
factors. Some research indicates that genetic factors are more important
to physical development, while environment and experience play a
greater role in shaping behavior. Other research, however, leaves the
nature-nurture issue unresolved. For example, considerable research
has focused on whether intellectual potential is inherited and fixed or
whether IQ can be raised or lowered by one's surrounding environment
or culture. So far there is no clear answer to this question.

Hereditarians espouse what is referred to as the epigenetic principle, that is, the belief that everything develops because of genetic programming. Thus, all human development is controlled by a set of
genetic blueprints or directions. This view is closely related to the discontinuous, or age-stage, theory, which we shall discuss later.

**Developmental psychologists observe and measure behavioral changes in
children—including those related to different types of preschool
education.**

Growth, Maturation, and Learning

Another important issue for child psychologists is the difference between growth, maturation, and learning. **Growth** is a biological increase in size, such as the enlargement of the body or any of its component parts, by an increase in the number of cells. An infant who is 20 inches long when born and later is 30 inches long is said to have grown 10 inches. Increases in head and heart size, arm and leg length and weight, and so on are generally referred to as results of the growth process.

Maturation is the development of cells until they can be fully and totally used by the organism. Maturation has many practical implications for those attempting to understand human behavior. For example, a 5-month-old infant cannot walk because the maturation of the necessary muscle and nerve cells has not yet taken place, even though the organs have been *growing.* The point at which an organism becomes mature enough to start conquering new developmental tasks is often referred to as the state of **readiness.**

Learning is a relatively permanent change in behavior resulting from experience. It does not include behavioral changes from injury, drugs, fatigue, or maturation. Learning depends on maturation because it cannot take place until appropriate maturation has occurred. For example, the ability to learn abstract concepts depends on both the growth and maturation of the cortical (brain) cells used for abstract thinking.

Concepts of Continuity and Discontinuity

Developmentalists must also determine whether behavior evolves in gradual and continuous or sudden and discontinuous ways. Continuous processes of change seem more evident in such phases of development as socialization and emotion, since evidence indicates they are gradually learned through interaction with the environment. On the other hand, discontinuous developments are based on internal biological states, which allow for distinct, age-related spurts in growth and development.

The continuous viewpoint stresses a slow methodical change or gradation occurring over time with less relationship to the individual's age. The concept is of a subtle flow of maturation. Some psychological theories, such as stimulus-response or conditioning models, are based on the continuous viewpoint in which organisms develop (for example, through reinforcement). This is a one-stage model of growth.

Discontinuous development theory emphasizes stages of development. The assumption is that before one stage or step can occur, the child must have emerged from a previous stage. Just as a house starts with the foundation and is built upward, so humans sit up before they creep, creep before they walk, and walk before they run. Stages of development are relatively sequential, with a definite order (no stage can be skipped), and are directly related to ages. The term *stages* refers to periods of characteristically distinct psychological functioning. Examples of discontinuous, age-stage theories are the psychoanalytic (Freudian) and cognitive-developmental (Piagetian) theories, which assume progression through successive stages, each of which represents a transformation of the previous stage and prepares the way for the next one. See Figure 1.1 for a diagrammatic comparison of continuous and discontinuous theories.

What Are Critical Periods?

One of the more intriguing areas of child psychology is the concept of the **critical** or **sensitive period.** There is increasing evidence that organisms are especially sensitive to certain external stimuli, but there is also evidence that some minimal sensory stimulation is needed during a specific time period if the organism is to develop normally. A critical period is a specific time when an environmental event will have its greatest impact on the developing organism. We will later see that those infants who for one reason or another are not left long in the care

Figure 1.1 Graph (a) illustrates the continuous theory of development. Here, we see a gradual increase in maturity during childhood and adolescence (learning theory view). Graph (b) represents the discontinuous developmental theories as proposed in the cognitive developmental theory of Jean Piaget and the psychosexual development theory of Sigmund Freud. Here we can see how "stages" of maturation exist at certain age levels.

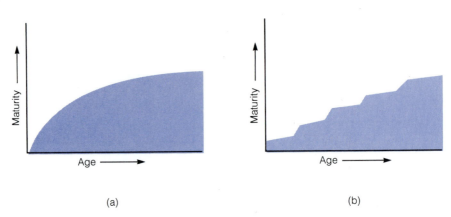

(a)   (b)

of one person may have difficulty experiencing and expressing warm human relations and feelings. In humans there seems to be a sensitive period between 6 and 16 months, when the infant "attaches" itself to the mother or caregiver. Before this period, babies can be handled by

Beware the Nonexistent Average

Periodically throughout this book, we refer to an *average* or *mean*, such as the average age for crawling, the average age for walking, or the average age for certain forms of language development or thought processes to occur. Unfortunately, the term *average* is frequently misinterpreted. Ask people to define it and they will probably tell you to add your figures and divide the sum by the number of scores involved. For example, when 100 test scores are added and the sum is 2,700, the average score is 27. *But what does 27 mean? What is the total range (highest and lowest) of scores? What is the highest score attainable? How did most people score?* Unless the average is placed in some meaningful context, it may lose some of its relevancy or even become meaningless. For example, if American families have an average of 2.7 children per family unit, does any family exactly fit this average? In this example, the average is a statistic about family size in general, and not a description of any single family.

Let's develop another hypothetical example to illustrate our point. If the average age for walking is 14 months, what does this actually mean? Suppose that 100 infants are observed daily until walking commences, with the results shown in Table 1.2.

While these hypothetical figures graphically illustrate the mean or average age (as well as the median or midpoint) for infants to take their first steps, there is no "average child."

Table 1.2

	Age in Months	Number of Infants Starting to Walk
	10	2
	11	8
	12	15
mean age for walking	13	20
	14	0
	15	20
	16	15
	17	8
	18	2

Although results other than the average have not been taken into consideration, it is possible that the parents may not realize this. Thus, 50% of the parents may become anxious, firmly believing that their children are below average because they were not walking by what the parents suppose is the prescribed time. In actuality, all of the children were walking within the normal **range** for this motor activity. This example should illustrate that averages and other variations of statistics exist as mathematical computations and are used to represent a group of children (or scores), not an individual child. ■

anybody, but during this period they become attached to one caregiver and dislike being handled by anyone else.

Active or Passive Behavior?

Another question about human development is whether people are either active or passive in relation to their environment. In other words, are children molded by environmental forces (for example, what happens *to* them as they develop), or do they seek experiences that they desire (for example, what do they *act on* as they develop)? This very important issue has generated much controversy and sparked numerous debates over the years.

Many environmentalists believe that environmental forces shape human behavior, much as rocks, sand, water, wind, and waves shape a piece of driftwood. One such passive school of thought is behaviorism, which emphasizes the importance of the environment and considers the surroundings to be crucial in the overall development of the individual. Theorists like B. F. Skinner maintain that behavior is passively learned from others. Rewards and punishments administered by others mold the child's responses.

Activist theories, on the other hand, suggest that individuals are not passive beings but are capable of governing and regulating their own development. Rather than picturing a piece of driftwood afloat, visualize it with a motor and rudder. Under these conditions, the organism can determine its own path in a self-directed way. Thus, activist theories stress our mental ability to seek from the environment the experiences and things that arouse our interest and meet our rational needs. This active role in exploring the environment is the foundation of Jean Piaget's theory of cognitive development.

Ethical Considerations: Protecting the Child's Well-being

Numerous difficulties confront researchers experimenting with humans, for they must not harm their subjects in any way. Some types of research may endanger a person physically or emotionally or even interfere with normal processes of development. When we experiment with people, ethical standards (the term *ethics* refers to a system of moral principles) must be foremost in our minds.

In the late 1960s, the American Psychological Association (APA) developed a code of ethical practices for research on humans. These guidelines have been studied, altered, and amended several times. The Society for Research in Child Development (SRCD) and the Division of Developmental Psychology of the APA have also devised ethical guidelines for research on children. Because of these guidelines, many research-oriented colleges and universities have an ethics committee that reviews and passes judgment on proposed experiments. Meanwhile, it has been recognized that children may pose greater problems to researchers than do adults.

Suppose that we want to observe and record the effects of punishment on learning certain tasks. Is it ethical to punish children under learning conditions for such a research project? If we wish to determine the effects of frustration on young children, is it ethical to subject them to tasks at which they are bound to fail? The obvious answer to some of these questions is "no," but not all questions can be so easily answered.

Extreme care must be taken when planning a child-oriented study or experiment. In support of this, the Division of Developmental Psychology of the APA has issued the following ethical standards:*

1. No matter how young the child, he has rights that supersede the rights of the investigator.

2. The investigator uses no research operations that may harm the child either physically or psychologically. Psychological harm, to be sure, is difficult to define; nevertheless, its definition remains a responsibility of the investigator.

3. The informed consent of parents or of those legally designated to act *in loco parentis* is obtained, preferably in writing. Informed consent requires that the parent be given accurate information . . . on the purpose and operations of the research, albeit in layman's terms. The consent of parents is not solicited by any claims of benefit to the child. Not only is the right of parents to refuse consent respected, but parents must be given the opportunity to refuse.

4. The investigator does not coerce a child into participating in a study. The child has the right to refuse and . . . should be given the opportunity to refuse.

5. When the investigator is in doubt about possible harmful effects of his efforts or when he decides that the nature of his research requires deception, he submits his plan to an *ad hoc* group of his colleagues for review. It is the group's responsibility to suggest other feasible means of obtaining the information. Every psychologist has a responsibility to maintain not only his own ethical standards but also those of his colleagues.

6. The child's identity [must be] concealed in written and verbal reports of the results, as well as in informal discussions with students and colleagues.

---

*From *Newsletter*, 1968, pp. 1–3. Copyright 1968 by the American Psychological Association, and reproduced by permission of the Division on Developmental Psychology.

7. The investigator does not assume the role of diagnostician or counselor in reporting his observations to parents or those *in loco parentis.* He does not report tests scores or information given by a child in confidence, although he recognizes a duty to report general findings to parents and others.

8. The same ethical standards apply to children who are control subjects, and to their parents, as to those who are experimental subjects. When the experimental treatment is believed to benefit the child, the investigator considers an alternative treatment for the control group instead of no treatment.

9. Payment in money, gifts, or services for the child's participation does not annul any of the above principles.

10. Teachers of courses related to children should present the ethical standards of conducting research on human beings to their students.

Thus, children as research subjects present the investigator with different problems from those presented by adult subjects. Our culture views children as more vulnerable to distress (although some evidence suggests that they are actually more resilient in recovery from stress). Because the young have less knowledge and experience, they may also be less able to understand what participation in research means. And the parent's consent to study the child is prerequisite to obtaining the child's consent. These are some of the major differences between research with children and research with adults (Irwin and Bushnell, 1980; Richarz, 1980).

The Science of Developmental Psychology

The term *psychology* is generally defined as the science of human and animal behavior. This broad definition encompasses every subfield of psychology. However, a few psychologists and many laypeople (including students) sometimes disagree with the use of the term *science*, stating that psychologists cannot predict the behavior of a person, at least not to the extent that a chemist or a physicist can predict how much a certain gas will expand at a given temperature or how fast an object will fall. But *science* has many definitions. It refers both to the techniques and methods (**scientific method**) used in experiments and to an organized and systematic body of knowledge. Developmental psychology qualifies as a science on both counts.

General Methodology: How Do You Study a Child?

Observation—The Key to Knowledge   The collection of data begins
when an observation is made, whether by unsophisticated means, such
as watching children at play, or by more technical processes, such as
recording brain waves on an electroencephalograph. Regardless of the
techniques employed, these methods fall under the general classification of observation. Theories, or even laws, can be formulated from
observations, provided, of course, that the data are supportive (Irwin
and Bushnell, 1980).

Although ideas may emerge following the observation of a solitary
incident, one must recognize the danger of generalizing from a limited
number of situations. A study of a single person assists us to understand only that person; it does not mean that other subjects will exhibit
identical behavior, or, if they do, that it will be for the same reason
(Matlin, 1980).

Simple observation of children at play can supply data for study.

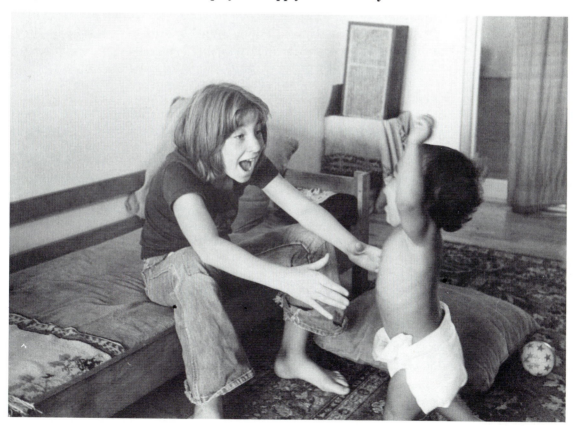

Even more hazardous than generalizing results from observation of a single subject is developing a theory without making any observations at all—what Sir Francis Bacon (1561–1626) disparagingly called philosophical presupposition. In *Novum Organum* (1620), Bacon stated that knowledge cannot be developed in the mind without some direct examination of the phenomena involved. He accused numerous thinker-philosophers of philosophical presupposition. In fact, he believed that most people's minds were filled with inaccurate generalizations that interfered with the attainment of knowledge.

In speaking on the dangers inherent in preconceptions or presuppositions, James Deese (1972, pp. 84–85) warns:

> The trouble with theoretical preconceptions in developmental studies is the assumption that a point of view is correct simply because it makes a sensible story. This is the problem of myth versus science. Even some highly developed and rigorous theories of developmental psychology require more data than they explain. A given theory may make a good story about how things got to be the way they are, but if it has little empirical content, it does not provide a plausible basis for action.

Although few of us would think of devising an unsupported theory in the area of physics or chemistry, people frequently make unfounded generalizations in the realm of human behavior. Although laypeople often cling to unfounded notions, professional psychologists must either avoid presuppositions or seek their validation.

Seeing the dangers in single-subject research methods (while acknowledging their significant role in psychology), researchers strive to test their suppositions on larger segments of the population and constantly seek new fields of information. Many graduate schools, for example, now have working agreements with nearby hospitals that enable researchers to study newborns within hours after birth. New techniques of study and evaluation, especially in such areas as electroencephalography (study of brain waves) and visual abilities (seeing objects, tracking moving objects, visual preferences, and so on), have been discovered and put to use.

Naturalistic Observation   Naturalistic observation is the examination of behavior under *normal* or *unstructured* (natural) conditions. Structured observation is an extension of naturalistic observation in which the researcher can administer simple tests. One-way windows enable a researcher to view children in natural settings without inhibiting their behavior. Both forms of observation differ markedly from **controlled experiments,** which require subjects to be placed in contrived and perhaps unnatural environments.

Some psychologists (Carlson, 1971) feel that results obtained from certain controlled experiments are of little value because the experiment itself may create unnatural behavior. Nevertheless, controlled experiments can be extremely valuable in gathering significant information. The fact remains, however, that the naturalistic method at least partially reduces the child's awareness of being observed, which should promote more natural behavior.

Baby Biographies   Historically, the earliest form of human observation was a **baby biography,** a day-by-day account of the development of an infant or young child. One of the earliest baby biographers, Johann Pestalozzi (1740–1827), a leading educator of his day, recorded three weeks of his 2½-year-old son's activities and later published the account. Included in the observations were comments on the role of the mother, whom Pestalozzi believed to be the most important educator in the child's life. He stated that behavioral patterns are first learned through the child's observation and imitation of the mother's actions. Today, many psychologists record children's behavior under varying circumstances and theorize on the important role of observational learning.

Figure 1.2 One-way windows afford observers opportunities to view children in a more natural setting.

Wilhelm T. Preyer (1841–1897), a physiologist, was interested in overall mental development. This interest was manifested in an account (later published as three separate books) of his son's development during the first four years of life, a baby biography that many psychologists consider a classic. Preyer, like Pestalozzi, observed behavioral patterns, socialization processes, and the child's tendency to imitate.

Charles Darwin (1809–1882) impressed many people with his interest in children, particularly in 1877, when he published a baby biography on the development of his first son. Darwin's special interests, however, interfered with his objectivity. In particular, most of his charts concentrate on what can be learned about the descent of human beings (and their emotions) by observing the infant develop into a child.

The following quotation shows the observational abilities of Darwin (Kessen, 1965, pp. 118–119):

During the first seven days various reflex actions, namely sneezing, hiccuping, yawning, stretching, and of course sucking and

Techniques of Naturalistic Observation

Frequently, students of child psychology are required to observe children's behavior in a number of different situations, such as in school, at play, or even in a grocery or department store. Whether observers are stationed behind one-way windows or simply attempt to keep out of sight, certain points should be kept in mind. Items to look for when observing individual children include physical appearance (body movements, facial expressions), speech, emotional reactions, and relationships with other children and adults. The following are general guidelines for observation:

1. Remain out of the way as much as the setting allows. When children know that they are being watched, they sometimes change their natural behavior, either shying away from strangers or suddenly showing off.

2. Use paper and pencil, tape recorder, or camera to record such factors as the physical setting and general activity of the child or children (lunch period, rest period, etc.).

3. After quickly scanning the scene and taking appropriate notes, focus on the activity of *one* child for at least 10 to 15 minutes. Observe play behavior, awareness of others, aggressiveness, passivity, and so on.

4. Refocus on the group at large, noticing other interactions, including any adult's behavior toward various children, to see if all children are treated identically.

5. Write your report immediately after finishing the observation, while the various scenes are still fresh in your mind (Carbonara, 1961). ■

G. Stanley Hall

screaming, were well performed by my infant. On the seventh day I touched the naked sole of his foot with a bit of paper, and he jerked it away, curling at the same time his toes, like a much older child when tickled. The perfection of these reflex movements shows that the extreme imperfection of the voluntary ones is not due to the state of the muscles or of the coordinating centres, but to that of the seat of the will. At this time, though so early, it seemed clearer to me that a warm soft hand applied to his face excited a wish to suck. This must be considered as a reflex or an instinctive action, for it is impossible to believe that experience and association with the touch of his mother's breast could so soon have come into play. During the first fortnight he often started on hearing any sudden sound, and blinked his eyes. The same fact was observed with some of my other infants within the first fortnight. Once, when he was 66 days old, I happened to sneeze, and he started violently, frowned, looked frightened, and cried rather badly: for an hour afterwards he was in a state which would be called nervous in an older person, for every slight noise made him start . . .

With respect to vision, his eyes were fixed on a candle as early as the 9th day, and up to the 45th day nothing else seemed thus to fix them; but on the 49th day his attention was attracted by a bright-coloured tassel, as was shown by his eyes becoming fixed and the movements of his arms ceasing. It was surprising how slowly he acquired the power of following with his eyes an object if swinging at all rapidly; for he could not do this well when seven and a half months old.

Most baby biographies were a step forward from the "armchair" philosophies and philosophical presuppositions that had dominated the past. The resulting interest in these accounts during the eighteenth and nineteenth centuries in turn helped give impetus to all subfields of developmental psychology, not just to the study of the early years of life. As more and more observations were made, simple techniques and testing devices were initiated, giving rise to a number of highly sophisticated observation and measuring techniques.

The Questionnaire as an Investigative Technique   Following the baby biography studies came the development of the questionnaire by G. Stanley Hall (1846–1924). Hall recognized the need for a more systematic study of children and for larger study samples. He felt a **questionnaire** could be used to discover the contents of children's minds. He became interested in children's thinking and developed a questionnaire designed to elicit pieces of knowledge from them. While it lacked the sophistication of modern questionnaires, it served its purpose well.

Hall's recognition as the father of child psychology is based not only on his questionnaire but also on numerous other contributions. He received the first American doctorate at Harvard and is generally credited with establishing the first psychological laboratory in the United States (1883) at Johns Hopkins University. He was the first American student in the first psychological laboratory (in its first year), founded in Leipzig by Wilhelm Wundt, the father of psychology. Hall was also the first president and the first professor of psychology at Clark University, an institution that would become famous for producing great psychologists. During his career, Hall was influential in shaping the careers of such notable psychologists as Lewis Terman, Arnold Gesell, and John Dewey.

Hall founded and initially financed the journal *Pedagogical Seminary* (since renamed the *Journal of Genetic Psychology*) in 1891. This periodical focused on the research being conducted with children. Hall's interest in genetics and evolutionary theory led him to study not only childhood but also adolescence. Possibly his most influential work is the two-volume *Adolescence: Its Psychology and Its Relation to Physiology, Anthropology, Sociology, Sex, Crime, Religion and Education* (1905, reprinted 1970).

Cross-sectional and Longitudinal Methods   The two basic approaches to studying developmental psychology are the cross-sectional method and the longitudinal method. The **cross-sectional study** obtains data

Establishing Rapport with Children

Whether subjected to simple or complex methods of observation, children must feel at ease in order to be unaffected by the observation and continue to act naturally, both in actions and words. Thus, if testing children is to be effective, it must take place in a friendly, nonthreatening atmosphere. If feasible, spend several sessions with a child to avoid unnecessary apprehensions or other behavior that might interfere with the results of the study.

Rapport with children is especially important if accurate responses are to be elicited. If a boy who fears failure is told that he is going to be tested to see how well he compares with classmates, he may fail miserably, not because of limited capabilities but because his anxiety has risen to a point that interferes with a normal or natural response. To avoid such failure, take the time to establish effective rapport and understanding.

In other situations and with different individuals, minimal anxiety can produce a higher degree of motivation and a higher test result. Part of the scientific method is knowledge of individual differences. ∎

from different groups of subjects (or even from a single subject) and compares it to identical studies performed on groups of subjects of a different age. A **longitudinal study** collects data on the same group of individuals over a long period of time (years and sometimes decades). Each technique has its advantages and disadvantages (Coladarci and Coladarci, 1980).

Let's examine these two research techniques by using an example to illustrate their application. Suppose that we want to obtain the average height of males and females for the first 25 years of life. It would be much quicker to use the cross-sectional method and measure the heights and weights of 1,000 newborn children, then collect appropriate data from 1,000 1-year-olds, from 1,000 2-year-olds, and so on. If we had enough assistants on our research team and lived in an area with sufficient population to supply us with 1,000 children having birthdays on any given day in each of 26 consecutive years, we might be able to measure a different age level each week. Our total time spent for collecting data would be 26 weeks, and we would have data from 26,000 different individuals.

If we used the longitudinal method, it would take us 25 years to obtain the equivalent set of data, and we might lose subjects through death, families moving, later refusal of subjects to continue participation, and so on. The significant advantage of the longitudinal technique, however, is that it allows us to follow such characteristics as intelligence, behavior problems, height, and weight over relatively long periods of time and enables us to ascertain developmental patterns.

An actual example of a longitudinal study may help clarify this method. The Fels longitudinal study undertaken in 1929 at the Fels Research Institute in Yellow Springs, Ohio, enrolled 89 subjects (45 females, 44 males) for participation in an 18-year study. Most of the subjects were enrolled in the program before birth. In this exhaustive study, children were repeatedly weighed, measured, and tested in an attempt to identify and assess developmental trends. At least twice a year, from birth to age 6, there were half-day visits by a professional interviewer to the home of mother and child. For the next six years, visits were on an annual basis. Mothers were interviewed annually to ascertain their attitudes toward their children. Each year, nearly all children between the ages of 2½ and 5 attended the institute's nursery for two three-week sessions. From ages 6 to 10, peer interaction was observed at the Fels Day Camp. Children were constantly rated on such traits as aggression, achievement, conformity, sociability, dependence, imitation, sex-role play, and language. A longitudinal study like this reveals how early traits and characteristics change or stabilize over time and how environmental influences affect these traits.

Table 1.3 summarizes the differences between the longitudinal and the cross-sectional methods. Whichever methodological approach is used, the data will only be as good as the measurement techniques used to obtain them and the conception behind their collection. These factors operate in any methodological design.

A more recent addition to the methodologies is the *short-term longitudinal method.* Using this less complicated method, a longitudinal study would last a maximum of five years and include investigations into fewer behavioral phenomena. This type of method takes less time, and there is less attrition of subjects and a greater likelihood that the original staff of investigators will carry out the entire project. An extension of this method is the *cross-sectional short-term longitudinal method,* a combination of the above methods. If one wishes to study certain personality traits developmentally—say, from ages 6 to 15—a ten-year longitudinal study would be in order. However, by doing simultaneous cross-sectional studies of two groups, one for ages 6 to 10 and

Table 1.3 Comparison between Longitudinal and Cross-Sectional Methods of Study

Factor	Longitudinal	Cross-Sectional
Method of procedure	Examines and reexamines same group repeatedly over the years.	Examines several groups (from different levels of development) simultaneously over a short time period.
Cost	Research is generally expensive.	Research is relatively inexpensive.
Time involved	Several years to several decades; frequent loss of contact with subjects.	Relatively little time—months, weeks, or even days.
Collection and use of data	Collection of data is as long as the experiment. Because much data are collected, much time is needed for interpretation.	Quick collection with rapid interpretation of results.
Personnel needed	Many people under capable researcher.	Relatively few (may need only one researcher).
Major advantage	Allows much data showing individual growth and developmental changes.	Large amounts of data can be gathered within a short period of time.
Major disadvantages	Requires much time and finance; loss of subjects by moving, death, etc.	Loses sight of individual changes; provides only a representative group of various ages, controls, etc.

the other for ages 11 to 15, the total study can be completed in five years. Hence the term *cross-sectional short-term longitudinal study.*

The Experimental Method: The Scientific Search for Facts

The **experimental method** in psychology is a series of steps by which the researcher tries to determine relationships between differing phenomena, either to discover principles underlying behavior or to find cause-effect relationships.

Each experimental investigation must follow a procedure that is relevant to the phenomenon being investigated. For example, studying schoolchildren and how they relate to authoritarian teachers would involve methods totally different from those employed to investigate the electrical activity of the brain after tranquilizers have been administered to a hyperactive child. However, the basic principles of experimental design remain the same. Regardless of specific experimental differences, certain common terms, definitions, and formats are universal to those using the experimental method.

Let's look at some of the universal parts of this design. The experimental method typically begins with a **hypothesis,** an educated guess made by the researcher. Suppose our hypothesis is that students will know more about the discipline of child psychology after a semester of study than they did before they enrolled. Before this hypothesis is tested on a large group of people—say, 1,000 undergraduate students— psychologists often employ a **pilot study.** A pilot study is a small-scale research investigation designed to discover problems, errors, or other obstacles that might develop when the large-scale study is undertaken. Discovering procedural problems while testing 10 or 20 subjects will save time, effort, and headaches when we start testing 1,000 subjects.

When psychologists are ready to begin their research, they choose two groups of subjects to prove or disprove the hypothesis. One group, called the **experimental group,** is subjected to special treatment and is carefully observed by the experimenter. The special treatment given to the experimental group is called the **independent variable.** In regard to our hypothesis, the experimental group is the group of students enrolled in child psychology classes, and the independent variable is the formal instruction in the discipline. The behavior affected by the independent variable (degree of knowledge acquired in class from the professor) is called the **dependent variable.**

Our other group of subjects, called the **control group,** is used primarily for comparison purposes. The control group does not receive the independent variable. In our example the control group of students will not get the formal instruction in child psychology that the experimental group receives.

To determine whether a hypothesis is correct, usually a pre-test and a post-test are administered to both the experimental and control groups. The pre- and post-tests in our study would seek to measure the students' knowledge of child psychology. Any changes would appear in the experimental group, especially when contrasted with the control group.

In the final phase of the experimental method, psychologists seek to draw **conclusions** and interpretations. They may use **correlational methods,** such as the analysis of the experimental events and the comparison of any relationships that might exist. A well-executed experiment should provide insight into a hypothesis, but the results may also raise many new questions and lead the researcher into other avenues of experimentation. Figure 1.3 is a diagram of the elements and steps in the experimental method.

Figure 1.3

THE EXPERIMENTAL METHOD

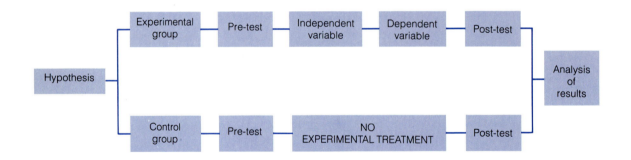

Summary

The field of developmental psychology studies the growth, maturation, and learning of an organism from conception to death. The three major divisions of the life span are childhood (0–12), adolescence (the teenage years), and adulthood (20 and up). The major areas encompassed by developmental psychology are physical growth and development, cognition (thinking), psycholinguistics (language development), and social-personality development.

Andrea, age 5

Psychologists must ask philosophical questions regarding the basic nature of the child. For example, are children born with predispositions toward evil behavior (original sin) or goodness, or do experiences with the environment shape their behavior? These questions and others like them lead to research designed to uncover some answers.

A fundamental controversy among psychologists is the heredity-environment (nature-nurture) issue. Child psychologists seek to define the relative contributions of each of these factors to overall behavior. Are biological factors (genetic predispositions and physiology) the major determinants of behavior, or do environmental factors (experiences) play the dominant role? Despite considerable research, the nature–nurture issue is unresolved. Many child psychologists today emphasize the interaction that takes place between genetic and environmental forces.

Epigenesis is the belief that everything develops according to genetic programming. Growth refers to a biological increase in size. Maturation is the cells' state of readiness to function after growth and chemical changes have occurred. Learning is a relatively permanent change in behavior that can occur only after growth and maturation have taken place.

Changes in behavior are thought to be either gradual and continuous (for example, socialization) or sudden and abrupt (for example, cognitive development). The former concept views children as developing from interactions and experiences with the environment. The latter considers developmental trends to be based on internal biological states (growth and maturation).

Critical or sensitive periods are points in the life cycle when an organism is especially sensitive to external influences. For example, the period between 6 and 16 months appears critical for children if they are to become "attached" to another human being and later on in life develop warm bonds of attachment to others.

The active-passive issue is the question whether children are passively shaped by their environment and simply react to it, or whether they actively seek out the environmental stimuli they desire.

Some aspects of developmental psychology present problems that do not have easy or concise answers. Ethical consideration of human rights and dignity disallow experiments that might provide information only by inflicting possibly irreparable damage on the subjects. The Division of Developmental Psychology of the American Psychological Association has been instrumental in developing ethical standards and research guidelines.

Developmental psychology is considered a science, and scientific methodology is applied to the study of the developing organism. Today's methods undoubtedly are more precise than the baby biographies of the past or the mass questionnaires originally developed by G. Stanley Hall. Perfecting techniques of naturalistic observation and learning how to establish rapport with children are critical skills that beginners in the field must develop.

There are two basic methods for accumulating data: the cross-sectional study, the quicker and easier method in which data are collected from many age groups simultaneously; and the longitudinal method, which follows developmental processes in the same persons over a period of years and thus allows for the perception of subtle changes that are missed by cross-sectional methodology. The experimental method is a systematic and highly sophisticated research approach designed to supply the researcher with the most accurate data possible.

Suggested Reading List

American Psychologist, Oct. 20, 1979, *34*, 10. This special issue focuses on current research and practice in child psychology. Topics include children's thought, children's social-emotional development, diagnostic and treatment services for children, and children in perspective.

Cartwright, C., and Cartwright, G. P. *Developing Observation Skills.* 2nd ed. New York: McGraw-Hill, 1984. This text focuses on, among other topics, the importance of observation, developing observation strategies, record keeping, and anecdotal records.

Irwin, D. M., and Bushnell, M. M. *Observational Strategies for Child Study.* New York: Holt, Rinehart and Winston, 1980. This book presents the fundamentals of observation, interesting historical material on child study, and structured lab assignments.

Nadelman, L. *Research Manual in Child Development.* New York: Harper & Row, 1982. This book is an excellent introduction to developmental psychology research. It presents a thorough overview and 15 detailed experimental projects that will help students develop an appreciation of research methodology.

Richarz, A. S. *Understanding Children through Observation.* St. Paul, Minn.: West, 1980. The strength of this text lies in its chronological approach to child study. The book's organizational framework allows the student to study development from birth to adolescence.

Chapter Two

Theories of Child Development

I had six theories about bringing up children, now I have six children and no theories.

John Wilmot, Earl of Rochester (1647–1680)

Introduction

Although psychology is a young science and developmental psychology is even younger, we are discovering new facts at an amazing rate. Indeed experimental data are being acquired so rapidly that it is becoming difficult to organize and integrate new and existing data. But this is true in any science when observations and experiments are made and data are continually collected. We call collected data *facts;* a fact is simply a statement of an occurrence.

Facts have been called the building blocks of a science; however, just as a pile of bricks does not make a house, a pile of facts does not constitute a science. A pile of facts is no good whatsoever, unless you can give it meaning. Thus we come to the role of theory. A **theory** is simply an attempt to explain a set of facts. In child development, theories attempt to answer such questions as: Why do children behave in certain ways? How can children be taught new behaviors? What underlying forces or motives produce behaviors? Facts can't explain processes, but theories can. Theories may also complement one another.

Frequently, however, different theories explain the same phenomena. The many theories of personality all try to explain human behavior and its underlying dynamics. Developmental theories attempt to explain the processes that take an individual from conception through adulthood. In this text, we will try not only to offer the facts but also to explain them with the most meaningful theory and apply the result to everyday life. Making the connection between theory and practice, however, is no easy task. Perhaps the most difficult obstacle developmentalists (or other scientists) face is the search for the vital linkage between a theory and the manner in which it can be success-fully implemented.

How does one view a child? This extremely difficult question will require you to examine your own orientation or perspective on child-hood. How you answer it will determine your view of the development of the human organism. As Robert Thomas (1984) suggests, your ideas can be likened to a lens through which to view children's growth. The theory you select will filter out certain facts and impose a pattern on those it lets in.

Like students taking a child development course, developmentalists do not agree on all the issues. While we often agree on some issues, we also often have our disagreements. However, developmentalists share the fundamental orientation of seeking to understand the nature of growth and development in children. This orientation has led to the development of numerous theories that have broadened our under-standing of the many facets of childhood (Crain, 1980).

Because an introductory course cannot consider every develop-mental psychology theory proposed, we will examine six widely recog-nized theories:

1. The *cognitive* school of thought, which emphasizes the child's developing mental capacities and the impact of these abilities on overall development

2. The *psychoanalytic approach*, which emphasizes the personality dynamics of the growing child

3. *Behaviorism*, which emphasizes the impact of the environment and its role in children's learning

4. *Social learning theory*, which emphasizes the role that imitation, modeling, or observational learning exerts on childhood behavior

5. The *ethology* approach, which focuses on relevant similarities between animal and human behavior

6. *Humanistic psychology*, which emphasizes each individual's uniqueness, inner potential, and striving for self-actualization

Analysis of these six theories establishes a foundation for the study of human development. While this chapter will provide an overview of these theories, each will be integrated and explored in greater detail in subsequent chapters. It will become increasingly obvious that these theories are intertwined with many aspects of human development. For example, each gives a unique insight into such developmental areas as attachment behavior, language development, sex typing, morality, per-sonality, and play behavior.

Cognitive Development Theory

Piaget's Theory of Cognitive Development

Our understanding of the cognitive developments in childhood has been considerably enhanced by the efforts of Swiss psychologist Jean Piaget. His unique theory of conceptual development is one of the most comprehensive to date. Although he did not attain true recognition for his work from the psychology community in the United States until the 1950s, Piaget is regarded today as a leading authority in the field of cognitive development.

While often referred to as a child psychologist, Piaget characterized himself as a genetic epistemologist (genetic means beginning; epistemology is the study of knowledge). Piaget asked how knowledge develops in the human organism. To answer this question, he had to study children and their mental processes. To Piaget, the term **cognition** was synonymous with intelligence, and he considered cognition to be a biological process, just like digestion. We might say that Piaget studied the "biology of thinking."

Piaget was not so much interested in what kinds of knowledge we learn as he was in how the brain processes or biologically digests the incoming information. His is an age-stage, or discontinuous, theory of development, which stresses the action of the mind on the environment. He viewed humans as self-generated and essentially rational and intellectual.

For example, Piaget had observed that different age levels yield different levels of comprehension and reasoning. A 3-year-old, for example, has rudimentary reasoning skills but can solve problems that escaped him or her at 2. Similarly, a 4-year-old may be able to deal with some concepts unsolved a year before yet be unable to keep pace with the thinking of a 5-year-old. All this led Piaget to believe that intellectual development proceeds in an orderly sequence characterized by specific growth stages. He postulated that these growth stages enable the child to develop certain concepts necessary for intellectual maturity. Consequently, Piaget believed conceptual development to be a building process, a series of qualitative intellectual advancements that can transport the child from a world of fantasy into a world of reality.

His explanation of this systematic process, the most important theme in all his writings, has provided psychologists and educators with a detailed and methodical analysis of cognitive development. In it, people, especially children, are viewed as developing organisms acquiring conceptual awareness as they pass through five orderly and progressive stages. At the base of these stages is an explanation of how

Jean Piaget

people interpret and store the vast amounts of stimuli to which they are exposed. These concepts now require our examination.

Conceptual Structure of the Mind   The design for mental growth, as proposed by Piaget, hinges on two important principles: organization and adaptation. Both will sustain an orderly, structured development of conceptual awareness and understanding.

Organization is the ability to order and classify new experiences, termed **schemata,** in the mind; it is a fundamental and innate process in all children. As the infant is increasingly exposed to new stimuli, the mind is able to construct a mental organization capable of categorizing and integrating these schematic elements into regular systems. Sensory stimuli objects and events are just two examples of schematic organization. This type of classification system constitutes the beginning of intellectual activity.

Adaptation gives the individual a meaningful understanding of the surrounding environment. It depends on the mental processes Piaget labels **assimilation** and **accommodation.**

Through assimilation, children perceive and interpret new information in terms of existing knowledge and understanding. Put another way, children attempt to explain new phenomena by referring to their current frame of reference. Assimilation is conservative in that its primary function is to make the unfamiliar familiar, to reduce the new to the old. A child who has been exposed only to cars, for example, may call a truck or bus a car, simply because *car* is the only word for vehicle stored in the child's mental organization. Along the same lines, a young child who has learned what a kitty cat is, may see a dog and call it a kitty cat. In learning theory, this is called stimulus generalization: responding to similar stimuli as though they were the same.

Through accommodation, children restructure their mental organization to include new information. Whereas the process of assimilation molds the object or event to fit the person's existing frame of reference, accommodation changes the mental structure so that new experiences may be added. Thus, if an incident takes place that does not correspond with an existing mental framework, individuals may revise their way of thinking in order to interpret that event. In the previous examples, children who effectively use accommodation skills will develop a new mental structure to categorize trucks or dogs after realizing that trucks cannot be put in the category of cars or that dogs belong in a category separate from cats. In learning theory this is called stimulus discrimination, defined as the ability to distinguish between different but similar stimuli.

Piaget's system involves two major divisions: structures and functions, which are both with the organism from birth. Structures, which include schemata, develop by means of the functions as the organism interacts with its environment. Functions—the innate components or biological givens—include the organism's tendency to organize information/perception (organization) and adapt to it by assimilation and accommodation.

The organism uses the functions to develop its cognitive structures by taking in new information and changing its representation of the world of structures. The development of thinking, therefore, relies on changes in the mental structures of the child. Indeed, the ability to change old ways of thinking in order to solve new problems is the true yardstick for measuring intellectual growth.

Assimilation and accommodation are always active, and there is a tendency to seek a balance between the two, which is called equilibration. The ultimate goal of equilibration is equilibrium, an ideal balance between assimilation and accommodation. Piaget noted, however, that this state is never reached and maintained, particularly not in childhood.

Piaget's Cognitive Development Theory: An Overview   The first stage of cognitive development proposed by Piaget (Table 2.1) is labeled **sensorimotor development** (ages 0 to 2). During this early phase of development, the infant exercises rudimentary sensory and motor awareness and functions almost exclusively by means of reflexive responses. In the beginning, limited cognitive activity takes place and little distinction is made between the self and the environment. By the end of the first year, however, meaningful interactions with surroundings have begun. For example, the infant may shake or strike a crib mobile if its movement proves interesting; when objects disappear from sight, the infant knows that, instead of disappearing totally (as it once thought), they remain permanent in reality.

During **preconceptual thought** (2 to 4), the child demonstrates an increase in language abilities, and concepts become more elaborate. Children are largely **egocentric** (self-centered) and view the world from their own perspective. Developing imagination abilities frequently promote a type of thinking called **animism,** the tendency to give life to inanimate objects. Thus, a tree may become a large animal or a fence post might be envisioned as a person. By the end of this stage, the world is increasingly represented by the use of mental images.

The **intuitive thought** stage (4 to 7) is a division of the preconceptual thought stage and is characterized by the development of refined perceptual sensitivity. This is seen in the child's ability to group objects on the basis of their similarities. Such reasoning, however, is limited to the child's perceptions of obvious physical appearances. For the most part, thinking is intuitive and many times impulsive. Finer discriminations of the world in general are still elusive. An example of this is the child's inability to understand the law of **conservation**: children cannot understand that an object can conserve its amount, weight, or mass when it is poured into a different-sized container, placed in a different position, or molded into a different shape.

By the time **concrete operations** (7 to 11) is reached, the child understands the law of conservation (see Chapter 7) and can perform and reverse various mental operations. The abilities to consider other viewpoints, classify objects and order them in a series along a dimension (such as size), and understand relational concepts (*A* is larger than *B*) is evident. However, a significant limitation of this stage is the child's inability to solve problems of an abstract nature.

Formal operations (11 to 15), sometimes called formal thought, is the final stage of Piaget's theory. Abstract thinking is now possible, and scientific problem-solving strategies emerge. When a problem is

Table 2.1 Piaget's Stages of Cognitive Development

Stage	Age	Significant Cognitive Developments
Sensorimotor development	0–2	Engagement in primitive reflex activity. Gradual increase in sensory and motor awareness. Little distinction made between the self and the environment, although meaningful interactions with surroundings and the establishment of object permanence characterize later phases of this stage.
Preconceptual thought	2–4	Increase in language and concept development. Child is largely egocentric. Animism is prevalent in thinking. Employment of mental images to represent the world is increasingly evident by the end of this stage.
Intuitive thought	4–7	Increase in perceptual sensitivity, although discrimination is based on obvious physical appearances. Child does not understand law of conservation. In general, thinking is intuitive in nature and frequently impulsive.
Concrete operations	7–11	Understanding of law of conservation and reverse mental operations. Objects can be classified and ordered in a series along a dimension (such as size), and relational concepts (*A* is larger than *B*) are understood. Abstract problems remain elusive.
Formal operations	11–15	Abstract thought and scientific reasoning. Problems are approached with advanced logic and reason. Individuals follow logical propositions and reason by hypothesis.

approached, a hypothesis is drawn and the individual develops several potential solutions. Advanced logic and reason accompany formal operations. Such thinking abilities herald the relinquishment of childhood mental operations and the emergence of mature adult thought.

Piaget's work has stimulated vast amounts of research around the world. The most noteworthy extension has come from Harvard's Lawrence Kohlberg, who has formulated a six-stage theory of morality based on the individual's developing cognitive awareness (see Chapter 16).

Psychoanalytic Theory

The psychoanalytic school of thought was originated by Sigmund Freud (1856–1939). Freud, like so many others of his day, came to psychology by other routes. While practicing medicine in clinics, he became interested in neurophysiology, especially the functions of the brain. He spent considerable time seeking to understand abnormal brain functions and mental disorders, a pursuit that would eventually bring him to the field of psychology.

Although many of his views are controversial, quite a few psychologists have been influenced by at least one of his ideas on child development. He devised a theory of personality (with the underlying dynamics of the id, ego, and superego) that has applications to the behavior of both child and adult. He also proposed psychosexual stages of development, a theoretical explanation of behavior that places great importance on the development and maturation of body parts and on early life experiences. One's past, he believed, plays an important role in determining one's present behavior. Furthermore, Freud's analysis of defense mechanisms has helped to explain how defensive behavior originates.

Freud perceived human beings' essential psychological nature as based on *desire* rather than *reason*. His focus in psychoanalysis was primarily upon people's passions, or emotions, and only secondarily upon their rational abilities or intellect. Freud's view of human nature relates to the doctrine of original sin, with the child perceived as being born with basic animal instincts operating at the unconscious level of thought. These instincts, or irrational needs, require immediate gratification. Development, therefore, partially depends on the transformation of the so-called animal desires into socially acceptable, rational behavior.

Freud's influence can be seen in the research of other psychologists, including his daughter Anna, who was one of the early investigators of children's play. He also stimulated the works of a number of

Sigmund Freud

neo-Freudians, particularly Erik Erikson, who devised a theory of personality that stresses psychosocial stages of development. We will look at Erikson's theory later in this chapter.

Freud's Theory of Personality

Freud developed a theory, or explanation, of how neuroses develop. This theory, in conjunction with his explanation of personality, describes the developmental stages through which a child must pass to reach adulthood and normal maturity. His developmental explanation, referred to as psychosexual stages of development, originated not from his direct study of children but from the extraction of information from adult neurotics, initially through hypnosis and later through the cathartic process termed *free association.* The only child Freud ever saw as a patient was Little Hans, and Freud saw him only once, conducting the remainder of his analysis by correspondence with Hans's father. This method raises serious questions about how much faith to place in the childhood events postulated in Freud's theory. Patients may be unable to recollect events that transpired years ago and, even if they can, their experiences may have no correlation with the experiences of more normal children.

Three Levels of Consciousness   One of Freud's major beliefs was that individuals are generally not aware of the underlying reasons for their behavior. He assumed that mental activity must occur at three levels of consciousness. The first level is called the conscious and includes whatever a person is thinking about or experiencing at any given moment. Information and immediate awareness are very fleeting: our conscious thoughts flow by like water in a stream. In fact, this phenomenon is sometimes called our stream of consciousness.

The second level of consciousness is called preconscious and includes all of a person's stored knowledge and memories that are capable of being brought up to the conscious level. For example: What is your home telephone number? Even though you were probably not thinking of your phone number, you could retrieve it from the preconscious level.

The third and largest level of consciousness is the unconscious, a vast area of irrational wishes, shameful urges, socially unacceptable sexual desires, fears, aggressive feelings, and anxiety-producing thoughts that have been repressed (pushed down to the unconscious to be forgotten). Because these feelings are very threatening to us, we keep them locked up in the unconscious. When we dream, these feelings and urges are sometimes released, but generally in so distorted a way that we do not recognize them. However, these beliefs, urges, desires, and so forth are all motivators of behavior and influence us in some way.

Personality Components: The Id, Ego, and Superego   According to Freud, the **id** is the original inherited system, the instinctive aspect of the personality triumvirate. The id contains the basic motivational drives for food, water, sex, and warmth. All emotions are housed in the id and add further dimension to what Freud described as "unconscious motivational forces."

The id contains the driving life force of an organism. One such dynamic force is the **libido,** which supplies libidinal energy. (Libido means lust or desire in Latin.) When this energy builds up, there is an increase in tension and unhappiness, which must be released by the organism. When the tension level is lowered, feelings of contentment and pleasure arise. The id also operates on the hedonistic principle, which is in many respects an extension of homeostasis (the tendency of the body to maintain internal equilibrium). Hedonism, often referred to as the **pleasure principle,** represents the organism's attempt to seek pleasure and avoid discomfort. The id's forces, operating at the unconscious level, drive the organism toward instant gratification of its primary needs. In this sense, biological needs such as hunger cannot be denied or deferred; without logic or ability to reason, an organism demands immediate gratification.

Freud believed that an infant operates solely at the id level for the first eight months of life until the ego commences its slow and gradual development. Until this time, the id is in total control of the child's behavior. Thus, when the internal tension level increases because of hunger pangs, soiled or wet diapers, gas bubbles, or other tension-producing stimuli, the infant will cry until the tension level is changed to an acceptable or pleasurable state.

The **ego** is the organism's contact with the external environment. Its purpose is to satisfy the desires or demands of the id and, later in life, the superego. As the ego develops, it learns to operate on the reality principle, which states that there are socially acceptable ways of satisfying needs. However, Freud views the reality principle as a "servant" of the pleasure principle and not as a separate or sovereign entity. According to Freud, the ego exists to further the aims of the id. Over a long time, socially acceptable behavior may prove to be more beneficial to the organism than behavior that produces instant gratification. Until this is learned, however, infants, toddlers, and preschoolers operate at a "gimme, gimme, gimme" level, wanting everything for themselves immediately and exhibiting little tolerance for more acceptable behavior. Ego maturity is in part the process of restraining the id's demands until they can be met according to the mores and values of one's culture.

The third component of the Freudian personality system is the **superego**, which appears when the child is approximately 5 years old. The superego consists of the internalization of the morals taught by one's religion, society, and family. The superego is similar to the id in making undeniable but largely unconscious demands on the ego. However, the superego also resembles the ego by virtue of its intent to exercise control over the id's urges. The child who steals without compunction because it is allowable according to his or her principles will suffer no emotional consequences for such an act or at best may intellectualize the possibilities of getting caught. The child whose values say theft is improper behavior and whose superego is sufficiently developed to operate on such a principle will most likely experience guilt or remorse. The opposite set of emotions originates from the ego ideal, the portion of the superego that makes one "feel good" for having behaved according to one's internalized principles.

Behavior, then, can be defined as the result of the interaction of these three personality components and their relationship to the outer world, each one seeking to attain a form of psychological satisfaction by directly influencing behavior (see Figure 2.1). Thus, when the id signals the ego that the body is in need of fluids, the ego, evaluating reality, attempts to choose an appropriate form of behavior to satisfy the id. This will be accomplished by conforming to acceptable social behaviors (such as not drinking from a puddle) and by adhering to standards within the superego (not stealing soda water).

Freud's Psychosexual Theory: An Overview   Freud has identified five stages of psychosexual development (Table 2.2). During the **oral stage**

Figure 2.1 The relationship of the id, ego, and superego to levels of awareness

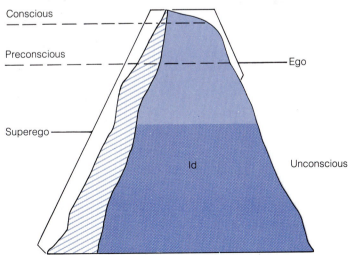

(0 to 2), the mouth is the primary source of pleasure. Enjoyment is derived from being fed or from sucking on a pacifier or one's thumb. Freud maintains that over- or undergratification of this need—and of others to follow—may lead to what he terms *fixation*. A fixation is a preoccupation with one particular aspect of psychosexual development (i.e., thumb sucking) that may interfere with or manifest itself in subsequent psychosexual stages. Thus, the child fixated at the oral stage, perhaps deprived of thumb sucking, may seek to fulfill this need later on in life. Such behaviors as smoking, gum chewing, or nail biting may be the individual's way of gratifying the oral need that was not satisfied earlier.

During the **anal stage** (2 to 3), the anus and the buttocks become the source of sensual pleasure. Satisfaction is derived from expelling or withholding feces, but external conflicts are encountered when toilet training begins. Freud maintains that the manner in which parents conduct toilet training, particularly the use of positive or negative reinforcement, may have consequences for the development of later personality traits.

Table 2.2 Freud's Psychosexual Stages of Development

Stage	Age	Psychosexual Development
Oral	0–1	Pleasure such as eating, sucking, vocalizing, etc. derived from oral cavity.
Anal	1–3	Pleasure derived from anal area, including retention and expulsion of feces. External conflicts may result when toilet training begins.
Phallic	3–5	Pleasure derived from manipulation of genital organs. Curiosity directed toward sexuality of self and others. Emergence of Oedipus and Electra complexes for males and females, respectively.
Latency period	6–11	Tranquil period of time between stages. Refinement of self-concept and increased peer group interaction. Emergence of coping or defense mechanisms.
Genital	Adolescence	Onset of puberty and discovery of new sexual feelings. Development of heterosexual attraction. Beginning of romantic love.

The **phallic stage** (3 to 6 or so) is characterized by interest in the genital organs. Pleasure is derived from manipulating one's genitals, and curiosity is directed toward the anatomical differences between the sexes. Children also have a tendency to develop romantic feelings toward parents of the opposite sex. The attraction of boys to their mothers is called the **Oedipus complex,** and the romantic feelings of girls toward their fathers is labeled the **Electra complex.**

The **latency period** (6 to 11) represents a rather tranquil period compared to the psychosexual turbulence of previous stages. However, there is an increased awareness of one's personal identity, surroundings, and the importance of social interaction. The latency period is also a time of ego refinement as the child seeks to develop socially acceptable character traits. Coping or defense mechanisms begin to develop as children attempt to avoid failure or rejection in the face of life's growing expectations and demands.

Freud's final psychosexual period is called the **genital stage** (the adolescent years). At this time, paralleling the onset of puberty, adolescents become interested in members of the opposite sex and have their first experiences with romantic love. Immature emotional interactions permeate the early phases of this stage, but in time people realize that they are capable of giving and receiving mature love.

Erikson's Psychosocial Theory

Erik H. Erikson

Erik H. Erikson (born 1902) is one of the foremost psychoanalytic scholars alive today. During his fascinating early life he created large woodcuts, especially of children, and taught art in Vienna, where he received a Montessori teaching certificate. He also studied with Anna Freud. Finally, he combined his two interests and published articles on the application of psychoanalytic theory to educational issues. He was later to study children at play, child-rearing practices, and the continual growth and developmental processes of the ego.

Of his many books, *Childhood and Society* (Erikson, 1963) is probably the best known, for in it he first presented and summed up his major theory. This theory converts the psychosexual theory of Freud to one of psychosocial stages of ego development. Erikson contends that the process of socializing the child into a given culture occurs by passing through innately determined sequential stages, or what he calls psychosocial development. Like Sigmund and Anna Freud, Erikson is concerned with ego development. However, while recognizing the individual's instinctual drives and interest in different parts of the body in a prescribed sequence, Erikson emphasizes the child's interactions with the environment. Thus, he views the ego, not the id, as the major driving force of behavior. Erikson also differs in his method of studying healthy rather than neurotic personalities to develop his theory.

Erikson also disagrees with Freud's emphasis on infantile sexuality. Owing to his anthropological training, Erikson perceived children's behavior as resulting more from societal influences than from sexual ones. His comprehensive theory of development encompasses the years from infancy through old age. For Erikson, the course of development is reversible, so that the events of later childhood can undo—for better or for worse—earlier personality foundations. For Freud, basic personality structure is essentially fixed by the age of 5. However, for both theorists, stages are related to ages in the sense that aging leads to movement to a new stage regardless of experience and regardless of reorganizations at previous stages.

Essential to Erikson's theory is the development of the ego and the ego's ability to deal with a series of crises or potential crises throughout the individual's life span. Each stage of life, according to Erikson (1963), has a crisis related in some way to an element in society. The development of personality begins with ego strengths that are present at birth; as the years pass, ego strength is accrued, one quality at a time. Each quality undergoes rapid growth at a critical period of development. Another key component of Erikson's theory is the epigenetic principle, which states that development is predetermined by genetic principles. Thus, Erikson—like Freud and Piaget—believes that development proceeds along a discontinuous or age-stage pathway (Erikson, 1968).

The first of Erikson's eight psychosocial crises (Table 2.3) is called **basic trust versus basic mistrust** (ages 0 to 1). During this stage, the nature of parental interactions with the infant is critical. If infants receive proper care, love, and affection, they develop a sense of trust. If these basic needs are not met, they become suspicious, fearful, and mistrusting of their surroundings.

During **autonomy versus shame and doubt** (1 to 3), developing motor and mental abilities give the child the opportunity to experience independence. If their growing urge to explore the world is encouraged, children grow more confident in themselves and more autonomous in general. However, if their developing independence is met with parental disapproval or discouragement, children may question their own abilities and harbor doubts about their own adequacy.

During the third stage, children experience the psychosocial crisis known as **initiative versus guilt** (3 to 5). Increasingly refined developmental capacities prompt the child to self-initiate environmental exploration and discovery. Parental reinforcement will encourage such initiative and promote purpose- and goal-directiveness. Parental restrictiveness, on the other hand, is likely to promote guilt whenever children seek to discover the world on their own.

Industry versus inferiority (6 to 11) is characterized by the child's desire to manipulate objects and to learn how things work. Such an industrious attitude typically leads to a sense of order, a system of rules, and an important understanding about the nature of one's surroundings. Inferiority feelings may result, however, if adults perceive such behavior as silly, mischievous, or troublesome.

The fifth psychosocial crisis, perhaps the most famous of Erikson's work, is **identity versus role confusion** (adolescence). The task at this time is to develop an integrated sense of self, one that is personally acceptable and, it is hoped, distinct from others. Failure to nurture an accurate sense of personal identity may lead to the dilemma of role confusion. This frequently leads to feelings of inadequacy, isolation, and indecisiveness.

The task of **intimacy versus isolation** (young adulthood) is to develop close and meaningful relationships with others. Having attained a sense of personal identity in the previous stage, individuals are now able to share themselves with others on a moral, emotional, and sexual level. Intimacy may mean marriage, the establishment of warm and nurturant friendships, or, of course, both. Those unable or unwilling to share themselves with others suffer a sense of loneliness or isolation.

Table 2.3 Erikson's Stages of Psychosocial Development

Stage	Age	Human Relationships Involved	Desired Outcome of Crisis
Trust vs. mistrust	0–1	Parents/caretaker	Hope
Autonomy vs. doubt	1–3	Parents/caretaker	Will
Initiative vs. guilt	3–5	Family	Purpose
Industry vs. inferiority	6–11	Neighborhood/school	Competence
Identity vs. role confusion	Adolescence	Peer groups	Fidelity
Intimacy vs. isolation	Young adulthood	Friends/spouse	Love
Generativity vs. self-absorption	Middle adulthood	Family interactions/job acquaintances	Care
Integrity vs. despair	Old age	All of mankind	Wisdom

(Based on Erikson, 1963)

Erikson's seventh stage is called **generativity versus self-absorption** (middle adulthood). The positive pole of this stage, generativity, means that adults are willing to look beyond themselves and express concern about the future of the world in general. The self-absorbed person tends to be preoccupied with personal well-being and material gains.

The final stage is **integrity versus despair** (old age). Those persons nurturing a sense of integrity have typically resolved previous psychosocial crises and are able to look back at their lives with dignity, satisfaction, and feelings of personal fulfillment. Those who have not successfully resolved previous crises are likely to feel a sense of despair. These individuals usually view their past lives as a series of disappointments, failures, and misfortunes.

See Figure 2.2 for a comparative alignment of Freud's and Erikson's developmental theories.

Behaviorism

Probably more attention has been paid to learning theory than to any other psychological process. Psychologists run rats through mazes, put pigeons and rats in Skinner boxes, and devise numerous experiments to measure human learning. While we have many experimental "facts," there are still many unanswered questions about what actually constitutes learning.

Some psychologists, especially learning theorists, feel very uncomfortable with theories of behavior that propose such abstract concepts as mental elements (for example, ego, conscience, and soul) or mental functions (for example, assimilation, repression, and cognition). Piaget, Freud, Erikson, and others who have studied mental life often present a somewhat untestable theory. Learning theorists often have misgivings about such mentalistic theory, and they have attempted to be more objective and "scientific." Stated bluntly, their credo is, "If you can't measure it, it doesn't exist." The first theorist to proclaim this position was John Broadus Watson, whose theory is known as **behaviorism.**

The school of thought known as behaviorism emphasizes that learning involves the interaction of the organism with the environment. Although one's genetic endowment influences the degree and rapidity of certain learning capacities, such as general intelligence and specific aptitudes and abilities, the organism's inherited potential is meaningless if there is no environment to provide it with enrichment and cultivation. Behaviorists maintain that it is through interaction with the environment that children learn various types of behaviors, such as how to get along with others, pass tests, or cope with a variety of everyday situations.

Pavlov and Classical Conditioning

A Russian Nobel-prize winning physiologist and a specialist on the digestive system, Ivan Petrovich Pavlov (1849–1936) was initially interested in the effects of saliva on food. Using dogs as subjects, Pavlov found that he could stimulate the salivary glands by placing food powder in the animal's mouth. The amount of saliva was then measured. To Pavlov's surprise, however, the dogs also began to salivate at the sight of their keepers, evidently in anticipation of the food stimulus. Motivated to seek an explanation for such responses (he initially used the rather ambiguous term *psychic reactions*), Pavlov embarked on a scientific pursuit that would eventually provide the field of psychology with a series of irrefutable principles concerning the nature of learning.

In his description of a learning process later to be labeled **classical conditioning,** Pavlov introduced a number of scientific terms that contrasted sharply with the vague terms that had been used in the past. He wrote that a reflex reaction was an unlearned response to a natural

Figure 2.2 Stages of Freud's and Erikson's personality theories

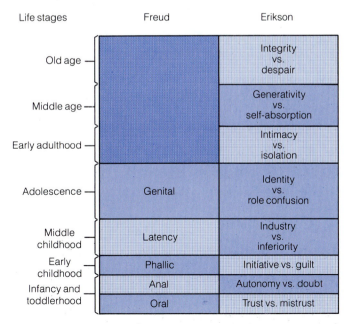

Life stages	Freud	Erikson
Old age		Integrity vs. despair
Middle age		Generativity vs. self-absorption
Early adulthood		Intimacy vs. isolation
Adolescence	Genital	Identity vs. role confusion
Middle childhood	Latency	Industry vs. inferiority
Early childhood	Phallic	Initiative vs. guilt
Infancy and toddlerhood	Anal	Autonomy vs. doubt
	Oral	Trust vs. mistrust

stimulus. For example, a dog will salivate (reflex) to food (stimulus) placed in its mouth just as an eye will blink (reflex) when a puff of air (stimulus) is directed toward it. Since a reflex is a natural, or unlearned, event, Pavlov named the reflex response to a natural stimulus an **unconditioned response** (he preferred the term *conditioning* to *learning*) and the natural stimulus an **unconditioned stimulus.** A neutral stimulus is one that does not elicit a response. Thus, we can diagram the relationship as follows:

Unconditioned ⟶ Unconditioned
Stimulus (US)   Response (UR)
(food powder)   (salivation)

Pavlov discovered that learning, or conditioning, will take place when a neutral stimulus is paired contiguously with the US. For example, when the ringing of a bell (neutral stimulus) was paired with food powder over successive trials, it eventually led to a conditioned response, the dog salivating at the tone of the bell. The model for a typical classical conditioning experiment can be diagramed as follows:

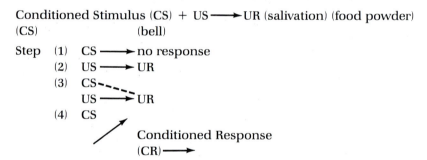

Conditioned Stimulus (CS) + US ⟶ UR (salivation) (food powder)
(CS)   (bell)
Step   (1)   CS ⟶ no response
       (2)   US ⟶ UR
       (3)   CS --.
             US ⟶ UR
       (4)   CS
                       Conditioned Response
                       (CR) ⟶

Pavlov also stated that the CR would eventually extinguish itself if reinforcement (US) ceased to be present. (Extinction differs from forgetting, which refers to the extinguishing of a response due to lack of practice over a period of time.)

Spontaneous recovery is an unusual phenomenon, which Pavlov discovered sometimes follows extinction. Even though a response has been extinguished through lack of reinforcement, a re-presentation of the CS will suddenly elicit the conditioned response although no reinforcement may be present.

Stimulus generalization is said to occur when the organism responds to similar stimuli just as it responded to the original stimulus. Thus, a dog will salivate to bells having tones approximating those of the original conditioned stimulus. The more nearly the new stimulus resembles the original conditioned stimulus, the stronger will be the response.

J. B. Watson

Stimulus discrimination is the ability to distinguish between two similar stimuli that have already produced stimulus generalization. Thus, a dog may be conditioned to salivate to one tone but not to tones that are slightly higher (or lower).

Watson, Father of Behaviorism

Children's behavior as a product of conditioning and learning experiences was brought into prominence by J. B. Watson (1878–1958). As a researcher, Watson was dissatisfied with the field of psychology because it strove to be a science yet was filled with introspective theorizing rather than experimental data. In his estimation, psychology should deal only with human behavior that could be accurately measured. What takes place inside an organism (thoughts, feelings, etc.) should be secondary.

In the early 1900s Watson read Pavlov's experiments and hypothesized that the conditioning process might be the answer to understanding all facets of behavior, normal or neurotic. Watson conducted several Pavlovian conditioning experiments, which led him to conclude that all behavior is the product of environmental learning.

Watson's classic experiment in the field of child psychology was conducted to illustrate how fears can be learned. Albert, a child of 11 months, was conditioned to fear the presence of a white rat. The rat (conditioned stimulus [CS]) initially produced no fear in the infant. However, the presence of the rat was accompanied by a loud noise (unconditioned stimulus [US]). After a number of trials in which the two stimuli were paired (CS and US), Albert reacted fearfully (conditioned response [CR]) to the sight of the rat alone. Then Albert began to generalize his fear to stimuli similar to the rat. Albert would cry and scream at the appearance of other white fuzzy objects, such as a rabbit or a man with a white beard (see Figure 2.3). This experiment helps to explain how children's fears—which often appear irrational and ill founded to adults—have a basis in fact (Watson and Rayner, 1920).

Through Watson's efforts behaviorism began to emerge as a total environmental science. He may best be remembered for a statement that was quoted in *Psychological Care of Infant and Child,* a child-rearing book published in the late 1920s. The statement reflects the importance he placed on the environment:

> Give me a dozen healthy infants, well-formed and my own specified world to bring them up in and I'll guarantee to take any one of them at random and train him to become any type of specialist I might select—a doctor, lawyer, artist, merchant, chief, and yes, even into a beggarman and thief regardless of his talents, penchants, tendencies, abilities, vocations and race of his ancestors. I am going

beyond my facts and I admit it, but so have the advocates of the contrary and they have been doing it for many thousands of years (Watson, 1928, p. 104)

Skinner and Reinforcement

The behavioristic school of thought was advanced in the 1950s by B. F. Skinner (born 1904), who concentrated on exploring the nature of reinforcement and reinforcing stimuli. Skinner devised elaborate problem boxes (popularly known today as **Skinner boxes**) for his experimental animals. The boxes were designed in such a way that a reward (food pellet) would be dispensed if a lever or button was correctly manipulated by the subject. Skinner found that through trial-and-error responses, animals could indeed learn to operate the proper mechanisms in the box to receive a reward. His theory, explaining the nature of this type of learning, has come to be known by several titles, including **operant conditioning, instrumental conditioning,** and **Skinnerian conditioning** (Skinner, 1951, 1957, 1961).

The emphasis in operant conditioning is on **positive reinforcement,** the notion being that a response followed by a reward is more likely to be repeated when the organism finds itself in a situation similar to the original one in which reinforcement occurred. Skinner reasoned that organisms are not normally under continuously paired stimuli from the environment. Although an organism learns to some

Figure 2.3 The generalization of fear, as displayed in Watson's classic experiment (after Watson and Rayner, 1920).

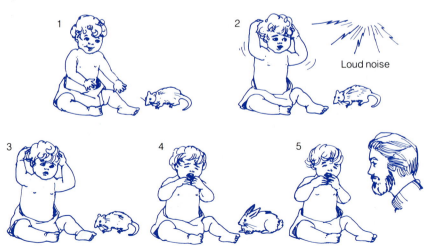

B. F. Skinner

degree through trial-and-error responses, Skinner postulated that true learning depends primarily on what behaviors are accompanied by positive reinforcement. However, Skinner stated that most behaviors are responses emitted by an organism when it has a choice of various responses. Skinner's view is that most responses are not associated with any stimuli; they simply occur. These instrumentally conditioned responses are called operants because they operate on the environment. The nature of these consequences Skinner believed to be critical, as they determined the future behavior of the organism.

Skinner's definition of learning is strictly operational; if behavior cannot be measured, no learning is assumed to have taken place. No assumptions can be made about internal cognitive states, since they are immeasurables:

> Skinner has been adamant in his rejection of mentalistic concepts, and this antipathy for mentalism can be seen in his definition of reinforcement. If the occurrence of a response increases or is strengthened by the subsequent presentation of a stimulus, then that stimulus is a reinforcement. In the Skinner-box, for example, the reinforcement stimulus is the food because it increases the rate of response. Note that Skinner's definition of reinforcement makes no mention of any state of the organism. He rejects as mentalistic any reinforcement concepts that demand an interpretation of the organism's internal state (Hunt and Sullivan, 1974, p. 161).

The Nature of Reinforcement in Operant Conditioning   While Skinner differentiates **reinforcement** into various types, one must remember his contention that learning is measured by overt muscular responses to a stimulus or stimulus situation. Skinner's concern is not with the growth and development of an individual or with inherited potential, but strictly with types of reinforcers and their effects on behavior. Here is a description of how positive and negative reinforcers differ from punishment:

> For Skinner, a positive reinforcement is a stimulus that, when added to a situation, strengthens the probability of the operant response. The food pellet received by the rat is a positive primary reinforcer contingent on the animal's response. Food and water are therefore classified as positive reinforcers. A *negative reinforcer* is a stimulus that, when *removed* from a situation, strengthens the probability of an operant response. . . .
> Skinner distinguishes negative reinforcers from punishment. When he speaks of positive or negative reinforcers, he is referring to stimuli that increase response probability either by their presence (positive) or absence (negative). In contrast, punishment decreases response probability. Punishment is usually applied after a response

to eliminate or suppress it. Skinner disagrees with this procedure of controlling behavior because the desired response is not occurring (Hunt and Sullivan, 1974, pp. 161–162).

Thus, the Skinnerian approach defines a **reinforcer** as anything that strengthens the probability of a response. The definition of reinforcement depends entirely on its effect on future behavior. There is no assumption of need reduction.

Primary and secondary reinforcers are two additional types of reinforcement. **Primary reinforcers** are satisfying stimuli related to primary, unlearned drives (food and drink are primary reinforcers related to the hunger and thirst drives).

A **secondary reinforcer** is a stimulus that is neutral to begin with but gains reinforcing qualities of its own when paired frequently over successive trials with a primary reinforcer. (This is called the conditioned stimulus in classical conditioning.) For example, if a light flashes every time the bar is pressed in a Skinner box, the light soon acquires reinforcement properties because it is paired with the resulting reward. Eventually, the organism will press the bar simply to see the light flash. For children, praise, approval, attention, or toys all represent secondary reinforcement.

Applied Aspects of Reinforcement   Positive reinforcement, **negative reinforcement,** and punishment are naturally occurring events in the lives of children, and as such play vital roles in determining behavioral patterns. In fact, some behaviorists believe they are the sole determiners of whether a stimulus-response (S-R) unit will become part of a child's repertoire of behavior. S-R learning refers to any solitary behavioral unit in which a stimulus is followed by one response. Most behaviors, however, are composed of a series of complex actions or a string of S-Rs. When a number of S-Rs are placed in a series, they are called a chain. Chains may consist of a series of nonverbal behaviors such as getting in a car, closing the door, fastening the seat belt, putting the key in the ignition, and placing the foot on the accelerator. Chains may also consist of verbal associations such as reciting the Pledge of Allegiance to the Flag or singing a song. Each link in a chain is learned from external cues and then placed in an appropriate position to produce the desired behavior. Chains represent a natural extension of S-R conditioning.

Shaping behavior, an outgrowth of operant conditioning, is the establishment of desirable chains by molding or developing a series of S-R situations into a desired behavioral pattern. A shaping technique called **successive approximations** is the step-by-step series of reinforcements that eventually produce a desired S-R behavior. Suppose that we wished to develop in a child behavior that has never previously been exhibited. Obviously, no "correct" behavior is present to be re-warded. Therefore, behaviors that are close to, or that *approximate*, the desired behavior are rewarded. The general response is rewarded each time it happens, until it becomes frequent. Thus, shaping and successive approximations represent the dispensing of reinforcements in order to refine a response gradually and produce a chain or behavioral pattern similar to the one desired.

Shaping and Reinforcement   J. B. Wolfe's classic experiment (1936) illustrates the shift from primary to secondary reinforcers. In his experiment, poker chips became "money" to chimpanzees. When a chimp inserted a chip into a vending machine, it received a grape. Initially, the poker chips were a neutral stimulus; but after the chimps were taught to insert them into the machine for a reward, they began to acquire reinforcement qualities. Wolfe discovered that he could teach the chimps to work for their poker chips even when the grape-vending machine was not present. While waiting for the vending machine to be returned to their cage, the animals would collect their chips in much the same way that people save coins.

The term *punishment* is incorrectly and frequently used interchangeably with such terms as *discipline, negative reinforcement,* and *nonreward situations.* Punishment or aversive conditioning does not imply negative reinforcement, and the two can be distinguished by their effects on behavior. As noted earlier, both positive and negative reinforcement increase the probability of a given response being repeated. However, it is highly questionable that punishment can completely extinguish an organism's response. It appears more likely that punishment brings about only a temporary suppression of a given behavioral response. When the threat of punishment is removed, the suppressed behavior may reappear (Estes, 1944). In fact, punishment has been found actually to increase resistance to extinction; instead of eliminating a response, punishment may lead to its greater persistence (Logan 1970).

As an attempt to extinguish behavior, punishment consists of adding an unpleasant stimulus (a spanking), sometimes called negative punishment, or removing a pleasant stimulus (no chocolate cake for dessert), sometimes called positive punishment. This differs from positive reinforcement, in which a reward is added to the situation, and negative reinforcement, in which an unpleasant stimulus is removed. See Table 2.4 for further clarification of punishment and reinforcement.

Punishment is a very significant aspect of our everyday behavior. Society punishes criminals, parents punish children, teachers punish pupils, and peers punish each other. How effective is punishment? Do criminals leave a penal institution rehabilitated? Does the child who is kept in after school for not doing homework suddenly change and become a dedicated student? Does one sibling stop picking on another because of punishment?

Almost without exception the answer to these questions is "no." As Logan's fieldwork (1970) implies, undesirable behaviors may be temporarily suppressed only to reappear hours or days later, perhaps with greater persistence and intensity. The child who behaves well in school will tend to continue to behave well, while children who behave badly in school will probably continue to behave badly as long as they remain in school (the stimulus situation). Usually, an improvement in behavior will be brought about by innate changes (maturation) or the discovery of a satisfactory behavior to replace the undesirable one.

For obvious ethical reasons, there is little experimental research about punishment and its effects on children, but it is generally recognized that punishment may have deleterious effects on the organism, especially in the realm of emotional development. Upon being punished by parents, children may exhibit an increase in arousal level, generally in the form of aggression outside the home (Sears, Maccoby, and Levin, 1957). Usually they become less aware of environmental happenings as they withdraw from the threatening situation. This response limits the child's ability to attend to and process education and personal information. Moreover, as in the case of Watson's experiment with the child Albert, negative emotions may become generalized and be extended from one situation to broader areas.

Social Learning Theory

Bandura and Observational Learning

Albert Bandura

Social learning theory maintains that most learning theories are built on structured laboratory situations, which often have few similarities to real-world learning. A great deal of human behavior involves the interaction of people, with multiple stimuli encroaching simultaneously on the individuals. Experiments involving puzzle boxes, mazes, and operant chambers may offer learning principles, but they hardly explain a child's table manners or sharing behaviors. In short, most laboratory experiments do not explain many aspects of social behavior.

Social learning researchers have devoted their time not to laboratory research but to direct observation of children's behavior in structured and unstructured situations. One such researcher, Albert Bandura, casts serious doubts on Skinner's theories of successive approximations as a means of explaining all behavior. Bandura does not dispute that shaping can occur, but he asserts that this is only a partial

Table 2.4 Model Depicting Punishment and Reinforcement Variables

	Added to Situation	Withheld from Situation
Pleasant Stimulus	Positive reinforcement	Punishment
Unpleasant Stimulus	Punishment	Negative reinforcement

explanation of behavior and that other aspects of learning are probably more important, for example, the imitation of cues emitted by others (Bandura, 1962).

Bandura states that verbal cues generally accompany other techniques of shaping and can serve as symbolic models to be imitated. He believes that imitation, modeling, and observational learning account for a great many of a child's behavioral patterns. Whether imitation is truly a form of learning is debatable. Some theorists (for example, Miller and Dollard, 1941; Skinner, 1953) have maintained that reinforcement of specific imitative responses leads to a generalized tendency toward imitation. In this fashion, they believe, many behaviors can be imitated without being reinforced. According to this view, imitation is a special kind of instrumental conditioning. Bandura, on the other hand, argues that imitation is a separate and distinct form of learning, requiring unique principles for its understanding.

In a unique series of studies, Bandura and associates have shown how, and under what conditions, observational learning occurs. In one study, 5-year-old children were brought one at a time into a room in which an adult model was playing with Tinker Toys. Suddenly the model turned to a large inflated Bobo doll and knocked it over, sat on it, and punched its nose. The model then let the doll up, only to smash it repeatedly on the head with a wooden mallet, throw it into the air, and kick it. During all this the model muttered, "Sock him in the nose, hit him down, throw him in the air, kick him, pow!"

Shortly after being exposed to this situation, the children were deliberately made angry by having attractive toys withheld from them. This part of the experiment was intended to enhance the possibility of an aggressive behavioral display. A second group of children was angered in the same fashion but was not exposed to the model.

When the experimenter left the room, toys were provided for each child to play with alone. Meanwhile, a group of "judges" hidden from the child's sight rated the resulting behavior. The children who had observed the model's behavior became aggressive, exhibiting behavior almost identical to that displayed by the model. They too punched the doll in the nose, walloped it with a mallet, and yelled "Kick him, pow!" and other phrases initially used by the model. This experiment emphasizes the fact that children not only learn certain behavioral patterns through observation but also learn them *without any external reinforcement.* In another phase of this experiment with the same experimental conditions, the children saw similar acts of aggression committed in an animated cartoon film. The results were very similar (Bandura and Walters, 1963).

Having thus established that learning can occur without reinforcement, Bandura designed a similar experiment to determine the exact roles of reward and punishment in influencing behavior. In this study, three groups of children viewed three different films of a model yelling at and punching the Bobo doll. However, one movie showed the model being punished for the aggressive behavior, the second film ended with the model being praised, and the third film ended with neither praise nor punishment of the model.

After the films were viewed, each child was left alone in a room. Children from the group that had seen the model being praised for aggressive behavior were more apt to behave aggressively than either of the other groups. The least aggressive group was the one that had seen the model being punished. However, in a later phase of the experiment, the children were told that they would be rewarded if they did everything the model had done in the film. Differences between groups immediately vanished. Thus, reinforcements administered to a model influence the performance, but not the acquisition, of initiative responses. However, the frequently contrived procedures used by Bandura make it uncertain exactly how much observational learning applies to everyday lives of children (Bandura, 1962).

While Bandura and others have criticized behaviorism, Skinner has not attempted to modify his position. This has forced some dissatisfied behaviorists to move toward the social learning theory position, and they have been joined by some cognitive psychologists who wish to study dimensions of behavior other than cognition. Thus, a revised social learning theory—what some call *cognitive social learning theory*—is arising (Mischel and Mischel, 1977).

This new school of thought emphasizes a number of general themes:

1. Each individual is continuously engaged in a two-way interaction between the self and the environment. In other words, you influence your environment as much as it influences you.

2. We can learn through observation without any immediate external reinforcement.

3. Learning and acquiring knowledge must be distinguished from performance. Reinforcement may not be essential in acquiring behavior; it is important in guiding and influencing our daily behaviors.

4. Our cognitive expectations and perceptions affect what we do, and our awareness of the consequences of such behavior influences our choice of behavior.

5. We are active processors of information and not the robot or mechanical being that the behaviorists would have us believe. Because of our cognitive processes, we engage in *self-regulation*, evaluating and controlling our behavior.

Thus, cognitive social learning theory is becoming broader, encompassing not only the original school of thought but also cognitive theory, behaviorism, and some ideas from humanistic theory (Mischel and Mischel, 1977).

Ethological Theory

Ethology is the study of human and animal behavior in natural settings. Initially influenced by the writings of Charles Darwin, this school of thought seeks to understand behavior in an evolutionary context and places considerable emphasis on the role that instinct plays in overall development. Notable contributors to ethology besides Darwin include Konrad Lorenz and John Bowlby.

Observing an organism in its natural setting enables ethologists to realize how a species adapts to its environment. Ethologists maintain that we cannot understand why birds build nests unless we see how this behavior protects them from predators in the natural environment. Similarly, we cannot hope to understand the development of children's social groups or status hierarchies unless we observe free play situations and appreciate how and why such socialization behavior emerges. Psychologists who restrict themselves to the laboratory study of animals and humans may miss critical aspects of behavior. Thus, ethologists engage in **naturalistic observation** (Crain, 1980).

Ethologists regard instincts as important aspects of behavior to study. Instincts have several dimensions. To begin with, instincts are released by a specific external stimulus. The rescuing behavior of a hen when her chicks are in danger is a reaction to the chicks' distress calls. Similarly, a young pheasant will rush for cover when it hears its parents' warning call, and a young jackdaw will follow its parents into the air only when they take off at a certain angle and speed. Such protective parental behaviors, although differing in content, are not so different for the human species (Crain, 1980; Thomas, 1984).

Instincts are **species-specific,** which means that particular behavior patterns are found only in members of a specific species. Instincts also include a fixed action pattern, such as fighting gestures, courtship behavior, or modes of following. Finally, as products of evolution, instincts have survival value for the species (Crain, 1980).

Lorenz and Imprinting

Ethologists maintain that, in addition to having instincts, some species have a *critical period,* which is a specific time when an environmental event will have its greatest impact on the developing organism. According to Austrian zoologist Konrad Lorenz and others, strong bonds of attachment develop between the caregiver and the young during the critical period. Lorenz has also suggested that imprinting is important for some species. **Imprinting** is an organism's rapid attachment to an object, usually its caregiver, and generally takes place shortly after birth. This type of behavior is easily observed among fowl, who attach themselves to and follow their mother just hours after birth.

Konrad Lorenz

Lorenz was interested in discovering whether imprinting would result if another stimulus was introduced during the critical period. To find out, he divided a number of Graylag goose eggs into two groups. One group was hatched by the mother, while the other group was placed in an incubator. After the goslings in the first group were hatched, Lorenz observed that they immediately followed the mother wherever she went. However, the goslings hatched in the incubator never had the opportunity of seeing the mother and attached themselves to the first moving object that they encountered, which happened to be Lorenz. Consequently, the goslings followed Lorenz; later in life, they even preferred his company to the company of other geese (Lorenz, 1952).

Other imprinting studies have had other dramatic results. For example, it was found that mallard ducklings exposed to a wooden decoy (equipped with a concealed tape recorder emitting duck sounds) hours after birth would follow it rather than their real mother. Other objects, including footballs and tin cans, have been successfully implemented during the critical period.

Several factors are related to the critical period and imprinting. Of paramount importance is the fact that the critical period varies from species to species. Imprinting can occur only during this relatively short time. The critical period for some species of ducklings extends from 13 to 16 hours after birth, while the critical period for puppies appears to be from 4 to 8 weeks after delivery. The critical period appears to be longer for rhesus monkeys, extending perhaps as long as the first six months of life (Harlow, 1971).

Another important dimension of imprinting is the amount of time spent in contact with the mother object. Longer periods of contact with the object during the critical period (and the earlier in the critical period the better) are more effective than shorter periods. Furthermore, such attributes as movement, color, and size seem to capture the attention of the organism more than do objects without distinguishing characteristics.

Whether a critical period exists in humans is difficult to assess. No conclusive answers to the question have been found. Humans are far more complex than other species and exhibit their own unique attachment behaviors. The issue is complicated by the fact that human infants cannot physically follow their caretakers.

This does not mean that the work of Lorenz and other ethologists has no application to the study of human behavior. On the contrary, we are beginning to see the relevancy of animal behavior to our own behavior in such areas as the establishment of territory, the expression of aggression, and the struggle for dominance. As already indicated, the field of ethology has helped psychologists better understand human attachment behavior. This is particularly evident in the research findings of ethologist John Bowlby (1980).

Humanistic Theory

Humanistic psychologists emphasize the uniqueness, individual potential, and inner drive of each child. Maximizing of individual self-concept and human potential in general are paramount in this school of thought. **Humanism** is often referred to as the "third force" in psychology because it challenges both environmental learning theories and psychoanalytic stances. Humanists contend that individuals are not exclusively controlled by either the external environment or the irrational forces of the unconscious. Rather, children are free and creative beings capable of growth and self-actualization.

Maslow and Self-actualization

Like the other schools of thought that we have discussed, humanistic psychology has been shaped by numerous contributors. Most notably,

Abraham Maslow has developed a theory of motivation stating that individuals are driven to attain uniqueness and the full development of their potentialities, capacities, and talents. The pinnacle of success is referred to by Maslow as **self-actualization.** To reach this goal, certain basic needs must first be satisfied (Maslow, 1968, 1970).

Maslow's Hierarchy of Needs   At the heart of Maslow's theory is the assumption that human needs (and consequently motivations) exist in a hierarchy, from the most basic to the most advanced. The further one progresses up this motivational pyramid, the more distinctly "human" one becomes. Higher motives will develop only when the more basic ones have been satisfied.

As Figure 2.4 shows, the most basic needs are for physiological well-being and safety. To fulfill these two needs, adequate rest, nourishment, and shelter must be found, and individuals must strive to achieve a sense of security. When these two needs have been satisfied, psychic energy can be directed to the need for belongingness and love. Belongingness may be defined as the need to be part of a group and to experience sharing. Esteem is the fourth level of the hierarchic pyramid. By this, Maslow means that individuals must receive feedback from others (in the form of respect and assurance) in order to realize that they are worthwhile and competent. The fifth need, self-actualization, means fulfilling one's individual potential in all its aspects. To reach the fulfillment of one's potential, all previous needs have to be met ade-

Figure 2.4

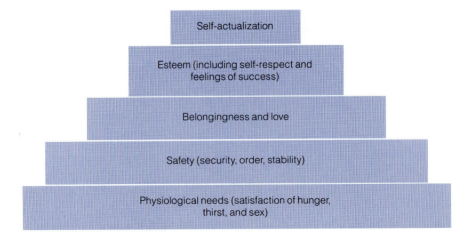

Abraham Maslow

quately. An essential component of self-actualization is freedom from cultural and self-imposed restraints.

Self-Actualization   The quest for self-actualization begins early in life. According to Maslow's **hierarchy of needs,** neither children nor adults can strive toward creativity unless their more fundamental needs have been met. The attainment of self-actualization also requires considerable ego strength, acceptance from peers, and self-respect. Self-actualization may not be attained until the middle years of adulthood. In the years before middle age, energy is frequently dissipated in many directions, including sexual relationships, educational advancement, career alignment, marriage, and parenthood. The need to achieve financial stability during the young adult years consumes considerable psychic energy. By middle age, though, many people have managed to fulfill most of these needs and can spare the energy to strive toward ego maturity.

Maslow has found that self-actualizers have unique character traits. Among other qualities, self-actualizers possess an efficient perception of reality, acceptance of self and others, spontaneity, direct problem-solving ability, autonomy, and a continued freshness of appreciation for their surroundings. Other characteristics include democratic character structures, brotherly love, creativity, and the ability to develop intimate personal relationships.

While Maslow's theory has focused for the most part on the adult personality, its basic thrust—and that of the humanistic approach in general—has recently been applied to children. More adults, especially educators, are beginning to realize the value of stressing individual uniqueness and helping youngsters to maximize their human potential. Carl Rogers, for example, has stressed the notion of establishing in children a positive acceptance of one's total being (Rogers, 1961). Such humanistic orientations in understanding early growth and development may help us create environments that nurture and foster the youngster's intrinsic creative forces (Crain, 1980).

Putting Theories Together

The theories discussed in this chapter have provided numerous answers about the nature of childhood behavior. However, we must stress that these theoretical positions do not have to be examined or weighed in an either-or manner. They are not mutually exclusive or independent of one another. Several of them may be operating at different times or under different conditions. For example, the fact that a child may be at a specific stage of Piaget's cognitive development theory does not mean that principles of reinforcement are not operating or that the youngster's acquisition of knowledge is not being shaped by observational learning. Thus, while each theory is an effort to explain behavior, it is not uncommon for two or more of them to be operating simultaneously.

This is the primary reason why many students and professors choose to be eclectic in developing their own theories. They pick and choose the bits and pieces of theories that they can accept and then develop their own theoretical judgments about child behavior. The primary responsibility of a textbook is to present all aspects of a theory objectively so that such judgments can be made. We hope that as you read this text, you will gain insight into the theoretical positions that are currently held by most developmentalists.

Finally, while each of the theories has broadened our horizons and uncovered new areas of exploration, we have not yet been able to answer all our questions about childhood development. Some issues remain elusive to theoretical explanation. For example, one seemingly unanswerable question is: What is the nature of a child's interaction with the environment? Psychoanalytic and behaviorist theorists view the child as maintaining a passive role and being continually shaped by the environment. Others, like Jean Piaget, believe children to be active participants in the environment, curiously seeking out the experiences and artifacts that interest them and avoiding those that do not. Still others believe the child's interaction with the environment to be a combination of these two positions. Issues such as these underscore the need for further investigation, as well as for reassessment of our "facts" and theories.

Summary

Andrea, age 6

This chapter has examined six contemporary theories of human development. Each emphasizes different aspects of growth and development, but all of them have enhanced our understanding of human development.

One of the leading schools of thought in contemporary developmental psychology is the cognitive approach. Swiss psychologist Jean Piaget has been most active in this area and has offered perhaps the most influential theory. He postulates that intellectual maturity is achieved through five orderly and distinct stages of development, including the sensorimotor stage (age 0 to 2), the stage of preconceptual thought (2 to 4), the stage of intuitive thought (4 to 7), the stage of concrete operations (7 to 11), and the stage of formal operations (11 to 15).

The psychoanalytic school of thought, initially proposed by Sigmund Freud and further developed by Erik Erikson, emphasizes the importance of personality development. Freud emphasized psychosexual stages of growth and the continual interaction of the id, ego, and superego. His psychosexual stages include the oral stage (infancy to toddlerhood), the anal and phallic stages (early childhood), the latency period (middle childhood), and the genital stage (adolescence).

Erik Erikson, a neo-Freudian, has postulated eight crises of personality development that must be resolved. Erikson's theory includes the stages of trust versus mistrust, autonomy versus shame or doubt (infancy and toddlerhood), initiative versus guilt (early childhood), industry versus inferiority (school-aged childhood), identity versus role confusion (adolescence), intimacy versus isolation (young adulthood), generativity versus self-absorption (middle adulthood), and integrity versus despair (old age).

Another school of thought is behaviorism, which has its roots in Pavlov's classical conditioning. The early experiments done by Pavlov on dogs inspired John Broadus Watson (father of behaviorism) to prove that humans could also be conditioned. His "Little Albert" experiment demonstrates his theory. More recently, behaviorism has been significantly modified and formulated by B. F. Skinner. Today behaviorism is synonymous with operant conditioning. The detailed experimentation of B. F. Skinner not only kept behaviorism alive but brought it to the forefront of American psychology. Skinner's investigations have clarified the nature of positive and negative reinforcement and have shed some light on punishment. Skinner's theories on conditioning have been named operant and instrumental conditioning. A practical extension of the Skinnerian reinforcement theory is called shaping behavior.

The research of Albert Bandura and other theorists has led to the development of the social learning school of thought. This approach to developmental psychology emphasizes observational learning, imitation, and modeling. Proponents of the social learning school maintain that individuals are very likely to copy the behaviors of others they have observed in the environment.

Finally, this chapter has dealt with the ethological and humanistic schools of thought. Ethologists devote great effort to studying animals and humans in their natural settings by means of naturalistic observation. Researchers such as Konrad Lorenz and John Bowlby have sought to demonstrate the applications that animal studies may have in our quest to understand human behavior. Humanists such as Abraham Maslow and Carl Rogers have emphasized individual uniqueness and strivings for self-actualization. Maslow has been particularly active in the latter area, developing a hierarchy of needs that progresses from basic needs to full self-actualization. Humanistic psychologists believe it is critical to create environments that foster a person's inner potential and creativity.

Suggested Reading List

Crain, W. C. *Theories of Development: Concepts and Applications.* Englewood Cliffs, N.J.: Prentice-Hall, 1980. One of the more comprehensive texts on theories. A clear writing style blends nicely with an outstanding overview of the major developmental psychology theories.

Thomas, R. M. *Comparing Theories of Child Development*, 2nd ed. Belmont, Calif.: Wadsworth, 1984. A well-integrated and careful comparison of the major theories in child psychology today. Especially well done are chapters on social learning theory, humanism, and operant conditioning.

Wadsworth, B. J. *Piaget's Theory of Cognitive and Affective Development*, 3rd ed. New York: Longman, 1984. A good presentation of Piagetian theory; includes many applied examples.

Chapter Three

Childhood through the Ages: A Psychosocial History

If you wish to study men, you must not neglect to mix with the society of children.

Jesse Torrey

Introduction

In today's society, most of the middle classes of Western civilization view infants and small children as little people that need aid, attention, and comfort whenever possible. Parental love, empathy, and understanding are viewed as essential ingredients in the care and treatment that children should receive. Yet, history reveals that these attitudes began emerging only during the last century. Before that time many youngsters were exposed to a childhood that could only be described as harsh, heartless, even brutal. Relationships between adult and child were more functional than loving (Suransky, 1982), and physical punishment of children was not disapproved (McCoy, 1983).

To comprehend and appreciate the nature of contemporary childhood, we must examine the various civilizations of humanity. By so doing, we will be able to examine the child in relation to historical, social, and cultural forces. This analysis will reveal that child-rearing practices reflect a society's place in time as well as its attitudes, beliefs, and customs. It will also help us understand how today's concept of childhood slowly evolved and gain a perspective on modern understanding, care, and treatment. As child advocates we may learn to avoid past mistakes, borrow what was good, and continue to examine modern child-rearing practices (Plumb, 1971; McCoy, 1983).

Past and Present Trends

One of the more interesting and obvious features about childhood as it existed in the past is that certain child-rearing practices appear to be recurrent. This is important, since child rearing is, at least in part, a practical extension of society's beliefs and viewpoints regarding the nature and purpose of youngsters.

The Child as a Miniature Adult

One recurrent practice was the training and indoctrination of young children into a designated skill. This training generally occurred between 6 and 9, when children were considered adults. Before the age of 6, children were viewed as infants and were left at home in their mother's care. An important facet of the child's household upbringing was learning the accepted mores, folkways, and basic rules of society—a process we now call **socialization.**

In many cultures the stage of childhood, between infancy and adulthood, simply did not exist. A baby outgrew infancy and either directly joined the adult world as a laborer or entered adulthood after a relatively short vocational training period. Consequently, children were frequently viewed (and portrayed in pictures) as miniature adults. In addition to working alongside grown-ups, children usually engaged in the same activities as adults, such as dancing, singing, or going to the market. Clothing was usually identical for adult and child.

Accounts of childhood, especially during the Middle Ages, pose semantical problems. The term *youth*, for example, generally signified the prime of life and in some cultures was immediately succeeded by old age. There were no terms for the developmental stages that we refer to today as middle childhood and adolescence. Interestingly, *infant* was a term applied not only to the newborn but to any child approaching "adulthood," which often commenced at age 7:

> In medieval society the idea of childhood did not exist; this is not to suggest that children were neglected, forsaken or despised. The idea of childhood is not to be confused with affection for children: It corresponds to an awareness of the particular nature of childhood, that particular nature which distinguishes the child from the adult, even the young adult. In medieval society this awareness was lacking. That is why, as soon as the child could live without the constant solicitude of his mother, his nanny or his cradle-rocker, he belonged to adult society (Aries, 1962, p. 128).

Education as a Luxury

The time of childhood did not begin to lengthen until the division of labor reached a level of complexity great enough to require increased education or training. Thus, the advent of more formal schooling helped to produce a new period of development in the child's life, and a second behavioral practice emerged: Children who came from wealthier families learned a skill or trade. In almost all cases, only boys received this formal education. For a long period, only wealthier families could afford formal and advanced educational experiences for their children.

From ages 6 to 9, most children, especially those born of peasant stock, were put to work in the fields or in the master's house, where boys learned the routines of farming or hunting for food and girls were taught cooking and weaving. At an early age, children of both sexes were expected to make meaningful and productive contributions to the household.

Figure 3.1 Education used to be regarded as a luxury. (The Bettman Archive, Inc.)

Emphasis on Male Physical Fitness

A third viewpoint and practice was the emphasis placed on the physical indoctrination of boys into manhood. While girls remained at home and were taught domestic skills, boys received rigorous physical training. The boys' entry into manhood was usually an elaborate, intricate, and sometimes painful ordeal. Such practice was designed to test the males' endurance and tolerance of pain. Initiation rites signifying formal induction into manhood are still practiced in some civilizations today, although in less brutal form (Plumb, 1971).

For many cultures, physical training meant instructing boys in the "manly arts." In addition to rigorous physical fitness instruction, boys received intense military instruction and training to prepare them for their roles in the many battles that virtually every country experienced. Heroes were (and sometimes still are) frequently made on the battlefield or in the sports arena. History's "boy" generals, emperors, kings, and athletes are testimony to the traditional emphasis on physical fitness and their recognition as adults in the community.

Infanticide

One of the more tragic recurrent behavioral practices was **infanticide,** the murder of babies, especially those deemed weak or deformed. Infanticide, which was practiced by several cultures, including Oriental, Greek, Spartan, and Roman civilizations, reveals how children were viewed as a practical commodity to the community. If a child could not serve the needs of the community, it was killed, either by the sword or by abandonment. Instances of infanticide still haunt us today. With alarming regularity, the media inform us of infants killed or abandoned by their parents.

Child Abuse

Infanticide is but one example of the harsh and often brutal treatment of children throughout history. Many civilizations believed in whipping and beating children, sometimes with instruments that we would associate with torture chambers. Beatings for youngsters began as early as infancy, persisted throughout childhood, and were frequently severe enough to shed blood or cause bruising (de Mause, 1975, 1974).

Why were children the objects of such brutality? Historians cite numerous reasons, including the caregiver's burning desire to foster such qualities as submissiveness, obedience, and reverence for adult demands and wishes. Another factor, though, has often been labeled the key contributing cause. Prior to the eighteenth century, children were perceived as "inherently sinful," that is, born with original sin.

Many parents believed that children were evil and that the devil had to be beaten out of them. Fortunately, such beliefs began to subside by the eighteenth century, and children began to receive more humane care and treatment as well as more love and affection.

Children of Ancient Times

Ancient Greece

Sparta   In the small, isolated Greek city state of Sparta, an ancestral tradition of military preparation and a strict social code prevailed. Children were brought up under rigid disciplinary measures and were viewed as necessary for the continued existence of Spartan civilization in the Hellenic world. Upon birth, parents had to have the child's health status examined by a council of elders. Babies pronounced in good health were adopted by the state but left in the mother's care until 7 years of age. If the child displayed any signs of physical weakness or deformity, however, infanticide was mandated.

In most families, boys and girls grew up together under the supervision of the mother, but in wealthy families, an older house slave cared for the young. Discipline and development of the mind and body began shortly after birth. Swaddling was not permitted by the state, since it was thought to hamper physical growth. Children left alone in the dark were not permitted to scream or cry out, and harsh punitive discipline was commonplace.

At 7 years of age, boys began receiving formal education, while girls remained at home. Removed to the state's barracks where they were issued light clothing and a straw bed, the boys of Sparta were divided into companies, usually of 60 members each. They underwent intense physical training to become disciplined and brave warriors. Subjected to the elements and frequently beaten with rods to develop their "masculinity" and endurance, they were driven to harden their bodies through calisthenics, running, and other vigorous forms of activity. This training continued until they reached 18, at which time they began two additional years of intense military training, which included an increased emphasis on skilled fighting and marching tactics. Upon completion of this advanced training, the Spartan warrior was subjected to ten years of active military service.

Athens   Like the Spartans, the Athenians examined infants at birth and left them to die of exposure to the elements if they were unfit or deformed. During early childhood the Athenians emphasized the importance of physical fitness; however, it took the form of gymnastics rather than military skills. Unlike the Spartans, the Athenians sought to educate the mind as well as the body. Greater responsibility and authority were given to the parents in regard to a child's upbringing. For example, the father, not the state, decided whether an infant should live or die, and Athenian parents were not required to send their boys away for military training.

The Athenian boy's formal education began at age 7, when the parents selected a teacher. Education concentrated on three primary areas: music, letters (reading, writing, and arithmetic), and gymnastics. Each of these, it was hoped, would stimulate and discipline the child physically and intellectually, enabling him to emerge as a well-integrated individual. At the age of 15, elementary education ended, and whether studies would continue became a financial issue; if a family was wealthy enough, the boy could further his education.

Ancient Rome

In Rome, the success of a marriage usually depended on the birth of a boy. Large families were encouraged, particularly during the rule of Augustus Caesar, who offered material rewards to the parents who could bring three children into the world. If this goal was attained, the mother was given full legal independence, and the father usually received some form of promotion in his career.

Like earlier civilizations, the Romans had no use for weak or deformed children, since they could not be counted on for future civilian manpower or service in the army. When such children were born, the parents generally decided upon infanticide, usually after consultation with five neighbors, who had to agree for the parents' sentence to be carried out. Until the fourth century A.D., neither public opinion nor the law found infanticide morally wrong.

The children of Rome grew up chiefly under the mother's care. At 6 years of age, however, a boy's father began to teach him to be a respectful citizen, to till the ground, and to carry arms. Fathers stressed physical fitness, teaching their boys to endure heat and cold and to survive physical hardships. Girls were instructed by the mother, learning primarily how to prepare food and make clothing.

Before the collapse of the Roman republic, some children (usually the wealthy, since Rome, unlike Greece, never established a national educational system) were placed under the individual supervision of schoolmasters. The manner in which the lessons of the day were handed down from teacher to student must have been difficult to endure. Beginning their school day shortly after dawn, pupils frequently fell victim to the corrective measures of canings or floggings with a leather whip. Only in later Rome, particularly under Quintilian (35–95 A.D.), was this brutal treatment prohibited.

Children of the Middle Ages (500–1400 A.D.)

Two important factors deeply affected child-rearing practices during the Middle Ages. The first was the belief that the child was inherently sinful. Because the church taught that all children were born wicked and sinful, it was considered not only justifiable but also right and appropriate to punish youngsters physically as often as possible. Adults believed that children who behaved badly were expressing the results of innate sin; consequently the devil had to be literally driven from the body. Parents who neglected their duty to punish their children earned the disapproval of their more-Christian neighbors who conscientiously beat the devil out of their kids. Thus, both children and adults were affected by the religious teachings of the day, and their alliance in the fear of Satan and the hope of salvation mirrored the social organization of the time (Kessen, 1978).

The second factor was the relinquishment or, in some cases, actual abandonment of their children by many parents. Many children were sold as slaves or abandoned to monasteries or nunneries. Most commonly though, relinquishment took the form of sending the infant or young child away to live with a wet nurse (a woman who breast-feeds other women's children) for two to four years. At the customary age of 7 the child was sent away again to receive some type of formal education or specialized training. Both practices, which were usually reserved for wealthier families, show how little time many parents spent in raising their young.

Children of the Renaissance and Reformation (Fourteenth through Seventeenth Centuries)

During the periods known as the Renaissance and the Reformation, children born in northern Europe experienced a social milieu undergoing sweeping religious, moral, and social changes, including vast increases in commerce and wealth, great intellectual advancements, and the establishment of protestantism. However, adults continued to view children as economic necessities, needed manpower to maintain maximum agricultural yield or continue a family trade or business. With skilled merchants in constant demand, many children were taught the practical aspects of a given trade. Many children were apprenticed— sent to live in homes of middle-class citizens willing to teach a particular trade—a practice that bears obvious similarities to the relinquishment custom of the Middle Ages.

The standard established school of the day had a wider variety of course offerings than previous schools. Although strict discipline still prevailed, particularly in the form of "whipping by the birch," students received an advanced and fairly diversified education. Over a period of nine to ten years, pupils studied the works of ancient classical writers, particularly Aristotle, Plato, and Cicero. Emphasis was placed on the arts, politics, geometry, ethics, and games and sports, which were recognized as an important aspect of the child's overall development.

Changing Perspectives on Childhood: From Inherent Evil to Inherent Goodness

By the eighteenth century, attitudes concerning the inherent qualities of children had begun to change. Two philosophers, John Locke and Jean Jacques Rousseau, offered new and challenging ideas on the nature of the child.

John Locke (1632–1704) viewed children in a new way, claiming that they were not inherently sinful but were products of societal influences that determined the qualities of goodness or evil. Concerning himself with the mind and mental attitudes, Locke emphasized that the most powerful shapers of childhood behavior were esteem and disgrace. By using these incentives, beating or chiding a child could be avoided. "Respect your child," Locke wrote, "reward him with praise and punish him with neglect or contempt and the child will behave accordingly."

Locke also theorized that infants have unformed minds that do not possess innate knowledge. The blank infant mind, termed *tabula rasa* by Locke, is a receptacle for sensory information. In this way, experiences are recorded and mental impressions are left behind. Locke further believed that the child was governed by strong passions or emotions. He maintained that it was the duty and obligation of rational members of society to create an environment capable of transmitting proper experiences to the child. He also felt that specific behaviors could be produced when parents and teachers supplied appropriate rewards. In addition, Locke stressed the importance of practice and drill in such learning tasks as math, scriptures, the alphabet, and even toilet training.

Jean Jacques Rousseau (1712–1778) viewed childhood as a positive rather than a negative state. He emphasized the importance of adult empathy, understanding, and compassion in meeting children's needs. Like Locke, Rousseau viewed children as unformed adults, born with no knowledge and having very little mental life of their own.

In 1762, Rousseau wrote the classic *Emile,* in which he voiced his observations and concerns about the nature of childhood and the treatment and education accorded to youngsters. In his tale of Emile, a young boy representative of all the children he had tutored, Rousseau described life stages from the first year of life to adulthood.

During the first year of life, Rousseau perceived the child as having no ideas, will, or habits. While adults generally attempted immediately to mold the unformed child, Rousseau believed that the child's own nature would guide him. During the second stage (ages 1–12), Rousseau believed that nature continued to provide the guidelines, and the role of a tutor was to prevent harmful influences, such as meddling adults, from influencing the child.

By the third stage (ages 12–15), Rousseau said, the mind is filled with many years of experience. During the early periods of this stage, Emile operated at a practical level of reasoning, but he progressed to a higher mental level and periodically applied abstract reasoning to quantity, number, and spatial tasks. Rousseau was opposed to pure book learning at this time, but he encouraged Emile to read Defoe's *Robinson Crusoe,* which he used as a lifetime model and inspiration for young Emile.

In the fourth stage (age 15 through adulthood), Rousseau encouraged Emile to widen his social contacts, gave him books to read, and imparted more formal instruction, confronting him with religious, ethical, and political issues. Because his tutor had prevented him from listening to adult opinion on these issues, Emile was now free to develop his own ideas. During the final stage (the early twenties), Emile traveled in order to learn of other cultures, married, and raised his son as he had been raised.

Emile was Rousseau's attempt to show that children are different from adults and should be treated as unique individuals. He emphasized that we must respect their rights, thoughts, and feelings. When children are allowed to follow nature's path of development, maintained Rousseau, they will seek out experiences that are important and beneficial. Strong in his belief that children were corrupted by the nature of the civilization into which they were thrust, and firmly against the rote style of learning prevalent in his day, Rousseau argued that children can learn more effectively through a process of reasoning, self-realization, and insight.

The ideas of Locke and Rousseau were progressive, and both managed to gain support from some factions and to provoke opposition from others. Denunciations came from those firmly convinced that the child was inherently sinful, such as colonial America's religious leader,

Jonathan Edwards. Rousseau's ideas aroused considerable controversy and rejection, including the condemnation of his works by the Parliament of France. Despite these criticisms, Rousseau's and Locke's views came to be shared by other philosophers and educators. Thus began a movement that would place the child in a new and more favorable perspective.

Children of the Eighteenth and Nineteenth Centuries

We now move our brief survey from eighteenth-century Europe to colonial America, where children were viewed less as evil creatures with only functional value and more as objects of love, care, and affection. To their customary responsibilities parents began to add sensitivity and understanding. However, they expected strict obedience from their children, who could expect harsh punishment for misconduct.

Physical abuse was no stranger to colonial America, and childhood at this time was a generally rugged experience full of physical hardships. Families were large, and children were expected to make

Figure 3.2 Home life in colonial America. Physical hardships abounded and everyone, children included, was expected to make contributions to the household. (The Bettman Archive, Inc.)

meaningful contributions to the household. As such, they were viewed as economic assets and vital components of the family enterprise.

The Impact of the Industrial Revolution

By the late nineteenth century, the old colonial family started to vanish as America experienced industrialization and urbanization. Families now seldom worked together as productive agrarian units as they once had. Children's functions changed, even in those families that remained on the farm. Mechanization gradually made farming an enterprise for adolescents and adults. In many middle-class families, the father now went off to work in an industrial setting, while the mother and children remained at home.

The industrial revolution thus brought about an important shift in role responsibilities within the family. Once partners in labor in colonial families, women were now assigned to the home and hearth. Employment outside the home and away from the family became the province of the male. It can be said that the industrial revolution brought about significant changes in sex role behaviors and expectations (Kessen, 1978).

The industrial revolution did not produce a role realignment in all families, though. In many lower-class families both parents and children (boys and girls) worked long hours, often leaving at dawn for the factories and returning home at sunset.

In general, we can see a major shift in the perception of children as America experienced its industrial revolution. Children had been needed hands on the farm and could be counted on to make worthwhile and productive contributions. Now they became economic liabilities, more mouths to feed. Work and family life became separate enterprises; families were consuming as units but did not produce as units (Saal, 1982).

As the industrial revolution continued, several other interesting childhood developments emerged. Children began remaining home in the family setting beyond the ages of 7 to 10. They also became the objects of a new type of sentimentality. Caring for children became a central concern, particularly for women. Many adults became committed to child-rearing and the concept of parenting. As children became older, school began to exert more influence on their lives. This latter point is part of a much larger theme that would have implications for children of the twentieth century; that is, parents again began to relinquish to other adults the guidance, instruction, nurturing, stimulation, and protection of their youngsters. Whereas the family was once the primary socialization agent, other institutions, such as schools, church youth groups, and Sunday schools, now played a role in the child's development.

Physical punishment of the child has been common throughout history, both at home and school. (The Bettman Archive, Inc.)

Child Labor in the Nineteenth Century

In the 1800s it was not uncommon to find 4-year-olds at work in the canning factories of New York State or to see 5- and 6-year-old girls working night shifts in southern cotton mills. Following the Civil War, the South was especially noted for using child laborers. One source (Osborn, 1980) proposes that nearly 80 percent of the mill workers during this time were 14 or younger. Overall, textile mills ranked high among the industries employing young children, as did glass factories, collieries, and wood-working plants.

Children as young as 8 or 9 worked over 12 hours a day; many never had the opportunity to see the sun rise or set. Little or no regard was given to their health and safety. Injuries and deaths were commonplace, especially in the mines, and food and water provisions were kept at a minimum. Children were beaten if their productivity slackened. At the end of each day, the children dragged themselves home with nothing but pennies to compensate their efforts.

By the mid 1800s, politicians in many states had become concerned with the child's welfare in such working situations and had enacted legislation to improve conditions. For example, in 1887 Alabama legislators passed a law that prohibited the employment of children

Figure 3.3 Child labor was widespread in factories and industries during America's early stages of industrialization. The hours were long, the working conditions hazardous, and the pay pitifully low. (The Bettman Archive, Inc.)

under 14 years of age for more than eight hours a day. New Jersey passed similar legislation in 1903, and other states followed. Despite the fact that such laws were slow in coming and not as far-reaching or restrictive as one might expect, this legislation marked the beginning of active efforts to protect children from exploitation. For thousands of children, it would put an end to bitter cries and nightmares associated with deplorable and frightening working conditions.

Contemporary Childhood

Like so many of their historical counterparts, the children of the twentieth century are shaped and molded by numerous cultural and family influences. In the early 1900s, democratic values became societal goals in this country, and we witnessed an increased trend toward caring and providing for our young. The education, health, and well-being of our children became goals of paramount importance. More than ever before, parents attached themselves emotionally to their children, retaining them as intimate members of the household for 16 or 18 years, rather than the 7 or 8 years customary in the past. The periods of infancy and early, middle, and late childhood began to be recognized as separate stages of development with unique needs. Consequently, the meanings of childhood and parenthood have changed, not to mention the sense of family (Solnit, 1976).

The Child and the Modern Family

The modern family is dramatically different from that of the past. One of the most striking changes is in family size. In 1790 the first census revealed that 36 percent of American households consisted of seven or more people: generally father, mother, and five or more children. Today there are just about two children per household, and many couples choose childless marriages. Demographers predict that by 1990 there will be approximately 60 million American homes with no children under the age of 15 (U.S. Bureau of the Census, 1984; Masnick and Bane, 1980).

Among the reasons for having fewer children are concern about overpopulation, greater numbers of women pursuing careers, the greater diversity of contraceptives now available, and the legalization of abortion. The primary reason for this decrease in family size, however, may be that the economic value of children has changed. Once an economic benefit, children have become an economic liability. Today, the total cost of housing, feeding, clothing, and educating one child through college is between $80,000 and $150,000 (Price, 1982). As schooling has lengthened, the financial drain may be prolonged to over 20 years, and there is no immediate, tangible return on the investment. Children today must be loved and wanted for reasons other than the work they can perform.

Another difference in the modern family is its mobility. In the past a person could expect to be born, raised, and die in pretty much the same geographical location. This physical permanence was caused by a number of factors, including the independent and self-sufficient nature of towns and villages and the fact that many children were groomed to take over the family enterprise. If one did venture away, it was usually for only a short distance to gain local employment.

The twin forces of industrialization and urbanization have created an increasingly mobile family unit today. The contemporary family is likely to change its residence as often as career and economic needs dictate. One source (Coleman, 1984) estimates that most modern American families move once every five years. This means that each year 15 million families, including 30 million children, must say goodbye to friends and adjust to new neighborhoods and schools. Adaptation and adjustment to such residential instability becomes an important challenge for children.

Rather than establish a residence on either the father's or the mother's side of the family, many families today settle down in a location largely determined by economic or career reasons. Moving away from one's network of relatives has changed the family's basic structure. The large, geographically stable family of the past frequently included parents, offspring, grandparents, and other relatives all living under the same roof (the extended family). Today's family is more likely to include only the parents and offspring (the nuclear family).

The modern family has also changed activities within the household. Perhaps the most pronounced change is the emergence of dual-career households. Many children today have both mother and father working outside the household. Mothers of preschool children and younger are currently the fastest-growing segment of the workforce (Zigler and Muenchow, 1983), and over half the mothers of school-age children work outside the home.

Other roles and activities within the family of the 1980s are also changing. Unlike the rigidly sex-stereotyped families of the past, modern families are more androgynous or unisexual in their orientation to domestic tasks. As a result, the operation of many homes today is based on mutuality and reciprocity. Whereas children once recognized the father as the sole authority figure and decision maker, today they see their parents sharing these responsibilities. This arrangement has obvious implications for such issues as discipline, sex education, and other child-rearing topics.

In light of rising divorce rates, our discussion of the modern family would be incomplete without some mention of marital dissolution. Marital disharmony and collapse did occur in the past, but it was rare. The ancient Hebrews and Greeks, for example, had provisions for divorce, as did the Romans. The settlers in colonial America were also entitled to divorce but rarely took advantage of this provision. Between 1639 and 1692, only 25 divorces were granted in the entire state of Massachusetts (Nass and McDonald, 1983). In contrast, it is now estimated that over 1 million children each year will see their parents' marriages end in divorce. Such children become members of blended families (stepfamilies) or live in a single-parent family. Either way, the challenge of adjustment is formidable.

Overall, this discussion has illustrated the many changes associated with the modern family. Let us add that the contemporary child is exposed to new social pressures and areas of uncertainty outside the family. Some child psychologists, such as David Elkind (1981a), feel that today's children are a hurried breed, pushed by adults to succeed and plagued with fears of failure. Others, such as Neil Postman (1982) and Marie Winn (1983), feel that the very concept of childhood is eroding. They see television as the primary culprit. Many children simply cannot escape the clutches of television. As a result, the once protective cocoon of childhood is penetrated by a vast array of violence, explicit sex, and other adult themes. This type of exposure robs many youngsters of their childhood and forces them to grow up before their time.

Persistent Problems and Trends

Many of today's children unquestionably have more advantages than children at any other moment in the past. The quality of life available to them is unsurpassed. Uncounted billions of dollars are spent on children's education, government programs, fashionable clothing, toys and games, and various types of recreation. In the United States, early childhood education programs are rapidly increasing and special education intervention for exceptional children is now part of many school systems. Whereas education was once restricted to children from affluent families, almost all children attend school today.

Children's general health is also better today than at any other point in history. This is largely due to the wider availability of health care, advances in medical science, better nutrition, and improved socioeconomic conditions. Medical science has been particularly effective in eradicating or markedly reducing many of childhood's major diseases. Smallpox, historically a dreaded disease responsible for the deaths of countless children, has now been eliminated worldwide. The vast majority of youngsters in the United States today are immunized against the major childhood diseases by the time they enter school.

Despite all the advancements of the twentieth century, however, today's children are still plagued with situations needing continued attention. Adequate medical care and social service intervention still escape the poor and underprivileged in this country. The poor are still especially vulnerable to acute and chronic diseases. Millions of American children remain malnourished. Infanticide, neglect, and abuse still exist in epidemic proportions.

In addition to these problems, modern children and their parents face hitherto unknown anxieties created by an increasingly complex society (LeMasters and DeFrain, 1983). The services and luxuries available today, in particular, are a mixed blessing. Much of what we consider the birthright of our children was simply unknown to our forebears. The issue of expectations and needs in childhood has changed significantly in scope and meaning (Suransky, 1982; Sommerville, 1982).

In the face of all this change, it is interesting to note that functional equivalents of earlier behavioral practices still persist. For example, while children are not sent out to wet nurses at birth or to be servants or apprentices at an early age, we do relinquish them to nurseries, teachers, camps, and babysitters for significant portions of their lives. Other outside sources, such as peers, video games, and extracurricular activities, draw children away from parents. This increasing influence of outside sources and the diminishing influence of parents are areas of concern for many (Brofenbrenner, 1981; Levine, 1981).

Another persistent behavioral practice is sex-role stereotyping. While gains have been made in deemphasizing sex-role stereotyping in contemporary society, traditional attitudes toward expected sex behaviors abound. Furthermore, sex discrimination in all phases of life has not evaporated. Traditional sex-role stereotyping appears to be a reflection of deeply rooted attitudes.

Finally, certain types of educational experiences are still available only to the wealthy. We do have public education, but the wealthy are often the only beneficiaries of diverse educational opportunities apart from the public sphere, including private nursery schools, preparatory schools, and college.

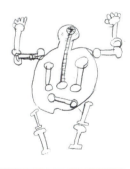

Kirk, age 6 years

Summary

The concept of childhood as we know it today is a fairly recent historical development. The study of childhood, as well as child-rearing practices, tells us much about a given society's overall attitudes, customs, and life conditions. This is true for past civilizations as well as for modern times.

In the past, childhood was frequently harsh and brutal, and children's work was usually equivalent to that of adults. Five behavioral practices appear to be consistent throughout most of history. These are training and indoctrinating children into their designated skills between the ages of 6 and 9, reserving formal education to children from wealthy families, emphasizing physical indoctrination of boys into manhood (especially physical training and weaponry skills), infanticide, and child abuse. These behavioral practices underscore the functional value placed on children throughout history.

Ancient civilizations such as Sparta and Rome attempted to breed young warriors to protect their nations. Others, like Athens, sought to stimulate their children intellectually. Physical fitness was strongly emphasized by all these civilizations, and all practiced infanticide on infants deemed weak or deformed.

Two developments characterized the Middle Ages. First, the child was believed to be inherently sinful. This justified physical punishment to "drive the devil" from the child's body. The second development was the parental practice of relinquishing or abandoning their children. The poor sold their children as slaves or left them for adoption; the middle-class and wealthy sent them to a wet nurse for their formative years and then apprenticed or sent them to school at age 7.

In the eighteenth century, the efforts of such figures as John Locke and Jean Jacques Rousseau gradually shifted social attitudes toward children, who began to be perceived as inherently good and the proper objects of parental attention and affection. In agricultural colonial America, children were economic assets as they worked with their parents to cultivate the land. The shift to urbanization and industrialization made children economic liabilities as work became an adult enterprise outside the family. Children who had to ease the economic plight of the family by working encountered deplorable and frightening working conditions.

The nineteenth century brought other changes to the concept of childhood. Youngsters increasingly remained home beyond the customary age of 7 to 9. More women became committed to the practice of child rearing, and school began to exert more of an influence on the lives of children. Parents again began to let other adults—such as educators, church, and civic group leaders—guide, instruct, and protect their young.

The modern family is smaller than its historical counterparts, highly mobile, and nuclear in scope. Furthermore, there is more than a remote possibility that both parents are working, a trend necessitating child-care assistance outside the home. In many contemporary households sex-role differences are deemphasized in favor of a division of labor and responsibilities based on mutuality and reciprocity. The high divorce rates in today's society are a key social problem facing the family of the 1980s.

Because of advances in medical science, wider availability of health care, better nutrition, and improved socioeconomic conditions, today's child is likely to be healthier than children at any other point in history. Medical science has conquered most of childhood's major diseases, but nagging problems still persist, including malnourishment, infanticide, neglect, and abuse. Poor, disadvantaged, and minority children are especially vulnerable to these problems.

Suggested Reading List

Aries, P. *Centuries of Childhood.* New York: Knopf, 1962. This book is written by one of the world's foremost authorities on the nature of childhood throughout history. Aries provides an extensive investigation into the philosophies, theories, and treatments of children through the ages.

Elkind, D. *The Hurried Child: Growing Up Too Fast Too Soon.* Reading, Mass.: Addison-Wesley, 1981. This thought-provoking book examines the pressures of modern life on the child. Especially interesting is Elkind's notion that we sometimes unwittingly pressure youngsters to succeed and promote fear of failure.

Kessen, W. *The Child.* New York: Wiley, 1965. Considered by many to be a classic of its kind, this book offers a compendium of writings by such early thinkers as Rousseau, Locke, Darwin, and Watson. The book is designed to give students a perspective on various views, attitudes, and beliefs regarding the developing child.

Postman, N. *The Disappearance of Childhood.* New York: Delacorte Press, 1982. One of Postman's many contentions is that today's electronic media—most notably television—have eroded childhood and integrated children into the grown-up world too soon.

Part Two
Infancy and Toddlerhood

Chapter Four

Prenatal Life

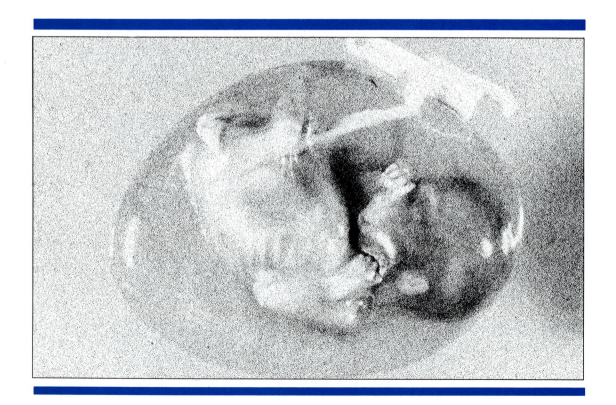

A babe in the house is a well-spring of pleasure.

Martin F. Tupper

Introduction

A child is born—we call it the miracle of birth. Yet far more remarkable than the birth itself is the process by which a single fertilized egg develops into a fully functioning infant—complete with arms, legs, nose, eyes, ears, internal organs, and an individual personality. The key to this magnificent story is a special code contained in the chromosomes located in the nucleus of each cell. This code, unique to every individual, is just now being understood by scientists. The chromosomes contain a "set of blueprints" that direct the cell to multiply itself many times and eventually become a fully developed organism. Each species of plant and animal and every individual within a species has a full set of directions locked inside its cells' nuclei. This genetic code is what makes a mouse different from a bird, a flower different from a tree, and siblings different from each other.

Because the field of psychology is mainly interested in the processes by which genetics affect behavior, most students need not know all the ongoing biochemical processes that occur in the cell. They should, however, possess a basic knowledge of the fundamental principles of **anatomy** and **physiology,** as well as an elemental understanding of **genetics** and **heredity** if they are to understand how a single cell develops into a complex organism.

Genetics: The Basics of Life

The Onset of Pregnancy

Alternately each month (approximately halfway through the 28-day menstrual cycle) one of the **ovaries** in the human female releases a mature egg, or **ovum**, which contains chromosomes. This discharged ovum begins a week's journey along the 4-inch **fallopian tube** into the uterus, where the uterine walls have been accumulating a large supply of blood vessels to nourish the egg should it be fertilized; if the ovum remains unfertilized, it continues past the uterus and degenerates (see Figure 4.1). Meanwhile, the uterine walls, gorged with blood vessels, also begin disintegrating, and the menstrual flow commences. However, if a **sperm** penetrates the ovum during an approximate 24-hour critical period while the ovum is in the fallopian tube, **conception** occurs (see Figure 4.2). The fertilized egg, containing its own 23 chromosomes plus the 23 chromosomes from the sperm, is now referred to as a **zygote.** It represents the onset of pregnancy and the genesis of a new life.

Figure 4.1 Graphic presentation of the relations existing between the cyclic events of the ovary and uterus and their relation to pregnancy. (Modified after Schröder in Arey, L. B. *Developmental Anatomy*, 8th ed. Philadelphia, Saunders, 1974.)

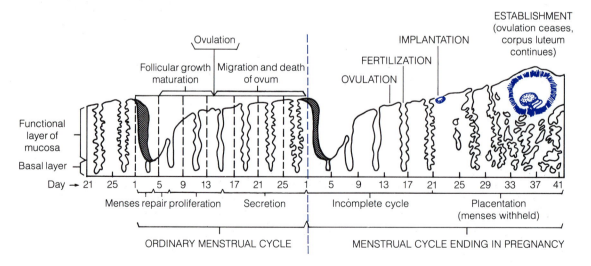

Multiple Conception: Twice upon a Time   Conception for the most part occurs when a single sperm cell penetrates the female ovum to create a zygote. As a result, a single child is conceived. However, more than one child can be created at one time, a phenomenon known as multiple conception.

Multiple conceptions are far rarer than singletons. Approximately 30,000 sets of twins are born in the United States each year. Twins occur approximately once in every 90 births; triplets about once in 9,300 births; quadruplets once in 490,000; and quintuplets once in every 55,000,000 births. In terms of cross-cultural differences, blacks give birth to the most twins, while Orientals give birth to the fewest.

These figures indicate that although the conception of twins is relatively infrequent, they are the most common of multiple births. Two major types of twins have been identified (Figure 4.3). **Identical** (monozygotic) **twins** result when a single fertilized egg splits after conception. Identical twins are genetically alike, including having the same physical characteristics such as sex, blood type, and eye color.

Fraternal twins (dizygotic) result when two female eggs are fertilized by two separate sperm cells. Fraternal twins are no more alike than

Figure 4.2 The first ten days from ovulation to implantation. (From Smith, D. W., Bierman, E. L., and Robinson, N. M., eds., *The Biologic Ages of Man*. Philadelphia, Saunders, 1978.)

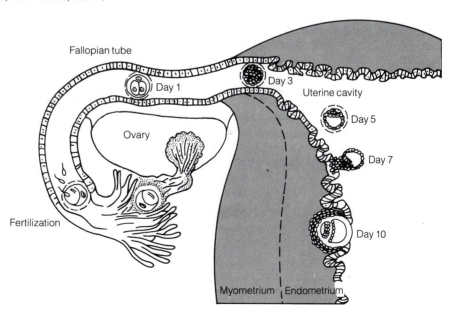

any two singletons born to the same parent. They may or may not be of the same sex, and each possesses individual characteristics. To determine whether twins are fraternal or identical, certain tests, such as fingerprinting or blood-typing, are undertaken (results should be the same for identical twins).

Cojoined (Siamese) twins are an obstetrical rarity. The ratio of Siamese to normal twin births is approximately 1 to 1,000. Siamese twins are always identical and usually female.

On the average, twins have a gestation period approximately 25 days shorter than normal. Almost half of all twin births are premature. The first twin is usually born head first, while the second is often a **breech** (buttocks first) **delivery** (Noble, 1980; Abbe and Gill, 1981).

Life in the Laboratory: The Test-Tube Baby   The concept behind the test-tube baby involves an intriguing medical procedure (see Figure 4.4) developed by British physicians Patrick Steptoe and Robert Edwards. First, an incision is made in the woman's abdomen. With a special device called a laparascope, an instrument designed by Steptoe, the physician is able to see inside the abdomen and remove the egg from the ovary. The egg is then placed in a dish, where it is fertilized with the male sperm. After this is done, the zygote (fertilized egg) is placed in

Figure 4.3 Fraternal twins (a) have separate placentas even though they come into close apposition. Identical twins (b) have one common placenta. (From Arey, L. B. *Developmental Anatomy*, 8th ed. Philadelphia, Saunders, 1974.)

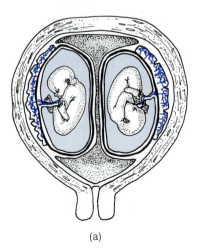

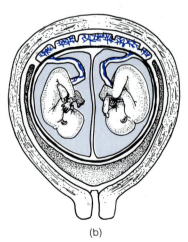

(a)   (b)

another dish of life-sustaining serum for approximately five days. Here it develops into a cluster of cells called a **blastocyte.** After the mother receives hormonal treatments to prepare the uterine wall for implantation, the blastocyte is placed in the uterus, where it embeds itself and continues its normal prenatal development. From conception in the laboratory, life continues in the womb of the mother.

Genetic Terminology

*   The biological symbol for male is ♂

*   The biological symbol for female is ♀

*   A **chromosome** (colored body) is a thin rodlike structure found within the nucleus. It contains small genetic units called **genes,** the true units of heredity.

*   A **dominant gene** is any gene that, when present, always expresses its hereditary characteristics. A capital letter is used to represent the dominant condition (e.g., B for brown eyes).

*   A **recessive gene** is a gene whose hereditary characteristics are present only when paired with another recessive gene. Its hereditary characteristics are not observable when paired with a

Figure 4.4 Fertilization of a test-tube baby. An ovum is removed from the ovary (1) and is fertilized in a dish (2). The resulting zygote is placed in a dish where it develops into a blastocyte (3), which is placed in the uterus (4).

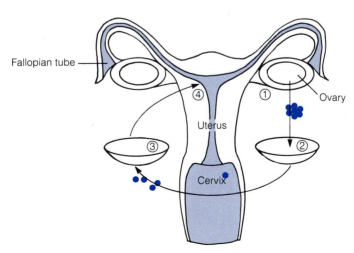

dominant gene. It is designated by the lowercase form of the letter that is used for dominance (e.g., b for hazel or blue eyes).

- **Homozygous** (sameness of genes) is the term for a condition in which both genes of a gene pair are identical for a given trait—both dominant or both recessive (e.g., BB or bb).

- **Heterozygous** (mixed or two types of genes) is the term for a condition in which each gene of a gene pair differs for a given trait (e.g., one dominant, one recessive gene, Bb).

- The visible, observable, or easily measurable appearance of an organism is its **phenotype.** A brown-eyed person is said to have a brown phenotype for eye color, while a blue-eyed person has a phenotype for blue eyes.

- The actual genetic makeup (gene pair) of an organism is his or her **genotype.** If the blue-eyed person has a bb gene pair, we can say his or her genotype is blue for both genes. When an organism exhibits a dominant phenotype we can only guess at the genotype. Are brown-eyed people genotypically BB or Bb? (They could be either.)

Figure 4.5 illustrates how genetic terminology is employed in charts known as **Punnett squares.**

Figure 4.5 In (a), all children born to this couple will have brown eyes but will be "carriers" (have recessive genes) for blue. In (b), two parents with brown eyes (their phenotype) may have a heterozygous genotype (Bb). If the recessive gene is present in an egg fertilized by a sperm carrying the recessive gene for blueness, the result can be a blue-eyed child. In theory, one-fourth of such children would have blue eyes.

♂ \ ♀	b	b
B	Bb genotype Brn. phenotype Heterozygous	Bb genotype Brn. phenotype Heterozygous
B	Bb genotype Brn. phenotype Heterozygous	Bb genotype Brn. phenotype Heterozygous

(a)

♂ \ ♀	B	b
B	BB genotype Brn. phenotype Homozygous	Bb genotype Brn. phenotype Heterozygous
b	Bb genotype Brn. phenotype Heterozygous	bb genotype Blue phenotype Homozygous

(b)

Cellular Organization

A **cell** is a living unit of organized material that contains a nucleus and is enclosed in a membrane. **Cytoplasm** is the substance found inside the cell but outside the nucleus; **nucleoplasm** refers to the substance found inside the nuclear membrane. Also in the cell are **ribosomes,** small particles in the cytoplasm that manufacture essential protein for the cell.

The **nucleus,** located in or near the center of the cell, is the control center for the cell's activity. Inside the nucleus are the chromosomes, which contain the directions for the cell's activity. Chromosomes occur in pairs, and the number varies according to species. For example, humans have 23 pairs of chromosomes per cell (46 chromosomes altogether). Only two types of cells exist in organisms, **somatic cells** and **germ cells.** The term *soma* means body; thus, somatic cells are the approximately one trillion cells found in the human body, *with the exception of the sex cells.*

In order for growth to take place, somatic cells undergo a process of division called **mitosis.** In mitosis, the chromosomes inside the nucleus pair up along its center; then, after duplicating themselves, they move to opposite poles. The original cell (and nucleus), called the parent cell, begins to pull apart while two new nuclei are formed to contain the new sets of chromosomes. Each of these new cells is called a daughter cell. The key fact to remember in mitosis is that the two new daughter cells are identical to the original parent cell and maintain the *same number of chromosomes* (see Figure 4.6). When a cell has its full quota of chromosomes, it is said to be in the **diploid state.** In the example given for somatic cells, the parent always has 23 pairs of chromosomes *(diploidy)*, and by mitotic division, the cells duplicate their chromosomes so that the daughter cells will also have 23 pairs,

Figure 4.6 Mitosis is the process in which the parent cell divides to become two daughter cells, each containing the original number of chromosomes.

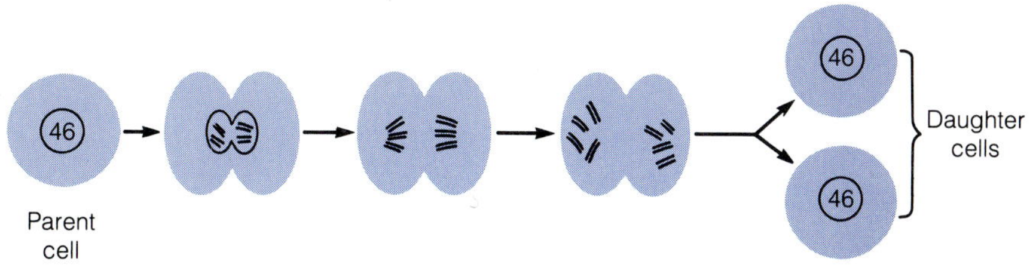

Parent cell

46   46

Daughter cells

which represents the diploid, or full species, number of chromosomes.

The second type of cell found in the human body is the germ cell, which undergoes division in the **gonads.** The gonads are the reproductive organs—the **ovaries** in the female and the **testes** in the male. Germ cells will become the cells of reproduction, or sex cells, but must undergo certain changes before they achieve their new state. The sex cells are called **gametes.** The male gamete is the sperm (which is produced from the germ cells in the testes), while the female gamete is the egg, or ovum (produced from the germ cells of the ovaries).

Cell division of germ cells is called **meiosis,** a series of divisions that takes a germ cell from the diploid state to the **haploid** state. *Haploidy* means that a cell contains only half the number of chromosomes that is natural for the species. Meiotic division, then, represents a parent cell (male or female germ cell) splitting into two daughter cells, the same process taking place in mitosis except that the chromosomes do not duplicate themselves. This leaves each daughter cell in the haploid state. Thus, meiosis in the male organism produces a sperm cell that

Figure 4.7 Sex is determined by the sperm cell.

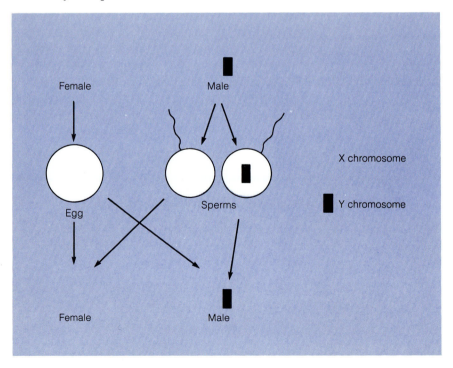

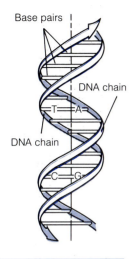

Base pairs

DNA chain

DNA chain

—T═══A—

—C═══G—

Figure 4.8 The DNA molecule.

contains 23 chromosomes, and in the female the final product of meiosis is an egg with 23 chromosomes. Conception occurs when the sperm fertilizes the egg and creates a single cell in the diploid state. This enables a cell to receive its full complement of chromosomes, complete with coded instructions for the development of a new generation.

How Sex Is Determined   Of the 23 pairs of chromosomes in every human being, one set of chromosomes is designated as the sex-determining pair. Female eggs contain 23 pairs including two large sex chromosomes, termed the **X chromosomes.** Each ovum contains one X chromosome. The male, however, has 22 pairs of chromosomes plus a "mismatched" set of sex chromosomes, an X similar to the female and a much smaller one called the **Y chromosome.** Sex is determined at the time of **fertilization** by the sperm that fertilizes the egg. Fertilization by an X-bearing sperm will produce a female. An egg fertilized by a Y-bearing sperm will produce a male. Figure 4.7 illustrates the possible combinations.

The Genetic Code: A Blueprint for Life

Now let's peer inside the nucleus to discover just what the genetic code entails. Under a microscope, the chromosome appears as a thin, colored, rodlike thread. A gene is simply a very small portion of a chromosome that has a very specific function. Unraveling the thread of the chromosome will reveal the structure called **deoxyribonucleic acid,** or more simply, **DNA.** The genes are the part of the DNA structure that carry hereditary instructions for the development of the organism.

The structure of DNA looks like a long spiral staircase or twisting ladder. This framework consists of alternate molecules of sugar and phosphate. The steps are composed of only four chemicals—**adenine** (A), **thymine** (T), **guanine** (G), and **cytosine** (C). Each step consists of two joined chemicals (see Figure 4.8). The chemical adenine will bond (link up) only with the chemical thymine, and guanine and cytosine will bond only with each other (Watson and Crick, 1953).

A gene is the segment of a chromosome that controls or influences inheritable characteristics. A gene represents a specific number of steps that, when activated, will eventually produce specific proteins or enzymes. Some genes are several hundred "steps" long, others several thousand. Although it is not known exactly how many genes are on a chromosome, a frequent estimate has been 20,000, which would give human beings approximately 460,000 gene pairs. Some theories even double this number, bringing the total closer to a million.

A gene is DNA material arranged in a specific fashion in order that an accompanying specific protein can be synthesized (manufactured)

(Beadle and Tatum, 1941). To make a long and complex story short and simple, this dormant genetic blueprint becomes active at an appropriate time. The activated gene duplicates itself, but with minor chemical alterations. Instead of being DNA, it is now **ribonucleic acid,** or **RNA.** More specifically, it is called messenger RNA because its purpose is to carry a genetic message (the code) outside the nucleus to a ribosome, a particle that synthesizes protein.

To comprehend what is about to happen, you have to understand that your body consists of protein from the top of your scalp to the tip of your toes. Protein is manufactured in the ribosomes, which produce almost a million different types of proteins by mixing various amino acids together. **Amino acids,** which exist in only 20 to 30 different varieties (no one knows for sure), are the true "building blocks of life." All protein in all life originates from amino acids.

The RNA delivers its directions to the ribosome, which then mix the appropriate amino acids according to the genetic instruction and send the results (protein) to the cytoplasm. When the cell is swollen with protein, mitosis takes place. Now two cells manufacture protein, divide, and so on. In nine months' time, in a similar way for every body part, a total of approximately seven pounds of protein is produced. In this very complex fashion a single cell becomes a human infant.

Genetic Individuality

To understand the nature of physical and psychological inheritance, it must be understood that during the process of meiosis, chromosomes line up opposite each other and then meiotically split into daughter cells. But keep in mind that most of the genes on one chromosome differ from the genes on the opposite chromosome. Although chromosomes do line up, there is no law requiring that they line up on the right or the left side. They may do either.

This means that the number of genetically different sex cells an individual can produce is 2^{23} or 8,388,608. In other words, the male can produce over 8 million genetically different sperm, and the female can produce the same number of different eggs. By calculating the various combinations of sperm penetrations of the egg, one finds that one couple (man and woman) can produce approximately 64 billion genetically different offspring without having two that are identical (identical twins being the exception).

Among other things, this means that in organisms as complicated as homo sapiens, heredity represents not only the passing on of certain characteristics but also the transmitting of individual differences. You may know of children in a family whose physical characteristics are as different as night and day. Yet some parents produce offspring whose appearances are almost mirror images of each other. The answer lies in

Table 4.1 Dominant and Recessive Characteristics

	Dominant Characteristics	Recessive Characteristics
Eye coloring	Brown eyes Gray, green, hazel Blue	Gray, green, hazel, blue eyes Blue Albino (pink)
Vision	Farsightedness Normal vision Normal sight Normal color vision	Normal vision Nearsightedness Night vision Color blindness*
Hair	Dark hair Nonred hair (blond, brunette) Curly hair Full head of hair Widow's peak hairline	Blond hair, light hair (red hair) Red hair Straight hair Baldness* Normal hairline
Facial features	Dimples in cheeks Unattached earlobes "Roman" nose Broad lips	No dimples Attached earlobes Straight nose Thin lips
Appendages	Extra digits Fused digits Short digits Fingers lacking one joint Limb dwarfing Clubbed thumb Double-jointedness	Normal number Normal Normal Normal length Normal proportion Normal thumb Normal joints
Other	Immunity to poison ivy Normal coloring (pigmented skin) Normal blood clotting Normal hearing Normal Normal Normal	Susceptibility to poison ivy Albinism Hemophilia* Congenital deafness Deaf mutism Amaurotic idiocy Phenylketonuria

*Sex-linked characteristics.

the fact that when both parents carry homozygous genes for a certain characteristic, the children will all be homozygous for that characteristic. If both parents have paired homozygous genes for blue eyes, black hair, and a "Roman" nose, all their children will have these characteristics. Parents who are heterozygous for various traits may have offspring without recognizable similarities. Table 4.1 indicates several dominant and recessive inherited characteristics. Heredity may result in familiar similarities as well as individual differences. We shall soon see that as early as the second month after conception some inherited physical characteristics are already emerging.

In this section, our attention has been focused on the various forms of gene action. So far, relatively simple examples of physical characteristics have been given. Behavioral traits, however, are more complex, and the more complicated an inherited characteristic is, the more difficult it is to study. Thus, we know more about the inheritance of apparently superficial traits, such as pigmentation, than we do about the inheritance of more complicated inherited characteristics, such as intelligence (Winchester, 1975).

Complex Types of Gene Action

Until now it has been implied that each gene has a definite and singular task, yet this is seldom the case. Instead, most physical and probably all behavioral characteristics are under the direction of **polygenes,** which work together with additive and/or complementary effects. Obviously, the more genes working together on a single task, the more difficult the research becomes.

Polygenes are responsible for building internal organs and controlling their cellular activity. Polygenes increase the number of individual differences in an organism's anatomical and physiological structure. In fact, since no two people are biochemically identical, each will react differently to similar biochemical environments (this includes not only drugs and medicines but also foods). This situation partially explains why some people can eat or drink certain foods or beverages that upset others. To understand polygenes, we must be aware of an individual's **constitution,** which is established by the polygenes.

There are studies mentioned throughout the text that suggest at least minimal evidence that we inherit predispositions toward certain behavior (e.g., Motulsky, 1978). Such studies indicate the *possibility* of many personality traits (aggressiveness, smiling responses, fear, shyness, moodiness) as being inherited. Even the activity level of newborn infants shows a behavioral range from total inactivity to hyperactivity or hyperkinetic activity, all of which may be genetically influenced. Periodically, we shall examine other evidence regarding the inheritability of behaviors.

Prenatal Development

The average full-term human pregnancy lasts 266 days after fertilization (280 days after the onset of the last normal menstrual period), although it is generally referred to as nine months. Using the more common, but slightly less accurate, nine-month description, the **prenatal period** can be divided into three equal segments, called *trimesters.* Each trimester is three months long. Although the new organism is both growing and developing throughout all phases of pregnancy, the trimester division is somewhat simplified by the following classification system: The first trimester is primarily characterized by differential development of basic structures, the second trimester is characterized by further development and growth, and the third trimester is predominantly one of growth (see Table 4.2).

The First Trimester

The First Month: Period of the Ovum or Germinal Period   After the egg has been fertilized, the zygote undergoes mitosis to become two cells. Ten hours later, these two cells again divide to become four cells. This process of cell division continues for approximately two weeks in what is called the **period of the ovum.** First, the rapidly multiplying ball of cells travels along the fallopian tube. While there is an increase in the number of cells, there is no increase in mass, since no source of nourishment is available to this group of free-floating cells. Thus, the cells can undergo mitosis but cannot increase their size.

On or about the fourth day, the cluster of cells reaches the uterus. It drifts about for another three or four days before embedding, or implanting itself in the spongy vesseled wall of the awaiting uterus. At this time the entire cluster of cells is no larger than the head of a pin. For another week this process of mitosis and implantation continues.

The Placenta   While the ovum is drifting about, it produces villi, hairlike growths that are able, through chemical activity, to attach them-

Table 4.2 Summary of Prenatal Development

Trimester	Major Characterization
First (0–3 months)	Begins development of all internal organs, appendages, sense organs.
Second (4–6 months)	Continues development and grows from 3″ to 1′ long and from 1 oz. to 1½ lbs.
Third (7–9 months)	Grows about 8″ in length, gains about 6 lbs.

selves to the lining of the uterine wall. These mechanisms of attachment are the beginnings of what will eventually become the **placenta,** or afterbirth—the membrane that allows nourishment to pass from mother to embryo and waste products to be channeled from embryo to mother.

There is no direct connection of blood vessels between mother and embryo. Substances are transmitted to and from the mother's and child's blood vessels through the placenta. Eventually the placenta will be connected to the fetus by the umbilical cord.

As the sole source of food, oxygen, and water for the unborn, the placenta must grow in relation to the organism's needs. Originally microscopic in size, it becomes 3 or 4 inches in diameter by the fourth month and at birth weighs about a pound and measures 8 inches in diameter. Figure 4.9 illustrates the exchanges that occur in the placenta.

The Amniotic Sac and Umbilical Cord   The **amniotic sac** is a transparent membrane completely enveloping the embryo except where the umbilical cord passes through to the placenta. Contained within the

Figure 4.9 Diagram of the fetal and maternal blood flow through the human placenta. (From Arey, L. B. *Developmental Anatomy,* 8th ed. Philadelphia, Saunders, 1974.)

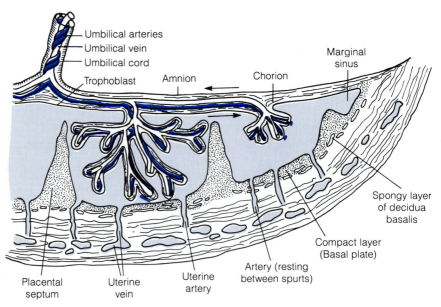

sac is **amniotic fluid,** which holds the embryo or fetus in suspension
and protects it not only from being jarred but also from any pressures
exerted by the mother's internal organs (see Figure 4.10). The fluid also
provides an even temperature for the fetus. By holding the fetus in
suspension, the fluid allows it free movement and keeps the mother
from being unduly jarred.

   The **umbilical cord,** or "body stalk," contains three blood vessels:
one vein carrying oxygenated blood from the placenta to the infant and
two arteries carrying blood and waste products from the infant to the
placenta. Since the umbilical cord is without nerves, severing and tying
it into the navel, or "belly button," at delivery is painless.

Embryonic Period   The **embryonic period** begins when the fertilized
ovum becomes well implanted in the uterine wall and the cells begin to
exhibit marked differentiation. The organism is called an embryo from
the beginning of cell specialization until the end of the second month
of pregnancy, the period from approximately two weeks to eight weeks
after fertilization.

**Figure 4.10 Longitudinal diagram of uterus showing relationship of fetus
to membranes. (Adapted from Arey, L. B. *Developmental Anatomy*, 8th ed.
Philadelphia, Saunders, 1974.)**

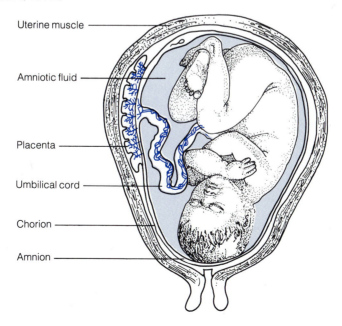

Four weeks after conception, the embryo measures only ³⁄₁₆ inch in length but is 10,000 times larger than the zygote. The specialization of cells produces an embryo that has a short, pointed, curled-up tail and a primitive umbilical cord through which it will eventually be nourished.

On day 18, the heart structure begins to appear (Moore, 1981) and by three weeks the heart is functional, undergoing muscle contractions, although it is not under neural control. The heart beats and blood pulsates through a small enclosed bloodstream that is separate from the mother's. There is also a backbone enclosing a spinal cord, and such internal organs as the lungs, liver, kidneys, and endocrine glands are also starting to develop. Moreover, the digestive system has begun to form. Small "buds" that will eventually become arms start developing on day 24, and on day 28 leg "buds" appear. Throughout development, the legs lag behind the arms (Moore, 1981).

The Second Month   As the embryo enters its second month, the rapid cell division and specialization that occurred during the first month continue to take place. By the end of eight weeks the embryo is about an inch long and weighs ¹⁄₃₀ of an ounce. Facial features and a neck are forming and the limbs are elongating, showing distinct division of knee and elbow, although they are less than ¼ inch long. More specifically, on about day 31 the shoulders, arms, and hands develop; on day 33, the fingers; and on days 34 through 36, the thumb. Underneath the tissue of the arms and legs, the long bones are forming and becoming padded with muscles.

The internal organs also continue to develop quite rapidly not only in form and structure but also in functional properties. The nervous system becomes functional, the kidneys are capable of removing uric acid from the bloodstream, and the stomach is capable of manufacturing some digestive juices. During these first two months the organism is especially vulnerable to environmental factors, especially mutagenic agents. Interference with the genetic code during this most critical period of development can cause irreversible abnormalities of any of the organs.

Although the organism is only an inch in length, it is already exhibiting some inherited characteristics. For instance, the ear lobes will already be attached or unattached, and the nose will have acquired a certain shape on day 37. These, as well as finger and toe shapes, are just a few of the inheritable traits that express themselves as early as the embryonic period.

Cephalocaudal and Proximo-Distal Development   **Cephalocaudal development** means a head-to-tail, or downward, progression of bodily

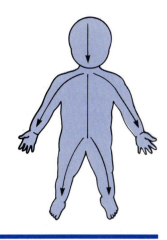

Figure 4.11 Arrows demonstrate cephalocaudal and proximo-distal development.

and motor skill growth. If we compare physical rates of development of the head, trunk, and legs, we find that the head grows the fastest. The trunk is next in overall rate of growth, followed by the legs. (This is true from conception through the full attainment of growth and development in young adulthood.) During the embryonic stage, the head and upper trunk develop before the abdominal area and the arms develop before the legs. (Motor skills involving the use of the upper body will develop before those using the lower body.) Infants can lift their heads before their trunks and can sit upright before they can walk.

Proximo-distal development implies that physical and motor skill growth takes place from the center of the body *outward.* For example, in the embryo and fetus, the trunk develops earlier than the shoulders or the arms, while fingers and toes develop at a much slower rate. Infants, young children, and even adolescents are capable of mastering motor skills that involve the central parts of the body before those requiring the use of peripheral parts. Thus, we typically develop the use of the shoulders and arms before we can master the use of the hands and fingers. Figure 4.11 illustrates cephalocaudal and proximo-distal development.

The Third Month   The end of the eighth week and the start of the ninth week mark the end of the embryonic period and the start of the period of the **fetus.** During this time, progressive maturation of both nerves and muscles takes place and leads to generalized movements in response to external stimulation. Fetal turning and rotation also occur as early as the ninth or tenth week (although the mother will be unaware of all this activity). These movements appear to mark the beginning of what some psychologists consider to be true, albeit reflexive, behavior. By the end of 12 weeks, the fetus can also kick, curl the toes and fingers, move the thumb, and even squint in response to external stimulation.

By the end of 12 weeks, the fetus is 3 inches long and weighs 1 ounce. Arms, hands, fingers, legs, feet, and toes are now fully formed. Even nails are developing on the 20 digits. Tiny tooth sockets, with the "buds" of future teeth, are present in the jawbone. The eyes, almost fully developed, have lids that remain fused.

By the end of this trimester, a very tiny but highly complex organism is in utero. (Figure 4.12 shows the organism's size from 2 to 15 weeks.) Other developments reveal how complex the organism has become. The nerves and muscles triple in number during the month. The heart can be heard by use of special instruments, the kidneys are operable, and sexual development reaches the stage where sex can be noted by a cursory examination. Meanwhile, the soft cartilaginous substance of the ribs and vertebrae turns to bone.

The Second Trimester

The Fourth Month   The second trimester is characterized not only by a continuation of the developmental processes but also by a rapid increase in growth. The fetus now approaches 7 inches in length and weighs approximately 4 ounces. The head is large in comparison to the rest of the body (see Figure 4.13). A strong heartbeat is present, along with a fairly well-developed digestive system. The eyebrows and genital

Figure 4.12 A graded series of embryos and fetuses drawn to actual size. (From Arey, L. B. *Developmental Anatomy,* 8th ed. Philadelphia, Saunders, 1974.)

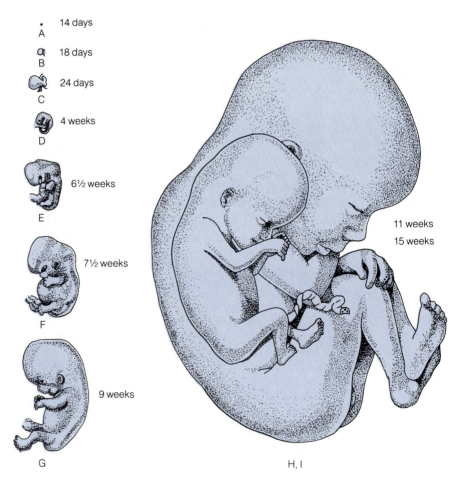

14 days
A

18 days
B

24 days
C

4 weeks
D

6½ weeks
E

7½ weeks
F

9 weeks
G

11 weeks
15 weeks

H, I

Figure 4.13 Fetus at the beginning of the fourth month.

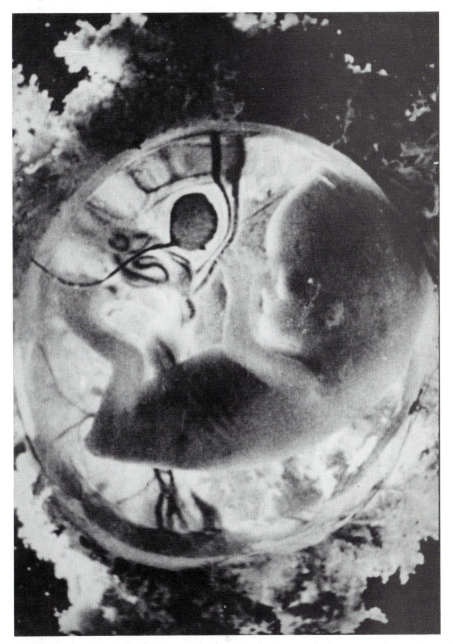

organs are quite noticeable. Because the fetus is now quite active, food, oxygen, and water intake increases. The placenta has increased from 3 inches to 4 inches in diameter, allowing for a more rapid exchange of nutrients and waste products between mother and child. The transparent fetal body is bright pink or red owing to the blood flowing through the circulatory vessels; there is no pigmentation in the skin.

Figure 4.14 Fetus in the fifth month, engaged in a common activity for this stage—thumbsucking.

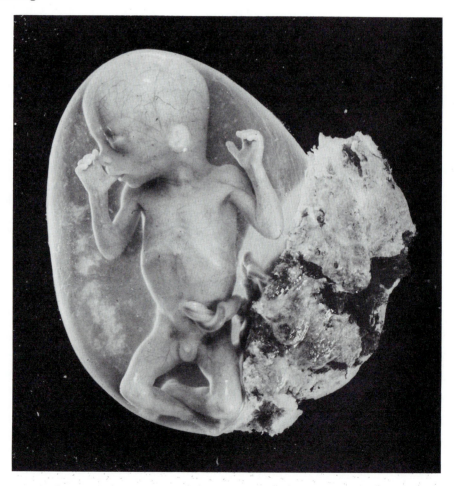

The Fifth Month   By the end of 20 weeks, a rapid increase in body size has occurred. The fetus is now 1 foot long and may weigh anywhere from 8 ounces to 1 pound, a considerable gain from the 4 ounces of 16 weeks earlier. There still being no production of melanin, the fetus remains bright red. The eyelids are still fused shut and a fine downy growth of hair, called **lanugo,** appears on the entire body. The skin is also usually covered with a wax-like substance called the vernix caseosa. It protects the fetus from the constant exposure to the amniotic fluid. The internal organs are rapidly maturing, with the exception of the lungs, which lag behind in development. The size and movement of the fetus are such that the mother is now very much aware of the ripplings and flutterings inside her. The fetus now has both sleeping and waking moments. During wakefulness there is crying, thumb sucking, and hiccuping, to say nothing of somersaults.

The Sixth Month   Just over a foot in length, the six-month fetus has started accumulating subcutaneous fat and now weighs up to 1½ pounds. Still wrinkled and red, it is a miniature baby. The eyelids have separated, tiny eyelashes can now be observed, and the fingernails extend to the end of the fingers. The fetus can now make a fist. **Ossification** (the hardening of bone) has started. There is a slim chance of survival should the fetus be born now.

The Third Trimester

The Seventh, Eighth, and Ninth Months   The third trimester, consisting of the seventh, eighth, and ninth months of pregnancy, is marked primarily by rapid gains in growth and weight. The fetus grows in length by 50 percent and gains nearly 6 pounds in the last three months. During the last two months the fetus gains an average of 8 ounces a week. In the seventh month the reflexes that will be seen at birth develop rapidly. Crying, breathing, and even thumb sucking are included in fetal behavioral patterns. As fetal growth increases (much of the weight gain is subcutaneous fat), the uterus becomes cramped, and movement is curtailed. Periods of sleep alternate with periods of activity.

Most organs rapidly reach a maturation level sufficient to allow them to operate independently of the prenatal environment. The capacity for independent respiration, however, depends on the maturation of the brain stem (**medulla oblongata**). Until there is appropriate neural function, respiration cannot occur. Thus, respiratory problems are among the major difficulties to be faced in keeping the premature infant alive.

Prenatal Environment

The organism, which is under genetic direction, is also influenced by its external and internal environment. The external fetal environment is the amniotic fluid. The more significant internal environment consists not only of the proteins and enzymes manufactured within the organism but also of a continuous inflow of nutrients, hormones, oxygen, chemicals, and other substances from the mother's bloodstream.

As noted, there is no direct connection between the blood vessels of mother and child. A "mixing" of blood in the placental region never occurs. Rather, molecules of many substances are released by the maternal bloodstream and pass through the placenta. These substances are generally assimilated by the fetal blood vessels within the umbilical cord. This makes the placenta an area of exchange. The environmental impact depends on what is exchanged in the placenta. Obviously, a physically healthy mother who is eating the proper foods for both herself and the fetus (something from the milk group, meat group, vegetables and fruits, and the proper amount of breads and cereals) will help provide a proper environment. In addition to maintaining a well-balanced diet, the mother should be free of disease and should receive prenatal care from a qualified physician or nurse midwife (Winick, 1981).

It is difficult to state exactly what constitutes a good prenatal environment. Until recently, very little was known about the prenatal environment and what affects the developing organism in a positive or negative way. Of course, experiments are performed on pregnant animals (e.g., Dunlap, Gerall, and Carlton, 1978), but what is true for the rest of the animal kingdom does not always apply to humanity. Since ethical considerations, namely the concern for human life, prohibit research on the effects of various drugs and other chemicals on humans, researchers usually accumulate data in retrospect. Should a child be born malformed, doctors attempt to ascertain what drugs, illnesses, or other factors could have affected the mother's system during the critical period when the embryo was most susceptible. Often knowledge consists solely of retrospective data and statistics.

The age of the mother is important when we consider what constitutes a good prenatal environment. Most experts agree that the best childbearing years are 20 through 35. For women over 35, the chances of the baby dying are almost one-third higher than for mothers in their early twenties. The baby's survival may also be less likely if the mother is too young. Mothers 17 years and younger appear more likely to deliver premature babies or infants with birth defects. Both older and younger mothers should receive special prenatal care (Sandler, Myerson, and Kindler, 1980; Jorgensen, King, and Torrey, 1980).

Miscarriage and Abortion

A miscarriage, or spontaneous abortion, occurs when a pregnancy terminates before the developing organism is mature enough to survive outside the womb. Physiologically, this happens when the embryo separates from the uterine wall and is expelled by the uterus. It is estimated that 10 percent of all pregnancies end in spontaneous abortion, usually during the first two or three months.

Vaginal bleeding from a pregnant uterus, with or without cramping, frequently signals the possibility of an abortion. But not all physicians agree that this means an abortion is inevitable, and few agree on the causes of spontaneous abortion. Precipitating factors that have been identified include severe trauma, abnormalities of the reproductive tract, maternal infections, and excessive drinking. Abortion is concentrated among very young women, with approximately one-third occurring among women under 19 years old, another one-third among women 20 to 24 years old, and the remainder among women 25 years old and older (Harlap and Shiono, 1980; Krannich, 1980).

Induced abortions should not be confused with spontaneous abortions. The former are deliberate external attempts to remove the organism from the uterus. Until recently, such abortions were illegal except in cases where a physician deemed the pregnancy harmful to the woman or in some cases of rape or incest. Nevertheless, women sought illegal abortions, which were frequently performed by unqualified and incompetent personnel using questionable procedures in unsanitary conditions.

In 1973, the Supreme Court ruled that any woman could obtain an abortion during the first six months of pregnancy. The court reasoned that this was the best way to ensure women's health and maintain their right to control their own bodies. The decision provoked ethical and moral objections from those opposed to induced abortion. Legal abortion remains a volatile issue, but since the decision, rates of abortions have been increasing steadily. In 1980, there were 1.55 million induced abortions in the United States (Tietze, 1981).

The Rh Factor: Incompatible Blood Types

Although a cure has been found, fetuses and newborns continue to die because their blood is Rh positive (Rh +) and their mother's is Rh negative (Rh −). Rh + is a genetically dominant trait; thus, the child of two Rh − parents or of an Rh − father and Rh + mother is not affected. The Rh factor comes into focus when the father is Rh + and the mother Rh −.

Positive and negative blood types are incompatible. It is common during the birth process for fetal blood to enter the maternal bloodstream during hemorrhaging. When the child is Rh +, this substance, foreign to the Rh − mother, is combated by the production of anti-bodies. During the first birth few if any antibodies are present, so the Rh factor is unimportant. When the mother becomes pregnant again, however, these antibodies pass through the placenta and cause erythroblastosis, a condition in which the antibodies attack the fetal blood cells, generally causing the fetus's death (see Figure 4.15).

Today, Rh immune globulin can be administered to the mother after the birth of each child, thus preventing the formation of antibodies and allowing an Rh incompatible couple to produce other healthy children. The globulin should also be given to Rh − women after an abortion or miscarriage.

Maternal Nutrition

In the course of nine months, the fetus must grow from a single cell to a highly complex being of approximately 7 pounds. The ability to develop normally depends on nourishment supplied by the mother.

Figure 4.15 While an Rh − mother is carrying an Rh + baby (a), some of the baby's Rh + blood enters the mother's body (b). Her body produces antibodies against this factor (c). When she carries a subsequent Rh + baby, the antibodies cross the placenta and attack the baby's red blood cells (d). If after birth, abortion, or miscarriage, it is determined that the baby's blood is Rh +, RhoGam, an anti-Rh antibody, is given to the Rh − mother within 72 hours. This suppresses the formation of anti-Rh antibodies and thus protects a future baby. The anti-Rh antibody cannot be given during pregnancy because it would pass through the placenta and damage the fetus's red blood cells. (From Blier, I. J. *Maternity Nursing: A Textbook for Practical Nurses,* 3rd ed. Philadelphia, Saunders, 1971.)

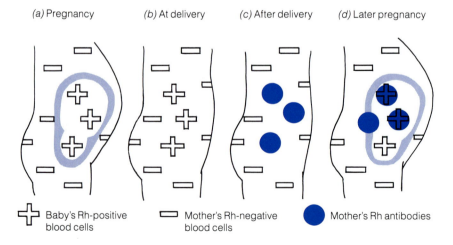

(a) Pregnancy   *(b)* At delivery   *(c)* After delivery   *(d)* Later pregnancy

Baby's Rh-positive blood cells   Mother's Rh-negative blood cells   Mother's Rh antibodies

Some reports claim that the most frequent cause of fetal death is malnutrition of the mother. Poor maternal nutrition may affect the fetus either directly by not meeting its nutritional needs or indirectly by increasing the mother's susceptibility to disease (Holt, 1982). Malnutrition can not only cause poor health, rickets, scurvy, physical weakness, miscarriages, and stillbirths but also produce mental subnormality (Kaplan, 1972). An interesting distinction has been drawn between two types of nutritional inadequacy: qualitative hunger (malnutrition caused by deficient supplies of vitamins necessary for normal growth) and quantitative hunger (insufficient amounts of food). Of the two, the former is more serious. Apparently, it is not how much the pregnant woman eats but what she eats that counts. In an earlier study, three researchers provided vitamins to half of a malnourished group of expectant mothers. Children born to mothers receiving the enriched diet scored significantly higher on intelligence tests at ages 3 to 4 than children born to the malnourished group (Harrell, Woodyard, and Gates, 1955). In fact, a seriously malnourished fetus may have up to 20 percent fewer brain cells than a normal fetus (Winick, 1976; Winick, Brasil, and Valasco, 1973). The mother's diet alone cannot be considered the only deleterious influence on prenatal development. Malnourished mothers frequently come from an environment of poverty, inadequate medical care, and inferior sanitation. These variables cannot be easily separated, which makes it exceedingly difficult to determine cause-effect relationships (Birch and Gussow, 1970).

The most serious damage (physical and mental abnormalities) occurs during organogenesis, the period of organ development occurring from the third week of pregnancy through the second or third month. Each organ has its own critical period, when it is most vulnerable to environmental forces.

Nicotine

Nicotine evidently affects development, but how much nicotine produces which prenatal effects is not known. Researchers have weighed and measured newborns of smokers and nonsmokers and found that the average baby born of a mother who smokes tends to be smaller than the baby of a nonsmoking woman (Meredith, 1975). But it is not known how or why this phenomenon occurs. An educated guess would be that the fetus of a nonsmoker receives its full quota of oxygen and nutrients, while a smoking mother, having various gases, tars, and nicotine in her system, passes them along through the placenta to the fetus at the expense of oxygen and/or other nutrients (Fried and Oxorn, 1980). Nicotine also apparently has other effects. It has been suggested that smoking not only increases the fetal heart rate (as it does in adult heavy smokers) but also may lead to fetal hyperactivity. In addition, women who are heavy smokers are more likely than nonsmokers to give birth to premature babies (Meredith, 1975). One study even indicates that women who smoke are more likely to give birth to malformed and stillborn infants (Naeye, 1978).

Maternal Emotions versus Maternal Impressions

There are many old wives' tales about how the pregnant woman's environment affects the fetus. For example, if a woman was frightened, it was believed that the child would be born with a birthmark shaped like the object that had upset the mother. Another belief was that happy mothers give birth to happy babies, while worried mothers have children who are emotionally upset. While there is no truth to these old superstitions, some closely associated biological factors must be considered.

Emotions (happiness, sadness, worry) do not directly influence the developing organism, but there is growing evidence that the **hormones** released when a mother is under great stress (anxiety) can affect both fetal and subsequent behavior (Crandon, 1979). For example, willing pregnant women can be tested and classified according to the degree of anxiety present: high or low. When the infants of these two groups of mothers are observed and tested, the results show that women subjected to severe or prolonged emotional stress during their pregnancy are more prone to give birth to infants who are hyperactive and irritable and who have low birth weights, feeding problems, and digestive disturbances. Furthermore, highly anxious women appear to have more spontaneous abortions and a higher percentage of premature infants, and they spend an average of five more hours in labor. They also tend to have more complicated and abnormal deliveries (Ferriera, 1969; Carlson and Labarba, 1979).

Drugs

Drugs pose another potential problem for the embryo and fetus. Again, research findings are limited to animal studies or human observation studies in which there are few controls. The specific effects of drugs vary depending not only on which drug is involved but also on the quantity used and the time during pregnancy when it is taken. If a pregnant mother is given a sedative during labor, the pattern of electrical activity in the infant's brain decelerates after birth. Excessive sedation can cause permanent brain damage or asphyxiation at birth. Addictive drugs, such as heroin and methadone, pass through the placenta readily, causing addicted mothers to give birth to babies who are also addicted. As a result, the newborn must suffer all the **withdrawal symptoms** (tremors, fever, convulsions, and breathing difficulties) that adults do when they "dry out." While most evidence indicates that no abnormalities exist in addicted infants, these babies are generally smaller than average; heroin babies, for example, seldom weigh more than 5½ pounds. In late childhood, these infants often show increasingly frequent disturbances of activity levels, attention span, sleep patterns, and socialization (Householder et al., 1982).

The fetal alcohol syndrome is caused by alcohol consumption during pregnancy. Research reveals that, like alcoholic mothers, mothers who consume moderate amounts of alcohol bear infants who are shorter than normal babies and often have subnormal IQs. Maternal alcohol use in midpregnancy is also related to poor habituation and low arousal in newborns. No one is sure how much alcohol is too much for the pregnant woman. Some authorities believe that even occasional drinking may be harmful, while others believe that moderate consumption is safe. Women who drink also have a higher risk of miscarriage than women who do not drink (Streissguth, Barr, and Martin, 1983; Steinhausen, Nestler, and Spohr, 1982; Harlap and Shiono, 1980; Kline, 1980).

Teratogenic Agents

A teratogenic agent is any substance that causes a change in the genetic code, which in turn produces an abnormality, anomaly, or malformation. Medical dictionaries describe teratogenic agents as being capable of producing monster children. It is important to distinguish between teratogenic agents (environmental substances) and inherited teratogenes (genes from one or both parents that will produce a mutant child through inborn errors of metabolism).

Teratogenic agents affect genes and protein production in several ways. They may damage genes and make them inoperable. Some agents can change the genetic code by bonding to a gene (or genes) and producing a mutant enzyme or blocking or destroying normal enzymes. More technically, teratogenic agents may act by agenesis (genes cease their protein production, and development halts), incomplete development (the failure of genes to complete development or growth already commenced), or developmental excess (overgrowth of the whole organism or any of its parts).

A teratogenic agent is especially dangerous during the development of an organ (organogenesis). For example, thalidomide, which affects the genes that control the development of the appendages, can do its damage only when the genes for arms and legs are "unzipping." During this time the gene is vulnerable, since it is in an unbonded state. With the thalidomide chemicals, there is probably a permanent bonding of thalidomide and the developmental gene resulting in agenesis. German measles (rubella), on the other hand, evidently enters the developmental code and produces mutant brain protein. The most dangerous time

Table 4.3 Possible Teratogenic Agents

Category	Causative Agent	Effect
Physical agent	Irradiation (X rays)	Malformation of any organ. The organ involved would depend on organism's state of development.
Infectious agent	Rubella (German measles)	Brain damage (mental retardation), sensory and cranial nerve damage (especially vision and hearing).
	Quinine (?)	Possible deafness and congenital malformations (not totally substantiated). Note: quinine water lacks sufficient quinine to be included in this group.
	Cortisone	Possible contribution to formation of cleft palate.
	Paint fumes (?)	Possible cause of mental retardation. Pregnant women would probably have to be in unventilated paint area for a substantial length of time to be affected.
Chemical agent	Thalidomide	Taken 21–22 days after conception, absence of external ears, cranial nerve paralysis; 24–27 days, agenesis of arms; 28–29 days, agenesis of legs.
	Vitamin A	Large doses taken throughout pregnancy, possible cleft palate, eye damage, congenital abnormalities.
	Vitamin D	Large doses taken throughout pregnancy, possible mental retardation.
	Alcohol	Heavy drinking, possible subnormal IQs.

for the developing organism is the first two or three months after conception, for this is the major developmental period, but deformations can occur at any time during development. Table 4.3 presents some suspected teratogenic agents.

Amniocentesis

Genetic and medical research have provided new diagnostic techniques for recognizing and identifying previously unknown genetic problems.

Amniocentesis, one of the more recent techniques, reveals some gross **chromosomal abnormalities** in the fetus. Amniotic fluid is sampled by inserting a hollow needle through the mother's abdominal wall into the amniotic sac and withdrawing amniotic fluid. This fluid contains discarded fetal cells, which can be observed, measured, and analyzed for size, shape, and number (see Figure 4.16).

This procedure has been used since the early 1960s. Presently, doctors and scientists can test for more than 50 chromosomal abnormalities (more than 1,600 known human diseases exist). Amniocentesis is generally used on pregnant women who are over 35 or have a family history of hereditary defects.

Some of these tests provide clear-cut answers. If an extra chromosome is found at chromosome site number 21, for example, the child will inherit a condition known as **Down's syndrome** (or **Trisomy 21**) and will be mentally retarded. A severe neurological disease, the Lesch-Nyhan syndrome, occurring in males, is characterized by **mental retardation,** involuntary writhing motions, and compulsive self-mutilation of the lips and fingertips by biting. In amniocentesis, the fetal cells are removed, cultured, and submitted to X-ray film. Normal cells absorb the radiation while Lesch-Nyhan cells remain free of radioactivity. Another rare condition, found mostly among Jews of northern European origin, is the Tay-Sachs disease, causing blindness, mental retarda-

Figure 4.16 The technique of amniocentesis. (*Scientific American,* November 1971, page 35.)

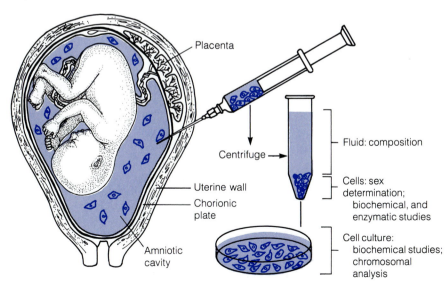

Placenta

Centrifuge →

Fluid: composition

Uterine wall

Chorionic plate

Cells: sex determination; biochemical, and enzymatic studies

Amniotic cavity

Cell culture: biochemical studies; chromosomal analysis

Table 4.4 Some Chromosomal Abnormalities

Name	Chromosomal Explanations	Risk	Characteristics
Down's syndrome or Trisomy 21 or Mongolism	3 chromosomes instead of a pair at position 21	1 in 700 or 1 in 1500 for women in their twenties	Mental retardation; fold in upper eyelid resembling Mongoloid races; short stature; wide round face; large tongue making coherent speech difficult
Trisomy 17 syndrome	3 chromosomes at position 17	?	Mental retardation; odd-shaped skull; webbed neck; low-set malformed ears; stubby digits; webbed toes
Trisomy 18 syndrome	3 chromosomes at position 18	1 in 3,000 live births, increases with maternal age	Severe mental retardation; feeble cry; low-set deformed ears; heart and kidney abnormalities; skeletal deformities; survival about 10 weeks
Cri du chat (cry of the cat) syndrome	Only 1½ chromosomes at position 5	Over 1%	Mental retardation; incomplete development of vocal cords, which gives the child's voice a meowing sound; round face; small cranium
Klinefelter's syndrome	XXY in position 23 (sex-determining chromosome)	1 in 400 male live births	Undeveloped males; small penis and testes; underdevelopment of body, pubic, and facial hair; frequently, female body contours and enlarged breasts; subnormal to retarded intelligence; frequently sterile
Turner's syndrome	XO in position 23 (one chromosome missing)	1 in 5000 females	Webbing of neck; short stature; hormonal abnormalities; failure of ovarian development (almost always sterile)
Triple X syndrome	Extra X sex chromosome at position 23	1 in 800 female live births	Often mentally retarded; increased chance of mental illness
XYY syndrome	Extra Y sex chromosome in position 23	1 in 250 males	Reportedly antisocial, aggressive, and criminal tendencies, but genetic potential may be buffered by environment; below average IQ; above average height; excessive acne

(Adapted from Baer, 1973; McClearn and DeFries, 1973; and Winchester, 1975)

tion, and early childhood death. This disease is caused by an enzyme deficiency which is detectable in fetal amniotic cells.

Other test results may offer only statistical data. Hemophilia, the inability of the blood to clot, is a simple example. For families that carry this disorder, if two XXs are found, the fetus (a female) will probably not have hemophilia. If the test reveals that the fetus is male, it can only be stated that there is a 50-50 chance that he will be a hemophiliac. Which X chromosome he inherited from the mother cannot presently be determined.

For women wishing to undergo amniocentesis, the 14th through 16th weeks of pregnancy seem optimal. There are sufficient fetal cells in the amniotic sac, which is large enough to lessen the likelihood of needle puncture injuring the fetus. This also allows time for a safe abortion, if desired (Kaye, 1981).

Summary

Sylvia, age 5

A sperm penetrates an egg as it travels along the fallopian tube and a new life commences. This single-cell zygote has received 23 chromosomes from the sperm and 23 chromosomes from the egg. These 46 chromosomes are located in the nucleus. Each chromosome consists of genes containing small units of information. DNA is the chemical substance that constitutes the chromosomes and their small "gene" units. Each gene is chemically arranged to contain a "code" and carries its genetic message (code) to "protein manufacturing plants" called ribosomes, which are located outside the nucleus in the cytoplasm. The genetic message is known as messenger RNA. Ribosomes synthesize the proteins (and enzymes) of which people are made, and the cells become the specialized organs and tissues that compose the human body.

Gestation is 266 days in the human, although it is more convenient to refer to pregnancy as having a nine-month duration. Most development occurs during the first trimester. In these three months, the body, head, arms, legs, nerve cells, heart, and other internal organs are formed. The second trimester is characterized by continued development and also growth. From weighing 1 ounce and being approximately 3 inches long, the fetus gains 1½ pounds and becomes over a foot long.

In the last trimester, all the organs, including the late-developing lungs, become operable. The fetus gains 6 pounds during the last three months and grows at least 6 inches longer. After nine months, the fetus is fully developed and is called a full-term baby.

While ethical and moral considerations greatly inhibit prenatal research (especially for humans), nevertheless considerable knowledge is available. The most desirable prenatal environment is provided by a woman in her twenties who is strong and healthy; has a well-balanced diet; and doesn't smoke, drink, or take supplemental drugs—at least not in excess.

Nicotine, alcohol, heroin, and other drugs have negative effects on the developing organism. Although maternal emotions do not affect the fetus, evidence indicates that hormones secreted while the mother is under stress may. Teratogenic agents, such as thalidomide or rubella, may produce abnormalities, anomalies, or malformation. Amniocentesis, a recent technique, allows medical authorities to detect chromosomal abnormalities by removing amniotic fluid and examining the fetus's genetic makeup.

Suggested Reading List

Moore, K. L. *The Developing Human,* 3rd ed. Philadelphia: Saunders, 1981. An authoritative and clinically oriented textbook on the anatomical and physiological development of the human embryo.

Nilsson, L., Furuhjelm, M., Ingelman-Sundberg, A., and Wirsen, C. *A Child is Born.* New York: Dell, 1977. The drama of life before birth unfolds in a most enjoyable and interesting fashion. Photographs by world-famous photographer Lennart Nilsson are combined with text to offer readers an understandable presentation of prenatal life. Also informative for prospective parents.

Rugh, R., and Shettles, L. *From Conception to Birth: The Drama of Life's Beginnings.* New York: Harper & Row, 1971. An extravagantly illustrated book showing all stages of prenatal development.

Chapter Five

The Neonate

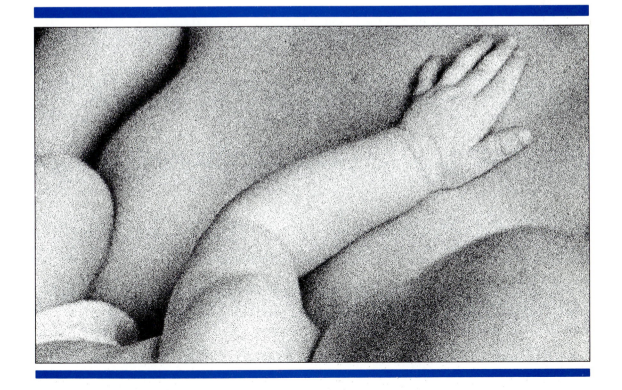

His own parents, he that father'd him and she that
had conceived him in her womb and birth'd him.
They gave this child more of themselves than that,
they gave him afterward everyday, they became
part of him.

Walt Whitman

Introduction

Following a relatively comfortable, unstimulating suspension in the
amniotic sac, the infant is suddenly squeezed through a comparatively
small birth canal into a world that stimulates virtually every sense organ
of the body. A barrage of stimuli follow—bright lights, noises, drops of
silver nitrate in the eyes, and injections into the muscles—all of which
constitute a most unpleasant welcome into the world. Since the organism is maturing from conception onward and environmental effects
begin long before we are born, birth may represent a less momentous
event for the baby than for the parents.

The term for a newborn infant is **neonate,** and it applies to the first
month of life (although sometimes its use is confined to the first week
or two). This is the transitory period from fetal to extrauterine life, the
period in which the newborn adapts, adjusts, and stabilizes in the
external world.

Labor and Delivery

Stages of Labor

By the end of the third trimester of pregnancy, the woman is ready to
give birth to her child. Physical development of the fetus is complete,
and most babies move into a head-downward position for delivery.

Some babies (approximately 5 percent), however, assume a breech position, meaning that the buttocks or the feet will move into the **cervix** (lowest part of the **uterus**) first. Buttocks first is called the frank breech position, and feet first is called the footling breech position. A **breech delivery** is more difficult than the normal headfirst delivery.

It is generally recognized that labor consists of three stages (see Figure 5.1). The first stage is the onset of rhythmic contractions of the uterus. Initially, the contractions are irregular, but they increase in strength and become regular as labor progresses. The duration of the first stage is an individual phenomenon and highly variable; it may last from 2 to 18 hours. First labors are generally longer than successive ones. At their peak intensity, first-stage contractions occur about every 3 to 5 minutes and last approximately 45 to 60 seconds. These contractions cause the cervix to open until full **dilation** is reached. When this occurs, the baby is able to move out of the uterus, and the next stage begins.

The second stage of labor is the delivery of the baby. The uterus now contracts to push the baby into the **vagina,** or birth canal, and out of the mother's body. This expulsive stage may last for about an hour and ends with a normal vaginal delivery. If the baby's position or size is a concern, or if the mother develops physical problems, a **cesarean delivery** may be performed. When this happens, the baby is delivered through a surgical incision made in the abdominal and uterine walls. About 15 percent of all births are cesarean deliveries (National Institute of Health, 1981).

The third and final stage of labor is the expulsion of the placenta. After the baby has been delivered, uterine contractions expel the placenta and the remaining portion of the umbilical cord. This stage lasts approximately 20 minutes.

Delivery Techniques

While some mothers continue to deliver their babies in a conservative medical and hospital setting, growing numbers of mothers now want a more informal setting in which family members can be present at birth. Most hospitals now encourage **natural childbirth** (giving birth without anesthesia) and admit fathers and other family members to the delivery room as well. (This is a major change in attitude from a decade or two ago when the expectant mother was anesthetized and isolated.) Analgesics (drugs that eliminate pain without making you unconscious) are available on request.

Some expectant couples who opt for natural childbirth (in either hospital or home) attend classes that stress special breathing exercises and relaxation responses. Practitioners of this approach reason that fears during delivery cause women to tense their muscles, which delays

116

**Figure 5.1
Labor and delivery: stages of the birth process. The birth process consists of three stages. In the first stage the uterus contracts rhythmically, which enables the cervix to open. During the second stage the uterus contracts and pushes the baby into the birth canal and out of the mother's body. In the third stage the placenta is expelled.**

Stage One: rhythmic contractions of the uterus

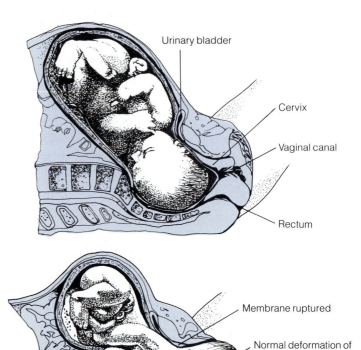

Urinary bladder

Cervix

Vaginal canal

Rectum

Stage Two: delivery of the baby

Membrane ruptured

Normal deformation of head by passage through birth canal

Stage Three: expulsion of the placenta

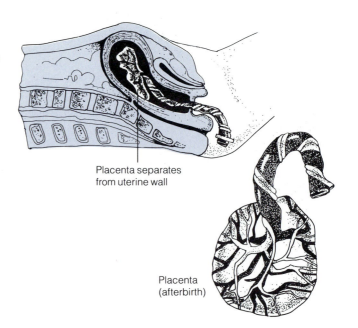

Placenta separates from uterine wall

Placenta (afterbirth)

the birth process and increases the mother's pain. If women know what to expect and learn how to relax, discomfort should be significantly reduced. Such preparation for birth was developed as early as 1940 by the English obstetrician Grantly Dick-Read.

The **Lamaze method** (named after Dr. Fernand Lamaze, a French **obstetrician**) is one of the most popular alternative approaches. In Lamaze classes, mothers learn about prenatal development and the stages of labor and are taught breathing techniques and muscular exercises. The Lamaze method and others like it are conditioned learning techniques, which teach the mother to replace one set of learned responses (fear, pain) with another (relaxation and muscle control).

Frederic Leboyer, a French obstetrician, has focused on the trauma of birth in his best-selling and controversial book *Birth without Violence* (1975). Childbirth, he feels, should be a gentle affair rather than a series of traumatic events for the newborn.

The **Leboyer method** for a more gentle arrival into the world offers a marked contrast to conventional childbirth procedures. The baby is born into a dimly lit delivery room that is kept relatively silent. Immediately after birth the infant is placed on the mother's stomach to be gently massaged, the belief being that tactile stimulation and contact soothe the baby. The infant is further soothed by a warm bath. Only after this is the baby given a routine medical examination.

Leboyer suggests that such transitional steps minimize the trauma of birth and the abrupt departure of the infant from the womb, but his ideas have not gained universal acceptance. Critics maintain that it is dangerous to postpone the examination of the neonate, especially when dim lighting may prevent the detection of vital life signs. Moreover, researchers have not been able to find any long-range benefits among infants delivered by the Leboyer method (Nelson et al., 1980).

More couples today opt for **home births** because of increased hospital costs and impersonal neonatal and postpartum care. Home births are often conducted by a licensed **midwife,** trained delivery specialists who provide qualified medical care to expectant mothers. Usually the midwife has earned a bachelor's degree in nursing and a master's degree in nurse-midwifery and works on a medical team consisting of a gynecologist and an obstetrician. The nurse-midwife spends a considerable amount of time with the mother before, during, and after the delivery and offers close personal attention in a relaxed and comfortable setting.

Rooming-in and birthing room hospital facilities are also increasing in popularity. Hospitals offering **rooming-in** allow the mother to care for the newborn in her own room. The infant is usually brought to the mother's room within the first few hours after birth and remains there (rather than in the nursery) during the duration of hospitalization. A **birthing room** offers a homelike and relaxed atmosphere within the hospital delivery unit. The mother experiences labor and delivery in this room rather than being rushed to the delivery room prior to birth. In some facilities, a birthing chair is available. A birthing chair allows the mother to sit up, a position in which gravity helps her deliver the baby.

The advantages and rewards to be reaped from these progressive concepts are numerous, including easy access for the father, greater attention and care directed to the newborn, earlier bonding, and the earlier opportunity for both husband and wife to assume their new role as parents.

Increasing numbers of hospitals allow fathers to share in the birth experience.

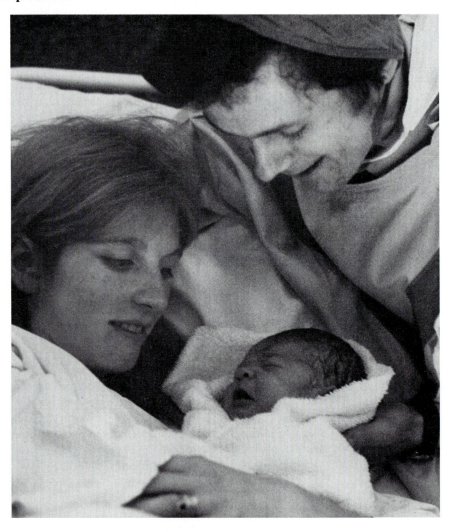

Neonatal Adjustment

Some researchers contend that the neonate must pass successfully through six overlapping stages to survive and achieve normal development in the external world. Briefly, step 1 (which occurs during labor) is adjustment to the stimuli of uterine contractions; step 2 consists of adaptation to foreign stimuli (sound, cold, light, etc.); step 3 is the change from dependence on placental oxygen to independent breathing; and steps 4 and 5 include the numerous and massive biological changes that occur as the neonate begins to use all of its own organs. The final step, which according to medical authorities is an especially crucial one, is the balancing (homeostasis) of all of the aforementioned physiological processes. This takes place throughout the first four weeks of life (Arnold, 1965; Desmond et al., 1967).

While neonates are going through the first steps of this transitional period, the hospital medical staff is taking measures to ensure their adjustment for survival. Respiration and heartbeat are the first concerns, with steps being taken to assure that respiration occurs as soon as the infant makes its appearance. As the head appears, mucus and fluids are wiped from the nose and mouth to assure normal respiration. After the full delivery is completed, the neonate is held in a head-down position, which prevents mucus and other matter (amniotic fluid, blood, etc.) from entering the respiratory passage. Gauze, or a small suction bulb, is generally used to clean out this matter, especially when a newborn has more than the normal amount of liquid present in the respiratory passage.

Contrary to popular belief, the birth cry does not occur simultaneously with the birth of the baby. Rather, the neonate gasps or cries shortly after the mucus has been removed and respiration commences. All that is required to stimulate crying is gentle rubbing of the neonate's back, which also promotes the drainage of liquids from the respiratory passage. The proverbial, but obsolete, slap on the buttocks not only is an unnecessary irritation but also can be dangerous to the infant.

Neonatal Tests, Checks, and Preventive Measures

Approximately one minute after birth and again five minutes later, a "score" is given to the infant based on a "systems check" designed to evaluate life signs. The **Apgar test** (named after the late Virginia Apgar, an internationally recognized specialist who concentrated on studying problems of the neonate) is a quick, simple, safe method of evaluating the neonate's overall condition.

The Apgar score is based on five life signs, which are listed in order of importance in Table 5.1. A score is given for each sign according to the degree of "life" present. By taking all of the vital signs of life into

Table 5.1 The Apgar Score

Sign	Score		
	0	1	2
Heart rate	Absent	Slow (less than 100)	Over 100
Respiratory effort	Absent	Slow, irregular, weak cry	Good strong cry
Muscle tone	Limp	Some flexion of extremities	Active motion
Reflex irritability	No response	Some motion	Vigorous cry and movement
Color	Blue, pale	Body pink, extremities blue	Completely pink

(Adapted from Apgar, 1953; Apgar and James, 1962.)

account, the newborn can be given an Apgar score in a surprisingly short time. A score of 7 to 10 indicates that the neonate is in generally good condition, whereas a score from 4 to 6 is considered fair. In the latter case, there will most likely be further clearing of the air passage and immediate administration of oxygen. A score of 0 to 3 indicates that the neonate is dead or in extremely poor condition. In the latter case, the child requires immediate emergency procedures (Apgar, 1953).

One additional factor to consider when evaluating immediate post-natal behavior is the amount of anesthesia the mother has received. What enters the mother's system also enters the fetal body; thus, a heavily drugged mother would have a less responsive child than an unanaesthetized mother. Table 5.2 lists some preventive measures that can be taken to safeguard the neonate after birth.

Prematurity

Since a mother can rarely pinpoint the exact day of conception, pre-maturity cannot effectively be defined in terms of days or months of gestation. However, ultrasound can be used to identify fetal size, and this, along with other tests, can help determine the age of the fetus. Most medical doctors define a **premature infant** as an infant who weighs less than 2,500 grams (5½ pounds) *and* is experiencing medical

Table 5.2 Other Neonatal Preventive Measures

Preventive Measure	Mode of Application	Reasons for Use
Vitamin K$_1$	Injection	Prevents hemorrhaging (from disease, circumcision, laceration)
Silver nitrate	Eye drops	Prevents contracting highly contagious gonorrhea in eyes and resultant blindness
Penicillin	Injection (optional)	Combats syphilis

Table 5.3 Birth Weight and Infant Mortality Rate

Birth Weight (grams)	Birth Weight (pounds)	Mortality Rate (per 1,000 live births)
1,000 or less	2 lb., 3 oz. or less	919
1,001–1,500	2 lb., 4 oz.–3 lbs., 4 oz.	548
1,501–2,000	3 lb., 5 oz.–4 lb., 6 oz.	207
2,001–2,500	4 lb., 7 oz.–5 lb., 8 oz.	58
2,501–3,000	5 lb., 9 oz.–6 lb., 9 oz.	19
3,001–4,500	6 lb., 10 oz.–9 lb., 14 oz.	9
4,501 or more	9 lb., 15 oz. or more	13

(Source: U.S. Department of Health, Education, and Welfare; Health Services and Mental Health Administration, National Center for Health Statistics.)

complications. Many neonates weigh well under 2,500 grams but, because there are no physiological problems, can develop normally with appropriate care. Any neonate weighing less than this will probably have at least some difficulty surviving, for a baby this tiny will not have reached a stage of sufficient development to survive independently (see Table 5.3). Premature infants often cannot breathe without aid or regulate their body temperatures. They also may lack the normal protective layer of subcutaneous fat.

Several studies indicate some factors that may contribute to prematurity. Premies are most often born to women who are nonwhite, come from poor neighborhoods, suffer from malnutrition, or are diabetics. It has also been discovered that premature infants are not always simply underweight. Relationships have been established between prematurity and cerebral palsy, epilepsy, hearing difficulties, and mental retardation (Kessner, 1973).

Inborn (Genetic) Errors of Metabolism

An **inborn error of metabolism** means that the body is either not producing a needed protein (or enzyme), producing too much of one, or producing a mutant enzyme that is toxic to the system. As early as 1909 it was noted that some people inherited metabolic errors that led eventually to severe physical and even mental problems. Although more metabolic errors have since been noted, this field of scientific investigation remains relatively unexplored. Consequently, with a few exceptions, little can be done to counteract such genetic defects.

Phenylketonuria (PKU), a fairly rare disorder (1 in 40,000 births), is one example of an inborn error of metabolism. This disorder is caused by the absence of the enzyme phenylalanine hydroxylase, normally found in the liver. The chemical phenylalanine is contained in milk and other common foods and is normally oxidized by the aforementioned enzyme. However, infants who receive two recessive genes for this enzyme are unable to produce sufficient amounts of it. The result is that phenylalanine builds up to an extremely high level and is converted into a toxic acid (phenylpyruvic acid) that can damage brain cells. It should be noted that a child with this disorder appears normal at birth and may continue to appear normal for a year or two before the toxic acid buildup produces obvious deterioration, mental retardation, and hyperactivity.

Hospitals require medical staffs to administer the Guthrie test (or a similar test), which is designed to determine whether phenylalanine is being oxidized properly. If it is not, the child is placed on a diet especially low in phenylalanine to prevent the chemical from building up to poisonous levels. As a precautionary measure, a PKU child must be kept on the special diet for many years, maybe even for life.

Reflexes and Lower Levels of Behavior

After undergoing necessary emergency, precautionary, or preventive measures, the neonate is given a complete physical examination. Measurement of body length and weight and the size of the head, as well as scrutiny for any deformity or abnormality, are all encompassed in this part of postbirth routine.

The other major life process that needs appraisal is the nervous system, particularly the brain. Although a neonate is born with all nerve cells present, most have not fully developed, so tests of the nervous system cannot predict the newborn's potential aptitudes or skills. They can, however, indicate normality or the presence of neurological problems.

What a Healthy Newborn Baby Looks Like

The baby's weight, unless well above the average of 7 to 8 pounds, will not prepare you for how tiny the newborn is. Top-to-toe measurement is between 18 and 21 inches.

A deep flush spreads over the entire body if the baby cries hard. Veins on the head swell and throb. You will notice no tears, as tear ducts do not function yet. The skin is thin and dry, and you may see veins through it. The baby's fair skin may be rosy red temporarily. Downy hair is not unusual. Some vernix caseosa (white prenatal skin covering) remains.

The head usually seems too big for the body. It may also be temporarily out of shape—lopsided or elongated—from pressure before or during birth. On the skull you will see or feel the two most obvious soft spots, or *fontanels*. One is above the brow, the other close to the crown of the head in the back. The scalp skin may be loose, and the brows may be wrinkled. A crop of thick hair or a bald head is normal. The face will disappoint you unless you expect to see pudgy cheeks, a broad flat nose with a mere hint of a bridge, receding chin, and an undersized lower jaw. The eyes appear dark blue or gray. You may catch one or both turning or turned to cross- or wall-eyed position. The lids are characteristically puffy.

The neck is short, and the trunk has small sloping shoulders, swollen breasts, large rounded abdomen, umbilical stump (future navel), and slender pelvis and hips. Genitals of both sexes seem large (especially the scrotum) in comparison with the scale of the hands to adult size.

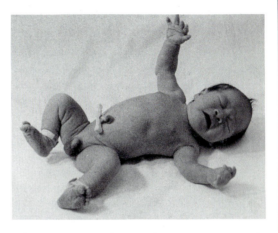

Newborn baby boy with legs still drawn up in prebirth position.

The hands, if you open them out flat from their characteristic fist position, have finely lined palms, paper-thin nails, dry loose-fitting skin, and deep bracelet creases at the wrists. The legs are most often drawn up against the abdomen in a prebirth position. Extended legs are shorter than you would expect, compared to the arms. The knees stay slightly bent and the legs are bowed.

The feet look more complete than they really are. An X ray would show only one real bone, located at the heel. Other bones are still only cartilage. ■

Source: From *American Baby for the Mother-to-Be and New Mother,* July, 1973.

Tests of the nervous system are generally checks of **reflexes,** the automatic responses to stimuli that do not involve higher brain functions. Neurological problems often involve the total nervous system, cortical areas as well as subcortical, or reflex, areas. Over time these subcortical reflexes will reach the cortical level (i.e., the automatic reflex will be lost, and the individual will have voluntary control over the behavior). By keeping records on an individual, the maturation of the nervous system can be traced and compared to normative data.

In addition to the major reflexes (see Table 5.4), approximately 15 other reflexes serve various protective, defensive, or survival functions in the newborn. For example, there are coughing, sneezing, gagging, and yawning reflexes; several reflexes of the eye; and the sphincter reflex.

Table 5.4 Major Reflexes Present at Birth

Reflex	Stimulus	Response	Meaning	Other Comments
Moro or startle	Any: loud noise, bumping crib, sudden loss of support, jerking blanket	Legs draw up, back arches, arms are brought forward in hugging or embracing motion; symmetrical movements	Absence indicates immaturity or edema of brain or brain damage. Presence indicates awareness of equilibrium	Basic reflex lost 3–6 months after birth. Can appear in modified form even in adult
Grasp or palmar; plantar	Any object placed on palms or soles	Hands grasp object with firm grip then let go, toes curl downward	Absence indicates neural depression	No thumb involved, reflex lost by 12 months. Infant can sustain own weight when lifted
Sucking (accompanies swallow reflex)	Touch lips	Sucking movements	Absence indicates immaturity, narcosis, brain injury, or retardation	Lost if not stimulated, generalized at first, but becomes more efficient as time goes by
Rooting	Touch cheek	Head turns toward touch	Prepares infant for sucking	Inexperienced mothers may touch cheek to turn baby toward nipple. Baby will root (i.e., turn the other way)

Aside from the sucking reflex, however, no continuity has been documented for the normal child between early reflexive behavior and significant social or cognitive behavior in later life.

Generalized or random movement that has little, if any, purpose frequently accompanies reflexes. Such generalized movements can be observed with the withdrawal reflex. When one foot is pulled, it will be withdrawn. However, a number of accompanying movements of arms, as well as the withdrawal of the other leg, are also part of the reflex action. With the partial exception of some reflexes, most behavior at the neonatal level is similar to the generalized state just described. For example, it has been found that infants make sucking movements when their hair is pulled. However, as the nervous system develops, the innate

Table 5.4 Continued

Reflex	Stimulus	Response	Meaning	Other Comments
Withdrawal	Heat (bottle), pin-prick (diaper)	Recoil from pain and cry	Absence indicates neural immaturity or damage	Protects against harmful stimuli
Babinski	Any foot (sole) stimulation	Fanning (spreading) of toes	Persistence indicates lack of myelination or other malfunction	Disappears at 4–6 months; convenient for noting cerebration progress
Swimming	Place in water	Can swim; head down, exhales slowly through mouth		6–12 months; child probably can make smooth transition to voluntary swimming
Swimming (out of water)	Flashing strobe lights, high temperature, electrical stimulation of the brain	Swimming motions even though not in water		Can occur at any age

reflexes diminish, and more specific responses occur. For example, although a loud noise will elicit the **Moro reflex** in the neonate (the whole body responds), less and less of the body responds as the infant becomes older, until finally only the head turns in the direction of the sound. The loss of certain reflexes is an indicator of normal neurological development.

Early Behavior: Sensory States

Most people, especially parents of newborn infants, tend to view neonates as helpless creatures of miniature proportions who are incapable of anything except crying, feeding, burping, sleeping, and excreting. As a result, parents of newborns often perceive their function in these terms: feed, burp and change the baby, and put the child in a crib to sleep most of the day. This view is incomplete because it overlooks a great deal of competent behavior exhibited by newborns, such as seeing, hearing, smelling, and feeling pain. Although not fully developed, the nervous system is capable of receiving input from varying stimuli via the sense organs. But, while neonates are capable of receiving many stimuli, some senses may be developed less fully than others and the responses to them are limited.

Neonates have few primary needs, but all those needs must be met for survival. The child obviously needs oxygen, and the air temperature should be no lower than 21°C (70°F). The need for food is limited to liquids during the neonatal period, although some pediatricians have been known to put children on cereal as early as the fourth day. Bottle feeders usually start eating food at 3 months and breast feeders at 5 to 6 months. Urination and defecation are also classified as primary needs, although initially they are simply reflex actions.

Another primary need is for sleep, and infants spend 18 to 20 hours a day in sleep. The various states of sleep and arousal and behavior during these "states" have been generally classified in Table 5.5, which offers a guideline for neonate behavior, at least during the first four days of life (Wolff, 1966).

As the weeks go by, infants increase the time they spend in alert inactivity. The average time spent in alert inactivity for the first week is 11 hours; this time is nearly doubled by the fourth week. During alert inactivity infants seem most receptive to stimuli from the environment. Because of this, tests of facilities, abilities, and the developmental status of the sensory system are more frequently administered during periods of alert inactivity. Tests have revealed, however, that not all activity ceases during sleep. From birth, infants display rapid eye movement

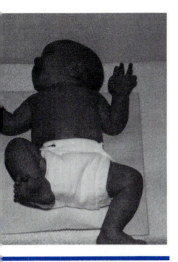

The Moro reflex, or startle response, is one of more than 20 reflexes found in the neonate.

(REM) during sleep; thus, even when newborns are asleep, their minds are active (Roffwarg, Muzio, and Dement, 1966).

Vision

Of all the senses, vision has been the most widely studied; hence, more is known about it than any other sense. At birth the eyes are functional, although not fully developed. Infants can see light and dark (pupillary reflex) and at least some degree of color. The immature portions of the eye include the optic nerve, eyeball muscles, and undeveloped cells for color vision. Although light can be received by the visual receptors, newborns cannot focus properly or coordinate the two eyes owing to lack of neural maturity (Bornstein, Kessen, and Wieskopf, 1976; Maurer and Maurer, 1976; Salapatek, 1975).

Newborns can fixate on a light and, within a few days, can even follow, or track, a moving light. Visual acuity improves markedly within

Table 5.5 States of Arousal

State or Degree of Arousal	Characteristic Behavior
Regular sleep	Regular breathing is probably due in part to need, plus little internal or external stimulation. Very little body movement is present. Infant does not respond to mild stimulation.
Irregular sleep	Breathing becomes more irregular, and body movement increases as infant makes the transition from regular sleep. Infant is more easily aroused by external stimuli.
Drowsiness	Infant shows little motor activity but is sensitive to external stimulation.
Alert inactivity	After basic needs are catered to, infant seems alert, relaxed, and may become attentive to specific stimuli.
Waking activity	Diffuse activity is provoked by a mild state of physiological need. Soft whimperings and gentle movements gradually become louder and more spastic.
Crying	Infant thrashes about. Loud crying or screeching is caused by noxious stimuli or a cycle of motility that suggests the more sensitive infants become, the more they cry; and the more they cry, the more sensitive they become.

(Adapted from Wolff, 1966.)

the next few weeks. In approximately a month's time, the lens can make the necessary accommodation for proper focusing and becomes able to focus on objects at varying distances. No adjustments are made during the early weeks, but after one month infants seem to have a natural focal point of 7½ inches. At 2 months infants begin to accommodate to greater distances, and at 3 months they can properly focus on both near and far objects. By the end of the fourth month infants apparently focus as well as adults (Salapatek, 1975). Developing cortical control during this time also enables infants to scan with greater efficiency (Bronson, 1982; Banks and Salapatek, 1981).

Psychologists, of course, are less interested in physiological development of the eye than in **attention,** which is the act of focusing on stimuli. Various kinds of apparatus measure how long an infant will fixate on an object. Studies show that given several stimuli to choose from, infants prefer a more complex pattern, such as the human face or bull's-eyes, over simple designs of circles or colors. In other words, the more complex the configuration, the longer the fixation time (Haaf, 1977). Other studies indicate that infants prefer areas of contrast, probably because the change stimulates the nerve cells. As Figure 5.2 shows, when infants are shown a triangle, they invariably fixate at an angle (Kessen, 1967). In another study on visual preference, researchers discovered that infants 2 to 4 months old will exhibit preferences when given choices of two or three checkerboard patterns but are incapable of dealing with as many as five (Greenberg and Blue, 1977). Figure 5.3 shows infants' fixation on different stimuli.

Figure 5.2 Kessen's experiments with newborns revealed that infants fixate at the vertices of triangles (blue lines). Note, however, the individual differences in fixation points. (From Salapatek and Kessen, 1966.)

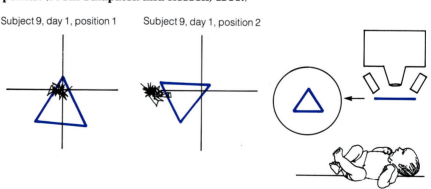

Subject 9, day 1, position 1   Subject 9, day 1, position 2

Audition

The presence of amniotic fluid and mucus in the auditory canal inhibits the reception of auditory stimuli at birth, but once the canal is clear, newborns respond to sounds in their environment. This is evidenced by changes in heart rates and bodily reactions to auditory stimulation.

Research suggests that neonates are more apt to respond to long and continuous tones than to shorter or intermittent sounds. They are also capable of detecting the locations of some sounds, although sounds directly ahead are perceived more accurately than those to the left or right (Bower, 1974; Ling, 1972). Newborns cry less when they hear soothing sounds such as a heartbeat or lullaby (Salk, 1962; Brackbill et al., 1967) and fuss or cry more when they hear a tape of another baby crying (Simner, 1971) or other high-pitched sounds.

Figure 5.3 Infants fixate for different times on varying stimuli. (From R. L. Fantz. *Visual Perception from Birth as Shown by Pattern Selectivity.* Copyright, The New York Academy of Sciences, 1965, Vol. 118. Reprinted by permission.)

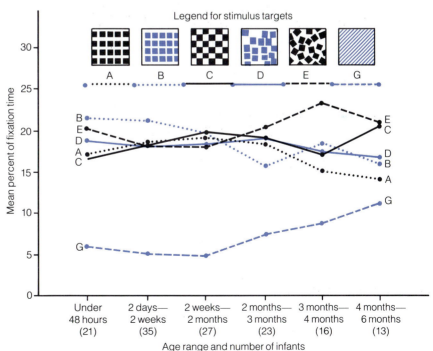

Although infants respond most readily to sound intensities, some studies reveal that they are also sensitive to variations in pitch. Infants exhibit more alert activity in response to high-frequency tones than to lower-frequency tones. However, low-pitched sounds (500 to 900 Hertz, or cycles per second) produce more reliable and persistent responses than high-pitched sounds (4,000 to 5,000 Hertz), such as the sound made by a whistle. Neonates are also believed to react more readily to pitch variations within the range of the human voice (Eisenberg, 1970; Eisenberg et al., 1964; Webster, Steinhardt, and Senter, 1972).

Interestingly, neonates can be soothed by a continuous sound and will habituate, or become accustomed, to noise. For example, researchers presented infants with a 10-second tone (200 CPS of 75 decibels) until the neonates exhibited no change in respiration, gross body movement, or foot withdrawal. Apparently, the babies became accustomed to the noise and exhibited some adjustment and adaptation. Such studies may explain in part why the sound of calm and gentle lullabies has such a soothing effect on newborns (Levanthal and Lipsitt, 1964).

In an attempt to determine their auditory-visual coordination, newborns were subjected to visual targets for tracking purposes. It was found that while they would track with their eyes, their tracking was uninfluenced by the addition of sound to the moving visual target. Thus there appears to be a "relative independence of auditory and visual perception during the neonatal period" (McGurk, Turnura, and Creighton, 1977). Recent research also indicates that the left side of a newborn's brain (the "hearing" side) shows more electrical response to speech sounds than the right (Molfese, Freeman, and Palermo, 1975).

Taste and Smell

Within weeks after birth, taste sensitivity becomes quite discriminatory. Neonates can distinguish between a number of solutions, including sweet and bitter (Lipsitt, 1980), and can even distinguish between certain types of sugar solutions. In one study the tongue pressure of 1-day-old infants sucking on a nipple was measured in relation to amounts of sugar concentrate added to the liquid being consumed. The infants' tongue pressure increased in direct relationship to the increase in sugar, leading the researchers to believe that taste sensitivity is quite well developed at birth (Desor, Maller, and Andrews, 1975; Engen, Lipsitt, and Peck, 1974; Nowlis and Kessen, 1976).

While the sense of smell is relatively weak immediately after birth, it apparently improves within the first few days. Researchers have found that babies can distinguish among several diverse odors and between differences in intensity. So, like the other senses, an efficient olfactory system is usually developed during the neonatal period (Acredolo and Hake, 1982; Alberts, 1981; Lipsitt, 1980).

Pain and Temperature Sensitivity

For the first few days, infants experience relatively little pain. Very young male babies undergo circumcision without anesthetic because of this insensitivity to pain. But sensitivity increases within a matter of days. In a study designed to investigate infants' pain sensitivity, electrodermal stimulation was administered to the foot region. As expected, the pain threshold was extremely low for the first few days of life and then rapidly increased (Lipsitt and Levy, 1959).

Although considerable individual differences are associated with thermal sensitivity, it is generally agreed that infants' sensory awareness and corresponding reactions are quite similar. Most infants can detect the extremes of hot and cold. Infants usually become less active when warm, while cold stimuli induce a more active state with increased breathing rates and bodily reactions.

Early Behavior and Individual Differences

Activity Levels

Behavioral differences exist among neonates from the moment they are born. Each child is born with a certain individuality, which influences the mother from the very start. Differences in **temperament,** notably crying and overt movements, are more noticeable than the subtler forms of behavioral reaction.

In one experiment, 30 neonates were tested with four different stimuli and rated according to their response. The four stimuli were a soft tone, a loud tone, a cold disk, and a pacifier. Some reacted vigorously to all stimuli, some reacted mildly to all stimuli, and others ranged in the middle. The newborns were tested on the second and fifth days after birth, and the individual differences expressed on the first testing were also present on the second testing (Birns, 1965).

Some infants are very active, others are passive, and most are somewhere in between. Some are very responsive to environmental stimuli, showing an interest in the world about them; others respond irritably to environmental stimuli; still others are placid and smile frequently. Suffice it to say that no two babies are exactly alike in their overall dispositions.

But this doesn't mean that children can't share certain general temperaments. On the contrary, research conducted by Alexander Thomas and Stella Chess (1977; 1980) shows that certain broad categories of temperament can be established. Thomas and Chess conducted a 20-year longitudinal study of 141 children, beginning when the subjects were 3 months old. They rated the subjects on nine temperament traits over the 20-year span. The traits included activity level, attention span, distractibility, adaptability, approach/withdrawal behavior to new environmental stimuli, regularity (in eating, sleeping, etc.), general responsiveness, mood, and general intensity of behavioral reactions.

The data gathered over the years revealed three types of temperaments:

1. The *easy child* is adaptable, mild, and cheerful. This youngster accepts schedules and routines and adjusts easily to changes in the environment. Approximately 40 percent of the children studied were categorized as easy.

2. The *difficult child* is intense in mood, slow in adapting, and has a tendency to withdraw from people. The difficult child frequently has temper tantrums, shows irregular eating and sleeping patterns, and is generally hard to live with. Approximately 10 percent of the children studied were labeled difficult.

3. The *slow-to-warm-up child* adapts slowly to environmental change and in general has a low activity level. These children demonstrate mild negative behavior, but positive behavior frequently evolves when parents are patient. About 15 percent of the youngsters studied fell into this category.

Neonates exhibit a wide variety of temperaments ranging from passivity through hyperactivity.

 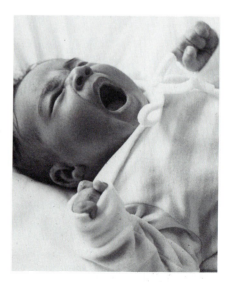

The remaining 35 percent of the children studied did not fit easily into these categories.

In the 65 percent that could be classified, many of the temperamental traits observed at birth were present in some form ten years later. Some had diminished over time, and some had become more prominent.

Studies such as this illustrate how we might inherit genetic behavioral predispositions, as well as how the environment affects our personality development. Knowledge of temperament may also help parents develop a style that promotes the most effective communication. A word of caution, though, about the total prediction value of temperament. Because temperament is modified by experience, motivation, environmental events, and a number of other variables, there is no guarantee that an infant will retain the same temperamental qualities throughout life.

Crying

Now let us examine some of the differences in crying behavior. After the birth cry, which one hopes is full of youthful vigor, the newborn will cease crying and will not cry again unless annoyed by hunger, wetness, or illness. In addition to general annoyance cries, there are the piercing cry of the baby with colic and the easily aroused, fussy cry of the hypertonic baby. Hypertonic infants are awake more than the average newborn, appear very active, and are startled and cry more readily than other newborns. There is no apparent reason for this behavior, except that hypertonics seem unable to relax like other neonates. Hypertonic babies can be calmed considerably by holding them securely and stroking them gently. Normally, nurses are the first to notice the hypertonic baby, and they should advise the mother accordingly. Otherwise, the mother may blame herself and become distraught and anxious, which can make matters worse.

Colic has many definitions, quite possibly because no one is quite sure what causes the problem. The causes may be physiological (immature digestive tract or nervous system, for example) or psychological (infant's awareness of the mother's anxiety). Regardless of the cause, colic generally seems to include acute distress in the digestive tract and loud, piercing cries.

The crying of an infant acts as a stimulus to the parent, usually producing some form of caregiver behavior. Variations of infant crying and the parents' perceptions of the sounds help to determine what caregiver behavior is produced. For example, infants that are considered temperamental often cry at a higher pitch and for longer durations than nontemperamental children (Lounsbury and Bates, 1982). It has also been demonstrated that adults who listen to these cries exhibit increased arousal of the autonomic nervous system and other physiologic changes, in heart rate for example, and show aversion toward the children (Wiesenfeld, Zander-Malatesta, and De Loach, 1981). In one experiment three groups of adults were studied: nonparents, parents of only one child (primiparous), and parents who had two or more children (multiparous). Each group listened to three types of taped cries (difficult, average, easy). Participants in this study were given a response sheet with four sections:

1. Reaction to cry: anger/irritation, sadness, spoiled, care for

2. Cry characteristics: urgent/not urgent, pleasing/grating, sick/healthy, soothing/arousing, piercing/not piercing, comforting/not comforting, aversive/nonaversive, distressing/not distressing, manipulative/not manipulative

3. Whether the cry sounded like that of their own infant

4. Probable cause of infants' crying ranked first, second, third, etc.: wet or dirty diapers, fatigue, wants attention, teething, hunger, too hot or too cold, pain, illness, fright, frustration

Nonparents and multiparous parents exhibited arousal levels in direct correlation to the type of cry; that is, they ranked difficult cries highest. Primiparous parents, however, ranked the average cry highest. The highest overall level of arousal was also exhibited by primiparous parents, followed by nonparents. The lowest level of arousal was seen in those parents who had two or more children. Fathers had higher irritation ratings and lower care ratings than mothers (Boukydis and Burgess, 1982).

Some personality theorists (e.g., Erikson) believe that emotion is transferred via action. Thus an anxious mother may make jerky motions that frighten the child (possibly a mild form of the Moro reflex and fear of falling). A number of researchers (e.g., Lakin, 1957) have made the somewhat similar finding that mothers who are overly anxious tend to have colicky babies.

Pediatric nurses working in hospitals are trained to listen for different types of cries. Table 5.6 illustrates their variety. Although it takes some practice, alert nurses will recognize the cry and communicate their knowledge of what it means to the mother. This helps to alleviate the mother's fears and establish a better mother-child relationship from the very beginning. Child rearing and parent training are two sides of the same coin. The socialization of children involves not only the influence of parents on their children but the ways in which children affect their parents through their unique temperaments.

Table 5.6 Varieties of Infant Cries

Type of Cry	Behavior	Meaning/Interpretation
Loud insistent cry	Leg flexion and kicking	Colicky pain
Fretful cry	Passing of gas and green stools	Indigestion
Fretful cry	Fingers in mouth, extremities flexed and tensed	Hungry
Whining cry	Little movement, listless	Ill, premature, very frail
Shrill, sharp-sounding cry	Much movement or too little movement	Possible injury

(Adapted from Fitzpatrick, Eastman, and Reeder, 1966.)

Parent—Infant Bonding

The early development of the child probably depends more on the parent-infant relationship than on any single other environmental factor. The first such interaction occurs shortly after birth when the neonate is cuddled on the prone mother's chest. As parent and infant spend time together they should establish a close relationship, which is called bonding. *Bonding* is defined as a "unique relationship between two people that is specific and endures through time" (Klaus and Kennell, 1976, p. 2). Since the term was first introduced in 1976 many studies have been undertaken to explain the bonding phenomenon, which some believe has a lasting effect on child development. Most of these studies have attempted to demonstrate the presence or absence of a "sensitive period," a limited period of time when the mother becomes attached to the neonate through such behaviors as gazing, fondling, kissing, smiling, and talking. If indeed the bonding phenomenon exists, it would behoove us to establish training clinics to teach mothers how to establish such bonds.

The concept of bonding is a warm, pleasant, and comfortable explanation of the early parent-infant relationship, but unfortunately the research evidence is not yet strong enough to support the existence of a sensitive period for parent-infant bonding (Goldberg, 1983; Chess and Thomas, 1982; Lamb and Hwang, 1982). What does appear to have more basis in fact is the development of attachment behavior, which is similar to bonding but occurs at about 8 months of age. We will fully explore attachment in Chapter 8.

Summary

Alice, age 7

Delivery of the newborn consists of three stages: rhythmic contractions of the uterus, delivery of the baby, and expulsion of the placenta. While large percentages of mothers continue to deliver their babies in conventional medical settings, growing numbers are pursuing alternative delivery techniques. Among these are the Lamaze and Leboyer techniques. Also discussed in this chapter were home births, rooming-in facilities, and birthing rooms.

The neonatal period, or the first two to four weeks of life, is characterized primarily by the newborn's adaptation and adjustment to the external world. Immediately after birth, measures are taken by the physicians and staff to ensure the neonate's survival. After respiratory and circulatory needs have been attended to, the Apgar test is performed to evaluate the infant's basic life processes. Other hospital procedures are preventive in nature, including the injection of vitamin K to prevent hemorrhaging and the use of silver nitrate in the eyes to combat gonorrhea.

Genetic errors of metabolism, which indicate that the body is not producing a needed protein, are difficult bodily disorders to deal with. Although phenylketonuria (PKU) can be kept under control by special diets, other imbalances are more severe and sometimes fatal.

Reflexes, specific subcortical responses to appropriate stimuli, are frequently accompanied in infancy by generalized random movements, such as those concomitant with the withdrawal and Moro reflexes. As the child's nervous system matures, generalized, more specific, and even learned responses accompany reflex reactions.

As infants become older, they spend less time in sleep and more time in responding to sensory stimuli and other types of alert activity. Hearing, smell, taste, and sensitivity to pain are immature at birth but begin to develop rapidly shortly thereafter. Extensive investigations into the visual abilities of the infant reveal that continual improvements are made in tracking, focusing, and selective attention capacities.

Behavioral differences among newborns exist in the form of cries, especially those of colicky and hypertonic babies, as well as the degree of activity or passivity exhibited. Research presented in this chapter reveals that three categories of temperament appear to persist over time: easy, difficult, and slow-to-warm-up.

Suggested Reading List

Brazelton, T. B. *Infants and Mothers: Differences in Development,* rev. ed. New York: Dell, 1983. This book explores the course of development, including variations, during infancy.

Kaye, K. *The Mental and Social Life of Babies: How Parents Create Persons.* Chicago: University of Chicago Press, 1982. Kaye does an excellent job of describing the nature of early parent-infant interaction.

Spock, B. J., and Rothenberg, M. B. *Baby and Child Care.* New York: Pocket Books, 1985. Dr. Spock's famous book is the standard how-to guide for all new mothers. This practical book is almost a "must" for understanding and meeting an infant's needs.

Chapter Six

Physical Growth and Development

Children learn to creep ere they can learn to go.

John Haywood

Introduction

Unlike the virtually helpless generalized movement of the neonate, the infant's movement consists of a complex hierarchy of specific muscular behaviors. Control over voluntary movement is evident in numerous forms of physical expression, including walking and prehensile abilities, which develop in a sequential fashion. Although there are individual differences among infants in rates of body growth and motor achievement, growth and maturation for the most part proceed in a definite order.

The sequence of development is to a great extent due to the gradual development of cells in the brain. Even though the neonate is born with 10 billion to 14 billion cells in the cortex, most of these cells are immature and not yet able to function. As the cranial bones enlarge, the brain cells grow, develop (mature), and become more chemically active. Until a cell reaches this physical and chemical level of maturity, learning cannot take place.

Development of the Nervous System

The nervous system consists of two parts, the central and peripheral systems. The brain and the spinal cord constitute the **central nervous system,** while the **peripheral nervous system** is a network of neural tissue that connects the brain and spinal cord with other parts of the body. Together, the central and peripheral nervous systems connect the body into a unified system under direct control of the brain.

The central nervous system grows very rapidly during the early years. By the first year, the brain has attained nearly 60 percent of its adult weight of approximately 3 pounds.

Brain function is a complex activity involving the interaction of its discrete parts. Let us say at the outset, though, that the parts of the brain do not develop evenly. Rather, its parts develop at different rates and follow unique timetables. Some parts of the brain, such as the cerebral cortex, experience both rapid and slow phases of development. We will spend more time on this topic later on in this chapter.

For convenience, the brain can be divided into three major parts: the forebrain, midbrain, and hindbrain (see Figure 6.1). The **forebrain** is the frontal and upper part of the brain and represents the largest of the three divisions. The forebrain contains the brain center responsible for conscious thought and higher-order behavior. It is the forebrain that

Figure 6.1 Major structures of the brain.

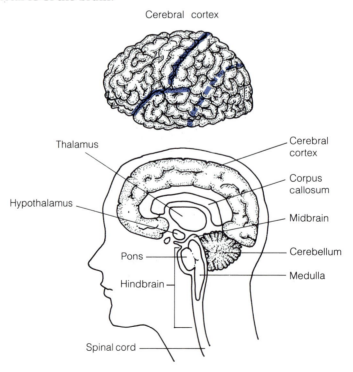

enables humans to surpass lower animal species in such areas as reasoning, speech, and complex patterns of muscle coordination.

The **cerebrum** is the largest portion of the forebrain and consists of a left and a right cerebral hemisphere. The cerebral hemispheres are connected by a bundle of nerve fibers called the **corpus callosum.** It is the corpus callosum that enables one hemisphere to know what the other is doing.

While the two cerebral hemispheres look very much alike, they differ greatly in function. The left hemisphere controls movement on the right side of the body, and vice versa. For example, if you scratch your head with your right hand, the left hemisphere of the brain is responsible for your movements. In addition, the left and right cerebral hemispheres control different functions. This type of hemispheric specialization is known as **lateralization** and emerges gradually during development. The left hemisphere is the site of language ability, systematic and logical thought (math, science, and so on), and writing, among other specializations. The right hemisphere controls primarily nonverbal functions, such as artistic or musical abilities, imagination, and the expression of emotion (Springer and Deutsch, 1985; Sperry, 1982).

The two cerebral hemispheres are covered by the **cerebral cortex,** which is grayish and wrinkled. The cerebral cortex has a number of important functions, including memory, concentration, problem-solving abilities, and muscle coordination. It is the last part of the brain to develop, continuing its growth beyond adolescence into adulthood.

The cerebral cortex is divided into four areas or regions called lobes. The **occipital lobe,** located at the back of each hemisphere, enables the brain to interpret the sensory information transmitted by the eyes. The **parietal lobe,** found at the top of each hemisphere, controls the sense of touch and transmits essential spatial information. The **temporal lobe,** located at the side of each hemisphere, is responsible for hearing as well as the storage of permanent memories. The **frontal lobe,** located behind the forehead and at the front of each hemisphere, regulates the sense of smell as well as body movement and control.

Two other parts of the forebrain are the thalamus and hypothalamus. The **thalamus,** located at the base of the cerebrum, relays nerve impulses from sensory pathways to the cerebral cortex. The **hypothalamus,** located beneath the thalamus, has a variety of functions, including the regulation of hunger, thirst, sexual functions, and body temperature. The hypothalamus is also a control center for pleasure and pain.

The **midbrain** is a connecting link between the forebrain and hindbrain. The midbrain controls movements of the eye muscles and relays visual and auditory information to higher brain centers.

The **hindbrain** is the lower portion of the brain and is responsible for bodily functions necessary for survival. The **medulla oblongata** connects the brain and spinal cord and helps regulate heartbeat, respiration, digestion, and blood pressure. The **cerebellum** controls body balance and coordination. The cerebellum grows rapidly during the first two years of life and attains almost full size by the fifth year of life. The **pons** (the Latin word for bridge) is located above the medulla. It acts as a bridge between the two lobes of the cerebellum. The **reticular activating system** runs through the hindbrain into the midbrain and part of the forebrain. It is involved in arousal, attention, and the sleep cycle.

The Principle of Readiness

A child's ability to perform a physical task is based not only on certain maturational phenomena in the brain but also on the muscular and skeletal systems. This state of maturation is often called **readiness**; until a child is "ready" to perform a task, no amount of training or encouragement will be much help. For example, it is often stated that a child does not learn to walk but matures to walk. This indicates a natural sequence of physiological events.

Thus, a child will walk only when all systems are developed; if any of the systems are immature, the child will be unable to walk, despite all the coaxing in the world. In fact, too much pressure may cause **frustration** and anxiety. This does not mean that an enriched or stimulating environment is not beneficial; just the opposite is true. Once the organism has reached a sufficient level of maturity, environmental enrichment can increase the learning of physical skills (Gottlieb, 1983).

Maturation and Myelination

The genetic code (DNA) sends instructions to all body systems producing specific sequential changes that are referred to as **maturation**. Until an organism reaches a certain level of maturation, no learning can take place. As systems mature, they become capable of an increase in behavior.

Generally, the major systems concerning psychologists are the nervous, **endocrine,** and muscular systems. The cerebral cortex of an infant has virtually the same number of nerve cells as an adult brain, but the infant's cells are comparatively small and undifferentiated. It is believed that these cells are present by the seventh month of prenatal development.

Thinking processes and motor reactions emerge at varying times because different areas of the cortex develop at different rates [see Figure 6.2(a)]. Even within given areas of the cortex, there are differences in neural maturation. For instance, the neurons in the motor area that control the arms and upper trunk of the infant are more advanced than those controlling the legs (cephalocaudal and proximodistal development) (Conel, 1939–1967).

The degree of maturity of **neurons** (nerve cells) is determined by a number of criteria, including size of cell, length of **axons** and **dendrites,** and degree of myelination. Myelination is the process by which the neuron develops an outside coating **(myelin).** This myelin sheath insulates the nerve cells and allows for the rapid transmission of electrochemical messages [see Figure 6.2(b)]. Prior to myelination, signals may dissipate themselves in the surrounding body fluids instead of following the neural pathway (Teyler, 1984; Morell and Norton, 1980). In time the connections between neurons increase, and signals follow the proper pathways.

The brain continues to develop at least into adolescence, if not beyond. Thus various modes of thinking, as well as sensory and motor processes, cannot be in an individual's repertoire of behavior until the necessary maturation has occurred (Brown and Wallace, 1980).

Figure 6.2 Different areas of the cortex mature at different rates. (a) Darker shadings indicate the areas that mature earlier, and the numbers indicate the sequence of development. In the diagram of a peripheral nervous system neuron (b), note how the myelin sheath insulates the nerve cell. (Based on data from Conel, 1939–1967.)

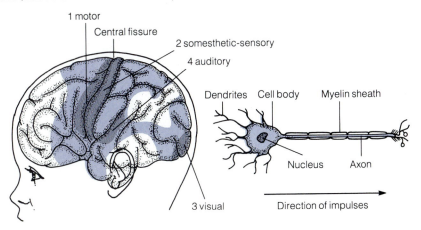

(a)   (b)

Locomotor Development

The rapid development of the motor cortex during the first year of life, particularly the area that controls the legs, paves the way for locomotor growth. **Locomotion** is defined as the progressive mobility of the child, and, like other facets of development, it unfolds in a sequence of stages. Its initial development begins at approximately 2½ months, the age at which infants can successfully raise their chests by means of arm support. At 4½ months, an infant can sit erect when supported, but there is no evidence of crawling behavior.

As the infant slowly acquires skills in using arms and hands, locomotion skills also develop. By 5 months, roughly the time when both hands are used together effectively, infants are able to roll over completely. By the age of 6 months, the infant makes the initial movements in forward mobility. By 8 months, crawling behavior emerges, and during the next one or two months infants attain considerable fluidity

Unsteady legs support the eight-month old infant.

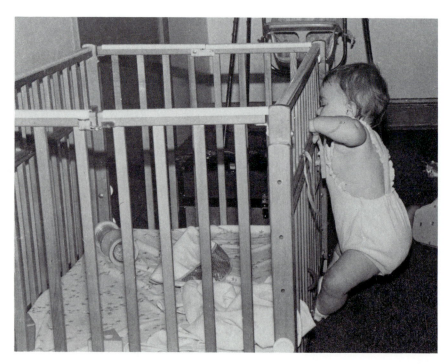

Walking facilitates early investigative behavior.

and coordination in crawling. At the same time, the arms and legs have the opportunity for exercise and development.

During the eighth month, the infant also gains the ability and strength to sit up and shift to a prone position; furthermore, the infant can stand when supported by an adult. Some children are also capable of pulling themselves up to a standing position.

Walking: From Infant to Toddler

By 13 to 15 months, the approximate age at which infants can consistently support their body weight, they are able to take their first step. When this time arrives, the toddler appears fragile and unsteady (but is soon found to be surprisingly durable); the legs are bowed and spread apart, with the weight usually on the inner part of the feet. The stomach is thrust forward, giving the youngster a rounded appearance; and the arms, used primarily for balance, are extended outward from the body.

Witnessing a toddler's early walking behavior is a memorable experience. In the beginning, all imaginable types of steps are displayed, including staggers, side steps, lurches, and backward steps. And even though children fall many times during the early phases, they pick themselves up with apparently limitless energy and determination.

An observer may estimate how much walking experience a toddler has by paying attention to four behaviors (Brazelton, 1974):

1. The stance and steps narrow as children gain locomotor experience.
2. More-experienced walkers recover fairly easily if their balance is threatened.
3. More-advanced toddlers develop other behaviors besides walking, such as turning, stopping, and picking up a toy.
4. While inexperienced walkers follow a somewhat devious and staggering path, experienced toddlers follow more direct lines.

It is important to mention that growing physical capacities blend with other developmental forces, including the cognitive prowess to master motor skills and the motivation to explore the environment, which Erik Erikson suggests is part of the toddler's quest for autonomy and initiative. Walking does present dangers, though, and parents must realize that the child is now able to explore and investigate areas that were previously inaccessible. It is a challenge to keep a constant eye on the busy explorer. Because it is common for children to reach and examine lamps, cords, bottles, and other potentially dangerous objects, such items should be kept out of the child's reach. Without curtailing the toddler's developing initiative, we want to safeguard the environment (Leach, 1983; Rubin, Fisher, and Doering, 1980).

Cross-Cultural Differences in Locomotor Development

Even though for most children walking occurs approximately by the age of 15 months, this figure is strictly an average, and averages (as discussed in Chapter 1) can be misleading. Toddlers may take their first steps months before or after this time. It should also be realized that many of the norms established for locomotion and other types of **motor skill** development are based largely on studies of children of Western cultures. Children from other parts of the world show differences in the attainment of certain skills, especially walking.

For example, it has been found that Ugandan infants acquire motor skills more quickly and easily than European or American infants. Most Ugandan babies are able to sit without support as early as 4 months and walk by 9 months, which places them considerably ahead of American schedules. Head control, muscle tone, and certain prehension abilities are also superior to those of American or European infants. This superiority appears greatest during the first year and then tapers off (Ainsworth, 1967; Kilbride, Robbins, and Kilbride, 1970; Tronik, Koslowski, and Brazelton, 1971).

The age of walking also appears to vary in European countries. An extensive study of more than 1,000 infants from five European cities revealed that toddlers from Stockholm and Brussels walked about a month earlier than youngsters from London, Paris, or Zurich. On the average, the accelerated children walked at 12½ months, while the others walked at 13½ months (Hindley et al., 1966).

What factors account for these cross-cultural differences in motor development? For African infants, a genetic explanation might be offered, especially since American black babies appear to be more advanced than American white infants in various phases of motor development during the first year (Bayley, 1965). However, this explanation is a controversial one among psychologists. A more widely accepted explanation is that African mothers encourage early head support and other types of muscle control. The Ugandan infant is frequently carried on the mother's back (with no means of head support) and also spends considerable time on the floor, which provides an environment for exploration and muscle exercise. Also noticeable are considerable social stimulation and conversation from mother to child, factors that may also heighten motor precocity (Ainsworth, 1967).

The differences that exist among European children are just as difficult to explain. Some have offered genetic explanations of the acceleration of children from Stockholm and Brussels, while others have emphasized such factors as nutrition and overall health. Still others feel that the accelerated children were given more opportunities for motor skill development. At best, the issue is an elusive one, and more precise information must be gathered.

The Development of Prehension

Prehension is defined as the ability to grasp objects between the fingers and opposable thumb. Similar to locomotion, prehensile development is affected by the rapid growth of the motor cortex during the first year of life. More specifically, the areas of the brain that control the arms and hands exhibit pronounced development.

Prehension is a difficult area to study. Most of the difficulty stems from the fact that the neonate is born with a **grasp reflex,** so that if an object is placed on the palm, the whole hand closes reflexively (a subcortical response). This reflex is quite different from the cortically controlled individual movements of fingers and thumbs that produce prehension. The grasp reflex disappears at approximately 4 months, and prehension does not occur until 5 to 6 months of age, following a sequential developmental pattern.

At first the infant has poor neuromuscular control and uncoordinated hand and eye movements. At 20 weeks, hand-eye coordination begins to improve as evidenced by fewer misdirected attempts to reach

The grasp reflex is present at birth and disappears at approximately 4 months.

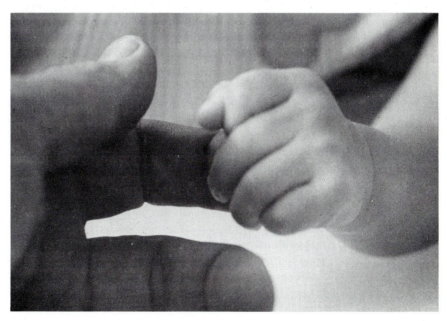

for objects. Although infants still have considerable difficulty maintaining a grasp on an object, they can direct arm movements more efficiently.

The first researchers to study prehension and reaching abilities believed that the total developmental sequence of these events was a result of maturational processes. Others have argued that hand-eye coordination involves a cognitive mapping of visual and motor schemes. In other words, reaching and retrieval behavior is learned as the infant observes the hand in the visual field. One study found that the reaching behavior of infants less than 3 months old did not seem to be disrupted when they could not see their hands as they reached for an object, but there was a definite disruption in 5½- to 6½-month-old infants in the same circumstances. It was hypothesized that the behavior pattern was disrupted in the older infants not by lack of visual feedback but by the infants' failure to meet their cognitive expectation of seeing their hands (Lasky, 1977).

By 5 months infants begin to use both hands simultaneously and become considerably more efficient in picking up objects. This phase of development not only increases hand-eye coordination but also gives the infant a wider range of different-sized objects to manipulate.

At 8 to 10 months, the approximate age when the thumb and fingers are used together consistently but still somewhat ineffectively, infants discover many new uses of the hands and arms. For example, they can support their weight on one arm while reaching for objects, and can also consistently pick up large and small objects with more and more coordinated movements (Ames, Ilg, and Haber, 1982).

Further challenges to the developing prehension abilities occur after the first year. Up to and including the walking stage, children use their hands for support; later they will be able to grasp objects from tables. Before infants can manipulate spoons, they go through a very sloppy period of direct hand-to-food-to-mouth self-feeding. This developmental stage increases the child's awareness of the motions and muscular coordination needed for self-feeding. If parents can tolerate the untidiness involved, spoon-holding skills will probably come more easily to the child.

See Figure 6.3 for some parallels in the development of locomotion and prehension.

Handedness

Handedness, the preference for and predominant use of one hand in such activities as throwing a ball, eating with a spoon, and scribbling, shows few signs of developing until the infant is at least 4 months of age. Observations of infants during the early months reveal no real

**Figure 6.3
Milestones in
motor skill
development.**

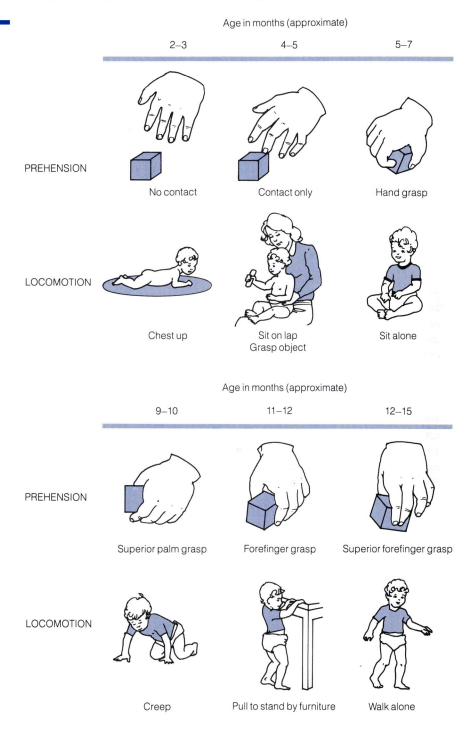

Age in months (approximate)

| 2–3 | 4–5 | 5–7 |

PREHENSION

No contact — Contact only — Hand grasp

LOCOMOTION

Chest up — Sit on lap / Grasp object — Sit alone

Age in months (approximate)

| 9–10 | 11–12 | 12–15 |

PREHENSION

Superior palm grasp — Forefinger grasp — Superior forefinger grasp

LOCOMOTION

Creep — Pull to stand by furniture — Walk alone

preference for either hand. Most infants are ambidextrous; that is, they show a preference for neither hand. What happens to produce handedness remains a puzzle to investigators. Handedness could be produced by either environmental determinants or genetic direction, but no watertight argument can be made for either reason. We find that when both parents are right-handed, there is a 92-percent chance that their offspring will be right-handed. If one parent is left-handed, it is estimated that there is an 80-percent chance of the offspring being right-handed. Should both parents be left-handed, the figure for right-handedness drops to 50 percent. These percentages might indicate a hereditary predisposition toward handedness, but there is plenty of room to speculate on environmental influence. For example, left-handed parents could be left-handed models that the child imitates (Longstreth, 1980; Hardyck and Petrinovich, 1977; Hicks and Kinsbourne, 1976).

Whatever the determinants for handedness may be, approximately 19 out of every 20 people are right-handed (95 percent), with the remaining person being either left-handed or ambidextrous (5 percent).

Handedness becomes apparent when the infant is 4 months old.

As we mentioned, a mild tendency toward handedness commences after 4 months. At first there is much fluctuation between unilateral and bilateral responses; the two hands work very closely together, but at about the age of 19 months, hand preference makes its appearance with an active hand and a passive hand. By 2 years of age, most children exhibit a definite preference, which is generally firmly established by the time a child enters school (Coren, Porac, and Duncan, 1981; Michel, 1981).

Because of their overwhelming numbers, right-handers enjoy certain advantages over left-handers. Left-handers, especially during the formative years, soon discover that they must adjust to a world designed primarily for right-handers. Learning to write is one of the biggest problems, since the left hand frequently smears letters that have just been written. Disadvantages for the left-hander continue to exist even after childhood. Tools, games, sporting equipment, doorknobs, and the handles of drinking fountains are all predominantly designed for right-handers.

This does not mean that left-handers cannot overcome such obstacles, nor does it imply that southpaws experience adjustment difficulties throughout life. On the contrary, left-handers appear to experience just as much success in life as right-handers. A study of over 7,000 right- and left-handed children detected no noticeable differences in such areas as school achievement, motivation, and intelligence. Apparently the left-handers had overcome with considerable success whatever obstacles initially confronted them in our predominantly right-handed world (Hardyck, Petrinovich, and Goldman, 1976).

Summary

Joy, age 7

Physical growth and development unfold throughout childhood in a sequential fashion, the result of the gradual development of brain cells. This chapter examined the manner in which the nervous system develops, including the central and peripheral systems. The central nervous system consists of the brain and spinal cord, while the peripheral nervous system is made up of neural tissue that connects the brain and spinal cord with other parts of the body.

The central nervous system develops very rapidly during the early years, although the parts of the brain do not develop evenly. The forebrain is the brain center responsible for conscious thought and higher-order behavior. Within the forebrain are the left and right cerebral hemispheres, connected by the corpus callosum. The left hemisphere controls movement on the right side of the body and vice versa. The left and right hemispheres also control different functions, a dichotomy known as lateralization. The left hemisphere controls such functions as language ability, logical thought, and writing, while the right hemisphere controls such nonverbal activities as artistic or musical abilities, imagination, and the expression of emotion.

The two cerebral hemispheres are covered by the cerebral cortex, the last part of the brain to develop. The cerebral cortex can be divided into four areas: the occipital, parietal, temporal, and frontal lobes. The thalamus and hypothalamus are two other parts of the forebrain. The thalamus relays nerve impulses from sensory pathways to the cerebral cortex, and the hypothalamus regulates, among other things, hunger, thirst, sexual functions, and body temperature.

The midbrain connects the forebrain to the hindbrain and controls eye-muscle movement as well as the transmission of visual and auditory information to higher brain centers. The hindbrain is the lower portion of the brain and controls the bodily functions necessary for survival. The medulla oblongata regulates heartbeat, respiration, digestion, and blood pressure. The cerebellum controls body balance and coordination, while the pons acts as a bridge between the two lobes of the cerebellum. The reticular activating system controls arousal, attention, and the sleep cycle.

Maturation, often called *readiness,* is based on the development of brain parts as well as the muscular and skeletal systems. Once the organism has attained a sufficient level of maturity, environmental stimulation can increase the learning of a particular physical skill. The fact that areas of the cortex mature at different rates accounts for the emergence of thinking processes and motor reactions at varying times. Maturation and readiness are greatly affected by myelination, the process by which a neuron develops an outside coating or sheath (myelin). Myelination allows for the rapid transmission of electrochemical messages.

Growth of the motor cortex during the first year of life enables locomotor skills to progress. Locomotion provides an example of the developmental nature of motor skills. The stages of head and chest support, rolling, and crawling all precede walking behavior, which emerges approximately between 13 and 15 months. However, this timetable is strictly an average, and there are cross-cultural as well as individual variations in motor skill attainment. Motor abilities at this age also blend with other developmental forces, including motivation, cognition, and the desire to establish autonomy and initiative. Factors that appear to accelerate motor skill development include parental stimulation, proper nutrition, and an environment that encourages muscular exercise.

Prehension, the ability to grasp objects between the fingers and opposable thumb, is also affected by the rapid development of the motor cortex during the first year of life. As neuromuscular control and hand-eye coordination improve, prehensile abilities also improve. By 8 to 10 months, the thumb and fingers are used together consistently. Handedness, the preference for and predominant use of one hand, begins to develop at approximately 4 months of age. Both environmental and genetic forces appear to be responsible for handedness. Right-handers constitute about 95 percent of the population and enjoy certain environmental advantages not available to left-handers. However, evidence suggests that most left-handers overcome these obstacles and exhibit no noticeable differences in such areas as school achievement, motivation, and intelligence.

Suggested Reading List

Caplan, F. *The First Twelve Months of Life.* New York: Bantam, 1981. One of the better books describing the growth and development of infants. Caplan combines readable narrative with much practical information.

Rubin, R. R., Fisher, J. J., and Doering, S. G. *Your Toddler.* New York: Macmillan, 1980. An applied overview of this important life stage.

Springer, S. P., and Deutsch, G. *Left Brain, Right Brain,* rev. ed. New York: W. H. Freeman, 1985. The authors explore the nature of hemispheric differences and their implications for human behavior. Of particular interest is a discussion focusing on handedness.

Thompson, R. F. *The Brain.* New York: W. H. Freeman, 1985. The physiology and functions of the brain are studied. This very readable book is filled with practical applications and numerous illustrations.

Chapter Seven

Cognition, Perception, and Psycholinguistics

Who knows the thoughts of a child?

Nora Perry

Introduction

Mental development increases significantly during the years of infancy and toddlerhood. By the end of the first year, most infants have developed the intellectual capacities to distinguish the mother and father from others in the environment, to understand simple associations, to designate an object or two by name, and to establish rudimentary attention and memory skills. Observers will also detect inquisitiveness about the world in general. By toddlerhood, language has become a vehicle for expression, and advanced cognitive processes enable children to understand simple problem-solving situations. Memory has become further refined, and children have begun to distinguish themselves as unique individuals in their rapidly expanding environment.

What factors account for these rapid developments? How do children learn to think and reason about their surroundings? What can be said about the manner in which they develop an understanding of the people, objects, and events in their environment? How do they develop the mental strategies necessary to engage in everyday problem solving?

These and a multitude of other questions have intrigued researchers for years, and the complexities of mental development have become an extremely active field of investigation. This field of research, known technically as **cognition,** encompasses the higher-order mental processes that deal with thinking, perceiving, and understanding. Simply stated, cognition is the intellectual activity of the individual.

Our approach in this chapter will be to examine four facets of cognitive activity. First, we'll investigate the advancements proposed by Jean Piaget within the sensorimotor stage of cognitive development. Then, we will turn our attention to the nature of early concept formation. Our third area of study will be changes in the major sense organs. Finally, we will examine the nature of linguistic development during the years of infancy and toddlerhood.

By toddlerhood, language has become a vehicle for expression.

Piaget's Stage of Sensorimotor Development

Jean Piaget labels the first two years of life the sensorimotor stage of cognitive development because most of the infant's learning abilities are directed toward the coordination of simple sensorimotor skills, including such activities as sucking or grasping objects and other fundamental actions. The sensorimotor stage has six substages, during which infants improve their construction and interpretation of the surrounding environment and advance their overall mental development.

Reflex Activities (0 to 1 Month)

In the beginning, the infant is capable only of primitive **reflex activities,** such as crying or sucking. This is due primarily to the undeveloped nature of the cerebral cortex. As the cranial bones enlarge, enabling brain cells to develop and become more chemically active, reflexes become more modified and efficient. For example, the sucking reflex is first directed toward all objects, but the infant later becomes able to discriminate between objects that are suckable, such as the breast or the bottle, and objects that are not. Piaget found this to be true in the case of his son, Laurent (Piaget, 1952, p. 26):

> The third day Laurent makes new progress in his adjustment to the breast. All he needs in order to grope with open mouth toward final success is to have touched the breast or the surrounding teguments with his lips. . . . As soon as his cheek comes into contact with the breast, he applies himself to seeking until he finds drink.

Primary Circular Reactions (1 to 4 Months)

If infants happen to produce a pleasurable behavioral pattern centered around their own bodies, they will repeat that behavioral pattern for its own sake. (In Piagetian terminology, *primary* means "on the body," and *circular* means "repeated.") For example, if sucking the hand is enjoyable, the infant will try to reproduce that action. During the period of **primary circular reactions,** marked by further variations and adjustments in the schemata, infants also begin to display signs of coordinating one action with another. This can be observed in coordination of the hand and arm, which may permit thumb sucking, or in efforts to look at whatever is grasped and reach for whatever is seen.

During this period infants take a great deal of interest in themselves. They frequently exhibit a preoccupation and fascination with their own arms, hands, legs, or feet and make careful investigations of simple body

**Infants are often preoccupied with their
hands and feet.**

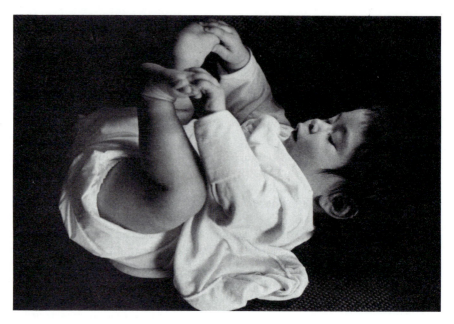

movements, such as the opening and closing of the fist. This form of
personal observation represents the infant's initial attempt at investigative behavior.

Secondary Circular Reactions (4 to 8 Months)

Reactions in this substage are secondary, or in the vicinity of the body,
and repetitious. Here, infants attempt to reproduce interesting events in
the external environment that were first caused by accident. The sides
of the crib, they discover, make a noise when kicked; shaken properly, a
rattle will make an interesting sound; and dropping an object to the
floor will make a thump. Gradually, infants become aware of the
changes that can be made, especially if a created event is amusing or
interesting. Thus, infants will continue to kick their legs to make a
dangling object move or to push a toy through the bars of the crib to
create an interesting fall to the floor.

     Another cognitive development occurring during the stage of
secondary circular reactions is the anticipatory or "power of association" effect, which in later life becomes an important aid to the under-

standing of cause-and-effect relationships. Infants slowly learn to associate events that occur at about the same time. Piaget observed this in his son, Laurent, especially during feeding time, when he associated a cradling position with being fed. As soon as he was in this position, he wanted contact only with his mother's breast.

Coordination of Secondary Schemes (8 to 12 Months)

Up to and during the early phases of the stage of **coordination of secondary schemes,** infants have difficulty understanding **object permanence,** the fact that objects continue to exist even if they are out of one's field of vision. If an object is hidden behind a pillow, for example, an infant will not search for it; an "out-of-sight, out-of-mind" principle seems to be in operation. After 8 months, however, an infant will attempt to search under and behind obstructions to recover a favorite object.

　　Several factors contribute to the development of object permanence. First, infants can make visual accommodations to rapid eye movements, which make possible the anticipation of the future position of objects and thus endow them with a certain degree of permanence. A second factor contributing to object permanence is what Piaget refers to as "interrupted prehension." If an infant has begun to reach for an object by making specific arm, hand, and finger movements, but does not succeed in capturing it, these prehensile movements will persist, enabling the infant to continue the pursuit. Another factor is the child's ability to reconstruct an invisible whole from a visible part. That is, if a

Permanence has not yet been achieved by this four-month-old infant; interest is lost when the object is concealed.

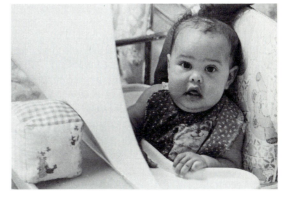

small portion of a partly hidden object is exposed, the child should recognize it as being part of a total object.

Piaget, however, cautions that some confusion about object permanence can still exist during this period. If a missing object has been found in a specific location, it is not uncommon for the infant to continue to search in this spot, even when the object has been placed elsewhere. Thus, true object permanence has not yet emerged.

In addition to the caution that Piaget stresses when analyzing developments in object permanence, it should also be mentioned that other views on the topic of object permanence have emerged. Not all agree on the level of infant competence described by Piaget in the establishment of object permanence. Some, such as Corrigan (1981) and Fisher and Jennings (1981), question whether infants have the ability to construct mental images of missing objects. They say infants may find missing objects by other means, such as knowing that adults are setting out to hide objects and watching where they are being hidden (a skill of at least equal sophistication).

Tertiary Circular Reactions (12 to 18 Months)

Tertiary circular reactions are reactions that occur in a repetitious fashion out in the environment. Because of their increased interest in

A Demonstration of Object Permanence

Before their first birthday, infants have difficulty understanding the principle of object permanence. A simple experiment with infants of 6 to 12 months illustrates the lack of this form of reasoning in early thought processes.

Select a small shiny object likely to capture the infant's attention, such as a coin, key, or ring. In plain view of the child, place the object in the palm of your left hand. Close both hands into fists, making sure that the fingers of the left hand hide the object from the infant's view. (During the initial trial, open both hands for several seconds in order to ensure that the infant knows in which hand the object lies.)

When given the opportunity to search for the missing object, the infant will undoubtedly seek to open your closed left hand. Repeat the process several times, each time hiding the object in the same hand.

Now, again in plain view, place the object in your right palm and, as in the initial trials, place both fists in front of the infant. Because the object is still conceived of as being in a specific location, that is, in the place in which it was first hidden and found, the infant will search your now empty left hand and ignore your right hand. Successful understanding of object permanence has yet to be developed. ∎

the changes that can be created in the environment, infants continue to develop primitive forms of reasoning. By the age of 12 months, infants display the beginnings of **trial-and-error learning** in solving simple problems, as illustrated in the following example (Piaget, 1969, p. 11):

> An object has been placed on a rug out of the child's reach. The child, after trying in vain to reach the object, may eventually grasp one corner of the rug (by chance or as a substitute) and then, observing a relationship between the movements of the rug and those of the object, gradually comes to pull the rug in order to reach the object.

Considerable attention is also directed toward understanding the construction of objects. Infants are genuinely concerned with how objects feel and how they are put together. This developmental phase may help to explain why infants of this age level are continually touching and fingering the face of the mother or father. This may be the infant's attempt to understand how the face is constructed (position of the nose, eyes, mouth).

Object permanence also develops further during this substage. In the hidden object experiment, infants no longer look for the object in the place where they first found it if they see its position being changed. If, however, the change is not visible, they continue to look for it in the first place. They still lack the ability to take into account displacements outside their immediate perception.

Invention of New Means through Mental Combinations (18 to 24 Months)

Before the second year is reached, children can form mental images that enable them to devise new ways and means of dealing with the environment. Piaget called this stage **invention of new means through mental combinations.** At this point, simple problems may be "thought out" before they are undertaken; furthermore, through "inner experimentation" new mental combinations may be formed to attain desired goals.

Infants are now capable of locating an unseen object, even when they have not observed it being moved, because they can infer its possible movements. The acquisition of this notion of invisible displacement completes the growth of object permanence and signifies the beginning of true conceptual thought. At the end of the sensorimotor stage, other noteworthy advances include the acquisition of fundamental sensory skills and motor responses, the establishment of anticipatory reactions, and the beginnings of mental flexibility. Such developments will supply the underpinnings of later cognitive stages.

Table 7.1 Summary of Developments during Sensorimotor Stage

Stage	General Description	Object Concept	Space
1 Reflex activities 0–1 month	Reflex activity	No differentiation of self from other objects	Egocentric
2 Primary circular reactions 1–4 months	Hand-mouth coordination; differentiation via sucking, grasping	No special behavior re: vanished objects; no differentiation of movement of self and external objects	Changes in perspective seen as changes in objects
3 Secondary circular reactions 4–8 months	Hand-eye coordination; reproduction of interesting events	Anticipates positions of moving objects	Space externalized; no spatial relationships of objects
4 Coordination of secondary schemata 8–12 months	Coordination of schemata; application of known means to new problems; anticipation	Object permanence; searches for vanished objects; reverses bottle to get nipple	Perceptual constancy of size and shape of objects
5 Tertiary circular reactions 12–18 months	Discovery of new means through experimentation	Considers sequential displacements while searching for vanished objects	Aware of relationships between objects in space, between objects and self
6 Invention of new means through mental combinations 18–24 months	Representation; invention of new means via internal combinations	Images of absent objects; representation of displacements	Aware of movements not perceived; representation of spatial relationships

(Adapted from Wadsworth, 1984.)

Concept Development

Critical to developing cognitive facilities is the establishment and refinement of concepts. A **concept** is a mental image that connects groups of objects and events having common properties. Concepts enable us to sort and categorize our daily experiences. As a result, concepts lie at the heart of cognitive functioning (Houston, 1981; Wessells, 1982).

The classification of concepts begins early in life, although the overall refinement process is often slow and difficult. As children are exposed to new information each day, they must either establish new concepts to represent this material or relate it to existing concepts. The difficulty of such a mental chore is best illustrated by an example. Consider, for instance, the concept "ball." After learning the correct verbal designation, children also have to learn that balls come in many different sizes, weights, and colors. Some bounce higher than others, and some, such as snowballs, don't bounce at all. Some are used in sports activities and can be pitched, dribbled, or rolled. The child will also learn that the word *ball* has other meanings, in such expressions as "having a ball," "ballroom dancing," or "the whole ball of wax." Like other developments, concepts are built up in stages as we shall see in the remainder of this section.

Shape and Size Concepts

To develop accurate concepts, children must first be able to distinguish among an object's properties. Among these properties are shape and size. As we discovered in Chapter 5, perception of shape and form begins to develop during the neonatal period. Newborns are especially attracted to novel patterns, including depictions of the human face. Infants are especially drawn to dark and light contrasting areas of faces, such as hairline and eyes. As scanning abilities become more mature, 6-month-old infants can also understand facial composition and detect whether facial elements presented in drawings are scrambled or correctly arranged (Bushnell, 1982; Caron et al., 1973; Lasky and Klein, 1980).

The accurate development of shape and size concepts relies considerably on **perceptual constancy,** the tendency of objects to appear the same under different viewing conditions. Because the retinal image changes when objects are examined from different standpoints, children may become confused in attempting to comprehend their actual size or shape. For example, when children grasp the notion of size constancy, a figure walking away or a boat disappearing over the horizon is not perceived as a miniature version of the actual object. By the same token, when shape constancy is understood, views from various angles will not distort our perception of the object's actual shape. For example, dinner plates on the table appear elliptical when viewed at a certain angle and distance, but shape constancy enables us to perceive them as circular. Surprisingly, infants show signs of recognizing size and shape constancy early in life. With age and practice, more accurate discriminations develop (Bower, 1981; Day and McKenzie, 1981).

In time, children become familiar with simple shapes and forms in their surroundings. Simple shapes, such as circles and squares, are learned first, while more complicated shapes, such as triangles and diamonds, are learned later. Not all shapes are easily detected by young children. Shapes having ambiguous dimensions or qualities are especially difficult to perceive. For example, when children between the ages of 3 and 6 were asked to identify a triangle, rectangle, and circle having illusory contours (see Figure 7.1), nearly all of the 6-year-olds could identify the shapes, but only half of the 3-year-olds could do so (Abravanel, 1982).

Size is another property of objects that must be learned. The notion of size is hard for children to grasp at first. Consider the toddler's difficulty in learning to understand how hollow cubes of varying sizes fit into each other. At first, the blocks may only be handled or stacked on one another. By age 2 or 3, however, children learn in a rudimentary way that the "little" ones can be placed inside the "big" ones. As they make contact with familiar objects, children gradually add a variety of size labels to their vocabularies (Stevens, 1981).

Spatial Concepts

Discrimination of space is a difficult cognitive advancement for young children. Primarily because of their inexperience as observers, children may fail to realize that an object can have different spatial appearances.

Figure 7.1 Shapes having ambiguous or illusory contours are difficult for the toddler to distinguish. (Abravanel, 1982.)

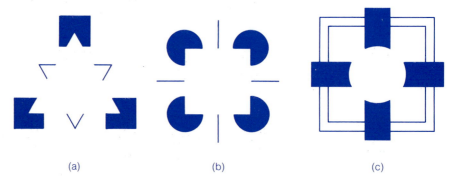

(a)   (b)   (c)

For example, they may have trouble telling whether a standard figure has been placed on the left or right or in front of or behind other objects. Similarly, deciding whether an object is right side up or upside down frequently results in confusion (Bower, 1981).

Much of the difficulty in understanding space is attributable to the fact that children lack the appropriate terminology for describing the different appearances of objects. They are also bound by an **egocentric,** or self-centered, view of the environment. However, as children learn correct terminology, move beyond an egocentric point of view, and become more aware of change in the environment, they are able not only to exhibit discrimination in regard to spatial orientations but also to acquire a general understanding of such appearances (Wishart and Bower, 1982).

Class Concepts

Class concepts are mental images that represent object categories. The early responses of children presented with object class problems strongly suggest that such concepts are difficult to grasp. To illustrate this, let us assume children are presented with a variety of blocks of different colors, shapes, and sizes. When asked to place these objects in some order, the children would most likely categorize them on a perceptual basis, by **seriation,** or chaining. That is, they would most likely classify the objects by placing red ones together, yellow ones together, similar shapes together, and so on. Although some part of grouping organization has been established, there is no separation into classes in the abstract sense. Rather, an object is categorized in relation to whether it "fits well" with another next to it. At this time there is little concern for less obvious differences.

The young child may also have difficulty understanding the relationship between subclasses and classes, known in Piagetian terminology as class inclusion. Suppose we presented a child with four red checkers and two black checkers and asked if there were more black or more red checkers. The child would have no difficulty answering this question. However, if we asked whether there were more red or more plastic checkers, the child would become confused and most likely be unable to answer the question correctly. Young children are unable to reason about parts and wholes simultaneously, but, as we shall see later, this cognitive advancement develops later in childhood (Winer, 1980).

Time Concepts

Children in the early years have a rather poor awareness of time. Usually they are able to associate daily activities with time and thus know about when dinner is served, when daddy comes home, or when they go to bed. In early speech patterns, children refer to their existence almost exclusively in the present tense. Only later, in most cases by age 3, are youngsters able to comprehend and use terms related to the past and the future.

Cognition and Memory

In relation to our discussion of Piaget, object permanence provides the basis for cognition and memory. Without memory, cognition would be virtually nonexistent for both children and adults. The ability to retain information from the past and apply it to present and future situations is clearly one of our most important capacities. Through memory, past experiences influence our present thoughts, plans, and actions (Norman, 1982; Klatzky, 1980).

Psychologists have distinguished three types of memory: sensory (or immediate), short-term, and long-term. **Sensory memory** refers to all the sensory stimuli to which an individual is exposed. Each day, we are constantly saturated with sensory stimulation. As a result, many impressions can be held only for short periods of time (less than a second). They are then subject to decay and replacement by new sensory impressions.

Short-term memory is often called the working memory. Its primary function is the advance organization of learning for transfer into long-term memory. Consequently, new information is stored only briefly.

Long-term memory is the storage system that enables individuals to retain large amounts of information in a relatively permanent way. As children become older, their selective attention enables them to place increasing amounts of relevant information into long-term memory. Children may need repeated rehearsal to pass information from short- to long-term storage. Usually, they also require coding, a process of compacting information so that it can be placed in appropriate long-term memory categories. Some information, however, passes directly from short-term to long-term storage, presumably as the result of its

Figure 7.2　Three types of memory storage.

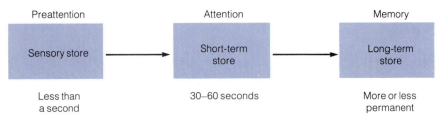

meaningfulness to, or impact on, the individual. Unlike short-term memory, long-term memory undergoes little or no decay. Figure 7.2 illustrates how information may be processed to become part of the long-term memory store. Note particularly how the sensory store may be held in reserve in a state of preattention, while the short-term store represents the actual attention span of the individual.

The Development of Memory during Childhood   During early child-hood, children are capable of holding only a few words or ideas in their minds. They frequently have difficulty in remembering events that have happened weeks, days, or even only hours earlier. This problem points to a lack of information in the long-term memory store. It is generally recognized that with age, memory exhibits significant gains.

Several factors account for this improvement in memory abilities. Children are able to increase their overall memory span as they grow older. The **memory span** refers to the number of items that can be held within the short-term store. Whereas the average 3-year-old can hold only three items in the memory span, this figure doubles for the 8- to 12-year-old (Case, Kurland, and Goldberg, 1982; Wilkinson, 1981).

An important factor contributing to improved memory abilities, as well as cognition as a whole, is metacognition. **Metacognition** is the individual's awareness of how a cognitive process can be applied to a mental task at hand. It also encompasses awareness of personal cogni-tive limits. The rehearsal of events so that they can be remembered and the use of other memory strategies to combat forgetting are examples of metacognitive abilities, although in some circles they are labeled **metamemory** skills.

Metacognition has other important parameters. Children will learn that paying close attention to objects and events and ignoring distrac-tions help improve memory. So do more efficient information-processing and organization abilities, not to mention heightened motivation. Children's understanding of these and other types of meta-cognitive processes steadily increases with age. The results are more refined and elaborate strategies for perceiving, storing, and retrieving environmental information [Flavell, 1981; Bjorklund and Hock, 1982; Miller and Weiss, 1981(a); Miller and Zalenski, 1982].

Sense Organ Development

The efficiency of children's sensory equipment continues to improve with age and practice. This improvement is due not only to the growing physical maturation of the sense organs but also to the increasing amounts of perceptual information that can be processed and the growing awareness of objects and events in the world. Consequently, toddlers are able to make remarkably fine discriminations among the sights, sounds, and other types of sensory stimulation around them.

Vision

The sense of sight develops rapidly during the early years. The visual system undergoes rapid changes after birth, so that by 4 months visual accommodation and focusing abilities are close to maturity. Similar acceleration is experienced with brightness sensitivity, which matures as early as 3 months. By 7 to 9 months infants can see small objects or details with increasing clarity (**visual acuity**), and by the end of the first year they can track remote objects as efficiently as adults. Research also reveals that infants have a very efficient perception of color at an early age. By 4 months they can perceive the visual spectrum of the primary color categories of red, yellow, green, and blue (Bornstein, 1981).

Depth Perception: When Seeing Is Believing   Accurate depth perception is an important visual development for young children. Without depth perception, a child would not be able to distinguish downward slopes, descending steps, or edges of precipices, all of which would severely retard the development of creeping, crawling, and subsequent walking abilities. However, psychologists have discovered that infants can perceive depth as early as the crawling stage. Apparently, when locomotion skills reach the stage at which depth perception is necessary for survival, infants can discriminate depth. Observations of children suggest that depth perception emerges even before the concept of two-dimensional space is understood. The latter perceptual immaturity can be observed as infants attempt to grasp pictures in magazines or story books. On being shown home movies, some children may even go behind the screen and become puzzled by their failure to find the rest of the bodies of the people in the film.

Infant depth perception can be tested by using a **visual cliff** apparatus, a split-level table designed with a "shallow" and a "deep" end. Quite simply, half the table is on one plane and ends abruptly, and the other half is located several feet below the "edge"; glass plating extends over the entire table. Both sides of the table are covered with a checkerboard design to show the "drop" between the two sides. Thus, an infant is able to see the differences in depth that exist in the table, although the glass surface is safe to crawl on if the subject desires.

Will infants trust their sense of touch (feeling the glass) more than their depth perception and cross to the deep end? Evidence compiled by Gibson and Walk (1960) indicates that infants do not; most crawling infants peer through the glass, sometimes pat it, or lean on it with their faces, but they simply do not venture over the deep end. Even when mothers stood at the deep end and tried to coax their babies across, 81 percent refused to move forward. Such findings illustrate the development and influence of depth perception at the crawling stage. This is evident not only in humans but also in other land animals, such as young rats, chicks, kittens, and kids. Nonland animals, such as turtles and ducks, however, have a different reaction to the visual cliff. Research discloses (Walk, 1978) that they show little if any hesitancy about crossing over to the deep side. Is it possible that the deep side of the visual cliff more closely resembles their natural surroundings?

Other studies have found that infants as young as 2 or 3 months exhibited differences in heart rate at the shallow and deep sides of the

As early as the crawling stage of development, infants refuse to cross to the deep side of the visual cliff.

table. The infants' heartbeats decreased when they were placed on the deep side, a reaction characteristic of humans pausing to pay close attention to new situations. At 8 months the infants' heartbeats increased, indicating an emotional reaction such as fear. Apparently the older infants, having greater experience in crawling and falling, were able to perceive the danger posed by the deep side (Campos et al., 1978; Campos, Bertenthal, and Caplovitz, 1982).

Audition

Hearing acuity also develops rapidly as association values of sounds are being learned. At 4 months, infants are aware of the sound of a familiar voice, crying, or novel sounds and will turn their heads in the direction of the sound (see DeCasper and Fifer, 1980; Rheingold and Adams, 1980; Martin and Clark, 1982). By 5 to 8 months, infants can distinguish different sound frequencies and make relatively fine auditory discriminations (Olsho, 1982).

Taste and Smell

The senses of taste and smell are both remarkably well developed at birth. Through direct contact with a multitude of tastes and odors, the child is able to differentiate and recognize these sensory stimuli. By the early years, children seem able to detect the same pleasant and unpleasant odors that an adult can. However, it must be recognized that there is a wide range of individual differences in taste and smell sensitivity (Ziporyn, 1982; Hubert et al., 1980).

Touch

Infants exercise their sense of touch considerably during the first year, exploring objects not only with their fingers but also with their tongue and lips. Skin contact and warmth provide acute stimulation for infants. During toddlerhood, touch is one of the most pleasurable of the child's sensations. Furthermore, the sense of touch adds a great deal to cognitive awareness during these years, especially when exploration of the sensations of hardness and softness, roughness and smoothness, and warmth and cold is at its peak. Learning environments for infants and toddlers should thus provide as many experiences as possible to increase touch sensitivity as well as the other major senses (see Cataldo, 1984; Honig and Laly, 1981; Jones, 1980).

Psycholinguistics

The development of language behavior, the process in which the individual passes from early stages of crying and babbling to spoken words and meaningful sentences, is an intriguing area of child psychology. Its study is known as psycholinguistics, which is a relatively new field of scientific concentration. **Psycholinguistics** includes the closely related areas of language, language development, mental imagery, cognitive development, symbolization, and speech. A glance at the topics explored in some of the psychology texts published in the 1980s reveals the growing interest in psycholinguistics among contemporary researchers (see Deese, 1984; MacNeilage, 1983; Nelson, 1983; Peters, 1982; Ziajka, 1981; Chomsky, 1980).

The student should realize that speech and language are different from each other. **Speech** is a concrete, physical act that consists in forming and sequencing the sounds of oral language. **Language** is the system of **grammar** rules and semantics that makes speech meaningful.

We should recognize two other important facts about language:

1. Language is a productive and creative system. While the set of words in a language (the vocabulary, or **lexicon**) is finite, the number of possible sentences an individual can create is unlimited. From any English sentence a new or longer one may be created. While there are dictionaries of words, no dictionary exists for sentences.

2. Many of the utterances encountered in everyday conversation are not perfectly grammatical. Because of slips of the tongue, changes of topic in midsentence, or false starts, the child may not be presented with high-quality information about language.

Both of these facts suggest that language consists of rules, or a set of patterns. These rules can be applied in situations that are not identical to those in which they were learned, and they can also be violated (Dale, 1976).

Language Centers of the Brain

Research has shown that the part of the brain that seems to be most directly associated with language and its subsequent development is the left cerebral hemisphere, since damage to the right hemisphere rarely produces any language disorders. Three areas in particular have been found to serve specific biological functions related to speech and language:

1. **Broca's area,** adjacent to the region of the motor cortex, which controls the movements of the lips, jaw, tongue, soft palate, and the vocal cords, coordinates these muscles in speech. Damage to this area produces motor aphasia and causes speech to be slow and labored, although language comprehension is still possible.

2. **Wernicke's area,** located in the temporal lobe, is believed to be related to language comprehension. When Wernicke's area is damaged, speech is fluent but has little content, and comprehension is usually lost, a condition termed *sensory aphasia.*

3. A nerve bundle called the **arcuate fasciculus** connects Broca's and Wernicke's areas. When damage occurs to this region, speech remains fluent but is abnormal; the individual employs meaningless phrases and although able to comprehend spoken or written words, is unable to repeat them.

Figure 7.3 depicts the language centers of the brain.

Theories of Language Development

How does a child learn to speak? What factors account for the infant's development of babbling, the emergence of the child's first word, and

Figure 7.3 Areas of brain associated with speech.

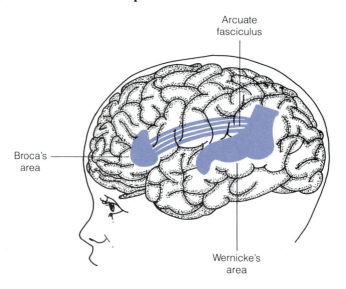

the ultimate fabrication of sentences? Certain theories have been proposed to explain the processes involved in language acquisition. These
include the innate, reinforcement, and social learning theories of language development.

Innate Theory   Noam Chomsky suggests that the human brain is pro-
grammed to enable individuals to create and understand language. He
refers to this system of programming as the language acquisition device
(LAD), which depends on mature cells in the cerebral cortex. Since the
cortex is not totally functional at birth, it must mature during the first
year if the child is to develop language skills. Chomsky (1980, 1968)
theorizes that this innate device allows the brain to perform cognitive
operations on the sounds received, enabling infants to follow grammar
rules and invent totally new sentences.

    Innate theory, then, views language development as a genetic phe-
nomenon. Chomsky also asserts that sentences are generated by a system of rules. These rules enable children to listen to language and
eventually to fabricate sentences. Chomsky focuses on analyzing entire
sentences rather than on how sounds and words combine to form
sentences. Sentence analysis is accomplished by examining two aspects
of the sentence: surface structure and deep structure.

    The **surface structure** is dictated by the rules of grammar and
consists of the actual words in a sentence. The **deep structure** is what
a particular sentence means to the individual, or the conceptual framework of the sentence. Several examples may clarify the distinction between the two types. Consider the following:

    The student attended the child psychology class.

    The child psychology class was attended by the student.

    While the two surface structures are obviously different, both sen-
tences mean the same thing. Both, to be more exact, have the same
deep structure. Now, consider the following sentences:

    They are eating apples.

    They are eating apples.

    While the surface structures are identical, these two sentences may
have different deep structures. The sentence could mean that the
people under discussion are in the process of eating some apples or the
apples are the type that people like to eat raw rather than the type used
for cooking. Understanding the relationship between the deep and surface structures of a sentence is called a **transformation.** Transformations include the realization that statements not only may be interpreted differently but also can be expressed in different tenses.
Although our example "The student attended the child psychology

class" dealt with the past tense, it could also have been expressed in other ways, such as: "The student attends the child psychology class"; "The student is attending the child psychology class"; or "The student will attend the child psychology class."

Chomsky maintains that certain aspects of deep structure are innate and universal among all natural languages. Surface structures are specific to each language. He also believes that children may learn to make correct transformations by first forming **kernel words:** words that can be strung together to make a statement, which is usually declarative. From these basic words children learn transformations and produce sentences.

The innate theory of language development poses numerous issues for students of psycholinguistics to ponder, the most prominent being whether language development follows a universal design. Since language production is viewed in part as a genetic phenomenon, and because Chomsky claims that certain aspects of the deep structure are universal, there are implications that children all around the world use the same language framework. Certain research supports Chomsky's hypothesis.

Children do follow the same universal patterns of speech sounds, such as cooing and babbling, before producing their first word. A number of researchers have also observed that children of different nationalities form early sentences that are grammatically similar. While individual languages (surface structures) vary from country to country, the underlying deep structures are remarkably uniform (see Table 7.2). From 1½ to 2 years, children everywhere acquire their native tongue and employ similar grammatical systems (Brown, 1973a, 1973b; Slobin, 1970).

This genetic interpretation of language development seems further supported by the fact that speech develops only when the child has reached a certain stage of physical maturation. Thus, language is seen as a product of biological development rather than environmental forces. This maturational hypothesis is favored by the finding that certain phases of language development correlate consistently with specific motor skill attainments (Lenneberg, 1967).

Although controversial (see Harman, 1982), Chomsky's ideas have affected many researchers. Conclusive support for Chomsky's views remains elusive, but psycholinguists are actively investigating the basic thrust of his theory. Such efforts will provide exciting research for years to come.

Reinforcement Theory   A viewpoint differing from Chomsky's theory of language development is offered by learning theorists, most notably B. F. Skinner, a psychologist known for his research in operant conditioning.

Table 7.2 Examples of Two-Word Sentences from Several Languages

Function of Speech	English	German	Russian	Samoan
Locate name	there book that car see doggie	Buch da (book there)	Tosya tam (there Tosya)	Keith iea (there Keith)
Demand	more milk give candy want gum	mehr Milch (more milk)	yeshche moloko (more milk)	mai pepe (give doll)
Negate	no wet no wash not hungry	nicht blasen (not blow)	vody net (water no)	le ai (not eat)
Question	where ball	wo Ball (where ball)	gde papa (where papa)	fea Punatu (where Punatu)
Possession	my shoe mama dress	mein Ball (my ball) Mamas Hut (mama's hat)	mami chashka (mama's cup)	lole a'u (my candy)

(Adapted from Slobin, 1970.)

Skinner (1957) theorizes that language acquisition is a form of operant behavior in which children add new words to their vocabulary primarily through three techniques called the *tact, mand,* and *echoic acquisition methods.*

The tact method is a system that enables children to learn new words through responses to stimulus objects in their surroundings. By responding to such stimulus objects as "mommy," "dog," or "toy," they are developing tacts, or names of familiar stimuli to which they wish to respond.

Through the mand (demand) method, a child acquires words simply because the words meet a need. Certain "deprivation conditions" exist and promote mands, which act as inducements for verbal responses. Thus, children will learn the word "food" and some of its subclasses, such as "candy," "cookie," and "meat," because they know that these names represent objects that satisfy their hunger. Other conditions, such as thirst and fatigue, cause children to learn other new words to verbalize needs.

Skinner's last method, the echoic, is verbal acquisition via imitation of adult speech. However, mimicry is not the only principle in operation here; the importance of positive reinforcement is particularly evident. When a child speaks appropriate words or uses correct grammar, parents usually provide a reward in the form of a smile or encouragement. Such reinforcement motivates the child to learn other new words.

Reinforcement theory has not yet provided many clear-cut answers about the nature of language development. One of the problems in this approach is that many adults pay more attention to whether children's speech patterns are factually correct than to whether their grammar is correct. For example, suppose a child sees you reading this book and asks, "That a book?" The natural inclination is to respond, "Yes it is." If you do that, though, you are responding to the truth of the proposition, not to the fact that the child's question was ungrammatical. Along the same lines, the child's question, "You a student?" may be approved because it is true, even though the child's question is grammatically incorrect.

Social Learning Theory   Social learning theorists suggest that children can acquire language by observing and imitating adults. In this sense, parents may serve as models, not only by offering remarks that the child can imitate but also by expanding on the child's utterances themselves. For example, if the child remarks, "Daddy work," the father may expand this by saying "Daddy is going to work now." Expansion and modeling are seen as enabling children to learn correct word designations and grammatical structures (Hoff-Ginsberg and Shatz, 1982).

Although social learning is considered important in language growth, it is not considered to be the pivotal factor in overall develop-

Table 7.3 Comparison of Major Language Development Theories

Innate Theory	Reinforcement Theory	Social Learning Theory
Genetic explanation of language development	Language growth influenced by reinforcement	Language growth influenced by observation and imitation of others
Presence of language acquisition device Analysis of deep and surface structures	Tact, mand, and echoic acquisition techniques	Emphasis on adult modeling and expansion

ment. The most dramatic evidence against imitation as an explanation of language acquisition is found in the language patterns of children who cannot speak but hear normally. One young boy in this category never had the opportunity to imitate adult speech. He did, however, learn to comprehend a language (Lenneberg, 1962). Such evidence supports the argument that the theory of social learning leaves unanswered many questions about language development. Table 7.3 compares the major theories of language development.

Is Early Language Stimulation Important?

Reinforcement of children's vocalization is important to language development.

"Patty cake, patty cake . . ." Infants and toddlers delight in the repetition of this rhyme and a wide assortment of other jingles and chants. Just how important are these verbal games, or for that matter, the adults' language stimulation of children in general? According to contemporary psycholinguists, they are very important. Environmental stimulation is viewed as a critical factor in the overall language development of the child. Children need to hear speech around them in order to realize their linguistic potential (Slobin, 1982; Cazden, 1981; Moerk, 1983; Ausberger, Martin, and Creighton, 1982; Faber and Mazlish, 1980).

The adult who talks (baby talk or adult talk) to the infant will encourage more sound production (number and variety) than the adult who provides no stimulation at all. Even though most babies will babble to some degree, reinforcement seems to have a great effect on the amount of vocalization. Furthermore, such early stimulation appears to have long-lasting linguistic and cognitive benefits (Stevens, 1981; Lewis and Coates, 1980; Masur, 1982; Barnes et al., 1983).

It should be recognized, though, that the infant's state of readiness greatly influences the effects of adult verbal stimulation. As babies develop and mature, they gradually gain control over muscles of the throat, mouth, and tongue. Brain cells also mature and enable the infant to associate and understand linguistic stimulation. As a result, infancy becomes a time for early sound production. Infants also exhibit a rather remarkable understanding of language and may be able to follow many simple instructions, such as clapping their hands to a nursery rhyme. These many positive reactions and benefits attached to adult interaction underscore the importance of providing children with early language stimulation.

Stages of Language Development

Before we begin our discussion of the stages of language, it is important to understand **phonology:** the speech sounds that are relevant to a language. We will briefly examine several of these speech sounds, including phonemes, morphemes, and vowels.

A **phoneme** is the smallest unit of sound and is thus the most fundamental element of a language. English has more than 40 such basic sounds, which are combined to form words. The sounds of *b* in *boy* or *th* in *thick* are phonemes. A **morpheme** is the smallest unit of a language that has recognizable meaning. Some words have one morpheme, while others have several. For example, the word *boys* has two morphemes; *boy* and *s*.

A distinction should also be made between vowels and consonants, the two major vocal sounds responsible for the production of the aforementioned language elements. A **vowel,** the most prominent sound in a syllable, is produced when the air flows freely through the mouth cavity as it passes over the vocal cords. A **consonant** is a speech sound characterized by constriction or closure at one or more points in the breath channel.

Keeping these basic speech sounds in mind, let us now discuss specific language stages. We will begin with crying, the earliest stage of vocalization.

Crying   When infants are born, the only vocalizations they make are referred to as cries. As discussed in Chapter 5, there are different varieties of cries, from whimpering to fussing to piercing and colicky. While some meaning is usually attached to certain types of cries, at first many parents have difficulty understanding the cause for the outburst or distinguishing among the many varieties. Even though crying cannot be called language, it is a viable form of communication since infants are conveying basic needs. In most instances, variations of the cry are the only vocalizations during the first six to eight weeks.

Cooing and Babbling   At approximately 2 months of age, infants begin to use a new type of vocalization called cooing. Cooing includes gurgling and mewing sounds and generally indicates that the infant is pleased, happy, or even excited. Although still not considered language because it follows no rules, cooing, like crying, is a form of communication.

Cooing occurs only after a certain amount of maturation because it involves muscular movements of the tongue that the infant cannot perform at birth. This innate behavior occurs in both normal and deaf children and diminishes at approximately 8 months of age.

At about 6 months of age, babbling begins to emerge a syllable at a time. While cooing consists of vowel sounds, **babbling** includes both vowels and consonants, which eventually become distinct ("ga," "ma"). Babbling is the first vocalization that bears any resemblance to speech; infants are for the first time making sounds that seem to arouse their interest. Early phases in this developmental stage are often accompanied by excitation and motor movement. The infant may lie quietly while listening to external sounds and resume babbling when the sounds stop. Because of all these factors, babbling leads to increased control of sound.

The Holophrase Stage   While infants present their parents with many diverse and exciting accomplishments, perhaps none overshadows the emergence of the first word. This milestone is eagerly anticipated and is a source of pride to both mother and father. After cries, gurgles, cooing, and babbling, there is something magical about the first word the baby says, especially since the child's initial words are often designations for the mother and father (or are taken to be such by the parents).

This milestone occurs between the ages of 12 and 18 months. Although there are variations in the types of words acquired (see Nelson, 1981; Peters, 1982), young children's early words appear to relate to food, toys, body parts, animals, and people and are primarily concrete nouns and verbs. One must not assume, though, that all words spoken are clearly understood by the child. Many words are initially learned through pure imitation, and the youngster does not know what they actually represent (McShane, 1980).

Psycholinguists refer to this period as the holophrase stage. A **holophrase** is a one-word utterance that represents an entire phrase. In time, a holophrase may become fairly complex in overall scope with each one-word utterance representing a complete sentence with its own structure. For example, the word *toy* may mean, "I want my toy," "My toy is in the corner," or "My toy makes funny sounds." In this sense, one-word utterances may reflect interesting semantics or underlying word meanings. Semantically, single-word expressions may mean the designated objects as well as the roles that these objects play in the child's environment. Understanding the various meanings of one-word expressions is a difficult task for adults, who frequently have to pay close attention to intonations, gestures, and facial expressions to understand what is being said.

Before and during the holophrase stage, a gap frequently exists between the words that a child can understand and those that can be verbally expressed. Known as the **receptive versus expressive lag,** this linguistic phenomenon means that even though words cannot be expressed, children can nevertheless understand words or directions spoken by adults. Thus, an infant of 11 months may be able to follow the directive, "Get the ball," yet lacks the linguistic ability to express the same sentence or even parts of it. In time, however, the discrepancy between **receptive** and **expressive language** will lessen. (See Figure 7.4 for an illustration of the rapid increase in vocabulary during infancy and toddlerhood.) Alert adults realize that a child's inability to express words does not automatically mean that he or she lacks understanding of the situation at hand. On the contrary, children know much more than their linguistic ability allows them to express (Clark and Hecht, 1983).

Early Sentences   Two-word utterances may begin to emerge by the age of 18 months. Previously used holophrases are now replaced by verbalizations resembling sentences. In many cases, these two-word utterances consist of single words that exist as separate entities, with separate intonations and pauses in between. In time they will be fused together and used in succession.

Knowledge of **syntax**—the rules for combining words into sentences—develops during the early phases of this stage. Sentence arrangements usually consist of **pivot words** and **open class words.** Pivot words are usually shorter than and slower in developing than open class words. For example, the word *go* may be acquired and later become a pivot word in such combinations as, "Car go," "Daddy go," or "Me go." The pivot word is usually, but not always, used in the second position of these sentences. Pivot words rarely exist as single-word utterances. Open class words, on the other hand, consist of any of a large number of words that are not considered pivot words. Most of the child's early growth in vocabulary occurs in the open class.

After using two-word verbalizations, toddlers begin to employ **telegraphic sentences,** which are characteristically short and simple and composed primarily of nouns and verbs. They contain the words neces-

Figure 7.4 Vocabulary gains during infancy and toddlerhood.

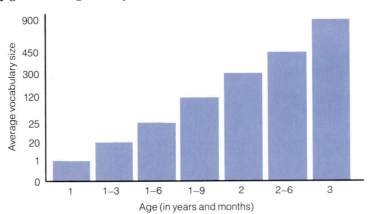

sary to convey the meaning and lack some words—including articles, prepositions, and conjunctions—as well as tense endings on verbs and plural endings on nouns. The following dialogue, between a father and his 2-year-old son, illustrates the concept of telegraphic sentences as well as the overall grammatical development up to this point. Note how even though the child's sentences are telegraphic, they transmit essential information:

Zachary: Eat now?

Father: Yes, now it's time to eat.

Zachary: Mommy home?

Father: No, Mommy will be working late tonight.

Zachary: Daddy eat too.

Father: Yes, I'm eating.

Zachary: Where's milk?

Father: It's right here. Would you like to start eating your rice?

Zachary: No. Too hot.

Father: Okay. We'll let it cool down some.

In addition to the fabrication of simple sentences, toddlers exhibit other remarkable language developments (see Table 7.4). Once restricted to crying as a basic form of communication, they now boast an average vocabulary of nearly 900 words. Knowledge of syntax and semantics increases daily as language becomes a vehicle for mental expression.

The Overregularization of Word Endings   Surprisingly, most toddlers are able to develop a variety of word endings. In the minds of many psycholinguists, this is due to the fact that children are adept at abstracting underlying rules of grammar. Thus, for example, they are able to pluralize nouns by adding an *s* and are able to place verbs in the past tense by adding *ed*. While such general rules permit inflections to be made with regular words, words that are exceptions (irregular words) pose difficulties to the young speaker. As a result, the rules for making nouns plural and verbs past tense are indiscriminately applied to irregular words. Thus, *foots* or *feets* may develop as an incorrect pluralization, and the *ed* ending may be applied to form such incorrect past tense words as *goed* for *went* or *doed* for *did*.

If you look beyond the obviously incorrect word, you'll see that the child has in fact mastered an important operating principle of the English language. That is, to form past tenses, one must add *ed*. The child has done this but has been fooled by the irregular nature of the English language.

Table 7.4 Speech and Motor Skill Developments

Age	Language Performance	Motor Performance
Birth	Cries	Little voluntary control
12 weeks	Coos, gurgles	Supports head when prone
16 weeks	Differentiates and responds to human sounds	Head self-supported
20 weeks	Vowel and consonant sounds	Sits if propped up
6 months	One-syllable babbling (ma, mu, da, di)	Sits
8 months	Reduplication (mama, didi) intonation pattern	Stands holding on
12 months	Understands some words	Walks when held by hand
18 months	Still babbles, 3–50 words, not many joined	Grasp fully developed; stiff gait
24 months	Vocabulary of 50 + words (especially nouns), uses two-word phrases	Runs, but falls; climbs stairs
30 months	Fastest vocabulary increase— new additions daily	Jumps; good hand-finger coordination
36 months	1,000 word vocabulary, 80% intelligible even to strangers	Runs on tiptoes, can ride tricycle

(Adapted from Lenneberg, 1967.)

This type of mistake is known as an **overregularization** and is evidence that children do not acquire a language through the exclusive use of reinforcement or imitation. Children could not have learned such words as *goed* or *doed* from adults because grown-ups do not use such overregularizations. Instead, children have created these words on the basis of overgeneralizing the operating principles they are learning (Schacter and Strage, 1982; Platt and MacWhinney, 1983).

Summary

The roots of mature thinking and reasoning begin to develop during the early years of childhood. Mental development, or cognition, is an extremely active field of exploration, and psycholinguists are providing

David, age 8

more and more information about this aspect of growth. This chapter explored four areas of mental activity: the cognitive advancements during Piaget's sensorimotor stage, concept developments, changes in the sense organs, and linguistic growth.

Piaget's sensorimotor stage occupies the first two years of life. The coordination of simple sensorimotor skills and reflex actions provide the undercarriage for this stage. Piaget identifies six substages within the sensorimotor stage: reflex activities (0 to 1 month), primary circular reactions (1 to 4 months), secondary circular reactions (4 to 8 months), coordination of secondary schemes (8 to 12 months), tertiary circular reactions (12 to 18 months), and invention of new means through mental combinations (18 to 24 months). Among the cognitive advancements emerging from the sensorimotor stage are the establishment of object permanence, the beginnings of mental representations, trial-and-error learning, and anticipatory behavior.

Closely associated with cognition are concept developments. The accurate perception of concepts relies heavily on perceptual constancy, which appears to develop remarkably early in life for both size and shape. Noteworthy developments in infancy and toddlerhood include progressively finer perceptions of shape and form, space, class, and time. Memory abilities are critical for the storage of environmental information. The three types of memory explored in this chapter were sensory (or immediate), short-term, and long-term. Of the three, long-term is the most resistant to decay.

Memory abilities gradually mature during childhood. One of the reasons for this improvement is an increase in the memory span, the amount of information that can be held in the short-term bank. Metacognition, the application of some cognitive process to a given cognitive task, also improves memory. Rehearsing events and employing various memory strategies to prevent forgetting are examples of metacognitive abilities.

Researchers have discovered that infants and toddlers are capable of making rather fine sensory discriminations. The sense of sight undergoes rapid development, particularly in regard to accommodation skills, brightness sensitivity, and acuity. Depth perception experiments using a visual cliff have shown that infants are equipped with this type of sensory awareness as early as the crawling stage. Other noteworthy perceptual developments occur in the senses of audition, taste, smell, and touch.

Psycholinguistics is the study of the processes through which an individual acquires a spoken language. Psycholinguistics is a fairly recent but very active field of study. Speech and language, while frequently used synonymously, are in fact quite separate. Speech is the act of producing vocalizations, while language is a system of grammatical rules and semantics that makes speech meaningful.

No single theory fully explains the nature of language development, although one proposed by Noam Chomsky, called innate theory, is quite influential among contemporary developmentalists. Chomsky's theory rests on the belief that language development is genetically determined through a system known as the language acquisition device (LAD). Chomsky proposes that language should be studied through generative analysis, an investigation of entire sentences rather than the component sounds and words. Sentences have two parts: surface structure (dictated by the rules of grammar) and deep structure (what a particular sentence means to an individual). Understanding the relationship that exists between surface and deep structures is known as a transformation.

Two other language development theories are the reinforcement theory popularized by B. F. Skinner and the social learning theory. Skinner believed that language is acquired through interaction with the environment, and social learning theorists believe that language is developed through a modeling process, either through imitation of adult remarks or by parents' expansion of their child's utterances.

Developmental patterns of speech and language follow a fairly stable sequence. Following the cooing stage at approximately 2 months, infants proceed to the babbling stage at approximately 6 months. Imitation appears to pave the way for the first word, which is generally spoken at between 12 and 18 months of age. Psycholinguists call the period of one-word utterances the holophrase stage. Toddlers can create two-word sentences at approximately 18 months and telegraphic sentences by the end of the second year.

By the end of toddlerhood, children have made remarkable gains in overall language development. Vocabulary gains are most rapid, as evidenced by the nearly 900 words that are acquired by the third year. Most toddlers have also attained some understanding of semantics (word meanings) and syntax (grammatical rules). The groundwork for later and more complex language growth has been established.

Suggested Reading List

Bower, T. G. R. *Development in Infancy,* 2nd ed. San Francisco: W. H. Freeman, 1981. Bower addresses himself to a wide assortment of topics related to infant perception and cognition, including space, distance, and object perception.

Brown, H. D. *Principles of Language Learning and Teaching.* Englewood Cliffs, N.J.: Prentice-Hall, 1980. This readable narrative of language acquisition includes techniques to stimulate linguistic growth.

Miller, G. A. *Language and Speech.* San Francisco: W. H. Freeman, 1981. A good overview of the nature of language. Miller provides the reader with an introduction to the properties of language, including its biological and social components.

Reese, H. W., and Lipsitt, L., eds. *Advances in Child Development and Behavior.* New York: Academic Press, 1982. This book of readings examines, among other topics, concept development and perceptual processes.

Chapter Eight

Personality and Social Learning

The first step, my son, which one makes in the world is the one on which depends the rest of our days.

Voltaire

Introduction

Successful personality and social adjustments are critical developmental challenges. These tasks begin during the years of infancy and toddlerhood and continue throughout life. During the first three years of life, personality and social developments are largely shaped by parents, especially the mother, who is the primary source of food, comfort, and attention. Yet it is only a matter of months before the entire family begins to exert molding influences on the child's developing personality.

It is from early interactions within the family that children develop a better understanding of themselves and their environment. Heightened cognitive powers blend with early personality and social forces to help young children realize that they are separate, unique individuals. These processes also combine to foster the development of such feelings as trust or mistrust, autonomy or self-doubt, and a wide range of other behavioral expressions.

This developing awareness of how individuals perceive themselves and others, including another person's thoughts and feelings, is known as **social cognition.** Social cognition, which requires the use of developing mental strategies to understand oneself and the general fabric of social relations, clearly shows how developmental processes are yoked together. Social cognition is an active field of study among contemporary researchers (see Rosenberg and Kaplan, 1982; Flavell and Ross, 1981; Higgins, Herman, and Zanna, 1981; Lamb and Sherrod, 1981).

The years of infancy and toddlerhood provide rich terrain for personality growth and the development of social cognition. After the dependency of the infant comes the toddler's ability to venture slowly into new and challenging situations with others. Family, peers, and other socialization agents influence the child in unique ways. Social experiences that are successfully met will generate positive self-regard; other occurrences are anxiety producing and ego threatening for the child. The manner in which each social situation is handled as time progresses will become a vital component of the child's developing personality and level of self-awareness (Maccoby, 1980; Kagan, 1981; Bronson, 1981).

This chapter will investigate the foundations of personality and social development that are established during infancy and toddlerhood. We will explore the theories of personality proposed by Sigmund Freud and Erik Erikson and examine the nature of early social experiences, including parent-infant interaction and the concept of attachment. Finally, we will examine emotional development during these early years.

Theories of Personality Development

Sigmund Freud's Theory

Readers will recall that Sigmund Freud proposed a five-stage theory of psychosexual development. The **oral stage** is of particular concern to us since it encompasses the first two years of life.

Freud suggests that the mouth is the primary source of satisfaction to the child during the first two years. The mouth and other sensitive body parts, such as the anus and the genitals, are referred to in Freudian terminology as erogenous zones. Freud states that the infant is "pleasure bent on sucking," and whether an advocate of Freudian theory or not, anyone who observes an infant sucking nipples, thumbs, fingers, or pacifiers has little doubt that much of the infant's interaction with the environment occurs through oral contact.

The oral stage can be further divided into the oral sucking and oral biting stages. Oral sucking is a stage of dependence in which the baby can only suck, while the oral biting stage (commencing at 18 months) is the point when the infant can also bite. It is possible that the latter stage occurs only in children who are frustrated when gratification is not immediate. The biting stage could thus be considered a form of aggressive behavior.

Satisfaction during the oral stage lays a foundation for the continuation of normal personality development. If the infant's needs are not gratified, or if they are gratified excessively, a fixation is said to occur.

The infant's interactions with the environment affect the development of his or her feelings of trust.

That is, oral needs continue to exist throughout life and may greatly influence behavior. Behavioral examples of oral fixation include thumb sucking; cigarette, cigar, and pipe smoking; and the manipulation of the lips with fingers or other objects such as pens or pencils. Other oral personality characteristics include overeating, greediness, and nail biting. However, research has not demonstrated any relationship between either frustration or overindulgence at the oral stage and these behavioral traits.

Erik Erikson's Theory

Unlike Freud, who emphasized psychosexual development, Erik Erikson emphasizes psychosocial stages of growth. The two psychosocial stages of importance to the present discussion are basic trust versus basic mistrust and autonomy versus shame and doubt.

Basic Trust versus Mistrust   The stage of **basic trust versus basic mistrust** occupies roughly the first year of life. Erikson stresses that during this time the infant develops physically as well as psychologically. Furthermore, the infant learns (in an unspecified way) to deal with the environment through the emergence of trustfulness or mistrust. Trust is a feeling that some aspects of the environment are dependable. Activities that may lead to such a feeling include feeding, tactile stimulation (cuddling, fondling, holding), and diaper changing.

The child's first relationship with the environment establishes a feeling of social trust or mistrust. Since the mother provides the child with the first social relationship, her task is to create a warm environment conducive to positive feelings. Trust, however, entails more than just physical reassurance (Erikson, 1963, p. 249):

> Let it be said that the amount of trust derived from earliest infantile experience does not seem to depend on absolute quantities of food or demonstrations of love, but rather on the quality of the maternal relationship. Mothers create a sense of trust in their children by that kind of administration which in its quality combines sensitive care of the baby's individual needs and a firm sense of personal trustworthiness. . . .

Trust forms the first building block in the infant's development: a sense of identity. Without the ego strength of trust, says Erikson, various behavior problems will arise (1963, p. 248):

An infant's feelings of trust should generalize from the caregiver to significant others—something that this child has not yet experienced.

In psychopathology the absence of basic trust can best be studied in the infantile schizophrenic, while lifelong underlying weakness of such trust is apparent in adult personalities in whom withdrawal into schizoid and depressive states is habitual. The reestablishment of a state of trust has been found to be the basic requirement for therapy in these cases.

Erikson points out that the ego qualities of trust and mistrust have been misconstrued as discontinuous traits, with one being good and the other bad. However, like the other so-called negative qualities, mistrust is not to be altogether avoided because life presents some very real dangers about which one should be apprehensive. Rather than viewing trust-mistrust as a dichotomy, Erikson sees it as a continuum on which it is desirable to be closer to the trust than to the mistrust end.

Parents who meet the baby's physical and psychological needs produce a happier, more contented infant, thus reciprocating parental enjoyment. Parents who have happy, trusting babies are apt to spend more time with them, which in turn establishes even more infantile trust. This phenomenon is termed the benign cycle. The vicious cycle occurs when a parent ignores the baby's needs. For example, rather than cooing and gurgling in trustful contentment, a hungry or wet infant whimpers, cries, and finally may scream as hunger pangs or skin irritations increase. The baby's screaming may irritate the parent, who becomes cross and handles the screaming infant roughly, which produces further annoyance in the infant. The vicious cycle eventually leads to an ego characterized by an uncomfortable and insecure relationship with the environment, resulting in a predominant sense of mistrust.

The emergence and growth of basic trust encourages the development of a variety of emotional responses, ranging from very pleasant to very unpleasant. The more severe the basic mistrust, however, the more limited the infant's repertoire of emotions. A child who is mistrustful of the environment may exhibit only anger, fear, distress, or apathy. This child may never learn how to respond to positive emotions such as love and warmth.

It is important to note the significant difference between Freud's and Erikson's theories concerning this early stage of development. Whereas Freud puts the emphasis on the quantity of oral pleasure felt by the infant, Erikson stresses the quality of care provided by the parents.

Autonomy versus Shame and Doubt   Erikson's second psychosocial stage of concern to us is **autonomy versus shame and doubt.** This stage occurs between the ages of 1 and 3 years. As the infant becomes increasingly aware of the surrounding environment, new interactions take place. Self-awareness has developed to the point where the child can now realize that the self is an entity separate from the environment, allowing the ego to develop further strengths or weaknesses. As perceptual skills develop and neuromuscular skills increase with maturation, the newly found self is aware both of its autonomy and of its vast limitations. Children attempt to assert themselves during this phase and frequently come into conflict with parental standards of behavior, leaving the psychological door open to feelings of shame and doubt. Thus developing physical abilities (walking, exploring the environment) intertwine with social interactions (parental standards) and personality dynamics (strivings for autonomy).

During this period, children desire independence; they want to have some say in decisions affecting their daily lives. For example, they may assert their autonomy by not eating at mealtime, by saying "no" to an adult's request, or by making demands at inappropriate times. This type of resistance is known as oppositional behavior, and many researchers (and parents) testify to its prevalency during the early years (see Haswell, Hock, and Wenar, 1982; Londerville and Main, 1981; Wenar, 1982). This behavior frequently leads to a harrowing experience for all concerned. The child's goals of autonomy are frequently thwarted, and the parent may become angry and even aggressive toward the little tyrant, producing doubt (Can I do things for myself?) and shame (Should I do things for myself?) in the child and possibly guilt in the parent.

This phase of development is all part of the socialization process, however, and strivings for autonomy are considered normal. Healthy autonomy will be the outcome if children encounter a reasonable balance between parental freedom and control.

Here again, the difference in emphasis between Freud and Erikson manifests itself. While Freud focuses on anal gratification, Erikson emphasizes the battle of wills between parent and child.

During the second year, autonomy emerges at higher levels (for example, a child strives for autonomy during the first year by resistance to being held), producing a conflict between independence and dependence. The child wants both, producing an ego struggle that may last months and even years until a comfortable compromise is reached. The emotions of shame and doubt may arise during this stage if the child is not allowed to develop freely. The parent who is intolerant and continually browbeats the child will raise an ashamed and doubtful child who lacks the independent spirit necessary for healthy autonomy. Jerome Kagan (1981) suggests that what 2-year-olds need is supportive guidance and understanding. Adults need to be sensitive to the toddler's desire to try out new behaviors. They must realize that toddlers need to test the validity of adult standards in order to develop an understanding of what will and will not be allowed. In the midst of such strivings, overbearing adults run the risk of crushing the child's emerging self-awareness.

Social Development

Humans are social animals, and the socialization process begins early in life. **Socialization** is the process whereby an individual learns to adapt and adjust to a given social environment. As we mentioned at the outset of this chapter, the process requires knowledge of oneself and others and what are called social cognitive powers. Children's social horizons expand gradually, from parents to siblings and soon to people outside the family. After their total dependence and social immaturity, children begin to develop social sensitivity and understanding, not to mention social responsibility and eventual maturity.

In this particular facet of our discussion, we will examine the nature of parent–infant interaction and the growth of attachment behaviors. Both of these extremely important facets of early development shape the growth of social relations.

Parent–Infant Interaction

As infants begin to spend more hours of the day awake, they usually have more interactions with parents, from the rituals of feeding, diaper changing, and other custodial chores to recreational and playtime activities. These early interactions are the seeds of social development for the infant.

Parent–infant interaction is important because adults can provide critical stimulation to the youngster's linguistic, cognitive, social, and physical capacities. Indeed, the lack of adult interaction and stimulation, a topic that we'll discuss momentarily, will retard growth in these areas. Through interactions with parents, infants also gradually develop a sense of the home's emotional climate. Interactions frequently reveal how parents feel about themselves and each other. Without question, the feelings parents have toward the child will also ultimately surface in direct or indirect ways (Roman and Raley, 1980; LaRossa and LaRossa, 1981).

Parents employ diverse techniques, styles, and mannerisms when they interact with infants. Generally speaking, adults behave differently with infants than they do with other adults. For example, many adults imitate certain aspects of the infant's behavior, such as smiling or cooing. Adults often employ exaggerated facial expressions such as raising their eyebrows and opening their eyes wide. Many adults also engage in varying degrees of baby talk in addition to employing exaggerated variations in intonation, pitch, and volume (Kaye, 1980; Fernald and Simon, 1984).

Attachment

While growing numbers of fathers share in child-rearing chores, the mother is usually the dominant influence in the infant's life. From the earliest feedings and handlings to verbal exchanges and eye contact, the mother has an unremitting influence on the infant's personality and social growth. During the early months the two will develop an affectionate bond that provides support and comfort to both. This bond between infant and caregiver is known as **attachment.**

Some researchers feel that attachment begins during the hours immediately following birth and that interaction between parents and infants intensifies the overall strength of attachment. However, as we stated in our discussion of neonatal behavior (Chapter 5), reactions to this point of view are mixed (see Lamb, 1982; Chess and Thomas, 1982; Herbert, Sluckin, and Sluckin, 1982; Marano, 1981), and no one has yet proved that such early attachment stimulation yields long-lasting results. However, we do know that generally speaking, bonds of attachment strengthen over time. To observe this, one has only to watch the intense and unblinking gaze of the infant toward the mother, the cling-

Bonds of attachment develop early in infancy.

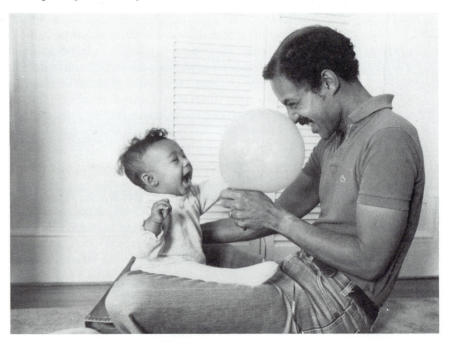

Mother's Milk or Formula?

The controversy over infant feeding alternatives has existed for years. For the female, this is perhaps one of the biggest decisions associated with parenthood.

Until formula feeding was perfected, there was no really safe and reliable substitute for breast milk. Now most mothers have a choice—and a chance to weigh the supporting evidence for each alternative. The proponents of breast feeding, supported by an international organization called the La Leche League (from the Spanish word for milk), maintain that this approach promotes close physical and psychological bonding between mothers and infants. League members assert that nursing is the "natural" way to nourish an infant and that it prevents most feeding problems, as well as constipation and some allergic reactions. The mother's milk also contains antibodies that will protect the infant from infectious diseases (Hirschman and Butler, 1981).

Many mothers feel as though they are giving part of themselves to their young and report a sense of inner peace during feeding times. This serenity may also have physiological support. It is generally accepted that breast feeding inhibits the mother's menstrual cycle, as well as the mood swings associated with menstruation. The apparent lack of irritability, tension, and restlessness frequently related to the menstrual cycle may enable nursing mothers to respond to the needs of the baby in a more relaxed and calm manner.

Bottle feeding is not without support. Proponents point to the greater mobility and freedom that bottle feeding offers to the mother after birth. Bottle feeding may also enable the father to become involved in feeding times and the mother to spend more time with her other children, who might resent the

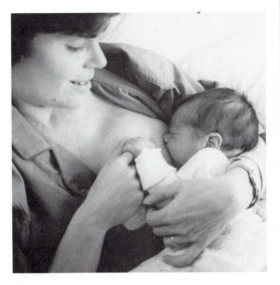

The arguments surrounding the advantages and disadvantages of breast feeding have existed for years.

continual contact that the breast-fed baby receives. In addition, some mothers find nursing physically annoying and painful, while others report a general dislike of the practice or a certain degree of social embarrassment.

There is no scientific evidence that either approach is more effective than the other. This may make the decision all the more difficult for the mother but may also relieve a sense of guilt for choosing one approach over the other. How to feed the infant is obviously an individual affair that must be carefully weighed. What appears more critical than the issue of the breast or the bottle is the manner in which the mother *relates* to the infant during feedings. Her warmth, care, and attention, while meeting life's most basic need, may well be more important than the approach chosen. ∎

ing behavior of a 2-year-old, or the upset face of a preschooler unexpectedly separated from mother. Witness, too, the intense reciprocal attachment behaviors from the mother to the infant as she tends to her child's needs.

We do not want to convey the impression that attachment is the exclusive domain of mother and child. Children are capable of developing different and separate bonds of attachment with the father or significant others. Many youngsters develop strong attachments to both parents, but it is not uncommon for a child to have a strong attachment to the mother but not to the father, or vice versa. The fact that attachment behavior can be directed toward either parent also has implications for the nurturance of trust and security. Such psychological reassurance need not always originate from the mother (Bowlby, 1980; Etaugh, 1980; Londerville and Main, 1981).

Attachment is considered to be a vital component of healthy personality and social functioning. Attachment promotes such positive behaviors and feelings as satisfaction, trust, security, and happiness. Its absence or disruption, on the other hand, can result in anxiety, anger, inner turmoil, and other problems. For example, insecurely attached children seem to be less adept in overall social relations than securely attached children. For some, absence of attachment results in grief and depression (Bowlby, 1980; Londerville and Main, 1981; Easterbrooks and Lamb, 1979).

Early as well as later social development appear to be affected by attachment experiences during the early years. Contemporary child psychologists feel that one's general outgoingness, social independence, and emotional investments in others may be traced to the outcome of these early social experiences. Also, we must not forget that our need for security, reassurance, or nurturance, while most intense during infancy and toddlerhood, is never really left behind. These are important needs even in adult life.

Theories of Attachment Behavior   Attempting to discover the origins and determinants of attachment has been a very active field of study. Moreover, contemporary research continues to supply us with many new thoughts and ideas about attachment (see Emde and Harmon, 1981; Sluckin, Herbert, and Sluckin, 1983; Field et al., 1981). The underpinnings of both past and present research are four major theoretical models of attachments: (1) ethological, (2) learning theory, (3) cognitive-developmental, and (4) psychoanalytical.

The ethological model has been influenced by such researchers as John Bowlby and Konrad Lorenz, who are engaged in the study of human and animal behavior called **ethology.** According to this school of thought, a human infant's social responsiveness develops largely through innate tendencies. A critical or sensitive period during the early months of life is said to make the infant especially receptive to the caregiver. During infancy, these innate systems are activated by the environment, and their expression elicits specific responses from the caregiver. Infant behaviors such as clinging and sucking promote close contact with the mother. Crying and distress capture the caregiver's attention, as do smiling and cooing. Later on, infants call their mothers and follow them, further strengthening the bond between the two. Combined, these behaviors promote physical nearness and attachment to the caregiver. History reveals that infants who can maintain this closeness have the best hope for survival.

Learning theory maintains that attachment is a learned rather than an innate process. Proponents of this viewpoint suggest that attachment can be broken into stimulus-response mechanisms, much like many other types of childhood behaviors. It is reasoned that the mother, who is initially a neutral stimulus, becomes a **secondary reinforcer** over time. Infants learn that the mother is the agent responsible for their **primary reinforcers,** such as tactile stimulation, milk, or warmth. Because she is continually associated with the dispensing of these primary reinforcers, and with the satisfaction of the infant's basic needs, her continual physical presence becomes important to the infant.

The cognitive-developmental view interprets attachment as an outgrowth of developing mental abilities. Attachment and proximity-seeking behavior develop because the infant is cognitively aware of the perceptual differences that exist between the mother and others in the environment. Attachment is further strengthened when the infant understands person permanence, a concept closely related to the Piagetian principle of object permanence. By age 2, infants realize that the caregiver can exist without being physically present in the same room. The child's ability to construct a mental image of the mother's distinguishing characteristics will result in more proximity-seeking behavior. In this way, cognitive and social behavior are said to be related.

Like the ethological approach, the psychoanalytic view emphasizes instincts. Attachment is perceived as an emotional relationship shaped by the Freudian concept of instinctual psychic energy. During the child's psychosexual stages of development, this energy is directed toward the mother because she is perceived as a source of pleasure and satisfaction. As the child's primitive needs are met during the oral and anal stages, bonds of attachment strengthen, and the mother is recognized as a "love object."

The Development of Attachment

Attachment does not just happen; it unfolds in a series of stages. Our knowledge of the course of attachment has been significantly aided by a longitudinal study of 60 Scottish infants during their first 18 months of life. The researchers interviewed mothers about various separation situations with their children and were especially interested in the timing of specific attachments. Their research reveals three basic stages of attachment (Schaffer and Emerson, 1964).

1. The first two months of life are called the asocial period. During this time the infant responds to both human and inanimate features of the environment. Infants respond to a variety of social and nonsocial stimuli, depending on the stimulation or satisfaction they provide.

2. The indiscriminate-attachment stage is characterized by the tendency to generalize attachment to all the people in the environment. At this stage infants regard humans as a generalized class of stimuli. Protests are directed not at people but at the cessation of an enjoyable activity, such as being put down or left alone. This stage lasts approximately until the infant's seventh month.

3. During the specific-attachment stage (from about 7 months to 1 year), the infant's preference is directed toward a specific person, in most cases the mother. Many of the babies studied made progressive attempts to seek the mother's presence and exhibited signs of protest and distress when they were put down or separated. Fear of strangers also begins to develop at this time.

Attachments to other persons in the environment, such as siblings, grandparents, and babysitters, will also take place. In Schaffer and Emerson's study, a clear-cut majority of the 18-month-old infants had specific attachments to several people other than the mother (see Figure 8.1).

The ages outlined by Schaffer and Emerson are approximations; cross-cultural investigations of attachment show wide differences in the overall development of attachment. For example, specific attachment may develop in Ugandan infants as early as 5 months, perhaps because of constant maternal contact (Ainsworth, 1967). Similarly, Guatemalan youngsters appear to exhibit separation anxiety earlier than American children (Lester et al., 1974).

There are also individual differences in attachment behavior. The quality or security of attachment, for example, can vary from child to child. According to Mary Ainsworth (1979), children can thus be classified as securely attached, anxiously attached, or avoidance attached:

- When placed in an unfamiliar situation with their mothers (a room they haven't seen before) **securely attached** infants typically turn to the mother for comfort but also make attempts to explore the environment. Securely attached infants show little anxiety when the mother is away for short periods of time. Upon the mother's return, these infants are happy and desire close contact with her.

- **Anxiously attached** infants do not explore the environment when they are placed in unfamiliar situations with their mothers. They are likely to be anxious and distressed when the mother is temporarily away and are ambivalent toward her when she returns. Upon her return, they may cling to the mother and then push her away.

- **Avoidance attached** infants are relatively unattached to their mothers and exhibit little anxiety or distress when left alone. Furthermore, they demonstrate little response when their mothers reappear. Many in this category ignored or avoided the mother upon her return.

Ainsworth maintains that these three types of attachment are the result of parenting styles. Securely attached infants usually have mothers who are responsive and sensitive to their needs. These mothers have succeeded in fostering a sense of trust and security in their children. The successful resolution of Erikson's stage of basic trust versus basic mistrust and the development of secure attachment illustrate the bridge that exists between personality and social growth. Mothers of anxiously attached infants tend to be insensitive and unresponsive to their children's needs. This holds true also for mothers of avoidance attached infants, although they also have a tendency to be

Figure 8.1 The course of specific attachment in infancy. (Adapted from Schaffer and Emerson, 1964.)

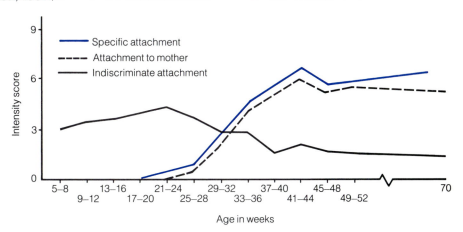

more rejecting, particularly when their children desire close physical contact.

Such findings stress the fact that infants need quality more than quantity in the attachment relationship. Parents who supply attention, sensitivity, consistency, and responsiveness to infant needs are most likely to promote the healthiest type of attachment. These are the psychological "vitamins" needed to sustain emotional security and satisfaction in the attachment relationship (Honig, 1981).

Clues to Developing Attachment Behaviors   In addition to the infant's desire to maintain contact and establish close proximity to the caregiver, there are several other visible clues to developing attachment behaviors. These clues include the infant's smiling responses and the expression of stranger and separation anxiety.

The **reflex smile** is the earliest type of smiling and occurs during the first few weeks of life. It is primarily physiological and may be the infant's response to a number of different stimuli, including internal stimulation (a bubble of gas in the stomach), feeding, or being stroked on the cheek. At this early age, reflexive smiles are not socially oriented.

Another type of smile, known as the **social smile,** appears somewhere around the second or third month. This is true smiling as we know it. The social smile can be evoked by the appearance or voice of a caregiver, any movement, and certain noises. Many infants smile, open their eyes wide, and make cooing noises at the same time. This is called a **greeting response.** Returning the greeting response may prompt the infant to continue the behavior (Lewis and Coates, 1980; Kaye and Fogel, 1980).

One other variation of smiling is the **selective social smile,** which appears at 5 to 6 months. Rather than smiling in an undifferentiated fashion, which is the case in the social smile, the infant now directs this response only to familiar social stimuli, such as the mother or other caregivers. Unfamiliar faces are detected quite readily at this age and generally cause withdrawal behavior.

Stranger anxiety may serve as another clue of infant attachment behavior. As we have suggested, after 6 months, infants attach themselves to a caregiver and express distress, wariness, and suspicion when a stranger is introduced. The infant is evidently able to detect a noticeable difference in the stranger's face, as compared with the mental image of the caregiver's features stored in the infant's developing mind. Growing levels of cognitive awareness are thus connected to stranger distress as well as the development of the social smile. As one might expect, overall distress levels are reduced when the primary caregiver is present and the stranger behaves naturally and approaches the infant with no sudden moves (Smith, Eaton, and Hindmarch, 1982).

Separation anxiety, which begins at approximately 12 months, is another possible indicator of attachment. Separation from the caregiver is likely to result in considerable infant protest and distress. However, the degree of protest and distress exhibited by infants is affected by the situation in which they are left. The child's familiarity with the environment as well as the child's possession of a favorite attached object both tend to reduce protest levels.

The Harlow Studies: Contact Comfort and Social Isolation

For Linus (of *Peanuts* fame) and children like him all over the world, security is a worn but comforting security blanket; for others it may be a huggable doll, teddy bear, or other stuffed animal. All these security-oriented objects seem to receive similar childhood attachment behaviors: they are clung to in times of peace as well as turmoil, they are stroked and hugged, and they usually end up each night cradled in the arm of the sleeping child.

Psychologists have long sought to understand why youngsters are drawn to objects that offer soft contact and comfort and how this behavior relates to attachment in general. Research conducted by Harry Harlow has provided some answers. Working with rhesus monkeys, Harlow devised a series of experiments to show how organisms are driven to seek contact and comfort and how these behaviors strengthen infantile attachment (Harlow, 1971; 1962; 1958; Harlow and Zimmerman, 1959; Suomi and Harlow, 1971). The fact that Harlow experimented with rhesus monkeys in his efforts to understand the **contact comfort motive** does not mean that his research has little or no relevancy to real life. When closely examined, Harlow's research and other related experiments have implications that may help explain the attachment behaviors that youngsters direct to security blankets and other love objects.

In Harlow's research two surrogate (substitute) "mothers" were built and placed in a cage; both were constructed of wire mesh, but one was covered with terry cloth. Each mother could be equipped with a nursing bottle (the nipple of which protruded through the "chest") and a light bulb behind the body to provide warmth for the infant.

The infant monkeys used in the study were divided into two groups; group A could receive nourishment from the nursing bottle placed in the wire mother, while group B could receive milk from the bottle of the cloth-covered mother. The monkeys in group A would feed from the wire mother, but gradually spent less and less time with her. Eventually, these monkeys would receive nourishment and then spend the intervening time with the more comforting cloth mother. Several infants clung to the cloth mother even while reaching over to feed from the wire mother. On the other hand, the infants in group B spent considerable time clinging to the soft covering of their cloth mother and almost never ventured to the other wire figure.

Harlow learned that the cloth mother also played a crucial role in reducing the infant's fear and anxiety. This was dramatically illustrated when a strange object (a mechanical teddy bear) was introduced. The infant invariably ran to the cloth mother and clung to her for security. After fear was reduced by this form of contact and comfort, the infant would venture short distances from the mother and eventually make attempts to explore the new object.

Harlow also explored the later behavior of those monkeys not benefiting from a real mother. He found that the absence of the mother severely hampered development, particularly in social and emotional areas. Although the monkeys reared with cloth mothers showed no overt problems in infancy, some were retarded later in life when compared with monkeys brought up by real mothers. In particular, the experimental monkeys became socially maladjusted, ignoring others and frequently passing time by biting and hugging themselves. Some females in the study group proved to be poor mothers, neglectful of and abusive to their young. However, when placed in the continual company of normal monkeys, the socially isolated monkeys began to recover from the effects of their experimental environment. This was

The Harlow experiments: research has shown that contact comfort is an important facet of normal emotional development.

 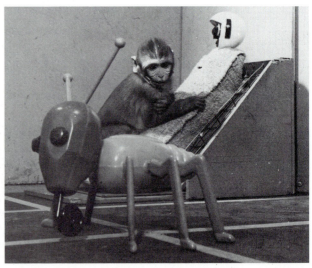

largely due to the fact that the normal monkeys encouraged social interaction and play behavior and discouraged solitary behavior.

The maladjusted behaviors observed by Harlow were probably caused by the fact that the monkeys studied had no real mothers to curtail clinging activities gradually and promote the development of autonomy. The contact in infancy that real mothers provide also promotes the formation and differentiation of facial and bodily postural expressions, a factor that may make later social interactions easier.

Harlow's research has provided us with fascinating dimensions to the overall concept of attachment behavior. His research indicates that satisfaction of the hunger drive alone does not promote the infant's attachment to the mother. Rather, the attachment to the mother is strongly promoted by the need to establish contact with something that can offer comfort, softness, and warmth. Thus, "mother love" may really mean tactile stimulation to a young infant.

Harlow's general findings apply to security blankets and other love objects as well. Some researchers, though, have provided us with more specific details about the role of these objects. For example, Passman and Halonen (1979) found that security blankets are very popular among children between the ages of 18 and 24 months and do help youngsters deal with anxiety and upsetting situations. When children were placed in a strange room without their mothers, play and exploratory behavior were less inhibited when the youngsters' blankets were put somewhere in the same room. In later research, when the mother was again absent, it was found that learning efficiency was greater for children who had security blankets present. Apparently the blanket was the best replacement for the mother.

In stressful situations, however, security blankets appear to have their limitations. For example, youngsters were placed alone with a researcher in a room where a strange clicking sound could be heard. Even the presence of the security blanket did not reduce their anxiety.

It should also be recognized that not all children are drawn to security blankets or similar objects. Adults should realize that they cannot just give youngsters a blanket and expect "security" to result. Some children are simply more prone than others to develop attachment behaviors toward these objects.

The need for comfort from such things as a security blanket or other love object can be surprisingly strong. Intense clinging, stroking the blanket, and even thumb sucking may be part of the overall behavior exhibited. In fact, thumb sucking often parallels security blanket behaviors. When youngsters use their blankets, the thumb or part of the hand is usually part of the experience. If one looks closely, the thumb and hand are working on the blanket itself as it is being held. If the security blanket is missing, children often suck their thumbs instead. Such behavior weaves together the oral need proposed by Freud and the need for trust and security emphasized by Erikson. In this way, the security blanket and the hand that holds it are the child's "companions," friends in a sometimes strange and threatening world.

Attachment Deprivation

The foregoing discussion has stressed the importance that quality caregiving has on attachment behavior. Thus far, though, we have not examined the effects that maternal absence has on human infants. What are the effects of infant attachment deprivation? Are they long-term or short-term effects? Must the effects always be negative? While Harlow's research provides us with some insight, studies of human infants experiencing actual attachment deprivation have enhanced our insight and knowledge in this area.

René Spitz (1945) was a pioneer in the study of attachment deprivation. Spitz compared infants in two institutions, a nursery school and a foundling home. The infants in the nursery school were cared for on a one-to-one basis, had toys to play with, and could see and hear other babies. This group displayed rapid gains in language and motor development. In the foundling home, however, 45 babies were cared for by six nurses, few toys were available, and barriers prevented the babies from viewing the surroundings. Stimulation and the opportunity to develop attachment were limited at best.

Spitz observed that the foundling-home babies were in a state of general depression, a condition characterized by sadness, lack of expression, and lethargic behavior. Furthermore, these children were more susceptible to disease, even though medical and sanitation conditions were almost identical in both institutions. Many of the foundlings experienced insomnia, a loss of appetite, and overall slowness of movement. In short, these children developed what Spitz labeled **failure to thrive.**

Another study concentrated on studying the long- and short-term effects of unsatisfactory and deprived relations between parent and child. Two groups of orphaned children were studied. The children in one group were raised by foster parents who provided care and understanding; the other children were raised in a foundling home without the individual treatment that the other group received. While the deprived institutional environment had long-term effects, such as retardation in social and emotional development, the length of time that an individual was institutionalized was a crucial factor. Those who were institutionalized for longer periods of time exhibited the most pronounced retardation (Goldfarb, 1943).

Other investigators have found that the potentially harmful effects associated with institutionalization do not necessarily persist in later life. One study compared infants in a Lebanon foundling home with noninstitutionalized infants. In the foundling home, adult-child interaction was limited during the first year, with the infants receiving little tactile stimulation other than that incidental to feeding and bathing. At 1 to 3 years, the children interacted in limited play groups (few toys available). At 4 years, they entered kindergarten.

To compare developmental rates, tests were administered to both institutionalized and noninstitutionalized children (between the ages of 4½ and 6 years). At the infancy level, the institutionalized babies were quite inferior to the control group in virtually every respect. In all likelihood, this was due to the limited learning opportunities available during the first year of institutionalization. However, in tests administered to the older children, the institutionalized youngsters were only slightly deficient in overall skills, leading the investigators to believe that retardation in the first year does not result in a generally poor performance at 4½ to 6 years, even when a child remains in a relatively restricted environment (Dennis and Najarian, 1957).

Supporting data are available in the findings of other researchers, such as Sayegh and Dennis (1965) and Skeels (1942). Their research showed that when institutionalized infants were given special attention—such as encouragement of prehension abilities, stimulation of interest in objects, or simply being placed in an upright position—a number of them exhibited marked improvement in developmental tests.

Thus several factors must be examined when investigating the overall effects of attachment deprivation. These factors include the age of the child when placed in institutional care, the amount of time spent in the institution, and the conditions of life preceding and following the experience.

Maternal Separation and the Israeli Kibbutz   The type of child-rearing practice in an Israeli kibbutz is in marked contrast to the American style of child rearing and offers another dimension to the issue of attachment and maternal separation. A **kibbutz** (from the Hebrew word for group) is a collective farm settlement where work and wealth are shared and children are reared communally away from their parents. The purpose of the kibbutz was to revolutionize Jewish society and prevent the development of social classes, an intention that still persists.

From shortly after birth until late adolescence, children are reared in group settings from nursery to high school. The group of children that one is born into remains the same, and as a result, close bonds of attachment usually develop. During infancy, a *metapalet* (a child care worker of the kibbutz) tends to the baby's basic needs. Parents visit the infant daily, and the mother returns as often as necessary to feed the child. When the infant is weaned from the mother, the metapalet assumes full responsibility for feeding the youngster. As children get older, they move to other living arrangements and come into contact with other metapalets and teachers.

By the time they reach adolescence, teenagers are part of the "youth movement," which exposes them to the kibbutz and communal sphere with more intensity. They are encouraged to formulate group decisions and develop more fully such capacities as cooperation and sensitivity toward others. By the end of their teenage years, members of the kibbutz work with adults and contribute to the economy.

How successful is the kibbutz pattern of child rearing? In the beginning, many criticized its approach by saying that the youngster would be deprived of parental care and nurturing, not to mention attachment and stimulation. Others felt that *kibbutzim* (children of the kibbutz) would be emotionally deprived. However, most evidence seems to indicate that kibbutzim grow up to be well adjusted and emotionally stable. They exhibit patterns of social attachment similar to those of children reared in the traditional American nuclear family, but they tend to be more cooperative and generous. Initially, kibbutz educators felt that this collective approach to child rearing would eliminate the patriarchal family structure and sex-role stereotyping. However, these goals have

Children of an Israeli Kibbutz.

not yet been attained (Rabin and Beit-Hallahmi, 1982; Maccoby and Feldman, 1972; Shapira and Madsen, 1974).

The Father's Role in Childrearing

Until recently, the role and impact of the father in such areas as attachment and infant care were overlooked. While the father's importance in the household was generally recognized, American society was "mother-centered" in its philosophy of child care. However, with more dual-career households and society's increasing deemphasis of sex role differences, this focus may be changing. The father's influence on various aspects of the developing child is now being recognized. Many contemporary researchers actively explore the father's role and have presented us with a wealth of information (see Pederson, 1980; Lamb, 1981; Parke, 1981).

We have learned in this chapter that children are capable of establishing strong bonds of attachment to both mother and father. Moreover, infants regularly turn to fathers in times of distress. What appears to be different in family relationships are the parental activities that foster attachment. The infant's more intense levels of attachment toward the mother may be attributable to her caregiving functions. Fathers offer other types of stimulation, such as play activities and the exploration of the environment (LaRossa and LaRossa, 1981; Fein, 1980).

Research clearly indicates that the father has strong influences on the child's overall emotional, social, and intellectual development. His presence and attention to his children has short- and long-term benefits. The absence of paternal care also seems to affect the development of the child. For example, academic achievement and IQ levels in children may be affected by the absence of a positive father-child relationship. Fathers can affect how well their children progress in school, which subjects they prefer, and even the kinds of occupations they eventually choose. Fathers also influence social and sex-role development by serving as role models and in their daily interactions (Parke, 1981; Radin, 1981).

Yet while the father's influence on the family cannot be overstressed, whether this influence is positive is another issue. This depends on a number of factors, including the father's involvement in child care and family activities, his upbringing, the quality of his other relationships, and the characteristics of his offspring [Lamb, 1982(c); 1983].

While many fathers look forward to child care, some resist the notion that they should spend more time with their children. Many feel that they are poorly prepared for parenting as it is, let alone for increased child-rearing responsibilities. In this vein, many fathers report considerable anxiety, confusion, and uneasiness over the multiple needs of their children (Spieler, 1982; Nannarone, 1983).

Let it be said, though, that anxiety and confusion over children's needs and parenting in general are normal for *both* fathers and mothers. Our society does not prepare adults for parenthood. The need for such preparation is especially obvious during infancy as parents anxiously tend to the intense, multiple needs of their offspring, who require numerous adaptations and adjustments by both father and mother (Waldron and Routh, 1981; Clark, 1981; Miller and Sollie, 1980).

Emotional Development

What Are Emotions?

Emotional reactions are variations or changes in arousal levels that may either interfere with or facilitate motivated behavior. **Emotions** are usually accompanied by physiological responses, such as an increase in blood pressure, heart rate, or muscle tension, and overt behaviors, such as facial expressions or body movements, as well as the individual's cognitive interpretation of the emotional state (Campos and Sternberg, 1981; Pribram, 1980; Brown and Wallace, 1980).

While this appears to be a fairly simple and straightforward description, emotions are not that simple. Emotions are highly complex states in children as well as adults. As a result, they are very difficult to define and categorize, although attempts have been made to do so (see Chapter 16). Exploring infant emotions is especially hard because there is no differentiated emotional responsiveness at birth. The researcher is often forced to apply broad labels to the infant's emotional behavior, such as "relative calm" or "diffuse excitement."

One might think that simple observation would reveal a number of different emotions in the infant. This is not the case; what seem to be outward signs of happiness, for example, may not correspond to the inner state of the infant. Crying or weeping may indicate, among other things, pain, hunger, or a state of general discomfort. With time, however, it is generally acknowledged that the infant's emotional behavior becomes increasingly differentiated (Izard, 1980, 1982; Lewis and Michaelson, 1983).

Crying

During infancy, the baby cries vigorously and with total bodily involvement, largely as a result of hunger or other internal discomfort. Other variables thought to be related to this behavior include fatigue and environmental tension. The caregiver's ability to soothe the baby and provide continuous stimulation during these emotional outbursts is critical in relation to the length and intensity of crying.

By the first birthday, the total amount of crying is generally reduced and bodily expressions are milder. As the child matures, crying is heard less and less frequently, and the reasons for crying vary with the situation. Crying can be caused by separation from the caregiver, unfamiliar and fear-invoking situations, physical pain, or even frustration when the child's goals are thwarted.

Laughter and Humor

Smiling and laughter become part of the youngster's emotional repertoire at an early age. As we discussed earlier, smiling is usually elicited by the sound of a human voice and may eventually indicate attachment to the caregiver. Interesting things, such as bright moving objects or the sounds of other people's voices, also trigger smiling.

Smiling and laughter may also be initiated by simple interaction with adults. For instance, the baby may smile, which prompts the mother to smile. The mother's smile may, in turn, motivate the child to smile again or laugh. Later on, laughter becomes associated with other

This infant can already play jokes on people.

types of stimulation (e.g., tickling) or with feelings of well-being. Games, stories, and television may also develop humor at an early age. Like other emotions, humor becomes more fully developed and widely diversified as childhood progresses and cognitive skills accelerate [see McGhee and Goldstein, 1983(a), (b)].

Fear

A controversial issue is whether fears are innate or the product of some form of learning experience. Fear of falling (including the Moro reflex) appears to be an inborn characteristic. On the other hand, infants' common fear of the dark seems to develop largely as the result of a conditioning process.

It is believed that certain factors contribute to children's early fears, especially the maturation level of the youngster. As children grow older,

A child's garden of fears.

their social environment expands considerably and exposes new areas of uncertainty and possible danger. However, what might have evoked fear at an early age may no longer do so as cognitive skills develop. For example, in early childhood, the youngster's fear of strangers decreases, but fear of imaginary creatures escalates. As with all emotional adjustments, children unquestionably need the support, guidance and gentle understanding of adults in overcoming fears (Schaefer and Millman, 1981).

Anxiety

Like fear, anxiety has its beginnings in infancy. **Anxiety** is a state of inner apprehension most often characterized as a response to a subjective rather than an objective danger. Two examples of this emotional reaction are stranger and separation anxiety, discussed earlier in this chapter.

As infants and toddlers expand their social environments, stressful situations arise. Parental demands, such as weaning, eating on a schedule, and toilet training, may contribute to anxious states. Especially stressful are crises such as divorce, abuse, or hospitalization. How to help children weather anxious and stressful situations has been an increasingly active field of study in recent years. Numerous suggestions are available in Chandler (1982), M. S. Miller (1982), Kuczen (1982), and McNamee (1982).

Anger and Aggression

Between the first and second year, the child may display signs of anger and aggression, an emotional reaction usually caused by frustration when attempts to reach a desired goal are blocked or thwarted. When such an obstacle develops, the child will react to remove the block. This reaction can be seen most readily when the child is threatened with the loss of the mother. Anger is often expressed for the first time when such a separation occurs.

Because the first two years produce a considerable number of demands on the child, angry behavior is fairly commonplace. Adjustment is particularly difficult for the infant and toddler when personal care and social training are involved. Outward-directed anger is frequently aimed at rigid demands in toilet training, dressing, and eating; interruptions in playtime activities; and being forced to go to bed. Frequent irritability in the child may have other causes, including bed-wetting, fatigue, or illness. Because of the frequent irritability in the age group, parents often refer to this stage of childhood as the "terrible twos" (Haswell, Hock, and Wenar, 1982).

Temper Tantrums: Understanding the Child's Angry Outbursts   The scene is probably familiar to parents of young children everywhere. A youngster is interrupted during a favorite playtime activity and told to go to bed. Another picks up a new toy in a store and is instructed to put it down because it is too expensive. Some youngsters may respond with a temper tantrum, a violent, outward-directed flow of anger. Temper tantrums are expressed in many ways, from crying and screaming to head banging and kicking. No matter how they are channeled, tantrums seem to express the same message: anger and frustration in having to adjust to the rituals and demands of grown-up life.

Temper tantrums are a normal phase of childhood development, yet they represent the ultimate in negative expression. While handling temper tantrums is an individual affair, most experts agree that giving in to the child's demands only reinforces this type of behavior and increases the likelihood of its future appearance. Getting angry and upset also serves as a reinforcer, since children can see that their behavior is taking its toll. Most experts suggest that ignoring the tantrum until it has extinguished itself and then talking to the child at a less emotional moment is an effective technique. In social situations, some parents prefer to remove the child firmly to a less public location to avoid social discomfort. Whatever course of action they choose, adults must use an approach with which they are comfortable and exercise consistency. Seeking to understand tantrums from the child's viewpoint and taking into account things such as irritability, fatigue, and adult demands may go a long way in dealing with this stormy stage of emotional development.

Summary

Kirk, age 6

During the years of infancy and toddlerhood, the child's personality and social growth are largely shaped by the family. From early interactions with parents, children develop a better understanding of themselves and their social surroundings. This type of growing awareness of oneself and the general fabric of society is called social cognition by contemporary developmentalists and is a very active field of research.

This chapter explored Freud's and Erikson's personality theories in relation to these early years. Freud refers to the first two years of life as the oral stage of psychosexual development and emphasizes the importance of oral gratification. Erikson stresses the importance of psychosocial relations, suggesting that sound personality growth at this time depends on the successful resolution of the basic trust versus basic mistrust and autonomy versus shame/doubt psychosocial crises.

Socialization is the process whereby an individual learns to adapt and adjust to a given social environment. Early parent-infant interaction represents the child's first social relationship. Attachment is an affectionate bond between infant and caregiver and is considered to be a vital component of healthy personality and social functioning. The four major theories of attachment are the ethological, learning theory, cognitive-developmental, and psychoanalytic models. The general progression of attachment includes asocial, indiscriminate, and specific stages.

The quality of attachment can vary from child to child. Mary Ainsworth's research indicates that children can be classified as having secure, anxious, or avoidance attachments. Of the three, secure attachments are the healthiest. Caregivers of securely attached children are usually responsive and sensitive to the child's needs and have promoted the Eriksonian notion of trust.

There are several visible clues to developing attachment behaviors. Smiling, for example, proceeds from a general and reflexive state to a selected response. Selected social smiles, which develop by approximately the sixth month, are reserved for familiar faces. Stranger anxiety, also developing by the sixth month, and separation anxiety, occurring approximately by the twelfth month, are two other clues to developing attachment behaviors.

Harry Harlow's comprehensive research clearly illustrates the importance of contact and comfort to attachment behaviors. Working with rhesus monkeys, Harlow discovered that attachment to the caregiver is prompted by the need to establish contact with something that offers comfort, softness, and warmth. This may help to explain why young children are drawn to security blankets and other "love" objects.

Harlow also found that the absence of a real mother hampers later social and emotional maturation, although this is not totally irreversible. Studies of institutionalized children support these findings. While institutionalization produces degrees of developmental retardation, social stimulation and an enriched environment undo many of the negative effects. When investigating the effects of institutionalization, critical factors to examine include the age of the child when institutionalized, the amount of time institutionalized, and the conditions of life preceding and following institutionalization.

A relatively recent research pursuit of child developmentalists is the father's role in child rearing. More fathers than ever before are participating in child care responsibilities. Studies indicate that the father is influential in shaping overall emotional, social, and intellectual growth. Whether the father's influence is positive depends on a number of factors, including his involvement in the home, his upbringing, the quality of his other relationships, and his children's characteristics.

Emotions are defined as variations in arousal levels that may either interfere with or facilitate motivated behavior. Emotions typically include physiological, expressive, and cognitive components. The measurement of emotions is especially difficult during infancy because of a lack of differentiation.

With age, though, emotions and how they are exhibited become increasingly differentiated, and this chapter explored some representative examples: crying, laughter and humor, fear, anxiety, and anger and aggression. Each of these emotions reflects a combination of cognitive, personality, and social forces. This mixture of developmental processes supports the notion that growth is an interrelated, rather than isolated, occurrence.

Suggested Reading List

Erikson, Erik *The Life Cycle Completed: A Review.* New York: W. W. Norton, 1982. Among the diverse topics is an exploration of Erikson's famous eight psychosocial crises, including the strengths and virtues emerging from each. This is a must addition to your psychology library.

Izard, E. E., ed. *Measuring Emotions in Infants and Children.* Cambridge, England: Cambridge University Press, 1982. This reader contains numerous points of view on the physiological, expressive, and subjective dimensions of emotion.

Kagan, J. *The Second Year: The Emergence of Self-Awareness.* Cambridge: Harvard University Press, 1981. Kagan thoughtfully describes the competencies that forge early levels of self-awareness.

Parke, R. D. *Fathers.* Cambridge: Harvard University Press, 1981. This is one of the better books about the influences of the father on the contemporary family.

Part Three
Early Childhood

Chapter Nine

Physical Growth and Development

The little ones leaped, and shouted, and laugh'd and all the hills echoed . . .

William Blake

Introduction

By the time youngsters reach early childhood, noticeable changes have taken place in their physical proportions and motor skills. The toddler's round, babylike contours have become more slender, largely due to a growth spurt that affects physical size as well as the preschooler's ability to engage in numerous and diverse types of physical activities. This latter development will affect muscular growth as well as the preschooler's general body build.

The growth spurt in early childhood, while not as great as that in infancy and toddlerhood, notably affects height and weight. By age 5, the average child stands 43 inches (about 3½ feet), a little more than double the birth length. The average weight is approximately 43 pounds, almost five times the weight at birth. Other significant developments associated with this growth spurt are increases in trunk and arm lengths (Corbin, 1980).

The preschooler's body also changes in other ways. By early childhood, most children have the full complement of 20 baby teeth. Shortly after the preschool years, teeth will begin to be lost. The muscle and skeletal systems continue to mature during this time, as do the digestive tract and respiratory system.

The head and brain approach their adult size during this time. More specifically, the head attains nearly 90 percent of its adult size, while the brain, growing in relation to cranial development, reaches 75 percent of its adult weight. The brain owes this rapid development to the fact that billions of nerve fibers have become increasingly myelinated and the dendrites in all layers of the cortex have increased in both size and number (see Figure 9.1). Such maturation processes increase the connectivity and transmission of nerve impulses, which are of paramount importance in more complicated brain functions, including motor control (Malina, 1982; Schmidt, 1982).

Factors Affecting Physical Growth

In addition to the physical developments characterizing the preschool years, certain other factors also affect the overall course of development and the eventual expression of physical change. One of these is the child's posture. Changes in postural dynamics contribute to the child's physical and emotional well-being since inefficient use of the body can lead to lack of muscle tone, a lowered threshold of fatigue, and less available mechanical energy.

Related to the influence of the posture is the manner in which the force of gravity affects the body (the center of the body being the trunk). The force of gravity affects the child whether sitting, standing, or running. Although the "battle" against the pull of gravity is more obvious in some children than in others, each child must maintain equilibrium in order to produce good posture and balance. As the child grows older and body proportions change, the center of gravity drops lower in the trunk, making it easier to maintain equilibrium in the standing position. Other factors affecting the course of physical growth are the strength of the bones, the firmness of the muscles, and the kinesthetic sense.

Proper amounts of rest and nutrition can also influence the overall course of physical development. Proper nutrition is as important during the preschool years as it is during all life stages. Generally speaking, the undernourished child is smaller, lags behind in many facets of development, and is more susceptible to illness and disease. This is as true for American children as it is for youngsters all around the world (Holt, 1982; Pipes, 1981; Stevens and Baxter, 1981; Endres and Rockwell, 1980).

Preschoolers also need sufficient opportunity to exercise their developing bodies. This is as important for the overall course of physical growth as it is for the development of small and large muscle skills. Many preschools, recognizing the importance of exercise and physical activity at this age, have included a diversity of movement programs in their curriculum planning. Such programs appear to enhance not only physical development, but also creative expression, confidence, and self-awareness (Sullivan, 1982; Hendricks and Hendricks, 1983; Torbert, 1980).

Figure 9.1 The growth of dendrites in the cortex. Compared to the first few months of life (left), dendrites increase in both size and number of connections (right) during the first five years.

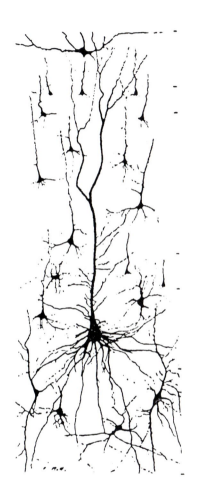
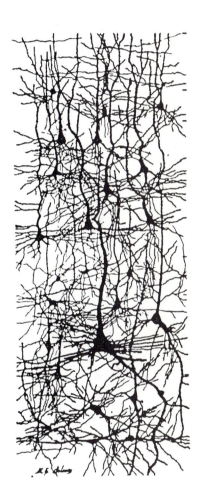

Life among the Giants: A Child's View of the Grown-Up World

A youngster stands on tiptoe to reach a faucet, hang a towel, or open a car door. Another appears to be engaged in a balancing act in a struggle to plop into a living room easy chair. Once settled, the child seems literally swallowed by the chair and her legs barely dangle over the edge. Other preschoolers show signs of utter exasperation as they

**Physical exercise enhances physical develop-
ment, creative expression, confidence, and
self-awareness.**

stretch to peer out of windows, wrestle with oversized household uten-
sils, or take giant steps to climb flights of stairs.

While these scenes may sound like part of a children's story, there
is more fact than fiction behind each portrayal. The scale of our grown-
up world in many cases dwarfs the young child. Adjusting to it is a
formidable task, which brings frustrations and problems. Although Erik
Erikson suggests that most young children are eager to exercise their
developing physical and mental skills, many find that their relative size
frequently creates difficult times. Not being able to master certain tasks,
combined with limited or discouraging feedback from adults, may produce the Eriksonian crisis of guilt or inferiority.

**The sheer size of our grown-up world often
dwarfs the developing child.**

The negative consequences of guilt or inferiority on developing personalities have also been stressed by Alfred Adler. Children who develop such feelings may seriously question whether they are capable of adjusting to the grown-up world; and they may even become reluctant to participate in new and different activities. Adler goes so far as to say that little or no adult feedback or guidance, coupled with successive failures on the child's part, may result in an **inferiority complex,** an acute awareness of one's weaknesses. Later in childhood, a youngster may combat an inferiority complex by employing the defense mechanism of **compensation.** Adler has stated that when compensation is used, children seek to overcome their failures or physical limitations in some areas by striving for success in others. All of this implies that children need understanding, support, and guidance as they seek to adjust and establish themselves in our grown-up world.

Motor Skill Development

In physical play characterized by such activities as running, tumbling, skipping, tricycle riding, block play, and artwork, the development of motor skills accelerates rapidly. Knowing what preschoolers are physi-

Preschoolers can usually ride a tricycle—a gross motor skill—before they can tie their shoes—a fine motor skill.

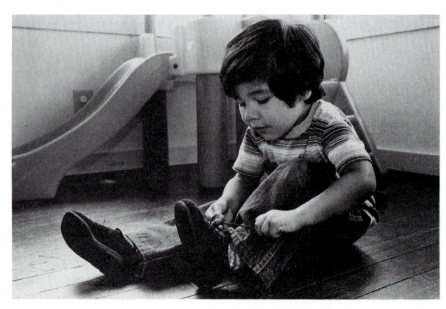

cally capable of undertaking and the degree of efficiency that they can exert, is important not only to parents but also to day-care facilitators and nursery school teachers, people who will be structuring the children's physical activities. Careful structuring of motor skill activities may help alleviate the frustration caused by a task that is too difficult or the boredom caused by a task that is too easy.

Advancements at this time are made in both gross (large) and fine (small) motor skills. **Gross motor skills** require the coordination of large body parts and include sliding down an incline, playing on a seesaw, and steering a wagon. **Fine motor skills** require the precise use of small body parts, most notably the hands. Fine motor skills include the movements necessary to complete a jigsaw puzzle, cut paper with a pair of scissors, or turn the pages of a book. Writing exercises, which may begin during the preschool years, also afford children the chance to nurture fine motor skills (Vukelich and Golden, 1984; DeFord, 1980).

Generally speaking, children gain mastery of gross motor skills before they acquire control over smaller muscles. Thus, most preschoolers can ride a tricycle before they can tie a shoelace or construct a detailed block tower with many small pieces. Physical activities should include a mixture of both gross and fine motor skill challenges. Sanoff (1982), Rowen (1982), Magg and Ornstein (1981), and Riggs (1980) offer numerous suggestions for such combinations.

A number of factors contribute to the ability to engage in more diversified motor skill activities. As we mentioned earlier, muscular development is rapid during this time. Prior to age 4, muscular development was proportionate to overall body growth; after this, muscle development accounts for approximately 75 percent of the child's weight gain. Other contributing factors are greater levels of overall body coordination and dexterity, spatial reasoning, knowledge of physical surroundings, and general body awareness [Williams, 1983; Wickstrom, 1983; Ridenour, 1980; Gallahue, 1982(a), (b)].

Each of these physical developments contributes to the child's many new motor skills. The number of such skills, as well as their diversity, becomes significant when we recall the limited physical abilities of the toddler. Table 9.1 lists some of the motor skill accomplishments of preschoolers and the implications of each.

Stages of Motor Skill Development

The attainment of motor skill mastery follows a fairly uniform pattern of development. While individual differences exist in the overall time frame needed to attain skillful mastery, a progression of stages lies at

Table 9.1 Motor Skill Development of Preschoolers

	Skill Characteristics		
Motor Pattern	3-Year-Old	4-Year-Old	5-Year-Old
Walking/ running	Run is smoother; stride more even. Cannot turn or stop quickly. Can take walking and running steps on the toes.	Run improves in form and power. Greater control, stopping, starting, and turning. In general, greater mobility than at age 3.	Has adult manner of running. Can use this effectively in games. Runs 35-yard dash in less than 10 seconds.
Jumping	42% rated as jumping well. Can jump down from 8-inch elevation. Leaps off floor with both feet.	72% skilled in jumping. Jumps down from 28 inch height with feet together. Standing broad jump of 8 to 10 inches.	80% have mastered the skill of jumping. Makes running broad jump of 28 to 35 inches.
Climbing	Ascends stairway unaided, alternating feet. Ascends small ladder, alternating feet.	Descends long stairway by alternating feet, if supported. Descends small ladder, alternating feet.	Descends long stairway or large ladder, alternating feet. Further increase in overall proficiency.
Throwing	Throws without losing balance. Throws approximately 3 feet; uses two-hand throw. Body remains fixed during throw.	20% are proficient throwers. Distance of throw increases. Begins to assume adult stance in throwing.	74% are proficient throwers. Introduction of weight transfer; right-foot-step-forward throw. Assumes adult posture in throwing.
Catching	Catches large ball with arms extended forward stiffly. Makes little or no adjustment of arms to receive ball.	29% are proficient in catching. Catches large ball with arms flexed at elbows.	56% are proficient in catching. Catches small ball; uses hands more than arms.

Adapted from Corbin, C. B. *A Textbook of Motor Development*. Dubuque, Iowa: W. C. Brown Co. Publishers, 1980.

the foundation of virtually all motor skills. This is true for gross as well as fine motor skills.

Three stages in particular have been identified: cognitive, associative, and autonomous.

1. In the cognitive stage the performer seeks to understand the motor skill and what it requires. Mental activity is essential at this point because certain strategies may be developed or the individual may try to remember how similar tasks were handled in the past.

2. The associative stage is characterized by trial-and-error learning, in which errors in performance are recognized and discontinued in the future. In this stage, the strategy changes from the "what to do" of the previous phase to "how to do it." Assistance in the form of instruction or practice in basic movements is needed for success to take place.

3. In the autonomous stage, performance is characterized by efficient responses and reduction of errors. Performers seem to become more "automatic" in making their responses, and the newly acquired activity is integrated with other skills (Schmidt, 1975; 1982).

These stages suggest that more advanced motor skills unfold in a fashion similar to the locomotion and prehension sequences of infancy and toddlerhood (see Chapter 6). Indeed, virtually every aspect of physical development seems to have an overall order in which visible changes follow one another with regularity. While early attempts are many times characterized by clumsiness and mistakes, later efforts are marked by fluidity. The end result is mastery of the mechanics underlying motor skills. In short, the individual has acquired accuracy of movement, precision, and economy of performance (Malina, 1982).

The Role of Rehearsal: Does Practice Make Perfect?

At one time or another we have all seen or heard of the supposed importance of practice, whether in the refinement of skills in bike riding, skipping, or ball throwing. Practice is the continual repetition of a motor skill, so that correct responses will emerge. But whether practice increases the efficiency of certain childhood motor skills is open to question. Not everyone is willing to accept the old adage that practice makes perfect.

Paramount in determining whether practice is beneficial is the maturational state of the child, or the readiness principle discussed earlier. Unless sufficient neurological maturation has occurred, certain

Assisting the Preschooler's Motor Skill Development

The preschool years are extremely active ones for children, who are now able to engage in playtime activities that were virtually impossible for them during infancy and toddlerhood. The ability to participate successfully in more physical and strenuous forms of activity depends not only on overall muscular growth and coordination but also on the child's self-confidence and self-assurance. Adults can help the preschooler develop these capacities in four ways:

1. Adults should be patient with the child. All motor skills require time and effort to develop. Although helpful encouragement is useful, adults should not push children past their limits. Furthermore, children should be allowed to set their own pace when developing a skill since they know best what they are capable of undertaking at a given time.

2. Adults should avoid comparing the child with other children. No two children develop at the same rate or exhibit the same degrees of proficiency in a motor skill. While some develop rapidly, others move slowly; while some become highly skilled in an activity, others may experience only mediocre success. In such instances, comparisons accomplish little, except possibly to produce anxiety and inferiority feelings in the child.

3. Adults should provide materials and an environment for optimal growth. Proper

Preschoolers are very active and need proper equipment and space to play to help them develop physically and mentally.

indoor and outdoor equipment, as well as the space in which to run and play, will help youngsters develop healthy minds as well as bodies. When selecting toys, adults should try to choose those that exercise small as well as large muscles.

4. Adults should realize that success in one motor skill area doesn't assure success in another. Most motor skills develop on an individual basis, each requiring special training and practice. The fact that the child has developed one skill, such as running, does not imply that he or she will be equally proficient in such skills as tricycling or ball throwing. ■

kinds of motor skills cannot be learned, and practice will not increase their chances of being expressed. In general, there is no guarantee that extended practice sessions or accelerated training always improves motor skill performances (Williams, 1983; Schmidt, 1982).

The role that experience can and does play should be stressed. Psychologists recognize that the child who participates in a wide variety of activities and engages in much exploration and experimentation with movement is more likely to learn a specific motor activity at an earlier age than one who has not had such experience. Thus, sufficient learning opportunities and adult encouragement are both important in the development of motor skills (Ridenour, 1980; Wickstrom, 1983).

Summary

Lauren, age 6

Early childhood brings noticeable changes in physical proportions and advancements in motor skill activities. By this time, preschoolers have doubled their original birth length and increased their birth weight five times. Other significant developments include the gradual maturation of the muscular, skeletal, digestive, and respiratory systems. The head and brain also approach their mature size. Brain growth occurs as the billions of nerve fibers become increasingly myelinated and the dendrites in all layers of the cortex increase in both size and number.

Certain factors appear to affect the overall course of physical development and the eventual expression of physical change. These factors include postural dynamics, the force of gravity, rest, proper nutrition, and the opportunity to exercise the developing body.

Preschoolers make significant advancements in gross and fine motor skills. Gross motor skills involve the coordination of large muscles and encompass such activities as running, tumbling, and tricycle riding. Fine motor skills require small muscle coordination and are needed to master such activities as playing with small blocks and drawing with a pen or brush. Generally, gross motor skills are mastered before fine motor skills. Numerous forces account for the overall improvement of motor skills at this time. These forces include the manner in which muscle development enables the child to participate in more activities and the greater levels of coordination, dexterity, spatial reasoning, knowledge of physical surroundings, and general body awareness.

Motor skill development adheres to a chronology of fairly predictable stages. These are the cognitive, associative, and autonomous stages. The autonomous stage indicates that the person has attained accuracy of movement, precision, and economy of performance with the motor skill at hand.

Whether steady practice guarantees the perfection of a motor skill is difficult to ascertain. Most contemporary experts feel that both maturation and environmental experiences account for motor skill efficiency. This chapter emphasized the importance of providing sufficient learning opportunities and adult encouragement when seeking to foster children's motor skill development.

Suggested Reading List

Ridenour, M. V., ed. *Motor Development: Issues and Applications.* Princeton, N.J.: Princeton Book Company, 1980. This text contains the latest research in motor development. Chapters focus on stages in motor development, programs to optimize development, and sex-role expectations in regard to the motor behavior of the young child.

Schmidt, R. A. *Motor Control and Learning: A Behavioral Emphasis.* Champaign, Ill.: Human Kinetics, 1982. Excellent analysis of many important areas of motor development.

Williams, H. G. *Perceptual and Motor Development.* Englewood Cliffs, N.J.: Prentice-Hall, 1983. Williams covers such areas as fine and gross motor skills, coordination, balance, and body awareness.

Chapter Ten

Cognition, Perception, and Psycholinguistics

Childhood is the sleep of reason.

Rousseau

Introduction

Cognitive and linguistic abilities develop significantly during early childhood. As we shall see, the progression of higher-order cognitive facilities is influenced heavily by the preschool child's continuing mastery of spoken language. The ability to use words and to understand the symbolic qualities that they represent gives the child's surroundings new meaning and significance. Spoken language is the essential link in communication between meaning and sound and the means by which one's thoughts are communicated to others. For these reasons, language and thought are closely related developmental processes and mirror the general mental activity of the child (Ault, 1983; Anderson, 1980).

The preschooler's conceptual attainment enables language acquisition to take important steps forward. In particular, language acquisition provides three important cognitive functions:

1. It enables the child to engage in "socialization of action" with other people and in acquisition of language and verbal exchange.

2. It stimulates the internalization of words, denoting the true emergence of thought, supported by internal language and a system of signs.

3. Perhaps most important, it assists in the internalization of action, so that rather than being purely perceptual and motor as it was previously, action can now represent itself intuitively through pictures and mental experiments (Dodd and White, 1980).

Cognitive development implies that preschoolers think in qualitatively different ways from infants or toddlers. Their thinking is more advanced—especially in terms of the refinement and elaboration of concepts—and is becoming more methodical and deliberate. They do not give up as easily on cognitive challenges, and they begin to nurture intrinsic motivation toward the tasks at hand. Furthermore, curiosity soars to new heights during early childhood. Thus, a number of developmental forces affect the course of cognition (Stipek, 1983; Gottfried, 1983; Bradbard and Endsley, 1982).

However, it must be recognized that preschoolers have a number of cognitive limitations. Paramount among these is the fact that their mental processes are largely dominated by perceptual processes of what seems to be, rather than of what logically must be. Preschoolers have not mastered the systems of logical operations that characterize the thinking of older children.

Similar to the structural framework established earlier in the book, we will begin our discussion by exploring Jean Piaget's theory of cognitive development. We'll then examine the nature of concept and sense organ development and, finally, the course of linguistic growth during the early childhood years.

The preschooler's progress in language acquisition assists in the internalization of action represented by pictures and words.

Piaget's Stage of Preconceptual Thought

The second stage of cognitive development as proposed by Jean Piaget is preconceptual thought. **Preconceptual thought,** occurring between the ages of 2 and 4, is part of the much longer preoperational thought stage, which encompasses ages 2 through 7. It is important to us because it focuses on the preschool years and is considered to be an active period of mental growth (Case and Khanna, 1981).

Like the stage of sensorimotor development, preconceptual thought provides a foundation for the emergence of later mature cognition. Cognitive activity in the preoperational period is greatly influenced by the preschooler's expanding environment and the ability to engage in self-directed activities. As new experiences are met, they are structured in accordance with existing schemes of thought or placed in new mental categories. In this fashion, the child's cognitive structures become more detailed and differentiated [Kuhn, 1981; Kamii, 1981(a)].

Several noteworthy cognitive developments occur during preconceptual thought. Most important is the ability to engage in symbolic functioning. Other developments include the growth of egocentrism, animism, artificialism, and immanent justice.

Symbolic Functioning

Symbolic functioning is the ability to differentiate signifiers (words, images) from significates (the objects or events to which signifiers refer). Symbolic functioning is an act of reference in which the child creates a mental image to stand for something that is not present. A signifier, such as the word *ball*, can be mentally created to represent the toy when it is not in the child's presence. Symbolic functioning thus increases the scope of the child's intelligence.

One clear-cut example of symbolic functioning takes place in children's play behavior. When children are able to create mental images to represent objects that are not present, they can engage in make-believe play. That is to say, they can select an object and imagine it to be whatever is desired; at this stage, the pretender knows exactly what is being pretended. A block of wood may become a car, boat, or airplane; a box may be a fort or castle.

The ability to engage in symbolic functioning develops gradually. Children are initially limited to single and simple representations of people, objects, or events. By the end of the preschool years, though, representations become more complex and include numerous details and characteristics (Nicolich, 1981; Case and Khanna, 1981).

A child at the stage of symbolic functioning can select an object, such as a block of wood, and imagine it to be anything.

Egocentrism

Egocentrism is a style of thinking that causes children to have difficulty in seeing any point of view other than their own. Children are incapable of putting themselves in another person's position, and their point of view does not allow them to separate themselves from the environment. Consequently, egocentrism will have implications for social relations as well as problem-solving situations requiring more than one point of view. The interference that egocentrism exerts on the preschooler's problem-solving abilities will be discussed later in this chapter.

Egocentrism may prompt children to reason that everything in the world is created for their own personal satisfaction. They do not realize that everyone else experiences the same phenomena that they do; their self-centered nature causes them to perceive the world with their own personal blinders. As viewed by egocentric children, then, snow is not a product of inclement weather but something to play in; music is "happy" because it puts them in a cheerful mood; and the family's new yellow car was bought because "it's my favorite color."

An egocentric quality is also visible in children's early language, particularly when two children in this age bracket are conversing. Since both children are so wrapped up in their own individual thoughts and feelings, neither has the capacity to "hear" what the other is saying, much less to understand the context of the speaker's thoughts. This type of egocentricity expressed in communication is known as **collective monologue.** In collective monologue children also often omit vital information because they fail to realize others may need this information to understand them. When children appear to be talking to one another they are doing little more than talking out loud to themselves. Figure 10.1 is an example of collective monologue.

We can compare the development of collective monologue with that of **parallel play,** a strikingly similar form of egocentricity that appears in children's playtime activities. Because of the inability of children to separate themselves from their own thoughts, playmate interaction is unlikely to occur. What appears to be two children playing together may actually be two children engaged in separate play.

Because children still have only rudimentary reasoning skills, their reasoning becomes even more egocentric during the preconceptual stage. Since they don't understand real-world concepts properly, children relate whatever they can to their personal experience. The interpretation of objects and events is based almost exclusively on assimilative powers; that is, children explain phenomena by consulting existing frames of reference. As a result, many conceptions are illogical, either because of the child's egocentrism or because of the child's very limited knowledge and understanding.

Whether all children are as egocentric in social relations as Piaget paints them is open to question. Some researchers (Black, 1981; Grasec and Arnason, 1982; Hobson, 1980) feel that preschoolers are capable of relinquishing an egocentric orientation to some degree and understanding the positions and feelings of others. In addition, contemporary research in the field of psycholinguistics proposes that preschoolers show some signs of taking the needs of listeners into consideration when speaking (Schmidt and Paris, 1983). Research also indicates that **prosocial** or helping behavior begins to emerge at this time, additional evidence that preschoolers can think beyond themselves to some extent [Honig, 1982(a); Grusec, 1981]. Findings such as this suggest that ego-

Figure 10.1 Two children engaged in collective monologue.

Egocentric speech can release tension and become an instrument of thought in planning the solution of a problem.

centrism may not be the driving force once thought, at least not in all spheres of expression.

Egocentric Speech: A Forerunner of Internal Thought?   According to Soviet psychologist Lev Vygotsky, the preschooler's egocentric speech and involvement in collective monologues are not just idle forms of talk. Such speech patterns represent an important stage in the internalization of "silent inner speech," the process whereby external language goes "underground" and is internalized as thought processes (Vygotsky, 1962).

Vygotsky maintains that language and thought develop separately during infancy but merge in early childhood, whereupon thought becomes verbal and speech rational. Vygotsky takes the position that language may well govern one's cognitive behavior and responses to the environment. While Piaget suggests that egocentric speech is basically no more than "thinking out loud" and usually is not directed toward anyone in particular, Vygotsky believes that it is a form of self-guidance and can assist the youngster in problem-solving situations.

Devising a series of problem situations for young subjects, Vygotsky found that egocentric speech increased markedly. For example, when getting ready to draw, one of Vygotsky's subjects discovered that a certain colored pencil was missing. Attempting to remedy the situation, the child became involved in the following egocentric speech: "Where's the pencil? I need a blue pencil. Never mind, I'll draw with the red one and wet it with water; it will become dark and look like blue" (Vygotsky, 1962, p. 16).

Vygotsky asserts that egocentric speech is not a mere accompaniment to the child's activity. Rather, it is a means of expression and can release tension. Eventually it becomes an instrument of thought in the proper sense—in seeking and planning the solution of a problem. One example recorded by Vygotsky illustrates how egocentric speech can also alter the course of an activity:

> A child of five and a half was drawing a streetcar when the point of his pencil broke. He tried, nevertheless, to finish the circle of a wheel, pressing down on the pencil very hard, but nothing showed on the paper but a deep colorless line. The child muttered to himself, "It's broken," put aside the pencil, took watercolors instead, and began drawing a *broken* streetcar after an accident, continuing to talk to himself from time to time about the change in his picture. The child's accidentally provoked egocentric utterance so manifestly affected his activity that it is impossible to mistake it for a mere by-product, an accompaniment not interfering with the melody (p. 17).

Vygotsky believes that his experiments illustrate developmental changes in the interrelation of activity and egocentric talk. Initially egocentric speech signifies the end result or the turning point in an activity, then it gradually shifts toward the middle and eventually to the beginning of a particular activity, in the process assuming a planning function and raising the child's acts to the level of purposeful behavior. What happens is similar to the fairly predictable stages in the naming of drawings. Children draw first, then decide what they have drawn. When they are older, they name their drawing when they are half-done. Finally, they decide beforehand what they will draw.

Thus, egocentric speech is conceived by Vygotsky as being quite communicative and goal oriented, existing as a stage between external speech and silent inner speech. Instead of being mere thinking "out loud," egocentric speech may be a forerunner of internal thought.

Animism

Animism is the tendency children have to attribute life to inanimate objects. Many preschoolers insist that objects have lifelike properties in the same sense that people are alive. In an attempt to understand and explain the nature of objects in the environment, children attribute thoughts and feelings to lifeless objects. Children of this age level, for example, feel that boats do not appear on lakes at night because they're "asleep"; the wind "sings" if you listen carefully; and trees "cry" when their branches are broken.

The concept of animism is evident in children's fairy tales; Geppetto's Pinocchio, Alice's Queen of Hearts, Dorothy's scarecrow, and Christopher Robin's toys are given human qualities and brought to life. Is it possible that in providing such stories to children, adults unwittingly contribute to the animism prevalent at this age?

Unfortunately, many adults fail to realize the animistic qualities attached to the child's selection of objects. A doll with thoughts and feelings may be thrown into a toybox by a heedless mother, or a favorite stone having animistic qualities may be maligned by a parent unaware of the fact that to the child the rock is alive. For children, this type of behavior is a personal blow to the world that they have created.

Artificialism

Artificialism is the notion that everything in the world, including natural objects and events, is designed by humanity. Since they reason that everything in the world is created for human use, children assume that humans must be responsible for all the creations in the world. The presence of objects and the occurrence of events are interpreted in light of this explanation; the sky is painted with a blue paintbrush; rain

DENNIS the MENACE

"YOU CAN ALWAYS TELL WHEN WINTER IS COMIN'...
THE TREES START GETTING UNDRESSED."

comes from giant watering cans; and mountains are built by strong
people who stack rocks together. One 4-year-old acquaintance of the
authors was convinced that thunder was caused by angels bowling.
Table 10.1 presents some of the types of responses preconceptual children give.

Immanent Justice

Immanent justice is the assumption that the world is equipped with a
built-in system of law and order. Children use this supposition to explain how justice and order are maintained. Whenever a wrong is committed or a misfortune occurs, the child concentrates on explaining
why things occur the way they do. Many of the interpretations are
characterized by egocentric overtones. A child who stumbles and falls

Table 10.1 Exploring Early Childhood Thought

	Sample Questions	Typical Answers
Egocentrism	Why does the sun shine?	To keep me warm.
	Why is there snow?	For me to play in.
	Why is grass green?	Because that's my favorite color.
	What are TV sets for?	To watch my favorite shows and cartoons.
Animism	Why do trees have leaves?	To keep them warm.
	Why do stars twinkle?	Because they're happy and cheerful.
	Why does the sun move in the sky?	To follow children and hear what they say.
	Where do boats go at night?	They sleep like we do.
Artificialism	What causes rain?	Someone emptying a watering can.
	Why is the sky blue?	It has been painted.
	What is the wind?	A man blowing.
	What causes thunder?	A man grumbling.

reasons that children are not supposed to run fast; children get burned with matches because they're not supposed to handle them; and children get spanked by their parents because grown-ups have to be mean sometimes. Many children are also taught that when misfortune strikes, it is "God's punishment," a unique variation of immanent justice.

Questions

In addition to the Piagetian concepts described, it is important to mention that preschoolers demonstrate growing levels of curiosity about their environment. They begin to ask a number of questions, many of the "why" variety. "Why" questions, if carefully studied by adults, are an excellent reflection of the child's cognitive state (Formanek and Gurian, 1980).

Most of children's why questions do not, from a superficial point of view, demand an answer. At this early age, a child may be asking a question merely for the sake of asking. The question may indicate pure astonishment without calling for an answer. The questions may be asked of no one and may simply be a roundabout way of stating something without risking contradiction. Very often, if children's questions are not answered immediately, they will not wait but answer the question themselves.

When attempting to supply answers to these questions, parents should try to understand the child's intent in asking them. Adult answers should be suitable for the child's frame of reference. Preschoolers often assume that physical events have psychological causes and vice versa. Thus, when the youngster asks "Why do the stars shine?" or "Why is the grass green?" he or she really wants to know their purpose and not their physical explanation. If an adult answers the question "Why do stars shine?'' by saying, "Because they are like fire," most children will be unsatisfied because they do not yet grasp the relation between heat and light. More importantly, the answer does not fit the intention of the child's question. What youngsters really want to hear is something like, "So that sailors can find their way home at night." Such an answer is sufficient for their current level of reasoning; in time they will be ready for more sophisticated explanations [Elkind, 1971; 1981 (b)].

Interestingly, it has been found that the types of questions adults direct *to* children also affect the course of cognitive development. Close-ended questions, those requiring a simple "yes" or "no" answer, are the least likely to stimulate children intellectually or encourage the use of representational abilities. Open-ended questions, on the other hand, move youngsters away from simple "yes" or "no" responses and require them to elaborate. Such questions encourage both cognitive and linguistic activity. Thus, whether receiving children's questions or directing their own questions to youngsters, adults are in a prime position to nurture cognitive growth (French and McClure, 1981; Bartlett, 1981).

Nurturing Cognitive Development

Children need challenging learning environments that nurture logical thought. These environments, at home and in early childhood education settings, allow children to explore at their own pace and according to their individual cognitive abilities. The notion that the classroom environment can be structured to accommodate and promote Piagetian learning principles, even at the preschool age, has attracted considerable research attention [see Byber and Sund, 1982; Kamii, 1981(a); Labinowicz, 1980; Saunders and Bingham-Newman, 1984].

One of the many suggestions given to help preschoolers is that adults need to contrive situations capable of stimulating curiosity and imagination. Hands-on experiences that encourage active exploration of the world are recommended. So too are simple science projects, especially those that demonstrate cause-effect relationships. These help foster flexible thought and provide children with the opportunity to observe and predict. Such challenges to the young mind promote a more logical analysis of the world as a whole and may help children overcome such illogical notions as animism and artificialism. Children's level of development limits their ability to assimilate new experiences, so such "challenges" should not greatly exceed the child's present level [Smith, 1981; Kamii, 1981(a); Benham et al., 1982].

As they learn, preschoolers should be encouraged to ask questions, reflect, and compare and contrast their experiences. Thinking and talking about what they are doing, with adults as well as their peers, enables children to share viewpoints and listen to the ideas of others. This will help preschoolers realize that there is more than one viewpoint, an awareness that may help them overcome the egocentrism prevalent at this time (Smith, 1981).

Concept Development

Concept development during the preschool years is greatly enhanced by developing perceptual abilities. **Perception** is the mental process that enables children to select and interpret relevant environmental information. While this important process varies from individual to individual, perception generally contributes to more complex aspects of mental operations. For example, children's growing ability to detect differences in size, shape, or space enables them to gain a broader understanding of the physical world in general. As a result, objects and events in their surroundings gradually acquire greater meaning and relevancy for the child (Wellman, 1982; Siegler, 1981).

Key factors that inhibit perception of environmental information during the preschool years are limited attention and attending skills. Correct selection of sensory information and a coordinated search for useful information are skills critical to accurate perception. Children, however, do not always pay attention to the aspects of a situation that attract adults. Children's attention spans and mental abilities are extremely limited, so they frequently avoid attending to information that they cannot comprehend. Consequently, a major task of adults working with young children is to teach what features of situations are important (Jackson, Robinson, and Dale, 1977; Stevens, 1981).

Concept development is affected not only by limited attention and attending skills but also by egocentrism. Such self-centeredness has implications for many facets of mental growth, and we will see how the failure to distinguish between one's own perceptions and the perceptions of others has important cognitive consequences.

Shape and Size Concepts

The discrimination of shape and size during childhood results from individual learning experiences and depends on a number of perceptual conditions, such as distance and the relation of one object to another. Although perceptual discrimination shows some advancement during early childhood, shape and size are still not fully understood.

For example, children are able to discriminate among sizes and shapes such as "big," "little," and "round," but they may not possess a true perception of these categories. Youngsters may not be capable of remembering the existence of these objects by their dimensions or characteristics unless forced to pay close attention to such details by the experimenter.

2½-year-old girl doing size sequence puzzle at nursery school.

Distance has a dramatic effect on the preschooler's perceptions; objects appear to change as they move away. A preschooler may think that a distant house becomes larger as it is approached, or that a mountain changes its shape when it is viewed from a new location. For example, a preschooler watched his mother depart on an airplane. As the plane gradually disappeared from view, the youngster turned to his father and asked, "Is mommy getting as small as that plane?"

The Development of Whole-Part Perception   When children see objects in their environment, how do they perceive these objects? Is it on the basis of the whole object, its parts, or both? To study this, children were shown a number of figures arranged to form larger objects, such as candy canes in the shape of a scooter or assorted vegetables and fruits forming a human. Children could conceivably perceive the various items as part of whole patterns (see Figure 10.2).

The researchers found that part perception, the tendency to recognize the parts and not the whole, accounted for 71 percent of the preschoolers' responses but fell off to 21 percent of the responses of 9-year-olds. Part and whole perception, the ability to perceive both part and total figures, increased from 11 percent for the preschoolers to 79 percent for the 9-year-olds.

Figure 10.2 Examples of whole-part drawings used to test children's perceptual tendencies.

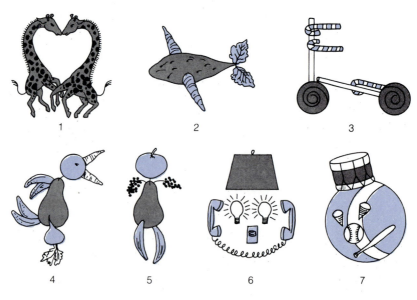

These findings indicate that, although children's perceptions are limited during the preschool years, the ability to see all contributing parts and the resulting wholes develops markedly by late childhood. Thus, as children grow older, they are able to have more comprehensive and refined perceptions of their surroundings (Elkind, Koegler, and Go, 1964).

Spatial Concepts

Understanding spatial relationships is especially important for a child's accurate interpretation of the environment. Like other perceptual challenges, growth in this area is limited during the early childhood years. Egocentrism hampers children as they seek to learn such spatial discriminations as "near," "far," and "down." More often than not, such terms are initially learned as they personally relate to the child—for example, "The toy is near me."

This egocentric point of view poses problems, especially in understanding relationships of distance and direction. To grasp these discriminations, preschoolers must learn to coordinate their self-centered points of view with other systems of reference. To appreciate how difficult this is for young minds, think of the problems preschoolers may encounter in discriminating left and right. After this has been mastered, imagine the difficulty in understanding left and right from another person's perspective—especially if that person is facing the child. This sort of difficulty in perspective-taking is evident in many situations, particularly those that require alternative points of view (Roberts and Patterson, 1983).

Adults can do a great deal to help preschoolers develop accurate spatial concepts. Precise terminology is always needed when referring to spatial relationships. It is equally important to provide situations that enable youngsters to see other spatial perspectives. Mirrors, for example, provide children with an opportunity to see different viewpoints. The same holds true for activities involving maps, the globe, or games requiring an analysis of spatial relations. Encouraging children to see more than one viewpoint by actively eliciting their perceptions is also valuable. For example, when viewing a particular situation, adults might ask "Does it look the same for me?" "How would that look if we moved away?" Such activities help reduce egocentrism and teach the child that there is more than one way to view the world.

Quantity Concepts

Although some advancements have been made in quantity discriminations, preschoolers frequently make quantity judgments on the basis of perception alone. In other words, they cannot make accurate quantity

Guiding Early Concept Development

The following suggestions may help adults guide early concept development:

1. No one perceives all features of a complex situation, and youngsters may pay attention to aspects of a situation that an adult might not notice.

2. "Paying attention" is an important facet of concept awareness. The best measure of children's attention to a lesson is whether the youngsters can demonstrate mastery of the information presented.

3. Youngsters often need to learn which features of a situation are important to learning or which aspects of a problem must be considered in order to respond correctly. The preschooler's egocentrism frequently distorts perception. Teachers can help children attend appropriately by simplifying the perceptual aspects of beginning lessons and consistently providing feedback on the accuracy of the children's responses.

4. Children may be bored by experiences that are insufficiently challenging, as well as by situations that are too difficult to comprehend. Since youngsters vary greatly in their sophistication in any situation, the best learning experiences are those that can be appreciated at several levels of difficulty.

5. Young children are less able than older children to control their own attention. The former also have difficulty planning and carrying out a systematic search for information, focusing attention on relevant information, and coordinating simultaneous attention to several aspects of a situation. Given these conceptual limits, teachers of young children need to be sensitive to the perceptual components of learning situations (Jackson, Robinson, and Dale, 1977). ■

discriminations independent of misleading perceptual cues. As we have observed in other instances, the problem is compounded by the preschooler's lack of the appropriate terminology for discriminating such quantities as "more" and "less" or "few" and "many." It is important to restate that even though children may use the correct terminology, this is no assurance that the related discrimination has taken place.

Adults may unknowingly confuse preschoolers by using ambiguous terminology. Terms such as *less, few, some,* and *many* are frequently bewildering, since they are used in so many different ways and contexts. Consider the problems caused by sentences like "Is there *much* left?" or "We need *some more* money." Such quantitative terms are very general, vague, and difficult for the child to fathom.

An important facet of quantity concepts is the notion of numbers. There is usually a significant gap between preschoolers' counting abilities and their ability to understand what is being counted. Preschoolers often use serial order but are unable to recognize figures. In addition, concepts of measure, simple addition, and fractional amounts are poorly understood by the preschooler. The development of number concepts depends on the child's ability to arrange a series of items according to their observable differences. For example, not until the age of 7 is the average child able to arrange a series of sticks, in order of increasing length. At this age, however, when one stick has been omitted from the series, the child can find the proper place for it (Kamii, 1982).

Once again, adults can take many steps to help the preschooler learn number concepts. Unfortunately, counting to 10, which is so often encouraged by adults, represents merely serial and rote memory rather than conceptual understanding. Educators suggest that children be given structured learning exercises that emphasize the quantities that numbers represent. Arranging groups of pencils or buttons in different patterns and having the preschooler count the items—as well as having the child pay attention to the perceptual differences in numbers—is an example of this approach. Or, at the dinner table after a child has watched a "Sesame Street" episode on the number 3, an adult might say, "Show me three beans (or three spoons)." Such exercises stress the qualitative aspects of numbers, not rote memory.

One other facet of quantity is the concept of money. In general, money is difficult for the preschooler to fathom. By the end of the early childhood years, however, the child has some understanding of what a penny, a nickel, and a dime are. The names of other coins are more elusive. This age also marks the time when the child realizes what the value of each coin is. By age 6, children are able to use money in crude mathematical transactions.

Time Concepts

We mentioned earlier that young children almost exclusively refer to the present before the future or the past. In addition, the preschooler has difficulty in distinguishing morning from afternoon and knowing the days of the week. In most cases, the youngster's understanding of time is bound by the immediacy or recency of situations (Harner, 1982).

Much like the problem encountered with quantity concepts, children are frequently confused by the adult's often vague time references. This includes such phrases as a "little while," "a bit," or "later on." While such references to time are a normal mode of expression, adults would be doing preschoolers a service if they did not always speak in such sweeping generalities. They might say "We'll leave in 30 minutes" or "after this (television) show is over."

When children develop a rudimentary understanding of time, they do so by relating events to certain hours of the day, such as the start of school and lunch periods. Egocentrism is apparent as children distinguish routines in the day that relate directly to themselves. Usually children learn hours first, followed by half hours and then quarter hours. Furthermore, most are able to name the days of the beginning and end of the week before they reach kindergarten, although days in the middle of the week may remain elusive. Also elusive to the child are different representations for the same time designations, such as "It is now 1:35" or "25 minutes to 2," or "We'll go on vacation in two weeks" or "the week after next." These different time designations for the same period require considerable thought and generally confuse the preschooler.

Sense Organ Development

Compared with that of the years of infancy and toddlerhood, little research has been done on sense organ developments during early childhood. However, we know that of all the sensory organs, the eye undergoes the most significant physiological changes during early childhood (see Figure 10.3). Although the young child's eye is hyperopic (a distant object's image falls behind the retina), this condition is easily overcome by rapidly developing accommodation skills, which refract the light waves properly. Later the eye becomes emmetropic, which allows images to fall on the retina without accommodation. However, if the eye develops in a myopic fashion, distant objects will be focused in front of the retina, leading to blurred vision. Such a condition, called **myopia,** can be corrected by glasses but may be undetected until the child undergoes an eye examination, either in the school setting or during a family visit to the optometrist.

Hearing acuity also shows marked gains during early childhood. Preschoolers exhibit increased sensitivity to different pitches and tones, and this sensitivity will continue to increase until age 12. Like children with sight problems, children experiencing auditory difficulties may have the condition for some time before it is detected; they do not complain since they know nothing else. A child is not usually tested for hearing until age 4 or 5. When hearing tests are made on younger children, appropriate background information about their behavior during auditory examinations must also be taken into consideration. When hearing problems are suspected, children should be diagnosed by a trained audiologist.

The senses of smell, taste, and touch are also well developed by early childhood. During this time, children are also better able to differentiate and distinguish between the vast amounts of incoming percep-

Figure 10.3 Changes in the eye during childhood.

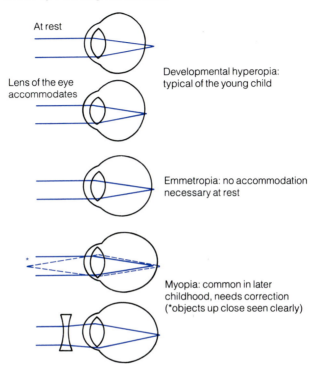

At rest

Lens of the eye
accommodates

Developmental hyperopia:
typical of the young child

Emmetropia: no accommodation
necessary at rest

Myopia: common in later
childhood, needs correction
(*objects up close seen clearly)

tual information. The preschooler's growing ability to remember and
attend to situations also provides new meanings and significance to
perceptual experiences. Thus, early childhood is a time of increased
perceptual sensitivity, discrimination, and selectivity.

Psycholinguistics

During the years of early childhood, youngsters acquire a basic mastery
of spoken language. This remarkable developmental process gains significance when one considers that the 18-month-old child knows about
25 words. Yet during the next three years, this figure rises to more than
1,800 words (see Figure 10.4). In addition to a vocabulary increase of
about 600 words per year, preschoolers exhibit marked advancements
in semantics and grammar (Cazden, 1981; Corrigan, 1983).

Figure 10.4 Vocabulary growth during early childhood.

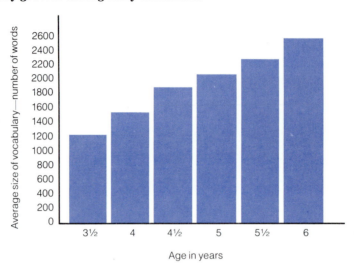

Most adults who have contact with children can attest that preschoolers become entertaining conversationalists with their developing speech skills. Preschoolers use language in a variety of different ways, whether in questions, dialogues, songs, or chants. For many, language also becomes a tool for experimentation, in rhythm and cadence activities, for example (Schwartz, 1981).

Does Adult "Baby Talk" Accelerate Preschool Language Growth?

A relatively new area in psycholinguistic research is the effect that adult baby talk has on the language development of children. Called **motherese** in some linguistic circles (because it's observed more frequently among mothers of infants), such caregiver speech is an attempt to simplify language for the child. Sounds are usually broken down and syllables duplicated, such as *bye-bye* for *goodbye* or *wa-wa* for *water*. Research in this area reveals that sometimes adults have a speech style as unique as that of the youngsters. When talking with children, adults often raise the pitch of their voices and use brief sentences with concrete nouns, diminutives, and terms of endearment (Fernald and Simon, 1984; Kaye, 1980; Ringler, 1981).

Does baby talk such as this help preschoolers refine language abilities? Not really, although it is at least an effort to stimulate the child verbally. This type of adult stimulation is better suited to the first year of

For Better or For Worse   by Lynn Johnston

life, when it does appear to have some beneficial value (see Gleitman, 1981). Children past the one-word stage still need adult input, but they respond more readily to language formulated in adult form than to language in simplified forms thought appropriate to the child's level. What does appear important in talking to young children is the speed of what is being said, as well as the clearness and conciseness of the message. Children need adults for accurate speech models; thus it is important that adults pronounce and use words correctly. This implies that adult use of baby talk during the child's first four years of life may well be a hindrance to language development, but so would speaking in an encyclopedic or diplomatic vein. There must be an optimum level of language complexity to challenge the child (Holzman, 1983).

Factors Affecting Language Development

Growth in language acquisition is considerably affected by a number of factors, most of which begin to exert their influence on the child's life during the preschool period. These factors include socioeconomic influences, the intelligence level and sex of the child, bilingualism, and whether or not the child is a singleton or twin.

Socioeconomic Level   The child's familial setting, particularly his or her socioeconomic level, is thought to have considerable influence on language growth. Many lower-class parents lack the grammar and vocabulary skills to act as satisfactory language models for their children. Children from upper-class homes have a tendency to acquire words at a faster rate and use more complex sentence structures [Honig, 1982(b)].

Other factors may account for the language differences that exist among social classes. The caliber and type of language directed toward the child will have an important effect on subsequent development. Lower-class parents have a tendency to stimulate their children verbally much less than middle-class parents do. Middle- and upper-class parents also emphasize proper grammar, feeling that its correct use reflects conscientious family training and upbringing. In addition, middle- and upper-class children are given more praise and affection when they use words correctly. Another possible reason that the language of the children of upper socioeconomic classes develops rapidly is the children's exposure to educational visual aids. The child who is surrounded by newspapers, magazines, encyclopedias, and television has a significant advantage over the child in a household that can offer few such aids [Schacter and Strage, 1982; Honig, 1982(b); Hess and Shipman, 1982].

While language differences exist among social classes, lower-class children are not linguistically inferior. In many cases, they possess their own dialect, a language style that differs from that of the middle and upper classes. Although these children possess a fully structured language, they are not bidialectal. Thus communication difficulties may originate from the vocabulary limitations of the dialect, not from the child's inability to handle the communication situation. This means that linguistic differences between social classes reflect differences in the rule systems of their languages (Schacter and Strage, 1982).

Intelligence Level   There seems little doubt that rates of language acquisition are also closely related to the general intelligence level of the child. Bright children usually begin to talk at an earlier age, acquire vocabularies at a more rapid pace, **articulate** more efficiently, and use longer and more grammatically correct sentences.

Sex   A somewhat controversial factor that may cause differences in language development is the sex of the child. On the average, girls seem to be more advanced than boys in overall language development. During the first year, there is little difference in the number of phonemes spoken, but after this time girls exhibit superiority in overall acquisition rates. Generally speaking, girls seem to be more articulate than boys and perform better in tests of grammar, spelling, and word usage. This superiority in language-based skills persists throughout life, which raises the question whether the phenomenon has biological or socialization causes (Springer and Deutsch, 1985; Demo, 1982).

Bilingual Background   It is not uncommon for a child to be brought up in a bilingual household, which can have interesting effects. In early studies, it was thought that attempting to learn two languages placed the child at a disadvantage and hampered overall linguistic growth. It is now felt that the effects of a bilingual home may depend on whether adults reprimand children for using their native dialect and insist that they speak standard English. Bilingualism is not a phenomenon solely related to language; it may also be a manifestation of cultural conflict.

Recent research also suggests that exposure to two languages and the subsequent proficiency in these two languages does not retard linguistic or cognitive development. Moreover, in some instances bilinguals may be cognitively superior to monolinguals. This is apparent in such areas as cognitive flexibility and creative expression (Garcia, 1980; Lambert, 1981).

Twinship   One other factor that should be mentioned is whether the child is born a singleton or a twin. Although research on this question has been limited, it appears that language growth in twins is frequently very different from that in singletons, particularly with regard to average length of responses and overall yearly word gains.

Experts maintain that a unique type of language called *twin speech* is employed by approximately 40 percent of all twins. The patterns of verbal interaction are highly private and unique to the communicators. For example, "tungay" may mean hungry and "nieps" could mean knife. Some of the sentences for older twins simply escape any translation, such as "Snup-aduh ah-wee diedipanna dihabana."

For the most part, twin speech develops because the siblings are together most of the time and slowly devise sounds to satisfy basic needs. Other explanations are that twins are verbally playful or, in some cases, left without adult verbal stimulation for longer periods of time than singletons. Twins usually discard this type of language pattern by the third year.

Twin speech is not the same as idioglossia, a more refined and complex type of twin talk. **Idioglossia** usually consists of a highly original syntax and vocabularies of several hundred words. Idioglossia has been known to persist into the middle years of childhood in severe cases, and it is just as comprehensible to the verbal partners as twin speech is.

Semantic Development

Semantic development is of great importance during all phases of childhood. As mentioned earlier, **semantics** is the study of how we use words to represent various external objects and events. More simply, it is the study of the word meanings in a language.

Psycholinguists are realizing that studies dealing with vocabulary acquisition must take into account accompanying word meanings.

There are several reasons why simply exploring vocabulary growth is inadequate:

- The mere presence of a word in the child's vocabulary does not tell an observer much about the meaning the word has for the child.
- Counts of vocabulary acquisition fail to take into account important relationships among word meanings, relationships that make a child's vocabulary more than a mere list of words.
- Vocabulary studies do not offer any information about the crucial process by which word meanings are formed into sentence meanings (Dale, 1976).

While the problem of learning word meanings begins with the child's first word, semantics becomes progressively more difficult for children as they grow older. By the preschool years, as we have seen, the youngster is faced with the task of learning the meanings and

Contemporary educators and psychologists recognize the many benefits literature offers to children.

interrelationships of more than 1,800 words. Understanding the sheer complexity of word meanings is a staggering challenge to the child's developing cognitive skills.

What processes underlie semantic development during the early years? Apparently, children first learn simple associations or semantic features about words and then add further dimensions to their new acquisitions. Perceptual features, such as size or shape, as well as functional qualities of objects, are usually learned early. There is no clear-cut evidence about whether perception or function emerges first. Over-extension of word meanings is also common in the early going; in this regard, the word *moon* may mean such objects as cucumber slices or grapefruit halves, as well as the spherical object in the night sky (Kay and Anglin, 1982; Dickson, 1981).

As time progresses, children acquire more abstract word meanings that are not directly perceptible. Thus, it might be said that semantics progresses from concrete to abstract word meanings (Tomikawa and Dodd, 1980).

The notion that concrete words are learned before abstract terms may help explain why young children have difficulty realizing that some words can have both physical and psychological meanings. For instance, if we ask preschoolers the meanings of *green* or *shady*, we would most likely get physically oriented explanations. That is, *green* is a color, and *shady* means protected from the sun. Older children presented with these words would supply extended meanings that imply psychological connotations. *Green* could mean an emotional state (green with envy), while *shady* might imply unreliability (a shady character). The child's initial limited semantic understandings of words may reveal why adult figures of speech or metaphors are translated literally by preschoolers. Can you understand why some preschoolers look skyward when we remark, "It's raining cats and dogs outside"?

Before closing our discussion of semantic development, it should be recognized that certain word meanings are simply more difficult to learn than others. Especially difficult is mastering the correct meaning of word pairs, such as *more* and *less* (Grieve and Dow, 1981). It seems as though one word of the pair is learned first and its meaning is overextended to apply to the other. For example, if preschoolers are asked whether one of two trees has more or less apples than the other, confusion usually results. Most preschoolers know the meaning of *more* but not of *less*; consequently, they respond to the latter in much the same way as they respond to the former (on the basis of the single concept of quantity). Similar difficulties are experienced for such word pairs as *before* and *after* (Trosberg, 1982), *front* and *back* (Levine and Carey, 1982), and *same* and *different* (Speer and McCoy, 1982). It's no wonder that many feel semantics is one of the more difficult aspects of language to master (Hudson, Guthrie, and Santilli, 1982).

Guidelines to Improve the Preschooler's Language Development

By responding to and encouraging young children's speech, adults can do a great deal to facilitate overall language development. Grown-ups can become active stimulants when they offer novel verbal learning situations to the child by playing jingle and rhyming games, reading aloud, or expanding upon their youngster's remarks. In addition, adults should consider the following suggestions.

Establish a Satisfactory Speech Model
Active steps should be taken to ensure that the child is learning from a good speech model. Adults should seek to provide the best possible instruction, pay careful attention to their speed of speech, and use clear and concise statements.

Encourage Verbal and Nonverbal Communication
Children need to communicate with others, either verbally or nonverbally, as with a smile, a gesture, a drawing, or a painting, or through music activities. Since each, in its own right, becomes a vital part of the

Providing something to talk about will aid the preschooler's language development.

communication process, these media should be supported and encouraged by adults. ▶

Soviet writer Kornei Chukovsky (1966), who has analyzed children's stories and the manner in which youngsters interpret them, has provided some humorous examples of childhood semantic confusion. On one occasion a visitor asked a child, "Does your sister go to sleep with the roosters?" The child replied, "No, she doesn't go to bed with the roosters—they scratch! She sleeps in the cradle!"

Another example arose when a child's grandmother said that winter was coming soon. The youngster immediately wanted to know, "Do you mean the winter has legs?"

Another incident involved a woman who returned home one night

Guidelines to Improve the Preschooler's Language Development, *continued.*

Provide Experiences That Will Make Words Meaningful
In order to talk, children must have something to talk about. Asking questions, providing toys, picture books, and pets or going on field trips supply youngsters with experiences to talk about.

Encourage Listening and Attention Skills
No matter how good a speech model is, children's articulation skills will not improve unless they listen effectively. Playing such games as "What is that sound?" or "What makes a loud sound?" helps improve children's listening abilities, as does paying attention to the sound and rhythm of nursery rhymes and jingles.

Encourage Speech as a Substitute for Action
In giving directions to children, adults can help ensure understanding by making sure that their speech patterns are approximately at the child's level of syntax. Substituting words for action also increases one's ability at self-expression. For example, the action of a child who is attempting to take a playmate's toy may be replaced by words if the parents remark, "Tell him what you want; maybe he will give it to you."

Use Exact Terminology and Talk with Children at Their Level
Adults can help the child immensely by being exact in their use of words. For instance, in referring to a tricycle a child is riding in the nursery school, "Your turn on the tricycle" establishes the temporary nature of ownership, whereas a careless reference to "your tricycle" may lead to a property problem. Equally important are respecting the language that preschoolers use and seeking to converse with them at their own level. Avoid complexity and confusion; correct a child's unclear words or lack of exact terminology without criticism; and take time to let children express themselves—don't rush them or answer for them (Landreth, 1972). ■

from her job and remarked, "The devil only knows what goes on." "Well, what goes on there?" asked her husband. Their 5-year-old immediately objected to the question, saying "She just said that the devil only knows. Is Mama a devil? She doesn't know!"

Some children humorously pretend that they cannot understand a particular adult idiom and attempt to teach adults to observe more closely the rules that they are teaching. Thus, if an adult complains in the presence of a child that his head is splitting, the child might say, "Then why can't I hear it split?"—expressing a negative attitude toward the odd way adults express their thoughts metaphorically.

Syntactic Development

One of the best indicators of children's overall intellectual growth is their insight into **syntax,** the use of proper sentence structure. Children's syntax provides a key to their logic and organization of thought; indeed, syntax and sentence structure are the guiding principles in children's effort to interpret the linguistic evidence that fluent speakers make available to them (Dodd and White, 1980).

After the telegraphic sentence stage of toddlerhood, children begin to fabricate sentences with fairly complex syntax. Compound sentences, formed by joining two or more simple sentences, begin to emerge by the preschool years. Such developments indicate that children are well on their way to mastering the syntax of their language.

It is striking how most children are able to grasp the notion of higher-order sentences, particularly the establishment of word classes and the rules for combining them. Being able to learn the proper location of words in a sentence is certainly one of the more remarkable features of growing children's speech. Another is their ability to develop past tenses, make words plural, and create negations. Each of these advancements is characterized by the child's awareness of linguistic rules. By listening to others, children extract the rules for putting language together. They first master simple linguistic rules and then move on to more complex ones, such as those that regulate complex syntactical structures (Slobin, 1982; Cazden, 1981).

Pragmatics

In addition to the points raised in this chapter, let us also acknowledge the fact that preschoolers' language reflects interesting pragmatics. **Pragmatics** refers to the manner in which language is used in a social context. It includes the use of a wide range of behaviors, including gestures, facial expressions, pauses, pointing, and turn taking. Pragmatic rules exist in every language, and for the most part adults start teaching these rules to children at a very early age. During early verbal interactions, for example, children learn to establish eye contact and pay attention to their partners (Dale, 1980; Bruner, 1980).

The pragmatic quality of preschoolers' language is more diverse than toddlers'. Turn taking and a greater range of expressions to convey messages characterize the preschooler's speech. There are also more complex styles of interaction between speaker and listener. For example, recent research suggests that preschoolers develop the ability to tailor their speech to the listener by expanding or deleting their sentences. They also know that when listeners move away they must raise their voices in order to be heard. Thus, in addition to grammatical rule awareness, preschoolers are also making gains in understanding the social implications of language use (Schmidt and Paris, 1983; Johnson et al., 1981).

Summary

Matthew, age 7

This chapter explored the nature of cognitive, concept, sense organ, and linguistic development during the years of early childhood. According to Jean Piaget, the preschool years represent the stage of preconceptual thought. Children at this time are able to engage in symbolic functioning, an act of reference whereby a mental image is created to represent objects that are not physically present. Piaget also proposes that preschool children are egocentric, a style of thinking that creates difficulties in problem-solving situations and social relations, although this latter area is subject to conflicting research findings. Piaget suggest that egocentrism is evident in preschoolers' language patterns, such as collective monologue, as well as in parallel play behaviors.

Other developments during preconceptual thought are, according to Piaget, animism, the tendency to give life to inanimate objects, and artificialism, the notion that everything in the world is designed by humanity. Also prevalent is immanent justice, the childhood notion that the world is equipped with a built-in system of law and order. Questions also abound during this stage, many of the "why" variety. Adults can nurture cognitive development by answering children's questions and directing their own questions to youngsters.

Concept development is enhanced by perceptual refinement, although children are still plagued by limited attention and attending skills, as well as by egocentrism. This chapter discussed developments in shape and size, spatial, quantity, and time concepts. The nurturance of each concept, coupled with advanced cognitive flexibility, enables children to perceive their surrounding environment more accurately.

Of all the sensory organs, the eye undergoes the most pronounced physiological changes during early childhood. In time, the eye becomes emmetropic, which allows images to fall on the retina without accommodation. If the eye develops in a myopic fashion (distant objects are focused in front of the retina), vision is blurred. Hearing acuity also shows marked gains during early childhood. In general, the preschooler exhibits marked gains in perceptual sensitivity, discrimination, and selectivity.

Overall language development reveals that preschoolers have added over 1,800 words to their vocabulary and developed a basic mastery of the spoken language. Several factors contribute to overall language acquisition, including socioeconomic influences, the intelligence and sex of the child, bilingual background, and whether the child is a singleton or a twin. The study of twin speech, including the complex variety known as idioglossia, is a relatively new research pursuit among psycholinguists.

The study of semantics, or the meaning of words, has received attention from psychologists because of its overall importance in language development. In the beginning, children usually learn the perceptual features of objects and then acquire more abstract meanings that are not directly perceptible. Because of the complexities in word meanings, semantics is one of the more difficult aspects of language development to master.

In contrast to the telegraphic sentences spoken by toddlers, the preschooler's multiword sentences have fairly complex syntax. The number of incomplete sentences declines steadily, and the preschooler displays a greater awareness of the proper use of past tenses, pluralizations, and negations.

The manner in which language is used in the social context also changes, an area of study known as pragmatics. Preschoolers use a wider range of expressions and engage in greater amounts of turn taking than their younger counterparts. They also show signs of expanding or deleting their overall verbal messages to accommodate the needs of their listeners. Such developments illustrate that in addition to understanding grammatical rules, children are realizing the social implications of language use.

Suggested Reading List

Cazden, C. B. *Language in Early Childhood Education*. Rev. ed. Washington, D.C.: National Association for the Education of Young Children, 1981. Part One of this readable and compact paperback examines the nature of preschool language experiences in the home and at school.

Formanek, R., and Gurian, A. *Charting Intellectual Development: A Practical Guide to Piagetian Tasks*. 2nd ed. Springfield, Ill.: Charles C Thomas, 1981. This text clearly identifies numerous Piagetian principles and discusses their implications for the course of mental growth.

Kamii, C. "Application of Piaget's theory to education: The preoperational level." In *New Directions in Piagetian Theory and Practice*, eds. I. E. Siegel, D. M. Brodzinsky, and R. M. Golinkoff. Hillsdale, N.J.: Erlbaum, 1981. This article details the educational implications of Piaget's theory for young children.

Wellman, H. M. "The foundations of knowledge: Concept development in the young child." In *The Young Child: Reviews of Research*, Vol. 3, eds. S. G. Moore and C. R. Cooper. Washington, D.C.: National Association for the Education of Young Children, 1982. Wellman provides excellent coverage of numerous facets of concept development in addition to what adults can do to foster this aspect of cognition.

Chapter Eleven

Personality and Social Learning

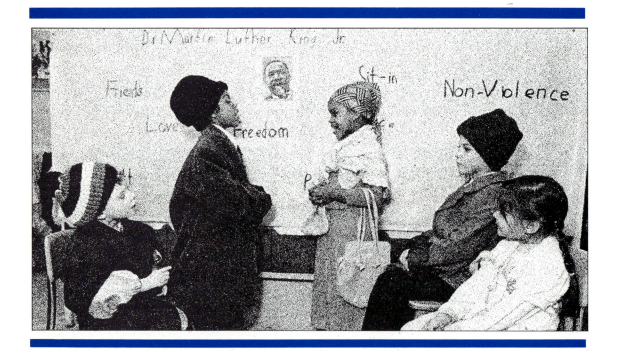

**The greatest poem ever known
     Is one all poets have outgrown:
The poetry, innate, untold,
     Of being only four years old.**

Christopher Morley

Introduction

During early childhood, youngsters expand their social horizons and develop considerable independence and autonomy. Once socially restricted and dependent, preschoolers become more involved with their environment and venture into new and challenging social situations with peers and adults. These new experiences—originating from the neighborhood, school, or other socialization agents—are integrated into the child's total sense of being and contribute immensely to developing personality and social awareness (Walsh, 1980; Blatchford, Battle, and Mays, 1983).

While in the midst of others, children emerge as individuals, gaining insight into their own unique personalities. Socially, children can observe what effects their behavior has on others, a developing cognitive power that enables them to nurture concepts of right and wrong. Insight and observations also enable them to begin to realize the rights and privileges of others. Moreover, social experiences help children develop a self-concept—that is, the manner in which they perceive themselves.

A number of factors related to the preschooler's personality and social development will be discussed in this chapter. We will continue our analysis of personality development and explore the theories of Sigmund Freud and Erik Erikson. Then we'll investigate the nature of sex-role and emotional development, relationships within the family, and interactions with the peer group. At the outset, let us continue to

261

2½-year-old children experimenting with social relations at nursery school.

stress that none of these areas develops independently of the others. All are intertwined and related, the result of the child's growing interaction and widened experiences with the environment.

Theories of Personality Development

Freud's Theory

According to Freud, early childhood is the time when youngsters go through the anal and phallic stages of psychosexual development. The **anal stage** (2 to 4 years) occurs when the child becomes aware of the body's processes of elimination. At this time, pleasure is derived both from the elimination of the feces and from their retention. Children are so fascinated by their excretions that they may peer into the toilet bowl to observe them or even handle them. This is also a time when many children engage in "toilet talk." Parents' reactions during this stage will determine the child's subsequent behavior. The adult's habits and attitudes toward orderliness, punctuality, possessiveness, and generosity are transmitted to the child during this stage. Parents who use such words as "dirty," "messy," or "bad" when referring to the process of elimination convey negative feelings to the child, who then may feel that this product of the body is "bad" and reason that he or she must therefore also be bad. Parents who force early toilet training may produce a child who is obsessively clean and neat, reflecting the parents' own rigidity and somewhat Victorian outlook on the body's natural functions. Conversely, parents who neglect toilet training may well be fostering a child who will later exhibit slovenliness, indifference, and other undesirable traits.

Many children of this age (the terrible 2s) resent adult authority and soon learn that although they can't hit, bite, spank, or yell at parents, there are two ways to retaliate: retention of feces and violent expulsion of them at inappropriate times. In Freudian thought, the child who is slow in being toilet-trained may actually not want to be trained, since this behavior now becomes an outlet for pent-up frustrations and hostilities.

The **phallic stage** (4 to 6 years) is Freud's third stage of psychosexual development. During this stage, the child's desires for gratification shift from the anal to the genital area. Pleasure is derived from manipulating and fondling the genitals, termed *childhood masturbation* by Freud. Once again, the manner in which the parents handle the situation will in part determine the child's future psychosexual development. Maturation and phallic awareness occur simultaneously with the child's social development in terms of imitation, identification, and sex-role typing. Freud notes that boys identify with their fathers and imitate paternal behavior because they have unconscious sexual feelings toward their mothers. The opposite could be said for girls. Freud called these patterns of sexual identification the **Oedipus complex** and the **Electra complex,** respectively.

For these complexes to be resolved, the sexual attachment to the parent of the opposite sex must be discontinued. Freud considered it quite natural for a strong bond to remain between daughter and father (and for girls to seek husbands like their fathers). But he believed that Oedipal feelings could become a more serious problem. A fixation at this stage could make a boy incapable of achieving the independence needed to function in modern society.

Erikson's Theory

The psychosocial crisis of early childhood proposed by Erik Erikson is known as **initiative versus guilt** (3 to 6 years). Having established a sense of trust and autonomy during the first few years of life, children now work to prove that they have a will of their own. They explore the environment and satisfy endless curiosity. Accompanying this high energy level are rapidly developing physical skills, an increased vocabulary, and the general ability to get around and do new and different things. All this adds up to an active child in pursuit of a variety of goals (Erikson, 1963, p. 255):

> There is in every child at every stage a new miracle of vigorous unfolding, which constitutes a new hope and a new responsibility for all. Such is the sense and the pervading quality of initiative. The criteria for all these senses and qualities are the same: a crisis, more or less beset with fumbling and fear, is resolved, in that the child suddenly seems to "grow together" both in his person and in his body. He appears "more himself," more loving, relaxed and brighter in his judgment, more activated and activating. He is in free possession of a surplus of energy which permits him to forget failures quickly and to approach what seems desirable (even if it also seems uncertain and even dangerous) with undiminished and more accurate direction. Initiative adds to autonomy, the quality of undertaking, planning, and "attacking" a task for the sake of being active and on the move, where before self-will, more often than not, inspired acts of defiance or, at any rate, protested independence.

As before, whether the balance is tipped toward initiative or guilt depends largely on the quality of children's interaction with their parents. If parents give children an opportunity to exercise physical skills, answer their questions, and encourage fantasy activity, a sense of initiative is likely to prevail. On the other hand, if the children feel that their questions are a nuisance and indulgence in fantasy is a waste of time, guilt is more likely to prevail.

Sex-Role Development

One of the most significant consequences of early identification trends is **sex-role** development, the process of socialization in which appropriate male and female behaviors are learned. This includes personality characteristics as well as attitudes and beliefs. Such social learning has its beginnings early in life and originates from a variety of sources.

Before we examine the overall nature of sex-role development during early childhood, a few terms need to be clarified. **Sexual identity** refers to the physiological differences that exist between males and females. **Gender identity** is the psychological awareness of being either a male or a female. It is generally accepted that this occurs by age 3. Sex or **gender roles** refer to those socially defined behaviors associated with being either male or female. Thus, in order to understand the total differences that exist between the sexes, one must take into account these physiological, psychological, and sociological processes [Eisenberg, 1982; Honig, 1983(b); Stockard and Johnson, 1979].

Theories of Sex-Role Development

How sex roles are learned during childhood has several explanations. These explanations are a reflection of the major theories of child psychology presented earlier. Once again we see that these theories have woven their way through yet another facet of child behavior (see Figure 11.1).

The Freudian explanation is that sex role development is the result of identification with the parent. **Identification** is the process in which the child uses parental behaviors as models. The boy assumes the father's sex-typed behaviors because of the Oedipus complex. The attributes of the father, perceived as being those which captured the love of the mother, are thus assimilated by the boy. Because of the Electra complex, girls emulate the mother's behavior, which is perceived as having captured the love of the father.

The social learning approach focuses on the manner in which boys and girls are reinforced for sex-typed behavior by the parents, who are

Figure 11.1 Three theories of sex typing (from Kohlberg, L. A. A cognitive-developmental analysis of children's sex-role concepts and attitudes. *Genetic Psychology Monographs*, 1966, 75, 128).

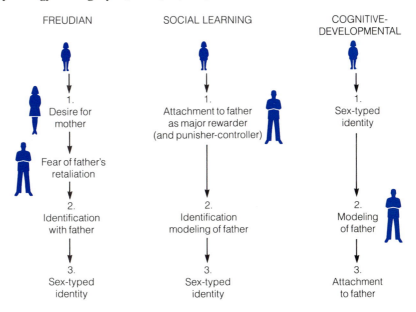

considered to be the major "rewarders" as well as "punishers" and "controllers." For example, girls are reinforced for engaging in "feminine" activities and not being aggressive, while boys receive encouragement for being the aggressors and for participating in more physical activities.

Cognitive-developmental theorists suggest that sex-role development emerges through the child's growing cognitive awareness of sexual identity. Early in life, boys and girls come to realize that specific roles, activities, and behaviors are appropriate for their own sex. As cognitive development increases, children are better able to understand those roles and behaviors. According to this interpretation, awareness of sexual identity leads to natural identification with the parent typifying the sexual role that the child has come to recognize.

Factors Influencing Sex-Role Development

From the very beginning, society exerts significant influences on the individual's sex-role development. In those segments of our society in which traditional sex-role stereotypes prevail, girls learn that they are to engage in domestic activities, have babies, and handle most of the responsibilities associated with child rearing. Boys, on the other hand, discover that being employed and providing economic support to the family will be their primary adult tasks. In those social environments that deemphasize traditional sex-role stereotypes, children learn instead that females and males are able to engage in similar types of activities.

It is no secret that sex-role stereotypes abound in society. Furthermore, such stereotypes are transmitted to the child at a very early age. Parents are largely responsible for this early teaching, which, for the most part, is accomplished through different treatment of the sexes. In general, girls are taught to be affectionate, gentle, and quiet, whereas boys are taught to be aggressive, independent, and active. Parents also teach sex-typed standards through their own behavior. Mothers are generally more nurturant and emotional, while fathers are typically more dominant, competitive, and unemotional [Plomin and Foch, 1981; Honig, 1983(b); Scanzoni and Fox, 1980].

Several important points should be made with regard to the transmission of sex-role stereotypes. Fathers appear more concerned than mothers about transmitting appropriate sex roles to their children. Furthermore, fathers often take more active steps to discourage cross-sex behavior in their children. Nontraditional parents are more likely than traditional parents to rear children who resist sex-role stereotyping and are more flexible in their overall views of masculinity and femininity (Langlois and Downs, 1980; Zuckerman and Sayre, 1982).

During playtime girls are frequently given dolls and play houses,

Sex-role stereotypes are transmitted to children at very early ages.

while boys often indulge in aggressive games, are given masculine toys, and avoid "sissy" play activities. Girls' behavior is usually more dependent, quieter, and less exploratory than boys', who play with toys that require more gross motor activity and are more vigorous and independent. Such sex-typed play is frequently supported and reinforced by parents (DiPietro, 1981; Fagot and Kronsberg, 1982; Muller and Goldberg, 1980).

As children drift toward peer groups of the same sex, they learn more about sex-role standards and behaviors. In fact, failure to comply with such expectations may be grounds for rejection by the peer group. The reinforcement of sex-appropriate behaviors from within the peer group also helps to explain the early sex-typed differences in children's play (Lamb, Easterbrooks, and Holden, 1980; Harris and Satter, 1981; Reis and Wright, 1982).

Teachers and other adults in the child's surroundings can also contribute to sex typing, as can the media. On television, for example, males are frequently cast as leaders, while females are portrayed as passive and submissive. With some exceptions, males outnumber females, and many programs lack a regular female character (Downs, 1981; Williams, LaRose, and Frost, 1981). The same degree of sex typing is evident in commercials (Feldstein and Feldstein, 1982). Adherence to traditional sex roles is also common in children's literature, where female characters are far outnumbered by males.

As a result of all these factors, children learn to behave in sexually appropriate fashions as taught by the vehicles of socialization, be it parents, peer groups, or playtime activities. Furthermore, these behaviors will become more deeply rooted as time progresses.

It should be pointed out that highly defined sex-role standards and expectations appear to be diminishing in the United States. Today, adults share roles previously labeled solely "feminine" or "masculine." There are many reasons for this turnabout. The similarity of early educational experiences for both sexes and the fact that males today engage in more "feminine" chores around the house (such as cleaning or doing the dishes) are contributing factors. Increasing numbers of women are employed outside the home, sometimes in jobs previously held by males (and vice versa), and more fathers are taking active roles in child rearing. We will discuss this topic more fully in Chapter 16.

Emotional Development

By the time a child reaches the preschool age, emotional reactions and patterns of expression are highly differentiated and distinguishable, a vivid contrast to the rather generalized responses that characterized the early years. Several factors account for this change. Growing levels of cognitive awareness enable children to perceive the environment in new and different ways. For example, the imagination abilities of the preschooler are responsible for the imaginary fears prevalent at this time. In general, cognitive advancements make youngsters more alert to emotional situations and more adept at expressing a wider range of feelings (Denny, Denny, and Rust, 1982; Harris et al., 1981).

Other factors affecting emotional expression at this time are new developmental challenges and expanding social horizons, such as the transition from the home to an early childhood education program and

THE FAMILY CIRCUS

"You be Honey and I'll be Sweetie."

more extensive involvement with peers. All told, emotional expression is intertwined with many other facets of development.

Fear

The fact that increased imaginative abilities affect emotional expression is best illustrated by children's fears. Because many objects and events cannot be understood or fathomed, they sometimes become magnified and distorted. Consider the bedtime rituals of many preschoolers. Some will not venture into a dark bedroom alone; others remain in the lit hallway while they search with groping fingers for the light switch on the wall inside the dark room. Others, caught in a classic **approach-avoidance conflict,** warily inspect the closet before bedtime, hoping not to find an imaginary creature. They know that they will not sleep peacefully until this dreadful task is done. Still others, after reciting their prayers, peer quickly underneath the bed, hoping that the mysterious unknown will not reach out and grab them before they can jump safely under the covers.

Fear of the dark and of imaginary creatures are but two examples of the preschooler's fears. Other objects of fears are death, certain animals, and physical perils such as drowning or fire. This variety of fears clearly illustrates the emotional susceptibility of the child.

A number of trends are evident in the overall development of fears. For example, as children grow older, girls are more susceptible to fear than boys, but boys report a greater variety of fears. Television and growing independence also contribute to preschoolers' fears. Children from upper socioeconomic classes tend to exhibit a greater number of fears related to personal health and safety than youngsters from lower-class environments, who report more fears of a supernatural variety. Television also contributes to children's fears with its frequent attempts to scare viewers (Moody, 1980; Wolman, 1978; Bauer, 1976). (Before television, fairy tales did the same thing.)

The attitudes of grown-ups may affect the manner in which children's fears are developed and expressed. Lack of understanding and empathy may hinder the child's attempts to overcome fear. Using fear as a method of discipline, mocking children's fears, or forcing youngsters to confront the feared object before they are emotionally ready are hardly appropriate or mature methods of assistance. Children need supportive guidance and gentle patience to overcome this hurdle of emotional life.

Anger and Aggression

The manner in which anger is expressed changes with age. After the second year, angry outbursts of an undirected physical nature, such as kicking and hitting, begin to decline. Temper tantrums, which started during toddlerhood, persist into the preschool years. The use of threats and insults tends to increase. Thus, while the amount of anger and aggression appears to remain stable, the child's manner of expressing it changes.

Two types of aggression need to be clarified. **Instrumental aggression** is aimed at acquiring objects, territory, or privileges. **Hostile aggression** is directed at another person with the intention of hurting that individual. Among young children, aggression is mostly of the instrumental variety (Maccoby, 1980).

Several factors influence outbursts of anger and aggression. Boys exhibit more overt displays of these emotions. This may be due to the fact that boys are expected to be more aggressive, a point we covered in our earlier discussion of sex-role development (Maccoby and Jacklin, 1980; Basow, 1980; Ullian, 1981).

The child's home environment is important to consider when examining aggressive behavior. In general, aggressive parents raise aggressive children, the former serving as models for this type of behavior.

Helping Children Deal with Fear

Understanding adults should realize that frightening and unhappy incidents may enter a child's life any day and create special fears. Although grown-ups neither can nor should protect the child from all fears, they can take certain measures when the child is afraid:

Respect Children's Fears
Adults take their own fears and apprehensions quite seriously, and they should similarly respect and understand children's fears of objects or events. Making fun of their fears or shaming them in front of others does not help children cope effectively with fear. Also, adults should never punish a child for being afraid.

Realize Children Will Outgrow Most Fears
Since some fears may take longer than others to overcome, adults should be patient in listening to the child and exhibit empathy and understanding. Achievements should be praised, no matter how small.

Allow Children to Become Accustomed to Fears Gradually
Adults should seek to build faith in children and their abilities. If heights are feared, let the child get accustomed to small elevations first; if dogs are feared, get the child acquainted

with a puppy as a starting point. This gradual adjustment to a feared stimulus is called desensitization. Another way to help children become accustomed to fears is imitation, or modeling. That is, fears might be overcome by watching someone else deal with the situation.

Try to Understand Fears in Relation to the Child's Overall Personality
Adults should observe how fears relate to the child's daily behavioral patterns. If strange sounds, sights, and sudden movements are characteristically feared, adults should help children avoid such situations as much as possible or assist the child gradually to develop means of dealing with such situations.

Become Familiar with Fears of Children at Different Ages
Adults will better understand most fears if they analyze their causes and underlying dynamics. If a fear involves a major situation, such as school, adults should take the time to analyze its origin and the circumstances that caused it. Adults should also set an example by dealing with their own fears rationally (Ilg, Ames, and Baker, 1981; Allen, 1982). ■

Other models for aggressiveness can be found on the television screen, where frequently the theme is "might makes right" [Parke and Slaby, 1983; Singer and Singer, 1980(a); Finkelstein, 1982].

The relation of imitation and aggression has been explored by Albert Bandura in a series of classic research investigations. In one of his studies (Bandura and Huston, 1961), preschoolers who were exposed to the sight of an adult aggressively knocking down a rubber doll and then being rewarded exhibited a strong tendency to imitate the behavior. In another study (Bandura, Ross, and Ross, 1961), the researchers sought to discover whether the sex of an aggressive adult model had any influence on the degree of aggressiveness of the child. After viewing the aggressive model, the children were subjected to a mildly frustrating situation and then left to play with several toys, including the doll that had been attacked earlier by the selected adult model. The children's behavior showed the boys exhibited more imitative physical aggression and identified with the actions of like-sex models more than girls did.

Hostile aggression by one 3-year-old boy against another.

This research strongly suggests that modeling and reinforcement influence the child's expression of anger and aggression. It also emphasizes the importance of suitable models for children, not only in the home but also in the playground and on television. As far as rewards are concerned, it is conceivable that aggression can be successfully manipulated through the proper use of meaningful reinforcers. Verbal approval, toys, and other forms of positive reinforcement given for nonaggressive behavior increase the chances that the behavior will persist. However, it must also be recognized that positive reinforcement directly following aggressive behavior, such as approval or attention from playmates for acting tough, also increases the likelihood that that behavior will persist (Hom and Hom, 1980).

In addition to being aware of the role that imitation and reinforcement play in anger and aggression, adults can do other things to promote nonaggressive behavior. For example, it is important not to give in to children's demands if they resort to aggressive behavior. Firmness is critical. Adults should try to understand how and why the child's anger originated. Careful observation of the events that triggered the outburst is important. The following observation is typical.

Sitting side by side with his younger friend in a sandpile in the neighborhood playground, a sandy-haired preschooler suddenly grabbed his playmate's toy truck. Yelling "You give that back!" the younger boy lunged for the truck, only to be pushed away by the aggressor. Quickly, the two were on their feet and shouting.

> "I'm gonna hit you if you don't give me my truck back!" the younger boy said.
> "You do," came the reply, "and I'll step on you!"
> "And I'll kill you!"
> "I'll cut your head off," shouted the sandy-haired youngster.
> "I'll cut your feet off," the other retorted.
> "See that?" the older boy said, making a mound of dirt and squashing it, "That's your head!"
> Not to be outdone, the other child picked up a stick and broke it. "That was your nose!"
> "Oh, you bad boy," said the boy with the sandy hair, "just for that I'm going to spank your fanny."

He picked up a branch lying nearby and began chasing the other boy. As they ran and slowly disappeared from sight at the far end of the playground, a distant voice could be heard trailing, "I'll get you, you bad, bad boy . . ."

If quarreling adults employed the same terminology, the situation would be described as a serious one, perhaps leading to fisticuffs and potential injuries. However, those who have carefully observed young children know that the above type of "argument" is common and representative of playtime behavior. (The same two preschoolers were observed playing in the same sandpile 15 minutes later.) Children's quarrels are fairly common, friendly sorts of interchanges that take place more often with close friends than with casual ones. Furthermore, most are brief. While they may appear to be serious, such outbursts simply reflect children's emotional immaturity and undeveloped social skills.

Family Influences on Child Development

As a cultural institution, the family not only transmits appropriate behaviors, knowledge, and values to children but also provides them with an emotional setting that makes them feel accepted and loved. It should be noted that the child must experience and learn to deal with negative emotions as well as the so-called positive emotions in order for psychological growth to occur. A favorable home environment and a positive emotional climate are critical influences in the child's personality and social development.

Certain factors in the child's interaction with the family are of particular importance during early childhood. For example, parental support, guidance, and fulfillment of the child's needs for security, trust, and understanding are extremely significant when one examines the quality of family relationships. Equally important are the methods of parental control in operation as well as relations with siblings. Sound personality and social growth, in general, are greatly affected by one's sense of identity and belonging to the family unit, not to mention the warmth and acceptance accorded by others (Westlake, 1981; Smith, 1982).

Methods of Parental Control

Parental control entails structuring the home environment so that children know what is expected and accepted. Control also implies the establishment of standards and limits for children's behavior and implementation of some degree of discipline.

Diana Baumrind's (1971) classic study reveals that parental control can be grouped in three broad categories: authoritarian, authoritative, and permissive. **Authoritarian** parents attempt to shape and control the behavior of their children by enforcing a set standard of conduct. Emphasis is placed on obedience and the use of punitive, forceful measures to enforce proper behavior. **Authoritative** parents also attempt to direct the child's activities, but do so in a more rational fashion.

Meaningful and realistic expectations are established for the child in these homes. Firm control is exerted, but verbal give-and-take is also stressed and parents attempt to convey to the child the reasoning behind their discipline. **Permissive** parents are usually nonpunitive and behave in an accepting and affirmative manner toward the child. Rules are very relaxed and parents exercise little control over their children's behavior.

It is important to realize that parents do not always fall into one category. Parents often mix their approaches in dealing with children. As far as overall effectiveness of each approach is concerned, the authoritarian and permissive styles appear to produce the least favorable results. Authoritarian parents generally allow little freedom of expression and dominate many aspects of the child's behavior. Frequently this method of control breeds conformity and submissiveness. Among older children, it may breed rebellion. Permissive parents, on the other hand, with their limited overall sanctions on behavior, have a tendency to nurture such child behaviors as selfishness and immaturity (Baumrind, 1971; 1980).

The authoritative method of control appears to produce the most favorable home climate. This democratic relationship has a tendency to foster such childhood behaviors as independence and self-confidence. Children reared in authoritative homes also have a tendency to be more cooperative and sensitive to the needs of others [Honig, 1982(a); Baumrind, 1980].

There are a number of current books and articles on the topic of parental control and discipline. Many authors [including Mitchell (1982), Silberman and Wheelan (1980), Dinkmeyer and McKay (1982), and Gilstrap (1981)] see the virtues of the authoritative style and have woven some aspects of it into their overall themes.

Birth Order and Sibling Relations

A question often directed to child psychologists is whether children's **ordinal position,** or **birth order,** in the family has any effect on their subsequent treatment or behavioral development. The question is difficult to answer because there is conflicting evidence.

Although research material has been gathered about birth order, clear-cut answers about its total effects have yet to be found. It is accepted by some that firstborns enjoy a favorable position in the family. Usually, they represent the center of attraction for the parents and monopolize their time. The parents of firstborns are usually young and eager not only to romp with their children but also to spend considerable time talking to them and sharing activities, something that tends to strengthen bonds of attachment (Dunn and Kendrick, 1982; Bank and Kahn, 1982).

Ten Steps to Effective Discipline

One of the more frequently expressed concerns among parents is how to discipline children effectively. Perhaps the first step is to understand exactly what *discipline* means. **Discipline** is the setting of limits in an effort to teach acceptable forms of conduct or behavior. The ultimate goal of discipline is to produce responsibility in children. Furthermore, children must learn that they are accountable for the consequences of their behavior. The following guidelines will assist adults confronted with the task of disciplining children:

1. *Realize that there are motivations for misbehavior.* Misbehavior doesn't just happen on its own; the child may be motivated in some way to engage in disruptive behavior. Some of the more common reasons for misbehavior include boredom and desires for attention, revenge, power, and control.

2. *Act with confidence.* Adults must believe in themselves and their ability to promote responsible behavior. They should adopt a take-charge attitude and handle disciplinary situations with self-assurance and confidence.

3. *Relate the discipline to the situation at hand.* Adults should focus on the central issue and not stray into unrelated problems. It is also important to tell children that it is the misbehavior that is being rejected, not them as individuals. Furthermore, adults need to explain why they are upset with the misbehavior ("You broke the vase, and I'm angry because it was special to me"). This helps to teach youngsters that misbehavior has implications for others.

4. *Be consistent.* Erratic discipline confuses children and seems unlikely to prevent similar problems in the future. If adults are going to discipline the child for one particular type of misbehavior, the recurrence of this misbehavior must also be disciplined. If there are two or more children in the home, discipline should be consistent among them as well.

5. *Don't make discipline a public spectacle.* Discipline can be a sensitive affair, especially among older children. Talking with children alone rather than in front of others reduces embarrassment and other painful emotions. Adults should also re-spect children's feelings after discipline ▶

Certain developmental characteristics and personality traits may be affected by birth order. For example, firstborns seem to perform better on early motor skill tasks than their younger **siblings.** Firstborns are also generally more successful in life and tend to be more conscientious and have higher levels of self-esteem. Firstborns also exhibit intelligence levels superior to those of siblings born later. In general, the more children in the family, the lower the IQ of each. The higher levels of achievement attained by firstborns may be due to their experiencing

Ten Steps to Effective Discipline, *continued.*

has been administered. Shame and guilt are fairly common reactions. Understanding adults do not attempt to increase the child's guilt after the situation has been confronted, and they are also open to whatever resolution the youngster wants to make.

6. *Avoid angry emotional outbursts.* No evidence exists indicating that yelling, screaming, or other emotional tirades promote effective discipline. In fact, it is conceivable that youngsters listen *less* when this sort of adult behavior occurs. Adults should take the time to organize their thoughts. When this is done, speech should be deliberate, controlled, and firm. Children also seem to listen better when adults talk *with* them, not *to* them.

7. *Establish limits in a clear, precise fashion.* Children need to know what is acceptable and what is not. Adults should spell out acceptable behavior limits so that there is no question about what misbehavior is or what it can encompass. Many children naturally test limits, which is all the more reason to be clear and consistent about behavioral expectations.

8. *Make the discipline fit the misbehavior.*

Adults need to examine the type and degree of disciplinary measure employed in relation to the misbehavior at hand. The discipline administered should be compatible with the nature of the misconduct and not too lenient or too extreme.

9. *Discipline should be as close in time as possible to the misbehavior.* Once adults have gathered their thoughts, discipline should be administered quickly. Children have a tendency to remember better and more clearly associate events occurring together in time and space. Misbehavior and discipline should be yoked together, the latter not being put off for hours or until day's end.

10. *Follow through at an appropriate time.* Discussing the disciplinary situation during a follow-up conversation often helps ensure that a lesson has been remembered. This does not mean dwelling on the misconduct or accentuating the negative; it implies that both adult and child have the opportunity to reflect on the issue and the role that discipline plays in creating a more harmonious living arrangement. ■

greater parental expectations and pressure for success (Malina, 1982; Zajonc, 1976; Pfouts, 1980).

On the other hand, being a firstborn may not be as advantageous as it might seem. Parents of firstborns may be inconsistent and inexperienced in child-rearing practices. Firstborns are usually punished more severely and rewarded more generously than siblings born later, thus creating an imbalance. Because the parents are eager to succeed and see clear-cut results—in mental abilities, for example—the firstborn is

Will birth order affect the development of this 5-year-old brother and his 4-year-old sister?

sometimes forced to succeed and strive for approval (Adams and Phillips, 1972; Kidwell, 1981).

Relations between siblings offer a unique slant to the topic of birth order. The arrival of a second child has a tendency to create anxiety for many firstborns, especially if they are preschoolers. Unsettled feelings may create **sibling rivalry,** a form of competition between children of the same family for the attention of the parents. If the former only child is old enough to perceive that the newcomer will be sharing the mother, there may be a considerable amount of jealousy exhibited during the early years (Kendrick and Dunn, 1980; Dunn, 1983).

Sibling rivalry is most likely to develop if parents exercise inconsistent discipline or are overindulgent toward a particular child. If little time has elapsed between births, older children will still receive their share of maternal attachment. If the interval is greater than three years, older children may develop interests outside the home, which will lessen their jealous feelings.

Although jealousy toward a new arrival is a completely normal emotion for the child, parents can take definite steps to make the adjustment period smoother. Making the child aware of the baby's arrival beforehand and attempting to convey the personal significance involved (having a new brother or sister) may prove particularly helpful. Allowing children to become involved with the infant's homecoming preparations can indicate to them that they are active and important in the family's activities. Later on, the proper attitude demonstrated by the parents can help minimize sibling rivalries. Parents should avoid showing any kind of favoritism or comparing one child with another.

It is not uncommon for sibling rivalries to persist for years, however. In fact, competition between siblings may be the norm rather than the exception. While it is recognized that the most intense sibling rivalry is between sisters, this may be due to the fact that females are more willing than males to express their rivalry openly (Bank and Kahn, 1982).

The degree and nature of sibling interaction vary greatly, not only from one set of siblings to another but also between the same siblings at different points in their lives. Some siblings become best friends, while others continue or come to detest each other. In some instances, love and hate may exist side by side in an uneasy equilibrium (Adams, 1981).

Siblings appear to have the most interaction and greatest influence on one another when they are close together in age. Significant age differences create physical and psychological distance between siblings. If they are similar in age, siblings may experience positive patterns of interaction, such as shared activities and interests, as well as negative patterns, including intense competition and a continual struggle for separate identities. These patterns of interaction usually intensify when siblings are of the same sex. Research also discloses that younger siblings more often than not try to imitate older siblings. They are far more likely to be followers of their older siblings, the latter often assuming the role of model and initiator (Bank and Kahn, 1982; Dunn and Kendrick, 1982; Dunn, 1983).

In most families, the oldest sibling is usually expected to assume some degree of responsibility for younger siblings. The fact that this expectation exists may help explain why firstborns are generally more adult oriented and responsible. Interestingly, older siblings in single-parent homes are often attachment figures for their younger counterparts (Stewart, 1981; Adams, 1981; Dunn, 1983).

While the study of sibling relations has not yet received as much attention as other aspects of family life, researchers today recognize its importance. As a result, many new and diverse thoughts are emerging on the topic (Lamb and Sutton-Smith, 1982). Sibling relations are recognized as a unique facet of the child's life. Furthermore, the attachment between siblings often transforms itself into a special bond that endures even after brothers and sisters have gone their separate ways in the world.

Child Abuse

Children do not always encounter harmonious family relations and domestic stability; many experience domestic disharmony and negative emotional climates. One family problem growing rapidly in recent years is child abuse, also known as the battered child syndrome. Each year, thousands of children are beaten, bruised, and maimed. It is estimated that as many as 2,000,000 children are abused annually. Even more shocking is the fact that several hundred children are murdered by their parents each year (Strauss, Gelles, and Steinmetz, 1980; Gelles, 1980).

Physical injury is only one type of child abuse. Other types include abandonment, neglect, emotional abuse, and sexual abuse. Understanding the total extent of all forms of child abuse is difficult since many cases go unreported each year. Some experts feel that we have under-

Figure 11.2 Divorce statistics [National Center for Health Statistics, (1982)].

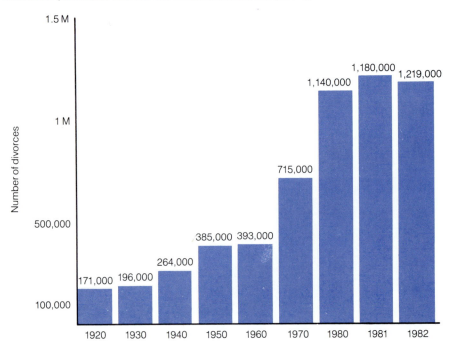

estimated the total scope of the problem and that abuse is increasing rather than decreasing (Martin and Walters, 1982; Williams, 1980).

In addition to physical injury, abused children frequently suffer social and emotional damage. Many are insecure, immature, and aggressive and have poor self-concepts. A large number of abused children also have low overall levels of self-confidence and self-reliance (Reidy, 1980; Straker and Jacobson, 1981; Kinard, 1980).

We are slowly obtaining a clearer understanding of the personality characteristics of the child abuser. Many seem to harbor feelings of hostility and aggression, and in most instances their anger is poorly controlled. Many also suffer from prolonged periods of depression and loneliness and are emotionally immature, compulsive, and generally distrustful. It is also believed that a sizable number of child abusers were abused themselves as children. Finally, child abuse seems to strike homes crippled by other social problems, including marital discord, alcoholism, and financial difficulty (Ulbrich and Huber, 1981; Gelles, 1980; Steele, 1980).

Through the efforts of concerned parties, programs designed to fight child abuse have developed all over the country, many of them sponsored by the federal government. Crisis centers, hot lines, public education programs, and group therapy sessions are a few of the recent approaches in the effort to curb the battered child syndrome. Of course, cases need to be reported and attention has to be directed to the social and emotional problems and pressures that trigger child abuse. This problem is going to require continued attention and assistance (Turner, 1980).

Family Dissolution and Reconstruction

Divorce rates are at an astronomically high level (see Figure 11.2). Today almost one out of two marriages ends in divorce. This means that half of us may experience a divorce firsthand, as either a child, an adult, or both [National Center for Health Statistics, 1981; Glick, 1980(a)].

Many of the homes stricken by divorce involve children. Nearly one million children will see their parents' marriage collapse. As one might expect, the problems encountered by and adjustments required of children of divorce are numerous. Some children feel personally responsible for the divorce; many are urged to take sides by their parents; and others bear the brunt of displaced parental aggression. Coping with the divorce may spill over to other aspects of the child's life and create additional problems, in schoolwork, for example (Wallerstein and Kelley, 1980; Hetherington, 1981; Berger, 1983).

Some people believe that a divorce should never occur while a couple still has dependent children at home. Advocates of this position realize that the stresses of marital discord may force children into roles that exact a tremendous emotional toll. Others feel that children are better off if unhappy parents get a divorce, ending the marital war and removing the children from the crossfire. Either course may pose problems for the children. If their parents stay together, they may be subjected to continual quarreling and tension; if their parents divorce, they may be brought up by a single parent beset by adjustment problems. The critical factors in the overall transition appear to be psychologically healthy parents with empathic attitudes, cooperation, and open lines of communication with their children (Kurdek, 1981; Wallerstein and Kelley, 1980).

In the aftermath of divorce, the child's custodial parent often remains single. In fact, the single-parent household is the fastest growing family form today. It is estimated that approximately 11.3 million children live in single-parent families. In the 1980s almost one out of every five families is of the single-parent variety (Furstenberg and Nord, 1982; Grossman, 1981).

Approximately 85 percent of all single-parent families are headed by women. Although the single-parent family often consists of a divorced mother and her children, divorce is not the sole reason for family dissolution. Single parents may also be separated, widowed, or never married. Some single parents have had their children naturally, others have adopted children.

Single-parent families report numerous problems, and financial difficulties top the list. Many single-parent families are poor, particularly if they are headed by a woman. Figures gathered in 1980 disclose that approximately 40 percent of female-headed single-parent homes were classified as living in poverty, while only 16 percent of male-headed single-parent families were (Payton, 1982; Johnson, 1980).

Care and supervision of the children is an additional financial problem for single parents who must work. Role realignment, loneliness, and stigmatization are other frequently reported adjustment problems. Both parent and child have to adapt to a changed family structure. These problems must be resolved if the family is to succeed. In addition, single parents must rid themselves of guilt associated with old ideas of parental responsibilities. Positive acceptance of one's new role and minimal guilt over one's new life are critical factors in meeting the challenge and determining the success of the single-parent family (Wallerstein and Kelley 1980; Miller, 1982).

If the parent having physical custody of the child remarries, a **blended** or **reconstituted family** is formed. Approximately 60 percent of all remarriages fall into this category. Another 20 percent of remarriages involve noncustodial parents. Overall, it is estimated that 6.5 million children live in blended families [Jacobson, 1980; Glick, 1980(b); Weingarten, 1980].

Blended families face their share of adjustments in attaining domestic solidarity and harmony. The successful assimilation of new family members and the definition of new family roles and relationships are especially difficult. So too is the issue of "turf," or who owns which possessions in the redesigned family network. In the face of such complex developments, children may experience divided loyalties (Visher and Visher, 1982; Kompara, 1980; Johnson, 1980).

Despite the energy required to meet these challenges, research indicates that stepchildren are generally a well-adjusted lot. Compared to children from natural families, most are just as happy and emotionally adjusted. Furthermore, they do as well in such areas as academic achievement and problem-solving resourcefulness (Skeen, Robinson, and Flake-Hobson, 1984; Santrock et al., 1982; Einstein, 1982).

Peer-Group Development

The Importance of Peer-Group Interaction

Being able to move from the family and interact with other children is an important step toward social maturity. Although early group interaction patterns are hardly representative of the social standards that adults consider acceptable, they give children opportunities to understand group interaction and the effect their behavior will have on others. Also, early group relationships endow the child with a growing sense of independence, competence, and emotional support. In addition, peer relations may provide more complex and arousing sensory stimulation than may be available at home, offer new models for identification, influence the development of a strong self-concept, and alter the character of children's play (Walsh, 1980; Hartup, 1980; Fine, 1981).

Initial contacts with other children evoke interesting reactions. No two children react in quite the same fashion. When brought to a playground for the first time, some eagerly seek the company of others, some scream to be taken away, and others passively watch the activity from a safe distance. When children become comfortable in the presence of others, their attempts at making further social contacts are frequently clumsy and awkward. Not having any previous group experience to teach them how to get along with their peers, children may resort to hitting, kicking, or spitting to achieve their ends.

Only experience teaches children that certain behaviors are socially acceptable and others are not; hitting other children may well release an inner impulse, but it will also cause the other child to strike back, run away, or cry. Throughout childhood youngsters gradually learn that the manner in which they relate to their peers will greatly influence the behavior they will be offered in return. Thus, cognitive awareness is an important dimension of peer-group development and socialization in general.

Peer-Group Dynamics

The preschooler's **peer group** is quite selective, consisting of individuals of the same approximate age. Bound by common play interests, group members tend to have an air of exclusiveness about them. "You can't play with us," is frequently heard. Acceptance into an established group may depend not only on newcomers' ability to accept and comply with the members' ritual and routines but also on the degree of friendliness that they exhibit. As Zick Rubin [1980(a)] writes, for children to be included and accepted, they must also include and accept.

Gender is also a qualifying dimension of peer-group acceptance. Unlike toddlers, whose playgroups lack sexual discrimination, preschoolers prefer playmates of the same sex. This facet of peer-group development is thus yoked to the sex-role developments brought out earlier. This trend will continue and intensify during the middle years

This group of peers is helping a friend learn to balance, illustrating the growing sense of emotional support that preschoolers experience.

of childhood, although it is more evident in males than females (Fu and Leach, 1980; Reis and Wright, 1982).

Other peer-group developments include the establishment of dominance hierarchies. Soon after the group forms, internal group processes classify one or a select few as leaders and the others as followers. Many times leaders are above average in intelligence, assertive, and well liked by others. Also emerging within the group are those children who will be regarded as popular or unpopular. Popularity is usually linked to friendliness, outgoingness, and the ability to cooperate [Hartup, 1983; W. Furman, 1982; Rubin, 1980(a)].

Compared to that of toddlerhood, the activity of the preschooler reflects interesting dynamics. A cooperative attitude is more evident, and preschoolers are more adept at sharing. The peer group is also able to develop more activities common to all members and engage in goal-directed behaviors. However, signs of emotional and social immaturity are still frequent. Selfishness, impatience, and disagreement punctuate many preschool interactions (Asher, Renshaw, and Hymel, 1982; Bell, 1981).

Peer-group dynamics are also influenced by adult intervention. Recent research has focused on the manner in which adults can help promote healthy peer relations and encourage overall social skill development. A fair portion of this research has centered on teaching children conflict management skills, maintaining positive peer relationships, enhancing interaction abilities and developing perspective-taking skills. Adult intervention is considered vital for the nurturance of such behaviors (Asher, Renshaw, and Hymel, 1982; Ladd, 1981; Howard and Barnett, 1981).

Peer-Group Influences on Behavior

As children participate in groups, their behavior begins to exhibit a number of changes, including a shift from dependent to independent behavior, an increase in prosocial behavior, and a growth in competitive spirit.

Dependency to Independence   **Dependency** is defined as a set of responses capable of eliciting positive attention from others. During infancy and toddlerhood, the manner in which the child is nurtured greatly affects the degree of dependency exhibited. Nurturance may take the form of the parent's positive reinforcement of the child's dependency, the eliciting of dependency reactions, or the conditioning of positive emotional responses to the nurturant adult. As children become older, a noticeable shift occurs in the frequency of dependent contacts with adults and the manner in which they are expressed. While toddlers are most likely to exhibit their dependent needs through physical means, older children need less physical reassurance. They still need psychological reassurance, though, and may seek it through a wide range of attention-getting and approval-seeking behaviors (Maccoby, 1980).

During early childhood, dependency is likely to shift from parents to peers. Certain noteworthy forces may determine whether dependency on one's parents persists. For instance, parents who are overprotective or inconsistent in their responses to dependency are likely to perpetuate dependency. Baumrind (1980) found that authoritative parents promote the most independent behavior in their children. It also appears that boys face stronger social pressures to become independent than girls. It is interesting to note that overly dependent children are likely to be rejected by or unpopular among their peers (Hartup, 1983; Asher, Renshaw, and Hymel, 1982).

Thus, while significant gains are made in the area of independence, children's behavior at this time is not without a dependent flavoring. Indeed, many children are emotionally dependent on their peers. We might say, then, that dependency still exists in many children, although its form and direction have changed.

Prosocial Development   Being sensitive to the needs and feelings of one's peers is an important facet of social development. Contemporary child psychologists call such peer sensitivity **prosocial behavior,** which encompasses cooperation, altruism, sharing, and helping others. In a broad sense, it might be referred to as good Samaritan behavior.

Prosocial behavior has been the object of considerable research, a fair portion of which has focused on the developmental trends that exist in its expression. Contrary to what we might expect, psychologists have found that the child's capacity to exhibit certain types of prosocial behavior begins early in life. For example, toddlers have been observed to share with others and even to demonstrate some insight into other people's emotional states and needs. Preschoolers may perform such prosocial acts as cooperating, comforting, and helping others. It is important to stress, though, that although the capacity for prosocial behavior appears to be established early, this does not mean that such behavior is consistently expressed. More consistent expressions of prosocial behavior usually do not transpire until later in childhood (Smith, 1982; Moore, 1982).

The child's early prosocial behavior appears to be greatly influenced by exposure to an adult model and certain social situations. Children are able to learn such skills as helping and cooperating by receiving adult guidance and positive reinforcement, by interacting with other children, and by observing adults and other children behaving in socially constructive ways. Children who are exposed to altruistic adults are likely to imitate their behavior, especially if the adult model is affectionate and nurturing. Other adult behaviors, such as vocal warmth, physical gentleness, and rational explaining of the consequences of actions, have been shown to elevate overall levels of prosocial behavior (Londerville and Main, 1981; Grusec and Arnason, 1982; Barnett et al., 1980).

Do American children differ in prosocial behavior from children in other cultures? This question is a difficult one to answer, but a look at cross-cultural child-rearing practices provides some insight. In Russia, Israel, Mexico, and China, for example, a high premium is placed on cooperation and the teaching of altruistic behavior. Parents and educators alike stress avoidance of interpersonal conflict and encourage cooperative interaction. The results of such training are evident in the high levels of prosocial behavior demonstrated by children in these countries. This doesn't mean that American children are not taught the same lessons and therefore automatically score lower on tasks involving

During early childhood, dependency is likely to shift somewhat from parents to peers.

prosocial sensitivity. But unlike youngsters from other lands, American children frequently lack universal, consistent teaching of altruism. American children often receive only sporadic commentary on prosocial behavior and limited structured opportunities to put such behavior into practice. It is conceivable that such opportunities would foster prosocial behavior [Honig, 1982(a); Bar-Tal and Raviv, 1982; Grusec, 1981; Rushton, 1980].

Development of Competition   The development of prosocial behavior is accompanied by the growth of competitive spirit. Most children initially experience competition as they vie against one another to reach some unsharable goal or as they strive for prestige or accomplishment. At one time it was maintained that males were clearly more competitive than females. More recent research, though, indicates that sex differences in competitiveness are unclear. Situational rather than individual factors appear to be critical in the expression of competition (Basow, 1980).

We do know, though, that a competitive spirit steadily increases in most children. For example, in a tug-of-war game among Mexican children, 4- and 5-year-old children were more cooperative than youngsters in the later years of childhood. These findings are consistent with another game situation in which preschoolers were far more cooperative than 7- to 9-year-olds. The older children, despite having opportunities to cooperate, chose to compete (Kagan and Madsen, 1971; Madsen, 1971).

Like prosocial behavior, competition may be learned through the process of reinforcement or through modeling (Sagotsky, Wood-Schneider, and Konop, 1981). A child who receives praise for winning a contest will be eager to compete again, even when the competition is irrational. Presumably, then, the child who does not receive praise for such behavior may learn other tactics (such as cooperation) to achieve the same goal (Nelson and Kagan, 1972).

Our society places a great deal of emphasis on competition. This is apparent in many facets of life, from sports to business. The emphasis on competition is especially obvious as schoolchildren compete for grades or class prizes. Even away from school, youngsters are thrust into competitive situations, such as the merit badge system in Boy or Girl Scouts. This is in marked contrast to the Russian school system, where individual competition is deemphasized and group goals encouraged.

While constructive competition is healthy, it is conceivable that our society often places the youngster in unfair competitive situations. Moreover, many of these goals can be reached with the emphasis on cooperation rather than competition. We will explore this topic more thoroughly when we present the advantages and disadvantages of organized sports in Chapter 17.

A Final Word on Peer Groups

Before closing our discussion, we need to examine how the child's personality and social development are affected overall by both peer and family influences. Without question, peer and family influences shape and mold the child to a great extent. But it must be recognized that peer and family influences are not separate forces. Rather, they are additive and interactive in their influence. While peer-group norms sometimes reflect the influence of adults, other times they reflect their own.

It should also be understood that peer and adult influences on the child are not always in harmony. While considerable consonance may exist, sometimes peer and family influences produce cross-pressures that can ultimately lead to conflict. Youngsters respond to such cross-pressures in extremely diverse ways. Psychologist Willard Hartup (1980; 1983) feels that sometimes the values and behaviors relative to the given situation seem to be crucial. At other times, the attractiveness of the peer group, the extent of contact with friends, the degree to which the peer group serves a reference function, and the adequacy of family adjustment are important factors. The broader milieu of the peer group, the amount of time children spend with it, and the number of interactions they have with its members tend to intensify the group's influence.

The purpose of these closing remarks is to stress the importance of viewing child development as an integrated process. Peer-group development is affected by numerous forces, including cognitive, personality, family, and emotional influences. None of these forces can be studied in a vacuum; the student of child psychology must look for the manner in which each affects the others.

Summary

During the preschool years children expand their social horizons and develop considerable independence. Sigmund Freud theorized that children pass through the anal and phallic sexual stages at this time. Erik Erikson's psychosocial crisis for this age group is that of initiative versus guilt.

Sex-role development is the process of socialization in which appropriate male and female behaviors are learned. The process of sex-role development has been subjected to Freudian, social-learning, and cognitive-developmental interpretations. Many factors contribute to overall sex-role development, including parents, play activities, peers,

Jacob, age 7

teachers, and the media. There is a trend in society today to downplay sex-role stereotypes and encourage more equality between the sexes.

The preschooler's emotional development is characterized by a greater differentiation of expression due to advances in cognitive awareness, wider social contacts, and new developmental challenges. Preschoolers exhibit many new fears because of their emotional susceptibility and because they do not properly understand many objects and events. Physical expression of anger declines, replaced by verbal displays of resentment. Preschoolers' aggression is usually of the instrumental variety; that is, it is aimed at acquiring objects, territory, or privileges. Hostile aggression, more characteristic of older children, is directed at another person with the intention of hurting that individual. Research discloses that imitation and reinforcement greatly influence the expression of aggression.

The youngster's interaction with the family has important influences on personality and social growth. Three types of parental control are authoritarian, which emphasizes obedience and the use of punitive discipline; authoritative, which is democratic and emphasizes the establishment of meaningful and realistic expectations for the child; and permissive, which is nonpunitive and exercises little, if any, control over children's behavior. Of the three methods, the authoritative style is regarded as the most effective.

Birth order and sibling relations are two other aspects of family life affecting the course of child development. Among other findings, first-borns tend to be more conscientious, intelligent, and successful than later siblings. However, they face certain obstacles, such as greater parental expectations and pressure for success. The study of sibling relations is a fairly recent research pursuit. Psychologists seem to agree that siblings have the most interaction and greatest influence on one another when they are close together in age. Under favorable conditions, siblings can develop a special bond that endures long after they have gone their separate ways.

Child abuse and divorce are two problems affecting many households. Child abuse, affecting as many as two million children each year, includes abandonment; neglect; and physical, emotional, and sexual abuse. In addition to physical injuries, it is recognized that abused children incur social and emotional injuries. Many abused children are immature, insecure, and aggressive and have low self-confidence and self-reliance.

Today divorce strikes nearly one out of every two marriages. Children need special attention in homes facing this problem. Many children feel responsible for the divorce, and some are persuaded to take sides or fear the brunt of their parents' aggression. What children need most during this difficult time are sensitive parents who keep lines of communication open. Escalating divorce rates have largely contributed to the rapid increase of two types of family structures, the single-parent family and the blended family.

The peer group during the years of early childhood is very selective and usually consists of individuals of the same sex and age. This chapter focused on some of the internal developments of the peer group, including dominance hierarchies and the establishment of leaders and followers. Popular and unpopular peer-group members also emerge at this time. While the peer group exhibits gains in such areas as cooperation and sharing, signs of social immaturity are frequent. Constructive adult intervention can nurture peer-group stability and harmony, but adults should not intervene unless necessary.

The peer group affords children the opportunity to expand their sense of independence, but dependency can linger in some instances. Prosocial behavior, or peer sensitivity, is evident at this age, although it will be more consistently expressed during middle childhood. Accompanying prosocial behavior is the growth of a competitive spirit among preschoolers. Competitiveness between children becomes more apparent as youngsters enter middle childhood.

Suggested Reading List

Hill, S., and Barnes, B. J., eds. *Young Children and Their Families: Needs of the Nineties*. Lexington, Mass.: Lexington Books, 1982. This book includes readings about many aspects of family life, including child abuse and parent-child interaction.

Perry, D. G., and Bussey, K. *Social Development*. Englewood Cliffs, N.J.: Prentice-Hall, 1984. This is a good overall analysis of children's social development. The authors devote separate chapters to child-rearing practices, aggression, prosocial development, and sex-role development.

Smith, C. A. *Promoting the Social Development of Children*. Palo Alto, Calif.: Mayfield, 1982. Smith covers such social behaviors as cooperation, friendship, conflict, and empathy and provides many strategies and activities to promote positive social behavior.

Chapter Twelve

Early Childhood Education

You can do anything with children if you only play with them.

Bismarck

Introduction

In 1855 society's growing interest in providing educational experiences for preschool children brought about the establishment of the first United States nursery school in the state of Wisconsin. Since that time, the growth of early childhood education in this country has been phenomenal. Today, approximately one-third of the nation's 3- and 4-year-olds are enrolled in some type of nursery school program. Figure 12.1 illustrates past and projected enrollment figures for the preschool population.

Early childhood education programs seek to provide programs and constructive learning experiences for 2-, 3-, and 4-year-olds. As a whole, these programs try to foster physical, linguistic, cognitive, personality, and social growth through a wide variety of learning experiences. Programs differ in structure and content. Because of differing philosophies regarding how best to educate the child, as well as changes and innovations to meet growing public need, the field of early childhood education has become increasingly complex in recent years.

Historical Events Shaping Early Childhood Education

The complexity of early childhood education today was generated by two key historical events in the fairly recent past. One, the "sputnik crisis," occurred when the Soviet Union launched the world's first satellite into outer space in 1957. It was labeled a crisis because Americans had assumed their country possessed superior technological knowledge. In the "race for space" during the 1950s, Americans firmly believed that they were far ahead of any other country's aeronautical space program. Americans were shocked to learn that the Soviet Union had scored a technological victory.

Figure 12.1 Projections of preschool enrollment (U.S. Department of Commerce, Bureau of the Census, unpublished tabulations, and U.S. Department of Health, Education, and Welfare, National Center for Education Statistics, *Projections of Education Statistics to 1988–89,* 1980).

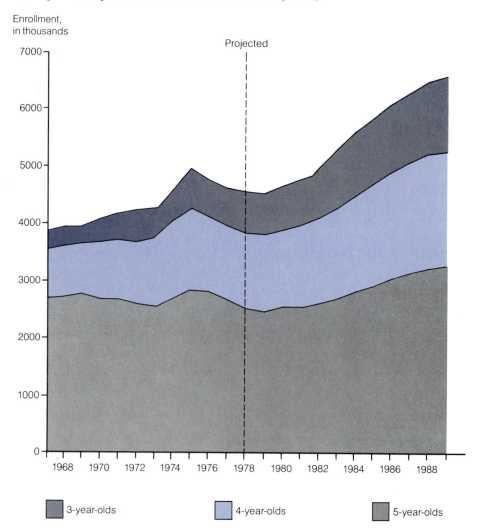

Politicians and educators in the United States began to ask many serious questions in the aftermath of sputnik. Many wanted to know how and why Russian technological skills, and those of other European countries, had advanced so rapidly. American schools began to compare themselves with European schools, especially in regard to the scientific and technical skills being taught. While colleges and universities were the focus of these questions, all grade levels, including early childhood education, were asked to give an accounting of their programs. And after the analysis, early childhood education teachers were asked to strengthen the cognitive aspects of their programs.

The second historical event, which took place in 1965, was the establishment of **Project Head Start,** a compensatory preschool program subsidized by the federal government. Project Head Start was introduced to help keep the blight of a deficient home environment from leaving a permanent impression on some of the country's children. Under the supervision of the Office of Economic Opportunity, federal grants were given to local community agencies capable of meeting basic outlined standards and implementing programs designed to improve the health of preschoolers and alleviate the prospect of school readiness deficiencies in disadvantaged children. Basically, Project Head Start consists of programs in education, medical and dental care, nutrition, social services, psychological services, parent education, and community volunteer programs.

Other types of programming have been added to Head Start since its inception in 1965. **Project Follow Through,** introduced in 1967, is a federally funded program designed to continue the services of Head Start to children in grades K through 3. Head Start now also includes **Project Home Start,** an outreach effort introduced in 1972 and designed to teach parents to stimulate their children educationally in the home. In 1982 Project Head Start also began a career development program for staff, parents, and administrators.

Thus, as a result of the sputnik crisis and Project Head Start a flurry of new and varied early childhood education programs came into being throughout the nation. Public and private institutions mushroomed as preschool education began to be recognized as an important foundation for later school experiences. The box on p. 296 displays the wide range of programs available today in preschool education.

Early Educational Intervention: Does It Work?

Since the development of Project Head Start in 1965, educators and psychologists alike have sought to determine whether early intervention and stimulation programs are effective and whether they produce any

Types of Contemporary Preschool Education Programs

Since many preschool education programs differ in their approaches in order to fulfill the needs of children and families, a classification may serve to explain the basic differences that exist among them. In addition to Project Head Start and other programs for the disadvantaged, Read and Patterson (1980) list the following types of major preschool programs:

Day-Care Centers

Once called day-care nurseries, these centers serve the needs of children whose parents are either employed or unable to care for their youngsters because of illness or other reasons. Although they initially had no planned educational programs, many of them have since been reorganized to meet the child's social, emotional, physical, and intellectual needs. The cost of day care varies considerably, but in many instances the centers charge fees on a sliding scale based on the family's ability to pay.

Laboratory Schools

College or university laboratory schools were among the earliest types of nursery schools in the country. The laboratory school focuses its energies on preparental education, teacher learning, and research studies. Sometimes mobilizing the resources of an area to meet the needs of young children, the laboratory school is usually financed primarily by the academic institution.

Programs for Handicapped Children

Some nursery schools employ qualified staff members who are capable of working with physical, mental, or emotional handicaps. Often these experts consider it important to have the handicapped child placed in a regular nursery school group, as when a blind child is enrolled in a group of sighted ▶

long-lasting gains. Although initial studies yielded uneven support, more recent evidence suggests that many participants in early training programs show gains in school performance as compared to nonparticipants. Furthermore, the differences between participants and nonparticipants appear to increase over time (Brown, 1977; Schweinhart and Weikart, 1977). Figure 12.2 illustrates the differences between participants and nonparticipants in preschool enrichment programs.

Results from similar compensatory programs have also provided considerable encouragement. For example, the Bereiter-Engleman program (1966) at the University of Illinois, which teaches the disadvantaged by using tangible rewards and punishments during language and other subject drills, has reportedly produced substantial IQ gains in its participants. The New Nursery School in Greeley, Colorado, working with 3- and 4-year-olds with Spanish surnames, operates on an auto-

Types of Contemporary Preschool Education Programs, *continued.*

children. With a trained person who understands the handicapped and can help the parents and the other children in the group deal constructively with the questions and anxieties a normal person inevitably feels, the experience may be a rewarding one for both the group and the handicapped child. In other situations, specially trained teachers work closely with psychiatrists to administer therapy to severely disturbed children, while some programs seek to fulfill the needs of the mentally retarded.

Cooperative Nursery Schools
A cooperative nursery school is organized by parents who employ a trained teacher to carry out the program. While sometimes obliged to use churches, community centers, or other buildings (well-established schools frequently have their own buildings) for their sessions, these schools are able to provide sound programs at somewhat lower enrollment charges than a private school.

Parent Education Programs
Some communities operate nursery schools under a parent education program, in which the parents actually participate and engage in "study discussion" sessions under the leadership of a professionally trained parent educator.

Private Nursery Schools
Although private nursery schools have experienced rapid growth gains in the recent past, their cost has restricted their services to wealthier families. When staffed by competent professionals, private schools provide excellent care for their pupils; unfortunately, very few states set up adequate standards or provide educational supervision for the private nursery schools within their borders. ∎

telic principle, so that the children engage in an activity for the sake and pleasure of the activity, rather than to obtain a reward or avoid punishment. The researchers in this program have reported mean improvements in IQ and other tests, such as the Peabody Picture Vocabulary Test (Nimnicht, McAfee, and Meier, 1969). Black children described as "deprived and diagnosed as mentally retarded" improved their overall IQs at the Perry Preschool Project in Ypsilanti, Michigan. For example, 3-year-olds gained an average of 27 to 30 IQ points, while 4-year-olds gained 17 to 24 IQ points (Weikart, 1967, 1969). Further success of the Perry Preschool Project has been reported in a more recent follow-up study (Schweinhart and Weikart, 1980). Other research studies conducted in the 1980s report similar positive effects of preschool programming (Ramey and Haskins, 1981; Lazar and Darlington, 1982; Collins, 1982; Beller, 1982; Deutsch et al., 1983).

Such positive findings support the belief that early intervention and enrichment programs play an important role in the development and nurturance of children's mental abilities. They also illustrate the impact of the environment in shaping human development, a concept presented in Chapter 1. Environmentalists are likely to use research evidence such as this when stating their position on the nature-nurture issue.

It must be recognized that contemporary educators are still gathering data on the topic of early intervention. Most agree that more exten-

Figure 12.2 The effect of a preschool enrichment program on children's school performance through the 8th grade (reprinted from Schweinhart and Weikart, 1977).

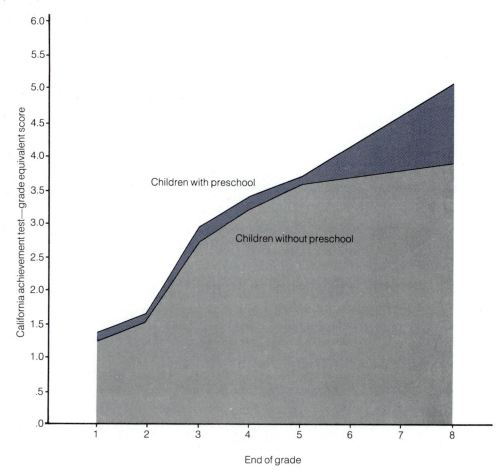

sive investigations are needed to assess the effectiveness of such educational programming. Given the importance of this issue and such initial positive findings, we will undoubtedly see a flurry of research activity in this area for years to come (Datta, 1983; Royce, Darlington, and Murray, 1983).

Goals and Objectives of Preschool Programs

Although early childhood education programs vary in location, size, and other details, their goals and objectives are not dissimilar. Experts in the field of early childhood education stress the importance of promoting social, self-help, and self-image skills. Equally important is the role of nurturing cognitive and linguistic abilities and, in general, learning readiness skills. At the heart of many programs today is the desire to heighten levels of self-sufficiency and independence (Morrison, 1984; Broman, 1982).

In striving to reach these goals, early childhood education programs seek to establish and maintain a healthy learning environment and provide positive guidance and discipline. The health, safety, and well-being of the preschooler are of obvious importance, as is the establishment of positive and productive relationships with parents (Click, 1980; Endsley and Bradbard, 1981).

The schedules and routines established by the preschool are the means through which goals and objectives are met. Although activities differ, the general thrust of programming is similar. Many schools offer a diverse mixture of free and structured play activities; creative play opportunities in art, music, and literature; and beginning subject area exercises in cognitive skills, letter formation, language skills, and so forth. Other activities may focus on small and large muscle skills, listening abilities, recitation, or special programs, such as nutrition and safety awareness. The overall length of the preschool program (full- or halfday sessions) determines the extent of these activities.

Many contemporary early childhood education programs offer microcomputers as part of their curriculum structure. While microcomputers have been successfully used among older children (see Chapter 16), their use among preschoolers is a relatively new development. Generally, microcomputer use can be a unique and challenging classroom tool when combined with sensitive and knowledgeable teachers. While it is generally recognized that computer use with children needs more in-depth study, results gathered so far describe numerous benefits and positive results. Among their many uses, microcomputers enhance fine motor skills, hand-eye coordination, symbolic representation abili-

A preschool structured activity: the class "train."

ties, and attention skills. They also give the child a sense of control, competence, and autonomy (Ziajka, 1983; Swigger, 1982; Titus, 1982).

In sum, early childhood education programs should offer an optimal learning environment. The goal of educators should be to teach whatever is necessary to keep youngsters' options open for further learning and help them learn whatever will enrich human experience. The preschool is one of the first steps in helping children to understand themselves, others around them, and the world in general (Day, 1983).

Working Mothers and Day-Care Centers: Good for Children?

The old adage that a woman's place is in the home is erroneous today, especially in regard to the growing number of women who are both mothers and wage earners. Statistics reveal a substantial increase of women in the labor force, indicating that mothers are breaking traditional role barriers and seeking more vocational involvement. The labor force now includes 56 percent of women with children under 6 years of age and 70 percent of women with youngsters between the ages of 6 and 18 (U.S. Bureau of the Census, 1982).

Numerous factors have encouraged women to return to work. Some mothers work because they are heads of households and need to support their families, some because they need to bolster their husband's income, and some simply because they want to work. Whatever the reason, someone must care for the children involved. While some mothers turn to relatives or babysitters for assistance, growing numbers are placing their youngsters in day-care centers.

Day-care centers are designed to care for youngsters of working parents or parents who are unable to meet the needs of their young. Day care offers the longest daily sessions, a time structure that accommodates the needs of the working mother. Some day-care centers specialize in infant care, offer meals, or even provide residential care. For children who spend considerable time at day-care centers, the facility may become a home away from home (Clarke-Stewart, 1982).

Day-care centers have aroused considerable controversy among child psychologists, educators, and parents. While such facilities offer protective care to children and enable both parents to work, concern is frequently voiced about the effects of day care on youngsters. Maternal separation and the disruption of attachment bonds to the caregiver are central issues for many. Some maintain that a full-time day-care center cannot provide this essential early social relationship, except under ideal conditions. Usually a child must share the attention of a day-care worker with other youngsters, and in the typical ten-hour center day, work shifts change at least once. Add to this vacations and job turn-overs, and a child may well have no special caregiver. Sometimes the parents compound the problem of the unhappy child by blaming the center and switching the child to another (White, 1981; Zigler and Turner, 1982).

Not everyone agrees on the potential negative effects of day care. Many feel that children are capable of adjusting well to day-care situations at an early age, and many also believe that these institutions offer rewarding learning experiences. The key to a successful experience appears to be finding the day care that best meets the child's needs. Above all, parents need to search for quality day care, a tedious chore but well worth the effort. Adults must search for centers with such positive features as low adult-to-child ratios, good nutrition programs, excellent sanitation conditions, and adequate staff training. A successful day-care experience goes beyond the center's qualifications, though. The parental warmth, acceptance, and care that the child receives in the home may greatly influence the youngster's response to the overall day-care experience (Peters, Hodges, and Nolan, 1980; Auerbach, 1981).

The Role of the Teacher

Whether program goals and objectives are met depends to a considerable extent on the teacher, who is in a unique position to promote positive learning experiences. Whether it be conducting a lesson plan, selecting play materials, or working with parents, teachers are instrumental in determining the effectiveness or ineffectiveness of a preschool program.

The teacher's personality, including basic outlook and convictions, is an important factor in influencing and shaping the child during the nursery school experience. And the manner in which the teacher interacts with the children in the class has important implications for their future social development. Of particular significance is the manner in which the teacher's guidance instills confidence and positive self-regard in the child (Marion, 1981; Tyler and Dittman, 1980).

Of course, different schools expect different things from their teachers. And just as no two students are alike, it can be said that no two teachers are alike. In some cases, teachers may be involved in all the major decisions related to the children and what they learn; in other

Teacher and pupils in a day-care center.

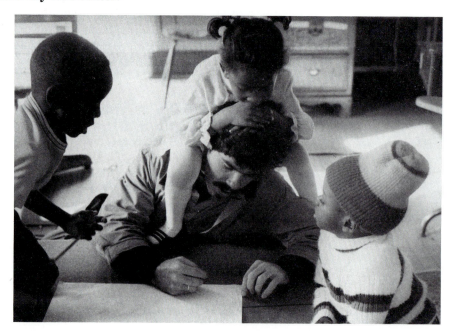

instances, teachers are told what to do. Some teachers emphasize the affective needs of the child, while others consider cognitive instruction their primary goal. Regardless of the approach taken, though, most emphasize the importance of establishing self-directed learning skills so that youngsters will be better able to handle the routines of kindergarten and later grade levels (Beaty, 1984; Morrison, 1984).

Teachers also differ in their overall classroom approaches and teaching styles. Some are authoritarian, others democratic, and still others permissive. Most are eclectic, though, in their teaching styles. That is, their teaching reflects bits and pieces of different styles and theoretical stances.

There are many teachers today who prefer nontraditional methods to traditional classroom guidelines. One of the more popular nontraditional preschool approaches is the Montessori method of instruction. The technique emphasizes freedom in the classroom, pupil individuality, and sensory awareness training. The **Montessori approach** has had a great deal of success, and many such schools are located throughout the nation.

Regardless of method of instruction, all preschool education teachers perform basic functions. Most experts agree that the primary functions include caregiving, building competence, providing emotional support and guidance, and instructing and facilitating learning. The caregiving function resembles that of the traditional maternal role and is expected to diminish as the children become older (Peters, Hodges, and Nolan, 1980).

The preschool education instructor does more than teach and present the school's program. The teacher also creates a favorable learning environment and helps preschoolers develop a sense of trust. The teacher's warmth, understanding, and support of children's strengths as well as their weaknesses are critical factors in the overall success or failure of the institution. The growth and development of preschoolers during these formative years are influenced and enhanced by the teacher's commitment to young children as well as his or her use of classroom strategies (Robison, 1983; Pierce and Pierce, 1982).

Preschoolers and Educational Television

While early childhood programs serve a large number of children today, not all preschoolers benefit from early schooling experiences. To reach those youngsters not attending preschool, a number of concerned individuals sought to design television programming of an educational nature. Since a sweeping majority of Americans had television, it was felt that educational broadcasting would be a unique and worthwhile learning tool.

One of the more widely publicized agencies to promote educational television was the Children's Television Workshop, an organization that sought to telecast a daily program that would be both entertaining and educational for young children. The results of its efforts were "Sesame Street," which appeared first in 1969, and "The Electric Company" in 1970, although the latter was aimed more directly at second-graders and the improvement of their reading ability.

Although other shows for young children had been aired ("Captain Kangaroo," "Romper Room," "Mr. Rogers"), "Sesame Street" was an entirely new concept in children's television. It combined attention-holding techniques, such as fast movement, humor, slapstick, and animation, with an educational curriculum that included recognition of the letters of the alphabet, the numbers 1 through 10, simple counting abilities, and vocabulary. Additions to the program in recent years have

One of the current educational programs on children's television is Mr. Rogers, which uses a slow, methodical pace (courtesy of Family Communications, Inc.).

been non-English-speaking characters, an increase in the use of Spanish, and the introduction of children who are exceptional in some way.

A study to investigate the educational effectiveness of "Sesame Street" examined approximately 950 children from five widely scattered areas of the country. The children were divided into a control group and an experimental group, the former not watching the show at all and the latter viewing it for six months. Parents of children in the experimental group were told about the goals and format of "Sesame Street," given material about the program, and visited each week by members of the research team. Both groups of children were pre- and post-tested to measure the specific teaching achievements of the program in eight main areas: knowledge of body parts, letters, numbers, forms, matching, relationships, sorting, and classification.

Observations made after the six-month period indicated that children who viewed the program displayed improvement in all eight areas compared to those who had not watched. While the most significant gains were among those who saw the show more than five times per week, improvements were found even in youngsters who watched only once or twice weekly (Ball and Bogatz, 1970).

In recent years, psychologists and educators have examined the different approaches and formats used in educational programming for preschoolers. The contrasting styles of "Sesame Street" and "Mr. Rogers," in particular, have been examined. Proponents of the lively, rapid-fire "Sesame Street" format like the manner in which it mentally stimulates the child. More specifically, it is felt that such an approach sustains attention and succeeds in presenting a wide range of important concepts (Lesser, 1979). "Mr. Rogers," on the other hand, offers viewers a much slower, more deliberate pace. Words are often repeated, and viewer interaction and participation are encouraged. According to supporters of "Mr. Rogers," this enables children to savor incoming information and consequently to process it more effectively. Such a deliberate and methodical pace may do more for developing the preschooler's attention span than introducing a multitude of short segments in the "Sesame Street" fashion (Singer and Singer, 1979; 1981).

While both "Sesame Street" and "Mr. Rogers" have been lauded for their programming efforts, investigations of their content and program format will undoubtedly give us a better understanding of the effects of educational broadcasting for preschoolers. The sheer educational nature of these and other similar types of programs, coupled with the positive results gathered thus far, is certainly gratifying to educators and parents alike. This is especially true in light of the questionable programming on television today, a topic covered in Chapter 16.

It is important to add that television experts continually stress the need for monitored television viewing hours and meaningful interaction between adult and child during and after broadcasting time. This is especially true during the preschool years. Adults need to help the child build on the concepts taught in order to reap the full benefits of educational television [Honig, 1983(a)].

Summary

Janis, age 9

Many youngsters today are enrolled in some type of early childhood education program. Because of continual changes and innovations, early childhood education has become increasingly complex and diversified in recent years. Two historical events, the "sputnik crisis" in 1957 and the development of Project Head Start in 1965, have shaped the growth of preschool education in America. Positive results have been gathered regarding the effectiveness of Project Head Start and other early intervention programs, but educators are still in the midst of evaluating total programming effectiveness.

While most early childhood education programs vary according to location or size, they share many of the same goals and objectives. Among the more common goals is the promotion of social, self-help, and self-image skills. The nurturance of cognitive and linguistic abilities, as well as general learning readiness skills, is equally important. Some preschools even offer exposure to microcomputers.

The teacher's personality, teaching style, and basic convictions are influential in shaping preschoolers' growth and development. It can rightfully be said that teachers' understanding of children and commitment to their profession and the learning climate they establish will largely determine the effectiveness or ineffectiveness of the preschool program.

Educational television is available to today's preschooler from such organizations as the Children's Television Workshop. Two of the more popular, though quite different, programs are "Sesame Street" and "Mr. Rogers." Research is still being conducted to determine the educational effectiveness of these and other programs. Most experts stress the importance of adult interaction and participation with children to reap the maximum benefits from television.

Suggested Reading List

Broman, B. L. *The Early Years in Childhood Education.* 2nd ed. Boston: Houghton Mifflin, 1982. Broman covers the theoretical essentials of preschool education and at the same time provides numerous practical tips to beginning teachers.

Morrison, G. S. *Early Childhood Education Today.* 3rd ed. Columbus, Ohio: Charles E. Merrill, 1984. One of the better introductory early childhood education texts on the market. Excellent coverage of Project Head Start, historical influences on the field, and kindergarten.

Robison, H. F. *Exploring Teaching in Early Childhood Education.* 2nd ed. Boston: Allyn and Bacon, 1983. A book loaded with classroom strategies and curriculum ideas for preschool teachers.

Chapter Thirteen

Imagination, Creativity, and Play

Out of chaos the imagination frames a thing of beauty.

J. L. Lowes

Introduction

Immersed in the business of play, 3-year-old Matthew pretended out loud that his toy bulldozer was clearing the way for a new road. Wobbling in her mother's high-heel shoes, 5-year-old Rebecca stood before a full-length mirror and admired her grown-up outfit of dress, hat, beads, and purse. She enjoyed imagining what it would be like to be a mommy someday.

While the above behaviors are situationally different, they are similar in terms of operating principles. Each is a way of transcending the ordinary and obvious features of the environment to perceive and interpret the world in novel and original ways. More specifically, some degree of imagination and creativity has been applied.

What Is Imagination?

Imagination is a mental process characterized by "as if" elements. These elements represent a modification of the environment that is based on experiences carried in the person's memory and involves some degree of imagery. Imagination may range from imitation of another person, to the make-believe use of materials, to participation in imaginary situations. Numerous terms are used interchangeably with *imagination,* including *fantasy, make-believe,* and *pretending* (Fein, 1981; 1982; Singer and Switzer, 1980; Singer, 1973).

Among children, imagination in play has a social quality in the symbolic sense. It has a tendency to involve interpersonal transactions, events, and adventures that encompass other characters and other locations in time and space. While a considerable amount of make-believe play occurs with other children (called **sociodramatic play**), the likelihood exists that additional invisible characters will be introduced or inanimate objects will be used to represent people or animals not present. Also, themes related to make-believe play are almost always flavored with a social quality. They are related in some way to the activities that characterize adult life or to adventures that children might have, either alone or with others (Singer, 1973).

Why the World of Make-Believe Is Important to Children

Engaging in some kind of make-believe play is a natural part of children's intellectual, social, and emotional development. Whether it be talking to themselves while pretending that someone else is in the room to listen, using a block for a car, or taking on different make-believe roles, children's imagination plays an important part of overall growth. The world of make-believe enables youngsters to incorporate the complex material they find around them into their own range of ideas. More specifically, make-believe play offers the following to children (Singer and Switzer, 1980):

Make-believe play exercises developing cognitive and linguistic skills.
When children talk to themselves, they may practice combinations of new words they have heard but do not quite understand. Imagination and a rich vocabulary tend to go together during early childhood. Make-believe play also enables the child to experiment and explore, important ingredients in developing cognitive ability.

Taking on a variety of roles during make-believe play helps children become more sensitive to the emotions of others.
Youngsters who are able to imagine themselves as someone else tend to be more tolerant and accepting of individual differences. Make-believe play also encourages children to understand the ideas and feelings of others.

Imaginative play encourages problem-solving behavior.
Sometimes a make-believe setup is an effective way to teach important concepts to children. For example, many teachers use an imaginary grocery store to teach addition, subtraction, division, and multiplication.

Imaginative play is a useful alternative to aggression.
Make-believe forms of aggression without the physical element are

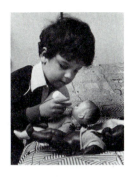

Early childhood play often reflects the pretend element.

far better than real-life episodes. Imaginary aggression also relieves a person's tension and frustration.

Imaginative play allows children to practice coping with a variety of life situations.

Imaginary games encourage youngsters to try out various kinds of roles and new experiences. For example, children who are not old enough to attend school often familiarize themselves with this situation by playing "class and teacher." In the process of experimenting with life situations, children can also express their emotions, including their fears and anxieties.

Imaginative play is enjoyable.

Children who engage in imaginative play are often happier than youngsters not involved in similar endeavors. Children involved in the world of make-believe have a tendency to smile more and display a wide range of positive emotions.

Children with active imaginations can amuse themselves and find it easier to wait when delayed or held back.

Imaginative children do not get as bored as nonimaginative youngsters; they find ways to amuse or entertain themselves. When required to wait, imaginative children protest less and show less impatience than nonimaginative youngsters.

What Is Creativity?

Creativity is best defined as a unique mental process that operates on a body of knowledge to develop a novel end product. While imagination and creativity are closely related, there is a difference between the two. Whereas the child's imaginative thinking might be "I *wish* that I could be ...," or "I *wish* that I could do ...," creativity moves into the sphere of "*What if* I could be ...?" or "*What if* I could do ...?"

The mental process of creativity includes the forming and testing of hypotheses and the ability to transmit the final result. The product or idea may be tangible, such as a better mouse trap or a work of art, or intangible, such as a philosophy or a new metaphysical concept. In many instances, creativity requires a search for new answers to old questions and application of mental flexibility, persistence, and insight.

Creativity is a concept that many people talk about but few understand. We hear of the need for creative teachers, thinkers, and leaders, as well as for creativity in nearly all aspects of human life. Yet when those who speak of this need are asked what they mean by it, they often cannot explain. Despite the recent scrutiny of many researchers (see Feldman, 1982; Mansfield and Busse, 1981; Tyler, 1983), the precise meaning and dimensions of creativity remain elusive. Many contend that the primary goal of education is to produce students who are creative and able to invent and discover, yet formal education seems to stifle creativity; most school systems seem to encourage mental conformity and discourage anything that might be construed as original thinking.

Creativity may result from unique ways of perceiving the world, from unusual thinking, or partly from personality characteristics of the individual. Creative people typically score high on tests of independence and internal control. They are inventive, determined, enthusiastic, and industrious. They enjoy novelty and diversity in their lives and are generally self-confident. Many creative people also have moderate levels of anxiety (Wallach and Kogan, 1971; MacKinnon, 1962; Davis, 1975).

To understand creativity, one must first realize that most people view the world in terms of a paradigm or mental set. When they are unable to unleash their thinking from that paradigm, their ability to arrive at new and different ideas and perspectives is limited. This type of mental block (which we all possess at one time or another) gives rise to such statements as "Why didn't I think of that?" or "That's so simple, why didn't someone think of it years ago?" or "No wonder I couldn't figure it out, the solution was right under my nose."

To explore creativity further, we must differentiate between two cognitive processes: convergent and divergent thinking. **Convergent thinking** is the mental process that singles out the one correct response to a problem. The following questions require convergent thinking: "What is the nickname of Ohio?" "How many states are in the United States of America?" "What is the boiling point of water?" In each instance, the mental operation consists of locating the correct information and giving the appropriate response.

Divergent thinking appears to be the central component of creativity. This mental operation is represented by the quantity and quality of different and novel responses with which a child responds. The following open-ended questions encourage divergent modes of thought: "In what ways are these two objects (a potato and a carrot) alike? List as many ways as you can." "How many uses can you think of for a brick?" "How many uses can you think of for a kitchen knife?" Instead of trying to arrive at one right answer, the mental operation is to pursue the problem along as many paths as possible.

Divergent thinking has several identifiable dimensions. One of these is ideational fluency. **Ideational fluency** refers to the flow and number of ideas that the child can generate. When asked any of the above questions (such as "How many uses can you think of for a kitchen knife?"), the child with little ideational fluency will respond with limited and typical answers (such as cutting meat, cutting bread, and cutting oranges). Conversely, the child with greater ideational fluency will probably list the more mundane uses and many additional ones (such as a dissecting tool, a fish scaler, a point for an underwater spear, a gift for grandmother, an arrow to be used with a miniature bow, a clam opener, a paper-shredding device for making confetti, a stick to toast marshmallows).

In addition to ideational fluency, divergent thinking encompasses associational, expressional, and word fluency. **Associational fluency** is the number of words one can name that can go with other words in terms of meaning. **Expressional fluency** is the ability to put words together to meet the requirements of a given sentence structure. **Word fluency** is the ability to find a variety of words to express a particular meaning or represent a particular concept. Divergent thinking also includes the ability to be original and flexible in the overall creative process (Guilford, 1959).

Myths about the Development of Creativity

To nurture creativity in children, parents, teachers, and other adults must overcome some persistent myths about this unique thought pro-

Creative art time for a group of 4-year-olds.

cess. According to Stephanie Dudek (1974; 1976), the following are some of the more popular myths:

1. Creativity is universal in children but rare in adults.

2. Creativity is innate and spontaneous.

3. As soon as the child starts school, the pressures to conform begin systematically to destroy creativity.

4. There are serious declines in creativity around the ages of 8 or 9 and then again around 11 or 12.

Dudek proposes that these myths have unfortunately been perpetuated by the existing literature and do not have a basis in fact. As far as the first two are concerned, one must realize that creativity is a mental process based on divergent thinking. It can exist among both young and old, although among adults the creative mode is different from that of children. It is partly innate and partly nurtured.

As far as the third myth is concerned, whether conformity crushes creativity largely depends on the school system. As children learn greater control and self-discipline, they develop a qualitative creativity style that is different from the free, uncontrolled expression of the younger child. This does not imply, however, that creative modes of thinking have been destroyed. What is important is the manner in which control

is taught and ultimately acquired by the child. A school system can either inhibit or encourage the growth of creative potential.

Dudek does not feel that there is a decline in creativity around the age of 8 or 9. What happens instead is that we start to see the earlier-mentioned change in self-expression. By this time, children are within Piaget's concrete operations stage, and they have usually mastered such concepts as seriation, transformation, reversibility, and causality. No longer chained to perceptual dominance, children employ more realistic and disciplined approaches as they interpret their surroundings. In artwork, for example, they draw more along the lines of what an adult sees; colors are more exact and details are elaborate. The overall organization is also more logical. While all of this may seem to result in more ordinary artwork, it is actually more complex and differentiated. Feeling, sensitivity, and imagination abound in artwork at this time.

At the age of 11 or 12, children are within Piaget's stage of formal operations. What is perceived to be another decline in creativity is instead the mastery of true conceptual ability. The foregoing skills are further elaborated and result in different modes of expression. At this time creativity usually unfolds in new imaginative and abstract ways. Children develop complex ways of viewing the world, including the testing of hypotheses and the combination of ideas. According to Dudek, these new abilities need to be perfected and transcended in years to come. Once again, the school system shoulders much of the responsibility for encouraging or discouraging creativity as an attitude and a developed skill.

What Is the Connection between Imagination and Creativity?

While imagination and creativity are regarded as separate mental processes, there is no mistaking the fact that they share common properties. For example, imagination and creativity embody unique and original ways of interpreting the environment. Both enable the child to experiment and explore, and both mirror spontaneity and self-expression.

It seems likely that early imaginative activity sows the seeds for later creative expression. In support of this hypothesis, one research study examined artistic creativity in college women and discovered that the more creative subjects had tended to engage in greater amounts of daydreaming during childhood (Helson, 1965). Another investigation (Schaefer, 1969) revealed that many creative high school students reported having an imaginary companion during childhood.

However, the foregoing does not mean that a clear, definite relationship exists between imagination and creativity. Jerome Singer (1973), among others, contends that while some connection between the two probably exists, more research is needed on the topic. We also need to examine more closely the forces responsible for initiating make-believe play and those nurturing later creativity. Moreover, we need to keep in mind that the nurturance and development of imagination and creativity are not an all-or-nothing situation; a person may be imaginative or creative in one area but not in others.

One other important stumbling block in analyzing the nature of imagination and creativity and whatever connections exist between them is the lack of adequate assessment devices. We will explore some laudable testing efforts later on in this book, but assessment devices seeking to measure creativity have not achieved total success. This is not unreasonable since, as we said earlier, we have yet to develop a clear definition of creativity. Thus measurement of imagination and creativity is a paradox. How do you devise a standardized way to measure a nonstandard behavioral product (Petrosko, 1978)?

There is considerable agreement on the importance of stimulating early imaginative and creative thought (see Singer and Singer, 1985; Segal and Adcock, 1981; Finley and Finley, 1982; Griffing, 1982; Chenfeld, 1983). Most experts agree that during early childhood youngsters explore the environment more freely, before being bridled by predetermined logic. In the process of exploring, children nurture a sense of curiosity. Curiosity often lies at the heart of imagination and creativity. According to Marilyn Bradbard and Richard Endsley (1982), curiosity sparks the child's motivation to question and experiment, not to mention the persistence to learn more about the world in general.

Developmental Trends

While make-believe behavior becomes evident during the preschool years, it actually begins during the first year or two of life. At that time, children may pretend that they're asleep when in fact they're well rested or hungry when seemingly sated. Such behaviors mark the beginning of **representational thought,** a cognitive capacity that enables children to construct mental symbols and images of environmental objects and events. Representational thought will pave the way for **symbolic play,** an activity in which children represent one thing as if it were another (Fein, 1982).

There appears to be a sequence of development behind early pretending. Prior to pretending, children demonstrate knowledge of the functions of real objects by gesture. They next pretend at their own everyday activities. As the youngster's ability to symbolize advances, pretending becomes decentered. This enables children to pretend at others' activities and apply pretend schemes to dolls and other substitute participants. Such play is then integrated into sequences. Early pretending is context dependent, apparently suggested by available objects. Toward the end of the second year, children begin to indicate verbally or nonverbally that pretend games are constructed mentally before action. This latter development suggests that pretend play is becoming more independent of available objects and context (Nicholich, 1981).

Advancement in cognitive development—namely, entry into the Piagetian stage of preconceptual thought—enables children's imaginative and creative spirits to take on new dimensions. One of the more noticeable trends is an elaboration of symbolic play. More specifically, the one or two representations characterizing the toddler's imagination give way to multiple representations. This means that play objects no longer are bound by a solitary characteristic. Instead, they acquire numerous intertwined and related dimensions [Case and Khanna, 1981; Field, Destefano, and Koewler, 1982; Singer and Singer, 1980(b)].

A 5-year-old acquaintance of ours was recently observed demonstrating the use of multiple representations. A devoted "Star Wars" fan, he was playing with a Luke Skywalker action figure. In the course of 20 minutes of pretend play, Luke "joined forces" with his friend Han Solo, "battled" Darth Vader in hand-to-hand combat, and "rescued" Princess Leah. His audible conversation was sprinkled with numerous characteristics of each person, such as the goodness of Luke and the evil of Darth Vader.

The need to have toys or objects bearing a close resemblance to the real world appears to persist, at least during the early phases of the preschool years. For example, a youngster will "fly" a pair of crossed popsicle sticks around the room but will not be satisfied with a single stick representing the airplane.

George Foreman and Fleet Hill (1980) maintain that this is not because children lack creativity. Instead, they say, children are very creative in the way that they represent those aspects central to the use of the missing object. Children are likely to think of representing the wings of an airplane because the wings represent the essence of the plane. The means of establishing the correspondence between that essence and the pretend object is therefore more complex, not less creative.

Often the use of more realistic toys affects the tempo of make-believe play. Many youngsters will not proceed with their pretending unless the right toy or prop is found. Whereas the rigidity of earlier pretending often originated from a ritualistic repetition of an action sequence, the rigidity now is often associated with the child's insistence on specific toys or props (Segal and Adcock, 1981).

However, let it be said that the requirement of likeness will begin to decline during these years. Children will begin to substitute dissimilar objects for lifelike objects and in time will need no object at all. The mental prowess behind such maneuvering is an excellent reflection of developing cognitive abilities (Fein, 1982; Griffing, 1982).

There are other dimensions to the preschooler's symbolic play. Preschoolers have better developed themes than toddlers do and pay more attention to detail, sequence, and continuity. Play sessions are also longer than before. Make-believe play sessions are preplanned, such as filling an area with toys beforehand in order to carry out a play idea. A dialogue similar to our earlier example is used both to establish the pretense and to describe the thoughts, feelings, and actions of the characters. Preschoolers talk not only *to* pretend characters but also *for* pretend characters (Segal and Adcock, 1981; Nicholich, 1981).

Sociodramatic Play

Another development at this time is the emergence of sociodramatic play. As defined earlier, sociodramatic play is the use of imagination or pretense with other children. In many respects, sociodramatic play is a reorganization of solitary symbolic play. Readers will recall that solitary play requires the child to imagine familiar or novel events. Sociodramatic play rests on this ability but also requires that a partner's imagination be taken into account (Fein, 1982).

Sociodramatic play may take the forms of imitation and identification of adult behavioral patterns. By becoming a doctor, parent, or law officer, children act out their inner desire to be like adults in what may be a valuable learning experience. Playing grown-up roles may help prepare children for later life, since many of the grown-up situations acted out are characteristic of the adult years. The following episode illustrates adult imitation by preschoolers.

Joshua and Karen were playing in the recreation room when David approached them with a doctor's kit in his hand. "I'm Dr. Adams," he announced, "is anybody sick today?"

"I'm sick," Karen said as she held her stomach. "Oh, I'm so sick."

David sat next to her and with his toy stethoscope listened most intently while he placed the instrument next to her head, chest, and back. He then looked inside her ears and mouth. "You're very sick," he said, "but if you're a good girl, I'll take care of you." He reached into his bag and from a bottle took two imaginary pills. "These will make your tummy all better . . . now take them like a big girl."

Karen stuck her tongue out and, with a wince, swallowed hard. "Oh Dr. Adams, I feel much better," she said. "Now I can go back to work."

David closed his bag and stood up. "That will be two dollars," he said, holding out his hand. "You pay me now."

Karen gave him the make-believe money, and David put it in his pocket, patting it to make sure it was there. As he departed, he announced that he had to go back to the hospital to help more sick people. "Oh, I'm so busy today," he remarked, "so, so busy."

Sociodramatic play at this time has other dimensions. In addition to the child's earlier described abilities to preplan and sequence make-believe activities, preschoolers' sociodramatic play involves the separation of the sexes. The themes used by both sexes are varied and elaborate, although the imaginative play of boys is often noisy, urgent, intense, and involves matters of life and death, whereas girls often pursue more nurturant or care giving themes. The themes for both boys and girls will persist throughout childhood. Both males and females are able to recognize the pretend element and employ such phrases as "Let's

3½-year-olds engaged in sociodramatic play, which in this case takes the form of imitation of adult behavior.

make believe," "You be the nurse," or "This is not really real." Finally, the roles being played require not only wearing the right costume but also taking on other characteristics and actions related to the role (Segal and Adcock, 1981).

Sociodramatic play offers many positive benefits to children. In a creative sense, it encourages children to use past experiences within the sociodramatic framework. Adjusting to the ideas of others also encourages a youngster's creavity. Intellectually, sociodramatic play encourages the use of cognitive powers, including linguistic ability, the power of abstraction, the widening of concept formation, and the acquisition of new knowledge. Sociodramatic situations also sharpen children's social skills. Finally, sociodramatic play encourages positive give and take, tolerance, and consideration of others. Thus, sociodramatic play weaves its way around many facets of growth and development (Smilansky, 1971; Rubin, 1980; Rubin and Everett, 1982).

Researchers once assumed that all children engaged in sociodramatic play and other varieties of pretending. However, there is evidence that low-income and working-class children engage in less sociodramatic and pretend play than middle-class youngsters. Numerous studies (see Sutton-Smith, 1983, for a review of the literature) point out that the play of the former group is often characterized by sensorimotor and kinetic activity. They proceed from motor play, through circumscribed and realistic imitative play, to rule games *without* the diverse imaginative activities that usually mediate between the two. This trend has been observed among low-income American children and youngsters from Israel, Asia, and North Africa.

Such a developmental pattern is said to result from the fact that children from lower socioeconomic settings have work tasks or family responsibilities imposed on them, creating a high level of physical activity. Middle-class children, on the other hand, have fewer demands on them in the form of household duties or work outside the home. It is conceivable that they have more opportunities to engage in sociodramatic play and the like, not to mention more adult encouragement. However, it is important to point out that this topic has sparked debate among child psychologists and not all of them agree with the aforementioned contentions (McLoyd, 1983).

Play and Socialization

For children under 3 or 4 years of age, play may be characterized primarily as activity that is exploratory and appeals to the senses and fundamental motor skills. The play of preschoolers, however, has new

Development of Cooperative Play Activities

Play behavior during early childhood is characterized as being nonsocial, primarily because of the child's egocentric or self-centered character. Since children are so involved in their own personal world, little if any interaction exists when they are placed in the company of other children in the same age bracket. In time, though, play acquires a more cooperative flavor. The following stages illustrate the progression of cooperative play.

Unoccupied Behavior
In unoccupied play, children are not actually engaged in play but are observing whatever events happen to catch their interest. When nothing of particular interest takes place, children may occupy themselves by doing other things, such as fondling the body, following an adult, or getting on and off a chair.

Solitary Play
Here, children play independently with their own toys and make no effort to interact with children nearby. Behavior at this point is egocentric, expressive of a self-centered attitude toward one's own activities.

Onlooker Behavior
Onlooker behavior is characterized by the observation of others and a gradual interest in what other children are doing. Yet, instead of joining a play activity, the child will spend considerable time asking questions of and listening to what is being said by the actual play participants. ▶

Social participation in play during early childhood (adapted from Parten, 1932).

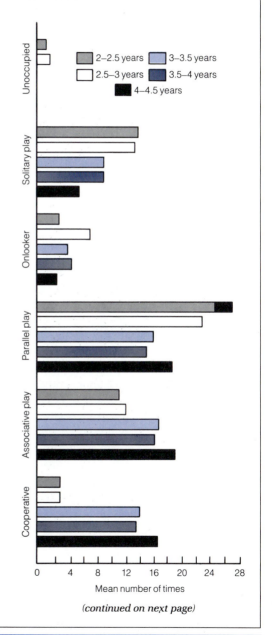

Mean number of times

(continued on next page)

Development of Cooperative Play Activities, *continued.*

Parallel Play
In parallel play, children play independently, but their play activities bring them into contact with other children. Since they are still basically egocentric and cannot yet comprehend and share the attitudes, feelings, and activities of others, they play alongside rather than with them.

Associative Play
At this point, children can interact and cooperate more with others than during previous stages. Play can be characterized also by sharing, borrowing, and lending of play toys.

Cooperative Play
This type of play, mostly characteristic of older preschool children, is confined to members of an organized play group. The play group itself is usually goal-oriented and is directed by one or two members, with group tasks being assigned to the other children. ■

qualities that reflect growth and development, particularly their desire to participate and become involved in more socially oriented activities, increased use of higher-order mental processes, and imitation of and identification with adult behavioral patterns. Contacts with social institutions other than the family, such as a nursery school, day-care center, or play school, may provide a myriad of new activities and facilitate overall play development.

Play is an important social activity throughout childhood because it is a means by which youngsters can better understand themselves and how they relate to others. For the preschooler, play groups enhance a sensitivity to the needs of others in addition to fostering a cooperative spirit. Play groups also help the child relinquish a singular, self-centered frame of reference. Overcoming egocentrism is one of the primary tasks of the early childhood years, although recent research suggests that the preschooler is not as egocentric as was once thought (Black, 1981).

The preschool play group is usually small, restrictive, and temporary (many groups dissolve after 10 or 15 minutes). This temporary quality is the result of a number of factors, including limited attending skills and impulsive desires to end activities prematurely in order to start something else (Corsaro, 1981).

Because of the play group's temporary quality, preschoolers are faced with the chore of entering new social gatherings on a fairly regular basis. Some may be better at this than others, perhaps because they are more outgoing, gregarious, and secure in overall relationships. The quiet, timid, or shy child may have a more difficult time (Zimbardo and Radl, 1981).

As a social vehicle, the play group will teach children that certain behaviors are expected and certain rules must be followed. Moreover, children will learn the importance of working toward group goals and sharing materials. Youngsters learn these social processes best by interacting with one another (and with adults in situations that warrant grown-up intervention and guidance) [Rubin, 1980(a)].

The extent to which adults should involve themselves in and structure playtime activities has received a fair amount of research attention. Many experts maintain that adults should provide guidance, support, and the environment for play but should be careful not to restrict children's freedom to play. Too often adults overinvolve themselves and overorganize play activities, which restricts children's spontaneity and free play spirit. While adult intervention has positive effects on the initiation and direction of play, it should be designed to minimize its obtrusive effects and avoid controlling all the choices of the child (Kleiber and Barnett, 1980).

Forms of Play

Virtually all types of play that preschoolers engage in (such as climbing, balancing, or manipulating blocks, or simple jigsaw puzzles) provide opportunities for them to develop muscular coordination. Children refine their motor skills during this period and develop more self-confidence as they master new play materials. Variation in performance is considerable, though, as it is with all motor skills. Preschool children often show a tendency to perform well in one area and do poorly in another. We must remember, too, that preschoolers generally have difficulty with tasks requiring fine muscle coordination (Malina, 1982; Wickstrom, 1983).

This means that some types of play will remain difficult and elusive. Interestingly, preschoolers can almost "sense" what types of activities are manageable and within reach. They learn—usually through trial-and-error behavior—that some activities are overpowering challenges to their developing physical capabilities, and they avoid these activities until a later time. Obviously, some activities develop motor abilities better than others, and adults should learn how to distinguish the difference [Gallahue, 1982(b); Foreman and Hill, 1980; Riggs, 1980]. Table 13.1 lists some of these desirable activities.

Table 13.1 Activities Promoting Motor Skill Development

Gross Motor Skill	Fine Motor Skill
Pulling a wagon	Using paintbrushes and crayons
Riding wheeled toys	Using hammer and peg sets
Running, skipping, and swinging	Playing with cars, trucks, and trains
Climbing trees, jungle gyms, and ladders; using seesaws	Playing with blocks
	Fingerpainting
Playing with inflated balls or dolls	Cutting with scissors; pasting
Digging with equipment	Using wooden building sets
Playing with beanbags, rubber horseshoes, sawhorses, and doll carriages	Assembling jigsaw puzzles or playing manipulative games

The child's use of imagination is a strong indication of originality and inventiveness. Toys, too, can provide an outlet for these traits. The desire to make toys alive with their own individual qualities (the Piagetian concept of "animism") illustrates this; for example, a doll may have its own thoughts and feelings; a chair may become a mysterious fort or castle; and a box may be turned into a car, complete with its own noisy engine. The child's play language, too, reflects the prevalence of animism during this stage of development. Youngsters may refer to a "sleeping" tree, the "happy" sun, or the "strong" mountains (Winner, McCarthy, and Gardner, 1980).

Summary

This chapter explored the nature of imagination and creativity and how they develop. Imagination is a mental process characterized by *as if* elements. These elements represent a modification of the environment based on some experiences carried in the person's memory and involve some degree of imagery.

Creativity is a unique mental process that operates on a body of knowledge in a way that results in a novel end product. It is characterized by *what if* elements, and its central component is divergent thinking. This mental operation is represented by the quantity and quality of a person's responses. Divergent thinking has numerous identifiable

Kirk, age 8

dimensions, including ideational, associational, expressional, and word fluency. Divergent thinking also includes the ability to be original and flexible in the overall creative process.

While imagination and creativity are regarded as separate mental processes, they have common properties. While it is conceivable that early imaginative activity sows the seeds for later creativity, more research is needed before definite conclusions are drawn. The accurate measurement and assessment of imagination and creativity are especially difficult for researchers.

The pretending of preschoolers includes more elaborate versions of symbolic play as well as sociodramatic play. Sociodramatic play is the use of imagination or pretense with other children. It is usually sextyped and often takes the form of imitation and identification of adult behavioral patterns. Sociodramatic play offers numerous benefits to children, including the stimulation of creative, cognitive, linguistic, and social sensitivity skills.

During the preschool years, play becomes more socially oriented, although incidents of social inexperience are still frequent. Play groups—small, restrictive, and temporary gatherings—help the child overcome a singular frame of reference and understand the needs and sensitivities of others. In addition to play groups, children at this time engage themselves in a wide range of activities involving small and large muscle skills. Imaginative play is also prevalent during early childhood.

Suggested Reading List

Bunker, L. K., Johnson, C. E., and Parker, J. E. *Motivating Kids through Play.* New York: Leisure Press, 1982. This paperback is written for adults who want to understand the everyday playworld of the child. The authors provide a good narrative of such topics as achievement motivation, goal setting, and independent play.

Shallcross, D. J. *Teaching Creative Behavior: How to Teach Creativity to Children of All Ages.* Englewood Cliffs, N.J.: Prentice-Hall, 1981. A good, practical discussion of what adults can do to encourage originality and spontaneity in children.

Singer, J., and Switzer, E. *Mind Play: The Creative Uses of Fantasy.* Englewood Cliffs, N.J.: Prentice-Hall, 1980. Jerome Singer is one of the leading researchers in the field of make-believe play. The book is delightful reading and covers a wide assortment of topics, from creative daydreaming to enriching your life through imagination.

Strom, R. D., ed. *Growing through Play: Readings for Parents and Teachers.* Monterey, Calif.: Brooks/Cole, 1981. A collection of 30 articles on many diversified aspects of play. Topics include the play of exceptional children, playground planning, advantages of solitary play, and the observation of play.

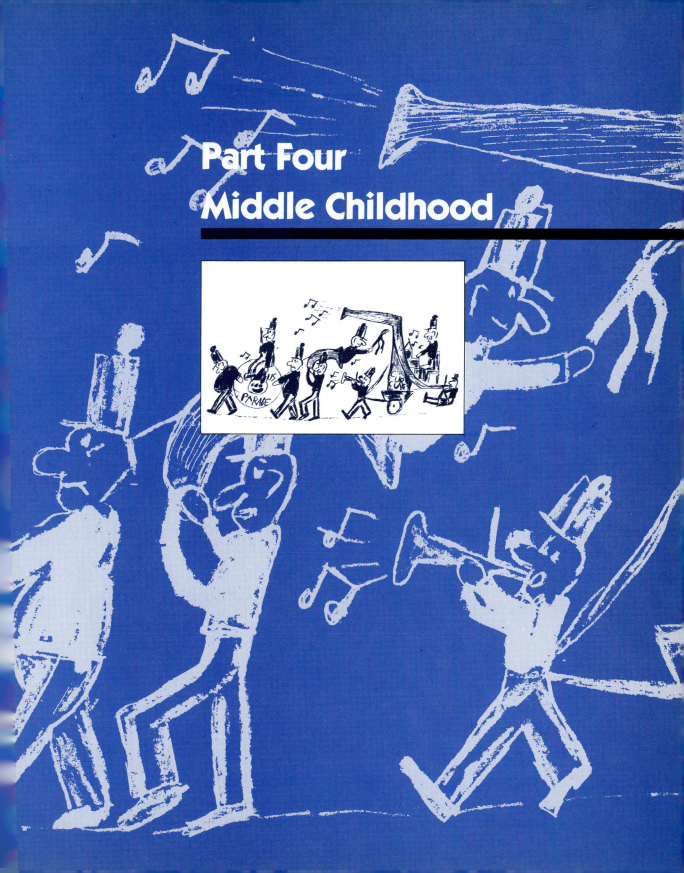

Part Four
Middle Childhood

Chapter Fourteen

Physical Growth and Development

I 'spect I growed. Don't think nobody never made me.

Harriet Beecher Stowe, *Uncle Tom's Cabin*

Introduction

On the whole, physical developments during middle childhood are slow but steady. As a result, year-to-year changes in size and proportion are less noticeable than the pronounced developments of the preschooler or toddler. This gradual physical change persists until the adolescent growth spurt.

Because bodily changes are less marked and physical size increases slowly, children gain control of and perfect motor skills they have been unable to master in the past. As a result, overall coordination, balance, and refinement in physical activities show an increase at this time. Such accomplishments affect children's physical and psychological self-concepts, not to mention their degree of acceptance into the peer culture.

Height and Weight Gains

Boys are taller than girls between the ages of 6 and 8; by age 9, differences in height are negligible; and past age 9, the average girl is taller than the average boy. This trend will persist until the adolescent growth spurt, when males catch up and then surpass females in height. On the average, children will add about 2½ inches to their height each year. By age 12, children have usually attained approximately 90 percent of their adult height.

Although girls weigh less than boys at birth, they are equal by age 8. By age 9, girls surpass boys in weight. As with height, however, males surpass females in weight during the adolescent growth spurt. During middle childhood, youngsters typically add approximately 5 pounds to their weight each year. By age 12, the average child weighs 80 pounds.

Remember that wide variations can exist in overall rates of physical growth and development. This becomes especially apparent when we look at the wide range of height and weight differences among elementary school children. Charts, tables, and other forms of normative data describing the growth of the "average" child must not be overused. While normative data are useful for comparisons, each child's growth pattern is unique. This is as true during middle childhood as it is during other stages of growth. Gains in height and weight can be affected by numerous variables, including nutrition, hereditary influences, endocrine balance, health care, exercise, and socioeconomic status. The progress of individuals should be charted in relation to their own rates of growth, not purely against the mass data available in the developmental tables.

The Secular Trend: Are Children Getting Taller and Heavier?

In the more prosperous parts of the world, children are reaching physical maturity at an earlier age, primarily because of improved nutrition and better health care. This means that children are taller and heavier than they were in the past and are entering puberty earlier.

This phenomenon is called a **secular trend,** and such a trend has been documented in America as well as all European countries (see

Figure 14.1 Earlier maturation rates have caused increased height gains in children over the years (from *Earlier Maturation in Man* by J. M. Tanner. Copyright © 1968 by Scientific American, Inc. All rights reserved.

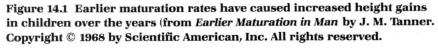
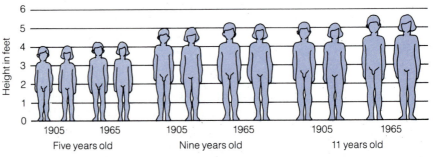

Tanner, 1968; 1978; 1981; Garn, 1981). For example, an analysis of children from Europe as well as the United States shows that in 1965 5-year-olds from average socioeconomic families were, as a rule, 2 inches taller than children of the same age in 1915; 9-year-olds were 3 inches taller; and 11-year-olds were 4 inches taller (see Figure 14.1). Similarly, the heights and weights of Canadian children in the 1950s were greater than those of children of the same age in 1946 (Tanner, 1968; Binning, 1958).

Does this mean that children will continue to become taller and heavier in the future? Apparently not, at least in more industrialized and prosperous countries where the trend seems to have gradually ceased. In more advanced nations, children are already receiving the care and treatment of which their predecessors were deprived. However, for youngsters from underprivileged nations or poorer sections of the community, the secular trend is likely to continue.

Changes in Proportion and Appearance

Despite the slow and gradual nature of physical change during middle childhood, this is a time when most youngsters lose the baby contours characterizing earlier years (see Figure 14.2). This change in physical

Figure 14.2 Changes in body proportions from infancy through adolescence. Note the changing physical appearance of the middle childhood youngster compared to other life stages.

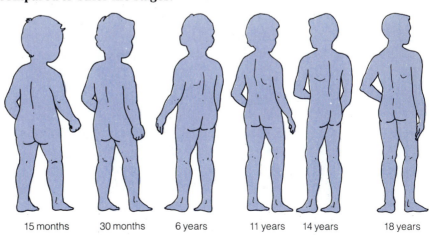

15 months   30 months   6 years   11 years   14 years   18 years

appearance, readers will recall, began during the preschool years. Generally speaking, rounded and chubby physiques give way to leaner overall appearances as fat layers decrease in thickness and change in overall distribution.

By age 6, the trunk is almost twice as long and twice as wide as it was at birth. As the chest broadens and flattens, the ribs shift from a horizontal position to a more oblique one. Contributing to the leaner appearance is a rapid growth spurt of the arms and legs. Throughout middle childhood, there are no marked sex differences in body proportions.

The facial structure also undergoes change during middle childhood. For example, the forehead tends to flatten and the nose grows. As permanent teeth replace baby or **deciduous teeth,** the jaw lengthens and becomes more prominent and the face enlarges overall. The first tooth is usually lost sometime during the sixth year, giving rise to the characteristic toothless grin of middle childhood. Girls generally lose their baby teeth earlier than boys. By age 11 or 12, both boys and girls have their permanent teeth rooted, with the exception of the second and third molars.

Muscular, Skeletal, and Organ Development

Muscle Growth

Throughout middle childhood boys have considerably more muscle tissue than girls, and girls have more fat than boys. Muscle growth tends to be extremely rapid; the muscle changes not only in composition but also becomes more firmly attached to the bones. Despite these advances, the muscles remain immature in function at times, as reflected in children's frequent awkwardness and inefficiency in movement, erratic changes in tempo, inability to sit still for long, and fatigability. Developing muscles are also more susceptible to injury from overuse (consider the large numbers of young baseball players suffering from "Little League elbow"). The fitness and development of the muscles depends not only on good physical care, rest, and activity, but also on their structure and the use made of them. Proper muscle and nerve development provides increasing steadiness of movement, speed, strength, and endurance.

Skeletal Growth

The skeleton continues to produce its centers of **ossification** (points at which ossification begins in a bone). Earlier, the child's bones were soft

Skeletal Development

The skeletal system progresses through a series of changes as it approaches mature size and form. Since the skeleton takes a long time to reach full maturity, it has characteristics that provide excellent examples of growth stages. At birth, for example, the skeleton lacks carpal, or wrist, bones and epiphyses, or centers of ossification at the ends of the bones. Whereas the primary centers of ossification are located in the shafts of the bones, or diaphyses, the epiphyses will produce smaller bones at the ends of the long ones. This can be seen in the X ray of the 2-year-old. Growth of the long bones terminates when the epiphyses and diaphyses unite. As one can see, this bone fusion is generally completed by age 18. When we speak of an individual's skeletal maturity, then, we are referring to the progress toward union of the epiphyses with the shaft of the bone.

(Reproduced from Greulich and Pyle, *Radiographic Atlas of Skeletal Development of the Hand and Wrist*, 2nd ed., Stanford, Calif., Stanford University Press, 1959.)

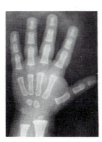
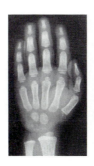
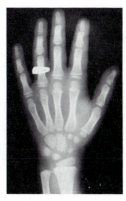
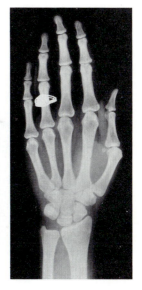

and spongy, consisting mostly of cartilage, but now minerals, particularly calcium and phosphorus, give hardness and rigidity to the bones. This process of bone development continues until the individual's twenties. The growth of the skeleton is frequently more rapid than the growth of muscles and ligaments. As a result, loose-jointed and gangling postures are not uncommon in middle childhood. Growth spurts are frequently accompanied by muscle aches. For many children, these "growing pains" are a very real phenomenon, caused by their developing muscles' attempts to catch up with their increased skeletal size.

Circulatory System

The **circulatory system** grows at a slow pace, although by the school years, the weight of the heart has increased to approximately five times its birth weight. The heart is now smaller in proportion to body size than at any other point in the person's life. The heart rate, relatively high during the early years, declines gradually during the middle years, and the blood pressure rises. The average pulse rate is from 85 to 100 per minute, the blood pressure 95 to 108 systolic and 62 to 67 diastolic.* The heart continues to grow until the end of the teenage years.

Nervous System

The brain nears its mature size and weight during the years of middle childhood. Accompanying these increases in size and weight is an increase in head circumference. The average circumference grows from 20½ to 21 inches between the ages of 6 and 12. The spinal cord has quadrupled in weight by age 5 and will have increased eightfold by the end of the teenage years.

Respiratory System

The **respiratory system** also grows and changes. The weight of the lungs has doubled by 6 months, tripled by 1 year, and increased almost ten times by the end of middle childhood. Rates of respiration decrease, shifting from 20 to 30 inhalations per minute during the preschool years to approximately 17 to 22 in middle childhood. In general, breathing becomes slower and deeper as the respiratory system works more economically and shows greater elasticity.

Digestive System

The maturation of the **digestive system** is reflected in fewer upset stomachs at this age and the youngster's ability to digest a wider range of foods. In general, the body's activities of secretion, digestion, absorp-

---

*Systolic and diastolic are terms used to designate blood pressure. Systolic pressure is the maximum pressure caused by the heart's contractions. Systolic pressure is compared to diastolic pressure, or the minimum pressure, which occurs when the heart muscle contraction relaxes. A healthy adult's blood pressure will be between 100 and 120 systolic and 60 to 80 diastolic.

tion, and excretion become more finely regulated. The school-age child can also retain foods for longer periods of time (which means that meals do not have to be served as often or as promptly), and calorie needs are not as great in relation to stomach size as they once were. Nutritional considerations are very important at this time since children need adequate protein and vitamins and not the "empty calories" offered in sweets, soft drinks, starches, and the like.

Motor Skill Development

Driven by the Eriksonian desire to establish initiative and industry, the school-age child is eager to participate in a diversity of both gross and fine motor skills. The success that a child experiences in motor skill activities depends on a number of factors, however, including rates of physical maturity, the cognitive skills needed to master the task, environmental opportunities to engage in physical activity, and degree of self-confidence. We must remember that children are still in the process of refining coordination abilities and mastering grace of movement. Improvement is gradual, and clumsiness and awkwardness can still be expected. The degree to which a motor skill is mastered may affect the child's sense of competence, achievement, and peer acceptance. Thus, beyond the physical dimensions of motor skills are implications for cognitive, personality, social, and emotional development.

Gross motor skill achievements are numerous during middle childhood. By age 6 most children can roller-skate, skip rope, and begin to ride a bicycle. By age 7, most have perfected running and jumping skills as well as the basic movements necessary for catching, throwing, and hitting a baseball. The developmental sequence of throwing is displayed in Figure 14.4.

Fine motor skill coordination, while lagging behind gross motor skill development, matures at a gradual and steady pace. As children gain control of their arms, shoulders, wrists, and fingers, they become adept at a wide range of activities. For example, by the end of middle childhood, most youngsters are proficient in such fine motor skills as building models, playing musical instruments, sewing, and creating detailed artwork. Advancements in fine motor skills also have practical, everyday value. Children now have the physical ability to tie their own shoelaces, fasten buttons, and dress themselves. They are more proficient in brushing their teeth, combing their hair, and bathing themselves. The simultaneous use of knife and fork at the dinner table is now possible. Advancements in fine motor skill development also enable elementary

Figure 14.3 The developmental sequence of throwing. Stage 1, the Anterior-Posterior Throw, occurs between age 2 and 3. It is characterized by an immature throw; movements of the arms and body are restricted to the anterior-posterior plane. Stage 2, Horizontal Arm and Body Movement Throwing, occurs roughly during the preschool years. Children learn to plant their feet together, throw with horizontal arm and body movements, and begin to rotate the body. Stage 3, Weight Transfer in Throwing, takes place between age 5 and 6. The child is now able to transfer weight from one foot to the other when throwing. Stage 4, Mature Overhand Throw, occurs usually after age 6. Not only do children transfer their weight, but they also take a step forward with the lead foot and use a fluid overhand motion (from Wickstrom, R.L. *Fundamental Motor Patterns*, 2nd ed. Copyright © 1977 Lea and Febiger Publishing Company, Philadelphia. Reprinted by permission).

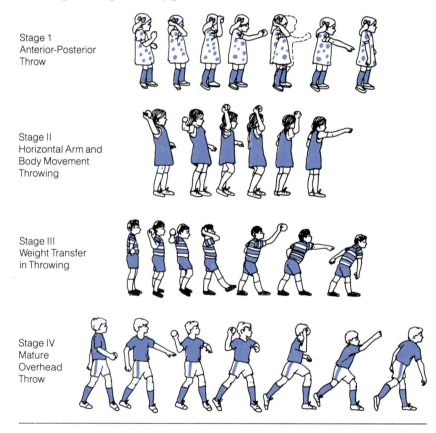

Stage 1
Anterior-Posterior
Throw

Stage II
Horizontal Arm and
Body Movement
Throwing

Stage III
Weight Transfer
in Throwing

Stage IV
Mature
Overhead
Throw

school children to refine their handwriting abilities (Kress, 1982; Williams and Stith, 1980).

The manner in which more-advanced motor skills are mastered has received considerable research attention (see Corbin, 1980; Williams,

Table 14.1 Components of Motor Skill Fitness and Developmental Patterns

Motor Fitness Component	Common Tests	Specific Aspect Measured	Synthesis of Findings
Coordination	Cable jump	Gross body coordination	Year-by-year improvement with age in gross body coordination. Boys superior from age 6 on in hand-eye and foot-eye coordination.
	Hopping for accuracy	Gross body coordination	
	Skipping	Gross body coordination	
	Ball dribble	Hand-eye coordination	
	Foot dribble	Hand-eye coordination	
Balance	Beam walk	Dynamic balance	Year-by-year improvement with age. Girls often outperform boys, especially in dynamic balance activities until about age 8. Abilities similar thereafter.
	Stick balance	Static balance	
	One-foot stand	Static balance	
Speed	20-yd dash	Running speed	Year-by-year improvement with age. Boys and girls similar until age 6 or 7, at which time boys make more rapid improvements. Boys superior to girls at all ages.
	30-yd dash	Running speed	
Agility	Shuttle run	Running agility	Year-by-year improvement with age. Girls begin to level off after age 13. Boys continue to make improvements.
Power	Vertical jump	Leg strength and speed	Year-by-year improvement with age. Boys outperform girls at all age levels.
	Standing long jump	Leg strength and speed	
	Distance throw	Upper arm strength and speed	
	Velocity throw	Upper arm strength and speed	

From *Understanding Motor Development in Children* by David L. Gallahue. Copyright © 1982 by John Wiley & Sons, Inc. Reprinted by permission.

1983; Schmidt, 1982; Ridenour, 1980). Most agree that motor skill mastery entails the ability to refine coordination and develop overall accuracy of response toward the task at hand. This means the gradual elimination of unnecessary movements and expenditures of surplus energy to develop economy of performance. Other researchers, such as David Gallahue [1982(b)], stress other factors behind motor skill development, including agility, balance, speed, and power (see Table 14.1).

As far as sex differences in motor skill development are concerned, boys are usually ahead of girls in such areas as running, jumping, and throwing. Such an edge, though, according to Corbin (1980), must be placed in a proper perspective. The fact that on the average boys have more muscle tissue and greater levels of overall strength gives them an advantage in such comparisons. It must also be realized that in studies in which boys are compared with girls, the outcomes (data) are facts. The question that remains unanswered is whether these factual differences result from genetic variance or from practice, environmental opportunities, "sexism," or other social and cultural factors.

Does Body Build Affect Personality Development?

Throughout childhood, youngsters become increasingly aware of their physical selves. This is accomplished not only by their awareness of the physical developments we have discussed, but also by their increasing efficiency in various motor skills. The degree of comfort with their changing physical appearance as well as their skillful execution of tasks have important implications for children's developing sense of self.

Regular physical activity is important during all of childhood.

Whether body build determines behavior has received research consideration from psychologists. One of the earliest researchers in this area was William Sheldon (1940; 1944), who attempted to classify specific body types and their respective personality characteristics. The result of his research was a three-way scheme for describing conditions found in body physiques (see Figure 14.4). These conditions are referred to as endomorphy, mesomorphy, and ectomorphy. All these conditions, he believed, are present in all of us, although in some individuals one of them may dominate the other two. **Endomorphy** is characterized by a round appearance, the result of large accumulations of fatty tissue. According to Sheldon, the endomorph is typically a happy-go-lucky sort, jovial, placid, and slow moving. **Mesomorphy** is characterized by a solid structure of bone and muscle, the more outstanding features being broad shoulders, strong legs, and an overall athletic appearance. Mesomorphs have a tendency to be aggressive, loud, direct, and action

Figure 14.4 Sheldon's classification of body types.

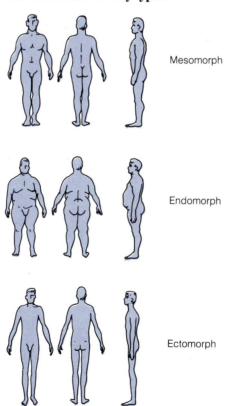

Mesomorph

Endomorph

Ectomorph

oriented. **Ectomorphy** is characterized by thin bones and generally weak muscles. Ectomorphs are usually sensitive and quiet individuals who are frequently shy and restless. It must be mentioned that Sheldon's theory is not as widely accepted today as it once was.

In general, it has been found that children like the mesomorphic body build best and the endomorphic build least. There is a tendency to view mesomorphs as the strongest, best looking, and healthiest when compared with the other builds. Furthermore, such perceptions appear to strengthen with age (Staffieri, 1967; 1972; Morrison et al., 1980; Jarvie et al., 1983).

Children's attitudes toward their developing bodies appear to exert influences on the developing personality. The satisfaction and acceptance individuals have with regard to their bodies may be related to such feelings as inner security or confidence, particularly when facing others in the environment. Being ridiculed or avoided on the basis of one's physical appearance, which often happens to obese children (see Wishon, Bower, and Eller, 1983), may produce considerable uneasiness.

A child's degree of self-acceptance may also be influenced by proficiency in motor skills. A relationship has been found between motor skill success and such behaviors as cooperation and attentiveness and feelings of security (Zion, 1965).

This discussion implies that one's physical development has implications for other spheres of growth. Difficulties may arise for children who feel that they are physically different from others, such as being shorter or taller, skinnier or fatter. Moreover, the inability to perfect a motor skill may promote insecurity, shyness, or feelings of rejection. Such differences may represent a potential threat to the child's social and emotional development and underscore the need for meaningful support and guidance from adults. Acceptance of one's physical self, including strengths as well as weaknesses, is a delicate facet of adjustment that tests the youngster during these important years.

Summary

Rates of physical growth and development during middle childhood are slow but steady. Because of the gradual nature of change, children are able to gain more control of their bodies and perfect those motor skills eluding them during earlier years. As a result, these years represent a time of greater physical coordination, agility, and refinement.

As far as specific physical developments are concerned, 12-year-olds have generally attained about 90 percent of their adult height and weigh approximately 80 pounds. Girls experience a height and weight advan-

Kirk, age 11

tage over boys after age 9, but boys catch up and surpass girls in these developmental areas during the adolescent growth spurt. This chapter stressed the wide individual variations that can exist in such developmental areas as height and weight.

The secular trend suggests that today's children in more prosperous parts of the world are taller and heavier and are reaching physical maturity earlier than their historical counterparts. This trend, documented in America as well as European countries, appears to be the result of improved nutrition and better health care. Once a given nation's nutritional and health standards reach peak levels, however, the secular trend ceases.

Middle childhood is a time when youngsters lose their babylike contours and acquire a leaner overall appearance. This is due primarily to the fact that fat layers decrease in thickness and change in overall distribution. The facial structure also undergoes change, including a general flattening of the forehead, an increase in nose size, and a lengthening of the jaw. By the end of middle childhood, the permanent teeth have replaced the baby (or deciduous) teeth with the exception of the second and third molars.

Muscle growth is rapid at this time. However, the muscles at times remain immature, and their developing quality makes them more susceptible to injury. The development of the muscles depends on good physical care, rest, and activity. The skeletal system also continues to mature, a process that will continue until the individual's twenties. In particular, mineral salts give hardness and rigidity to the bones, a process called ossification. It is not uncommon for skeletal growth to be more rapid than muscle development, causing "growing pains" in some cases.

This chapter examined changes in the circulatory, nervous, respiratory, and digestive systems. The weight of the heart increases five times, the heart rate declines, and the blood pressure rises. The brain nears its mature size and weight, and the spinal cord quadruples in weight. Changes in the respiratory system include a slower and deeper breathing rate. The digestive system's ability to secrete, digest, absorb, and excrete becomes more finely regulated. The child is able to digest a wider range of foods and can retain foods for longer periods of time.

Gross and fine motor skills rapidly accelerate during the elementary school years. Proficiency in motor skills involves other spheres of growth, including cognitive, personality, social, and emotional development. Most experts agree that motor skill mastery hinges on the ability to refine overall coordination and the accuracy of response, not to mention the implementation of agility, balance, speed, and power. While boys are ahead of girls in many facets of motor skill development, such findings must be carefully explored and not generalized. Numerous factors beyond the pure data gathered need to be taken into account, including the superior physical capacities of the male in such testing situations, genetic variance, practice, environmental opportunities, "sexism," or other social and cultural factors.

The sense of a physical self is achieved throughout the course of childhood by the youngster's growing awareness of bodily changes and efficiency in various motor skills. An attempt to classify body physiques and their respective personality characteristics was undertaken by William Sheldon, who devised the system of endomorphic (round), mesomorphic (muscular), and ectomorphic (thin) body builds. Most children prefer the mesomorphic body build. As far as motor skill proficiency is concerned, individuals adept in this area have been found to be self-confident, secure, calm, and cooperative. Acceptance of one's physical self during childhood is an important area of adjustment and may require the assistance of supportive and understanding adults.

Suggested Reading List

Corbin, C. B. *A Textbook of Motor Development.* 2nd ed. Dubuque, Iowa: William C. Brown, 1980. An abundance of useful charts, tables, and developmental norms combined with a readable description of motor skill development.

Gallahue, D. L. *Understanding Motor Development in Children.* New York: Wiley, 1982. Gallahue covers many aspects of motor skill development, including motor fitness and the skills needed for team sports.

Lowrey, G. H. *Growth and Development of Children.* 7th ed. Chicago: Year Book Medical Publishers, 1978. Chapters of particular significance deal with the role of nutrition in normal growth, skeletal and organ development, and energy metabolism.

Williams, J., and Stith, M. *Middle Childhood.* 2nd ed. New York: Macmillan, 1980. The authors provide good coverage of virtually all facets of change in this interesting description of middle childhood.

Chapter Fifteen

Cognition, Perception, and Psycholinguistics

Childhood is the sleep of reason.

Rousseau

Introduction

As we have seen, the human mind continually organizes and classifies information to deal with it more effectively. By middle childhood, youngsters are able to reason about many new and challenging situations and express themselves with heightened levels of linguistic proficiency. The content of school learning coupled with mental development enables them to experience many new accomplishments and achievements.

School-age children are clearly better able than younger children to reason about the world in general. Words and symbols, for example, acquire new meaning and become increasingly important to mental processes. The school-age child will gradually learn to deal with many variables simultaneously in deliberate and systematic problem-solving situations, such as the manipulation of speed and distance variables to solve mathematical problems. This systematic ability to understand and manipulate multiple variables or dimensions of the environment is considered an important cornerstone of intellectual functioning (Case, 1980; Paris and Lindauer, 1982).

There are certain cognitive limitations during middle childhood, though. While school-age children become generally more systematic and objective and possess keener judgment than their younger counterparts, abstract concepts remain elusive. This is especially evident when such concepts are completely outside the youngster's experience or cannot be grasped by analogy. We must also recognize that the cognitive accomplishments of middle childhood are only emerging and may not develop evenly in all content areas. There are also significant differences in cognitive functioning between younger and older school-age children. While general comments can be made about the nature of cognitive growth (and other facets of development) during middle childhood, we can't forget that wide differences exist between the 6-year-olds and 12-year-olds (Feldman, 1980).

Our analysis of mental growth during middle childhood will follow the structure of earlier chapters. First, we'll examine Jean Piaget's theory of cognitive development, more specifically the intuitive and concrete stages. Then we'll continue with our observations of concept development and the implications concepts have for overall cognitive functioning. The development of problem-solving abilities and the nature of cognitive styles will then be examined. The final facet of this discussion will concern itself with the school-age child's growth in linguistic abilities.

Piaget's Theory of Cognitive Development

Intuitive Thought

Intuitive thought is the third stage in Jean Piaget's cognitive development theory and occurs between the ages of 4 and 7. Coupled with preconceptual thought (2 to 4 years), it is a substage of the lengthier preoperational thought stage, which bridges ages 2 through 7.

Intuitive thought bears its title because it is characterized by immediate perceptions and experiences, rather than by deliberate and methodical thought. The egocentrism of the preschool child tends to change because of the cognitive advances at this time. The mental structures that emerge at each stage of development free children from a lower form of egocentrism but trap them in a higher form of the same style of thinking. The form found at this stage is an egocentrism of symbols and the objects they represent.

Centering   A distinctive trait of intuitive thinking is **centering,** the tendency to concentrate on a single outstanding characteristic of an object while excluding its other features. Reasoning may be distorted by this selective attention. For example, if presented with two identical glasses of a liquid, a child would agree that each contained the same amount. But, if the liquid were presented in containers of a different shape or size, the child would deny that each contained the same amount. Children's preoccupation with the outstanding perceptual feature of the problem (the different appearances of the liquids) causes them to overlook more important characteristics (the shape and size of the two containers). Thus, their cognitive activity is dominated by limited perceptual inspection rather than evaluation and exploration of all aspects of the stimulus (Wadsworth, 1984; Furth, 1981).

Transductive Reasoning   Up to and often including the intuitive thought stage, children may employ neither **inductive** (particular to the general) nor **deductive** (general to the particular), but **transductive reasoning,** which means that they tend to reason from particular to particular without seeking a generalization common to both. Sometimes, this type of reasoning may be correct, as in the statement, "Mommy's got her hair up in curlers; she must be going out with Daddy tonight," but often it is based on some functional property that merely links objects or events, as in the remark, "I haven't had my nap, so it isn't afternoon."

Transductive reasoning is a good illustration of the cognitive limitations present during this stage, particularly the youngster's intuitive tendencies to perceive the world. Rather than examining events in a systematical fashion, children often seek to make statements of implication, even though no relationship exists between events.

Transformational Reasoning   In **transformational reasoning** an individual observing an event having a sequence of change can appreciate how one state transforms itself into another. To illustrate, consider the following. If asked to draw the successive movements of a pencil falling from an upright position to a final horizontal state, the sequence of change would be very obvious to us, and we would most likely draw something resembling Figure 15.1.

Figure 15.1 The falling pencil problem. Transformational reasoning enables the individual to draw the successive movements of a falling pencil in a fashion similar to this.

When asked to observe the pencil falling and then depict the sequence of change, children within the intuitive thought stage encounter difficulty. Rather than understanding the concept of total change, they restrict their attention to each successive state as it occurs. This cognitive limitation prevents them from grasping the concept of succession or chronology. As a result, most can depict only the initial and final positions of the pencil. Related to our previous discussion, this also means that thought is also transductive. In other words, children reason from particular to particular without seeking the generalization common to both.

Reversibility   An important limitation in children's reasoning during intuitive thought is the inability to reverse mental operations. **Reversibility** is the capacity to trace one's line of reasoning back to its origin. It is regarded by Piaget (1963) as a crucial feature of mature cognition.

The inability of youngsters to reverse mental operations is clearly illustrated in the following experiment. A preoperational child is presented with three colored wooden beads strung on a wire, as illustrated in Figure 15.2. The beads are then placed inside a tube, which obstructs the child's view. After they are hidden, the child is asked which color bead will be the first to emerge through the opposite end (A). Even preschool children have little or no difficulty in solving this portion of the problem.

However, when the beads are pushed back into the tubing so that they emerge from the same end they entered (B), children are quite unable to predict the order in which they will reappear. Furthermore, if the entire device is turned 180° (C), and the subjects are asked to state in which order the beads will emerge in either direction, utter confusion results. One child remarked that since one color came out first in the first trial and another color appeared in the second, it was the third color's turn to come out first. According to Piaget (1967), the conceptual ability to predict object reversal correctly will not fully develop until later in the school years.

Figure 15.2 A wooden-bead reversibility problem of the sort employed by Piaget.

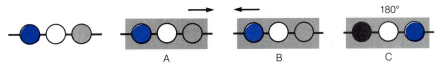

Concrete Operations

The fourth stage of Piaget's cognitive development theory is labeled concrete operations. **Concrete operations** occurs between the ages of 7 and 11 and heralds a new level of awareness and understanding. At this time children begin to think and reason logically about their environment and perform actions mentally that previously had to be carried out in actuality. It is a time when cognition can be used on a consistent level. Children in this stage do not understand certain things, but they no longer give the impression of understanding something and moments later reveal total ignorance.

The challenges of the elementary school will stimulate the child's overall cognition. School activities such as mathematics, including manipulating, sorting, and counting, will nurture such cognitive skills as reversibility, seriation, and conservation. Science projects will gradually introduce the child to the methodical and systematic procedures for gathering facts. Expanding social horizons in general will further enable children to appreciate the viewpoints, sensitivities, and opinions of others (Castaneda, Gibb, and McDermit, 1982; Jacobson and Bergman, 1980; Walsh, 1980).

Yet while cognitive functioning soars to new heights during the concrete operations stage, children are not yet prepared to deal with **abstractions.** Thinking is bound to the immediate and physical, as indicated by the name of this stage. Children cannot analyze their own thoughts or think about problems in the future. They can reason about what is, but they cannot construct what may be.

Conservation   The logical operations of the child are evident in the classic Piagetian conservation experiment. **Conservation** means that the amount or quantity of a matter remains the same despite changes made in its outward, physical appearance. In other words, even though the distribution of matter changes, it nonetheless conserves its properties.

Younger children are confused by the fact that the same matter can have different appearances, as in the problems posed by the same amount of liquid occupying different levels in dissimilar containers. This is due not only to centering but also to lack of understanding that matter can change in one outward dimension without changing in other dimensions.

By the concrete operations stage, children can understand that matter remains the same despite changes made in outward appearances. Children have learned not only to **decenter,** but also to reverse their mental operations. This means that children understand that matter can have its original condition restored after changes have been made in its appearance. Most children would agree that two balls of clay are the same size when they have similar shapes; however, if one ball were flattened, the young child would reason that the flattened ball contained more clay because of its longer appearance, or that the round ball had more clay because it was fatter. The older child can reason that the flattened ball of clay can be remodeled into the original ball and that liquid poured back into its original container will regain its original level. They know that matter has been conserved despite trans-formations and do not need to check it by repeating the operation.

How children learn to conserve has been a hotbed for research activity. In fact, since the 1960s there have been more than 200 articles on some facet of conservation (Siegler, 1983). Among other things these studies have revealed that children's understanding of different types of conservation, such as conservation of liquid or mass, does not occur at the same time. This means that children may have grasped number conservation but not conservation of weight or volume (Pinard, 1981). Table 15.1 illustrates the various types of conservation that exist and the approximate ages at which they are grasped by the child.

Classification   Concrete operations is a time when children are able to understand the concepts of subclasses, classes, and class inclusion.

This intuitive-level child demonstrates a lack of understanding of the principles of conservation.

Table 15.1 Judging the Levels of the Child's Response on Piagetian Conservation Tasks

Conservation Tasks	Approximate Age Reached	Establish Equivalence	Transform or Rearrange	Conservation Question and Justification
Conservation of number: Number is not changed despite rearrangement of objects.	6–8		Change shape of one string	Will an ant have just as far to walk, or…?
Conservation of length: The length of a string is unaffected by its shape or its displacement.	6–8		Rearrange one set	Are there the same number of red & green chips or…?
Conservation of liquid amount: The amount of liquid is not changed by the shape of the container.	6½–8½		Transfer liquid	Do the glasses have the same amount of water, or…?
Conservation of substance (solid amount): The amount of substance does not change by changing its shape or by subdividing it.	7–9		Roll out one clay ball	Do you still have the same amount of clay?
Conservation of area: The area covered by a given number of two-dimensional objects is unaffected by their arrangements.	8–10	Grass / Garden	Rearrange one set of triangles	Is there still the same amount of "room" for planting or…? / Is there still the same amount of grass to eat or…?
Conservation of weight: A clay ball weighs the same even when its shape is elongated or flattened.	9–11		Change shape of one ball	Do the balls of clay still weigh the same or…?
Conservation of displacement volume: The volume of water that is displaced by an object depends on the volume of the object and is independent of weight, shape, or position of the immersed object.	11–14		Change shape of one ball	Will the water go up as high or…?

(Adapted from Labinowicz, 1980.)

Demonstrating the Principle of Conservation

Piaget's research studies investigating conservation abilities are relatively easy experiments to duplicate. To observe the developmental stages through which this principle is attained, it is necessary to test children between the ages of 6 and 10.

For conservation of substance, begin by showing the child two identical balls of clay, asking if the two contain identical amounts. (The best way to ask this is "Does this one have more, or does this one have more, or do they both have the same?") If the child says they do contain the same amount, roll one of the balls into the shape of a sausage and ask if they still contain the same amount. According to Piaget, children under 6 are most likely to respond that the amounts of clay now differ, reasoning that because the sausage shape occupies more space, it must therefore contain more clay. (You might employ some even younger subjects and record their reactions for comparison purposes.) Between ages 7 and 9 the typical response is that each still contains the same amount, an indication that the law of conservation has been grasped.

Once you have tested for conservation of substance, consider examining for conservation of liquid. Start with two identical glasses, and pour an equal amount of liquid into both. Do they appear the same to your subjects? If so, change the size or shape of one of the containers and fill them again. Are your subjects fooled by the appearance (level) of the liquid? Have they failed to decenter? Between ages 6½ and 8½, this facet of conservation should be mastered, although individual differences must be considered.

Do your subjects follow the prescribed sequence of conservation described in this chapter? If some of your subjects have mastered liquid but not substance conservation, why do you think this is so? Does "coaching" your younger subjects affect the outcome of your experiment? Questions like these illustrate some of the many dimensions of conservation and why this facet of children's thinking has attracted the attention of child developmentalists for years. ■

Earlier, these concepts created considerable confusion (see Chapter 7). When presented with four red checkers and two black checkers and asked whether there were more red or more plastic checkers, young children are confused. Unlike the younger children, however, school-age youngsters realize that three classes of checkers exist—red, black, and plastic—and that one element can belong to two classes at once. Therefore, since all the checkers are plastic, there are more plastic checkers because there are six checkers and only four are red. Such an awareness is an important dimension of cognition because it facilitates proper organization and classification skills. Moreover, it relinquishes children from a solitary, perceptual point of view (Winer, 1980; McCabe et al., 1982; Cameron and Goard, 1982).

Seriation   **Seriation** is the ability to order objects according to size. This is yet another concept that eludes younger children but is understood by those within the stage of concrete operations. To test seriation, children are typically given sticks of varying lengths and asked to arrange them from smallest to largest.

Prior to concrete operations, children have not grasped the true notion of a series. For example, 5- and 7-year-olds align the tops of the sticks but pay no attention to the bottoms. Their understanding of more than one relationship is obviously limited, and they are often driven by intuition and trial-and-error behavior. Older children, though, order the sticks without having to resort to trial-and-error behavior. They are deliberate and methodical, employing such strategies as searching for the smallest stick, then the next smallest, and so on. They understand the task before they begin and can mentally order the series for successful construction (Wadsworth, 1984; Gallagher and Reid, 1981). Figure 15.3 illustrates the manner in which children attempt to seriate.

Rules of Logic   Thinking during concrete operations is flavored by **logic** and reason, but only when applied to the physical world. Mental operations enable the child to understand the following rules:

Closure: Any two mental structures (also called elements or operations) can combine to form a third structure (for example, $3 + 4 = 7$).

Reversibility: For any structure, there exists an opposite operation that cancels it (for example, $3 + 4 = 7$, but $7 - 4 = 3$).

Associativity: When multiple structures are combined, it does not matter what the order of combination is (for example, $3 + 4 + 7$ is the same as $4 + 7 + 3$).

Identity: Certain actions leave the structure unchanged (for example, $4 + 0 = 4$).

While the above rules of logic appear to extend only to mathematical operations, they also have other applications. For example, we saw earlier how reversibility is an important dimension in solving conservation tasks. That is, the level of a liquid will change when it is poured into a different-size glass, but we can restore the first level by pouring it back into the original container. Associativity is an important consideration in understanding classes and subclasses. The child will learn that the order in which the subclasses are combined will not affect the outcome of the overall class. Identity is applied in conservation tasks. Children who have grasped the notion of identity and the broader concept of conservation know that the outward appearance of a matter can be altered but the properties remain the same.

Figure 15.3 The development of seriation (adapted from Wadsworth, 1984).

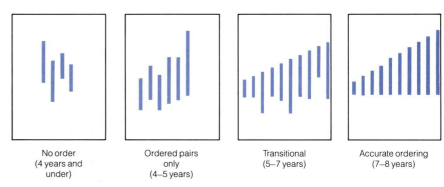

| No order (4 years and under) | Ordered pairs only (4–5 years) | Transitional (5–7 years) | Accurate ordering (7–8 years) |

Number Conservation and Counting Abilities   How proud we are when children learn to count. Rightfully so, since early training paves the way for more detailed and complex numerical challenges. Yet during the early going we must realize that even though children know the names of numbers, this does not mean they have grasped a true number concept. The understanding of numbers is a gradual process [Kamii, 1981(b); 1982; Ginsburg, 1982].

True number concepts involve more than the memorization of a label; they involve understanding what a number truly represents, which implies knowing that the number of objects in a group remains the same, or is conserved, no matter how the objects have been arranged. When such an understanding is reached during concrete operations, children have taken a significant step forward in cognitive development. Judgment is now based on reason rather than perception. Piaget takes particular delight in recounting the story of a young boy's discovery of number conservation (1964, p. 12):

> He was seated on the ground in his garden and he was counting pebbles. Now to count these pebbles, he put them in a row and he counted them, one, two, three and up to ten. Then he finished counting them and started to count them in the other direction. He began by the end and once again found he had ten. He found this marvelous. . . . So he put them in a circle and counted them that way and found ten once again.

It is not surprising that before attaining the concept of number conservation during concrete operations, young children may be able to count without knowing what numbers actually stand for.

Figure 15.4 Books for children often seek to teach the conceptual properties of numbers in innovative fashions.

Teaching the conceptual properties of numbers and mathematics as a whole to the young child has generated a flurry of educational strategies (see Burton, 1984; May, 1982; Benham et al., 1982; Castaneda et al., 1982; Cruishank, Fitzgerald, and Jensen, 1980). See Figure 15.4 for an example. Educational games and educational television also seek to teach number concepts in innovative fashions. Such teaching strategies help youngsters move beyond the **rote learning** of numbers. Moreover, it appears to promote a state of readiness for more advanced mathematical challenges.

Concept Development

Concepts become increasingly refined and detailed during middle childhood. As the children's environment expands, concepts will link objects or events with common properties. As a result, children's surroundings acquire an organized and meaningful quality and are no longer an assortment of unrelated and confusing experiences. This prompts many developmentalists to regard concepts as critical and essential features of cognition (see Wessells, 1982; Smith and Medin, 1981; Houston, 1981; Matlin, 1983).

Concept development continues to be greatly enhanced by the maturation of perceptual abilities. Attention and attending skills steadily improve. School-age youngsters pay more attention than pre-schoolers to environmental events and are better able to focus on the critical features of a situation. In other words, they can concentrate on needed information and ignore irrelevant information. They also know that attention is affected by numerous variables, including one's motivation and external distractions [Miller and Weiss, 1981(b); Miller and Zalenski, 1982].

Perception also becomes more economical. That is, youngsters learn to detect the characteristics that distinguish one object from another. Children also learn to understand why certain features of objects remain constant. Like the subjects in Piaget's study of the law of conservation, older children become economical in their perceptions when they realize that different shapes contain the same amount of matter and that the same quantity of liquid may be carried in different-sized containers.

Size and Shape Concepts

Children's ability to understand size and shape concepts and how they relate to the environment rapidly increases. Perceptions such as the identification of middle size, size in relation to distance, or recognition of certain forms in changed or strange surroundings greatly improves. As far as the latter is concerned, children can now detect shapes with ambiguous or illusory contours (Abravanel, 1982). Such perceptual advancements indicate that children are more selective and specific in their overall interpretation of the environment. The perceptual constancy earlier established also enables individuals to see sizes and shapes as unchanging, even though the distance and angle from which they are viewed change (Goldstein, 1980).

Spatial Concepts

Older children can also recognize that objects in the environment occupy certain spatial positions and have relationships with other objects. By middle childhood youngsters begin to indicate some comprehension of perspective. However, because of lingering egocentrism, they may make mistakes about how an object might look under different viewing conditions, as Piaget illustrated in a unique experiment. Three models of mountains were put on top of a table, and a doll was alter-

Figure 15.5 Model mountains observed by children from different viewpoints to test their egocentric concepts (adapted from J. Piaget and B. Inhelder, *The Child's Conception of Space.* London: Routledge & Kegan Paul Ltd, 1948. Copyright © 1948, Routledge & Kegan Paul Ltd. Reprinted by permission of the publishers).

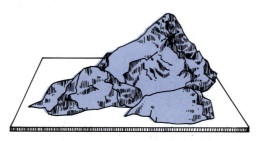

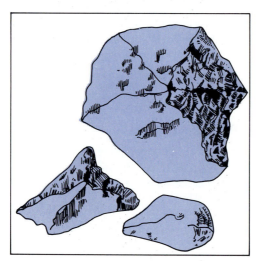

nately placed on different sides of the same table (see Figure 15.5). Children were asked to select the cutouts or pictures that showed how the doll viewed the mountain from its various angles. Until approximately age 7, children were unable to understand that the mountains could look different from different viewpoints; the children's spatial concepts were limited to their own egocentric visual perspective (Piaget and Inhelder, 1956).

Relational Concepts

Reasoning about relations such as left or right also emerges during middle childhood. This type of concept creates considerable confusion among younger children. Suppose a preschooler was sitting opposite you and you asked her to raise her right hand and then her left. Chances are, this could be accomplished without difficulty. Trouble would begin, though, if you asked her to point to *your* right and left hands. Like most children her age, she would most likely point to the hands opposite her own. In other words, she would label your right hand "left" because it's opposite her own left hand.

By the middle years, however, children attain a relational conception of right and left and are able to distinguish between their own right and left arms and those of individuals standing opposite them. It is often maintained that the perception of left-right is harder to learn than other relational orientations, such as up-down or front-back. Adults may be reminded of the confusing quality of this concept when they are placed in situations requiring a relational orientation. For example, teaching children how to tie their shoes or knot a necktie is difficult for many of us, especially when standing opposite the youngster.

Quantity Concepts

Children's understanding of quantity exhibits marked gains during the school years. They begin to understand and manipulate numbers and recognize parts, wholes, and units. Most children of this age grasp the durability of numbers and are not harnessed to a mere functional and nonverbal understanding of them.

As a result of such heightened levels of awareness, children acquire quantity concepts rapidly. By age 8, most children can add, subtract, multiply, divide, and deal with simple fractions. These number concepts can also be applied to a wide range of measurement situations, such as weight, length, area, and volume.

Related to the child's growing awareness of numbers is an understanding of money. While a 5-year-old's understanding of money is restricted to the identification of pennies, nickels, and dimes, school-age children realize the value and worth of coins and understand complex money combinations. Moreover, they seem to have an understanding of "indeterminate" money concepts, such as a "few" dollars, "several" coins, or "some" money.

Time Concepts

Time concepts develop gradually. Clock time is mastered during the early school years, as are the days of the week, months of the year, and seasons. During middle childhood youngsters develop the capacity to reflect on what they did yesterday and anticipate what they're going to do tomorrow. Some time concepts remain elusive, though, such as years, dates, and the notion of historical chronology as a whole. These concepts will not be truly understood until late childhood.

The Concept of Death

One of the more difficult concepts for the child to understand is death. For many children, as well as adults, death is a mysterious phenomenon. It is also a situation most youngsters are likely to encounter at some point during childhood. Rare is the child who has not experienced the death of a pet, neighbor, relative, or friend.

Children's understanding of death reflects developing cognitive awareness. During infancy and toddlerhood they show little understanding, but by the preschool years, ideas about death become more numerous and detailed, and death-related thoughts and experiences show up in songs, play, and questions. Many preschool children conceive of death as partial, reversible, and avoidable, and because of their egocentricity, many view themselves as living forever (DeSpelder and Strickland, 1983; Lonetto, 1980).

During middle childhood, more information is acquired about death, but the new ideas are often applied illogically. For example, school-age children often reason that death happens only to the elderly. They want to know about death's physical qualities, including what happens to the body and the nature of death-related illnesses. This preoccupation with death's physical qualities parallels the concrete quality evident in other cognitive spheres. By later childhood most youngsters have developed the notion that all people die, including themselves (Kübler-Ross, 1983; Stillion and Wass, 1980).

Children's developing awareness of death is greatly influenced by adults. How adults handle the topic is critical. Experts in the field recommend gradually introducing the youngster to the topic throughout childhood rather than initiating discussions after a death strikes close to home. Explanations should take the youngster's cognitive and emotional states into consideration (E. Furman, 1982; Wass and Corr, 1982; Knowles and Reeves, 1983; Lonetto, 1980).

In the final analysis, adults can do much to help children develop healthy attitudes toward death. Children need to learn that death is an expected part of the life cycle, not an unrelated occurrence. Seeking to comprehend death, rather than denying or repressing it, adds an important dimension to one's life. If this is done, the young may learn to live their lives with full appreciation of their finiteness and of the limits on their time here (Kübler-Ross, 1983; Shneidman, 1985; Kastenbaum, 1981).

Development of Problem-Solving Abilities

The successful application of cognitive facilities to problems is one of the distinguishing features of the mature mind. Problem-solving abilities improve with age and in time become more systematic and sequential. This methodical approach entails (1) definition of the nature of the problem and the solution sought, (2) development of a strategy or set of strategies to reach the solution, (3) implementation of the decided course of action and application of internal and external resources, and (4) monitoring and evaluation of the progress made toward the solution (Wessells, 1982; Hayes, 1981).

There are a number of reasons for children's overall improvement in problem-solving abilities, including the cognitive advancements described in this chapter and the curriculum challenges of the elementary school. Problem-solving abilities are also enhanced by the child's work habits in general. As children grow older, most develop not only persistence and concentration but also independence in working on problems [Stipek, 1983; Fisher et al., 1980; Miller and Weiss, 1981(a); Eisner, 1982].

Advancements in problem-solving abilities also reflect developing memory abilities and metacognition as a whole. Readers will recall (Chapter 7) that metacognition refers to the application of some cognitive process to a selected cognitive task. Children become more adept at organizing, searching for, and retrieving the information that has been encoded or placed in memory storage. Also developing are metacognitive skills designed to encourage **retention** and **retrieval,** sometimes called "metamemory" skills. Examples of these skills are rehearsal and **elaboration,** the technique of expanding verbal or visual material to increase the number of ways it can be retrieved. Other noteworthy metacognitive advancements include the growing ability to see one's efforts as the primary cause of the problem's outcome as well as to judge how well one is actually performing in solving a given problem (Kail and Hagen, 1982; Pressley, 1982; Stipek and Weisz, 1981; Saxe and Sicilian, 1981).

It might also be pointed out that competence and proficiency in problem solving are influenced by the youngster's intrinsic motivation. **Intrinsic motivation** means that the child undertakes an activity such as problem solving for the rewards or pleasures derived from activity itself. While intrinsic motivation is limited in early childhood, it increases as youngsters grow older. Children learn to enjoy problems or situations that are challenging and responsive to their actions. In their quest for mastery of the environment, children develop an ever-

How to Help Children Become Better Thinkers

There is much that adults can do to foster the growth and development of the youngster's problem-solving skills and thinking abilities during middle childhood. Since intrinsic motivation is an important facet of mental development, children need mental challenges to nurture curiosity, mastery of the environment, and a sense of competence. When working on problems, children also need to learn the merits of a deliberate, methodical approach. Adults should encourage the youngster to reflect on the material at hand and think about the accuracy and quality of answers before they are given (Stipek, 1982).

Adults should also encourage children to develop as much independence as possible in problem-solving situations. They need to be patient with trial-and-error learning. Jumping in and solving the problem for a child may produce the answer but frequently promotes dependency. Moreover, it robs the child of benefiting from a mistake or experimenting with multiple problem-solving approaches. Adult feedback, encouragement, and praise

help to strengthen desired problem-solving strategies, not to mention the motivation to succeed (Deci and Ryan, 1982; Pittman, Boggiano, and Rubble, 1983).

School-age children can also be groomed to question more deeply and analyze the learning material at hand. While children need to acquire the cognitive advancements described in this chapter, they also need to develop genuine thought, not a mindless recitation of facts. In short, children need to learn how to think. According to James Alvino (1983) certain philosophical questions can be directed to children to help them think and rethink ideas. They should also sow the seeds for later analytical reasoning skills. As grown-up as they sound, these questions (which emerged from the Institute of Philosophy for Children, founded by Matthew Lippman of Montclair State College) have been incorporated in the curricula of thousands of elementary school systems.

1. *"Why?"* This requests an explanation of the basis for the youngster's response. ▶

increasing interest in things that can be explored or investigated (Gottfried, 1983; Deci and Ryan, 1980).

Cognitive Styles

There are significant differences and variations in how children evaluate problems. The characteristic ways in which information is organized and solutions to problems are found are referred to as **cognitive style.** Put another way, cognitive style represents the general pattern of behavior that an individual applies to cognitive tasks (Kogan, 1983).

How to Help Children Become Better Thinkers, *continued.*

2. *"If that is so, what follows?"* This requires the child to elaborate, extrapolate, and draw a valid hypothetical or causal inference.

3. *"Aren't you assuming that . . . ?"* This asks the child to explain the premises on which the statement or argument is based.

4. *"How do you know that?"* This calls for more information from the child, for a source of the information given, or for the youngster's explanation of the line of reasoning.

5. *"Is the point you are making that . . . ?"* This question asks the youngster to confirm the adult's comprehension of the main point.

6. *"Can I summarize your point as . . . ?"* This is similar to the previous question but requires the child to confirm the adult's restatement or condensation of the main point.

7. *"Is what you mean to say that . . . ?"* This rephrasing requires children to interpret their own statements and be certain of the meaning.

8. *"What is your reason for saying that?"* This is basically a request for the rationale behind a judgment as well as the justification for it.

9. *"Doesn't what you say presuppose that . . . ?"* This points out assumptions that may be hidden in the child's argument and requests that children defend their assumptions.

10. *"What do you mean when using that word?"* Such a question asks for the precise meanings and contextual use of words.

11. *"Is it possible that . . . ?"* This offers other possibilities and points out possible contradictions and inconsistencies in the child's argument.

12. *"Are there other ways of looking at it?"* This calls for alternative perspectives and an examination of the child's objectivity and impartiality.

13. *"How else can we view this matter?"* This places an emphasis on open-mindedness and mental flexibility. It also gives the child a chance to be creative. ■

Cognitive styles vary from child to child. Some children may examine the minute details of stimulus objects, employing what is referred to as an **analytic style.** Others employ a **superordinate style** and look for shared attributes among objects. A **functional-relational style** means that a group of objects or events are linked because they have some sort of interactional value. Finally, **functional-locational orientation** represents a cognitive style in which classification is based on a shared location (Kogan, 1983; Kagan and Kogan, 1970).

To examine these modes of cognitive style, children between 6 and 11 were presented with a series of pictures in a set (see Figure 15.6) and asked to tell which two of the figures were alike or went together in some way. Older children were more likely to use superordinate or analytic styles. With the superordinate style, for example, the two shirts would be paired in set (b); the analytic style would mean pairing the watch and ruler in set (a) because both are used for measurement. Children aged 4 to 6 tend to classify the pictures with a functional-relational style. For example, pairings are made because the match lights the pipe in set (c) or the man wears the watch in set (a) (Kagan et al., 1964).

Conceptual Tempos: Impulsivity versus Reflectivity

In addition to cognitive style, children differ in their **conceptual tempo,** the manner in which they evaluate and act on a problem. **Im-**

Figure 15.6 Picture sets designed to test children's cognitive styles. Subjects were asked to select two pictures in each group that are similar in some way (from J. Kagan et al. "Information processing in the child." *Psychological Monograph,* **1964, 78. Copyright 1964 by the American Psychological Association. By permission).**

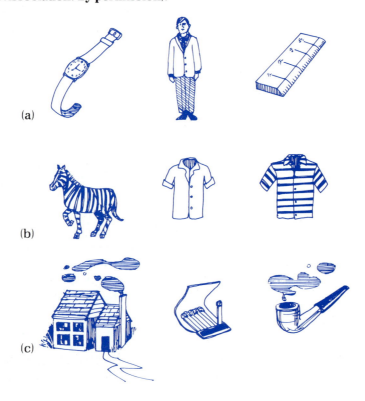

pulsive children usually accept and hurriedly report the first idea that they can generate, giving little consideration or thought to its accuracy. Others are **reflective** in their deliberations, spending longer periods of time considering various aspects of a hypothesis. Reflective, attentive children are more apt to be analytic in their cognitive style than impulsive youngsters.

Our knowledge of impulsivity and reflectivity has been greatly enhanced by Jerome Kagan and his colleagues (Kagan, 1965; 1966; Kagan et al., 1964). In a typical test designed to measure conceptual tempo, children are shown pictures from the **Matching Familiar Figures Test** (see Figure 15.7). In the test, the child is asked to match a standard figure with one of six variants. The subjects' scores are measured by the time it takes them to select the appropriate figure and the number of errors made in the process. Generally, the faster the children make their decisions, the more mistakes they make. Older children typically take longer to offer their first answer and make fewer errors. Children exhibiting reflective behavior in this test appear to be reflective in other situations too. For example, they tend to wait for longer periods of time before answering questions, make fewer incorrect guesses on reading tests, and make fewer errors in reading textual material.

Other studies have generally supported Kagan's research and found other interesting dimensions of conceptual tempo. One investigation (Toner, Holstein, and Hetherington, 1977) revealed that conceptual tempos can be measured to some degree in children as young as 3 years of

Figure 15.7 Test items designed to measure impulsiveness-reflectivity. Subjects are asked to select from each group of six variants one that is identical to the uppermost standard figure (from Kagan, 1965).

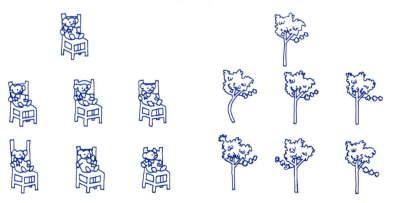

age. Another study (Cohen, Schleser, and Meyers, 1981) disclosed that among younger school-age children, those classified as reflective were more apt to understand conservation. Impulsive children were more likely to react in a preoperational fashion.

One possible cause of a child's reflective attitude is **anxiety** over making a mistake, although research offers conflicting results on this topic. Some feel that a strong fear of error may foster reflective attitudes. Children usually want to be correct and will try to avoid whatever mistakes they can. Conversely, for reasons not clearly understood, impulsive children do not appear to become upset over their mistakes and therefore respond quickly. Research has revealed that American schoolchildren become more reflective with age than do children of other cultures. This may be true because the American value system encourages children to avoid mistakes and the humiliation of being wrong [Kagan, 1971(b); Duryea and Glover, 1982].

Psycholinguistics

During middle childhood overall psycholinguistic development continues to be rapid. By 6 years of age, children know virtually all the letters in the alphabet, recognize the printed form of a handful of words, and can understand diverse concrete terms. School-age children also increase their ability to use words as vehicles of expression. While the basic language acquisition process is completed earlier in childhood, most youngsters have made the linguistic refinements necessary for verbal fluency by the age of 10 (Moskowitz, 1978).

The path to linguistic competency is by no means an easy one for children. Youngsters must learn to use language as a vehicle of expression. They must find the proper words to exchange information, describe their feelings, and convey their needs. Language will be the means through which children present evidence to support their perceptions and conceptions of the world. Moreover, language will bridge the development of two other forms of communication, writing and reading.

Vocabulary and Semantic Development

Consider the progress the developing child has made in vocabulary acquisition. At the end of the first year, only a handful of words are known. By the third year, the number of words in the child's vocabulary jumps to approximately 900. The 6-year-old has a vocabulary of about 2,600 words. By the time children enter sixth grade, it is estimated that they have a reading vocabulary of nearly 50,000 words. Suffice it to say that word acquisition is very rapid during these years. The staggering number of words learned is a reflection not only of growing linguistic competency, but also of cognitive growth, particularly of the skills needed to remember such a multitude of new acquisitions (Kail, 1984; Schank, 1982).

But while vocabulary acquisition is rapid, comprehension of word meaning and the interrelational value of words are slow to develop. Several reasons account for these lags. As far as word meanings are concerned, the abstract qualities of many words are still beyond the cognitive reasoning skills of the school-age child. There is a restriction to the physical qualities of words much as there is a cognitive restriction to the physical qualities of the environment. The abstract qualities of certain semantic features help explain the difficulty youngsters have in understanding the interrelational value of words. Nothing in the superficial form of sentences implies underlying semantic regularities. Compared to syntactic abstractions, which are systematically related to surface structure through transformations, the semantic relations between surface and deep structures are unsystematic. For example, no general relationship exists between the phonemic forms of *school, uncle,* and *spaceship* and the meanings of these words (McNeil, 1970).

School-age children have difficulty with the abstract qualities of many words.

As children grow older, they become more accurate in defining words and can understand abstract relationships between words. They are also able to name an agent when an action has been given. For example, if asked "What burns?" children can give an appropriate answer. They can also understand word pairs that eluded them earlier, such as *before-after*, *big-little*, and *wide-narrow*. Instead of learning the part of the meaning that is common to both words as they once did, children now understand the part of the meaning that distinguishes the two words (Donaldson and Wales, 1970; Moskowitz, 1978).

Syntactic Development

During the school years, the use of incomplete sentence structures declines, while compound and complex sentences increase. In fact, most children appear to be using adult grammar. They show continuing mastery of three basic rules behind complex sentence formulation:

1. A sentence consists of a noun phrase and a verb phrase.

2. A noun phrase consists of an article and a noun.

3. A verb phrase includes a verb and a noun phrase.

While there are many more rules to be learned, these three are used repeatedly in the creation of sentences (G. Miller, 1981).

Children show a substantial increase in the number of adjectives, adverbs, and conjunctions employed and the ability to understand the use of proper names, pronouns, and prepositions. Such advancements pave the way for the structural and functional changes in syntax evident at this time. As they learn more about sentence structure, children acquire more devices to convey different functions. Similarly, as they learn more about function, children extend the uses to which different structures can be put (Clark and Clark, 1977).

Grasping the notion of syntax is no easy chore, especially in light of our complex system of language rules. The need to couple the semantic qualities of words with an understanding of sentence construction illustrates the complicated dynamics behind learning a language. Seeking to understand this complex process, including the relationship of language to memory and thought, has always been, and continues to be, an intriguing area of study (see Howard, 1983; Reed, 1982; G. Miller, 1981).

Pragmatics

We learned in the last developmental section (Chapter 10) that in addition to semantic and syntactical understanding, children must learn the pragmatics of a language, that is, how the language is used in social contexts. As they move beyond their egocentric shells in problem-solving situations, children also transcend egocentric styles of communication and increasingly take listeners into account.

In addition to the changes in pragmatics previously discussed, including the greater use of gestures, pauses, and facial expressions, school-age children are more adept at turn taking during conversations. They also show a greater facility in adapting information to fit the listener's needs and adopting the listener's point of view if the situation warrants it.

The communication patterns of school-age children include other advancements in pragmatics. For example, conversations contain a more meaningful exchange of questions and answers. While younger children do ask questions, they often have trouble listening to the answers (Patterson and Kister, 1981). School-age youngsters use questions as a spontaneous means of obtaining information. Formulating a question, asking it, and listening to the answer involve a unique social exchange that improves with age.

In some instances, children learn the pragmatic qualities of language through rote memory. This appears to be especially true for socially proper expressions such as "Please," "Thank you," or "I'm sorry." Such expressions place no obligations on either speaker or listener, but they are often considered essential to the smooth functioning of society. They may or may not reflect the speaker's real feelings, but they express the feeling expected within a particular society for a particular situation. Because of this, they are often difficult to explain or justify to young children, and many parents do not attempt to do it. Their concern is usually purely social: "Say thank you to your grandmother"; "Tell John that you're sorry." Not until school age and even later do youngsters understand why such expressions are employed and their social significance (Clark and Clark, 1977).

Language Dialects

Not all children speak the same language. Nor do they all employ the same slang or grammatical styles. Variations in language, known as a **dialect,** can exist. Dialects are based on the same general language but differ in the verbal details and expressions chosen by the speaker.

Factors influencing dialect differences include:

1. *The profession or occupation of the speaker.* People employed in different occupations not only talk about different topics but also frequently employ different words for the same thing. For example, the words *forecast, prognosis,* and *prediction* all have similar meanings, but according to the occupational status of the speaker, one meaning is associated with the weather, another with medicine, and the last with science (Dale, 1976).

2. *The age of the speaker.* This is particularly noticeable in these days of the **generation gap.** One age group may coin new words or phrases and contrive new meanings for existing words and phrases. (Working with children quickly alerts adults to age dialect differences. Recently, one of the authors was informed that *fantastic* and *great* were outdated; the more fashionable words were *radical* and *awesome.*) Age differences are preserved by the tendency of speakers to continue using the language they learned when young, even though the language as a whole may have changed since then.

3. *Geography.* In parts of the United States, for example, *r* is not pronounced at the end of words or before a consonant; thus, *par* rhymes with *pa*, and *startle* with *throttle.* Understanding certain words may be difficult when listening to geographical dialect differences. Moreover, in different parts of the country, different words are used to refer to the same object. *Stoop*, for example, is often used for *porch* in the Northeast, and the words *hotcake*, *pancake*, and *griddle cake* are each used in specific geographical regions. Similarly, *grinder* is the designation for a particular kind of large sandwich in the Northeast, but elsewhere the same type of sandwich is called *hoagie*, *sub*, *wedge*, or *hero.*

4. *Social class.* Social class differences in language become more pronounced when society is stratified. The middle and upper classes frequently employ carefully organized and highly structured sentences, while the lower classes use sentences that are syntactically simple and terse. Whereas the middle and upper classes usually provide an elaboration of words, the lower classes often do not elaborate to make their meanings clear. For example, the former may say, "Please be quiet because your father is sleeping," while the latter might say, "Be quiet."

    Whether lower-class language patterns are deficient compared to those of the middle and upper classes has sparked considerable interest (see Feagans and Farran, 1982). Many feel that rather than being deficient in language skills, lower-class people merely have different linguistic patterns adapted to their respective social class. Their language is not only functional and fluent but also complete, with its own vocabulary and rules of grammar (Schacter and Strage, 1982; Hilliard and Vaughn-Scott, 1982).

Black English

The fact that certain nonstandard speech styles are functional rather than deficient is best illustrated by the dialect known as **Black English.** Most sociolinguistic research has focused on the speech of black people of lower socioeconomic classes, largely because this group has been a general focus of attention during the last 25 years. Because not all black people speak in this style, *Black English* refers to a social dialect, not a racial one, and is used mostly by people at lower socioeconomic levels.

Although Black English differs from standard English, this does not mean it is inferior. On the contrary, Black English has its own rules of grammar, vocabulary, and structure (White, 1984; Hale, 1981; Folb, 1980). The verb *to be*, for example, is used as an auxiliary verb to indicate different tenses in standard English, but not in Black English. The languages of many West African tribes, which correspond to Black English, have a tense referred to as the habitual, which is not found in standard English. The habitual tense is used to express action that is always occurring, and it is formed with a verb that is translated as "be." Thus, "He be coming" should be taken to mean something similar to "He's always coming," "He usually comes," or "He's been coming." To form the habitual tense in English, Black English speakers use the word *be* as an auxiliary. Thus, sentence constructions read "He be doing it," "My momma be working," or "He be running."

The Black English speaker does not employ verb changes (inflections) to indicate the past tense. For example, a speaker of standard English may ask "What did your brother say?" and the speaker of Black English may respond "He say he coming." As one can see, the verb *say* is not changed to "said." This style of talking of the past is like the Yoruba, Fante, Hausa, and Ewe languages of West Africa.

The manner in which plurality is expressed is another difference between standard English and Black English. Instead of saying "those boys" or "two dogs," the Black English speaker will talk of "them boy" or "two dog." Still another contrast is in gender. Speakers of standard English are often confused to find that the nonstandard vernacular often uses only one gender of pronoun, the masculine, and refers to women as well as men as "he" or "him." "He's a nice girl" or "Him a nice girl" are common (Seymour, 1973).

Thus, on closer inspection Black English is found to be highly structured and meaningful rather than deficient. Misunderstanding of the grammatical patterns of the disadvantaged black's speech frequently leads many nonblacks to conclude that no grammar exists—a very wrong judgment indeed.

Also, Labov and Cohen (1967) found lower-class blacks capable of perceiving and understanding the meaning of many English terms even though they were not able to reproduce the language in its standard form. Another study (Labov, 1970) revealed that young blacks who were classified as linguistically retarded in standard language test measures could engage in nonstandard English conversations and express themselves quite adequately. However, their poor performance in tests could not be attributed to the language in which the test was given. Administering the Stanford-Binet test in Black English or standard English had no effect on the IQ scores at the third- or sixth-grade levels (Quay, 1974).

While Black English is the normal mode of speech for thousands of children and adults, it is also one of the country's biggest educational problems. Children who speak Black English frequently experience immense difficulty in learning to read, since books are written in standard English. Teachers, too, sometimes make matters worse with their attitudes toward Black English, a factor that may lower the student's self-concept, since self-expectations are influenced strongly by the expectations of others. To add to educational difficulties, black children are tested for skills in cognitive development that require forms of cognitive awareness, learning styles, and language comprehension derived from white middle-class experiences. When the youngsters fail in these tasks, many assume that the children are inferior in overall cognitive development (Hale, 1981; Hilliard and Vaughn-Scott, 1982; Freeman, 1982).

The status of Black English in the educational arena will be a persistent theme in the literature for years to come. Educators need to come to grips with the central issue of how to best structure the classroom for those children whose primary language is not standard English. More general efforts need to be directed toward raising the public's awareness of Black English as a whole. More people need to realize that although Black English differs from standard English in form, it is not necessarily deficient (Markham, 1984; Smitherman, 1981; Smith, 1980).

Summary

Kirk, age 11

The school-age child demonstrates significant gains in cognitive and linguistic development. Jean Piaget proposes two stages of cognitive development for us to consider at this time: intuitive thought (4 to 7) and concrete operations (7 to 11). Intuitive thought is a substage of the much longer preoperational thought stage. Limitations in cognitive reasoning during this time include centering, transductive and transformational reasoning, and inability to reverse mental operations.

Concrete operations is a time when children reason more logically about their environment. This reasoning is evident in the youngster's ability to decenter and understand the principles of conservation. This chapter explored the fact that conservation exists in many different forms, such as liquid or mass, and that understanding these various dimensions does not occur at the same time. Children in the stage of concrete operations also understand the concepts of classification and seriation, as well as basic rules of logic, including the notions of closure, reversibility, associativity, and identity.

The child's growing understanding of the environment is also reflected in concept development. Concepts continue to be critical components of overall cognitive activity. Among the concept refinements discussed were those relating to size and shape, space, relation, quantity, and time. We also explored the manner in which children learn about death, an elusive concept for children. The true abstract quality of death is not usually understood until the teen years.

Problem-solving abilities improve throughout middle childhood. Ultimately, problem solving will follow a methodical approach: definition of the problem, development of strategies to reach a solution, application of internal and external resources, and monitoring and evaluating of progress. Problem-solving abilities are enhanced by the school-age child's cognitive advancements, the curriculum challenges of the elementary school, better work habits, improved memory abilities and metacognitive strategies, and the development of intrinsic motivation.

Cognitive style refers to the characteristic ways in which the individual organizes information and finds solutions to problems. Among the cognitive styles explored were analytic, exploring the minute details of stimulus objects; superordinate, looking for shared attributes; functional-relational, linking objects or events on the basis of some interactional value; and functional-locational, classification on the basis of a shared location.

In addition to cognitive style, children's problem-solving strategies are affected by conceptual tempo. *Conceptual tempo* refers to the manner in which one evaluates and acts on a problem, and it includes impulsivity and reflectivity. Impulsive children usually accept and hurriedly report the first idea they get. Reflective children take more time when confronted with problem-solving situations and are deliberate in their appraisals. This chapter stressed the importance of promoting reflective behavior as well as methodical and deliberate problem-solving strategies.

The school-age youngster has made the linguistic refinements necessary for verbal fluency. By the sixth grade, the average child has a reading vocabulary of nearly 50,000 words. However, the abstract quality and interrelational value of certain words may still elude the child. The use of incomplete sentence structure declines during middle childhood while that of compound and complex sentences increases. Structural and functional changes in syntax become evident at this time. Three rules are behind many of the more complex sentences created by the child: (1) a sentence consists of a noun phrase and a verb phrase; (2) a noun phrase consists of an article and a noun; and (3) a verb phrase includes a verb and a noun phrase. As knowledge of sentence structure increases, children acquire more devices to convey different functions. As more is learned about function, children extend the uses to which different structures can be put.

Pragmatics, how language is used in social settings, also reveals developmental changes. In addition to using gestures, pauses, and the like when they talk, school-age children are more adept at taking turns during conversations, adapting information to meet the needs of the listener, asking meaningful questions, and supplying relevant answers. Some pragmatic qualities of language are learned through rote memory, and it is not until later childhood that the social significance of such verbal devices is learned.

Variations in language are known as dialects. Numerous factors influence dialects, including one's profession or occupation, age, geography, and social class. The fact that people speak differently does not mean that their language is deficient. This is best illustrated by examining the speech style known as Black English. Although Black English differs from standard English, it has its own rules of grammar, vocabulary, and structure. The educational status of Black English, particularly its application to the classroom, is currently being debated.

Suggested Reading List

Matlin, M. *Cognition.* New York: Holt, Rinehart & Winston, 1983. A very good overview of the study of cognition. Of special interest are discussions related to concept formation and problem solving.

Miller, G. A. *Language and Speech.* San Francisco: W. H. Freeman, 1981. This introduction to language covers many diverse topics in a very readable and enjoyable fashion.

Wadsworth, B. J. *Piaget's Theory of Cognitive and Affective Development.* 3rd ed. New York: Longman, 1984. Wadsworth explores each of Piaget's stages of cognition, as well as the implications of intellectual and affective development. Many useful tables, figures, and applied formulations are included.

White, J. *The Psychology of Blacks: An Afro-American Perspective.* Englewood Cliffs, N.J.: Prentice-Hall, 1984. White devotes an entire chapter to psychological themes in black language, oral literature, and patterns of expression.

Chapter Sixteen

Personality and Social Learning

Children need models more than they need critics.

Joseph Joubert

Introduction

The years of middle childhood are an active period of personality and social development. During this time, the interaction between the child and society, which constitutes socialization, expands and becomes more complex. Observers of this age group will see that youngsters wish to be with others and that social relations acquire many new dimensions, whether in peer-group relations, school activities, sports, or family activities.

As social horizons expand, children learn that they must adjust their behavior to meet the numerous expectations and demands of society. This is an ongoing process and requires adaptability. Socially acceptable or tolerable behavior in toddlers, such as clinging dependency, may not be acceptable in school-age youngsters. Modification of behavior is necessary to meet the changing expectations of society.

Youngsters gain insight into themselves and their developing personalities from the social relations of middle childhood. More specifically, the child's sense of personal awareness or self-knowledge grows through interactions with others and from inferences about personal experiences. While certain degrees of self-awareness were evident earlier in life, they were frequently based on the youngster's physical qualities or possessions. Children are now likely to include in their self-appraisals other facets of themselves, such as how they are perceived by others and their general competencies (Perry and Bussey, 1984; Harter, 1983; Damon and Hart, 1982).

All of the foregoing implies that cognitive facilities join forces with personality and social functionings, a blending of developmental forces evident in other life stages. In particular, the developing powers of social cognition enable children to perceive more accurately both themselves and the perspective of others in their environment. One of the many benefits of improved social cognitive skills is that school-age children become more skilled in interpersonal relations. Friendships acquire more depth and children are better able to understand the thoughts and sensitivities of others. Their maturing social perceptions are evident in other ways, too. For example, they can now distinguish cooperative situations from competitive ones or trustworthy, kind, and unselfish people from untrustworthy, unkind, and selfish ones.

We'll begin this examination of personality and social learning with our ongoing analysis of Freud's and Erikson's developmental theories. Next we'll turn our attention to moral, sex-role, and emotional development. Finally we will examine family influences on child development and the nature of peer relations at this time.

Theories of Personality Development

Freud's Theory

Sigmund Freud labels the middle years of childhood as the latency period in psychosexual development. This stage of development is characterized by a tapering off of biological and sexual urges. In fact, it is a tranquil period of transition for the child.

Children do grow and acquire new skills during this quiescent time, even though there are no prominent instinctive urges within the child. This is a time for continued ego identity formation, including ego strengthening and methods for protecting the self against life's failures and frustrations, called coping mechanisms.

Freudian Coping Mechanisms **Coping mechanisms** are patterns of behavior that relieve anxiety. We have all heard references to anxiety at one point or another: Mary has test anxiety, Stewart is anxiously awaiting the company's decision, or Phillip is always anxious and uptight. **Anxiety,** a most unpleasant emotion, is a reaction of inner apprehension often described as a response to a subjective, rather than an objective, danger. Put another way, it is psychological rather than physical pain. In many instances, anxiety originates from the conflicts we face in life.

We use coping mechanisms to try to deal with the pain and turmoil of such threatening situations as failure, mistakes, and accidents, and

As children grow older, they increasingly use
coping mechanisms.

they may succeed in freeing us from some anxiety. By middle childhood, coping mechanisms are used with surprising frequency. With age,
these mechanisms become more elaborate and intertwined with the
child's overall personality. However, coping mechanisms are, at best,
temporary; they do not resolve underlying conflicts. In some cases,
coping mechanisms produce automatic and rigid reactions that enable
the individual to avoid, rather than deal with, anxiety. Such patterns of
behavior tend to distort reality.

Although coping mechanisms are a normal behavioral expression
and do have some beneficial value, they should not be used to excess.
When they are used excessively, such as in the case of the perpetual
excuse maker or cover-up artist, then troubles begin. As we are
assaulted by the problems of daily life, coping, or defensive, behavior
yields few, if any, long-lasting solutions. The child or adult who relies
too heavily on coping mechanisms makes of life a defensive battle,
which historically is not a winning strategy.

It has often been said that coping mechanisms deal with the symptoms rather than the causes of problems. Just as taking two aspirins for
a headache or a sleeping pill for insomnia does not expose the roots of
the problem, continually using a coping mechanism does not deal with
the need or frustration that causes the anxiety. Thus, while coping
mechanisms can be useful, their adjustive or maladjustive quality depends on how often the child uses them.

Types of Coping Mechanisms   Just as anxiety exists in all shapes and
sizes, so do coping mechanisms. Coping behaviors are highly individualized and will differ from person to person and from situation to
situation. In this sense, it is possible that no two people use the same
coping device in the same manner. There are, however, some standard
types of coping behavior.

Rationalization is one of the most common coping mechanisms. Rationalization is the attempt to justify and provide logical reasons and explanations for one's failures or shortcomings. The youngster who is unable to make the Little League team, for example, may attempt to rationalize this failure by claiming that the games are boring. Or to avoid a spanking after breaking some dishes, the rationalizing child may say it never would have happened if someone else had not stacked them so high. In its simplest form, rationalization is common excuse making.

Projection is the attributing of one's difficulties or failures to someone else. In order to guard against unfavorable self-evaluations, motives that are found personally unacceptable are attributed to others. A child who happens to be caught copying or cheating, for example, may attempt to defend the act by saying that everyone else in the class was guilty of the same misconduct or that the teacher is to blame for not taking adequate safeguards against cheating.

Displacement is the redirection of pent-up hostile feelings toward people or objects less dangerous than those that initially aroused the emotion. Displacement can be seen in a young girl who, after committing a misdeed, has been spanked by her father. Obviously, she cannot return the blow without deepening her predicament. Instead, she may seek other channels for her internal hostile feelings, such as kicking a ball or spanking a doll. Displacement may also explain why so many adolescent bedroom doors are slammed shut following family disagreements.

Children frequently resort to **denial of reality.** To protect the self, children may refuse to perceive the existence of hurtful situations. For example, a youngster may continually deny that a beloved relative has passed away or older children may deny to their parents that they are doing poorly in school even though they are failing four courses.

Many children seek to substitute a successful or rewarding activity for failure in another kind of activity. This coping mechanism is called **compensation.** The unathletic boy who cannot successfully compete in sports may find satisfaction in a hobby. An unattractive girl may try to excel in her studies or become the school's best dresser.

Interestingly, parents employ a type of compensation when they seek to satisfy their own ambitions through their children. A mother who experienced a deprived childhood may go out of her way to give her children the best of everything. A father who always wanted to go to college but never had the chance may continually urge his child to pursue higher education. This type of compensation may satisfy the parent's needs, but whether it meets the child's needs is questionable.

Regression is a retreat to earlier developmental periods to escape the anxiety of a situation. This coping mechanism is quite apparent when a new baby arrives home from the hospital, and an older child regresses to infantile behavior. In an effort to regain the parental attention that has been displaced by the new arrival, a child may regress to babylike behavior, such as bed-wetting, thumb-sucking, or crawling. It is conceivable that in the child's mind, earlier developmental stages represented security.

To avoid expressing unwanted and perhaps objectionable desires, a child may learn to substitute opposing desires. This coping mechanism is known as **reaction formation.** Growing children who are anxious about their passivity and dependency, for example, may exhibit a type of reaction formation by behaving in an aggressive and assertive fashion in the company of peers.

Finally, escape and withdrawal are two interrelated coping mechanisms that children use to avoid threatening or undesirable situations. They are attempts to avoid or put off doing an unpleasant task, such as presenting an oral report in class or washing dishes.

Erikson's Theory

Erikson's fourth stage of development is called **industry versus inferiority.** This psychosocial stage occupies all of middle childhood (6 to 12) and, as such, parallels Freud's latency period.

Children who are anxious about being passive and dependent may behave aggressively in the company of peers—a reaction formation.

Helping Children Understand Coping Behaviors

Everyone needs feedback on his or her behavior, and children are no exception. It is important for children to be aware of their coping behaviors, especially if defensiveness is common. The importance of objective adult feedback and meaningful guidance cannot be overstressed here. Parents, teachers, guidance counselors, and other adults are in strategic positions to observe children and help them develop personal awareness. The following suggestions are offered to adults trying to help youngsters understand their coping behaviors:

Examine Your Own Coping Mechanisms.
Seeking to understand our own coping mechanisms and why we use them may provide meaningful insight into children's defensive behavior. While adult coping mechanisms are more refined than children's, the fundamental design is remarkably similar.

Respect the Struggles, Turmoils, and Disappointments Characteristic of Childhood.
An empathic adult can appreciate the many anxious situations that confront the child throughout life. Because coping mechanisms are learned forms of behavior, children need models more than they need critics. Shaming the child or making fun of coping behavior accomplishes nothing and should be avoided.

Try to Teach the Child That Both Success and Failure Are Part of Life.
While everyone wants to succeed, few succeed all the time. Failure and disappointment should not be reasons for negative self-regard; learning to accept them is an important part of growing up.

Try to Understand Why Coping Mechanisms Are Used, Especially Those That Are Used Excessively.
This requires not only patience and gentle understanding but also careful observation of the events that triggered the coping device. Verbalization of the situation should be encouraged after the anxiety of the event has diminished. It should be stated to the child that while defending against and retreating from unpleasant situations are normal reactions, learning to face struggles head-on avoids reality distortion and nurtures a more accurate sense of self.

Avoid Comparisons with Other Children.
Children rarely employ coping mechanisms or accept the consequences of negative situations in exactly the same fashion. It is unfair to say such things as, "You're always making excuses. Mary doesn't behave like you!" Such comparisons downplay the child's individuality and accomplish little, except possibly to produce further feelings of anxiety and inferiority.

Try to Understand Coping Mechanisms as Part of the Child's Whole Personality.
Coping mechanisms do not exist as separate behavioral phenomena; they frequently reflect significant aspects of the child's total personality. Adults should try to be aware of such areas as accuracy of **self-concept,** level of self-esteem, insecurities, and emotional sensitivities. ■

Source: Turner, 1981(b).

During this stage, children have reached a point in their cognitive development at which they can understand more about the world around them. School-age children attempt to understand and build or make things that are practical to them. **Play** intermingles with work; play becomes productive, and the product is important to the child's **self-esteem.** However, the child who fails frequently at productivity may soon feel inferior and even worthless. In their quest for positive self-regard and esteem, children unquestionably need the support and guidance of adults. This notion is held by others as well as Erikson (see Clemes and Bean, 1981; Swayze, 1980).

Competence is needed, regardless of the culture. In American society, industry is expected in the classroom, while in simpler societies, industry is required in the field, in the tying of fishnets, spear throwing, and other forms of activity. This time is one of schooling (in or out of the classroom) and continued socialization, particularly in ways that can lead to competence in adulthood.

The industrious child takes pleasure in the accomplishment of new and different goals. For the school-age child, these accomplishments may range from winning a Monopoly game to becoming a member of a sports team, participating in a school play, or earning good grades. Each goal attainment generates further motivation toward both more and new industrious behavior. However, there is an obvious risk that youngsters may lose self-esteem because of failure (Erikson, 1963, p. 260):

> The child's danger, at this stage, lies in a sense of inadequacy and inferiority. If he despairs of his tools and skills or of his status among his tool partners, he may be discouraged from identification with them and with a section of the tool world. To lose the hope of such "industrial" association may pull him back to the more isolated, less tool-conscious familial rivalry of the oedipal time. The child despairs of his equipment in the tool world and in autonomy, and considers himself doomed to mediocrity or inadequacy. It is at this point that wider society becomes significant in its ways of admitting the child to an understanding of meaningful roles in its technology and economy. Many a child's development is disrupted when family life has failed to prepare him for school life, or when school life fails to sustain the promises of earlier stages.

Moral Development

Moral development is the process whereby individuals learn to adopt standards of right and wrong. While standards of conduct vary from culture to culture, every society has established some type of behavioral

rules. During early childhood, a sense of morality is born when youngsters realize that certain behavioral patterns are classified as "good" and
are sometimes rewarded by their parents, while some actions are
considered "bad" and are frequently accompanied by punishment. As
children become older, morality begins to encompass a complex set of
ideas, values, and beliefs (Carroll and Rest, 1982).

To understand the nature and meaning of morality, including such
factors as guilt, shame, lying, discipline, and religion, we must examine
the manner in which morality unfolds throughout the course of childhood. Two psychologists in particular, Jean Piaget and Lawrence
Kohlberg, have attempted to explain the developmental aspects of
morality. In this section we shall examine their theories of how a foundation for developing morality is laid during childhood.

Piaget's Theory

Jean Piaget contends that all morality consists of a system of rules
handed down from adults to children. Through training and practice,
children learn to respect these standards of conduct. More importantly,
their understanding of right and wrong is shaped by developing cognitive awareness.

In order to obtain an understanding of how moral concepts develop
in children, Piaget constructed pairs of stories and asked children to
describe which of the two was "naughtier." For example, one pair of
stories concerned two children who accidentally cut holes in their
dresses, each in a different manner. The first child wanted to help and
surprise her mother by cutting out a pattern of material for her; in the
process, the girl cut a big hole in her own dress. The second girl took a
pair of scissors from her house to play with while her mother was away
one day. Not knowing how to use them, she cut a small hole in her
dress.

In the first of a second set of stories, a little boy named John is
called to dinner. As he opens the dining room door, the door slams into
a tray holding 15 cups, which was totally obstructed from his view
when he entered, and all the cups are broken. In the other story, a
little boy named Henry wants to get some jam from the cupboard while
his mother is away from the house. Climbing on a chair to reach for the
jam, he knocks over a cup and breaks it.

In follow-up conversations, Piaget found that young children felt
that the first story in each set was "naughtier," simply because a larger
hole was made in the dress and more cups were broken. Good intentions and accidents were ignored by these subjects, who were affected
only by the total property value of each mistake. Older children, however, considered the second stories to be worse because, as Piaget explains, older children have begun to judge right and wrong behavior on
the basis of motives.

The development of morality appears to follow a sequential pattern. Before age 5, in a stage called the **premoral stage,** the child has little awareness of any rules. Some moral judgments begin in a stage that Piaget calls **moral realism.** In this stage (generally from 5 to 10 years of age), a child receives rules from parents without being totally aware of or understanding their reasons. Rules are viewed as sacred and untouchable, and the purpose of punishment is atonement for sins.

Not until the stage of **moral relativism** does the child become aware of the meanings of rules and the reasons for them. At this point (after age 10), children begin to view rules as products of mutual consent and respect related to certain principles. Their moral reasoning has a social, cooperative, logical quality.

Younger children best realize the seriousness of wrongdoing if the punishment fits the act. Justice to them is based on an "eye for an eye, a tooth for a tooth," so the pain felt by the transgressor must be proportional to the pain inflicted on others. Older children believe that punishment should put things into perspective. On hearing the story of a boy who broke his little brother's toy, younger children generally say that the boy should be deprived of his own toys for a week. Older children recommend that the boy should give the brother one of his own toys (reciprocity) or pay to have the toy fixed (restitution).

Piaget's early writings succeeded in launching a wave of research into the topic of morality. He has gained support over the years, most notably for his notion that morality is closely allied with cognition (see Krebs and Gillmore, 1982). Modern researchers (such as Surber, 1982) have also found that younger children judge wrongdoing on the basis of harm done rather than on the intent or motivation of the offender. Yet for some, Piaget's research leaves room for doubt and some unanswered questions. For example, his suggestion that morality is established by the preadolescent years is criticized by those who feel that moral development is a longer and more elaborate process. In fact, some feel that mature moral reasoning doesn't unfold until the adulthood years (Colby et al., 1983). Other critics maintain that Piaget's theory fails to take into account cultural and socioeconomic differences among children (Boehm and Nass, 1962; Harris, 1970; Lickona, 1976).

Kohlberg's Theory

Inspired by the work of Piaget, Harvard's Lawrence Kohlberg [1976; 1981(a), (b)] has provided a more detailed structure in formulating a theory of children's moral development. Like Piaget, Kohlberg feels that morality is developed in a series of stages. Both agree that children's successive stages of morality result from the cognitive restructuring of their experiences, not from a set of graded lessons taught by adults. Kohlberg, however, believes that moral development is a more complex and longer process than Piaget does. More importantly, Kohlberg sees the various stages as closely related. He suggests that development is characterized by increasing differentiation and that each stage takes into account everything that took place at previous stages.

Kohlberg's theory consists of six stages categorized within three major levels: the preconventional level (0 to 9), the conventional level (9 to 15), and the moral principles level (16 onward). Figure 16.1 charts these major levels as they compare to Piaget's stages. Each of Kohlberg's levels consist of two stages. Let's turn our attention to the preconventional level in light of our present analysis of middle childhood.

At the level of **preconventional morality,** children have little conception of what socially acceptable moral behavior is, but during this level's two stages, they begin to display signs of initial moral behavior. In the first stage, called **obedience and punishment orientation,** children begin to follow rules in order to avoid punishment. During this initial stage, youngsters conform to rules imposed on them by authoritarian figures. True rule awareness, as we know it, has not been established; children's moral conduct is based largely on fear of punishment associated with rule violations. Like Piaget, Kohlberg maintains that at this time judgment of the seriousness of a violation depends on the magnitude of the wrongdoing.

In the second stage, called **naively egoistic orientation,** children reason that by taking the right action, they usually earn some tangible

Figure 16.1 Piaget's and Kohlberg's stages of moral development.

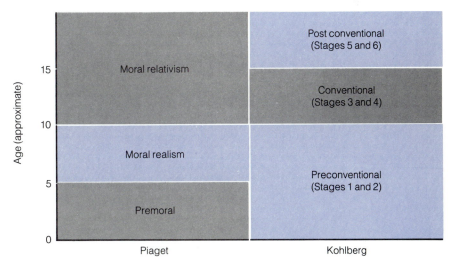

reward. Kohlberg feels that a sense of reciprocity is in operation here; that is, children will do the right thing not only to satisfy their own needs but also to satisfy the needs of others. If the latter is the case, they reason that some sort of "return favor" will be in order.

Measuring Moral Reasoning

A technique known as the Kohlberg Moral Judgment Interview is used to measure an individual's level of moral development. The technique consists of asking the person to react to several moral dilemmas. Attention is focused on the reasoning behind a person's response. The following is one of the more popular dilemmas, and Table 16.1 charts typical responses according to all of Kohlberg's moral stages.

In Europe a woman was near death from cancer. One drug might save her, a form of

Table 16.1 Stages of Moral Development

Levels	Stages	Illustrative Reponses to Story of Heinz Stealing the Drug
Level I: Preconventional level	Stage I: Obedience and punishment orientation	It isn't really bad to take it—he did ask to pay for it first. He wouldn't do any other damage or take anything else and the drug he'd take is only worth $200, he's not really taking a $2,000 drug.
	Stage 2: Naively egoistic orientation	Heinz isn't really doing any harm to the druggist, and he can always pay him back. If he doesn't want to lose his wife, he should take the drug because it's the only thing that will work.
Level II: Conventional level	Stage 3: Good boy/nice girl orientation	Stealing is bad, but this is a bad situation. Heinz isn't doing wrong in trying to save his wife, he has no choice but to take the drug. He is only doing something that is natural for a good husband to do. You can't blame him for doing something out of love for his wife. You'd blame him if he didn't love his wife enough to save her.

While moral development is shaped by various influences through-out Kohlberg's stages (we will discuss and critique the later stages in Chapter 20), certain influences are critical during the early years. The disposition of the parents and the encouragement of dialogues on value

Measuring Moral Reasoning, *continued.*

radium that a druggist in the same town had recently discovered. The druggist was charging $2,000, ten times what the drug cost him to make. The sick woman's husband, Heinz, went to everyone he knew to borrow the money, but he could only get together about half of what it cost. He told the druggist that his wife was dying and asked him to sell the drug cheaper or let him pay later. But the druggist said "no." The husband got desperate and broke into the man's store to steal the drug for his wife. Should the husband have done that? Why? ■

Table 16.1, *continued*

Levels	Stages	Illustrative Reponses to Story of Heinz Stealing the Drug
Level II: Conventional level *(continued)*	Stage 4: Law and order orientation	The druggist is leading a wrong kind of life if he just lets somebody die like that, so it's Heinz's duty to save her. But Heinz can't just go around breaking laws and let it go at that—he must pay the druggist back and he must take his punishment for stealing.
Level III: Postconventional moral principles	Stage 5: Contractual legalistic orientation	Before you say stealing is wrong, you've got to really think about this whole situation. Of course, the laws are quite clear about breaking into a store. And, even worse, Heinz would know there were no legal grounds for his actions. Yet, I can see why it would be reasonable for anybody in this situation to steal the drug.
	Stage 6: Conscience or principled orientation	Where the choice must be made between disobeying a law and saving a human life, the higher principle of preserving life makes it morally right—not just understandable—to steal the drug.

issues, such as role-playing situations, are important for the foundation of sound moral principles. Also, the more children participate with others, either in social groupings or in institutional settings, the greater their chances of developing social responsiveness. The opportunity to interact with others seems to help youngsters appreciate differing social perspectives.

Other Theoretical Perspectives on Morality

In addition to the cognitive-developmental aspects of moral reasoning popularized by Piaget and Kohlberg, there have been other noteworthy attempts to define and explore morality. In this area, as in others, awareness of child psychology's major schools of thought and their differing viewpoints is critical. For example, Freudian theory views moral standards as the largely unconscious products of irrational motives and the need to keep antisocial impulses from levels of consciousness.

Moral development can be enhanced through group discussion.

As a result, Freudian research has focused on the guilt that results when moral standards are transgressed. Behaviorists, on the other hand, define morality on the basis of particular acts and avoidances that are learned through the use of reward and punishments.

Social learning researchers seek to discover whether imitation of adults plays a role in the child's developing morality. For example, in an experiment similar to the Piagetian project, 5- to 11-year-olds were told stories designed to elicit moral reactions. The types of reactions were in turn recorded by the experimenters.

The children were then divided into three experimental groups. In two of the groups, the children heard an adult express a moral opinion (about a similar story) contrary to the children's initial responses in the pretest period. Furthermore, the adult's response was approved by the experimenter. In one of these groups, the children received approval each time they adopted the adult's style of thinking and deviated from their own; in the other group, the children received no reinforcement when they deviated from their initial thinking. Children in the third group, not exposed to any adult model, received approval from the experimenter when their thinking differed from that of the initial trial period.

When this portion of the experiment was completed, the children were taken into another room and were asked to respond to similar stories without the adult present. On the whole, children who were exposed earlier to adult models were most likely to change their original opinions and adopt a style similar to the grown-ups'. Whether the child had been given approval mattered very little (Bandura and McDonald, 1963).

Sex-Role Development

We learned in Chapter 11 that sex-role development begins early in life. For some, this socialization process begins at birth, when the infant is swaddled in a pink or blue hospital blanket. As time goes on, children receive different sex-typed behaviors from their mothers and fathers. Mothers are typically more nurturant and affectionate and indulge in cuddling, kissing, and stroking their children. Fathers, on the other hand, display affection through other channels, such as engaging in outdoor activities, roughhousing, and sharing hobbies and sports. Many parents openly worry that their boys are too feminine and their girls too masculine. No wonder children have established at an early age a fairly clear picture of what society thinks is appropriate sex-role behavior.

By middle childhood, youngsters exhibit a strong preference for sexually separate groups, in the process assuming sex-appropriate mannerisms, recreational patterns, attitudes, and values from the surrounding adult culture. By the middle years, most children have a rather extensive knowledge of sex-role stereotypes, and these standards become even more deeply rooted over time (Tavris and Wade, 1984; Fu and Leach, 1980; Basow, 1980; Harris and Satter, 1981).

Sex-Role Stereotypes: Separating Myth and Fact

How much of what we hear about sex-role stereotypes is true? Are girls really more emotional than boys? Are boys generally more physically active than girls? Is there a difference between the sexes in displays of aggression? Research undertaken by Susan Basow (1980) shows that many of the sex-role stereotypes abounding in society are untrue. Some, however, such as males being superior to females in quantitative skills, are founded in fact. Others, including sex differences in competition and cooperation, are unclear and really depend on the situation. Basow's analysis and summary of research focusing on sex differences reveal the following:

Physical
Anatomy: Females have a uterus, ovaries, a clitoris, and a vagina.

Males have testes, a penis, and a scrotum. Males tend to be bigger and more muscular.

Processes: Females mature faster, have slower metabolism.

Differences in sensation are unclear; females may be more sensitive to touch, pain, and visual stimuli. Hormonal production is cyclic in females after puberty (ovulation and menstruation); it is mostly continuous in males.

Brain organization: Females may have less localization of function than males and may be cognitive specialists.

Vulnerability: Males are more vulnerable to disease, physical disorders, and early death.

Activity level: There are no differences in the amount of activity, although differences in type of movements and activities are found.

Cognitive
Learning and memory: No difference.

Intelligence: No difference in level of intelligence.

Verbal: Females tend to excel up to age 3 and after age 11.

Quantitative: Males tend to excel after age 12.

Visual-spatial: Males tend to excel after age 8.

Analytic: No difference.

Concept mastery: No difference.

Cognitive style: Differences are unclear.

Creativity: No difference with nonverbal material; females tend to excel with verbal material. ▶

Children of this age generally perceive sex roles in much the same fashion as adults. In addition, they have developed an understanding of which stereotyped occupations go with which sex. Research also reveals that boys and girls will increasingly segregate into sex-typed play activities (Gettys and Cann, 1981; Reis and Wright, 1982).

Children's growing cognitive awareness and expanding social horizons contribute to sex-role development. Cognitive skills enable them to

---

Sex-Role Stereotypes: Separating Myth and Fact, *continued.*

Personality and Temperament
Self-description: Females are more people-oriented; males are more achievement-oriented.

Emotionality: No difference during childhood.

Fears: The evidence is contradictory; females report more fears.

Social Behavior
Communication patterns

Verbal: Males dominate.

Nonverbal: Males dominate; females may be more sensitive to cues.

Person-centered interactions

Dependency: No difference depending on the definition used.

Affiliation: No difference during childhood. After adolescence, females tend to be more interested in people.

Empathy: No difference depending on experience and the person.

Nurturance: No difference depending on experience.

Altruism: No difference depending on the situation and the person.

Power-centered interactions

Aggression: Males tend to be more aggressive after age 2.

Assertiveness: Differences are unclear; depends on the situation and the person.

Dominance: Differences are unclear; males may be more dominant depending on the situation.

Competition and cooperation: Differences are unclear; males may be more competitive depending on the situation.

Compliance: No difference depending on the situation and the person from whom compliance is required.

Sexual Behavior
Response: No difference; females are capable of multiple orgasms.

Interest: Males express more and have more experiences. Meaning of sex may be different for males and females.

Response to erotica: No difference.

Homosexuality: Reported more in males.

Masturbation: Reported more in males. ■

understand and associate behaviors appropriate to their sex. This is another illustration of the link between cognition and social development. Exposure to a growing number of role models and to television and other media, including advertisements, also transmits sex-role behaviors to the child (Wehren and DeLisi, 1983; Shepard-Look, 1982; Hess and Grant, 1983; Courtney and Whipple, 1983; Downs, 1981).

A growing number of psychologists are voicing concern over the manner in which sex-role stereotypes permeate our society. They maintain that rigid and conventional standards of masculinity and femininity may be maladaptive to the child. In this sense, traditional sex-role stereotyping is thought to restrict the human personality and its growth throughout the life cycle.

A girl in wood shop, learning to use the saw—an example of efforts being made to overcome sex-role stereotypes.

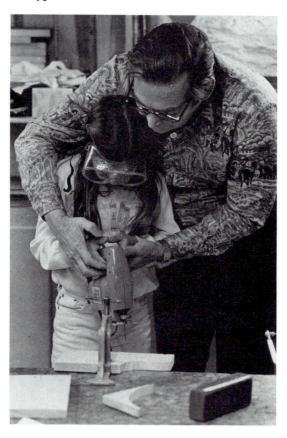

To combat rigid sex-role expectations, a relatively new concept in the field of socialization has emerged. According to this concept, called **androgyny,** possessing both male and female personality traits is not only beneficial but also important. Androgynous individuals define themselves as human beings rather than as males or females. Personality traits are not compartmentalized by sex. Being nurturant, assertive, sensitive, dominant, affectionate, and self-sufficient are seen as proper for both men and women.

Sandra Bem [1974; 1975; 1981(a), (b)] is among the researchers exploring the concept of androgyny. She maintains that the androgynous personality encompasses many positive character traits and abilities. Androgynous individuals appear to be more competent and to possess higher levels of self-esteem than individuals who adhere to traditional sex-role behaviors. Furthermore, the former seem to be more effective in dealing with their surroundings, are generally more secure with themselves, and are less anxious. Androgynous individuals are also more flexible in their behavior than sex-typed people (Wiggins and Holzmuller, 1981).

Although the field of androgyny is controversial, such research findings suggest that moving away from rigid sex-role typing has implications for growth and development. Proponents feel that removal of sex-typed behavioral constraints and expectations would allow individuals to develop all aspects of their personalities more fully and to demonstrate the best qualities of both sexes. Children, especially, would benefit from a more tolerant acceptance of their total selves, instead of continually being made aware of how they should behave. As a result of this type of philosophy, such statements as, "Big boys shouldn't cry" or "Girls should act like ladies" may be heard less frequently in years to come.

Emotional Development

With age, children exhibit varying amounts of emotional maturity. Emotional maturity is characterized by a change from helplessness to independence and self-sufficiency. Maturity implies progressive stages of growth and the overall acquisition of emotional flexibility. The emotional maturity of the school-age child is also characterized by greater emotional differentiation.

Because of greater emotional differentiation, school-age children express a wide range of feelings. They get mad, are afraid, harbor feelings of jealousy, and exhibit frustrations. They also show love and affection,

giggle with delight, and shiver with excitement. Of course, one important chore during childhood is learning appropriate and inappropriate
times for showing emotions. Healthy emotional expression usually
means not feeling guilty about what one feels but conveying it in a

The Differentiation of Emotional Expression

There is little question that the emotions of school-age children are more complex than those of younger children. Indications are that they will become even more diverse as time goes on. The diversity of our emotional repertoire has attracted the attention of psychologists such as Robert Plutchik (1980), who has classified the basic human emotions. His classification may help students see the range of mature emotional expression. Plutchik

Table 16.2 Plutchik's Eight Primary Emotions and Their Functional Value

Primary Emotion	Function	Functional Description
Fear	Protection	Behavior designed to avoid danger or harm, such as running away or any action that puts distance between an organism and the source of danger.
Anger	Destruction	Behavior designed to eliminate a barrier to satisfaction of an important need. This includes biting, striking, and various symbolic acts of destruction, such as cursing or threatening.
Joy	Incorporation	Behavior that involves accepting a beneficial stimulus from the outside world, as in eating, grooming, mating, or affiliation with members of one's own social group. Such actions have the effect of nurturing the individual.
Disgust	Rejection	Behavior designed to expel something harmful that has been ingested, such as vomiting or, at times, defecation. This behavior is believed to be associated with feelings of contempt and hostility and with sarcasm, all of which are essentially a rejection of other people or their ideas.
Acceptance	Reproduction	Behavior designed to provide contact with sex for the purpose of perpetuating one's gene pool. Expressions of

controlled manner and in socially acceptable ways. What determines the degree of emotional control, appropriate times, and acceptable channels will be the child's overall level of maturation and the emotional norms of society (Williams and Stith, 1980).

The Differentiation of Emotional Expression, *continued.*

maintains that there are eight primary emotions: fear, anger, joy, disgust, acceptance, sadness, surprise, and anticipation. He suggests that these emotions have evolved from the function each serves. Each of us has inherited the capacity for these eight emotions even though life experience may teach us when to be emotional. Table 16.2 displays Plutchik's eight primary emotions and their functional value. ■

Table 16.2, *continued*

Primary Emotion	Function	Functional Description
Acceptance *(continued)*	Reproduction *(continued)*	this function include sexual signaling, courtship rituals, and sexual intercourse.
Sadness	Reintegration	Behavior associated with the loss of someone who has provided important nurturance in the past. In such circumstances, the individual sends signals that encourage the return of the lost individual or attract a substitute. Expressions of this function include crying, emission of distress signals, and "babyish" behavior.
Surprise	Orientation	Behavior associated with a new, unfamiliar stimulus: a loud noise, a strange animal, or a new territory, for example. The organism must quickly reorient the body and stop what it is doing so that the sense organs can take in information about the novel stimulus.
Anticipation	Exploration	Behavior designed to bring the organism into contact with many aspects of its environment. Getting to know one's neighborhood permits a form of mental mapping that enables the animal to anticipate and deal with future challenges to its survival.

From Plutchik, 1980, p. 73.

Sex-role stereotyping has a great deal to do with the nature and quality of emotional expression. While all children need outlets for their emotions, sex-role stereotyping often prevents this. For example, boys are often taught not to cry or show fear, and girls aren't generally allowed to be physically aggressive. Boys who cry may be called sissies, and aggressive girls are often called tomboys. Such stereotyping prevents children from experiencing and accepting their total feelings, as well as from expressing all their emotional needs. With these points in mind, let's turn our attention toward some of the emotions that have been studied during middle childhood.

Anger and Aggression

The physical qualities attached to anger and aggression persist through the school years, including such overt outbursts as shoving, kicking, and hitting. Children also learn that anger can be expressed through other channels. For example, anger can be released verbally by arguing, name calling, insulting, and swearing. Children also learn to bury their anger and express it through passive and sullen means.

School-age children tend to engage in greater amounts of hostile aggression. **Hostile aggression** is aimed at another person with the intention of hurting that individual. Such behavior usually results when individuals feel that they have been threatened, unjustly accused, or intentionally hurt. Note the connection to growing cognitive awareness. The child has to think about the intentions or motives of another, something younger children have difficulty doing. This is different from **instrumental aggression,** which is more common among younger children and is directed at acquiring such things as toys or play space. Regardless of the form it takes, many researchers today (see Eron, 1980) regard aggressiveness as a learned form of behavior. Also, research studies almost always show that boys are more aggressive than girls (Maccoby and Jacklin, 1980).

Fear

During middle childhood there is a decline in fears related to body safety, such as sickness and injury, and in fear of dogs, noises, darkness, and storms. There is no significant decline in fears of supernatural forces, such as ghosts and witches. Most new fears at this time are related to school and family, an obvious reflection of expanding social boundaries. Fears of ridicule by parents, teachers, and friends increase, as do fears of parental disapproval and rejection (Wolman, 1978).

Joy, Happiness, and Humor

Joy and happiness are pleasurable emotional states. A diversity of situations arouse joy and happiness, including the satisfaction of curiosity and the development of new abilities and accomplishments. Curiosity toward, and mastery of, the elementary school environment can produce pleasurable states within the child (Gottfried, 1983; Deci and Ryan, 1982). Other sources of joy and happiness include being with friends and loved ones, surprises, treasured gifts and possessions, and the challenge of doing something new.

Humor is closely related to joy and happiness. Jokes are especially savored by the school-age youngster. Although preschoolers enjoy hearing jokes, their understanding of them is limited. Cognitive facilities beyond the preschooler's capacities are needed to understand such elements as subtleties, punch lines, the use of puns and incongruities, and general delivery. Younger children also have trouble telling jokes, which requires considerable cognitive mastery and linguistic fluency. Because of their many cognitive components, jokes and children's humor as a whole are regarded as a mirror of the developing mind [McGhee, 1980; McGhee and Goldstein, 1983(a), (b)].

As far as specific types of jokes are concerned, school-age children delight in knock-knock jokes, "one-liners," and puns. They also enjoy off-color jokes dealing with things that are slightly if not entirely taboo, such as sex and body functions (Williams and Stith, 1980). Other research indicates that some children prefer humor that contains aggressiveness and hostility (McCauley et al., 1983).

Love and Affection

Love is regarded as a sentiment, a complex state of feelings with many abstract qualities that will not be totally understood until a state of cognitive maturity has been reached. However, children learn about love early in life, usually when bonds of attachment are formed with parents. From attachments, children create their first definitions of themselves, their self-worth, and self-acceptance. Youngsters who receive love from their parents come to accept themselves as being important objects of affection for someone else. Those children who have been given love and affection are capable of giving love in return (Orthner, 1981; Dinnage, 1980).

The manner in which love is expressed changes with age. Preschoolers are likely to express love through physical means, such as hugging and kissing. School-age children still do this, but they also learn that love can be expressed in other ways, such as by sharing and

talking. The relinquishment of an egocentric point of view and heightened sensitivity toward others help to develop the child's capacity to
love during middle childhood, and love and affection are expressed not
only to family and friends but also to animals.

**Children who are raised with love are able to
give it to others.**

The masculine and feminine roles that children learn will be an important determinant of their definition of love and an even greater influence on how they express it (Cox, 1984). If, for example, it is deemed unmasculine for a male to display tenderness, then tenderness may not be a part of the male's style of love.

Empathy

Empathy is the ability to sympathize with or share the emotions of others. It is an important quality of emotional maturity, and evidence indicates that it steadily increases with age. Acts of kindness, helping others, and supplying reassurance are quite evident by middle childhood (Burleson, 1982).

While such behavior was evident earlier in childhood, it had a tendency to be sporadic. Now, it is expressed more consistently and for many will become more deeply rooted as time goes on. Among the reasons for this is the fact that older children not only better understand the needs of others but also have developed a concept of responsibility toward others. Moreover, it is conceivable they have come to learn the benefits of empathy as they have learned the benefits of altruism and sharing (Peterson, 1983; McGinnis and Goldstein, 1984).

Family Influences on Child Development

The fact that children now attend school full-time, have greater interaction with their peers, and display heightened levels of independence places the family in a new perspective. Children still need and rely very much on their parents, but their contacts with the outside world have expanded. As a result, their social relationships with other adults are considerably broader, including, for example, interactions with teachers, den mothers, coaches, or summer camp leaders.

The negotiation of new social boundaries and the parents' reactions to the youngster's strivings for independence make these years especially challenging. Fired by the Eriksonian desire for industry, most children want to spend more time away from the family. This threatens many parents, who need to be assured that this is a completely normal phase of child development and that they will remain special and unique in the wake of these social strivings. It is interesting to note that amidst these desires for social independence, many school-age children periodically tend to slip back to dependency, although usually in private and on their own terms. This age also marks the time when many want to spend more time alone doing private things or to keep secret what they do both within and away from the family.

Children's greater interactions with others enables them to bring back to the home an abundance of social experiences, whether it be tales about school or sports exploits or neighborhood news. Their increasing powers of social cognition also enable them to compare their home environment with those around them. As a result, what other children have or do is weighed against what they have or are allowed to do, a comparison likely to breed a fair number of questions and possible disagreements with parents. (How many parents have heard, "Everyone else does it, why can't I?") Parental values and standards are also tested when children bring home ideas, language, and attitudes different from those taught at home.

Experiencing a Favorable Home Environment

Youngsters need to experience a favorable home climate throughout all of childhood, but this is especially true during the school years. Children unquestionably need the support and guidance of parents as they seek to meet the challenges of this age. This is as true for achieving personal independence as it is for other facets of growth, such as developing a sense of morality, establishing healthy relations with siblings, learning appropriate sex roles, and building self-esteem.

Favorable home environments provide warmth and acceptance to children, employ consistent measures of discipline, encourage competence, and respond to children's growing needs. Healthy patterns of child development depend on the degree to which parents love, communicate, and seek to understand the needs of their offspring. Given such an environment, children are apt to become emotionally stable, cooperative, and happy. The unloved or rejected child, on the other hand, often becomes resentful, quarrelsome, lonely, and insecure (Evoy, 1982).

Charles Thompson and Virginia Rudolph (1983) stress the importance of nurturance and loving support in parent-child relations. They contend that among other outcomes, children from nurturing families are likely to communicate more openly, be more honest with others, and adjust more readily to life's demands than children from nonnurturing homes. In addition, children from nurturing families know that their parents regard them as special individuals and will listen to them when they talk. Furthermore, they know that their ideas will not be devalued.

A harmonious family life and a positive emotional climate are also evident in those homes sharing responsibility. Dolores Curran (1983) maintains that shared responsibility is a critical ingredient of healthy family relations. By sharing responsibility, children learn to believe in their capacity to make a contribution. They also learn that each person counts in the family and makes a difference. Curran maintains that shared responsibility includes, but goes beyond, responsibility for everyday chores and obligations. Responsibility also encompasses, for example, responsiveness to other family members' feelings and getting along with, and looking after, one another. Shared responsibility also tends to breed other positive traits, such as affirmation, respect, and trust.

Maladaptive Patterns of Family Life

Research discloses that a child's maladaptive behavior may be caused by the general family environment as well as the youngster's relationships with one or both parents. Although there is no blueprint or model of the "ideal" family, James Coleman (1984) identifies five maladaptive patterns of family life that have a negative effect on children's growth and development.

1. *The inadequate family.* The inadequate family is unable to cope with the ordinary problems of everyday life. It lacks the psychological and physical resources for meeting the demands made on it. This family frequently fails to provide children with security and safety. It also has difficulty steering children toward the development of essential competencies.

2. *The disturbed family.* While disturbed families have many different pathological patterns, they have three common characteristics. First, the parents are often struggling to maintain their own equilibrium and are unable to generate needed love and guidance for their children. Second, the children are often tangled in their parents' emotional problems, which

hinders their own emotional development. Third, the children are exposed to constant emotional turmoil, irrationality, and poor parental models.

3. *The antisocial family.* The antisocial family espouses values not accepted or taught by others. Parents may either overtly or covertly engage in behaviors deemed unacceptable by society. Such misbehavior may often place them in trouble with the law. Obviously, such antisocial behaviors as lack of concern or dishonesty are unsuitable role models for children.

4. *The abusive family.* The abusive family (see Chapter 11) is characterized by lack of caring. Abusive behavior may include abandonment; neglect or failure to provide; and physical, emotional, or sexual abuse.

5. *The disrupted family.* Desertion of the family by a parent, usually the father, is the most common cause of the disrupted family. Desertion causes feelings of rejection, financial troubles, and an assortment of other difficulties. Should the remaining family not reorganize effectively, children often suffer in their development. ■

The Family and Television

The contemporary child rarely escapes the clutches of television programming since a television is available in nearly every home in America. Television has changed family life more than any other technological innovation of the twentieth century. Families often plan their schedules to accommodate television, sometimes even scheduling meals and social activities around or in front of "the tube" (Liebert, Sprafkin, and Davidson, 1982).

In the average family, television is turned on each day for a period of 6 to 7 hours. For children under age 6, the average viewing per day is about 2½ hours. From age 8 until early adolescence, viewing time increases to almost 4 hours per day and then begins to level off. By the end of high school, the average individual will have devoted about 12,000 hours to school but 15,000 hours to television. For the child born in the 1980s, more hours will be spent watching television than in any other single activity besides sleep (Liebert, Sprafkin, and Davidson, 1982; Steinberg, 1980; Moody, 1980).

Think carefully about the above statistics, particularly in relation to our analysis of the contemporary family. These figures mean that the daily activity of the American household can now be divided into three fairly equal parts: 6 to 7 hours of television viewing, 9 hours of work or school, including transportation back and forth, and 8 hours of sleep. To say that television has become part of the American lifestyle is an understatement.

Televised Violence   Few issues related to television have aroused more concern or sparked more debate than televised violence and its effects on children. Among psychologists and educators, the study of televised violence has been a hotbed of activity for almost 20 years. Research activity among contemporary investigators indicates that this interest pervades the 1980s [see Eron, 1982; Eron et al., 1983; Huesmann et al., 1983; Singer, 1983; Singer and Singer, 1981; 1980(a); Morton and Acker, 1981; Milavsky et al., 1982].

Television programming for children contains a considerable amount of violence, with cartoons invariably the guiltiest culprit (see Cramer and Mechem, 1982). Moreover, most research findings show that televised violence has increased markedly in the last decade. For example, one investigation revealed that in the course of one program hour there is an average of nine acts of physical aggression and almost eight instances of verbal aggression (Williams, Zabrack, and Joy, 1982).

What effect does viewing violence have on children's behavior? Two major theories currently offer answers to this question. The **social learning theory** maintains that children will imitate aggressive behavior when they are exposed to it on television. The **catharsis theory**

DENNIS the MENACE

" GOOD OL' TELEBISION...YOU CAN ALWAYS DEPEND ON IT TO BE THERE WHEN YOU NEED IT. "

proposes that watching aggressive behavior on television provides a vicarious outlet for the viewer's own aggressiveness. Televised aggression thus enables viewers to drain off or discharge their aggressive tendencies.

Support for the social learning interpretation has been steadily growing. Although there is some support for the catharsis explanation (see Feshbach and Singer, 1971), many psychologists today maintain that among children there is a significant relationship between watching excessive violence and aggressive behavior. This has been the central finding of numerous studies, including a ten-year study conducted by the National Instutite of Mental Health (1982). The NIMH study cited "overwhelming evidence" supporting the existence of the above relationship.

Televised violence has other effects on the viewer. Seeing repeated acts of violence tends gradually to desensitize the viewer to aggression. Over time, even one's level of physiological arousal toward violence declines, indicating that one has become hardened to violence and aggression (Thomas, 1982; Geen, 1981).

Benefits of Television   In spite of its potentially harmful effects, television can provide a wealth of information and positive experiences. As we discussed in Chapter 12, advancements in educational television have proved beneficial. Television programming such as this can enhance a number of developmental areas, including language abilities, concept formation, reading skills, and prosocial development (see Singer and Singer, 1983; Rice, 1983; Liebert, Sprafkin, and Davidson, 1982). In other spheres, television, when not overused, can provide wholesome entertainment and relaxation.

Children and Television: Promoting Healthy Viewing Habits

Adults can do much to help children develop healthy television viewing habits. Most experts maintain that controlling the amount of time children watch television and the kinds of programming they watch is a step in the right direction. More specific recommendations and suggestions include the following:

1. *Familiarize yourself with children's television.* To evaluate children's television programming and provide guidance to youngsters, become familiar with the range of shows available. Sample a cross-section of programs and critique each. A single Saturday morning should be an eye-opener.

2. *Balance a child's television needs against other needs.* A legitimate concern among adults is that television often detracts from other important facets of childhood. Balance television viewing against these other important activities, including play, reading, exploring, socializing, family interaction, and studying.

3. *Decide on a schedule for television viewing.*

Monitor the amount of time children spend in front of the television set. Establish daily schedules specifying the hours of the morning, afternoon, or evening when television viewing is permissible. Many experts today feel that between 10 and 15 hours of television viewing per week is acceptable.

4. *Select good television programs for children.* Quality programming is available to children if one takes the time to look for it. Educational television, in particular, offers a multitude of programs for youngsters of different ages. Steer children toward suitable documentaries, music, and classic stories.

5. *Help children distinguish between make-believe and real life.* Young children, especially preschoolers, have difficulty understanding that the fantasy depicted on television cannot happen in real life. As a result, many are convinced of the extraordinary powers of their favorite superheroes, for example. Many also ▶

With such positive potential, television is a powerful teacher capable of enhancing the quality of life for individuals and society. It is our most powerful communication tool, and without question it is here to stay. Therefore it is important to examine continually television's role in our lives. As Alice Honig [1983(a)] aptly states, television can be used for violence, for crass commercialism, or for instruction and for enhancing and enriching lives. Clearly we must take charge of television and harness its potential rather than let it control our lives. By so doing, we can make television an ally and not an adversary.

Children and Television: Promoting Healthy Viewing Habits, *continued.*

perceive the violence depicted in cartoons as acceptable and amusing since the victim always gets up and comes back for more. Try to help children differentiate between fantasy and fact and see the world as it really is.

6. *Observe how children's behavior is affected by television.* Too much television can overstimulate the child and cause mood shifts, including general irritability. Excessive amounts of television can also cause eyestrain and headaches. These negative reactions underscore the need to monitor television viewing time.

7. *Express disapproval of television violence and other negative elements.* Children need to know that important adults in their lives do not like violence. They should learn that there are many ways to reach a desired goal in life other than through a path of senseless destruction. In addition, speak out against television programs that downgrade members of a societal group or depict unfair sexual stereotypes.

8. *Seek to expose the deception in television advertisements.* Products advertised on television are not always as glamorous or perfect as they appear. Children must learn that advertising strategies can sometimes be misleading.

9. *Share television viewing time with children.* More families need to share what television brings into their lives. Arrange time to watch family programs with children and explain sensitive programming topics, hatred, tragedy, loss, or sorrow.

10. *Follow up on the positive qualities of television programming.* Try to expand and integrate into children's lives the positive lessons reaped from television. This applies to educational programs, as well as to important life lessons portrayed in other programming endeavors. ■

Adapted from Honig, 1983(a); Kelley, 1983; Moody, 1980.

Peer-Group Development

Sharing experiences with friends and being a member of a peer group are important dimensions of social relations. By middle childhood, increasing amounts of time are spent with peers, especially close friends. Peer relations combine with the family and the school to become a powerful agent of socialization (Howes, 1983; Hartup, 1983).

Friendships

A friend is one of life's greatest treasures. In order to have friends and promote close ties with special people, children must acquire such desirable social skills as empathy, cooperation, and sensitivity. True **friendship** will require that children forgo some of their own personal desires and adopt the perspectives of others. Thus, just as egocentrism must decline in order for children to make advances in cognitive development, it must decrease even further for children to reach heightened levels of social maturity. Declining egocentrism will help pave the way for other changes in childhood friendships, such as improved conflict resolution skills, more meaningful exchanges of information, and a more systematic exploration of differences. Each of these is regarded as necessary for the establishment of more meaningful patterns of friendship (Gottman, 1983; McGuire and Weisz, 1982; Furman and Bierman, 1983).

Robert Selman's (1981) analysis of friendships throughout childhood reveals certain developmental stages. Friendships during the preschool years, called the "playmateship stage," depend on the child's feelings at the moment, the physical presence of the other youngster, and the availability of toys or other resources. Friendships during the early school years are characterized by what Selman calls the "one-way assistance" stage. During this stage, a friend is someone who has come to fill a need, such as the provision of toys or companionship.

By the later school years, children enter the stage of friendships called "fair-weather cooperation." Friendships at this time acquire a flavoring of reciprocity and mutuality. This stage bears its name because arguments and disagreements still punctuate friendships and tend to suspend the relationship. It is only during late childhood or early adolescence that friendships encounter smoother sailing and acquire more consistent expressions of mutuality and supportive understanding. Selman labels this final stage "intimate and mutually shared relationships." The notion that older children's friendships are characterized by mutuality and reciprocity is a consistent theme in the literature (Youniss, 1980; Newcomb and Brady, 1982; Howes, 1983; Rubin, 1980; Diaz and Berndt, 1982).

Children are drawn to friends of the same sex, a trend persisting from earlier years. Interestingly, boys' and girls' friendships have several unique differences. While both boys and girls center their friendships around shared activities and interests, boys are typically more competitive and girls more cooperative. Boys have a tendency to downplay the intimacy or closeness of their relationships. Boys are also more oriented to groups while girls are attracted to one-to-one friendships. Furthermore, girls tend to be more expressive to one another than boys (Rubin, 1980). Their attraction to the emotional bond that friendships offer will spill over into the adolescent years (Richey and Richey, 1980; Coleman, 1980).

Peer-Group Dynamics

Peer groups that develop during the middle years are individual in structure, cohesive, and centrally motivated. Each group represents a separate and unique sociological phenomenon. However, certain generalizations concerning their development can be made.

For example, peer groups continue to be highly selective. Newcomers are accepted on the basis of similar sex, race, social status, and age. Physical attractiveness also appears to be a requirement for acceptance among some peer groups (Schofield and Francis, 1982; Schofield and Whitley, 1983; Vaughn and Langlois, 1983; Schofield, 1981; Finkelstein and Haskins, 1983).

Peer groups arise to satisfy definite needs, such as a desire to escape adult supervision or to be in the company of like-minded individuals. They typically establish a **hierarchical structure,** a division of their members into leaders and followers. While a hierarchical structure can be seen in groups of younger children, it is more stable and durable among older children.

Invariably, the peer group consists of children who are popular and well liked and those who are unpopular. What factors determine popularity? One of the most consistent themes in the literature is that popularity is determined not by the quantity of time children spend with their peers but by other, deeper factors. For example, popular children tend to be bright, friendly, and cooperative. Less popular children tend to be overly aggressive and often inappropriate in their behavior. Popular children usually have good group entry skills; that is, they enter group activities without having a disruptive effect. Finally, the popular child, in contrast to the less popular one, possesses more of the personality traits judged desirable by members of his or her sex (Hartup, 1983; Dodge et al., 1983; Asher and Hymel, 1981; Putallaz and Gottman, 1981).

Youngsters who are rejected or unpopular frequently face negative consequences. For some, the loneliness accompanying rejection may persist into adulthood. Others may develop more severe problems, such as neurosis or delinquent behavior (Hojat, 1982; Cowen et al., 1973; Roff, 1974).

Peer Relations and Conformity

Observe any group of elementary school children during a recess period or play situation, and you will probably see one of the more interesting phenomena of early social development: **conformity** to the peer group. While waging a battle to impress and be accepted by others, and at the same time striving to avoid rejection, children want to conform to the norms established by the peer group. This has a number of effects, from similar modes of dress, language, and hairstyles to similar activities and mannerisms. Any parent of a middle childhood youngster can testify to the growing levels of conformity at this time. If the adult ventures to ask why a particular toy or type of clothing is desired, the typical reaction is, "because everyone else has one."

Although conformity to peer-group pressure is especially evident at this time, the presence of individual differences should be stressed. Generally, girls appear to display higher degrees of conformity than boys. Status in the group and personality factors such as dependency also affect the degree of conformity a group member may display [Hartup, 1970(a); Shaffer, 1979].

Studies designed to measure conformity have repeatedly shown that children will go along with the group, even against their own better judgment. Children tend to pattern their answers after others' responses to a problem-solving situation. They are likely to conform even to obvious wrong answers, and the more uncertain they are of a cognitive problem, the more likely they are to conform (Miller and Brownell, 1975).

School Influences on Child Development

Entrance into school brings children into a new and complex social environment. Most children eagerly anticipate attending elementary school and each year look forward to the classroom's developmental challenges. Youngsters will have to adjust to new routines and demands, task-oriented behavior, conformity to authority, and impulse control, to name but a few challenges children face each year in school (Stewart and LeCompte, 1980).

Table 16.3 Significant Social Developments during Middle Childhood

Age	Social Developments
6	Egocentrism still present at this time inhibits meaningful social relationships. Interactions with other children in the family are often competitive, but vary according to the child's ordinal position in the family. Although friendships are sometimes erratic, 6-year-olds often establish a best friend, with whom they spend a good deal of time. Movement toward same-sex friends is most prevalent.
7	Increased sense of self and heightened sensitivity to others enhances social relationships. However, this heightened sensitivity makes the youngster acutely aware of shortcomings, failures, and criticisms. Consequently, brooding, feelings of shame, and negativism may be common. Advanced interpersonal skills allow the 7-year-old to become a better listener; growing evidence of empathy and understanding of the needs of others is present.
8	Noticeable separation between the sexes, even to the point where the opposite sex is excluded from group activities. However, the 8-year-old's attitude toward members of the opposite sex is a mixture of attraction and hostility, a pattern that will be seen again in early adolescence. At this age, most children are friendly and cooperative. Also there is social curiosity about other people, evidenced by the child's attentiveness to adult conversations and eagerness to observe at grown-up gatherings.
9	Heightened self-confidence and emotional security bolster social relationships. Close friendships started earlier are strengthened, but a dichotomy of the sexes still exists. Much overt hostility between boys and girls. Organized games and other structured social activities begin to emerge.
10	Organized social activities continue to attract the attention of the child, and a diversity of interests emerge. Most 10-year-olds do not resent spending time with family rather than friends. A new admiration and respect for one's parents emerge. Interpersonal relationships and communication skills continue to increase.
11	A new level of maturity (the plateau between childhood and adolescence) frequently requires a redefinition of one's sense of self, as well as one's social relationships. Choices of friendships are now based on mutuality of interest and temperament rather than on proximity. Although friendships grow in number at this time, one or several intimate relationships are established. Interest in the opposite sex begins, although girls are likely to be more interested and vocal about their interest than boys.

(Adapted from Elkind, 1978)

The Influence of the Teacher

Many children become attached to, or are awed by, their teacher, not only because the teacher acts in many respects as a substitute parent but also because the teacher conveys to the child the assurance that adult authority is trustworthy and that the school environment is safe, stimulating, and satisfying. In fulfilling these and other needs, teachers exert strong influences on the child's behavior. In the process of instruction and the manner in which it is delivered, teachers transmit their personal attitudes and beliefs to their pupils (Walter and Ashton, 1980).

Teacher behaviors have an effect on pupil performance. On the whole, teachers are effective when they demonstrate warmth, understanding, support, and compassion toward their students. Successful elementary school teachers are generous in their appraisals of behavior and are warm, empathetic, and friendly in their social relationships. They also indicate a strong preference for nondirective classroom procedures. Conversely, unsuccessful teachers are less favorable in their expressed opinions of pupils, less satisfactory in emotional adjustment, and more critical and restrictive in their appraisals of the behavior and motives of others. Teachers who exhibit genuineness, warmth, and friendliness in their dealings with children, rather than punitive and authoritarian techniques, also encourage favorable behavior, particularly constructive and conscientious attitudes toward schoolwork and less aggressive behavior (Walter and Ashton, 1980).

Although their main task and responsibility is to teach academic subjects, teachers are also responsible to some extent for the psychological well-being of pupils. So teacher behavior directly relates to the student's self-concept and peer acceptance. Teachers are in a prime position to serve as role models, as well as reinforcers, of children's social interaction. The examples they set, the tone they establish for peer relations, and the feedback they give to children are important influences (Rutter, 1983).

Methods of Classroom Control

Children are also exposed to different types of classroom control, from traditional types of leadership to more liberal approaches. Three general types of classroom control have been identified: democratic, authoritarian, and laissez-faire.

Authoritarian leadership has a tendency to produce two major types of social atmosphere, aggressive and apathetic. Studies have shown that there are higher incidences of irritability and aggressiveness toward fellow group members in atmospheres created by authoritarian and laissez-faire leadership than in democratic climates. In addition, authoritarian teachers tend to foster high interpersonal tension. Authoritarian classes are also often lower in task-related suggestions by the members; whenever authoritarian leaders are absent for short periods,

Children must learn new routines if they are to adjust to new social environments.

work motivation among students has a tendency to decline [Hartup, 1970(b)].

Students taught by democratic and laissez-faire teachers often make more frequent requests for attention and approval than do students in authoritarian classrooms. Although interpersonal friendliness does not usually vary as a result of teaching styles, democratic and laissez-faire classes seem to have more of a "we" feeling than their authoritarian counterparts. Finally, the absence of democratic teachers for short periods of time does not appear to affect the task-oriented efforts of the class [Hartup, 1970(b)].

Deciding which type of classroom climate and control to establish may be one of the most difficult chores for the beginning teacher. Certainly formal education and likes and dislikes of various approaches will determine the emotional climate to some extent. So, too, will the relationship between the children's temperamental characteristics and the teacher's reactions to them (Elias, 1980; Pullis and Cadwell, 1980).

Most experts agree that no general prescription can tell teachers what choices to make in terms of classroom control. A teacher with a strong personality can, to some degree, persuade students to subscribe to his or her values. But such a teacher may also arouse feelings of opposition in students whose values are not the same. Classroom harmony usually depends on the match between the **values,** temperaments, and personalities of the children and those of the teacher (Glassberg, 1980; Kagan and Lang, 1978).

Classroom behavior is partly dependent on the type of classroom control the teacher uses.

Microcomputers in the Classroom

An exciting development in elementary school education in recent years has been the addition of microcomputers. More schools than ever before are making microcomputers part of their curriculum, and their use has given a new dimension to teaching strategies, not to mention the nature of the child's schooling experience. Many people hail microcomputers as the teaching tool of our time and an essential part of America's educational future (Schuelle and Kins, 1983; Watts, 1981; Papert, 1980).

Consider the rapid growth of microcomputers in the public school system. In 1982 the number of microcomputers in use was approximately 100,000, nearly triple the number in use between 1980 and 1981. This means that today almost 40 percent of all elementary schools have microcomputers in their buildings. More than 60 percent of public school districts have at least one school using a computer for instruction. Couple this with the 9 percent (approximately) of American households owning a home computer and you'll begin to see why children are very much a part of our computer revolution (Ziajka, 1983; Magarrell, 1982; Titus, 1982; Nilles, 1982).

Microcomputers have a variety of uses in the classroom. They can help teachers keep track of attendance, lesson plans, grading, assignments, inventories, and a multitude of other tasks. They can teach reading, writing, arithmetic, and spelling. They can be used for drill and testing, tutoring, simulations to develop problem-solving skills, or individualized pacing of the curriculum. As children grow older, more advanced uses are available, and their functions become even more diverse (I. Miller, 1981).

Beyond their functional qualities, what benefits do microcomputers offer children? Many experts feel that microcomputers offer children an active style of learning that avoids mental drudgery. The educational programs themselves are often lively and colorful. Furthermore, microcomputers can adapt to each child's learning pace, offering limitless patience to slow learners but establishing a rigorous routine for bright children (Walker, 1983; Swigger, 1982).

Microcomputers have other benefits as well. Microcomputer use helps improve hand-eye coordination and develop fine motor skills. They also encourage independent learning and provide children with immediate reinforcement. That is, children can see the results of their efforts instantly, not hours or days later. Even partial solutions offer the user some degree of accomplishment. Microcomputers also offer children control and mastery of their environment. This sense of control becomes evident as children learn to write programs. Moreover, as they teach the computer to think, youngsters explore how they themselves think (Papert, 1980).

Microcomputer use appears to have social benefits as well, including the encouragement of cooperative behavior. Often computers are a catalyst for group activity and problem-solving strategies. Alan Ziajka's (1983) observations of children bears this out. In one classroom setting he observed the microcomputer serving as a bonafide interest center. Its presence encouraged children to work together, share ideas on what to do next, and help one another. In the process he observed children making extensive use of oral language, even sprinkling it with a little computer jargon.

Let it be said, though, that microcomputers are far from being universally accepted in the educational sphere. While many educators laud their merits, many others question whether microcomputers actually increase learning or are truly more effective than traditional classroom teaching strategies. Many are concerned that some schools are jumping on the bandwagon without thoroughly examining all the facets of microcomputers (Brady and Hill, 1984; Nilles, 1982; Walker, 1983).

What are the drawbacks of microcomputers? One of the most frequently heard complaints is high purchase prices, a criticism that raises the related issue of school equity. About 80 percent of our richest, largest school districts have microcomputers, while only about 40 percent of poorer school districts do. Maintenance, service, and software are also expensive. And the limited information about what school systems are doing and purchasing has further muddied the waters (Billings, 1981; Nilles, 1982; Turkington, 1982).

Many teachers feel threatened by computers. Some fear losing their jobs or being upstaged by computers. Most overcome these anxieties once they're exposed to the microcomputer and realize its value as an educational tool. Of course, many must be reassured that microcomputers are a supplement to conventional education, not a substitute for it (Walker, 1983).

There is some concern about the time, money, and effort needed to orient teachers to microcomputer education. In particular, adults working with microcomputers have to develop **computer literacy,** the knowledge and skills needed to function in a computer-oriented society. Children cannot become computer literate without computer literate teachers. This means that teachers must make a commitment to orient themselves to microcomputers (Riedesel and Clements, 1985; Bell, 1983; Bradley, 1983; Watts, 1981).

Because we are only beginning to understand how to use microcomputers, it would be easy for school personnel to look foolish around them. Also, since new products and systems are being created in such profusion, with such speed, and with so little standardization, it is nearly impossible for schools to implement systematic, long-term planning. Finally, programs for teaching explicit, formal models can be created fairly readily with existing techniques. However, it is much more difficult to use microcomputers to teach subject matter that involves intuition, judgment, improvisation, and creativity (Walker, 1983).

Thus while microcomputers have many positive features, their total worth has yet to be assessed. The drawbacks and concerns cited need to be explored. More research needs to be done, particularly since investigations to date have used very small groups and have maintained few standard research controls (Brady and Hill, 1984).

Summary

Kirk, age 10

Personality and social relations acquire many new dimensions during the years of middle childhood. Freud refers to these years as the latency period of psychosexual development. Freud perceives this as a quiescent period, although ego identity continues to unfold. In particular, many children of this age devise and refine coping mechanisms.

Coping mechanisms are patterns of behavior concerned with relieving anxiety. This chapter explored the more common types of coping mechanisms. Rationalization is an attempt to provide logical reasons for one's failures or shortcomings, and projection is attributing one's difficulties or failures to someone else. Displacement is redirection of hostile feelings to people or objects less dangerous than those creating the anxiety. Denial of reality is refusal to perceive the existence of hurtful situations. Compensation is finding a successful or rewarding activity that can be substituted for failure in another activity. Regression is a retreat to an earlier developmental level, and reaction formation is substituting an opposite behavior for an unacceptable behavior. Escape and withdrawal are interrelated ways of avoiding threatening or undesirable situations.

Erikson's psychosocial crisis of middle childhood is labeled industry versus inferiority. This stage parallels Freud's latency period and represents Erikson's fourth psychosocial crisis in his overall theory. During this stage, children strive for competence as their social worlds expand. Life accomplishments are important for the child's developing self-esteem. Failure, on the other hand, promotes feelings of inadequacy and inferiority.

Moral development is the process whereby individuals learn to adopt standards of right and wrong. Piaget and Kohlberg have proposed two of the more popular theories of moral development. Both theories employ a cognitive-developmental base and propose that mature morality is directly linked to mental functioning. Thus, if one is cognitively immature, moral reasoning is also immature. Piaget's analysis of morality includes the premoral stage (0 to 5), a period marked by little rule awareness, moral realism (5 to 10), a time when children receive rules but do not fully understand their purpose, and moral relativism (10 onward), a point at which the underlying meanings of rules are understood.

Kohlberg elaborates Piaget's work into a more detailed structure. He proposes three major levels of moral development, each consisting of two substages. Of concern to us in this chapter is the preconventional level (0 to 9). The substages that make up the preconventional level are obedience and punishment orientation and naively egoistic orientation. During the obedience and punishment substage, moral conduct is largely based on fear associated with rule violations. Like Piaget, Kohlberg suggests that for children of this age the seriousness of a violation depends on the magnitude of the wrongdoing. In the naively egoistic orientation, children reason that if they choose the right moral action they will get a tangible reward.

This chapter also examined other theoretical interpretations of morality. Freudian theory regards morality as the unconscious product of irrational motives and the need to keep antisocial impulses from levels of consciousness. Behaviorists view morality as particular acts and avoidances learned through reward and punishment. Social learning theorists examine the role that modeling or imitation plays in shaping one's moral behavior.

Sex-role development increases during middle childhood owing to growing cognitive awareness and expanding social horizons. This chapter examined both the unfounded nature of many sex-role stereotypes and the concept of androgyny. Androgyny is the relatively new notion of viewing people as individuals rather than typecasting them as males or females. Personality traits, in particular, are not compartmentalized by sex.

School-age children display more emotional maturity than their younger counterparts. Emotions become more specific and sophisticated at this time. Children learn to express anger in a multitude of ways, and aggression changes from instrumental to hostile forms. Fears related to the supernatural are characteristic of the school-age child, as are fears of ridicule, disapproval, and rejection.

Joy and happiness are pleasurable emotional states elicited by a variety of causes, including accomplishment, curiosity, the development of new abilities, and a host of other positive experiences. Humor, related to joy and happiness, is a good example of an emotional expression directly affected by one's state of cognitive awareness. Love is a complex state of feelings including emotion. While it is still expressed physically by the school-age child, youngsters of this age learn that it can be conveyed through other means, such as by sharing or talking. Empathy is the ability to sympathize with or share the emotions of others. Evidence indicates that empathy steadily increases with age.

The family continues to be an important agent of socialization for children, although they spend more time outside the home. As in other developmental stages, youngsters need the support, guidance, and nurturance of parents to meet the challenges of middle childhood. Favorable home environments foster warmth, acceptance, love, and open communication. Moreover, effective parents employ consistent measures of discipline, encourage competence, respond to the child's growing needs, and seek to teach the concept of shared responsibility. Five maladaptive patterns of family life are: inadequate, disturbed, antisocial, abusive, and disruptive. Each has a negative overall effect on the child's growth and development.

Television viewing is widespread in American homes. The effect of televised violence, in particular, has attracted the attention of researchers. Two main theories have emerged: social learning and catharsis. Social learning theory, the more widely accepted, maintains that children will imitate aggressive behavior when exposed to excessive amounts of it on television. The catharsis viewpoint suggests that watching aggressive behavior on television provides a vicarious outlet for the viewer's own aggressiveness.

Children spend increasing amounts of time with their friends during middle childhood. The acquisition of such social skills as empathy, cooperation, and sensitivity enables children to develop bonds of friendship. By late childhood, friendships have begun to be characterized by mutuality and supportive understanding. Peer groups continue to be highly selective and usually discriminate on the basis of sex, race, social status, and age. Popularity in the peer group is linked to intelligence, friendliness, cooperation, and group entry skills. While there are individual differences within the peer group, pressure to conform is especially evident during middle childhood.

The final portion of this chapter examined school influences on child development. Teachers greatly influence the degree of success children experience in school. Successful teachers are in control of their subject matter but are also empathetic, genuine, warm, and friendly in their dealings with children. Of the methods of classroom control presented, children tend to react more favorably to democratic structures than to authoritarian or laissez-faire structures. However, classroom harmony usually depends on the match between the values, temperaments, and personalities of the children and those of the teacher.

Microcomputers in the classroom are a fairly recent development in education. Today almost 40 percent of all elementary schools have microcomputers. In addition to their functional qualities, microcomputers offer a wide range of benefits to children. Among other benefits discussed in this chapter, microcomputers encourage independent learning, provide immediate reinforcement, offer children control of their environment, and encourage cooperation among youngsters.

Not all educators laud the merits of microcomputers, though. Critics point out their high cost and the fact that microcomputers have yet to be totally proven in the classroom. Moreover, many teachers feel threatened by microcomputers and balk at the time and effort needed to develop computer literacy. Another criticism is the difficulty microcomputers have in teaching subject matter involving intuition, judgment, improvisation, and creativity. Despite the criticism, enthusiasm abounds for microcomputers in the classroom. We are certain that, in years to come, we will see a flurry of research about their role in education.

Suggested Reading List

Hartup, W. Peer Relations. In *Carmichael's Manual of Child Psychology,* ed. P. H. Mussen. New York: Wiley, 1983. An up-to-date analysis of the research on peer relations for the serious student wanting a sophisticated coverage of the topic.

Perry, D. G., and Bussey, K. *Social Development.* Englewood Cliffs, N.J.: Prentice-Hall, 1984. A good exploration of many facets of social development. Separate chapters cover such topics as social cognition, morality, sex differences, and peer relations.

Rubin, Z. *Children's Friendships.* Cambridge: Harvard University Press, 1980. An authority on the topic explores the dynamics of friendships and how they change throughout the course of childhood.

Tavris, C., and Wade, C. *The Longest War: Sex Differences in Perspective.* 2nd ed. New York: Harcourt Brace Jovanovich, 1984. Chapter Six of this paperback explores how children learn sex-role differences.

Thomas, J. L. *Microcomputers in the Schools.* Phoenix, Ariz.: Oryx Press, 1981. This carefully edited collection of articles covers a wide array of topics, including computer literacy, implications of microcomputers for teachers, and how microcomputers affect children.

Chapter Seventeen

Imagination, Creativity, and Play

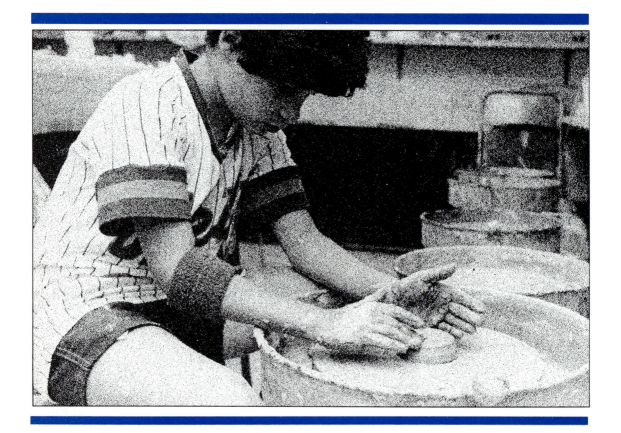

To stop playing is not to grow up; it is to cease living authentically.

William A. Sadler, Jr.

Introduction

As children get older, they are able to distinguish between pretending and the real world. After age 5, they can easily slip from fantasy to reality and back again. This is especially true if role playing is involved; children can completely submerge themselves again when the situation warrants it (Butler, Gotts, and Quisenberry, 1978).

The imagination of school-age children become more inner and private. They still enjoy sociodramatic play but tend to prefer quiet solitude and do not reveal their fantasies. This internalization of make-believe is generally caused by fear of ridicule or embarrassment or more direct social pressure. On the whole, society frowns on talking out loud, and when children enter school, they learn the demands of the class-room require quiet attention to the teacher. So they increasingly internalize their imaginative communications (Singer, 1975).

This does not mean that school-age children are less imaginative and creative than their younger counterparts. As we shall see, they are simply changing their mode of self-expression. New forms of make-believe expressions in school-age children testify to this, as do new creative accomplishments in such areas as play, art, and literature.

Imaginary Companions

Not long ago, children who reported having imaginary companions were thought to be hallucinating and dangerously removed from reality. Today it is believed that invisible playmates are a completely normal phase of childhood development. Furthermore, imaginary companions are created by large numbers of children, not just a handful of youngsters.

Maya Pines' (1978) review of the literature discloses that most imaginary companions are created between the preschool years and middle childhood. Children who have invisible playmates seem to be more cooperative, less aggressive, better able to concentrate, and more advanced in language skills than children without such companions. The language skills advantage is attributed to "dialogues" with the playmate. Boys invariably choose male imaginary companions, while girls may pick either males or females. Segal and Adcock (1981) maintain that imaginary companions are often duplicates or mirror images of their creators.

Imaginary playmates are true "companions" in every sense of the word. They are steadfast, loyal, and always available. Some come and go as the child needs them to fill various roles. They talk a lot and listen even more. They corroborate a youngster's stories, share accounts of how unfair the world is, and offer unfailing support.

These mental companions are not indications of insecurity or withdrawal, although there is cause for concern if their creators abandon the real world, cannot form human ties, or prefer their imaginary companions to real people. In most cases, invisible playmates fill "empty spaces" in children's lives. Most children with imaginary companions are firstborns or only children; often they have no real playmates of the same age (Singer, 1975).

Many feel that the creative genius behind such mental inventions is overwhelming. It takes an extremely creative mind to conjure up the right kind of "friend" at the right time, someone who is always available, always willing, and always ready with exactly the right thing to say (Pines, 1978).

Daydreaming

As indicated earlier, middle childhood is a time when make-believe play is carried out mostly in the form of private imagery. Daydreaming also develops at this time and persists throughout life. Daydreams are a form of wish fulfillment that enables the individual to circumvent space and time and explore the possibilities of life (Singer and Switzer, 1980).

Most children daydream, sometimes as a means of escape and other times to bring excitement, adventure, or pleasure into their lives. In the privacy of their own make-believe worlds, children can imagine limitless possibilities for themselves. In daydreams a child can be a star athlete, a central figure in an outer space odyssey, or a television star.

Daydreaming is regarded as a completely normal form of mental activity. In fact, it is maintained that daydreams enrich a person's thoughts and lead to more creativity and better emotional health. Of course, individuals must learn to build into their daydreams a self-checking system that keeps them from becoming overly involved in their inner worlds. Successful daydreaming lies in the individual's ability to shift smoothly from external awareness to inner concentration (Singer and Switzer, 1980; Martindale, 1981).

Many people believe that daydreaming leads to increased creativity.

The Measurement of Creativity

As we have expressed earlier, creativity is a difficult mental process to define, let alone measure. However, during the last 30 years, tests designed to measure various aspects of creativity have become increasingly sophisticated. Most tests used today involve the measurement of divergent thinking and place a premium on the number of responses a child can give. Some are problem-solving tests and require the child to provide a correct solution to a given situation. This type of test involves both divergent and convergent thinking in a trial-and-error problem-solving process. Problem-solving tests are often tricky, primarily because only one correct answer exists and frequently only one cognitive path leads to it. Other types of creativity tests are nonverbal in scope (see Figure 17.1).

Figure 17.1 Nonverbal tests of creativity (from *Modes of Thinking in Young Children: A Study of the Creativity–Intelligence Distinction* by Michael A. Wallach and Nathan Kogan. Copyright © 1965 by Holt, Rinehart and Winston, Inc. Reproduced by permission of Holt, Rinehart and Winston, Inc.).

Pattern meanings. Tell what each card looks like to you.

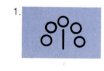
1.

3.

5.

7.

The line meaning test. What does each incomplete drawing bring to your mind?

1.

3.

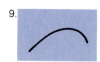
9.

Unique response	Common response
1 "Lollipop bursting into pieces"	Flower
3 Foot and toes	Table with things on it
5 Five worms hanging	Raindrops
7 Three mice eating a piece of cheese	Three people sitting around a table

Unique response	Common response
1 Squished paper	Mountain
3 Squeezing paint out of a tube	Piece of string
9 Fishing rod bending	Rising sun

Is There a Link between Creativity and Intelligence?

Because of the differences found in the types of divergent thinking that children display, researchers have attempted to find a relationship between **intelligence** and creativity. Does the fact that children score high on tests of divergent thinking indicate that their **intelligence quotient (IQ)** is also high? Should this ability be considered as one more dimension of intelligence and be incorporated into tests for IQ measurement?

Numerous researchers (see Getzels, 1975; Richards, 1976; Guilford, 1950) believe that divergent thinking is one aspect of intellect. They also maintain that creativity embraces several intellectual abilities that are not tapped by traditional intelligence tests (see Torrance and Wu, 1981). Thus, tested creativity is unrelated to tested intelligence, although both are types of cognitive activity.

While there are some individuals who have above-average intelligence and are also creative, most research indicates that there is little relationship between the two. It is not uncommon to find two children who have equally high IQs and exhibit unique talents in understanding abstractions or analyzing complex situations but differ radically in creativity and ability to generate diverse ideas or develop novel end products.

A study conducted by Michael Wallach and Nathan Kogan (1967) illustrates the manner in which creativity and intelligence operate with each other. The researchers examined 151 fifth-grade children, administering tests of both creativity and intelligence. Such a testing situation made it possible for the subjects to score high on one part and low on the other, high on both, or low on both. The researchers' analysis of the findings as well as observations of the children themselves revealed four combinations of creativity and intelligence:

High creativity-high intelligence
These children tended to have long attention spans, both control and confidence, and good concentration skills. Of the four groups, this was regarded as the superior one.

High creativity-low intelligence
These children tended to have poor concentration skills and had trouble paying attention in class. They also exhibited disruptive classroom behavior and had poor opinions of themselves. They were often in conflict with themselves and harbored feelings of unworthiness and inadequacy.

Low creativity-high intelligence
Children in this category were the least disruptive in the classroom.

They tended to be conformists, and although they did well in school, they feared failure. Most were hesitant about expressing their opinions.

Low creativity-low intelligence

These youngsters did not do well in school but sought to compensate socially. Compared with children of low intelligence but high creativity, these youngsters were more self-confident, less hesitant, and more extroverted.

Wallach and Kogan propose that the combination of creativity and intelligence has important implications in the child's life. These mental dimensions affect academic performance as well as social relationships and self-appraisal. Knowledge of the two dimensions may help teachers meet the needs of children. Such assistance may range from helping the low creativity-high intelligence child relax in the face of classroom challenges to working with the high creativity-low intelligence child to bolster overall levels of self-confidence.

Nurturing Imagination and Creativity

Parents, teachers, and other adults can play key roles in the development of children's imagination and creativity. Parents especially can exert significant influences and set the stage for creative expression. A warm and accepting family climate that nurtures close ties with all members appears to be especially conducive. Parents in such households tend to bring out a child's natural sense of wonder and imaginative abilities.

More specifically, parents need to accept their children and be open to the questions they ask. Imagination is stimulated when parents are available to share in discoveries and accomplishments. The provision of abstract rather than realistic toys, especially during early childhood, encourages imagination. Imaginative and creative children also tend to come from homes that monitor television viewing and provide a wide variety of family activities and exposure to new situations. Providing psychological "space," or standing back at appropriate times, gives the child added freedom to explore and express (Finley and Finley, 1982; Shmukler, 1981; Shallcross, 1981).

In the classroom, teachers need to foster environments that promote creativity. E. Paul Torrance [1962; 1965(a), (b); 1972; 1980], maintains that creativity can and should be taught in the classroom. He feels that the basic components of creativity—fluency, flexibility, originality, and imagination—can be increased by encouraging children to explore the unusual or different. Problems encouraging insight and ingenuity and "brainstorming" as many ideas as possible toward a given problem are highly recommended by Torrance.

Torrance feels that the educational system frequently, if not generally, discourages divergent thought, by teaching children that there is only one correct answer to a question, only one way to set up their notebooks, and only one way to do a math problem or correctly spell a word, for example. Torrance believes we all are born with the ability to use both convergent and divergent thought. Unfortunately, only convergent thought seems to bring positive reinforcement.

For example, in high school one of the authors, while browsing through a dictionary, discovered that the word *tricky* could also be spelled *tricksy* and proudly used the newly discovered spelling in an English paper only to have the teacher circle it for a misspelled word. More recently, after helping a school-age daughter with a problem in division, the same author was surprised to be told that it was done "the wrong way." "The teacher said we can't do it that way," the daughter explained. Torrance says that children will need substantial prodding to be creative simply because they have undergone so many experiences like these. It's not so much teaching creative thinking as it is allowing an unused thought process to resurface.

In learning opportunities having legitimate options or possibilities, children need to hear less of, "This is the way" and more, "How would you approach this problem?" Such teaching strategies will encourage the youngster to truly think and explore the world of possibilities. Although they may never become Einsteins, Rembrandts, or Picassos, children will discover their own special brand of imagination and creativity.

Forms of Play

While youngsters often play alone at this age, they also continue to seek out the company of other children. Neighborhood and school interactions are the more popular play groups, and they further encourage cooperative forms of play endeavors. By learning how to share and be responsible to one another, following the directions of a leader, developing self-confidence in a group setting, and coping with success and failure, children come to understand what a group is, how it operates, and how they can interact with it. As a result of these developments, the play group is able to structure its own activities. Children within the group setting are also likely to demonstrate advances in sensitivity toward others, as well as increasing amounts of prosocial behavior. These social advancements typically increase as group experiences become more diverse (Fine, 1981; Holmberg, 1980; Orlick, 1981).

To suppose that the elementary school play group is characterized by internal stability and smooth sailing is incorrect. Throughout all of childhood, group relations are fraught with the potential for disagreement or conflict. Middle childhood is no exception. While younger children are more likely to dispute the possession of a toy or object, elementary school children are likely to experience disagreements over which activities to undertake, which children can play, and who has created group disharmony. It is the task of the group members to resolve group disharmony. Conflict resolution is an important phase of interpersonal development, and the play group affords children the opportunity to try out potential solutions, strategies, and decision-making skills (Asher, Renshaw, and Hymel, 1982).

Earlier we mentioned that adult intervention can have positive effects on the initiation and direction of play. Conflict management within the play group is an area that can benefit from the assistance of

Play helps children develop social skills and learn about cooperation.

capable adults. Successful intervention techniques include providing conflict resolution strategies, giving feedback on behavior, and offering reinforcement when conflicts are reduced (Ladd, 1981; Youniss, 1980).

As children get older, seeking entry and gaining acceptance by the play group become increasingly important. The skills used by children to accomplish these goals greatly contribute to developing social knowledge. Rejection by one's playmates, on the other hand, will cause children to experience the bitter taste of social alienation. Continual rejection during childhood may create adjustment difficulties for the individual in later life (Asher and Renshaw, 1981; Hartup, 1980).

Youngsters in middle childhood have a broader range of group entry skills than younger children. Older children usually approach a play group in a nondisruptive way, observe the group's activity, and then copy it. It is not uncommon, though, for children to meet with initial resistance when they seek to join a group's activity (Corsaro, 1981).

Unpopular children, however, have more difficulty joining play groups. They are likely to make more initiation attempts than popular children and are more likely to be rejected. This may be due, in part, to the fact that during their initiation attempts they call considerable attention to themselves and divert attention from the activity at hand. Popular children, instead, cause fewer distractions. They also tend to enter the play group's conversation with greater ease (Putallaz and Gottman, 1981).

Learning the "Rules of the Game"

Organized games, such as marbles, hide and seek, tag, or London Bridge, not only bring children into contact socially with one another but also teach them that certain rules and codes of conduct are expected to be upheld. Children learn to understand and follow rules of games in four stages.

In the first stage, roughly the years of toddlerhood, children have no concept of rules; they react in any fashion they desire to an object associated with a game. Before 5 years of age, the second stage, the child's conception of rules is largely individual. Although there is some imitation of codified rules, most often a game will be played without any attempt to "win." At the incipient cooperation stage (7–8), the child attempts to unify and obey the "rules of the game." At this point, winning becomes important, and children realize that in order to win, they must all follow the same rules. By the fourth, or rule codification, stage, each player has developed not only an actual code of the rules but also an understanding of the attitudes of others. Participants recognize a system of conduct, ostracize cheaters, and accord recognition to those who excel (Piaget, 1932).

Play and Sex Typing

While children begin to exhibit sex-typed play in the preschool years, it becomes more evident during the middle years. Elementary school youngsters readily identify and state a preference for play activities that are appropriate to, and characteristic of, their sex. Boys typically involve themselves in physical and independent types of play, while girls are less physically oriented. Many toys for boys require more physical types of expressions, while toys intended for girls do not (Maccoby, 1980; Pitcher and Schultz, 1983).

An interesting aspect of sex-typed play is that boys seem to be more aware of sex differences than girls and avoid playing with objects that might be labeled feminine or "sissy." Girls seem to be willing to engage in male-oriented activities. Although both sexes congregate in sex-typed play groups, boys seem to hold more rigid, stereotyped beliefs than girls (DiPietro, 1981; Fagot and Kronsberg, 1982).

Many parents encourage their children to engage in sex-typed play. Fathers, in particular, seem to be more vocal about the selection of sex-appropriate toys and play behaviors. Further pressure to engage in sex-typed play emerges from the peer group, an increasingly important source of social approval and reinforcement (Langlois and Downs, 1980; Lamb, Easterbrooks, and Holden, 1980).

There is some evidence that the traditional classification of "masculine" and "feminine" forms of play may be changing. Society's attempt to promote a more androgynous definition of the sexes may reduce the gap between male and female activities. Although girls still engage in "feminine" activities, they now also enjoy types of play previously cast as "masculine," such as track and field competition, basketball, golf, and softball.

Girls are now involved more in organized sports activities than ever before. Schools are enlarging their programs and encouraging females to participate more actively and more competitively. Furthermore, success in sports and the accompanying social prestige no longer appear to be the exclusive domain of the male (Murphy, 1983).

Team Sports

Team sports are important during middle childhood. Being members of a team, whether in baseball, football, wrestling, or soccer, enables children to develop their physical and mental prowess and also introduces them to competitive team contests. Competing as team members helps children learn to make contributions as members of a group with a common goal.

Team sports can cause frustration in some children, though, particularly when they become overeager to prove themselves on the playing field. Striking out with the bases loaded, having to sit on the bench, or experiencing defeat is difficult for children, especially if they have never dealt with such situations before. Adults therefore must help foster proper attitudes toward sports.

Adults must pay special attention to the varied needs of the child competing at the organized level. For the child, organized sports require a considerable amount of coordination, dexterity, teamwork, and concentration. Organized sports can be said to represent the major developmental processes of childhood. That is, they require the successful integration of physical, cognitive, social, and emotional forces. While these processes are required in virtually all forms of play, team sports appear to require a more rigorous application and successful integration of all these forces.

There are many children who fear failure and humiliation within the framework of team sports. Unfortunately, many parents dismiss these apprehensions and fears and force children to participate in sports. As a result, many youngsters feel anger, resentment, anxiety, or even a loss of self-confidence. Some may experience the Eriksonian notion of inferiority prevalent during this stage of childhood.

In additon to appreciating psychological needs, adults must work closely with children to help develop skills needed for competitive play. Good instruction usually embodies the elaboration of a skill for a specific age, not the acceleration of a child through many different skills. Careful attention must also be given to the fact that success in one facet of the game does not automatically ensure success in all other phases. It must be realized, too, that behind this type of training must lie a framework of such mental qualities as determination, dedication, and concentration (Murphy, 1983).

How Important Are Winning and Finishing First?

While thousands of people point out the positive aspects of organized team sports for children, relatively few have pointed out the weaknesses. The following are a few examples.

It was the bottom of the sixth inning, the pitcher wound up and threw the ball, which the batter swung at and lined to right field. At the crack of the bat, the little boy playing right field came rushing in. But as the ball's trajectory dropped off rapidly, it hit the ground and rolled between the boy's legs. Rather than quickly turning and retrieving the ball, the boy turned to his father, who was standing along the right-field fence. Amidst the cheering and the jeering of fans and the screaming of his teammates, he said "I'm sorry Daddy. . . ."

In an "official" ballpark, a child slides into second base. "You're out!" cries the umpire, simultaneously jerking his thumb in the "out" position. Parents shout their approval or disapproval, and possibly a coach emerges from the dugout to complain; but, with head bent down, the child automatically trots back to the bench without (overtly) questioning the umpire's decision. The umpire is an adult and represents authority. Authority has spoken.

In a "sandlot" game, a child slides into second base. "You're out!" screams the shrill voice of the second base player. "I was safe by a mile!" yells the runner. Suddenly players from both teams are gathered around second base while a heated argument rages.

One difference between these latter two illustrations is that the second group is permitted to work out the problem, allowing the participants to learn various socialization processes. In many respects, the children playing unorganized ball may develop a rudimentary sense of justice, learn to give and take, and devise ways to work out problems by themselves and get along with others. This does not mean that children in organized sports will not learn the same valuable rules of life. Rather, the question seems to be which method of social learning is more efficient and valuable for the child.

These examples are hardly isolated ones. Many games and sports overemphasize competition and winning. Children frequently are taught to view everything as a race, contest, or fight. With the high premium frequently placed on being first, we need to examine the psychological implications of competitive play. Under stress, what is the price that children pay for winning?

While striving to do one's best is to be encouraged, adults need to teach children that winning is not the sole purpose of organized sports. Too often winning becomes so important to children that the enjoyment of playing the game becomes secondary to the stresses and pressures of finishing first. This might be cured by placing more emphasis on overall skill development than on winning (Smith et al., 1983).

Every sport has its share of good and bad coaches. Little League coaches especially have fallen under public scrutiny. Those poorly trained to work with children are frequently labeled "macho coaches." They cherish winning above all else and often have a destructive influence on children flung into the middle of competition. Also destructive are parents, particularly fathers, who use their children's sports contests to fulfill their own stifled athletic dreams or relive past glories (Beisser, 1980; Simon and Martens, 1983).

Adults should try to expose children to more than one or two primary sports. Children should participate in a representative number of competitive as well as noncompetitive sports and leisure activities.

THE FAMILY CIRCUS®

"We made it up ourselves. You don't need nine
guys on a team, or grownups, or uniforms. . . .
It's like baseball, only better!"

Personal fulfillment, enrichment, and relaxation are possible through a
wide range of different activities, not just those found in the sports
arena.

Summary

By middle childhood, youngsters can distinguish between pretending
and reality. The imagination of the school-age child also becomes more
private. Some school-age and even younger children create imaginary
companions, invisible playmates who seem to fill empty spaces in their

Sylvia, age 12

lives. Imaginary companions are regarded as a normal phase of child development and reflect considerable originality and creativity. School-age children also begin daydreaming, a form of wish fulfillment that enables the individual to circumvent space and time and explore life's possibilities.

In this chapter we examined how researchers have sought to measure creativity. This is a difficult task, but measurement devices have become increasingly sophisticated in recent years. Most tests used today involve the measurement of divergent thinking and place a premium on the number of responses a child gives. Tested creativity is unrelated to tested intelligence, although both are types of cognitive activity. Most research indicates that little, if any, relationship exists between creativity and intelligence.

Imagination and creativity need to be nurtured in the child. E. Paul Torrance has been especially outspoken on this topic. He urges teachers to design their classrooms so that student originality, ingenuity, and insight can surface. Teaching strategies tapping into creative potential encourage children to think and explore the world of possibility.

Middle childhood is a time for increasing amounts of peer group interaction through play. While gains are made in the form of such social skills as altruism, cooperation, and the development of group goals, conflicts within the group are still frequent. Adult intervention in the form of coaching, feedback, or reinforcement helps children resolve internal group strife.

Play behavior within the group or in solitary play endeavors continues to reflect sex typing. Children readily identify with and participate in those activities characteristic of their sex, although current social efforts to downplay traditional sex-role typing appears to be prompting more unisexual play behaviors.

Team sports are also popular during middle childhood and afford children the opportunity to experience both competition and cooperative contribution to group goals. As with all play activities, team sports require effective adult intervention in the form of proper instruction, supportive understanding, and provision of a climate for enjoyment.

Suggested Reading List

Peppler, D. J., and Rubin, K. H., eds. *The Play of Children*. New York: Carger, 1982. This collection of readings examines many aspects of play, including pretending and the relationship between play and creativity.

Piers, M. W., and Landau, M. *The Gift of Play.* New York: Walker, 1980. A thorough account of play with special emphasis on how it influences cognitive and social development.

Strom, R. D., ed. *Growing through Play.* Monterey, Calif.: Brooks/Cole, 1981. An assortment of 30 articles analyze the types of behaviors promoted by play.

Part Five
Adolescence

Chapter Eighteen

Physical Growth and Development

Youth is the time to go flashing from one end of the world to the other, both in mind and body.

Robert L. Stevenson

Introduction

Adolescence, from the Latin word *adolescere,* meaning "to grow into maturity," is the life stage between childhood and adulthood. It is a period marked by numerous and complicated developmental tasks and physical, psychological, and emotional changes. Adapting to these changes places great demands on the teenager, in some instances causing anxiety, apprehension, doubt, and even guilt. Yet one cannot deny that adolescence is also a time of happiness, growing independence, new and exciting perceptions of the world, and satisfying social relationships.

While growth during the elementary school years is relatively calm, during adolescence males and females experience pronounced physical developments that change them from children to sexually mature young adults. This point in development, during which biological changes begin to give the first indications of sexual maturity, is known as **puberty.**

The period of time that precedes puberty (referred to technically as **pubescence**) is characterized by a rapid growth spurt, which involves increases in height and weight as well as in skeletal growth. For females the growth spurt generally begins between ages 8½ and 10½, whereas for males it takes place between the ages of 10½ and 16. The peak of the growth spurt is between 12 and 13 for females and at approximately 14 for males (Tanner, 1981).

In addition to these differences between the sexes, the timing of the growth spurt and the essential maturation of sexual characteristics are influenced by other factors. The most prominent of these is the secular trend. Readers will recall our earlier discussion (Chapter 14) of the secular trend, which is the tendency for children in more prosperous parts of the world to grow taller and heavier than preceding generations. This means that the adolescent growth spurt begins earlier and the timetable for attainment of physical and sexual maturity is more accelerated. However, as mentioned earlier, the secular trend ceases to have an impact when a given nation's health and nutritional standards reach an optimum level (Garn, 1980; Tanner, 1981).

The Physiological Foundations of Puberty

Hormones are largely responsible for the onset and nature of growth during puberty. Prior to puberty, a part of the brain known as the hypothalamus stimulates the pituitary gland. The **pituitary gland,** often called the master gland because of its central role in the coordination of the endocrine system, then stimulates other glands. Figure 18.1 illustrates the glands of the endocrine system.

Figure 18.1 The glands of the endocrine system.

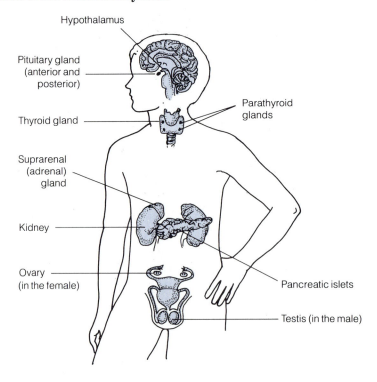

Most experts agree that puberty begins when the pituitary gland secretes increased amounts of the **human growth hormone (somatotrophic hormone).** This causes a rapid increase in body development and signals the onset of the adolescent growth spurt. At the same time production of thyroxin and and adrenalin increases to match the increase in cells or total body weight.

The pituitary gland also releases **gonadotrophins,** hormones that stimulate the testes and ovaries (parts of the endocrine system called the gonads). The testes and ovaries, in turn, secrete their own sex hormones. The male sex hormone is testosterone, and the female sex hormones are estrogen and progesterone.

Testosterone is secreted from cells within the testes and directs the development of the genitals, growth of pubic hair, and other features of sexual development. **Estrogen** is secreted by the follicles of the ovary and controls, among other phases of growth, the development of the uterus, vagina, and breasts. **Progesterone** aids in the development of the uterine wall, particularly its preparation for implantation and development of the ovum and of placental development after implantation has taken place. Progesterone is also thought to be influential in breast development during pregnancy.

While the bodily mechanisms that terminate puberty are not fully understood, it is believed that high levels of sex hormones in the bloodstream are largely responsible. Once a particular phase of physical or sexual development is complete, these high levels of sex hormones signal the hypothalamus to cease further production of a given hormone (Doering, 1980; Higham, 1980).

Physical Developments

Females reach physical maturity earlier than males and experience an initial height superiority between the ages of 11 and 13. By the age of 15, however, males begin a period of rapid development that enables them to surpass girls in overall height (Figure 18.2). During peak years of growth, males gain from 3 to 5 inches, whereas females add 2 to 4 inches to their height. Because the rate of growth is greater in the legs than in the trunk, many adolescents have a leggy and gangling appearance. By age 21, most males reach the plateau of their adult height, whereas for females this occurs at age 17 (Petersen and Taylor, 1980; Chumlea, 1982).

By age 11 both sexes exhibit a noticeable increase in weight, averaging between 10 and 14 pounds during peak years of development. Weight gain is proportionately greater than the height gain; consequently the individual has a stocky appearance.

The skeletal structure increases in length, weight, proportion, and composition. Girls exhibit more rapid skeletal development than boys; their bone structure reaches mature size by age 17. Boys reach this mature stage of development almost two years later. Skeletal weight for both males and females increases throughout puberty but appears to be more marked in males (Katchadourian, 1977).

The rapid growth of the facial bones may temporarily thicken and coarsen the features. Among males especially, the mouth widens, the nose projects more, and the jaw becomes more prominent. This results in a more muscular and angular face. Females, on the other hand, add a layer of fat that tends to soften facial features.

Primary and Secondary Sex Characteristics

In addition to the physical developments discussed above, primary and secondary sex characteristics also undergo change. **Primary sex char-**

Figure 18.2 Physical changes in adolescent males and females. The range of years during which the changes occur are indicated by the shaded bars (based on statistics from Tanner, J. M., *Growth at Adolescence*, 2nd ed. Oxford: Blackwell, 1962, and Tanner, J. M., *Education and Physical Growth*, 2nd ed. New York: International Universities Press, 1978).

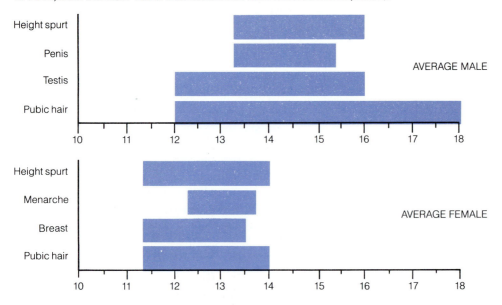

In the early stages of puberty, girls develop more rapidly than boys.

acteristics are physiological features related to the sex organs. For males, these organs include the penis and the testes, and for females they are the ovaries, uterus, clitoris, and vagina. **Secondary sex characteristics** are not directly related to the sexual organs but nevertheless distinguish a mature male from a mature female. Examples of secondary sex characteristics are the development of a beard in males and breasts in females. The gradual maturation of the primary and secondary sex characteristics signifies the end of childhood and the onset of sexual maturity.

Male Sexual Development

For most males the testes begin to accelerate in growth approximately by age 12. Individual variations in development, however, account for different rates of growth. By the end of adolescence, the penis has reached adult proportions. The scrotum and testes have also reached mature proportions and have dropped to their proper adult location (Morris and Udry, 1980).

When the male reproductive organs become mature, **nocturnal emission,** the ejaculation of semen during sleep, may be experienced. Most boys experience nocturnal emissions some time between the ages of 12 and 16. A perfectly normal phase of development, nocturnal emissions are frequently caused by sexual excitation in dreams or by some type of physical condition, such as a full bladder or pressure from pajamas.

The development of pubic hair begins between the ages of 12 and 14, usually starting at the base of the penis and extending upward. Two years after the beginning of pubic hair growth, axillary (underarm) and facial hair appear. Chest hair in boys appears in late adolescence and continues growing throughout young adulthood. It is often taken by boys to be the ultimate sign of virility, even more so than pubic hair.

A definite sequence exists in the development of the moustache and the beard. The downy hairs at the corners of the upper lip become noticeable and begin to extend over the entire upper lip. This slowly forms a moustache of fine hair, which becomes coarser and more heavily pigmented with age. Later, hair begins to appear on the upper part of the cheeks and the midline below the lower lip. Finally, it develops on the sides and border of the chin, as well as on the upper part of the face just in front of the ears.

Other secondary sex characteristics that appear in males during puberty are increased activity of the sweat glands and marked voice changes. Voice changes, which are due primarily to a rapid increase in the length of the vocal cords, are greater in males than in females (Katchadourian, 1977; Petersen and Taylor, 1980).

Female Sexual Development

Sexual development in females includes the development of the breasts and sexual organs, the appearance of pubic hair, the onset of **menarche** (the first menstrual period), the continuing development to the adult stage of breasts and pubic hair, and the characteristic widening of the hips, believed to be due to the influence of estrogen on the growth centers of the pelvic bones.

Breast development begins for most females between ages 10 and 11, but it can begin as late as age 14. The breasts develop from bud to mature size over a span of about three years. At about the same time, the uterus and vagina begin to mature. By the end of the adolescent years, the internal organs of reproduction have reached their adult status.

Female pubic hair usually begins to appear after the breasts have begun to develop but before the onset of menarche. Appearing first on the outer lips of the vulva, by the end of adolescence pubic hair is dark, curly, and coarse and has formed a triangular pattern over the **mons** (Morris and Udry, 1980).

Most North American girls experience the onset of menarche by age 12, the normal age range being from 10 to 15 years. This event is the most clearly defined sign of sexual maturity in females. It appears to have other implications as well. Females who have reached menarche appear to have a clearer sexual identification than females of the same age who have not experienced menarche (Rierdan and Koff, 1980).

The median age of menarche varies from 12 to 18 throughout the world (see Figure 18.3). Although this indicates a mature stage of uterine development, it may not mean that the female has attained her total reproductive capacity. The early menstrual cycles, which for some females are more irregular than later ones, often occur without **ovulation.** There is frequently a period of adolescent sterility, lasting 12 to 18 months after menarche (Tanner, 1981).

The sex hormones are also mainly responsible for the changes that transform the girl's body from the shape of childhood to the distinguishing contours of womanhood. Early in puberty, the pelvis widens, an important change when one considers that reproduction usually requires the passage of a baby's head through this bony ring. At the same time, the laying down of more subcutaneous fat around the pelvic girdle exaggerates the breadth of the hips. Fat is also deposited in such areas of the body as the shoulder girdle, back, abdomen, and legs. As the breasts develop, the apparent depth of the chest is increased and further enhanced by growth changes in the bony and muscular structures of the chest beneath the breasts.

The Relationship between Physical and Psychological Development

A primary reason for considering biological change is the influence it may have on the way adolescents perceive themselves. Preoccupation with the changing physical self is common. As we described in Part Four, during middle childhood youngsters express concern about their changing physical appearances, most notably body build. The adoles-

Figure 18.3 Cross-cultural comparison of the age of menarche and its decline over the years (from J. M. Tanner, *Growth at Adolescence*, 2nd ed. Oxford: Blackwell Scientific Publications. Redrawn for *Scientific American*, 1973, 229, p. 40. By permission).

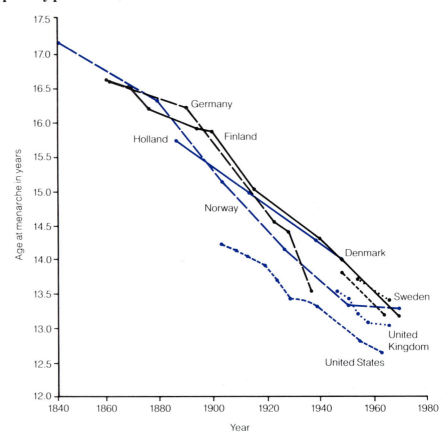

cent faces further adjustments to the changes brought on by the growth spurt, as well as the overall maturation of sexual characteristics. How teenagers react to such changes will greatly affect the manner in which they ultimately evaluate themselves (Petersen and Taylor, 1980; Adams, 1980; Higham, 1980).

Certain aspects of physical change may promote psychological discomfort. For example, the leggy and gangling appearance described earlier may be a source of anxiety, as may the rapid hand and foot development that contributes to a rather disproportionate appearance. When these developments are coupled with such other physical adjustment problems as acne, awkwardness, and voice breaks, it is no wonder that teenagers sometimes feel uncomfortable about their changing physical selves. In general, though, the adolescent's preoccupation with physical traits declines with age (Cramer, 1980).

Teenagers continue to pay attention to general body images, a physical type of appraisal begun during middle childhood. Adolescents do not want to be skinnier or fatter than their peers. Many still prefer the mesomorphic body build (see Chapter 14) and tend to view obesity with disdain. Among males, the desire to have a mesomorphic build is undoubtedly heightened by the cultural emphasis placed on physical strength and muscular development (Morrison et al., 1980; Blyth et al., 1980).

Another factor that may produce self-consciousness is whether an adolescent is an early or late maturer. Because physical development is an individual phenomenon, adolescents differ in overall rates of growth (see Figure 18.4). Adolescents generally report higher levels of personal satisfaction and more positive feelings about themselves when they mature before prescribed times. Furthermore, early maturation has been linked to success in other areas. Early maturers tend to be more independent, self-confident, self-reliant, and adept in overall social adjustments (Gross and Duke, 1980; Wilen and Petersen, 1980). They seem to be more popular and have a greater capacity for leadership than late maturers, who frequently have poorer self-concepts, are overly concerned with matters related to social acceptance, tend to be immature, and frequently resort to attention-seeking behavior.

Although their overall social adjustment is smoother, it is possible that early maturers encounter other problems. Early maturers have much less time to adjust to physical change than late maturers. This

Figure 18.4   There are wide variations of 13-year-old boys and girls in body shape and size.

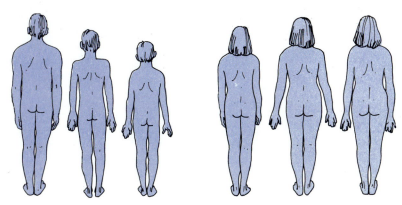

seems especially true for females experiencing early onset of menarche, which may produce more confusion and anxiety than among late maturers experiencing the same physiological event. The external harmony often exhibited by the early maturer may sometimes be accompanied by internal disharmony (Livson and Peskin, 1980).

**Growth spurts may give the adolescent a leggy
or gangling appearance.**

There is no mistaking the fact that today's adolescents are physically capable of having sexual relations earlier than their predecessors. However, a mature body is not always accompanied by a mature mind, and many teenagers begin having sexual relations before they are psychologically ready. This applies to both males and females, but the consequences for females are greater when the issue of childbearing is considered. Statistics show that there are increasing numbers of teenage pregnancies today, many with mothers under 16 (Nye and Lamberts, 1980; Garn, 1980).

This is a good example of how growth in one area (physical maturity) may affect development in other spheres (sexual behavior). It also underscores the need to teach teenagers about the changes in their developing bodies, which includes sharing information about the psychological and physiological risks of adolescent pregnancy. Such efforts may help to reduce the increasing numbers of ill-prepared teenage parents.

Motor Skill Development

Because physical growth during adolescence is generally disproportionate and uneven, one might expect motor skill development to lag behind during the adolescent years. However, most adolescents exhibit steady improvements in strength, **reaction time,** and coordination. Males continue to surpass females in overall motor skill development, largely because of their larger muscles and ability to develop more force per gram of muscle tissue (Tanner, 1981; Petersen and Taylor, 1980).

Males are generally more proficient in such areas as accuracy in speed of responses and overall body control. This proficiency may be demonstrated in the areas of running, throwing, and other tasks requiring varying degrees of physical endurance. Researchers agree that strength and dexterity increase rapidly between the ages of 12 and 16 (Maccoby and Jacklin, 1974).

Such findings must be placed into proper perspective since much of the research conducted was done before the current increase in athletic activities among female adolescents. Furthermore, even though males surpass females in overall ability to perform certain athletic tasks, this may be due primarily to the vast amounts of time that males devote to developing and practicing these skills. Physical prowess depends considerably on exercise and training, which in turn depend on personal motivation, social expectations, and practical opportunities. The

Adolescents exhibit steady improvements in motor skill development.

fact that males have received more encouragement in this regard has contributed greatly to the gap in physical ability between the sexes (Petersen and Taylor, 1980; Katchadourian, 1977).

Summary

Sylvia, age 13

Adolescence is a life stage marked by pronounced physical growth and development. A growth spurt typically precedes puberty and the attainment of sexual maturity. The growth spurt involves increases in height, weight, and skeletal growth. Females usually experience the growth spurt earlier in life than males.

For the most part, hormones determine the course of puberty, which begins when the hypothalamus stimulates the pituitary gland, which in turn sends signals to the gonads in the form of gonadotrophins. The gonads then secrete their own sex hormones; testosterone for males, estrogen and progesterone for women. The sex hormones are responsible for the development of primary and secondary sex characteristics.

Primary sex characteristics are physiological features related to the sex organs themselves. Secondary sex characteristics are characteristics that distinguish a mature male from a mature female. Examples of secondary sex characteristics are beard development and lowering of the voice in males and breast development in females. The sequence for the development of both primary and secondary sex characteristics is fairly predictable, although individual variations can exist.

Physical change during adolescence is related to other parameters of development. Teenagers' inner reactions to physical changes and treatment of the adolescent by others affect psychological and social development. In general, it is normal for adolescents to be preoccupied with physical traits, including body build. Researchers maintain that this preoccupation declines with age.

Considerable research has focused on the consequences of early and late maturation. In general, early maturers report higher levels of personal satisfaction and more positive feelings about themselves than late maturers. Early maturers also tend to have better self-concepts and are more adept at making social adjustments. However, the shorter amount of preparation time for physical changes may breed anxiety and confusion among early maturers. Late maturers, on the other hand, appear to have the advantage of adjusting gradually to physical change.

Motor skill development and coordination, in addition to strength and speed of reaction time, has been found to increase steadily during adolescence. While males continue to surpass females in motor skills, this superiority is most likely the result of time that males have traditionally devoted to develop and practice these skills. Most research studies showing male superiority were conducted before the current interest in athletics among females. This factor must be taken into consideration when evaluating existing research on this topic.

Suggested Reading List

Doering, C. H. The endocrine system. In *Constancy and Change in Human Development*, eds. O. G. Brim, Jr. and J. Kagan. Cambridge: Harvard University Press, 1980. The nature of the endocrine system, including implications for puberty, are covered in this article.

Petersen, A., and Taylor, B. The biological approach to adolescence: Biological change and psychological adaptation. In *Handbook of Adolescent Psychology*, ed. J. Edelson. New York: Wiley, 1980. The authors provide a good, clear contemporary analysis of physical growth during adolescence and the psychological ramifications involved.

Tanner, J. M. Growth and maturation during adolescence. *Nutrition Review*, 1981, *39*, pages 43–55. One of the world's foremost authorities on growth and development explores physical change during adolescence.

Chapter Nineteen

Cognition

Youth, being indeed the philosopher's tabula rasa, is apt to receive any impressure.

Richard Brathwaite

Introduction

By the time adolescence is reached, the ability to acquire and use knowledge nears maximum capacity. Furthermore, teenagers are likely to improve their thinking in both quantitative and qualitative ways. In a quantitative sense, mental abilities have reached a high level of proficiency and have become greatly differentiated. Qualitatively, changes in problem-solving strategies and overall thought processes over time bring the adolescent considerable mental flexibility.

In relation to Jean Piaget's theory of cognitive development, adolescence marks the onset of formal operations. **Formal operations** is the crystallization and integration of all previous cognitive stages. Past developments now combine with formal operations to create a tightly organized and highly systematic mental whole (see Figure 19.1). Furthermore, thinking becomes extremely rational and will continue to develop throughout adulthood as these refined mental strategies are applied to greater numbers of problem-solving situations.

It must be recognized, though, that not everyone reaches such lofty heights of cognitive reasoning. As in other areas of development, age is no guarantee of maturity. In support of this, it is estimated that only 40 to 60 percent of college students and adults will attain formal operations (Keating, 1980; Super, 1980; Keating and Clark, 1980).

It is equally important to point out that the attainment of formal operations is not an all or none situation. Individuals may attain peak levels of mental functioning in certain areas and not in others. Also, some individuals, such as the very **gifted,** may demonstrate more precision and greater flexibility in certain skill areas or even in overall cognitive operations. There may also be sex differences in cognitive performance. Males seem to perform better on tests of mathematical reasoning and visual spatial problems; females tend to excel in tasks involving verbal abilities. All of this suggests the wide range of individual variations in cognitive functioning (Keating and Clark, 1980; Hogan, 1980; Benbow and Stanley, 1980; Springer and Deutsch, 1985).

The individual is now capable of thinking about the past, present, and future and can deal effectively with problems of a hypothetical nature. Moreover, when confronted with a problem, adolescents can formulate a number of possible answers while working toward the solution. Compared to earlier stages, the thinking of the adolescent now resembles that of a scientist.

Perhaps the best word to describe the mental processes in this phase of cognitive development is *flexibility*. The individual's cognitive maturity allows mental adaptation to the task at hand, thus enabling the adolescent to benefit and learn from previously developed concepts and mistakes made as a growing child. Thinking is flexible also because the adolescent can now apply a diversity of logical thought processes to the problem at hand, including the use of inductive and deductive reasoning powers.

To illustrate the changing character of adolescent cognition as well as its overall flexibility, we will examine several key accomplishments,

Figure 19.1 All of Piaget's stages are interrelated. To arrive at formal operations, there must be a total integration of all developmental stages.

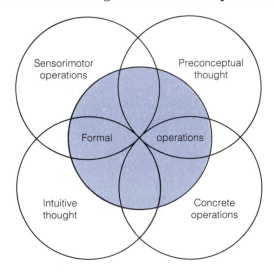

including advancements in abstract thinking, problem solving, and literary understanding. We will also explore adolescent egocentrism, which has a tendency to distort cognitive functioning at this time.

Abstract Thinking

In early stages of cognitive development, children are limited in their understanding of abstractions or relationships between abstractions. **Abstractions** are subjective concepts or ideas apart from one's objective analysis of the tangible environment. While objective reasoning skills are needed to solve concrete problems in science or math, for example, abstract reasoning powers are needed to understand what can't be seen.

When confronted with abstract concepts during childhood, youngsters generally depend on the physical or concrete properties of these concepts. The ability to move beyond the physical properties of the environment and understand abstractions has enormous implications for cognitive development at this time. No longer is the individual shackled to current or recent concrete experiences. Whereas the child can only reason about what is, the adolescent can imagine what may be.

Adolescents can also think about ideas and propositions that may violate reality (Keating, 1980). For example, they can transcend the fanciful quality of such hypothetical problems as: "If a red cat had green kittens, could we say that a green kitten had a red mother?" They can understand what is wrong with the statement: "John's feet are so big that he has to put his trousers on over his head." Whereas younger children would argue that such situations can not exist or are just too silly to be true, adolescents overlook these things and instead systematically work toward a solution.

The ability to engage in abstract thought, coupled with the capacity to deal with the future, is reflected in the teenager's personality and social development. Individuals are now able to think more realistically about their identity and future, including occupational and social roles. They may experiment with these roles just as they would experiment with hypotheses about physical events. Furthermore, adolescents are able to generate many new ideas about themselves and about life in general. They can debate a variety of moral and political issues, such as whether wars can ever be moral, whether abortions should be legal, whether there are basic inalienable human rights, and what an ideal community would be like. Teenagers can consider these issues from a variety of perspectives and see how the issues themselves are related to a larger set of social relationships. In this way cognitive advancements affect numerous other aspects of development (Miller, 1983).

Problem-Solving Abilities

Approaching problems by attempting to imagine all the possible relationships is a characteristic feature of the mature mind. The adolescent is able to accept data or propositions as purely hypothetical and tentative and then test them against available evidence. While younger children frequently accept initial answers to problem-solving situations as true, adolescents make deductions on a hypothetical basis. Unlike children, adolescents can make analyses of the full range of possibilities inherent in a problem before adopting one of them.

During adolescence, cognitive abilities improve in both quantitative and qualitative ways.

This means that adolescents can now employ **deductive logic,** or reasoning from a set of premises to a conclusion, which Piaget calls **hypothetico-deductive reasoning.** They are also able to make use of **inductive logic,** which means starting with specific, individual experiences and proceeding to general principles.

Syllogisms provide a good example of deductive logic. For example, if given the premises (1) Socrates is a man and (2) all men are mortal, adolescents in the stage of formal operations can conclude that (3) Socrates is a mortal. Deductive logic requires us to deal with more than one aspect of a problem at a time. In this example, for instance, we must keep in mind that Socrates is a man and that all men are mortal. As time goes on, individuals are able to approach even more complex syllogisms. For example: "I am a man. If Larry's son is my son's father, what relationship am I to Larry?" (To avoid frustration, the answer is "Larry's son.")

Adolescent use of inductive logic can be seen in Piaget's classic pendulum problem (Inhelder and Piaget, 1958). The experiment involved a wooden stand, various string lengths, and assorted weights (see Figure 19.2). After the swing of the pendulum was demonstrated, children and adolescents were shown how to vary the length of the string and how to push the weights with varying degrees of force. Then, each subject was asked to predict which was the more important determinant in increasing the pendulum's frequency of oscillation (the speed of the swings)—the string length or weight size. This is considered a test of inductive logic, because the subject starts with specific instances and is asked to figure out a general principle. (The correct response is that the string length determines the speed.)

Children in the preoperational, intuitive, and concrete stages of development had difficulty in providing the correct solution, although older children demonstrated greater facility in reasoning. The difficulty experienced by the children was due largely to their lack of a systematic and logical approach for investigating potential determinants of oscillation. Most of the younger children insisted that increased weight was the cause of speed changes. Older adolescents, however, were able to examine the problem objectively and to realize that there might be several possible explanations for differences in oscillation frequency (weight, string length, force), each of which they tested systematically. During this process, each hypothesis was examined objectively until the correct solution was discovered, at which time conclusions were drawn. Logical mental maneuvers such as these represent the essence of formal operations.

A more recent experiment (Siegler, 1981) also sought to explore the use of adolescent logic in problem-solving situations. In this experiment, subjects were shown a balance scale that operated like a seesaw (see Figure 19.3). Their task was to balance the seesaw. To attain a state of balance, different weights could be hung on the balance's pegs at varying distances from the fulcrum. There were two important dimensions, then, in balancing the seesaw: how much weight was on each side of the fulcrum and the distance of the weights from the fulcrum.

Children not in the stage of formal operations typically considered only the weight on each side of the fulcrum. If the weights were unequal, they surmised that the side with the heavier weight would descend regardless of counterbalancing distances from the fulcrum. In

Figure 19.2 In Piaget's pendulum problem, subjects are asked to predict which is the more important determinant in increasing the speed of the pendulum's swings: string length or weight size (from *The Growth of Logical Thinking from Childhood to Adolescence: An Essay on the Construction of Formal Operational Structures* by Barbel Inhelder and Jean Piaget. Translated by Anne Parsons and Stanley Milgrim. Copyright © 1958 by Basic Books, Inc. By permission of Basic Books, Inc., Publishers, New York).

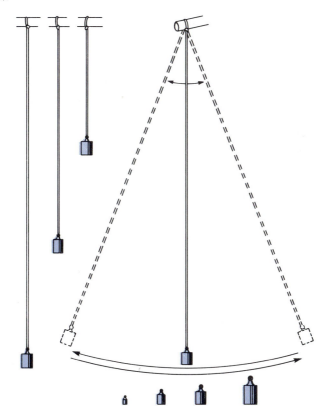

Figure 19.3 The balance scale employed by Siegler (1981). Subjects were asked to balance this device by considering two important dimensions: how much weight is on each side of the fulcrum and the distance of the weights from the fulcrum.

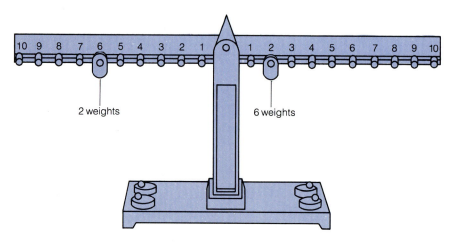

2 weights   6 weights

general, the children reasoned that the seesaw would balance if the weight amounts were equal.

Adolescents involved in the experiment were more apt to consider not only the dimension of weight but also the distance of the weights from the fulcrum. Unlike the limited responses of the children, the teenagers' responses revealed an obvious scientific and systematic analysis of the problem.

Experiments like this clearly illustrate that adolescents carefully explore all features of problem-solving situations and employ hypotheses that are logically more complex and more flexible and mobile than those of younger children. By testing predictions from each hypothesis, they arrive at correct solutions to problems with systematic deliberation. Such problem-solving approaches will bring new levels of insight to such academic subjects as calculus and physics, not to mention scientific inquiry in general [Flexer and Roberge, 1980 (a),(b); Ault and Vinsel, 1980].

Literary Understanding

Formal operations is also a time for heightened levels of literary understanding. Mature cognition enables adolescents to develop greater insight into literary ideas, to question what is being read, and to be generally more receptive to new facts and ideas.

An older, yet nonetheless relevant, research investigation (Peel, 1960) revealed the manner in which children and adolescents (ranging in age from 8 through 15) develop literary understanding. In the study, the following passage about Stonehenge was read to the subjects:

> Stonehenge is in the south of England, on the flat plain of Salisbury. There is a ring of very big stones which the picture shows. Some of the stones have fallen down and some have disappeared from the place. The people who lived in England in those days we call Bronze Age Men. Long before there were any towns, Stonehenge was a temple for worship and sacrifice. Some of the stones were brought from the nearby hills, but others we call Blue Stones we think came from the mountains of Wales (Peel, 1960, p. 422).

After reading the passage and showing the subjects a picture of the Stonehenge site, researchers asked several questions, including whether the subjects felt that Stonehenge served as a temple or a fort and what might have happened to some of the stones that were missing from the site.

The younger children answered with rather flat, matter-of-fact statements. For example, a 7-year-old remarked that Stonehenge was a temple because "people lived in it." A 9-year-old said "it might have been to stop the enemy charging through." When asked why, the response was, "because it looks like it. The bricks would stand up, the enemy could not force through quick enough, and they'd be killed."

When asked where the missing stones were, one 7-year-old stated, "They've fallen down. People have rolled them somewhere." When asked for a reason, the child said, "so they could live in them." When a 9-year-old was asked the same question, the response was, "They must have sunk into the ground." Even when told that men searched for the stones by digging in the area, the child stated, "They must have been used by people who came after." In this way, the children stated an initial hypothesis and adhered to it, even to the point where they rationalized conflicting evidence to support their viewpoint. They did not differentiate between their hypothesis and the facts, assuming instead that both had the same priority. This lack of differentiation between thought and reality is characteristic of Piaget's concrete operations stage.

The adolescents, however, treated the material in a more flexible fashion, leaving their minds open to whatever possibilities could explain the situation. They tried to alter the interpretation to fit the facts rather than the reverse. The response of a 14-year-old, when asked if Stonehenge could have been a fort, reflects these more mature reasoning abilities (Peel, 1960, p. 124): "I doubt it. I shouldn't think so. It does

Adolescents gain insight into literature as their cognitive powers mature.

seem rather small. You wouldn't need a fort in the middle of Salisbury Plain. It's deserted. There's not many people about. There's not likely to be any trouble around there."

As this example illustrates, adolescents verbalize their conclusions tentatively and differentiate thought from reality. Because they are aware of the difference between their own guesses and the facts of a case, adolescents give higher priority to facts than to hypotheses. Moreover, in many of the responses recorded, they frequently used material from the actual literary passage to support their judgments.

Contemporary research findings tell us that other aspects of literary understanding increase as cognitive powers mature. For example, advanced cognitive reasoning enables teenagers to digest a greater range of symbols, metaphors, word meanings, and characterizations. Historical chronology can now be grasped, and literary techniques that confused younger readers, such as the use of irony and abstract concepts, are better understood. Adolescents also respond to a wider range of humor, including riddles, cartoons, and subtle forms of expression (Parr, 1982; Demorest, Silberstein, and Gardner, 1981; McGhee, 1980; Couturier, Mansfield, and Gallagher, 1981).

Much of this advancement in literary understanding is due to the fact that formal operations releases readers from a singular, concrete interpretation of printed or spoken words. Furthermore, their ability to engage in systematic analysis of facts and abstract reasoning opens new horizons for thought. This is as true for editorial cartoons as it is for such books as *Alice in Wonderland* or *Huckleberry Finn*. When such understanding emerges, the adolescent's interest in such courses as English or literary appreciation may soar to new heights.

Adolescent Egocentrism

Adolescence is accompanied by a significant increase in self-consciousness. Teenagers exhibit a great deal of concern over what other people think about them. This type of thinking—being able to conceptualize one's own thought in addition to being preoccupied with the thoughts of those in one's surroundings—is responsible for what is known as **adolescent egocentrism.** Individuals in this age bracket are unable to differentiate between the objects toward which the thoughts of others are directed and those that are the focus of their own concern. Thus teenagers feel that others are obsessed with the same feelings and perceptions as they are.

Our understanding of adolescent egocentrism has been greatly influenced by the research of psychologist David Elkind [1967; 1980;

1981(b); Elkind and Bowen, 1979]. Since his initial findings in the 1960s, researchers have generally acknowledged the existence of adolescent egocentrism. Furthermore, Elkind's ideas have spurred a diversity of other thoughts on the topic (see Muuss, 1982; Adams and Jones, 1981; Enright, Shukla, and Lapsley, 1980).

There appear to be two related consequences of adolescent egocentrism. The first is the tendency of adolescents to construct an **imaginary audience** for themselves in social situations. Because they anticipate the reactions of others to themselves, they feel that they are continually the focus of attention or on center stage. The perceived existence of the imaginary audience usually intensifies during potentially threatening social situations, such as having to speak in front of the class or walking into a crowded cafeteria alone. The tendency to create an imaginary audience may partially account for a wide variety of teenage behaviors and experiences.

The construction of such an audience may also help to explain the self-consciousness that is particularly prevalent at this age. When one is self-critical, one assumes that the audience is critical as well. This is particularly painful since adolescents believe that other people are as acutely aware of their cosmetic and behavioral blemishes as they are. Desire for privacy and reluctance to reveal the self may well be the adolescent's reactions to feelings of being under continual scrutiny by others.

A second consequence of adolescent egocentrism is the creation of a **personal fable.** Personal fables are fantasies that adolescents construct and tell about themselves. They feature prominently in diaries, which are often written for posterity in the conviction that the teenager's life experiences have universal significance. Within the secret pages of a diary, one may discover among other subjects an adolescent's "personal" relationship with God or grandiose schemes for improving society. Poetry, paintings, and the great American novel are other forms of personal fables. Many teenage girls become pregnant partly because in their personal fable pregnancy happens to others, not to them, so they take no precautions. The conviction that one leads a charmed life may lead, for example, to reckless driving.

The personal fable, like the imaginary audience, is overcome when adolescents are able to see themselves and others in a more realistic light. When this happens, individuals can establish true, rather than self-interested, interpersonal relationships. When they share confidences and establish relations of mutuality, teenagers discover that others have similar feelings.

While teenagers are frequently self-critical, they are often self-admiring as well. When this happens, their imagined audience assumes the same admiring stance. Such adolescent egocentrism can be observed in behavior toward members of the opposite sex. Before going on a date, a boy may spend hours in front of a mirror combing his hair or flexing his muscles, while his date may become engrossed in applying her makeup or trying on clothes. Both are immensely preoccupied with the dramatic impression they will make when the evening begins. When the two adolescents eventually meet, each is more concerned with being observed than with observing or interacting with the other. Vanity and conceit, two traits frequently attributed to adolescents, may thus derive from lingering egocentrism [Elkind, 1981(b)].

Many teenage girls become pregnant because they take no precautions; they believe pregnancy happens only to others—a "personal fable."

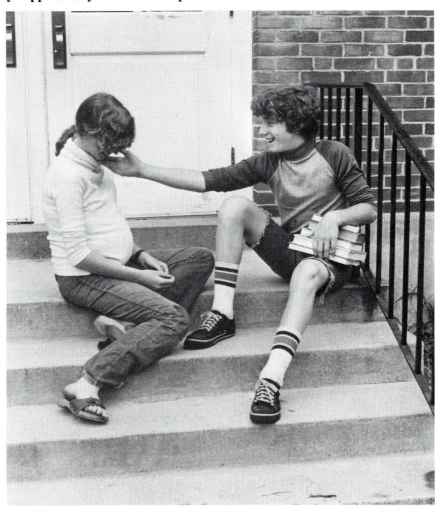

Summary

Sylvia, age 13

Cognitive advancements during adolescence are both quantitative and qualitative in nature. Jean Piaget refers to this time as formal operations, the fifth and final stage of his cognitive development theory. Formal operations represents the crystallization and integration of all previous cognitive stages.

Not everyone reaches formal operations, and success in one facet of this stage does not imply success in all areas. Generally speaking, thinking during this stage is characterized by flexibility, deliberation, and systematic methodology. Cognitive functioning in formal operations resembles scientific thought.

One of the more striking advancements in adolescent cognition is the ability to engage in abstract thought. Abstract thinking involves the use of subjective concepts or ideas, and it enables the individual to move beyond a concrete, physical analysis of the environment. Abstract thinking also enables adolescents to think about ideas or propositions violating reality.

Advanced problem-solving abilities develop through the use of deductive and inductive logic. Deductive logic, called hypothetico-deductive reasoning by Piaget, involves reasoning from a set of premises to a conclusion. The ability to understand syllogisms during adolescence is a good example of emerging deductive logic. Inductive logic implies starting with specific, individual experiences and proceeding to general principles. The classic Piagetian pendulum problem, which can be solved by adolescents, is a test of inductive logic.

Literary understanding reaches new heights during formal operations. Advanced cognitive ability enables teenagers to develop greater insight into what is being read and to appreciate a wider range of literary techniques. More specifically, mature literary understanding is facilitated by abstract reasoning skills, the systematic analysis of facts, and the relinquishment of singular and concrete interpretations of words.

Adolescence is frequently accompanied by considerable self-consciousness. David Elkind refers to such self-concern as adolescent egocentrism. Two consequences of adolescent egocentrism are the imaginary audience and the personal fable. The imaginary audience occurs when teenagers feel they are under the close inspection and scrutiny of others. Personal fables are untrue stories adolescents construct about themselves that usually reflect ill-founded beliefs and a conviction of personal uniqueness. The prevalence of both the imaginary audience and the personal fable diminishes after the adolescent years.

Suggested Reading List

Keating, D. P. Thinking processes in adolescence. In *Handbook of Adolescent Psychology*, ed. J. Adelson. New York: Wiley, 1980. A thorough overview of cognitive functioning during the teenage years. Keating provides a fine summary of Piaget's formal operations stage.

Phillips, J. L., Jr. *Piaget's Theory: A Primer*. San Francisco: W. H. Freeman, 1981. Chapter Five of this compact and well-written paperback focuses on the formal operations stage. Phillips includes a good assortment of Piagetian experiments.

Sigel, I. E., Brodzinsky, D. M., and Golinkoff, R. M., eds. *New Directions in Piagetian Theory and Practice*. Hillsdale, N.J.: Erlbaum, 1981. A diverse assortment of essays designed to show readers the nature of contemporary Piagetian research activity.

Chapter Twenty

Personality and Social Learning

Youth is wholly experimental.

R. L. Stevenson

Introduction

Personality and social development acquire new dimensions during the adolescent years. Observers of this age group will discover that teen-agers demonstrate heightened levels of self-awareness and intensified desires to be accepted by their peers. Establishing a personal sense of identity; examining one's values, beliefs, and attitudes; and developing personal and intimate social relationships are all important. The latter provide an outlet for new feelings and experiences, a source of support and security, and a mirror to one's own generation.

Personality developments in adolescence affect and are affected by social growth as they are in other stages of life. This means not only that the accuracy, stability, and acceptance of the self-concept affect the nature and degree of social relationships but also that feedback and reinforcement of others influence how adolescents ultimately perceive themselves. Other developmental forces also blend with personality and social growth. Heightened social cognitive skills, for example, give teen-agers the mental prowess to examine themselves and others around them with greater understanding and awareness. Adolescents' accept-ance of their changing physical selves and achievements in other de-velopmental areas will affect sexual interests and social development, particularly if the teenager is an early or late maturer.

When studying overall personality and social development during adolescence, we must focus on several key areas and their significance. Our first chore will be to examine the theories of personality proposed by Freud and Erikson. We will then study the manner in which morality and family relationships change at this time. Finally, we will concentrate our attention on peer group interaction, including heterosexual relationships and sexual behavior.

Theories of Personality Development

Freud's Theory

For Sigmund Freud, adolescence is marked by the psychosexual dynamics of the **genital stage.** Unlike Erikson's ongoing interpretation of personality functioning, the genital stage represents Freud's last stage of development.

Developing intimate social relationships is extremely important to adolescents.

Freud proposes that the genital stage is a turbulent time for the adolescent. The biochemical upheaval associated with the growth and development of primary and secondary sex characteristics makes youths acutely aware of the erotic zones of their bodies.

Unlike the early pregenital stages, in which each period marked the onset of a new conflict, the genital stage witnesses a revival of old conflicts, particularly the Oedipus complex. Thus, Freudians view adolescence as recapitulating infantile sexuality. Although adolescence is seen as a distinct era in psychosexual growth, this does not violate Freud's belief in the all-important role of experiences during the first few years of life. A novel feature of the genital stage is the sublimation of Oedipal feelings through expression of libido by falling in love with an opposite-sex person other than one's parent. Such psychosexual desires, according to Freud, will affect sexual behavior and heterosexual development in general. We will discuss both of these areas later on in this chapter.

Erikson's Theory

In Erikson's analysis of adolescence, the fifth stage of his psychosocial theory is called **identity versus role diffusion.** It is perhaps the most publicized of his eight stages of life. With the onset of puberty and genital maturity, the youth realizes that childhood has disappeared and adulthood is approaching. Because of this, the ego must reevaluate reality, and in so doing, teenagers become most conscious of the ideas and opinions of others. They also become increasingly concerned with their skills and self-perceptions, especially in terms of society's occupational prototypes. During this stage all previous stages should blend into an integrated ego (Erikson, 1963, p. 261):

> The integration now taking place in the form of ego identity is, as pointed out, more than the sum of childhood identifications. It is the accrued experience of the ego's ability to integrate all identifications with the vicissitudes of the libido, with the aptitudes developed out of endowment, and with the opportunities offered in social roles. The sense of ego identity, then, is the accrued confidence that the inner sameness and continuity prepared in the past are matched by the sameness and continuity of one's meaning for others, as evidenced in the tangible promise of a career.

When integration fails to occur, the result is some form of role diffusion. The eternal adolescent questions of "Who am I?" and "What is my purpose in life?" indicate ego confusion and consequent attempts to integrate various roles and experiences. The teenager's dilemma is to choose a possible **role** to identify with: to be rugged and masculine like a cousin, jolly and humorous like a sibling, warm and affectionate like a parent, perceptive and intellectual like a grandparent, or athletic and worldly like some other relative. Meanwhile, adolescents often develop subcultures with which they also identify. They become clannish and accept very little deviance in dress, thought, or behavior. This intolerance toward others is a temporary defense against role diffusion until the time when the ego can successfully develop a sense of identity.

James Marcia (1980) proposes that an individual can possess one of four identity statuses. **Identity achievement** means that a person has gone through an appraisal of values and choices in life and has made a commitment to some goal or occupation. **Identity moratorium** means the individual is in the process of rethinking values and goals and is in the midst of an identity crisis. No commitment has yet been made to any goals or values. **Identity diffusion** means the person has not even begun an examination of any goals or values. Finally, **identity foreclosure** means that goals have been established by others, usually parents, and the individual chooses not to question or even examine these impositions. These four types of identity possibilities add a unique dimen-

Adolescents often develop subcultures that accept little deviance in dress, thought, and behavior—a defense against "role diffusion."

sion to Erikson's theory and show that the concept of identity is a multifaceted, rather than singular, psychological concept.

We mentioned at the outset that growth in one area is frequently affected by growth status in other developmental areas. This appears to be the case when we examine the effect of mental development on identity formation. The attainment of Piaget's stage of formal thought facilitates identity formation during adolescence. However, this does not mean that an adolescent in the stage of formal thought automatically achieves identity status. There is no guarantee that placement in one stage ensures predictable status in another. However, we can say that certain cognitive capacities in operation at this time, namely the ability to engage in abstract thought, enable the teenager to differentiate and integrate identities and new role behaviors into the self-system (Bernstein, 1980; Leadbeater and Dionne, 1981).

Moral Development

In adolescence the quest for acceptable moral standards of conduct intensifies. Earlier developmental stages charted by Lawrence Kohlberg were characterized by the child's conformity to rules in an effort to avoid punishment or to obtain personal reward (see Chapter Sixteen). The adolescent now seeks to develop a set of ethical principles that will govern and direct personal behavior.

Kohlberg's Theory

As individuals approach adolescence, they reach Kohlberg's level of **conventional morality** (ages 9 through 15), where they learn the nature of authority, not only in the family but also in society. During the third stage, known as the **good boy–nice girl orientation,** there is considerable conformity, since children realize they must live up to rules in order to win praise or approval from others. Identification also occurs during this phase, usually with emotionally important persons. Eventually, conforming behavior leads to an internal awareness of rules and behavior, which fosters a sense of respect. Identification now shifts to institutions of society, such as church or school. This fourth stage of moral development is known as the **law and order orientation.**

Between stages four and five, an intervening stage may occur. Its central ingredient is deep questioning of the validity of society's definition of right and wrong. This rejection of conventional morality was once interpreted as a regression to stage two (see Chapter Sixteen), but it is now felt that it represents self-realization rather than selfish functioning. Subjects at the conventional level use moral terms, but use them interchangeably with *wish.* Subjects at stage "four-and-a-half," in contrast, question the validity of general moral terms. Many are inclined to omit the word *moral* from their vocabulary, as they see no objective sense in which one thing is morally better than another (Kohlberg and Turiel, 1973).

At the last major level of Kohlberg's theory, **postconventional morality** (age 16 onward), the individual's morality reaches a mature state. In the fifth stage, the **contractual legalistic orientation,** teenagers personally select moral principles to guide their behavior and are careful not to violate the rights and wills of others. In the sixth and final stage, the **universal ethical principle orientation,** the development of a true conscience enables individuals to choose behavior that best respects the dignity of others as well as their own. Researchers have found that this last stage is difficult to distinguish from the preceding one. Even Kohlberg himself questions whether the fifth and sixth stages can be effectively separated. Not everyone reaches the postconventional level of morality, just as not everyone attains Piaget's stage of formal operations (Colby et al., 1983).

Kohlberg in Retrospect   Without question, Kohlberg's theory of moral development has been influential among contemporary psychologists. It has attracted the attention of researchers in the field and has gathered considerable support in the process. Most psychologists agree that certain cognitive developments clearly underlie progression of morality from level to level (Saltzstein, 1983; Fisher, 1983; Krebs and Gillmore, 1982; Walker, 1982; Page, 1981).

However, some developmentalists feel that the invariant sequence hypothesis is too restrictive. There is evidence that Kohlberg's last three stages represent alternative types of moral maturity rather than a progressive sequence. It has also been suggested that a difference exists between moral judgment and moral behavior. In particular, some have found a weak relation between what is said and how one actually behaves (Kupfersmid and Wonderly, 1980; Maccoby, 1980; Blasi, 1980).

Kohlberg's theory appears to have cross-cultural applications. Examination of moral responses of subjects from Taiwan and Mexico, for example, indicates that their overall development roughly parallels the maturation rate of American subjects (Kohlberg, 1969) (see Figure 20.1). Studies in India and other nations also support the chronology of Kohlberg's stages (Parikh, 1980; Edwards, 1982).

When analyzing Kohlberg's theory, it must be recognized that morality is affected by other factors, including uncertainty about how to resolve a moral conflict and ego identity status. Exposure to moral arguments and involvement in role-playing exercises appear to advance the level of moral reasoning. On the whole, subjects prefer moral reasoning that is more sophisticated than their own. Emotions also have a role in determining moral judgments, an area not examined by Kohlberg. Each of these factors appears to be critical in considerations of overall level of moral reasoning (Krebs and Gillmore, 1982; Rest, 1981, 1983; Shweder, 1981).

One other factor worthy of our attention is that Kohlberg's theory of moral development does not take sex differences into account. Carol Gilligan (1982) maintains that females employ different reasoning from males when confronted with moral issues. More specifically, females tend to be concerned with relationships and responsibilities while males typically center their responses around rights and rules. Because Kohlberg's stages of moral development are primarily structured on the basis of rules, females often fail to reach the zenith of moral functioning. Gilligan argues that the current sequence is therefore an inaccurate model to assess female moral development.

Adolescence and Postconventional Morality: Is Age a Guarantee of Maturity?   Postconventional morality is the zenith of Kohlberg's developmental theory; but do adolescents automatically enter this stage because they have reached the prescribed age? Unfortunately not, since

Figure 20.1 Kohlberg's theory of moral development from a cross-cultural perspective. Although middle-class urban boys from Mexico and Taiwan lag slightly behind American boys, the stages of moral development are remarkably similar. At the bottom of the graphs are levels I (preconventional), II (conventional), and III (postconventional) (Kohlberg, 1969).

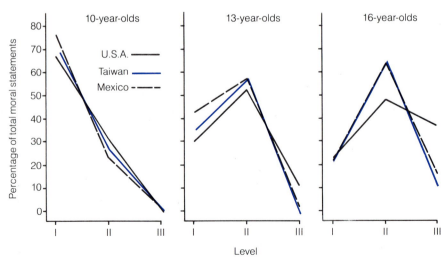

age is no guarantee of maturity, particularly in regard to cognitive and moral development. Furthermore, the attainment of formal thought does not guarantee that mature morality will automatically unfold (Walker, 1980).

The notion that age is no guarantee of postconventional morality has been explored by numerous researchers, including Kenneth Keniston (1970). In his survey of adolescent morality, he discovered that only 36 percent of those surveyed had attained postconventional styles of expression. Even though this percentage may be dishearteningly small, Keniston is optimistic that many more young people in the future will demonstrate Kohlberg's zenith of moral development.

Keniston believes that several factors will account for this increase in advanced moral development:

- Steering clear of the institutions of adult society, rather than joining the labor force and entering into early marriage. College-bound students have been shown to exhibit higher levels of moral development than youths who were not headed for college.

- Confrontation with relativistic points of view held by professors and fellow students. Such confrontation may cause students to abandon simple dualistic thinking about right and wrong and seek a relativistic concept of morality and truth. Later, personal commitments may be made within a relativistic universe.

- Discovery of corruption, hypocrisy, and duplicity in the world, particularly if these traits are found in those who originally taught the concepts of conventional morality. Not all individuals react in the same fashion when such a discovery is made; some may be pushed to attain higher stages of moral development, others may react with a temporary regression that leads to moral cynicism.

In evaluating the meaning of the highest levels of moral development, somewhat of a paradox exists. On one hand, Kohlberg identifies moral reasoning with men such as Gandhi or Martin Luther King: historic figures who were devoted to the highest personal principles and considered to be moral leaders of their day and age. On the other hand, particularly during the past two decades, the college-age generation has learned to view abstract personal principles with considerable mistrust—as a part of ideology in the highly pejorative sense, not in the Eriksonian sense. Unfortunately, they have seen that such principles may lead to zealotry, dogmatism, fanaticism, and insensitivity.

Whether the highest stages of morality lead to destructive zealotry or real ethicality depends on the extent to which moral development is matched by developments in compassion or empathetic identification with others. In this respect, danger does not lie in high levels of moral development but in the absence of love for fellow human beings.

Family Influences on Adolescent Development

The adolescent's desire to be independent has important implications for family life. Parents at this time are confronted with the task of redefining child-parent relations and gradually increasing the teenager's responsibility. Many parents realize for the first time that their offspring will soon be moving on and establishing their own independent lifestyles and living arrangements. How the two forces—the adolescent's desire for greater autonomy and the parents' reactions to such strivings—blend will greatly determine the emotional climate of the home during this time (Carter and McGoldrick, 1980).

While many parents handle the challenges of this stage, some do not fare as well. Part of the problem is that they resist granting adult status to their children. Rather than promoting responsible behavior, they overprotect their children and promote dependency. Some do not let go of their teenagers because they dread the thought of the next phase of family life, the "empty nest" stage. While the empty nest has numerous positive consequences, many parents have difficulty imagining what life would be like without children in the home (Borland, 1982).

Creating effective communication patterns between parent and adolescent is an important task at this time, as is establishing management and control of teenage behavior. The latter task has, of course, been going on since early childhood, but it may now reach a new level of intensity. Parents want to convey their own standards and values, but there are conflicting ideas about what is the most effective type of authority. The swiftly changing values and standards of society further complicate the problem for contemporary parents.

Methods of Parental Control

As discussed in Chapter Eleven, one method of classifying parental control is by authoritarian, authoritative, or permissive style. In the authoritarian family setting, parents play a dominant role in establishing the conduct or behavior allowed. Such parents frequently emphasize respect for authority, work, and the preservation of order and traditional structure. Disciplinary measures are predominantly harsh and forceful.

The authoritarian method of control often produces rebellion in teenagers and a power struggle between parent and adolescent. Such strict parental domination, with no room for give and take, also fosters dependency, submissiveness, and conformity. Other problems develop

Adults in the family must create and maintain effective communication patterns with the teenagers to help maintain a healthy emotional climate in the home.

if the parent mixes the authoritarian style with physical punishment. The use of excessive physical punishment tends to create maladjustment in many areas of personality and social development. In particular, it is likely to promote lower levels of self-reliance and confidence and higher levels of immaturity and aggressiveness (Reidy, 1980; Kinard, 1980).

Authoritative methods of parental control, in which the adolescent is consulted on family matters, given a fair share of autonomy, disciplined in a primarily verbal way, tend to be the most effective and rewarding. Authoritative parents are more democratic, allow adolescents ample opportunity to make their own decisions, but retain final authority.

In permissive households, parents provide high levels of emotional support to their offspring but exert little control. Adolescents from these homes are frequently allowed to come and go as they please. When permitted to behave as they desire, however, adolescents may become selfish, insecure, and immature. Sometimes adolescents interpret their parents' lack of assertiveness as lack of caring even though the reverse may be true.

Martin Hoffman (1980) offers three complementary or parallel parenting styles:

1. **Power assertion** is essentially the same as the authoritarian approach. It places an emphasis on parental domination and the use of forceful discipline.

2. **Love withdrawal** occurs when parents emotionally remove themselves from the adolescent. Characteristic behaviors include the refusal to listen, silence, or walking away during an exchange.

3. **Induction** parallels the authoritative approach. It includes reasoning with the adolescent, explaining the consequences of behavior, and democratic decision making.

Which style of parental control do adolescents prefer? A study by Glen Elder (1963) sought to address this issue. Teenagers at the junior high and high school levels were asked to describe how decisions (rules of conduct, expectations) were made in their household and how they were explained. In addition, the subjects were asked to what degree they would want to be the type of persons their mothers and fathers were.

It was found that authoritarian parents, unlike authoritative ones, maintained a policy of imposing rules of conduct and expectations without explanation. Independent decision making on the part of the teenager was extremely limited. Permissive parents provided more explanations but showed relatively little interest in the decisions the adolescents attempted to make. Authoritative parents not only ex-

plained their reasons for making decisions but also encouraged teenagers to arrive at solutions with them. Self-confidence and independence were higher in this group than in the other two, which were
characterized by dependency and a general lack of confidence. Because
authoritative parental control was perceived as being fair and legitimate,
adolescents of this group became the more autocratic, or authoritative,
grown-ups. In addition, adolescents who perceived their parents as
democratic were most likely to be motivated to comply with parental
wishes.

Another study, which was concerned with parent-youth relationships in five nations, revealed that there have been pronounced
increases in authoritative methods of control over the last 40 years in
the United States, Great Britain, and West Germany. Several factors may
account for this trend: the rapid urbanization of these nations; the
middle-class population's greater exposure to the mass media, increased education, and higher incomes; and historical events, such as
wars, that gave youths the opportunity to become more involved in
family decision making (Elder, 1968).

Adolescents prefer households that are regulated on the basis of
honesty, fairness, and mutuality. Consultations between parents and
teenagers on issues of mutual concern and opportunities for teenage
autonomy appear to foster the healthiest emotional climate. Parent-
adolescent relations are likely to prosper with such operating principles, and the personal growth of each party is likely to flourish as well
(Larson, 1980; Kelly and Goodwin, 1983).

The Generation Gap: Myth or Reality?

Teenagers have a knack for telling parents about the distance that exists
between their two age groups. They may remark that their parents are
"over the hill" and that their ideas are "outdated" or "out of step" with
the times. Teenagers use different slang and catchphrases, and often tell
adults that certain words and expressions just aren't used anymore and
are a sure giveaway of a person's age. The same is true for everything
else, from hairstyles and clothing to preferences in music.

No discussion of parent-adolescent relations is complete without
some mention of the generation gap. The **generation gap** is the difference in values, attitudes, and behavior between two generational groups
such as parents and adolescents. But is the generation gap an inevitable
part of parent-adolescent relations, or is it more of a myth?

The values, attitudes, and beliefs of today's teenagers are different
from those of adolescents 10 or 20 years ago. As they seek to nurture
accurate self-concepts, teenagers have to develop their own beliefs,
which may include their perceptions of right and wrong, moral and
immoral, and important and unimportant. To do this, they must look

around and examine the views of their own generation and compare their beliefs with numerous societal agents. As young adults, they will learn that several environmental factors influence their value system, including parents, peers, schools, and the media. Usually, these societal agents present generational changes and differences in attitudes and convictions.

The acquisition of suitable standards of living is a difficult task for teenagers. Since childhood, youths have incorporated their parents' values as their own, but teenagers are quick to realize that times have changed since their parents' youth. While some will adopt parental viewpoints without question, many hesitate to do so. The desire to be independent and newfound cognitive skills, which enable the adolescent to analyze the world more fully, may promote a more questioning attitude than ever before.

Do age differences contribute to the creation of contrasting points of view? Is a generation gap almost certain to develop between young and old? Not necessarily. In fact, most researchers today regard the generation gap as largely a myth. More often than not, differences that exist between parent and adolescent are ideological, not generational. Moreover, adolescents and parents are likely to agree on more issues than one might expect. While they might overtly differ in such areas as dress or mannerisms, both groups are surprisingly similar in such areas as attitudes and fundamental values (Hamid and Wyllie, 1980; Coleman, 1980).

Parent–Adolescent Conflicts

The psychological climate of the home is extremely important in all the phases of child development. By the adolescent years, the overall climate of the home environment may be affected not only by the method of control employed but also by the degree to which parents and teenager seek to understand one another. Lack of understanding and empathy between parents and teenager is likely to disrupt family harmony and breed conflicts.

The conflicts that exist between parents and teenagers are numerous and diverse. Some of the common reasons cited for such conflicts include sexual behavior, dress, and drugs. Other frequent reasons for conflict include issues centered on school performance, friendships in general, and the use of the family car.

Males are more likely than females to disagree with their parents. This may be partly due to the fact that females tend to be more susceptible than males to parental influences. In general, females tend to view parental rules and expectations as fair and lenient (Kandel, 1980).

Given the points raised in the preceding discussion, it stands to reason that certain approaches to conflict resolution are better than

**The reasons for conflicts between parents
and teenagers are numerous.**

others. Open discussions, democratic decision making, and parental
explanations of the reasons for certain rules are sensible approaches to
resolving domestic disputes. So too is seeking to understand and
appreciate the position of the other party. The ability to take the perspective of another person into account is higher in homes fostering
support, nurturance, and affection (Adams et al., 1982).

The Desire for Independence

The urge to break away from the "semipassive" family relationships that
characterized earlier childhood and to move toward independence
seems to be prevalent among adolescents. Thus, one of the more difficult tasks of adolescence is striving for independence while at the
same time maintaining harmonious relations with parents (Sullivan and
Sullivan, 1980).

In their quest for independence, many adolescents are motivated to
escape both adult authority and social conformity. However, whether
teenagers actually avoid the latter is open to question, especially if they
seek the exclusive shelter of the peer group. Sometimes the pressure to
conform to group expectation is just as great, if not greater, than the
pressure to conform at home. Adolescents may also find that their
desire to be with others tends to promote a new type of dependency
(Josselson, 1980).

Seeking independence and adult status may place adolescents in a
conflicting situation. On one hand, they can no longer be treated as
children; on the other hand, they are not yet considered adults. It is not
clear when they pass from adolescent to adult status. Our culture, unlike others, has no rites of passage or formal initiation ceremonies that
signal the individual's emergence into adulthood. Complicating the
issue is the fact that many adolescents have attained only token independence. For example, they may be allowed to dress as they desire or

go where they please, but there is no guarantee that they have attained psychological or emotional autonomy. Furthermore, some adolescents may simply have acquired privileges in exchange for their compliance with parental ideals and wishes. This type of trade-off causes many adolescents to settle for ritual signs of independence. Consequently, many forfeit true psychological growth.

The adolescent's desire to be independent is influenced by several factors, including sex differences. Males express a greater urge to be free than females. The measure of independence achieved is clearly related to other areas of development, especially the integration of the concept of the future, upward mobility aspirations, and general achievement strivings. The manner in which adolescents seek to attain autonomy is also influenced by psychosocial maturity. Teenagers with low levels of psychosocial maturity seek to show their independence through rebellious behavior and the persistent testing of parental rules. Those with high levels of psychosocial maturity tend to internalize parental expectations, a factor that promotes a more peaceful quest for autonomy (Bernard, 1981).

In some instances, the teenager's striving for independence can produce heated conflicts. Households offering little give and take en-

The desire to be independent is often demonstrated through hairstyles.

counter the roughest going. Authoritative parents appear to weather this aspect of family life most effectively. Viewing the adolescent's strivings for independence as normal rather than threatening, authoritative parents are likely to foster cooperative independence and mature forms of responsible behavior.

Malparenting: "If I'm Not Happy, Whom Should I Sue?"

Malparenting was unheard of by our forebears, but it has caused headlines in recent years. This concept has added a new twist to child rearing and shed new light on the age-old issue of household harmony, and it represents a social trend that may make proponents of family unity shudder.

Take the case of Mrs. Laura Sumey (no pun intended) of Tacoma, Washington. The mother of two teenage daughters, Mrs. Sumey had a history of personal problems, including a broken marriage and several nervous breakdowns. In 1979, her daughters sued her under a Washington State law that states "when families are in conflict, a child can petition the court for an alternative residence." For Mrs. Sumey, this law led to several complex and controversial issues. Her older daughter ran away from home in an effort to escape Mrs. Sumey's strict supervision. Her second daughter, equally distraught, tested the legal system by petitioning for another residence.

While she was merely trying to correct her children, Mrs. Sumey found that, in others' opinion, her child-rearing techniques left much to be desired. The state agreed that in the best interests of all, the daughters should be placed in other homes, and Mrs. Sumey should be required to pay more than $100 each month for her older daughter's room and board.

This case study is not an isolated incident; on the contrary, many lawsuits have been brought against parents for various reasons. One successful lawsuit was leveled against a father who had continually physically abused his teenage son. A California youngster was also victorious in a malparenting lawsuit because his mother neglected and emotionally deprived him in addition to offering no parental support during times of stress. As one New York metropolitan lawyer says, such legal action represents a whole new type of courtroom battle.

The issue that we want to consider here is whether children should be allowed to sue their parents, other people, or even groups and organizations if they feel unhappy, discontent, or inadequate in dealing with a society as complex as ours. It is becoming fairly clear that other societal organizations are just as vulnerable as the family to such legal action. Some students have successfully brought lawsuits against teachers or entire school systems, maintaining that they were not adequately prepared in a given academic area.

Parents have also gotten into the act. Some have sued a religious group, such as the Unification Church, after it purportedly persuaded their children to join its ranks. Some parents have even had their children kidnapped and sent for "deprogramming." Ironically, while some parents were seeking lawsuits against the church, their children were suing them.

Are we becoming a nation of plaintiffs? Is legal action the course that should be taken? What is the role of government in regard to child rearing, parenting, and other aspects of socialization? If young adults who feel that they were deprived or mistreated are suing their parents, what is considered effective parenting? Do proven guidelines for effective parenting exist?

The issue becomes even more intricate. Since each child is a unique individual with different needs and different parental expectations, how can parents know the needs of each child? If parents are indeed held responsible and lawsuits are successfully brought against them, may parents in turn sue their own parents? Many experts agree that we learn many of our own child-rearing techniques from our parents. These are just a few of the questions pertinent to this complex and delicate contemporary issue.

Adolescent Runaways

Family conflicts and adolescent strivings for independence do not always end on happy notes; many teenagers run away from home. Some 750,000 choose this course of action, most between the ages of 15 and 17. There are slightly more male runaways than females, and while adolescent runaways come from all ethnic and social levels, most are from white suburbs. A majority leave home because of destructive family situations or a secret personal problem, such as pregnancy. While some travel only a short distance from home and return in less than a week, three out of ten stay away for longer periods. Some never return home (Nye, 1980).

Adolescents become runaways for several reasons. Some leave the home to escape pressure and conflict. Others run away to freedom; some of these are drawn to drugs, sex, or escape from routines in general. Finally some runaways are, in actuality, throwaways. In the face of intolerable parent-adolescent relations, many teenagers are encouraged, and in some cases forced, to leave home [Johnson and Carter, 1980; Turner, 1981(a)].

Care and treatment for runaways have improved significantly in recent years, although many runaways still go unreported. Family therapy is frequently part of the overall treatment program. In cases involving parental abuse or lack of parental cooperation, authorities may place the teenager in a foster home. An important step in combating this problem has been the establishment of tollfree hotlines that give runaways information about temporary shelter and enable them to send messages to their parents if they desire [Turner, 1981(a); Wodarski and Ammons, 1981].

Peer-Group Development

As the adolescent gropes for a sense of personal identity and the need to be accepted and recognized, the peer group becomes a critical agent of socialization. For many, security is found among friends who share the same feelings, attitudes, and doubts. Teenagers turn to their peers for approval of various activities and behaviors (Kandel, 1980).

This is not to say that a dichotomy suddenly develops between peer and parental influences. Indeed, most peers come from the same social class as the teenager's family and are thus likely to share the same

The peer group is a critical agent for socialization.

values. Furthermore, while adolescents rely on peers for ordinary day-to-day decisions, they tend to lean toward parents in more critical matters. The perceived competence of parents and peers, though, is a critical element in determining the adolescent's eventual choice between the two (Larson, 1980).

Interaction with the peer group, like socialization in general, is affected by growing social cognitive skills. In particular, advanced mental abilities enhance levels of interpersonal awareness. For instance, individuals can now empathize and take on the perspectives of others. As a result, teenagers are more sensitive to the needs of others and can also make psychological inferences about people, a cognitive capacity eluding them before (Barenboim, 1981; Elkind, 1980).

Because they do not want to be perceived as different from others, adolescents adhere closely to established peer-group norms. Eager to attain social acceptance, adolescents will pay close attention to current fads in dress and hairstyle and popular activities. They are also acutely aware of the type of behavior that will earn peer approval (see Table 20.1). As far as peer approval is concerned, females are more concerned than males with popularity and group acceptance. The desire for social acceptance is also more pronounced among middle and upper classes than among lower socioeconomic classes (Sebald, 1981).

Types of Peer Groups

Because the adolescent subculture is extremely diverse, there are different types of peer group relationships. While some adolescents become involved in highly structured and organized groups, others become members of less formal and conventional gatherings.

The smallest type of peer group, **friendship** is best described as the pairing off of two individuals who are likely to be similar in temperament and personality. Friendships in early adolescence center predominantly around shared activities and interests. Friendships of older adolescents also contain these common denominators but are differentiated by a strong emotional bond and psychological commitment between partners. In general, females are more attracted to the emotional bonds that close friendships offer (Coleman, 1980; Richey and Richey, 1980; Tesch, 1983; Berndt, 1982; Hunter and Youniss, 1982).

Cliques are similar to friendships in that individuals share common interests and exhibit a strong emotional attachment toward one another. The clique is small in number and highly exclusive, usually consisting of adolescents with similar socioeconomic backgrounds, attitudes, and beliefs.

Similar to the clique, but larger in size, is the **crowd.** Although the crowd is more impersonal and lacks the strong bonds of attachment

Table 20.1 Criteria for Peer Popularity*

	Males	Females	Total
1. Conforming (in activity, speech, attitude, dress, interest)	37	55	47
2. Being friendly, courteous, and getting along with others	40	40	40
3. Being yourself, being an individual	18	20	19
4. Having a good personality	10	20	14
5. Having a sense of humor, being cheerful, being fun to be with	11	12	11
6. Being cool	11	8	9
7. Helping, caring, and taking an interest in others	0	17	8
8. Being trustworthy, honest	11	5	8
9. Being good looking	4	10	7
10. Having money	4	0	2
11. Having good reputation	2	2	2
12. Not being gay	0	4	2
13. Keeping up with fashions	0	2	1
14. Exhibiting antiestablishment behavior	2	0	1

*Rankings and percent distribution of adolescents' answers to the question "What is expected of a teenager by his or her friends in order to be popular with them?" The study was conducted among 100 high school students of both sexes in Phoenix, Arizona.

From H. Sebald, "Adolescents' Concepts of Popularity and Unpopularity. Comparing 1960 with 1976." *Adolescence*, 1981, *16* (61), 189.

that cliques offer, it has rather rigid membership requirements. Being a member of a clique is often a prerequisite for crowd membership. Distinguishing features of crowds are heterosexual interaction and emphasis on social events such as athletic contests and dances.

The Development of Adolescent Cliques and Crowds

One of the more extensive investigations of adolescent peer group structures was undertaken by Dexter Dunphy (1963), who studied urban adolescents ranging from 13 to 21 years of age. His fieldwork revealed that cliques and crowds develop through five distinct stages during the teenage years (see Figure 20.2).

In the first stage, preadolescents socialize in unisexual cliques. Each clique remains isolated from those of the other sex. The second stage is characterized by a movement toward **heterosexuality** in group structure. Interaction between the sexes, however, is considered to be "daring" and is usually undertaken only when same-sex members are present, presumably because of the support and the sense of security they lend.

During the third stage, cliques become quite heterosexual and the first dating takes place. Usually one-to-one interaction is initiated by upper-status members of each clique. While dating places the adoles-

Figure 20.2 Stages of group development in adolescence (Dunphy, D. C. The social structure of urban adolescent peer groups. *Sociometry,* **1963, *26,* 230–246).**

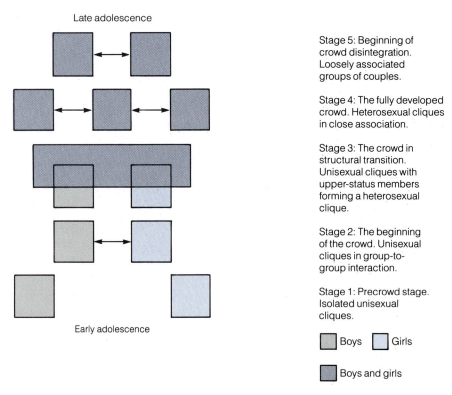

Late adolescence

Stage 5: Beginning of crowd disintegration. Loosely associated groups of couples.

Stage 4: The fully developed crowd. Heterosexual cliques in close association.

Stage 3: The crowd in structural transition. Unisexual cliques with upper-status members forming a heterosexual clique.

Stage 2: The beginning of the crowd. Unisexual cliques in group-to-group interaction.

Stage 1: Precrowd stage. Isolated unisexual cliques.

Boys   Girls

Boys and girls

Early adolescence

Stages of group development in adolescence

cent in an entirely new social sphere, membership is still retained in the unisexual clique, the result being that the adolescent now becomes a member in two intercepting cliques.

The fully developed crowd characterizes the fourth stage. At this point, cliques still exist within the larger crowd framework, but their membership now includes both sexes. At the last stage, occurring in late adolescence, crowds begin to disintegrate as the adolescent's need for support and larger group activities lessens. When this change takes place, cliques have a tendency to reappear and become important again. Couples who are going steady or who are engaged exemplify this phase of development.

Adolescent Dating

Dating generally begins during the teenage years. Dating is especially popular in the United States, and American teenagers begin dating earlier than teenagers in other countries. This precocity is largely due to encouragement of early heterosexual interactions in the school system or at social functions and to the influence of mass media. This exposure and prompting, coupled with the perceived importance of dating, exerts significant influences on the adolescent's personality and social development.

Dating serves a number of important functions. It is a social vehicle that enables teenagers to learn more about themselves and how they are perceived by others, including strengths as well as weaknesses. Thus, dating helps adolescents to develop their identities. Dating also teaches the importance of sensitivity, mutuality, and reciprocity and enables the adolescent to experience love and sexual relations within mutually acceptable limits. Finally, dating is the process through which one may ultimately select a marriage partner.

The complexion of dating has changed over the years. In the past, dating was a structured and formal affair, profoundly affected by traditional sex-role stereotyping. The male usually took the initiative to ask the female out, provided transportation, and absorbed the expenses. Although traditional behaviors still exist, dating is more casual today, and growing numbers of couples share expenses and the transportation involved. Some females even take the initiative to ask the male out (Bell and Coughey, 1980; Murstein, 1980).

Certain sex-role standards persist in dating and sexual behaviors. The male, many times eager to prove his manhood (to himself and later to his peers as he narrates his sexual exploits), frequently makes the first move toward sexual intimacy on a date. The female, on the other hand, is expected to be less sexual and curtail the advances of her date. The notion that males desire sex earlier in the dating relationship than females is a persistent theme in the literature (Knox and Wilson, 1981; Allgeier and McCormick, 1982).

In general, females start dating earlier than males. They also have different attitudes about dating. Although anxious about dating during the early stages of adolescence, females tend to exhibit deep understanding, sensitivity, and emotional involvement toward their partners by late adolescence. Males, meanwhile, tend to deemphasize the emotional and intimate features of the relationship. Such differences support our earlier finding that female friendships in general are characterized by an intense, emotional bond (Selman, 1981; Coleman, 1980).

Adolescents look for certain qualities in a date. Physical attractiveness is equally important for both males and females, as are personality and compatibility. How prestigious a date is appears to be more important for females. This latter consideration might be linked to the fact that females, more than males, view dating as a way to increase their popularity and status in the peer group. Finally, both males and females value honesty and the degree to which a partner can bring companionship and enjoyment to a relationship [Hansen and Hicks, 1980; Rubin, 1980(b)].

More serious dating may lead to going steady (also simply called "seeing" or "going with" someone). Although the meaning of this type of relationship varies from couple to couple, going steady generally implies a rather permanent relationship in which both parties refrain from dating others. In general, going steady is more common today than in the past and it also begins earlier in the lives of teenagers. Many teenagers go steady as early as age 16 (Bell and Coughey, 1980).

Compared to random, casual dating, going steady has its share of advantages. One of the more practical benefits is that dates are assured, which promotes a sense of security in many adolescents. Going steady also encourages independence and practice with interpersonal communication skills. In this sense, going steady teaches adolescents the importance of openness, feedback, and conflict resolution skills, all important prerequisites to marriage.

There are disadvantages to going steady, too. Exclusive dating arrangements reduce the adolescent's heterosexual experiences and many times remove the teenager from same-sex peers, which may restrict the adolescent's overall social development. Going steady also promotes the escalation of physical intimacy, which often leads to sexual intercourse before the partners are ready for it. This in turn increases the risk of teenage pregnancy and premature marriage.

Sexual Behavior

Few topics about adolescent heterosexual development arouse more general interest and curiosity than sexual behavior. This interest has led

Dating enables teenagers to find out more about themselves.

to a flurry of publications on the topic. The most consistent research finding is that today's attitudes toward sex have become more relaxed and tolerant. Studies repeatedly uncover the fact that American society has moved from an antisex to a prosex orientation, the latter becoming quite obvious in teenage dating patterns. These liberal attitudes are part of the so-called sexual revolution America has been experiencing over the past 20 years (Singh, 1980).

While today's sexual attitudes have become more liberal, it is incorrect to assume that all sexual behavior is equally liberal. It is true that we are experiencing a convergence of liberal sexual attitudes and behavior, but not everyone partakes in permissive sexual activity, and not everyone believes in such behavior. Therefore, actual sexual behavior and the principles motivating sexual activity need to be examined more carefully (Hyde, 1982; Mahoney, 1983).

In this respect, four basic principles or moral standards underlying sexual behavior have been proposed (Reiss, 1960; 1981).

1. The **abstinence standard** means that it is wrong for both unmarried males and females to engage in sexual intercourse.

2. The **double standard** asserts that males can have sexual relations before marriage but women are expected to remain abstinent.

3. **Permissiveness without affection,** also called "recreational sex," means that sex by itself without emotional attachments is acceptable.

4. **Permissiveness with affection** implies that sexual relations are acceptable if accompanied by emotional attachment between partners.

Of these four guiding principles, permissiveness with affection is the most popular today, for adults as well as adolescents. In a survey of over 300 older adolescents questioned about their sexual standards, results clearly indicated that the more emotionally involved a person was in a relationship, the more likely increasing levels of physical intimacy were regarded as appropriate (Knox and Wilson, 1981).

Interestingly, many adolescents have migrated to the permissiveness with affection standard after initially holding abstinent views on sexual relations. Adolescents (and adults) are least likely to favor the double standard and the permissiveness without affection values. The double standard is viewed as demeaning to women. Rejection of this standard may well be part of the social movement against sexual inequality.

Research reveals that adolescents can be quite conservative about certain aspects of sexual activity. This was shown in a study designed to elicit adolescents' moral judgments of sexual situations. When asked about the morality of having sex with many partners, the respondents tended to regard such behavior as immoral or sinful. While premarital sexual relations were viewed as tolerable, a succession of partners was not (Robinson and Jedlicka, 1982).

It should be recognized that sexual attitudes are shaped by numerous social agents. For example, the peer group wields a significant influence, perhaps more than parents. Other important influences are the media and schooling, particularly with regard to the nature and extent of sex education. Religious instruction also influences the course of attitude development. In relation to this, regular church attendance tends to promote sexual guilt and diminish sexual permissiveness (Jorgensen, King, and Torrey, 1980; Inazu and Fox, 1980; Gunderson and McCary, 1980).

The adolescent's need to manage his or her sexuality is of importance not only to the teenager but also to parents, educators, and other concerned adults. Knowing how the sex drive manifests itself and affects behavior during these years may help adults provide effective guidance and understanding.

Masturbation   **Masturbation** is defined as the manipulation of one's own sex organs to produce pleasure. Once regarded as a sinful and forbidden activity, masturbation today is generally recognized as a normal form of sexual expression. Research evidence indicates that by age 21 masturbation has become almost universal, especially among males. This means that experiencing masturbation is the norm while the failure to masturbate by this time is the exception (Gold and Petronio, 1980).

It is estimated that nearly 70 percent of all males and about 40 percent of all females masturbate by age 15 (Dreyer, 1982). It should be realized that these and other findings on sexual behavior may be influenced by a number of factors. For example, females may be reluctant to admit such behavior. Nonetheless, such high percentages coupled with the fact that they will further increase with age, show how widespread masturbation is.

Masturbation tends to provoke feelings of guilt and anxiety, although this appears to be less true now than in the past. Guilt may originate from perceived social disapproval or misgivings about achieving sexual pleasure through self-stimulation. Many teenagers will not admit to their peers that they engage in masturbation.

Another source of anxiety may be the fantasies imagined during masturbation. Since many of the teenager's fantasies involve people they regularly encounter, such sexual associations may promote guilt and even embarrassment. Yet another source of guilt may develop between adolescents and their families. After masturbating, some teenagers may have difficulty in passing themselves off as "normal" human beings, especially to parents. Managing both sexual feelings and family attachments may thus be difficult for the sensitive adolescent.

Petting   **Petting** is physical contact that does not involve union of the genitalia but is a deliberate attempt to effect erotic arousal. Petting is one of the more common sexual activities during adolescence, for both males and females. Although females do engage in petting, however, they usually do it in a conservative fashion. Many have been taught to resist the sexual advances of the male, but many females also know that allowing some sexual intimacy, such as petting, will enhance their popularity among males.

The actual numbers of teenagers who engage in petting is unknown. However, researchers estimate that about half of all 15-year-olds have engaged in some form of light petting (above the waist). About 20 percent have experienced heavy petting (below the waist) by this same age (Dupold and Young, 1979; Vener and Steward, 1974).

When petting should occur in the overall time frame of dating produces different reactions from males and females. A study of older adolescents found that females want this type of sexual intimacy delayed until at least after the fourth date. Only one-third of the males surveyed felt this way; in fact, almost one-third believed that petting should occur on the first date (Knox and Wilson, 1981).

Premarital Intercourse   Research supports the fact that a greater percentage of today's teenagers are engaging in premarital intercourse than in the past. A comparison of Alfred Kinsey's classic studies of male and female sexual behavior (Kinsey, Pomeroy, and Martin, 1948; Kinsey, Pomeroy, Martin, and Gebhard, 1953) with more recent investigations will illustrate this point. When Kinsey conducted his research, he discovered that approximately 20 percent of all females and about 40 percent of all males surveyed had experienced sexual intercourse by the time they were 20. More contemporary research shows significant increases in the percentages reported by Kinsey and his colleagues. In fact, a glance at the findings reveals that it is not uncommon to find approximately 50 percent of the females surveyed and about 70 percent of the males engaging in premarital intercourse before age 20 (Kantner and Zelnik, 1980; Clayton and Bokemeier, 1980; Bell and Coughey, 1980; Robinson and Jedlicka, 1982).

Certain factors affect the rates of premarital coitus. As the aforementioned statistics imply, rates will increase as adolescents get older. Actual frequency of premarital coitus is also greater among adolescents from lower socioeconomic groups who do not attend college than among college students from higher socioeconomic groups. Rates are also greater for adolescents who do not attend church on a regular basis. Finally, blacks engage more frequently in premarital coitus than whites (Lamer and Housker, 1980; Clayton and Bokemeier, 1980; Inazu and Fox, 1980).

Males generally want sexual intercourse before females do during the dating relationship. Almost half the males surveyed in one study felt that intercourse was appropriate by the fifth date in contrast to about 25 percent of the females surveyed. Does this mean that individuals should circle their calendars and set their watches in anticipation of the fifth date? Hardly. This is strictly an average and should not be taken out of context. It is interesting, though, that this general desire on the part of males to initiate and of females to delay this aspect of sexual intimacy is similar to our earlier findings on petting (Knox and Wilson, 1981).

Adolescents report a variety of reasons for engaging in sexual intercourse. Among males, the motives include the desire to prove their manhood, explore the unknown, relieve pent-up sexual desire, and the fact that they are in love and will be married soon anyway. Female reasons include satisfaction and the need for sexual activity. Many adolescents believe that premarital sex may help them develop the capacity to make the sort of emotional adjustments needed in marital relationships and may test the capacity of two people to make satisfactory sexual adjustments after marriage.

A number of reasons are also given by adolescents for not engaging in sexual intercourse. For females, two of the more common reasons are the fear of pregnancy and the guilt over loss of virginity. This is also a source of anxiety for males as far as responsibility is concerned. For both sexes, other reasons for refraining include the fear of being caught by parents and the fear of contracting a sexually transmitted disease.

Teenage Promiscuity and Sexually Transmitted Diseases   The sexually active teenager's concern over contracting a venereal disease is a legitimate one in light of today's alarming statistics. Compared to other segments of the population, teenagers are especially vulnerable. While individuals between the ages of 20 and 24 have the highest incidence rate of sexually transmitted diseases, teenagers between the ages of 15 and 19 are the next highest group (NIAID, 1981).

The three most serious sexually transmitted diseases are gonorrhea, syphilis, and genital herpes. **Gonorrhea** is the most common of the three and affects more than one million individuals each year. This makes the incidence of gonorrhea almost as frequent as that of the common cold. **Syphilis** is the least prevalent of the three, owing largely to the success of penicillin treatment. However, syphilis still claims an estimated 150,000 new victims each year (Masters, Johnson, and Kolodny, 1982; NIAID, 1981; Silber, 1981).

Genital herpes has created much public concern in recent years. An estimated 10 million Americans currently suffer from genital herpes, with 500,000 new cases reported each year. Because a cure for genital herpes has not yet been found, the number of cases continues to spiral upward (Gotwald and Golden, 1981; Hamilton, 1980).

Despite their general concern over contracting a sexually transmitted disease, too many adolescents become victims. There are several reasons for such high rates. The sheer increase in the overall sexual activity of teenagers makes the risk factor greater. In addition, the pill has become the major birth control method, replacing the condom, which offered some protection against infection. Another reason is that adolescents are frequently unaware of the symptoms and treatment available for sexually transmitted diseases, which means that more emphasis must be placed on prevention and upgrading the adolescent's awareness of the magnitude and severity of sexually transmitted diseases.

Adolescent Pregnancy   Adolescent pregnancies are rapidly increasing in the United States. Approximately one million adolescent girls become pregnant annually. Of this total, about 600,000 give birth to their babies. With birth rates for older women declining, statistics reveal that one out of every five new mothers today is a teenager. Perhaps the most shocking statistic is that approximately one out of every ten teenagers will become a mother by the age of 18 (Nye and Lamberts, 1980).

There are many reasons why these figures are so high. The liberal sexual attitudes and behavior of today's youth culture are quoted most often. The misuse of contraceptives or the absence of any birth control is another contributing factor. Some adolescents do not care about the consequences of their sexual behavior; others become pregnant because they want to have a baby (Kelley, 1981; Oskamp and Mindick, 1981; Strahle, 1983).

Teenage pregnancies pose numerous problems. One of the most tragic statistics is that the younger the mother, the greater the chances of infant death. Teenage mothers are more apt to have premature births than older mothers and are more likely to experience labor and delivery complications, including toxemia and anemia. The babies themselves frequently suffer from neurological problems and birth defects. Children of teenage mothers also tend to have lower IQs and perform more poorly in school than children of older mothers (Broman, 1981; Chilman, 1980).

In addition to physical problems, psychological, emotional, and economic difficulties go hand in hand with teenage pregnancies. Dropping out of school to take on the responsibility of baby care requires a major reorientation that many teenagers fail to make. Even for those mature enough to meet the challenges of decision making, and most have difficulty accepting the reduction of freedom that accompanies childbirth. Lack of finances is also a problem in most teenage marriages, a factor that increases the risk of child abuse. All these factors may help explain why teenage marriages coupled with the birth of a child are likely to end in divorce (Walters and Walters, 1980; Sahler, 1980; Nye and Lamberts, 1980).

Teenage pregnancy is a social problem that needs attention from everyone. Most experts believe that we need to place a greater emphasis on sex education, especially birth control methods and their accessibility. Making parents aware of the problem and encouraging

Teenagers who keep their children need help completing their education and achieving vocational skills.

communication between adults and adolescents are also being stressed. Sex education at home, in addition to the emotional support that parents can offer to their offspring, is also critical (Byrne, 1983; Fisher, 1983).

Finally, those teenagers who decide to keep their children need help as well. Programs must focus on the needs of both mother and child. Attention should be directed toward increasing the educational level of teenage parents, especially the mother, in addition to upgrading vocational skills (Schneider, 1982; Brown, 1982; Montgomery and Leashore, 1982).

Summary

George, age 15

During adolescence teenagers exhibit heightened levels of self-awareness and strong strivings to be accepted by the peer group. Several significant developmental theories have focused on the nature of change during adolescence. Sigmund Freud emphasizes the psychosexual dynamics taking place during the period known as the genital stage, while Erik Erikson maintains that adolescents must resolve the psychosocial crisis of identity versus role diffusion. Lawrence Kohlberg proposes that adolescents typically reach the stage of post-conventional morality, a period marked by the careful selection of, and adherence to, personalized moral principles.

One of the primary tasks of adolescence is the establishment of satisfactory family relationships. Parents employ a number of methods to control their offspring, the most popular being the authoritarian, permissive, and authoritative styles. Of these, the authoritative approach has proven to be the most effective in teaching responsibility, in handling discipline, in resolving family conflicts, and in handling the adolescent's strivings for independence.

The peer group becomes an important agent of socialization during the teenage years. Adolescents typically come into contact with a wide range of peer groups, including friendships, cliques, and crowds. Research presented in this chapter illustrates how five fairly predictable stages characterize clique and crowd development.

The most distinguishing feature of social development is the adolescent's interest in heterosexual relations and the subsequent emergence of dating. Dating is especially popular and begins earlier in the United States than in other countries. Dating serves a number of important functions, including the opportunity to refine one's identity and to develop such capacities as understanding, empathy, and sensitivity. Dating today is less structured and formal than in the past. However, traditional sex-role standards persist.

It is generally recognized today that attitudes about sex have become more liberal. Of the four moral standards regarding sexual behavior, permissiveness with affection is the most popular. Contemporary research findings reveal increasing numbers of teenagers engaging in such sexual behaviors as masturbation, petting, and intercourse. Sexually transmitted diseases and teenage pregnancy are two of the more serious problems resulting from the increase in adolescent sexual activity. The rising incidence rate of each has generated concern from many segments of the population.

Suggested Reading List

Adelson, Jr., ed. *Handbook of Adolescent Psychology*. New York: Wiley, 1980. A good assortment of articles on many key aspects of adolescent development. Contributors include, among others, David Elkind, Martin Hoffman, and James Marcia.

Allgeier, E., and McCormick, N., eds. *Gender Roles and Sexual Behavior*. Palo Alto, Calif.: Mayfield, 1982. This book of readings succeeds in providing a thorough analysis of how gender roles influence sexual behavior, including that of adolescents.

Byrne, D., and Fisher, W. A., eds. *Adolescents, Sex, and Contraception*. New York: McGraw-Hill, 1981. A diverse collection of readings focusing on many aspects of teenage sexuality, including birth control, pregnancy, and the problems adolescent parents have in child rearing.

Rathus, S. A. *Human Sexuality*. New York: Holt, Rinehart & Winston, 1981. Rathus covers the dynamics of adolescent sexual behavior in Chapter Nine of this well-written text.

Chapter Twenty-One

Problems of Adolescence

Custom and convention govern human action.

Pyrrho

Introduction

Not all teenagers successfully resolve the developmental tasks of adolescence. When faced with the complexities and pressures of modern society, some feel futile or hopeless. Many are simply incapable of dealing with the life demands placed on their shoulders and react to this developmental stage with a mixture of self-defeating behaviors.

In recent years, a number of adolescent maladjustment problems have received attention from psychologists. All have grown in alarming fashion and have generated a great deal of public concern. These problems are juvenile delinquency, drug abuse, teenage suicide, and anorexia nervosa.

Juvenile Delinquency

Juvenile delinquency is behavior on the part of youths 18 and under that society deems unacceptable. Delinquency includes acts by youths that would be considered crimes if committed by adults. It also encompasses violations of ordinances that apply only to children and youths, such as curfew regulations, school attendance laws, and restrictions on the use of alcohol and tobacco. Children variously designated as being beyond control, ungovernable, incorrigible, runaway, or in need of supervision may also be considered delinquent.

Perhaps a glance at a fairly recent statistic will illustrate the manner in which juvenile delinquency has increased. In 1960 the majority of people arrested in this country were over 25 years of age. In 1980, over half of those arrested were 24 or younger (see Figure 21.1).

Collected data give us a fairly accurate profile of today's juvenile delinquent. For example, rates of delinquency are highest for teenagers between the ages of 15 and 16. By age 18, delinquent behavior is likely to decline. The young adolescent generally commits the less serious forms of delinquency, such as vandalism or running away from home. The older adolescent is more likely to commit such serious offenses as drug abuse or truancy. More violent crimes, such as aggravated assault or forcible rape, are more characteristic of individuals over 18 (Federal Bureau of Investigation, 1980; U.S. Bureau of the Census, 1982).

Statistics also show that there are more black and male juvenile offenders than white and female ones. Males at one time heavily out-numbered females in number of offenses, sometimes as much as 5 to 1. Today, it is closer to 3 to 1. There is a notable difference, though, in the types of delinquency committed by males and females. Males are more likely to be reported for burglary and car theft. Females tend to be charged with running away from home, ungovernable behavior, and sex offenses (Gold and Petronio, 1980; Hindelang, 1981).

Figure 21.1 Persons arrested—Percent by age: 1961 to 1981 (U.S. Bureau of the Census, *Statistical Abstract of the United States.* **Washington, D.C.: Gov't. Printing Office, 1982).**

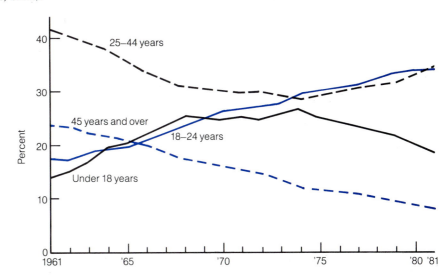

Conditions and Factors Affecting Delinquency

In addition to gathered statistics, psychologists have uncovered a number of conditions and factors related to juvenile delinquency. Certain elements of family life have been found to affect this problem. For example, many juvenile delinquents have emerged from broken homes. Domestic settings stricken by divorce, death, desertion, or a lack of affection and understanding can produce great stress in the child, not only before and during separation but also during subsequent social development (Haskell and Yablonsky, 1982; Canter, 1982).

The degree of affection exhibited by the parents toward the adolescent is one consideration. In homes where the individual is exposed to warm and affectionate relationships, delinquency is rare. Conversely, when parents, especially fathers, offer little affection or reject their children, there is a strong likelihood of rebellious or delinquent behavior. Thus, the psychological absence of the father from the home can contribute as much to delinquency as his physical absence would (Gold and Petronio, 1980; Stott, 1982).

Methods of parental discipline may also contribute to delinquency. Rates of delinquency are higher when parents employ abusive and hostile measures of discipline. Adolescent rebelliousness and defiance are likely to be fostered by whippings, beatings, and other types of physical punishment. Hostile behavior on the part of adolescents may persist throughout adult life, especially when they start their own family lives. Those who were abused have a strong tendency to employ similar violent techniques (Gelles, 1980; Youngerman and Canino, 1983; Ulbrich and Huber, 1981).

Another unfavorable family condition is unstable parental behavior. Delinquent youths are more apt to have one or both parents exhibiting maladjustment problems. These problems include emotional disorders, alcoholism or other drug dependencies, antisocial attitudes, and sociopathic tendencies. When these problems are combined with patterns of rejection and hostility, delinquent behavior may result in the children (Cavan and Ferdinand, 1981; Stott, 1982).

Other conditions and factors occur outside of the family and are equally important to examine. Economic deprivation almost always goes hand in hand with juvenile delinquency. When economic deprivation is joined by such factors as low education, high unemployment, and overcrowding, rates of juvenile delinquency escalate.

While rates of delinquency are higher among urban lower socioeconomic classes, it would be incorrect to assume that rural middle and upper socioeconomic classes are free of this problem. The notion that juvenile crime is restricted to inner-city youth is especially erroneous. Delinquency is fairly commonplace in rural and well-to-do neighborhoods. In fact, some of the biggest annual crime increases among juve-

niles were in rural communities with populations of less than 25,000
(Adler, Bazemore, and Polk, 1980).

Middle- and upper-class juveniles break the law for a variety of
reasons, including a desire to attain recognition or peer pressure. More
affluent delinquents may be the product of inadequate parenting or
emotional neglect. In general, though, middle- and upper-class delinquents become involved in less serious offenses such as disturbing the
peace or minor traffic violations. More serious offenses, such as aggravated assault, are more likely to be committed by lower-class delinquents (Cavan and Ferdinand, 1981).

**Many factors can lead to delinquent behavior—from problems and
conditions in the home to peer pressure and the desire for recognition.**

Although delinquent acts are sometimes carried out alone, more often than not they are committed in the company of others. Delinquents usually seek out the support of friends with similar interests. The unsatisfactory home life described earlier often heightens the delinquent's need to be accepted and gain peer recognition.

The peer group of the delinquent frequently transforms itself into a gang. The **gang** of the juvenile delinquent is a formally organized group with between 10 and 15 members, whose primary purpose is illegal activity. In general, delinquent gangs can be divided into two broad categories. One type agrees with the materialistic values of society but chooses illegal methods to obtain what it wants. For the most part, members of this type of gang are emotionally stable. The second type of gang is violent and often operates in a psychopathic manner. In addition to its antisocial stance, this type of gang continually wages war with other gangs and uses violence as a form of emotional gratification (Haskell and Yablonsky, 1982).

Characteristics of the Juvenile Delinquent

To provide delinquents with guidance, it is important to be aware of their personality makeup and other characteristics. Certain patterns of behavior appear to be common. Many delinquents feel deprived, insecure, and defiant; most deliberately set out to break the law (Gold and Petronio, 1980; Cavan and Ferdinand, 1981). Many juvenile delinquents are excitable and impulsive and have low levels of moral development and deviant values. Delinquents harbor poor self-concepts due to past failures in family, school, or other social situations. These inadequacies frequently produce defensive behavior, including ambivalence toward authority, hostility, and frequent destructiveness (Gold and Petronio, 1980; Stott, 1982; Haskell and Yablonsky, 1982).

Some delinquents have lower levels of intelligence than nondelinquents, indicating that they may be unable to foresee the probable consequences of their actions or to understand their significance. This factor is seldom viewed as a determining one in predicting delinquency, however, since low intelligence appears to be significant in only 5 percent of incidents of delinquent behavior (Coleman, Butcher, and Carson, 1984).

Providing Assistance for the Juvenile Delinquent

Past efforts to help the troubled adolescent have shown that effectively preventing and treating delinquency are formidable and difficult tasks. Despite numerous attempts and different approaches, clear-cut answers have yet to be found. The low success rate of rehabilitation programs is as alarming today as it was in the past.

In some cases, the juvenile justice system itself is part of the problem. The labeling process of court hearings and the inadequate corrective measures of juvenile rehabilitation institutions are especially vulnerable to criticism. Some institutions resemble training grounds for criminals. By placing juvenile offenders in the midst of other delinquents who model and reinforce each other's behavior, jail-like institutions do more harm than good.

A variety of programs and strategies have been attempted, including group and family therapy, behavior modification, alternative vocational and educational settings, group homes, and more intensive social service intervention. Unfortunately, none of these has solved the problem. Contemporary experts argue that most approaches are applied to youths who already have serious problems and are thus too late to do much good.

Future efforts need to begin much earlier and emphasize prevention. In addition to therapeutic intervention, preventive measures must emphasize alleviation of slum conditions, provision of adequate educational and recreational opportunities for the disadvantaged adolescent, education of parents, and the delineation of a more meaningful and relevant social role for the teenager (National Commission on Youth, 1980; Gold and Petronio, 1980; Coleman, Butcher, and Carson, 1984; Safer, 1982).

Drug Abuse

Drugs have been used throughout history to induce happiness, alter moods, or create intoxication. Today, a variety of drugs serve a wide range of medical and recreational purposes. Many drugs serve as chemical shelters against the stresses and insecurities of modern life. Millions of Americans today cannot sleep, wake up, or feel comfortable without drugs. Many do not realize, don't care, or will not admit that they have become dependent on drugs.

The use of mind-expanding drugs by vast numbers of middle-class youths and adults is the novel feature of the problem. In a sense, all drug users are behaving like good American consumers. The mass media constantly advise us to satisfy our emotional needs with material products, particularly those involving oral consumption of some substance. Our society depends on the willingness of the American public to turn to things rather than people for gratification. Who doubts "better living through chemistry"?

Types of Drug-Taking Behavior

Among the misinformed, it is common practice to label the drug user as an "addict." Such a label is incorrect, as is labeling the individual who takes a drink an "alcoholic." In order to understand drug-taking behavior, certain terms need to be clarified.

Contemporary physicians and health professionals prefer to apply the term *dependence* for an individual who continually takes a drug. Furthermore, there are two types of dependence: psychological and physical. **Psychological dependence** is said to exist when the effect of a drug becomes such an important facet of an individual's life that the person needs it to function.

The use of drugs alters the user's perception of reality and may interfere with social and emotional development.

Physical dependence also occurs when the use of a drug becomes necessary for a person to function. However, unlike psychological dependence, this condition is characterized by unpleasant physical effects in the absence of the drug. These unpleasant effects, called **withdrawal symptoms,** can include nausea, cramping, excessive sweating, and diarrhea.

Drug tolerance is said to have developed when a person needs greater amounts of a drug in order to obtain the original effects of that drug. Repeated and prolonged use of a drug produces tolerance.

All drugs can be classified by the nature of their effect on the central nervous system. This is equally true for drugs that stimulate and those that depress. See Figure 21.2.

Alcohol

The use of alcohol is widespread among both adults and teenagers, and its increasing use has aroused concern in both public and private sectors of the population. Overall, it is estimated that 75 percent of American males and 66 percent of American females drink. Among teenagers, it was found in one study that approximately 90 percent had tried alcohol by their senior year of high school (Gallup, 1981; Johnston, Bachman, and O'Malley, 1980). Figure 21.3 charts the use of alcohol among individuals by age and sex.

Alcohol is accepted in most societies and is rarely regarded as a drug, but it can be so categorized because it affects the central nervous system. Alcohol numbs the higher brain centers. As the concentration of alcohol in the blood increases, progressive impairment of normal brain functions gradually reduces one's awareness of and response to stimuli from the outside (Schlaadt and Shannon, 1982; Julien, 1981).

Alcohol initially reduces inhibitions and tensions, giving the individual an expansive feeling of well-being and sociability. Larger amounts, however, interfere with complex and higher-level thought processes and may impair motor coordination, balance, speech, and vision. Alcohol is also capable of blunting pain and in larger amounts induces sedation and sleep.

Heavy drinkers tend to be impulsive, unstable in their behavior, and unpredictable. This is why the drinking of alcohol is one of the traditional reasons juveniles are taken into custody after breaking the law. Regular users of alcohol also run the risk of **alcoholism.** In the United States, approximately 8 to 10 percent of males and 2 to 4 percent of females can be described as alcoholics at some point in their lives (Gallup, 1981).

Why are adolescents attracted to alcohol? Adolescents as well as adults use alcohol to be more sociable and to reduce anxiety or build courage in difficult situations. Whether alcohol actually does relieve tension and anxiety is subject to question (Peyser, 1982). Conformity to peer pressure and the desire to appear more grown-up are other popular explanations. Since drinking is associated with adult role behavior, it may symbolize the attainment of adult status. It is known that adolescent drinking patterns are influenced by others in the community. Examples set by parents and other adults need to be examined when seeking to understand the teenager's drinking behavior (Tomaszewski,

Figure 21.2 Drug classifications and the effect on the central nervous system (Dr. Robert W. Earle, Department of Pharmacology, College of Medicine, University of California at Irvine. Reprinted by permission).

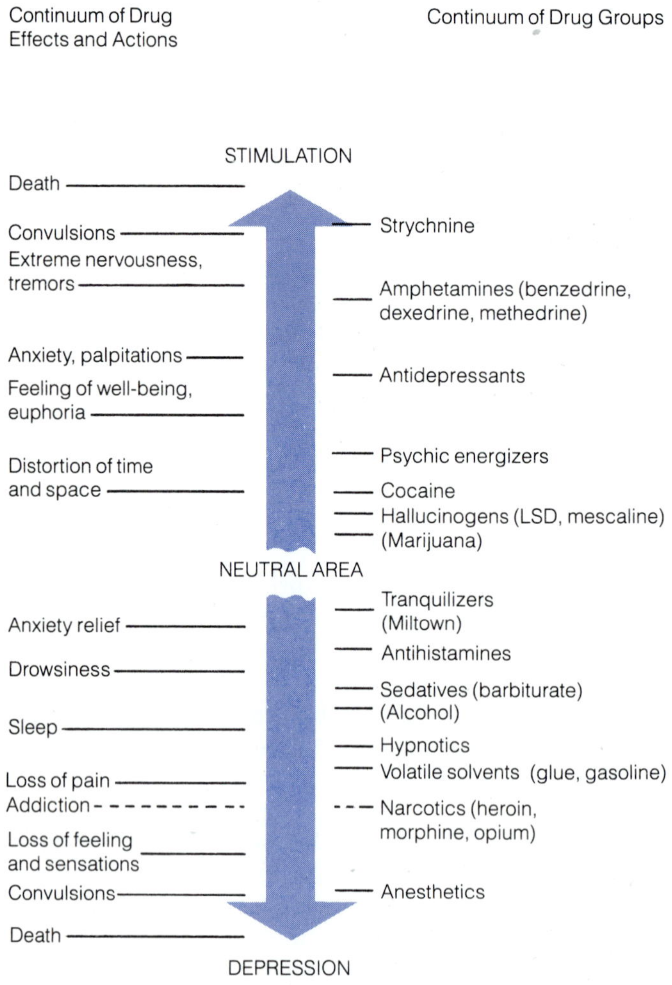

Continuum of Drug Effects and Actions   Continuum of Drug Groups

STIMULATION

Death

Convulsions ——————————— Strychnine
Extreme nervousness, tremors ———————

_____ Amphetamines (benzedrine, dexedrine, methedrine)

Anxiety, palpitations ———— Antidepressants
Feeling of well-being, euphoria ———————

Distortion of time and space ——————— Psychic energizers
——— Cocaine
——— Hallucinogens (LSD, mescaline)
——— (Marijuana)

NEUTRAL AREA

——— Tranquilizers (Miltown)
Anxiety relief ——————
——— Antihistamines
Drowsiness ——————
——— Sedatives (barbiturate)
——— (Alcohol)
Sleep ————————
——— Hypnotics
——— Volatile solvents (glue, gasoline)
Loss of pain ——————
Addiction – – – – – – – – – Narcotics (heroin, morphine, opium)
Loss of feeling and sensations
Convulsions ——————— Anesthetics
Death ————————

DEPRESSION

Strickler, and Maxwell, 1980; Brook, Whiteman, and Gordon, 1983; Hawkins, 1982; Koop, 1983; Segal, Huba, and Singer, 1980).

Hallucinogens

Hallucinogens are drugs capable of producing a hallucination. Many of the reasons adolescents give for turning to hallucinogens are the same as those for using alcohol. In addition, many adolescents take these drugs because they're curious. In certain social circles use of drugs other than alcohol is a status symbol. Some use hallucinogens because they're faster acting and more potent than alcohol. Others use them as a symbol of rebellion or as a way to escape boredom, conflict, or stress.

Of course the decision to turn to hallucinogens does not mean that alcohol is abandoned. Many adolescents use one or the other depending on the nature of the social setting; in some circles, it is not unusual to be offered the choice of a joint or a drink. Many adolescents mix alcohol and other drugs, even though they may be aware that some

Figure 21.3 Current alcohol use among youth by age and sex (adapted from P. M. Fishburne, H. I. Abelson, and I. Cisin, *National Survey on Drug Abuse: Main Findings, 1979*. Washington, D.C.: National Institute on Drug Abuse, Government Printing Office, 1980, pp. 94–96).

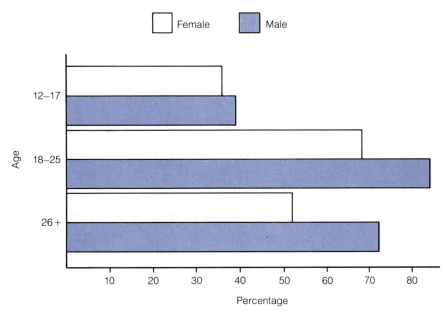

combinations, such as alcohol and barbiturates, can be lethal (Leavitt, 1982).

Marijuana   Next to alcohol, the most frequently and widely used non-medical drug is **marijuana.** While surveys vary from region to region, it has been estimated that the number of Americans who have tried marijuana at least once in their lives may be as many as 43 million. Of this figure, 16 million are regarded as regular users (Kaufman, 1982).

Marijuana use is extensive among adolescents. One study found that 60 percent of the respondents had tried it at some point in their lives and almost 50 percent had smoked it during the prior year (Johnston, Bachman, and O'Malley, 1980). Yet some researchers believe that its popularity has peaked among high school students and is now declining (see Figure 21.4). Concern over marijuana's adverse effects appears to be the primary reason for this trend (National Center for Health Statistics, 1982).

Marijuana is obtained from a mixture of the tops, leaves, seeds, and stems of female hemp or cannabis plants. This plant grows wild and is

Figure 21.4 Frequency of marijuana use by high school seniors, according to sex: United States, 1975–80 (adapted from National Center for Health Statistics: *Health, United States, 1982.* Public Health Service, Washington. U.S. Gov't Printing Office, 1982, p. 19).

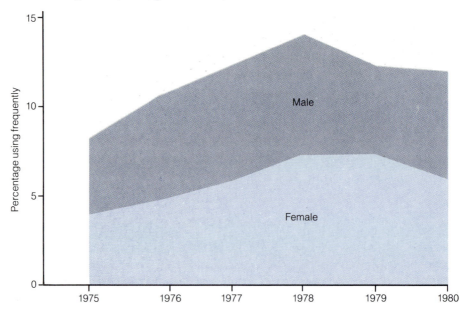

usually found in the temperate or semitropical climates of the world. The active ingredient of marijuana is tetrahydrocannabinol (THC), which varies in amount and subsequent strength. The strongest grade of marijuana is known as hashish. In recent years, more careful cultivation has produced marijuana with 6 to 10 times as much THC, resulting in much greater potency (Cotman and McGaugh, 1980).

In the United States, marijuana is most frequently smoked either in the form of cigarettes or in a pipe. The smoker retains the deeply inhaled smoke as long as possible in order to enhance absorption across the alveolar capillary bed. Most experts agree that marijuana has the greatest effect on the central nervous system and the cardiovascular system. It is felt that marijuana does not produce physical dependency (Julien, 1981).

The behavioral effect of marijuana is mostly determined by the dosage and by the personality of the user. The average person generally experiences a sense of relaxed well-being or exhilaration and an increased sensitivity to sounds and sights. Time, distance, vision, hearing, hand-leg reactions, and body balance may be slowed or distorted. The user may become drowsy or have an illusion of increased physical and mental capacities.

Marijuana increases the heart rate moderately, but does not seem to affect the respiratory rate, blood sugar, or pupil size. It tends to cause bloodshot, itchy eyes; a dry mouth; and increased appetite. When severely abused, marijuana produces lethargy and passivity and may cause high blood pressure and even lung cancer (National Academy of Sciences, 1982).

Recently, marijuana has been found useful for certain people afflicted with medical problems. For example, marijuana sometimes helps to combat the nausea and loss of appetite that cancer patients experience after chemotherapy or radiation treatments. Marijuana also seems to help patients suffering from glaucoma, a painful eye disease that can cause blindness.

LSD and Other Hallucinogens   Marijuana is only a mild hallucinogen; others have far greater potency. Most were originally of the plant variety and are capable of changing perceptions of the world and oneself. Also known as psychedelic drugs, this group includes mescaline, psilocybin, and LSD, the most widely known of all.

Discovered by the Swiss biochemist Albert Hoffman, **LSD** is an alkaloid synthesized from lysergic acid, which in turn is a component of some natural alkaloids or ergot (a parasitic fungus that grows as a rust on grain, particularly wheat and rye). Compounds containing lysergic acid can also be found in certain species of morning glory, produced apparently by the plant rather than by the parasitic fungus. Odorless, tasteless, and colorless, LSD operates rapidly and produces marked changes in behavior. Research has shown that an amount smaller than a grain of salt can produce hallucinations.

Affecting cells, tissues, and organs, in addition to exerting an influence over the transmission of neural impulses in the lower brain centers, LSD produces profound physiological and psychological reactions. Its effects, like those of other drugs, depend on its potency, the user's personality structure, and the social and psychological context in which it is taken.

During the mid-1960s, LSD reached its peak of popularity. Its use among adolescents and young adults has steadily declined, largely because of increased awareness and apprehension about "bad trips," "flashbacks," and brain damage or chromosomal defects.

Stimulants: Amphetamines

Amphetamines, including cocaine, benzedrine, dexedrine, and methedrine, are placed in the category of stimulants because they act on the central nervous system. Amphetamines produce many reactions, including constriction of peripheral blood vessels; increase in blood pressure and heart rate; relaxation of the smooth muscles of the stomach, intestines, and bladder; and suppression of appetite. Because of their appetite suppressive effect, amphetamines have been widely used in weight reduction programs. Amphetamines produce feelings of energy and alertness and relieve depression.

Although amphetamines do not create physiological dependence, tolerance develops rapidly. When this happens, mouthfuls of pills are required to produce the stimulating effect. Those with greater tolerance levels may stop taking pills and inject methedrine—considered to be the strongest of the amphetamines—directly into the veins (Davison and Neale, 1982).

Such overdoses cause increased blood pressure, enlarged pupils, unclear and rapid speech, and confusion. For some, the racing world created may be "out of control" and lead to temporary psychosis characterized by panic, delusions, and hallucinations. When the drug wears off, individuals frequently "crash" by sleeping for long periods. Afterward, they are highly irritable, belligerent, and impulsive (Coleman, Butcher, and Carson, 1984).

Cocaine has increased in popularity in recent years. An estimated 25 percent of all adolescents have experimented with it. Cocaine produces effects similar to those of other amphetamines and in mild doses creates a sense of euphoria and heightened levels of energy and alertness. Heavier doses and prolonged use, though, can produce hostility, withdrawal, paranoid feelings, and even collapse and death (Van Dyke and Byck, 1982; National Institute on Drug Abuse, 1982).

Depressants: Barbiturates

Barbiturates, referred to as "downers," were designed primarily to induce sleep and provide relaxation. Barbiturates exist in a variety of forms, including Nembutal and Seconal (Valium and Librium, although not barbiturates, have similar effects). Barbiturates can produce physiological dependence and are frequently used as a means of suicide. Tolerance to the effects of barbiturates as well as withdrawal symptoms have been reported among heavy users of this drug.

Barbiturates are nonspecific in their effects and are capable of depressing a wide range of functions, including the central nervous system and the skeletal, smooth, and cardiac muscles. Depending on the dosage, the effects of barbiturates on the central nervous system range from states of mild sedation to coma. When prescribed at normal clinical dosage levels, they depress the respiratory system and cause slight blood pressure and heart rate decreases. Usually prescribed as sleep medication, the continued use of barbiturates paradoxically increases sleep disturbances (Julien, 1981).

With high dosages, the aforementioned reactions are accentuated and activities of the smooth muscles of the bladder and uterus are depressed. In addition, high dosages also cause stimulation of a hormone in the kidney, which in turn decreases the flow of urine. The enzyme system of the liver is also affected, and morphological changes will take place in the liver if high dosages continue.

It is not uncommon for heavy drug users to take barbiturates as supplements to other drugs. Barbiturates are addictive and are especially dangerous when taken in conjunction with alcohol. Barbiturates are also frequently used to moderate the stimulating actions of amphetamines or to accentuate the actions of heroin. Habitual use promotes drowsiness, mental confusion, and the loss of muscular coordination. In addition, the withdrawal symptoms of barbiturates may be particularly severe, often including delusions, hallucinations, and even coma.

The Addicting Narcotics: Opium and Its Derivatives

In its raw state, opium is a milky substance obtained from the flower pods of a particular species of poppy. The pain-killing and sleep-inducing effects of opium have been known for over 4,000 years. It is extensively cultivated in China, India, Turkey, and Iran.

Morphine, named after Morpheus, the Greek god of sleep and dreams, is the best known derivative of opium. Discovered in 1805, morphine was introduced primarily as a pain killer, but, like opium, is highly addictive. Morphine may be taken orally or by injection.

Heroin, another derivative, is almost five times as powerful as morphine and is the drug choice of virtually all narcotics addicts because of its potency and ability to produce euphoric effects. Of all these drugs, heroin is the most physically addictive and accounts for more deaths than any drug except alcohol (Cross and Kleinhesselink, 1980).

Heroin initially produces a feeling of relief and euphoria that lasts for a few minutes. The next several hours are characterized by a "high," during which the individual is usually in a state of well-being but is lethargic and withdrawn. Following the euphoric and lethargic stages is a negative phase, which produces a strong desire for more of the drug. When deprived of the drug, heavy users begin to experience withdrawal symptoms, which increase in severity if the drug is withheld. Restlessness, excessive sweating, nausea, severe abdominal cramps, vomiting, and delirium are a few of the symptoms exhibited by addicts during withdrawal (Sideroff and Jarvik, 1980).

Adolescent Suicide

At an age when they should have everything to live for, about 5,000 teenagers and young adults, or about 13 a day, commit suicide each year. Besides accidents, the leading cause of death among young people is suicide. Perhaps the most shocking statistic, though, is that since 1960, the suicide rate among adolescents has increased 300 percent (Colt, 1983). Figure 21.5 illustrates suicide mortality rates by sex, race, and age.

Victims range from the happy-go-lucky types, who give no clear clues before acting, to classic loners, who are screaming silently for help. Adolescent suicide attempts are unplanned and impulsive for the most part since many want to get help rather than die (Grueling and DeBlassie, 1980; Giffin and Felsenthal, 1983).

The number of teenage suicides may be greater than statistics indicate because many attempts fail and many medical examiners routinely list questionable deaths—especially for teenagers—as accidents. Hanging, shooting, and taking poison are common suicide methods (Weiner, 1980).

Suicide victims come from many different backgrounds, but statistics reveal a significant increase among minority youths. Males outnumber females in the number of suicide deaths reported each year, but females outnumber males in suicide attempts, and there has been an increase in completed suicides among females in recent years (Neuringer and Lettieri, 1982; Weiner, 1980).

What might motivate teenagers to take their own lives? One persistent theme is depression; many have a pervasive feeling of worthlessness, apprehension, and hopelessness. Other probable causes are the loss of love objects and the stress that sometimes occurs in family life. Many suicide victims are rejected youths who receive little affection or attention. Most feel socially isolated from the rest of the world (Colt, 1983; Grueling and DeBlassie, 1980; Konopka, 1983).

The magnitude of the problem has prompted many different segments of society to investigate preventive measures. Detection and identification of conflict and stress are vital and require the collaboration of parents, teachers, counselors, and other concerned adults. Improving the quality of human relations and enhancing educational and employment atmospheres are important too. The establishment of community resources, such as halfway houses, shelters, hotlines, and adolescent

Figure 21.5 Suicide mortality rates by sex, race, and age (adapted from U.S. Bureau of the Census, *Statistical Abstract of the United States, 1980.* Washington, D.C.: Government Printing Office, 1980, p. 188).

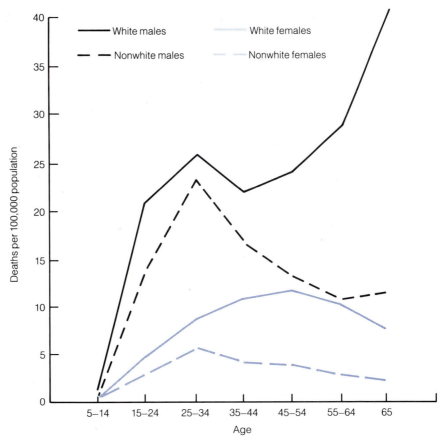

Table 21.1 Drugs and Their Effects

Drugs	Often Prescribed Brand Names	Medical Uses	Dependence Potential: Physical	Psychological
Opium	Dover's Powder, Paregoric	Analgesic, antidiarrheal	High	High
Morphine	Morphine	Analgesic	High	High
Codeine	Codeine	Analgesic, cough suppressive	Moderate	Moderate
Heroin	None	None	High	High
Meperidine (Pethidine)	Demerol, Pethadol	Analgesic	High	High
Methadone	Dolophine, Methadone, Methadose	Analgesic, heroin substitute	High	High
Other Narcotics	Dilaudid, Levitine, Numorphan, Percodan	Analgesic, antidiarrheal cough supressant	High	High
Barbiturates	Amytal, Butisol, Nembutal, Phenobarbital, Seconal, Tuinal	Anesthetic, anticonvulsant, sedation, sleep	High	High
Methaqualone	Optimil, Parest, Quaalude, Somnafac, Sopor	Sedation, sleep	High	High
Tranquilizers	Equanil, Librium, Miltown, Serax, Tranxene, Valium	Anti-anxiety, muscle relaxant, sedation	Moderate	Moderate
Cocaine	Cocaine	Local anesthetic	Possible	High
Amphetamines	Benzedrine, Biphetamine, Desoxyn, Dexedrine	Hyperkinesis, narcolepsy, weight control	Possible	High
Phenmetrazine	Preludin	Weight control	Possible	High
LSD	None	None	None	Degree unknown
Mescaline	None	None	None	Degree unknown
Psilocybin-Psilocyn	None	None	None	Degree unknown
PCP	Sernylan	Veterinary anesthetic	None	Degree unknown
Marijuana Hashish Hashish Oil	None	None	Degree unknown	Moderate

Tolerance	Duration of Effects (in hrs)	Usual Methods of Administration	Possible Effects	Effects of Overdose	Withdrawal Syndrome
Yes	3 to 6	Oral, smoked	Euphoria, drowsiness, respiratory depression, constricted pupils, nausea	Slow and shallow breathing, clammy skin, convulsions, coma, possible death	Watery eyes, runny nose, yawning, loss of appetite, irritability, tremors, panic, chills and sweating, cramps, nausea
Yes	3 to 6	Injected, smoked			
Yes	3 to 6	Oral, injected			
Yes	3 to 6	Injected, sniffed			
Yes	3 to 6	Oral, injected			
Yes	12 to 24	Oral, injected			
Yes	3 to 6	Oral, injected			
Yes	1 to 16	Oral, injected	Slurred speech, disorientation, drunken behavior without odor of alcohol	Shallow respiration, cold and clammy skin, dilated pupils, weak and rapid pulse, coma, possible death	Anxiety, insomnia, tremors, delirium convulsions, possible death
Yes	4 to 8	Oral			
Yes	4 to 8	Oral			
Yes	2	Injected, sniffed	Increased alertness, excitation, euphoria, dilated pupils, increased pulse rate and blood pressure, insomnia, loss of appetite	Agitation, increase in body temperature, hallucinations, convulsions, possible death	Apathy, long periods of sleep, irritability, depression, disorientation
Yes	2 to 4	Oral, injected			
Yes	2 to 4	Oral			
Yes	Variable	Oral	Illusions and hallucinations (with exception of MDA); poor perception of time and distance	Longer, more intense "trip" episodes, psychosis, possible death	Withdrawal syndrome not reported
Yes	Variable	Oral, injected			
Yes	Variable	Oral			
Yes	Variable	Oral, injected, smoked			
Yes	2 to 4	Oral, smoked	Euphoria, relaxed inhibitions, increased appetite, disoriented behavior	Fatigue, paranoia, possible psychosis	Insomnia, hyperactivity, and decreased appetite reported in a limited number of individuals

From Schlaadt, R. G., and Shannon, P. T. *Drugs of Choice.* Englewood Cliffs, N.J.: Prentice-Hall, 1982, pp. 260–262.

clinics, are important steps in prevention, crisis intervention, and follow-up care that helps the victim cope with reality (Davis, 1983).

Anorexia Nervosa

**Anorectics place
an unrealistic
importance on
being thin.**

Anorexia nervosa is a type of self-imposed starvation that affects growing numbers each year. It is often considered a teenager's disorder
because it affects adolescents, usually females, more than any other
age group.

Anorexia nervosa is different from **bulimia,** another type of eating
disorder. Whereas **anorectics** refuse to eat, bulimia is characterized by
gorging with excessive amounts of food and then inducing vomiting
and/or using large doses of laxatives. Bulimia (from a Greek word meaning "ox hunger") is often called the binge-purge disease (Hawkins, Fremouw, and Clement, 1983).

For most anorectics the problem begins innocently enough: the
individual wants to lose weight and look trim and fit. However, the
desire to lose weight becomes an obsession and the body image becomes distorted. As this drastic type of dieting goes on, many sufferers
fail to eat at all, some resort to daily laxatives, and virutally all deny their
eventual emaciated appearance. Anorexia nervosa is a condition severe
enough to cause serious malnutrition, complications of metabolic and
endocrine functions, and the cessation of menstruation in females.
Deaths resulting from anorexia nervosa range from 5 to 20 percent of all
patients (Schleimer, 1981; Maloney and Klykylo, 1983).

In a majority of cases, anorexia nervosa afflicts members of the
upper and middle classes, perhaps because of the emphasis these
groups place on fitness and leanness. It also has a tendency to strike
individuals with above-average intelligence. Anorectics tend to be per-
fectionists who feel they must be in complete control of themselves,
even while they are starving. The typical patient has a distorted view of
reality, a sense of inadequacy, experiences sexual conflicts, and may
suffer from severe depression bordering on a suicidal level (Richardson,
1980; Hendren, 1983).

Anorexia nervosa is frequently preceded by obesity. During the
starvation period, victims frequently induce vomiting and suffer from
constipation. In addition to the cessation of menstruation, the development of secondary sex characteristics is curtailed in adolescent girls.
Males experience diminished sexual interest and, in some cases, impo-
tence. Both sexes have extremely high activity levels (Schleimer, 1981).

The treatment and cure of anorexia nervosa are usually a long and
complicated process. Behavior modification has been somewhat effec-

tive; other techniques include individual psychotherapy and the use of insulin to induce weight gain. Sometimes intravenous or tube feeding is necessary when individuals are too weak to eat. Anorectics treated in a psychiatric ward have the poorest prognosis for cure and the highest percentage of deaths (Richardson, 1980).

Treatment also includes family therapy as well as helping anorectics eat at regular intervals and establish some self-sufficiency. Psychotherapy should aim at helping patients develop more effective problem-solving strategies, higher levels of self-esteem, and greater body awareness. Thanks to the efforts of concerned researchers, as well as the Anorexia Nervosa Aid Society, understanding and treatment of this disorder has improved markedly over the past decade and seems likely to improve further in the future (Levenkron, 1982; Halmi, 1983; Anyan and Schowalter, 1983; Neuman and Halvorson, 1983).

Summary

Sarah, age 16

Four problems related to the teenage culture—juvenile delinquency, drug abuse, suicide, and anorexia nervosa—have grown at alarming rates during recent years.

Juvenile delinquency is behavior on the part of adolescents that society deems unacceptable. While delinquency is more prevalent in low socioeconomic neighborhoods, middle- and upper-class suburbs are far from free of the problem. A number of factors contribute to juvenile delinquency, including broken homes and a general lack of affection and warmth from parents. Many delinquents are physically beaten as children; many have feelings of rejection and harbor poor self-concepts; many are also impulsive, defiant, and ambivalent toward authority.

In many respects, our society has become drug dependent. Psychological dependence occurs when the effect of a drug becomes such an important part of a person's life that he or she cannot function without it. Physical dependence is similar to psychological dependence but includes withdrawal symptoms that occur when the drug is removed. Drug tolerance is said to develop when, after continued use, greater amounts of a drug are needed to obtain the original effect. All drugs can be classified by the nature of their effects on the central nervous system.

Many adolescents consume large quantities of alcohol. Alcohol may initially reduce inhibitions and tensions for some users. Consequently, many teenagers view alcohol as a way to enhance their overall sociability. Peer pressure and curiosity also prompt many teenagers to consume alcohol. Physiologically, large quantities of alcohol interfere with higher-level thought processes and impair motor coordination, speech, and vision. Heavy drinkers tend to be impulsive and unstable in their behavior. Overall, 8 to 10 percent of American males and 2 to 4 percent of American females can be described as alcoholic at some point in their lives.

Many of the reasons that adolescents give for using hallucinogenic drugs are the same as those for consuming alcohol. Next to alcohol, marijuana, a mild hallucinogen, is the most frequently used nonmedical drug. Among the general population, nearly 16 million Americans are regular users of marijuana. Recent research, however, suggests that marijuana use among adolescents may have peaked in popularity. Teenagers today appear to be more aware of marijuana's potentially harmful effects.

Amphetamines, or stimulants, include benzedrine, dexedrine, and cocaine. The latter is especially popular today. Barbiturates, also called depressants, include Nembutal and Seconal (Valium and Librium have similar effects). Of the addicting narcotics, opium, morphine, and heroin are the most widely known. With the exception of alcohol, heroin causes the most drug-related deaths.

Teenage suicide is reaching epidemic proportions in contemporary society. After accidents, suicide is the leading cause of death among young people. Precipitating causes are diverse, but commonly reported factors are feelings of depression and worthlessness, the loss of a love object, and alienation. Measures to help curb this problem include crisis intervention programs, improved environmental conditions for the adolescent, and greater community resources such as halfway houses and hotlines.

Anorexia nervosa is a type of self-imposed starvation that afflicts teenagers more than any other age group. Anorexia nervosa is different from bulimia, which is characterized by excessive eating followed by self-induced vomiting and/or heavy use of laxatives. Anorexia nervosa is most common among females and begins as an effort to lose weight, but leads to malnutrition, physiological complications, and emaciation. Treatment for anorectics sometimes includes intravenous or tube feeding, psychotherapy, behavior modification programs, and the use of insulin to induce weight gain.

Suggested Reading List

Haskell, M. R., and Yablonsky, L. *Juvenile Delinquency*. 3rd ed. Boston: Houghton Mifflin, 1982. A thorough and detailed account of virtually all aspects of juvenile delinquency.

Newman, G., ed. *Crime and Deviance.* Beverly Hills, Calif.: Sage, 1980. Chapter Five deals with a wide range of issues related to youth crimes and delinquency.

Scarpitti, F. R., and Datesman, S. K., eds. *Drugs and the Youth Culture.* Beverly Hills, Calif.: Sage, 1980. An excellent examination of contemporary adolescent drug use. The 14 contributors to this text describe patterns of drug consumption, current trends, and prevention and treatment programs.

Chapter Twenty-Two

Imagination, Creativity, and Play

The art of a person is a mirror of the mind.

Jawaharlal Nehru

Introduction

The imaginative and creative spirit of the adolescent is kindled by the cognitive advancements of Piaget's formal operations stage. Thinking at this time is logical and rational, and problems are approached in a systematic fashion. As a result of these advancements, teenagers are able to employ imagination in new and different ways.

For example, teenagers are able to think about the future and reflect on the past through the powers of imagination. They can envision themselves in future roles or relive happy moments. Illustrative of the fantasy prevalent at this time is the "imaginary audience" concept discussed earlier. Adolescents' power of imagination enables them to engage in creative writing, as well as to experience vicariously the exploits of literary characters. Also, for many, creative talent gives artwork new dimensions, including abstract qualities.

In general, the adolescent can approach schoolwork with an abundance of original ideas and thoughts. It is not uncommon, though, for adolescents to forgo their creative thoughts in favor of the accepted fact or standard answer. This continues and in many respects intensifies an earlier trend.

High schools, colleges, and society as a whole place a tremendous premium on being "right." This, of course, is a legitimate demand in situations or disciplines requiring a single, precise answer. But in settings offering some degree of choice or possibility, the individual should be encouraged to be innovative and original.

The heightened sensitivities of teenagers often prompt them to supply the desired or conventional response. Many fear rejection or failure (see Wolf and Larson, 1981) and do not want to be labeled different or "strange," because of an original thought. They firmly believe that to be different implies that one is deficient in some respect. The desire to conform with others during adolescence is another driving force often curtailing the creative expression of the teenager. Also, the high premium placed on finishing first or at the top of one's class compels many adolescents to supply only the expected answers.

What is needed are more high school and college classrooms willing to develop the divergent thought processes of students. Teachers need to value creative thought and encourage teenagers to mentally manipulate objects and ideas. They also need to respect unusual ideas and, if possible, provide opportunities for creative thought that are not necessarily evaluated [Torrance, 1965(b), 1966].

Stages of the Creative Process

The attainment of formal operations enables thinking processes to emerge in a unified flow. The creative thinking process is no exception. Regardless of the field in which a person does creative thinking, there appear to be five steps or stages through which most creative thinkers proceed. The first stage, preparation, occurs when the individual first formulates the problem to be solved. Suppose a person was asked to write a story that takes place on or in the ocean. The individual would probably prepare by doing some brainstorming. Maybe the person would make a list of concepts by using divergent thinking and ideational fluency. An amazing array of different ideas might be found, including: whaling; pirates of yesteryear; modern pirates; marijuana smuggling; the historical smuggling of rum; a shark attack; a beach party in Florida; a scuba diving adventure; the life of a fisherman; and underwater science fiction. Once the person has decided on the type of story, library research might help to develop ideas and produce the correct vocabulary.

By this time, days, weeks, or months may have passed with no plot discovered. Many ideas may have been generated for background setting or characters, but the problem isn't solved. At this point, it is put to rest for awhile. This is the second stage: incubation. During incubation, thoughts that had been interfering with the development of a story line fade, and unconscious mental processes begin to work, leading to the third stage: illumination, or the "aha!" experience. At this time an idea has been developed for the solution. During the fourth stage—evaluation—new ide~~ are tested to see if they "work." If an idea is unsatisfactory, as many "aha!" ideas are, one usually backs up to the first or second stage and waits for further illumination. If the new idea is satisfactory, one enters the fifth stage: revision. Meanwhile, there may be other problems to solve besides the main plot, perhaps a subplot or the nature of one or more of the characters. Thus, a person may be at the revision stage on one part of the story, at the incubation stage on another aspect, and even back at the library doing more preparation on yet another part of the story (Wallas, 1926).

Daydreams and Fantasies

Adolescence offers a rich terrain for daydreaming and fantasizing. Indeed, most of us can conjure up the popular image of the teenager staring idly off into space actively engaged in the contemplation of future heroics or romances. The adolescent moodiness that so bedevils parents may also reflect the teenager's private world of daydreaming.

Both high school and college teachers need to value creativity and encourage teenagers to think individually.

The Benefits of Daydreams and Fantasies

Daydreams and fantasies are extensions of the childhood capacity for play. Provided that individuals do not get so immersed in a fantasy world that they miss important clues from the outer one, daydreams offer numerous benefits.

Daydreams Can Often Help One to Plan a More Effective Future
People can mentally rehearse actions that they wish to take in the future and review past action. By so doing, they can often decide what has been or will be constructive and effective or destructive and self-defeating.

Fantasies Can Help One to Become More Sensitive to the Moods and Needs of Others
We are told that we cannot understand other people unless we "walk a mile in their shoes." This kind of empathy dictates an active imagination. Fantasies enable people to put themselves in another's position, in the process gleaning an understanding of that person's emotions and sensitivities.

Daydreams and Fantasies Can Help One Learn More about Himself or Herself
Imagination often helps people uncover hidden facets of themselves. As individuals get to know themselves better, it is conceivable that they'll adopt more appropriate methods of living.

Variations of Daydreaming and Fantasies Can Help One Reduce Stress
People with high blood pressure, ulcers, or migraines have been urged by physicians to use meditation techniques for relaxation.

Among the most effective of these techniques is an organized system of daydreaming or fantasy.

Fantasy Can Enhance One's Creativity in Daily Living, Not to Mention Artistic and Scientific Expression
Fantasy is an indispensable ingredient in virtually any kind of artistic or scientific endeavor. New and unsuspected vistas are often uncovered when an idea is stretched to its outer limits.

Fantasy Can Help One Gain Control of Undesirable Habits
A variety of psychological techniques encourage people to combine relaxation with controlled fantasy to abandon unwanted habits and impulses. Such techniques have been successfully used with a variety of problem areas, including excessive smoking, overeating, and nailbiting.

Daydreams and Fantasies Can Heighten One's Enjoyment of Art, Literature, Music, and the Like
Virtually all forms of artistic expression require people to add their own imagination to that of the artist.

Fantasizing Can Help One Avoid Boredom
Fantasies and daydreams can be put to work to overcome boredom during idle moments. Moreover, such imaginative powers help people amuse themselves and overcome impatience. ■

(Adapted from Singer and Switzer, 1980.)

An adult directive to do a chore or get at homework may produce moodiness because it has interrupted private sequences of pleasurable or anticipatory fantasies (Singer, 1975).

The daydreams and fantasies of teenagers differ from those of children. School-aged children tend to have fantasies involving some degree of action or adventure. By the teenage years, fantasies shift to themes involving achievement, romance, and sex (Gottlieb, 1973).

As mentioned earlier, daydreams and fantasies are important mental activities. Many experts contend that an individual's life can be vastly enriched by daydreaming for a few minutes every day. Sitting quietly for a short time and letting memories, wishes, and impressions mentally surface often enables one to relax. When a few moments have elapsed, one is often able to attack immediate problems with new vigor (Singer and Switzer, 1980).

Forms of Play

By the time the individual reaches adolescence, recreational interests change, owing primarily to a shift in values and a shortage of time. For the most part, recreational activities become less strenuous and physical, except for people who pursue sports and other active interests throughout adolescence. There is also a marked increase in the intermingling of the sexes, which has been lacking throughout most of childhood. For many, the heterosexual friendships and recreational activities of adolescence are a valued counterpart to same-sex recreational pursuits (Wright and Keple, 1981).

Parents are much less involved in structuring, directing, or taking part in the recreational pursuits of their children, who are increasingly independent and involved with peer group interests. The peer group plays a significant role in determining the type and duration of activities to be undertaken. However, not all adolescents sever family ties and rely exclusively on the peer group for recreational purposes. Many adolescents, typically those from close-knit and nurturant homes, enjoy family-oriented recreational activities. Popular forms of family recreation include backyard sports, camping, boating, and indoor games.

Because of growing levels of physical, cognitive, and social maturity, adolescents typically enjoy a wide range of recreational activities. These activities also tend to be introspective, egoistic, and considerably more serious. Among adolescent activities are competitive and noncompetitive games and sports, dancing, and musical pursuits.

Adolescent recreation often involves the peer group and is unstructured.

In addition to structured activities, many adolescents opt for unstructured, or leisure, pursuits. Leisure implies the freedom to choose nonactivity outside the constraints of school, work, family, or other social obligations. This means that the person can choose whatever is desired without being monitored by external forces. Thus, leisure is associated with intrinsically motivated and unrestrained activity. Leisure activities at this time include reading, pursuing hobbies, and watching television. Television viewing hours often peak during the adolescent years and then decline (Murray, 1980).

The Computer Game Revolution

Computer games have attracted unparalleled interest among adolescents. Both home and arcade games offer a new twist to the field of electronic technology and add a new dimension to the realm of recreational activities. Sales of computer games has been nothing short of

phenomenal, increasing nearly 500 percent in the last 15 years (Nilles, 1982; Logsdon, 1982).

When first introduced, computer games brought an onslaught of negative reactions. Many felt that these games would produce glassy-eyed zombies. Some likened the games to television and proclaimed that these customized electronic gadgets would keep children and adolescents from other more meaningful activities. Others feared that computer games would promote lethargy, passivity, and dullness (McWilliams, 1982; Nilles, 1982).

Investigations into the nature and effects of computer games have tempered much of this initial anxiety. Some findings are critical of certain aspects of the games, such as the overabundance of violent themes or the risk of overindulgence or video addiction. Most of the findings, though, have been quite favorable. Computer games have been shown to enhance attention, inductive reasoning, decision-making and problem-solving skills, and resource management (I. Miller, 1981; Spivak and Varden, 1981).

In reaction to the criticism that computer games resemble television and therefore promote passivity and lethargy, proponents argue that the two electronic devices produce very different reactions. While television promotes passive viewing, computer games demand active player participation and interaction (Nilles, 1982).

Realizing the enormous popularity of this type of recreational pursuit, many schools are now using computer games as stepping stones to advanced computer use in the classroom. The use of such games, modified for educational purposes, is being advocated by increasing numbers of educators and students. The results thus far have been gratifying. Students of the computer age are finding that the educational computer game is another electronic tool that will help them learn without drudgery (Billings, 1981; Levin, 1981).

Leisure time is frequently spent listening to popular music.

Summary

Kelly, age 17

The cognitive advancements inherent in Piaget's formal operations stage fuel the imaginative and creative development of the adolescent. However, it is not uncommon for teenagers to forgo creativity in favor of the accepted fact or standard answer. Many sacrifice creative thinking because they fear that their ideas will be rejected or ridiculed. Adolescence marks the emergence of a true sequence behind creativity: preparation of an idea, incubation, illumination, evaluation, and revision.

Computer and video games have become popular in recent years; research shows that they can help teenagers increase their problem-solving abilities.

Daydreams and fantasies are popular mental activities during the teenage years.

During the adolescent years, individuals generally pursue activities of a less physical and strenuous nature, although some continue with competitive sports programs. In general, adolescent play reflects increasing cognitive, physical, and social maturity. Furthermore, it bears a more serious and introspective quality. Some adolescents opt for leisure activities, recreational pursuits characterized chiefly by their freedom from constraint. Computer games are also very popular. Contemporary research indicates that the benefits of computer games outweigh their drawbacks. Among other findings, these games have been found to increase such cognitive capacities as attention, problem solving, and inductive reasoning skills. Many school systems are using modified versions of computer games as stepping stones to advanced computer use.

Suggested Reading List

Hendry, L. B. *Growing Up and Going Out: Adolescents and Leisure.* Aberdeen: Aberdeen University Press, 1983. The adolescent's use of leisure and play is discussed in terms of age, gender, social class, and educational attainment.

Pepler, B. J., and Rubin, K. H., eds. *The Play of Children.* New York: Karger, 1982. This reader examines a number of issues, including parallels between language and symbolic play and the relationship between play and creativity.

Singer, J. L., and Switzer, E. *Mind Play: The Creative Use of Fantasy.* Englewood Cliffs, N.J.: Prentice-Hall, 1980. Among many diverse topics is a thorough explanation of adolescent imagination.

Glossary

abstinence standard   A moral standard asserting that it is wrong for both unmarried males and females to engage in sexual intercourse.

abstraction   A subjective concept or idea apart from one's objective analysis of the tangible environment.

accommodation   According to Piaget, the restructuring of mental organizations so that new information or previously rejected information may be processed.

adenine   One of the four nucleotide bases of the DNA molecule; it bonds with the base thymine.

adolescence   The life stage that begins with puberty and encompasses approximately the entire teenage years.

adolescent egocentrism   Being able to conceptualize one's own thought in addition to being preoccupied with the thoughts of those in one's surroundings. Two types of adolescent egocentrism are the imaginary audience and the personal fable.

adrenal gland   A gland of the endocrine system located near the kidneys.

affiliation need   The desire to be with other people.

alcoholism   A disorder characterized by physiological dependence on alcohol.

allele   Any of several alternative genes at a given chromosomal locus.

amniocentesis   The removal of fluid from the amniotic sac so that chromosomes of the fetus may be analyzed.

amniotic fluid   A liquid that holds the embryo or fetus in suspension and protects it against jarring and from any pressure exerted by the mother's internal organs.

amniotic sac   A transparent membrane completely enveloping the embryo or fetus, except where the umbilical cord passes through to the placenta.

amphetamine   A drug that serves as a stimulant and acts on the central nervous system. Examples of amphetamines are cocaine, benzedrine, dexedrine, and methedrine.

anal stage   The second stage of psychosexual development theorized by Freud. During this period, children's erotic feelings center on the anus and on elimination.

analytic style   A type of cognitive style in which objects are categorized according to their similar components or properties.

anatomy   The branch of biology that studies the structure, position, location, and shape of some biological object.

androgen   The sex hormone that regulates the male secondary sex characteristics. Androgen is also found in lesser amounts in females.

androgyny   Having both masculine and feminine personality traits.

animism   According to Piaget, the tendency of children to give life to inanimate objects. Animism is most prevalent between the ages of 2 and 7.

anorectic   A person suffering from anorexia nervosa.

anorexia nervosa   A severe diminishment of appetite, particularly among teenagers. This disorder is more common in females than in males and is believed to have psychogenic origins.

anxiety   A state of inner apprehension most frequently characterized as a generalized fear of a subjective danger.

anxiously attached   A type of attachment described by Mary Ainsworth. Anxiously attached infants, among other characteristics, do not explore the environment when placed in unfamiliar situations with their mothers. They are usually distressed when the mother is temporarily away and ambivalent when she returns.

Apgar test   An evaluation of the newborn's basic life processes, administered approximately one minute after birth and again five minutes later. The life signs tested are heart rate, respiratory regularity, muscle tone, reflex irritability, and coloration.

approach-avoidance conflict   A situation in which the individual is confronted by a situation having both positive and negative aspects.

arcuate fasciculus   An area of the brain that plays a significant role in producing meaningful speech.

articulate   Produce words and sounds vocally.

artificialism   The childhood notion that everything in the world, including natural objects and events, is designed by human beings.

assimilation   Perceiving and interpreting new information in terms of existing knowledge and understanding.

associational fluency   A dimension of divergent thinking. Associational fluency is the number of words one can name that can go with other words in terms of meaning.

associativity   The fact that the order of combination doesn't matter when multiple structures are combined.

attachment   An affectionate bond between infant and caregiver.

attention   The act or process of focusing on a stimulus or stimuli.

authoritarian control   An attempt to control behavior by enforcing a set standard of conduct. Emphasis is placed on obedience and punitive discipline.

authoritative control   An attempt to control behavior by establishing democratic, meaningful, and realistic expectations.

autonomy versus shame and doubt   The second of eight psychosocial crises proposed by Erik Erikson.

autosome   Any chromosome other than a sex chromosome.

aversive conditioning   A form of learning that is brought about through the use of negative reinforcement or some type of punishment.

avoidance attached   A type of attachment described by Mary Ainsworth. Infants having this type of attachment are relatively unattached to their mothers and exhibit little anxiety or distress when left alone.

axon   The long and slender portion of a neuron that extends outward from the cell body. The axon carries the electrochemical impulse from the dendrite to the end plates.

babbling   A stage of early language development, beginning approximately by the sixth month. Babbling first emerges a syllable at a time and will include both vowels and consonants.

Babinski reflex   A major reflex present in the newborn. When the sole of the foot is stimulated, the toes fan outward.

baby biography   A day-by-day account of the development of an infant or child.

barbiturate   A depressant drug that induces sleep and provides relaxation. Examples are Nembutal and Seconal.

base   A nonacid that has an excess of OH ions and a pH greater than 7.

basic trust versus basic mistrust   The first of eight psychosocial crises proposed by Erik Erikson.

behavioral genetics   The study of inherited behavior.

behavioral predisposition   A term implying that one has a tendency toward certain behavioral characteristics, given certain environmental conditions.

behaviorism   A school of thought emphasizing that an organism's behavior is a product of conditioning and learning experiences. Emphasis is on the organism's observable behaviors.

behavior modification   The control of behavior by employing the principles of conditioning.

birthing room   For the parents of newborns, a room offering a homelike and relaxed atmosphere within the hospital's general delivery unit.

birth order   *See* Ordinal position.

Black English   A social dialect used mostly by black people at lower socioeconomic levels.

blastocyte   A hollow sphere of cells that form after conception and attach themselves to the uterine wall.

blended family   A family in which one or both spouses have children from a previous marriage; also called a reconstituted family.

blending action   A type of biochemical activity in which no one gene dominates the other; rather, the two proteins manufactured by the ribosome mix together.

breech delivery   Delivery of the baby buttocks or feet first.

Broca's area   A portion of the brain, located adjacent to the motor cortex, which controls the muscles involved in speech. Damage to this area produces motor aphasia and causes speech to be slow and labored.

bulimia   An eating disorder characterized by gorging oneself with excessive amounts of food and then inducing vomiting and/or using large amounts of laxatives.

catharsis   The release or discharge of pent-up emotional feelings.

cell   A living unit of organized material that contains a nucleus and is enclosed in a membrane.

centering   The tendency to concentrate on the outstanding characteristics of an object while excluding its other features.

central nervous system   Part of the nervous system that consists of the brain and the spinal cord.

cephalocaudal development   Physical growth that takes place from the head downward.

cerebellum   A part of the hindbrain controlling body balance and coordination.

cerebral cortex   The surface layer of the cerebrum.

cerebrum   The largest portion of the forebrain. The cerebrum consists of a left and a right hemisphere, connected by the corpus callosum.

cervix   The lowest part of the uterus.

cesarean delivery   The delivery of the baby through a surgical incision made in the mother's abdominal and uterine walls.

chromosomal abnormalities   Occurrences that affect the number of genes and/or chromosomes for a given species.

chromosomes   Thin rodlike structures in a cell that contain the essential mechanisms for directions of the cell's activity.

circulatory system   The cardiovascular system consisting of the heart, blood vessels, and the lymphatic system.

classical conditioning   A fundamental type of learning theory originated by Pavlov, also referred to as respondent conditioning. In this form of conditioning, a subject responds to a previously neutral stimulus after it has been effectively paired with the unconditioned stimulus that originally produced the response.

clique   A small peer group characterized by social exclusiveness and a strong emotional bond among its members.

closure   The fact that any two mental structures can combine to form a third structure.

cognition   The intellectual activity of the individual. The mental process involving all aspects of thought and perception.

cognitive dissonance   An inconsistency or conflict in one's thoughts, beliefs, attitudes, or behavior, resulting in a tension state that the individual is motivated to reduce.

cognitive style   The manner in which an individual organizes information and discovers solutions to problems.

collective monologue   A type of egocentric communication characterized by inability to listen effectively to what others are saying.

compensation   Finding a successful or rewarding activity that can be substituted for failure in another kind of activity.

compulsion   An irrational desire to engage in ritualistic acts.

computer literacy   The knowledge and skills needed to function in a computer-oriented society.

concept   A mental image formed to represent an object or event.

conception   The union of the male sperm with the female ovum, creating a zygote.

conceptual tempo   The manner in which one evaluates and acts on a problem.

conclusions   In research studies, what an experimenter interprets the data to mean.

concrete operations   The fourth stage of Piaget's theory of cognitive development, occurring approximately between ages 7 and 11. The stage marks a time when cognition is used consistently and the child can reason logically in new and challenging situations.

conformity   Change in an individual's behavior in response to the actions or pressures of others.

conservation   The recognition that the amount or quantity of matter remains the same despite changes made in its outward physical appearance.

consonant   A speech sound characterized by constriction or closure at one or more points in the breath channel.

constitution   A term referring to the physical and mental makeup of an individual.

contact comfort motive   According to Harry Harlow, the desire among infants to seek objects offering softness and warmth. Contact and comfort from such objects are said to strengthen attachment behaviors.

contractual legalistic orientation   Kohlberg's fifth of six moral development stages. This stage is grouped under the major division or level known as postconventional morality.

control group   A group of subjects in a research study who receive the same treatment as the group being experimented upon, except that they do not receive the stimulus (independent variable) under observation.

controlled experiments   An experimental situation in which the subject is placed in a structured and perhaps unnatural environment that can be manipulated by the experimenter.

conventional morality   Identified by Lawrence Kohlberg, a stage of moral development in which children (9 to 15) learn the nature of authority, not only in the family but in society in general. Substages include the "good boy–nice girl" orientation and the "authority and social-order maintaining" orientation.

convergent thinking   The mental process concerned with gathering information relevant to a problem and then producing a single response to the problem.

coordination of secondary schemes   The fourth of six substages constituting Piaget's sensorimotor stage of cognitive development. This substage occurs between the ages of 8 and 12 months.

coping mechanisms   Patterns of behavior that relieve anxiety.

corpus callosum   A bundle of nerve fibers connecting the left and right cerebral hemispheres.

correlation   The relationship between any two events, frequently expressed as a number between +1.00 and −1.00. Different statistical procedures are used to discover degrees of relationship.

correlational method   Method of observing and comparing naturally occurring events for whatever relationships may exist.

creativity   A unique mental process that allows an individual to operate on a body of knowledge in such a way that a novel end product is developed.

critical (or sensitive) period   A point in the early life stages of an organism at which strong bonds of attachment are established with the mother or other caretaker.

crossing over   The tendency of chromosomes to exchange genes prior to cell division.

cross-sectional study   A method of investigating developmental trends based on the comparison of groups who differ in age at a given time.

crowd   A group of people larger than a clique but less personal and lacking strong bonds of attachment but having rather rigid membership requirements.

cytoplasm   Protoplasm found inside the cell but outside the nucleus.

cytosine   One of four nucleotide bases that compose the DNA molecule. It is always linked with the base guanine.

decenter   The ability to examine all aspects of a problem rather than one outstanding perceptual feature.

deciduous teeth   The milk teeth or temporary teeth. Also called baby teeth. They usually appear at six months and are lost by the end of six years.

deductive reasoning   Reasoning from a set of premises to a conclusion. Called by Piaget hypothetico-deductive reasoning.

deep structure   The conceptual framework or meaning of a particular sentence.

dendrite   The portion of the cell body of a neuron that receives electrochemical impulses from other neurons.

denial of reality   A defense mechanism characterized by the individual's refusal to perceive the existence of hurtful situations.

deoxyribonucleic acid (DNA)   The chemical substance that constitutes chromosomes and genes.

dependency   A class of responses that are capable of eliciting positive attending and ministering responses from others. During early childhood, the manner in which the child is nurtured will greatly affect the degree of dependency exhibited.

dependent variable   The change, if any, brought about by the independent variables in experimental studies. Changes appear in the experimental group, especially when contrasted with the control group.

depression   An emotional state characterized by feelings of dejection and worthlessness.

developmental psychology   A general term encompassing the psychology of childhood, adolescence, and all the remaining years of the human life span.

dialect   A regional variation of a language.

diaphyses   The primary centers of ossification located in the shaft of the bones.

diastolic   The relaxation that exists between heart beats. Diastolic is compared to systolic pressure to measure one's blood pressure.

digestive system   The system responsible for breaking down food, mechanically and chemically, so that it can be absorbed by the body.

dilation   The widening of the cervix caused by contractions during labor.

diploid state   The condition of a cell having its full quota of chromosomes.

discipline   The setting of limits in an effort to teach acceptable forms of conduct or behavior. The ultimate goal of discipline is to produce responsible behavior.

displacement   The releasing of pent-up hostile feelings onto objects less dangerous than those that initially aroused the emotion.

divergent thinking   A mental operation represented by the quantity and quality of different and novel responses that an individual can offer.

DNA   *See* deoxyribonucleic acid.

dominant gene   A gene that always expresses its hereditary characteristic.

double standard   A moral standard asserting that males can have sexual relations prior to marriage but females are expected to remain abstinent.

Down's syndrome   Referred to as Trisomy 21, a chromosomal abnormality in which there is an extra chromosome on the 21st position. Children afflicted with this disorder have, among other characteristics, the Mongol eye flap, round heads, and mental retardation.

drug tolerance   A condition that results when a person needs greater amounts of a drug in order to obtain the original effects of that drug.

dyad   A two-person group.

ectomorphy   A body build characterized by a slender appearance.

ego   In the psychoanalytic school of thought, the part of the personality that serves as a rational agent and mediator between the id and the superego.

egocentrism   A style of thinking that causes children difficulty in seeing any point of view other than their own; self-centeredness.

elaboration   The technique of expanding verbal or visual material to increase the number of ways that it can be retrieved.

Electra complex   According to Freud, the romantic feelings a girl has for her father and aggressive feelings for her mother. The Electra complex is prevalent during the phallic stage of psychosexual development.

embryonic period   A period of prenatal development beginning when the ovum becomes well implanted in the uterine wall and the cells begin to exhibit marked differentiation.

emotions   A variation or change in one's arousal level that may either interfere with or facilitate motivated behavior.

empathy   The ability to sympathize with or share the emotions of others.

enactive period   The first stage of cognitive development postulated by Jerome Bruner. During this time, the child interacts with the world through motor actions and responses.

endocrine system   A system of glands that secrete hormones into the bloodstream and have effects on other body organs.

endomorphy   A body build characterized by large accumulations of fat.

epiphyses   Centers of ossification at the ends of the bones.

estrogen   Female sex hormone that regulates the menstrual cycle and maintains secondary sex characteristics.

ethology   The study of human and animal behavior in natural settings, including the role that instincts and biologically inherited responses have on growth and development.

experimental group   A group of subjects in an experimental study who receive a special stimulus or treatment, the effect of which is under observation.

experimental method   A series of steps by which the researcher tries to determine relationships between differing phenomena either to discover principles underlying behavior or to find cause-effect relationships. The method is characterized by control and repetition.

expressional fluency   A dimension of divergent thinking. Expressional fluency refers to the ability to put words together to meet the requirements of a given sentence structure.

expressive language   The language that a person can verbally express.

extinction   Conditioned elimination of response by the withdrawal of reinforcement.

failure to thrive   A condition observed by René Spitz among children deprived of attachment. In addition to being depressed, sad, and lethargic, these children experienced insomnia, loss of appetite, and slowness of movement.

fallopian tube   Either of two tubes that extend from the ovary region to the uterus. Also called uterine tube.

fertilization   The union of the egg and the sperm.

fetus   The human organism in the womb from approximately the third prenatal month until birth.

fine motor skills   Motor skills requiring the use of small body parts, most notably the hands. Examples include writing and sewing.

fixed interval schedule   A type of partial reinforcement in operant conditioning in which the organism receives reinforcement after a fixed amount of time has elapsed.

fixed ratio schedule   A type of partial reinforcement in operant conditioning in which the organism receives reinforcement after a predetermined number of correct responses have been made.

forebrain   The frontal and upper portion of the brain. The forebrain consists of the cerebrum, cerebral cortex, corpus callosum, thalamus, and hypothalamus.

formal operations   The final stage of Piaget's theory of cognitive development, occurring between the ages of 11 and 15. The stage is characterized by systematic reasoning abilities and the successful integration of all past cognitive operations.

fraternal twins   Twins conceived when two ova are released simultaneously by the female and both are penetrated by male sperm cells. Also referred to as dizygotic twins.

frequency distribution A set of measurements arranged from lowest to highest (or highest to lowest) accompanied by a count of the number of times each measurement occurs.

friendship The pairing off of usually two individuals who are likely to be similar in temperament and personality and share common interests.

frontal lobe An area of the cortex that controls the sense of smell as well as body movement and control.

frustration An emotional reaction that usually results when attempts to reach a desired goal are blocked or thwarted.

functional-locational orientation A cognitive style in which classification of stimulus objects is based on some type of interactional value.

functional-relational style A cognitive style in which classification of stimulus objects is based on their interactional value.

gamete A reproductive cell, either the female ovum or the male sperm.

gang An aggregation of peers who band together and become involved in illegal activities.

gender identity The psychological awareness of being either a male or a female.

gender roles Those socially defined behaviors associated with being either male or female.

generalization The tendency to respond to a related group of stimuli in a similar manner. At a cognitive level, the ability to find the same generalized properties in otherwise different things.

generation gap Differences in values, attitudes, and behavior between two generational groups such as parents and adolescents.

generativity versus isolation The sixth of eight psychosocial stages proposed by Erikson.

genes Biological units contained in the chromosomes, the fundamental transmitters of hereditary characteristics.

genetics The science of heredity.

genital herpes A sexually transmitted disease.

genital stage As theorized by Freud, the stage of psychosexual development at which normal and mature sexual behavior is attained.

genius An individual who possesses abilities that have high social significance within a given culture.

genotype The actual genetic makeup (gene pair) of an organism.

germ cells The cells frequently referred to as sex cells, or gametes.

gonadotrophins Hormones that are produced by the pituitary gland and stimulate the testes and ovaries.

gonads The reproductive organs: the ovaries in the female and the testes in the male.

gonorrhea A sexually transmitted disease affecting more than one million individuals each year.

good boy–nice girl orientation Kohlberg's third of six stages of moral development. This stage is grouped under the major division or level known as conventional morality.

grammar The study of words and their function in the sentence.

grasp reflex A major reflex present in the newborn. When an object is placed on the palm, the newborn grasps it with a firm grip. The thumb is not involved, and the grasp reflex starts to diminish at 4 months.

greeting response A response usually accompanying an infant's social smile. The greeting response consists of opening the eyes wide and making cooing sounds.

gross motor skills Motor skills requiring the coordination of large body parts. Examples are running, tumbling, and climbing a ladder.

group test An intelligence test that can be administered to a group of individuals by one administrator.

growth Physical changes in the body or any of its parts because of an increase in cell number.

guanine One of the four nucleotide bases that compose the DNA molecule. It is always linked with the base cytosine.

hallucinogen A drug capable of producing illusions, delusions, or hallucinations.

handedness An individual's hand preference.

haploid state   A genetic condition in which a cell contains only half the number of chromosomes that are natural for its species.

heredity   The tendency of parents to transmit certain characteristics to their offspring.

heterosexuality   Attraction to members of the opposite sex.

heterozygous   Descriptive of a genetic condition in which both gene pairs in an organism differ for a given trait (one dominant, one recessive).

hierarchical structure   A division of group members into leaders and followers.

hierarchy of needs   According to Abraham Maslow, a series of human needs, from the most basic to the most advanced. The needs, in ascending order, are physiological, safety, belongingness and love, esteem, and self-actualization.

hindbrain   The lower portion of the brain responsible for those bodily functions necessary for survival. The hindbrain consists of the medulla, cerebellum, pons, and part of the reticular activating system.

holophrase   The one-word stage of language development that transpires between 12 and 18 months.

home births   The delivery of a baby in the parents' home rather than in a hospital. The delivery is often conducted by a licensed nurse-midwife.

homozygous   Descriptive of a genetic condition in which both genes are identical for a given trait (two dominant or two recessive).

hormone   A product of the endocrine glands secreted into the bloodstream.

hostile aggression   A type of aggression directed at another person with the intention of hurting that person.

human growth hormone   A hormone that will cause a rapid increase in body development, particularly the adolescent growth spurt; also called the somatotrophic hormone.

humanism   One of child psychology's major schools of thought. Humanists such as Abraham Maslow and Carl Rogers stress the importance of helping children to maximize their uniqueness and potential in life.

hypothalamus   Part of the forebrain that regulates hunger, thirst, sex, and body temperature. The hypothalamus is also a control center for pleasure and pain.

hypothesis   A prediction of the solution of a problem.

hypothetico-deductive reasoning   *See* deductive logic.

iconic stage   The second stage of cognitive development theorized by Jerome Bruner. Thinking is characterized by the use of mental images.

id   According to the psychoanalytic school of thought, the instinctual part of the personality, which is concerned with the immediate gratification of motives.

ideal self   The type of person one would like to be.

ideational fluency   A term referring to the flow and number of ideas that an individual can generate.

identical twins   Twins that occur as the result of the zygote splitting into two separate but genetically identical cells. Also referred to as monozygotic twins.

identification   The process in which individuals perceive themselves as being alike or similar to other people and behave accordingly. During childhood, parents become initial models for identification.

identity   In Piagetian research, an awareness that certain mental actions may leave other mental structures unchanged.

identity achievement   According to James Marcia, going through an appraisal of values and choices in life and making a commitment to some goal.

identity diffusion   According to Marcia, the failure to examine any goals or values.

identity foreclosure   Marcia's idea of having life goals established by others.

identity moratorium   Marcia's notion of rethinking values and goals, which often leads to an identity crisis.

identity versus role diffusion   The fifth of eight psychosocial crises proposed by Erik Erikson. Identity versus role diffusion occupies the teenage years.

idioglossia   A refined and complex type of twin talk. Although frequently incomprehensible to listeners, this speech style consists of highly original syntactical structures and conveys meaning to the communicators.

imaginary audience   A consequence of adolescent egocentrism. Teenagers imaginatively feel they are continually the focus of attention.

imagination   A mental process characterized by "as if" elements. These elements represent a modification of the environment that is based on some experiences carried in the person's memory and involves some degree of imagery.

immanent justice   The childhood assumption that the world has a built-in system of law and order.

imprinting   An organism's rapid attachment to an object (generally its caretaker); usually takes place shortly after birth.

impulsive   A conceptual tempo characterized by a hurried response and little, if any, consideration of the accuracy of the response.

inborn error of metabolism   A disorder due to the body's not producing a needed protein (or enzyme), producing too many of them, or producing a mutant enzyme that is toxic to the system.

independent variable   A stimulus administered to the experimental group of subjects but not to the control group.

induction   A disciplinary style that includes reasoning, explanation of behavioral consequences, and democratic decision making.

inductive reasoning   Reasoning from specific, individual experiences and proceeding to general principles.

industry versus inferiority   The fourth of eight psychosocial crises proposed by Erik Erikson. Industry versus inferiority occupies all of middle childhood.

infanticide   The killing of babies deemed mutant, deformed, or unwanted.

inferential statistics   Statistics designed to test a representative sample of the total population, results of which are then extrapolated.

inferiority complex   A feeling of inadequacy or unworthiness.

inhibition   The forgetting or blocking out of a learned response.

initiative versus guilt   The third of eight psychosocial crises proposed by Erik Erikson. Initiative versus guilt occurs between the ages of 3 and 6.

instrumental aggression   A type of aggression aimed at acquiring objects, territory, or privileges.

instrumental conditioning   Learning a response to attain positive reinforcement or to avoid punishment.

integrity versus dispair   The eighth and final stage of Erikson's psychosocial theory.

intelligence   A broad term that encompasses an individual's proficiency in a wide variety of intellectual areas, including problem solving, number abilities, vocabulary, and so on.

intelligence quotient (IQ)   The ratio of an individual's chronological age to mental age, as measured by an intelligence test.

intimacy versus isolation   The sixth of eight psychosocial stages proposed by Erikson.

intrinsic motivation   Undertaking an activity for the reward or pleasure derived from that particular activity.

introjection   The process of assimilating the attributes of others or incorporating external values and attitudes into one's own ego structure.

intuitive thought   The third stage of Piaget's cognitive development theory, occurring approximately between ages 4 and 7. The child's thought patterns are bound by immediate perceptions and experiences rather than by flexible mental functions.

invention of new means through mental combinations   The last of six substages constituting Piaget's stage of cognitive development. This substage occurs between 18 and 24 months.

isolationism   In early artwork development, the tendency of the child to create shapes and forms as independent markings on the paper.

juvenile delinquency   Behavior on the part of youths 18 and under that society deems unacceptable.

karyotype   A special treatment of cells during their division that allows researchers to observe, measure, and compare the treated chromosomes with normal chromosomes to check for suspected imperfections.

kernel words   Words that can be strung together to make a statement that is usually declarative.

kibbutz   A collective farm settlement where children are raised communally and apart from their parents.

Klinefelter's syndrome   A chromosomal abnormality in which males have two normal X chromosomes plus the Y (XXY). Those afflicted have small external male sex organs but the general contour of a female and are sterile.

lactation   The secretion of milk by the female breast.

Lamaze method   A natural childbirth approach emphasizing a conditioned learning technique in which the mother replaces one set of learned responses (fear, pain) with another (relaxation, muscle control).

language   The system of grammatical rules and semantics that makes speech meaningful.

lanugo   A fine downy growth of hair appearing on the entire body of the fetus and newborn.

latency period   The fourth stage of Freud's psychosexual theory in which the individual's sexual urges become calm.

lateralization   Specialization of the left and right cerebral hemispheres.

law   A statement of fact or facts that describes a sequence of events that occur with unvarying uniformity under precise conditions.

law and order orientation   Kohlberg's fourth of six stages of moral development. This stage is grouped under the major division or level known as conventional morality.

law of effect   The learning principle postulated by Edward Thorndike, which states that responses leading to satisfying results will have a tendency to be remembered and repeated.

learning   A relatively permanent change in behavior as the result of experience.

learning disabilities   A perceptual or communication disorder that prevents or hinders the individual from processing information.

Leboyer method   Proposed by French obstetrician Frederic Leboyer, this technique emphasizes a gentle delivery of the baby as well as the establishment of a peaceful and soothing delivery room environment.

lexicon   One's vocabulary.

libido   According to Freud, energy, which is basically sexual, that serves the basic human instincts.

locomotion   The ability of an organism to move from place to place; to walk.

logic   The use of formal rules applied to reasoning.

longitudinal study   A study in which the researcher repeatedly collects data on the same group of individuals over a long period of time.

long-term memory   A storage system that enables individuals to retain information for relatively long periods.

love withdrawal   A disciplinary style in which parents emotionally remove themselves from their offspring.

LSD   Lysergic acid diethylamide, a hallucinogenic compound produced from ergot.

marijuana   A hallucinogenic drug obtained from a mixture of the tops, leaves, seeds, and stems of female hemp or cannabis plants. The strongest grade of marijuana is known as hashish.

masturbation   The stimulation of the genital organs to climax by self-manipulation rather than sexual intercourse.

maternal drive   Motivation to protect and care for one's young.

maturation The development of body cells to full maturity, at which time they are fully and totally used by the organism.

mean The arithmetical average attained by adding scores and dividing their total by their number.

measures of central tendency Scores that closely approximate the middle or average as opposed to the extremes. The mean, median, and mode are the most common measures of central tendency.

median The middle score obtained by arranging scores in numerical order and locating the point above which half fall and below which half fall.

medulla oblongata A part of the hindbrain that connects the brain and spinal cord and regulates heartbeat, respiration, digestion, and blood pressure.

meiosis The process of germ cell division.

memory span The number of items that can be held in one's short-term memory bank.

menarche The first menstrual period.

mental retardation An intellectual subnormality or deficiency; usually denoted by an IQ of 70 or below.

mesomorphy A body build characterized by a sturdy, athletic appearance.

metacognition A person's awareness of how a cognitive process can be applied to a selected mental task.

metamemory A person's awareness of how a memory strategy can be employed to prevent forgetting material at hand.

midbrain The connecting link between the forebrain and the hindbrain.

midwife A person who usually holds a bachelor's degree in nursing and a master's degree in nurse-midwifery and works on a medical team consisting of a gynecologist and an obstetrician. Midwives often conduct home births.

mitosis The process of somatic cell division.

mode The single score that occurs with the most frequency.

mons Elevated fatty tissue over the pubis region in the female.

Montessori approach An educational program emphasizing the adaptation of schoolwork to the individual child, sensorimotor training, and freedom in the classroom.

moral development The process through which individuals learn to adopt the standards of right and wrong established by the culture in which they live.

moral realism According to Jean Piaget, a stage of morality in which children between the ages of 5 and 10 perceive rules without total awareness of why they exist.

moral relativism According to Jean Piaget, a stage of morality in which children 10 years of age and older view rules in relation to the principles they uphold.

Moro reflex A major reflex present in the newborn. Any loud noise or loss of support will cause newborns to draw the legs up, arch the back, and fling the arms. Also called the startle reflex.

morpheme The smallest unit of a language that has recognizable meaning. The word *boys*, for example, has two morphemes, *boy* and *s*.

motherese A language style employed by adults, more often the mother, when speaking to young children. Motherese consists of shortened sentences, easy words, the duplication of syllables, and an increase of voice frequency.

motor skill The ability to coordinate the bodily movements that enable an individual to execute a particular physical task.

mutagens Agents such as X rays or radiation that are capable of producing mutations in the DNA molecule.

mutation A gene error or dysfunction that produces a change in the characteristic that the gene determines. Mutations may be positive, negative, or neutral.

mutual respect stage In the Piagetian design of moral development, the point at which children become aware of the meanings of rules and the reason for their formation.

myelin   A white fatty substance that covers many nerve fibers of the body. Nerves that are covered with myelin transmit their electrochemical messages at a more rapid rate than nonmyelinated nerves.

myopia   A condition of nearsightedness.

naively egoistic orientation   Kohlberg's second of six moral development stages. This stage is grouped under the major division or level known as preconventional morality.

natural childbirth   A method of childbirth avoiding the use of anesthesia and allowing both husband and wife to play an active role in the delivery of the baby.

naturalistic observation   The examination of behavior under normal or unstructured conditions.

negative reinforcement   In instrumental conditioning, an unpleasant stimulus is taken away from a subject following a desired response. This is done in order to strengthen that particular response.

negative transfer   The interference of a previously learned task with the learning of a new task.

neonate   A term for the newborn infant during the first few weeks of life.

nervous system   All the neurons in the body that carry electrochemical signals either to the central nervous system (CNS—brain and spinal cord) or from the CNS to the body (autonomic nervous system—ANS—or peripheral nervous system—PNS).

neuron   A cell of the nervous system that transmits information in the form of electrochemical impulses.

nocturnal emission   The ejaculation of semen during sleep.

nucleic acid   Substance found in the chromosomes, mitochondria, and cytoplasm of all cells.

nucleoplasm   Protoplasm found inside the nuclear membrane.

nucleus   The control center for the cell's activity, located in or near the center of the cell.

obedience and punishment orientation   Kohlberg's first of six stages of moral development. This stage is grouped under the major division or level known as preconventional morality.

object permanence   The mental ability that enables one to realize that objects exist even if they are out of one's field of vision.

obsession   A persistent unwanted idea.

obstetrician   A physician who treats women during pregnancy and childbirth.

occipital lobe   An area of the cortex enabling the brain to interpret the sensory information transmitted by the eyes.

Oedipus complex   According to Freud, the romantic feelings a boy has for his mother and the fear of the father's retaliation. The Oedipus complex is prevalent during the phallic stage of psychosexual development.

ontogeny   The course of development of a particular organism.

open class word   A word in early sentence structure that is connected to pivot words. Pivot words rarely exist as single word utterances and are usually in the first position of early two-word sentences.

operant conditioning   *See* instrumental conditioning.

opium   An addicting narcotic obtained from the flower pods of a particular poppy species. Its derivatives include morphine and heroin.

oral stage   The initial phase of psychosexual development theorized by Freud. During this period infants seek gratification from stimulation of the mouth.

ordinal position   A child's place in the family, such as being the first-born or second-born.

ossification   The process through which minerals, particularly calcium and phosphorus, are deposited in the bone.

ovaries   The two female sex glands that produce egg cells (ova) and sex hormones.

overregularization   The extension of a grammatical rule to situations in which it does not apply—for example, *goed* instead of *went*.

ovulation   The release of the egg from the ovary.

ovum   The female egg or germ cell.

parallel play   A variation of egocentrism expressed in young children's playtime activities. Because children between 2 and 4 are fundamentally self-centered and unable to separate themselves from their thoughts, playmate interaction is restricted.

parietal lobe   An area of the cortex controlling the sense of touch and the transmission of essential spatial information.

peer group   An individual's associates, usually of the same age and status.

perception   The process of being aware of and interpreting stimuli in the environment.

perceptual constancy   The tendency of an object to remain the same under different viewing conditions.

period of the ovum   In early prenatal development, the process of cell division that continues for approximately two weeks after fertilization of the ovum.

peripheral nervous system   A network of neural tissue that connects the brain and the spinal cord with other parts of the body.

permissive   A style of parental control characterized by a nonpunitive orientation and relaxed rules and regulations.

permissiveness with affection   A moral standard asserting that sexual relations between unmarried persons are acceptable if accompanied by emotional attachment between partners.

permissiveness without affection   A moral standard asserting that sex between unmarried persons without emotional attachments is acceptable; also called recreational sex.

personal fable   A consequence of adolescent egocentrism. Teenagers are convinced of their personal uniqueness and construct stories about themselves that are not true.

petting   Physical contact between a male and a female that does not involve union of the genitalia but is a deliberate attempt to effect erotic arousal.

phallic stage   According to the Freudian psychosexual theory of development, a period characterized by genital manipulation and attraction for the parent of the other sex.

phenotype   The visible, observable, or easily measurable appearance of an organism.

phenylketonuria (PKU)   A mutation that prevents the body from manufacturing an enzyme capable of reducing phenylpyruvic acid, a substance toxic to the central nervous system.

phobia   A persistent and abnormal fear.

phoneme   The most fundamental element of a language. The sound of *b* in *big* or *th* in *thick* is a phoneme.

phonology   The study of phonemes and other sounds made in speech.

physical dependence   A condition in which the absence of a drug produces unpleasant side effects.

physiology   The science concerned with the functions of living matter.

pilot study   An experiment tested on a very small sample in order to assure, among other things, that the equipment is operable, that the researcher feels confident of the experimental procedure, or that the subjects understand the directions.

pituitary gland   The gland that secretes hormones that stimulate the production and release of hormones by other endocrine glands; often called the master gland.

pivot word   A word that is usually small in size and is connected to open class words. Pivot words are usually used in the second position of early two-word sentences.

placenta   The organ that allows nourishment to pass from mother to embryo and fetus and waste products to be channeled from embryo and fetus to mother.

play   Spontaneous behavioral patterns that emerge when one engages in an unstructured activity solely for the pleasure that it offers.

play therapy   A technique to help diagnose and treat childhood behavioral disorders.

pleasure principle   According to Freud, the tendency of individuals to seek pleasurable experiences and avoid unpleasant ones.

polygenes   A number of genes that work together with additive and/or complementary effects.

pons   A part of the hindbrain bridging the two lobes of the cerebellum.

population   A statistical term that applies to all individuals within a selected group.

positive reinforcement   In instrumental conditioning, a pleasant stimulus that is given to a subject following a desired response to strengthen that particular response.

positive transfer   A condition in which the learning of one task aids in the learning of another.

postconventional morality   Kohlberg's third major division or level of moral development, occurring from age 16 onward. Stages within this level include the contractual legalistic orientation and the universal ethical principle orientation.

power assertion   A disciplinary style that emphasizes parental domination and forceful discipline.

pragmatics   The manner in which language is used in a social context.

preconceptual thought   The second of Jean Piaget's five cognitive development stages. Preconceptual thought occurs between the ages of 2 and 4.

preconventional morality   The initial phase of moral development occurring during the early childhood years. As theorized by Lawrence Kohlberg, substages within this period include "obedience and punishment orientation" and "naively egoistic orientation."

prehension   The ability to grasp objects between the fingers and opposable thumb.

premature infant   A newborn infant weighing less than 2,500 grams (5½ pounds).

premoral stage   According to Jean Piaget, a stage of morality where children 5 and under have little, if any, awareness of rules.

prenatal period   The time between conception and birth.

primary circular reactions   The second of six substages comprising Piaget's sensorimotor stage of cognitive development. This substage occurs between 1 and 4 months of age.

primary reinforcers   Satisfying stimuli related to primary, unlearned drives. Food and drink are primary reinforcers related to the hunger and thirst drives.

primary sex characteristics   Sex characteristics that relate directly to the sex organs—the penis and testes in the male, and the ovaries, clitoris, and vagina in the female.

principle of invariance   *See* conservation.

principle of reversibility   Realizing that objects can have their original condition restored after changes have been made in their physical shape or arrangement.

problem   In research terminology, the defining of an issue or question toward which research can be directed.

procedure   An explanation and description of the apparatus used in a research experiment so that it can be duplicated for future use.

progesterone   A female sex hormone that aids in the development of the uterine wall, particularly its preparation for implantation of a developing ovum and in placental development after implantation has taken place.

Project Follow Through   A federally funded program established in 1967 designed to continue the services of Project Head Start to children in grades K–3.

Project Head Start   A federally funded compensatory preschool program established in 1965.

Project Home Start   A federally funded program established in 1972 designed to teach parents to stimulate their children educationally at home.

projected animism   In early artwork, the tendency of children to attach humanlike qualities to objects they draw.

projection   The defense mechanism of mentally placing one's difficulties or failures on someone else.

prolactin   A hormone secreted by the pituitary gland into the bloodstream of females, which begins the production of milk for newborns.

prosocial behavior   Being sensitive to the needs and feelings of others.

protoplasm   The entire living substance that constitutes a cell.

proximo-distal development   Growth from the center of the body outward.

psycholinguistics   The study of the developing communication processes of the child from early stages of crying and babbling to spoken words and meaningful sentences. Psycholinguistics include the closely related areas of language, mental imagery, cognitive development, and symbolization.

psychological dependence   A condition in which the effect of a drug becomes such an important facet of an individual's life that it is needed for the person to function.

puberty   The point in the life span at which sexual maturity is attained.

pubescence   The period of time that proceeds puberty.

Punnett square   A diagrammatical means of computing the possible genotypes and phenotypes for any given characteristic.

questionnaire   A set of systematic questions designed to obtain information from a population; also called an inventory.

random sampling   A method of drawing a sample so that each member of the population has an equal opportunity of being selected.

range   In statistics, the spread between the highest and lowest scores.

rationalization   The attempt to justify and provide logical reasons and explanations for particular patterns of behavior.

reaction formation   The defense mechanism of substituting an opposing attitude for an unwanted and perhaps objectionable desire.

reaction time   The interval between the introduction of a stimulus and an individual's response.

readiness   A state of maturation that enables a child to perform a task.

receptive language   The language that a person can understand.

receptive versus expressive lag   The discrepancy, if any, that exists between what a person can understand and what the person can express verbally.

recessive gene   A gene the hereditary characteristics of which are present only when it is paired with another recessive gene.

reconstituted family   *See* blended family.

reflective   A conceptual tempo characterized by a careful and deliberate approach to problem solving.

reflex   The automatic elicitation of a specific response without the involvement of higher brain functions.

reflex activities   The first of six substages constituting Piaget's sensorimotor stage of cognitive development. This substage occurs during approximately the first month of life.

reflex smile   The earliest type of smile, occurring during the first few weeks of life. This smile is primarily physiological and is usually the infant's response to a number of different stimuli, including internal stimulation (a bubble of gas in the stomach), being fed, or being stroked on the cheek.

regression   A defense mechanism characterized by the individual's reverting to behavioral responses characteristic of earlier developmental levels.

reinforcement   The process of strengthening an organism's response. In classical conditioning, the unconditioned stimulus serves as the reinforcement, while in instrumental conditioning, the use of a reward constitutes the reinforcement.

reinforcer   Anything that strengthens the probability of a response.

representational thought   A cognitive capacity that enables one to construct mental symbols and images of environmental objects and events.

repression   The tendency to push from levels of awareness experiences, thoughts, or impulses associated with severe anxiety.

respiratory system   The system responsible for breathing. The system consists of the lungs, bronchi, pharynx, larynx, tonsils, and nose.

respondent conditioning   *See* classical conditioning.

results   The facts collected in a research study without any commentary.

retention   The mental ability that allows an individual to retain information from the past.

reticular activating system   A part of the hindbrain controlling arousal, attention, and the sleep cycle.

retrieval   The process of bringing stored memories into consciousness.

reversal learning   Learning the opposite of what was previously learned.

reversibility   The ability to trace one's line of reasoning back to where it originated.

ribonucleic acid (RNA)   A substance formed by DNA, it carries genetic messages to the ribosome for the manufacturing of specific proteins.

ribosomes   Small particles in the cytoplasm that manufacture protein under the direction of DNA.

role   A type or pattern of behavior that one is expected to follow in a given social position.

rooming-in facility   For the parents of newborns, a facility allowing the parents to care for their baby in the mother's hospital room.

rooting reflex   An early reflex response of babies that includes head turning movements and sucking attempts when the cheek is touched.

rote learning   Learning by memorization without regard for meaning.

sample   A group of individuals who represent a part of a larger population.

schedule of reinforcement   A term referring to the manner in which reinforcement will be administered to the subject.

schemata   Organized patterns of thought. Sensory stimuli, objects, and events are a few examples of schematic organizations.

scientific method   The testing of hypotheses concerning natural events and relationships.

secondary circular reactions   The third of six substages constituting Piaget's sensorimotor stage of cognitive development. This substage occurs between 4 and 8 months.

secondary reinforcer   A stimulus that was previously neutral but when paired frequently over successive trials with a primary reinforcer gains reinforcing qualities of its own.

secondary sex characteristics   Sex characteristics that are not related directly to the sex organs but distinguish a mature male from a mature female.

secular trend   A pattern of physical growth and development whereby children in more prosperous parts of the world are taller and heavier and enter puberty earlier than youngsters from less prosperous nations. This is due primarily to improved nutrition and better health care.

securely attached   A type of attachment described by Mary Ainsworth. Securely attached infants, among other characteristics, will explore the environment and show little anxiety when the mother is away for short periods of time. Upon the mother's return, securely attached infants are happy and desire close contact with her.

selective social smile   A type of smile appearing approximately between 5 and 6 months of age. The selective social smile is directed only to familiar figures, such as the mother or other caregivers.

self-actualization   According to Abraham Maslow, the fullest development of one's potentials, capacities, and talents.

self-concept   The manner in which individuals perceive themselves.

self-esteem   A feeling of personal worthiness.

semantics   The study of meaning in a language.

sensorimotor development   The first stage of cognitive development (0 through 2 years) outlined by Jean Piaget. Learning activities at this point are directed toward the coordination of simple sensorimotor skills.

sensory memory   The part of the memory system that receives and holds all incoming sensory stimuli for a fraction of a second. They then decay or are transferred to short-term memory.

separation anxiety   A distress reaction expressed by infants upon separation from the caregiver. Separation anxiety occurs approximately by 1 year.

seriation   Ordering objects according to size or other dimensions.

sex-linked characteristics   Inherited characteristics carried by the genes of the X and Y chromosomes.

sex-role development   The process of socialization in which appropriate male and females roles are learned.

sexual identity   The physiological differences that exist between males and females.

shaping behavior   The establishment of desirable chains by molding a series of stimulus-response situations into a desired behavioral pattern.

short-term memory   The temporary retention of information. Unlike the long-term memory store, short-term memory is affected considerably by interference and interruption.

sibling   A brother or sister.

sibling rivalry   A form of competition between children of the same family for the attention of the parents.

skeletal maturity   The progress toward union of the epiphyses with the shaft of the bones.

Skinner box   A problem box designed for experimental animals. The box is designed so that a reward (food pellet) is dispensed if a lever or button is correctly manipulated by the subject.

Skinnerian conditioning   *See* instrumental conditioning.

social cognition   The awareness of how individuals perceive themselves and others, including another person's thoughts and feelings.

social learning theory   One of child psychology's major schools of thought. This view proposes that children's behavior is influenced by observing and copying others.

socialization   The process of learning how to behave in a socially approved manner.

social smile   A type of smile emerging by the second or third month of life. The social smile may be evoked by the appearance or voice of a caregiver, movement, or certain noises.

sociodramatic play   Imaginative or make-believe play shared with a partner.

somatic cells   Cells in the human body, with the exception of the sex cells.

somatotrophic hormone   *See* human growth hormone.

species-specific   Particular behavior patterns found only among members of a specific species.

speech   A concrete, physical act that consists of forming and sequencing the sounds of oral language.

sperm   Male germ cell, or gamete.

spontaneous recovery   In conditioning, a process in which a learned response occurs after apparent extinction.

startle reflex   *See* Moro reflex.

stimulus discrimination   The level of learning that allows one to distinguish among two or more stimuli.

stimulus generalization   Responding to similar stimuli as if they were the same.

stimulus-response (S-R)   A theoretical view that all behavior is in response to stimuli from the environment; sometimes called the "mechanical man" theory.

stranger anxiety   A distress reaction expressed by infants when unfamiliar people are introduced. Infants show stranger anxiety after the sixth month of life.

successive approximations   The step-by-step series of reinforcements that eventually produce a desired stimulus-response behavior.

superego   According to Freud, the part of one's personality that represents societal expectations and demands.

superordinate style   A cognitive style in which the classification of stimulus objects is based on shared attributes.

surface structure   Sentence structure that is dictated by the rules of grammar.

symbolic functioning   An act of reference in which a mental image is created to stand for something that is not present.

symbolic play   A type of make-believe play. The child represents one thing as if it were something else.

syntax   The rules for combining words into sentences.

syphilis   A sexually transmitted disease.

systolic   The greatest force caused by the heart's contraction. Systolic pressure is compared to diastolic, the relaxation phase that exists between heart beats.

telegraphic sentences   A type of sentence used by children at approximately 2 years. Telegraphic sentences include only the words necessary to give meaning. Connecting words are usually omitted.

temperament   The general disposition of a person, such as cheerful, easy to please.

temporal lobe   An area of the cortex responsible for hearing as well as the storage of permanent memories.

tertiary circular reactions   The fifth of six substages constituting Piaget's sensorimotor stage of cognitive development. This substage occurs between 12 and 18 months.

testes   The primary male reproductive organs.

testosterone   The primary male hormone that is secreted by the testes.

thalamus   Part of the forebrain that relays nerve impulses from sensory pathways to the cerebral cortex.

theory   A formulation of apparent relationships that have some degree of verification and supportive evidence.

thymine   One of the four nucleotide bases of the DNA molecule; it bonds with the base adenine.

transductive reasoning   Reasoning from particular to particular without generalization.

transformation   Understanding the relationship that exists between the deep and surface structures of a sentence.

transformational reasoning   The ability to appreciate how one state transforms itself into another when an event has a sequence of change.

triad   A three-person group.

trial-and-error learning   An individual's attempt to find an answer to a problem that has no clear-cut solution.

triple X syndrome   A female chromosomal abnormality that produces mental retardation, menstrual irregularity, and premature menopause.

trisomy 21   *See* Down's syndrome.

Turner's syndrome   A female chromosomal abnormality (only one sex chromosome) distinguished by a webbed neck, short fingers, and short stature. No secondary sex characteristics appear at the time of puberty (X0).

umbilical cord   The "body stalk" containing three blood vessels: a vein carrying oxygenated blood from the placenta to the infant and two arteries carrying blood and waste products from the infant to the placenta.

unconditioned response   The response that an organism will exhibit prior to the beginning of the classical conditioning procedure (that is, salivating when food powder is placed in the mouth).

unconditioned stimulus   A stimulus that causes an unconditioned response (for example, an electrical shock and withdrawal).

unconscious motives   Motives that individuals are unaware of but still affect their behavior.

universal ethical principle orientation   Kohlberg's sixth stage of moral development. This stage is grouped under the major division or level known as postconventional morality.

uterus   A thick-walled, hollow, muscular organ in which the fertilized egg develops into an infant.

vagina   A short muscular tube in females that extends from the uterus to an exterior opening, also called the birth canal.

validity   The ability of a test to measure what it intends to measure.

value   A principle or ideal of intrinsic worth.

variable   An experimental condition that can be measured or controlled during an experiment.

variable interval schedule   A type of partial reinforcement schedule in which the organism is reinforced after a variable time period.

variable ratio schedule   A type of partial reinforcement schedule in which the organism is reinforced after a variable number of correct responses.

verbal learning   A learning situation that involves the use of words either as stimuli or as responses.

visual acuity   The ability to see small details.

visual cliff   A testing apparatus designed to measure depth perception in infants and animals.

vital capacity   The quantity of air that the lungs can hold.

vowel   The most prominent sound in a syllable.

Wernicke's area   A portion of the brain, located in the temporal lobe, that is responsible for the comprehension of speech.

withdrawal symptoms   Unpleasant side effects, such as nausea and cramping, that are caused by the absence of a drug.

word fluency   A dimension of divergent thinking. Word fluency is being able to find a variety of words to express a particular meaning or represent a particular concept.

X chromosome   A sex-determining chromosome. Females have two X chromosomes, whereas males have one X chromosome and one Y chromosome.

Y chromosome   A sex-determining chromosome. When paired with the X chromosome, a male offspring is produced.

zygote   A cell formed by the union of the male sperm and the female ovum; the fertilized egg.

References

Abbe, K. M., and Gill, F. M. *Twins on Twins.* New York: Crown, 1981.

Abravanel, E. Perceiving subjective contours during early childhood. *Journal of Experimental Child Psychology,* 1982, *33,* 280–287.

Acredolo, L. P., and Hake, J. L. Infant perception. In *Handbook of Developmental Psychology,* ed. B. B. Woolman. Englewood Cliffs, N.J.: Prentice-Hall, 1982.

Adams G. R. The effects of physical attractiveness on the socialization process. In *Psychological Aspects of Facial Form,* ed., G. W. Lucker, K. A. Ribbens, and J. A. McNamara. Craniofacial Growth Series Monograph no. 11. Ann Arbor, Mich.: Center for Human Growth and Development, 1980.

Adams, G. R., and Jones, R. M. Imaginary audience behavior: a validation study. *Journal of Early Adolescence,* 1981, *1,* 1–10.

Adams, G. R.; Jones, R. M.; Schvaneveldt, J. D.; and Jenson, G. O. Antecedents of affective role-taking behavior: adolescent perceptions of parental socialization styles. *Journal of Adolescence,* 1982, *5,* 1–7.

Adams, R. L., and Phillips, B. N. Motivation and achievement differences among children of various ordinal birth positions. *Child Development,* 1972, *43,* 155–164.

Adams, V. The sibling bond: a lifelong love/hate dialectic. *Psychology Today.* June 1981, 32–47.

Adler, C.; Bazemore, G.; and Polk, K. Delinquency in non-metropolitan areas. In *Critical Issues in Juvenile Delinquency,* ed. D. Shichor and D. H. Kelley. Lexington, Mass.: Lexington Books, 1980.

Ainsworth, M. D. S. *Infancy in Uganda.* Baltimore: Johns Hopkins Press, 1967.

———. Infant-mother attachment. *American Psychologist,* 1979, *34,* 932–937.

Alberts, J. R. Ontogeny of olfaction: reciprocal roles of sensation and behavior in the development of perception. In *Development of Perception,* ed. R. N. Aslin, J. R. Alberts, and M. R. Petersen. Vol. 1. New York: Academic Press, 1981.

Allen, J. E. *Helping Children Overcome Fears.* West Lafayette, Ind.: Purdue University Cooperative Extension Service, 1982.

Allgeier, E., and McCormick, N., eds. *Gender Roles and Sexual Behavior.* Palo Alto, Calif.: Mayfield, 1982.

Alvino, J. Philosophical questions help children think and rethink ideas. *Gifted Children Newsletter.* December 1983.

American Psychological Association. *Newsletter.* 1968, 1–3.

Ames, L. B.; Ilg, F. L.; and Haber, C. C. *Your One Year Old.* New York: Delacorte, 1982.

Anderson, J. R. *Cognitive Psychology and its Implications.* San Francisco: W. H. Freeman, 1980.

Anyan, W. R., and Schowalter, J. E. A comprehensive approach to anorexia nervosa. *Journal of the American Academy of Child Psychiatry,* 1983, *22,* 59–62.

Apgar, V. A proposal for a new method of evaluation of the newborn infant. *Current Research in Anesthesia Analgesia,* 1953, *32,* 260–267.

Apgar, V., and James, L. S. Further observations on the newborn scoring system. *American Journal of Diseases of Children,* 1962, *104,* 419–428.

Aries, P. *Centuries of Childhood.* Trans. R. Baldick. New York: Knopf, 1962.

Arnold, H. W., et al. Transition to extrauterine life. *American Journal of Nursing,* 1965, *65,* 77–80.

Asher, S. R., and Hymel, S. Children's social competence in peer relations: sociometric and behavior assessment. In *Social Competence*, ed. J. D. Wine and M. D. Smye. New York: Guilford Press, 1981.

Asher, S. R., and Renshaw, P. D. Children without friends: social knowledge and social skill training. In *The Development of Children's Friendships*, ed. S. R. Asher and J. M. Gottman. New York: Cambridge University Press, 1981.

Asher, S. R.; Renshaw, P. D.; and Hymel, S. Peer relations and the development of social skills. In *The Young Child: Reviews of Research*, ed. S. G. Moore and C. R. Cooper. Vol. 3. Washington, D.C.: National Association for the Education of Young Children, 1982.

Aston, A. *Toys That Teach Your Child: From Birth to Two.* Charlotte, N.C.: East Woods Press, 1984.

Auerbach, S. *Choosing Child Care: A Guide For Parents.* New York: E. P. Dutton, 1981.

Ault, R. *Children's Cognitive Development.* New York: Oxford University Press, 1983.

Ault, R., and Vinsel, A. Piaget's theory of cognitive development. In *Developmental Perspectives*, ed. R. L. Ault. Santa Monica, Calif.: Goodyear, 1980.

Ausberger, C.; Martin, M. J.; and Creighton, J. *Learning to Talk is Child's Play: Helping Preschoolers Develop Language.* Tucson, Ariz.: Communication Skill Builders, 1982.

Baer, A. S., ed. *Heredity and Society.* New York: The Macmillan Co., 1973.

Baker, D. *Functions of Folk and Fairy Tales.* Washington, D.C.: Association for Childhood Education International, 1981.

Ball, S., and Bogatz, G. A. *The First Year of Sesame St.: An Evaluation.* Princeton, N.J.: Educational Testing Service, 1970.

Bandura, A. Social learning through imitation. *Nebraska Symposium on Motivation.* Lincoln, Neb.: University of Nebraska Press, 1962, 211–269.

———. *Aggression: A Social Learning Analysis.* Englewood Cliffs, N.J.: Prentice-Hall, 1973.

Bandura, A.; Grusel, J.; and Menlove, F. Vicarious extinction of avoidance behavior. *Journal of Personality and Social Psychology*, 1967, *5*, 16–23.

Bandura, A., and Huston, A. Identification as a process of incidental learning. *Journal of Abnormal and Social Psychology*, 1961, *63*, 311–318.

Bandura, A., and McDonald, F. J. Influence of social reinforcement and the behavior of models in shaping children's moral judgement. *Journal of Abnormal and Social Psychology*, 1963, *67*(3), 274–281.

Bandura, A.; Ross, D.; and Ross, S. Transmission of aggression through imitation of aggressive models. *Journal of Abnormal and Social Psychology*, 1961, *63*, 575–582.

Bandura, A., and Walters, R. *Social Learning and Personality Development.* New York: Holt, Rinehart & Winston, 1963.

Bank, S. P., and Kahn, M. D. *The Sibling Bond.* New York: Basic Books, 1982.

Banks, M., and Salapatek, P. Infant pattern vision: a new approach based on the contrast sensitivity function. *Journal of Experimental Child Psychology*, 1981, *31*(1), 1–45.

Barenboim, C. The development of person perception in childhood and adolescence: from behavioral comparisons to psychological constructs to psychological comparisons. *Child Development*, 1981, *52*, 129–144.

Barnes, S.; Gutfreund, M.; Satterly, D.; and Wells, G. Characteristics of adult speech which predict children's language development. *Journal of Child Language*, 1983, *10*(1), 65–84.

Barnett, M. A.; King, L. M.; Howard, J. A.; and Dino, G. A. Empathy in young children: relation to parents empathy, affection, and emphasis on the feelings of others. *Developmental Psychology*, 1980, *16*, 243–244.

Bar-Tal, D., and Raviv, A. A cognitive-learning model of helping behavior development: possible implications and applications. In *The Development of Prosocial Behavior*, ed. N. Eisenberg. New York: Academic Press, 1982.

Bartlett, J. Selecting an early childhood language curriculum. In *Language In Early Childhood Education*, ed. C. B. Cazden. Washington, D.C.: National Association for the Education of Young Children, 1981.

Baruch, D. *One Little Boy.* New York: Delta Books, 1964.

Baskin, B. H., and Harris, K. H. *More Notes From A Different Drummer: A Guide to Juvenile Fiction Portraying the Disabled.* Ann Arbor, Mich.: Bowker, 1984.

Basow, S. S. *Sex Role Stereotypes: Traditions and Alternatives.* Monterey, Calif.: Brooks/Cole, 1980.

Bauer, O. H. An exploratory study of developmental changes in children's fears. *Journal of Child Psychology and Psychiatry*, 1976, *17*, 69–74.

Baumrind, D. Current patterns of parental authority. *Developmental Psychology*, 1971, *4*, 1–103.

———. New directions in socialization research. *American Psychologist*, 1980, *35*, 639–652.

Bayley, N. Comparison of mental and motor test scores for ages 1–15 months by sex, birth order, race, geographical location and education of parents. *Child Development*, 1965, *36*, 379–411.

Beadle, G. W., and Tatum, E. L. Experimental control of developmental reaction. *American Naturalist*, 1941, *75*, 107–116.

Beaty, J. J. *Skills for Preschool Teachers.* Columbus, Ohio: Charles E. Merrill, 1984.

Beisser, A. The American seasonal masculinity rites. In *Jock: Sports and Male Identity*, ed. D. F. Sabo and R. Runfola. Englewood Cliffs, N.J.: Prentice-Hall, 1980.

Bell, R. R. *Worlds of Friendship.* Beverly Hills, Calif.: Sage Publications, 1981.

Bell, R. R., and Coughey, K. Premarital sexual experience among college females, 1958, 1968 and 1978. *Family Relations*, July 1980.

Bell, T. E. Computer literacy: the fourth "R". *Personal Computing*, May 1983, 4–11.

Beller, E. K. The Philadelphia study: the impact of preschool on intellectual and socioemotional development. In *As the Twig is Bent: Lasting Effects of Preschool Programs.* Hillsdale, N.J.: Erlbaum, 1982.

Belmont, L., and Marolla, F. A. Birth order, family size, and intelligence. *Science*, 1973, *182*, 1096–1101.

Bem, S. L. The measurement of psychological androgyny. *Journal of Consulting and Clinical Psychology*, 1974, *42*, 155–162.

———. Sex-role adaptability: one consequence of psychological androgyny. *Journal of Personality and Social Psychology*, 1975, *31*, 634–643.

———. Gender schema theory: a cognitive account of sex-typing. *Psychological Review*, 1981(a), *88*(4), 354–364.

———. The BSRI and gender schema theory: a reply to Spence and Helmreich. *Psychological Review*, 1981(b), *88*(4), 369–371.

Benbow, C. P., and Stanley, J. C. Sex differences in mathematical ability: fact or artifact? *Science*, 1980, *210*, 1262–1264.

Benham, N. B.; Hosticka, A.; Payne, J. D.; and Yeotis, C. Making concepts in science and mathematics visible and viable in the early childhood curriculum. *School Science and Math*, 1982, *82*(1), 45–56.

Bereiter, C., and Engleman, S. *Teaching Disadvantaged Children in the Preschool.* Englewood Cliffs, N.J.: Prentice-Hall, 1966.

Berger, S. *Divorce Without Victims: Helping Children Through Divorce With A Minimum of Pain and Trauma.* Boston: Houghton Mifflin, 1983.

Bernard, H. S. Identity formation during late adolescence: a review of some empirical findings. *Adolescence*, 1981, *16*, 349–358.

Berndt, T. J. The features and effects of friendship in early adolescence. *Child Development*, 1982, *53*(6), 1447–1460.

Bernstein, R. M. The development of the self-system during adolescence. *Journal of Genetic Psychology*, 1980, *136*(2), 231–245.

Billings, K. Microcomputers in education: now and in the future. In *Microcomputers in the Schools*, ed. J. L. Thomas. Phoenix, Ariz.: Oryx Press, 1981.

Binning, G. Earlier physical and mental maturity among Saskatoon public school children. *Canadian Journal of Public Health*, 1958, *49*, 9–17.

Birch, H. G., and Gussow, J. D. *Disadvantaged Children: Health, Nutrition and School Failure.* New York: Grune & Stratton, 1970.

Birns, B. Individual differences in human neonates' responses to stimulation. *Child Development,* 1965, *36,* 249–259.

Bjorklund, D. F., and Hock, H. S. Age differences in the temporal locus of memory organization in children's recall. *Journal of Experimental Child Psychology,* 1982, *33,* 347–362.

Black, J. K. Are young children really egocentric? *Young Children,* 1981, *36*(6), 51–55.

Blasi, A. Bridging moral cognition and moral action: a critical review of the literature. *Psychological Bulletin,* 1980, *88,* 1–45.

Blatchford, P.; Battle, S.; and Mays, J. *The First Transition: Home to Preschool.* Atlantic Highlands, N.J.: Humanities Press, 1983.

Blyth, D. A.; Simmons, R. G.; Bulcroft, R.; Felt, D.; Van Cleave, E. F.; and Bush, D. M. The effects of physical development on self-image and satisfaction with body image for early adolescent males. In *Handbook of Community and Mental Health,* ed. R. G. Simmons. Vol. 2. Greenwich, Conn.: JAI Press, 1980.

Boehm, L. The development of conscience: a comparison of American children of different mental and socioeconomic levels. *Child Development,* 1962, *33,* 575–590.

Boehm, L., and Nass, M. Social class differences in conscience development. *Child Development,* 1962, *33,* 565–574.

Borland, D. A cohort analysis approach to the empty-nest syndrome among three ethnic groups of women: a theoretical position. *Journal of Marriage and the Family,* 1982, *44,* 117–129.

Bornstein, M. H. Human infant color vision and color perception, reviewed and reassessed: a critique of Werner and Wooten. *Infant Behavior and Development,* 1981, *4,* 119–150.

Bornstein, M. H.; Kessen, W.; and Weiskopf, S. The categories in hue in infancy. *Science,* 1976, *191,* 201–202.

Boukydis, C. F. Z., and Burgess, R. L. Adult physiological response to infant cries: effects of temperament of infant, parental status, and gender. *Child Development,* 1982, *53,* 1291–1298.

Bourisseau, W. S. To fathom the self: appraisal in the school. In *The Child and His Image, Self Concept in the Early Years,* ed. K. Yamamoto. Boston: Houghton Mifflin, 1972.

Bower, E. M. *Early Identification of Emotionally Handicapped Children in School.* 3rd ed. Springfield, Ill.: Charles C. Thomas, 1981.

Bower, T. G. R. *Development in Infancy.* San Francisco: W. H. Freeman, 1974.

———. *Development in Infancy.* 2nd ed. San Francisco: W. H. Freeman, 1981.

Bowlby, J. *Attachment and Loss.* Vol. 3. New York: Basic Books, 1980.

Brackbill, Y.; Adams, G.; Crowell, D. H.; and Gray, M. L. Arousal level in neonates and older infants under continuous auditory stimulation. In *Behavior in Infancy and Early Childhood,* ed. Y. Brackbill and G. G. Thomson. New York: Free Press, 1967.

Bradbard, M. R., and Endsley, R. C. How can teachers develop young children's curiosity? In *Curriculum Planning for Young Children,* ed. J. F. Brown. Washington, D.C.: National Association for the Education of Young Children, 1982.

Bradley, B. Machines don't dehumanize: people do. An interview with Herbert Kohl. *Classroom Computer Learning,* 1983, *4*(2), 20–28.

Brady, E. H., and Hill, S. Young children and microcomputers. *Young Children,* 1984, *39*(3), 49–61.

Brazelton, T. B. *Toddlers and Parents.* New York: Dell, 1974.

Brofenbrenner, U. Children and families: 1984? *Society,* 1981, *18,* 38–41.

Broman, B. L. *The Early Years in Childhood Education.* 2nd ed. Boston: Houghton Mifflin Co., 1982.

Broman, S. H. Long-term development of children born to teenagers. In *Teenage Parents and Their Offspring,* ed. K. G. Scott, T. Field, and E. Robertson. New York: Grune & Stratton, 1981.

Bronson, G. W. *The Scanning Pattern of Human Infants: Implications for Visual Learning.* Norwood, N.J.: Ablex, 1982.

Bronson, W. C. *Toddlers' Behavior with Agemates: Issues on Interaction, Cognition, and Affect.* Norwood, N.J.: Ablex, 1981.

Brook, J.; Whiteman, M.; and Gordon, A. S. Stages of drug abuse in adolescence: personality, peer, and family correlates. *Developmental Psychology,* 1983, *19*(2), 269–277.

Brown, B. Long-term gains from early intervention: an overview of current research (mimeograph). Presented at the 1977 annual meeting of the American Association for the Advancement of Science, Denver, Feb. 23, 1977.

Brown, R. The development of the first language in the human species. *American Psychologist,* 1973(a), *28,* 97–106.

———. *A First Language: The Early Stages.* Cambridge: Harvard University Press, 1973(b).

Brown, S. V. Early childbearing and poverty: implications for social services. *Adolescence,* 1982, *17*(66), 397–408.

Brown, T. S., and Wallace, P. M. *Physiological Psychology.* New York: Academic Press, 1980.

Bruner, J. S. The social context of language acquisition. The Witkin Memorial Lecture, presented at Educational Testing Service, Princeton, N.J., May 1980.

Bunker, L. K.; Johnson, C. E.; and Parker, J. E. *Motivating Kids Through Play.* West Point, N.Y.: Leisure Press, 1982.

Burleson, B. R. The development of comforting communication skills in childhood and adolescence. *Child Development,* 1982, *53*(6), 1578–1588.

Burns, R. C. *Self-Growth in Families: Kinetic Family Drawings Research and Application.* New York: Brunner/Mazel, 1982.

Burns, R. C., and Kaufman, S. H. *Kinetic Family Drawings.* New York: Brunner/Mazel, 1970.

Burton, G. M. *A Good Beginning: Teaching Early Childhood Mathematics.* Menlo Park, Calif.: Addison-Wesley, 1984.

Burtt, K. G., and Kalkstein, K. *Smart Toys for Babies from Birth to Two.* Cambridge, Mass.: Harper Colophon, 1981.

Bushnell, I. W. Discrimination of faces by young infants. *Journal of Experimental Child Psychology,* 1982, *33*(2), 298–308.

Butler, A. L.; Gotts, E. E.; and Quisenberry, N. L. *Play as Development.* Columbus, Ohio: Charles E. Merrill, 1978.

Butler, D. *Babies Need Books.* New York: Atheneum Publishers, 1980.

Buytendijk, F. *Wesen Und Sinn Des Spieces.* Berlin: K. Wolff, 1934.

Byber, R. W., and Sund, R. B. *Piaget for Educators.* 2nd ed. Columbus, Ohio: Charles E. Merrill, 1982.

Byrne, D. Sex without contraception. In *Adolescents, Sex, and Contraception,* ed. D. Byrne and W. A. Fisher. Hillsdale, N.J.: Erlbaum, 1983.

Cameron, C. A., and Goard, C. Procedural factors in children's class inclusion. *Journal of Genetic Psychology,* 1982, *140*(2), 313–314.

Campos, J. J.; Bertenthal, B. I.; and Caplovitz, K. The interrelationship of affect and cognition in the visual cliff situation. In *Emotion and Cognition,* ed. C. Izard, J. Kagan, and R. Zajonc. New York: Plenum, 1982.

Campos, J. J.; Haitt, S.; Rampsay, D.; Henderson, C.; and Svejda, M. The emergence of fear on the visual cliff. In *The Origins of Affect,* ed. M. Lewis and L. Rosenblum. New York: Wiley, 1978.

Campos, J. J., and Sternberg, C. R. Perception, appraisal, and emotion: the onset of social referencing. In *Infant Social Cognition,* ed. M. Lamb and L. Sherrod. Hillsdale, N.J.: Erlbaum, 1981.

Canter, R. J. Family correlates of male and female delinquency. *Criminology,* 1982, *20*(2), 149–167.

Carbonara, N. T. *Techniques for Observing Normal Child Behavior.* Pittsburgh, Pa.: University of Pittsburgh Press, 1961.

Carlson, D. B., and Labarba, R. Maternal emotionality during pregnancy and reproductive outcome: a review of the literature. *International Journal of Behavioral Development,* 1979, *2*(4), 343–376.

Carlson, R. Where is the person in personality research? *Psychological Bulletin,* 1971, *75,* 203–219.

Caron, A. J.; Caron, R. F.; Caldwell, R. C.; and Weiss, S. J. Infant perception of the structural properties of the face. *Developmental Psychology*, 1973, *9*, 431–434.

Carroll, J. L., and Rest, J. R. Moral development. In *Handbook of Developmental Psychology*, ed. B. B. Wolman. Englewood Cliffs, N.J.: Prentice-Hall, 1982.

Carter, E. A., and McGoldrick, eds. *The Family Life Cycle: A Framework for Family Therapy.* New York: Gardner, 1980.

Case, R. The underlying mechanism of intellectual development. In *Cognition, Development, and Instruction*, ed. J. R. Kirby and J. B. Biggs. New York: Academic Press, 1980.

Case, R., and Khanna, F. The missing links: stages in children's progression from sensorimotor to logical thought. In *Cognitive Development*, ed. K. W. Fischer. New directions for child development, no. 12. San Francisco: Jossey-Bass, 1981.

Case, R.; Kurland, D. M.; and Goldberg, J. Operational efficiency and the growth of short-term memory span. *Journal of Experimental Child Psychology*, 1982, *33*, 386–404.

Castaneda, A. M.; Gibb, E. G.; and McDermit, S. A. Young children and mathematical problem-solving. *School Science and Math*, 1982, *82*(1), 22–28.

Cataldo, C. Z. Infant-toddler education. *Young Children*, 1984, *39*(2), 25–32.

Cavan, R. S., and Ferdinand, T. N., *Juvenile Delinquency.* 4th ed. New York: Harper & Row, 1981.

Cazden, C. B. *Language in Early Childhood Education.* Rev. ed. Washington, D.C.: National Association for the Education of Young Children, 1981.

Chandler, L. A. *Children Under Stress: Understanding Emotional Adjustment Reactions.* Springfield, Ill.: Charles C. Thomas, 1982.

Chenfeld, M. B. *Creative Activities for Young Children.* New York: Harcourt Brace Jovanovich, 1983.

Chess, S., and Thomas, A. Infant bonding: mystique and reality. *American Journal of Orthopsychiatry*, 1982, *52*(2), 213–222.

Chilman, C. S. Social and psychological research concerning adolescent childbearing: 1970–1980. *Journal of Marriage and the Family*, 1980, *42*, 793–806.

Chomsky, N. *Language and Mind.* New York: Harcourt Brace Jovanovich, 1968.

———. *Rules and Representation.* New York: Columbia University Press, 1980.

Chukovsky, K. *From Two to Five.* Berkeley, Calif.: University of California Press, 1966.

Chumlea, W. C. Physical growth in adolescence. In *Handbook of Developmental Psychology*, ed. B. B. Wolman. Englewood Cliffs, N.J.: Prentice-Hall, 1982.

Clark, A., ed. *Culture and Childrearing.* Philadelphia: F. A. Davis, 1981.

Clark, E. V., and Hecht, B. F. Comprehension, production, and language acquisition. *Annual Review of Psychology*, 1983, *34*, 325–349.

Clark, H. H., and Clark, E. V. *Psychology and Language: An Introduction to Psycholinguistics.* New York: Harcourt, 1977.

Clarke-Stewart, A. *Daycare.* Cambridge: Harvard University Press, 1982.

Clayton, R. R., and Bokemeier, J. L. Premarital sex in the seventies. *Journal of Marriage and the Family*, 1980, *42*, 759–775.

Clemes, H., and Bean, R. *Self-Esteem.* New York: Putnam, 1981.

Click, P. *Administration of Schools for Young Children.* Albany, N.Y.: Delmar, 1980.

Cohen, R.; Schleser, R.; and Meyers, A. Self-instructions: effect of cognitive level and active rehearsal. *Journal of Experimental Child Psychology*, 1981, *32*, 65–76.

Coladarci, A. P., and Coladarci, T. *Elementary Descriptive Statistics: For Those Who Think They Can't.* Belmont, Calif.: Wadsworth, 1980.

Colby, A.; Kohlberg, L.; Gibbs, J.; and Lieberman, M. A longitudinal study of moral judgment. *Monographs of the Society for Research in Child Development*, 1983, *48* (1, serial no. 200).

Coleman, J. C. Friendship and the peer group in adolescence. In *Handbook of Adolescent Psychology*, ed. J. Adelson. New York: Wiley, 1980.

———. *Intimate Relationships, Marriage, and Family.* Indianapolis, Ind.: Bobbs-Merrill, 1984.

Coleman, J. C.; Butcher, J. N.; and Carson, R. C. *Abnormal Psychology and Modern Life.* 7th ed. Glenview, Ill.: Scott, Foresman, 1984.

Collins, R. C. *The Impact of Head Start on Children's Cognitive Development.* Washington, D.C.: Administration for Children, Youth and Families, Office of Human Development Services, May 1982.

Colt, C. H. Suicide in America. *Harvard Magazine.* September/October, 1983.

Commons, M. L., and Richards, F. A. A general model of stage theory. In *Beyond Formal Operations: Late Adolescent and Adult Cognitive Development,* ed. M. L. Commons, F. A. Richards, and S. Armon. New York: Praeger, 1982.

Commons, M. L.; Richards, F. A.; and Armon, C. *Beyond Formal Operations: Late Adolescent and Adult Cognitive Development.* New York: Praeger, 1984.

Commons, M. L.; Richards, F. A.; and Kuhn, D. Systematic and metasystematic reasoning: a case for levels of reasoning beyond Piaget's stage of formal operations. *Child Development,* 1982, *53,* 1058–1069.

Conel, J. L. R. *The postnatal development of the human cerebral cortex.* Vols. 1–8. Cambridge: Harvard University Press, 1939–1967.

Coody, B. *Using Literature with Young Children.* 3rd ed. Dubuque, Iowa: Wm. C. Brown, 1983.

Coody, B., and Nelson, D. *Teaching Elementary Language Arts.* Belmont, Calif.: Wadsworth, 1982.

Corbin, C. B. *A Textbook of Motor Development.* 2nd ed. Dubuque, Iowa: Wm. C. Brown, 1980.

Coren, S.; Porac, C.; and Duncan, P. Lateral preference behaviors in preschool children and young adults. *Child Development,* 1981, *52,* 443–450.

Corrigan, R. The effects of task and practice on search for invisibly displaced objects. *Developmental Review,* 1981, *1,* 1–17.

———. The development of representational skills. In *Levels and Transactions in Children's Development.* New directions for child development, no. 21. San Francisco: Jossey-Bass, 1983.

Corsaro, W. A. Friendships in the nursery school: social organization in a peer environment. In *The Development of Children's Friendships,* ed. S. R. Asher and J. M. Gotlman. New York: Cambridge University Press, 1981.

Cotman, C. W., and McGaugh, J. L. *Behavioral Neuroscience.* New York: Academic Press, 1980.

Courtney, A. E., and Whipple, T. W. *Sex Stereotyping in Advertising.* Lexington, Mass.: D. C. Heath, 1983.

Couturier, L. C.; Mansfield, R. S.; and Gallagher, J. M. Relationships between humor, formal operational ability, and creativity in eighth graders. *Journal of Genetic Psychology,* 1981, *139*(2), 221–226.

Cowen, E. L.; Pederson, A.; Babigan, H.; Izzo, L. D.; and Trost, M. A. Long term follow up of early detected vulnerable children. *Journal of Consulting and Clinical Psychology,* 1973, *41,* 438–446.

Cox, F. D. *Human Intimacy.* St. Paul, Minn.: West, 1984.

Crain, W. C. *Theories of Development: Concepts and Applications.* Englewood Cliffs, N.J.: Prentice-Hall, 1980.

Cramer, P. The development of sexual identity. *Journal of Personality Assessment,* 1980, *44*(6), 601–612.

Cramer, P., and Mechem, M. B. Violence in children's animated television. *Developmental Psychology,* 1982, *3*(1), 23–39.

Crandon, A. J. Maternal anxiety and obstetric complications. *Journal of Psychosomatic Research,* 1979, *23*(12), 109–111.

Cross, H. J., and Kleinhesselink, R. R. Psychological perspectives on drugs and youth. In *Understanding Adolescence,* ed. J. F Adams. 4th ed. Boston: Allyn & Bacon, 1980.

Crowder, N. A. *Introduction to Genetics.* Garden City, N.Y.: Doubleday, 1967.

Cruishank, P. E.; Fitzgerald, D. L.; and Jensen, L. R. *Young Children Learning Mathematics.* Boston: Allyn & Bacon, 1980.

Cullinan, B. E. *Literature and the Child.* New York: Harcourt Brace Jovanovich, 1981.

Curran, D. *Traits of a Healthy Family.* Minneapolis, Minn.: Winston Press, 1983.

Dale, P. *Language Development: Structure and Function.* 2nd ed. New York: Holt Rinehart & Winston, 1976.

―――. Is early pragmatic development measurable? *Journal of Child Language*, 1980, *1*, 1–12.

Damon, W., and Hart, D. The development of self-understanding from infancy through adolescence. *Child Development*, 1982, *53*, 841–864.

Datta, L. We never promise you a rose garden, but one may have grown anyhow. In *As The Twig is Bent: Lasting Effects of Preschool Programs.* Hillsdale, N.J.: Erlbaum, 1983.

Davis, G. A. Care and feeding of creative adolescents. In *Studies in Adolescence*, ed. R. E. Grinder. New York: Macmillan, 1975.

Davis, P. A. *Suicidal Adolescents.* Springfield, Ill.: Charles C. Thomas, 1983.

Davison, G. C., and Neale, J. M. *Abnormal Psychology: An Experimental Approach.* 3rd ed. New York: Wiley, 1982.

Day, B. *Early Childhood Education.* 2nd ed. New York: Macmillan, 1983.

Day, R. H., and McKenzie, B. H. Infant perception of the invariant size of approaching and receding objects. *Developmental Psychology*, 1981, *17*, 670–677.

DeCasper, A. J., and Fifer, W. P. Of human bonding: newborns prefer their mother's voices. *Science*, 1980, *208*, 1174–1176.

Deci, E. L., and Ryan, R. M. The empirical exploration of intrinsic motivational processes. In *Advances in Experimental Social Psychology*, ed. L. Berkowitz. Vol. 13. New York: Academic Press, 1980.

―――. Curiosity and self-directed learning: the role of motivation in education. In *Current Topics in Early Childhood Education*, ed. L. G. Katz. Vol. 4. Norwood, N.J.: Ablex, 1982.

Deese, J. *Psychology as Science and Art.* New York: Harcourt Brace Jovanovich, 1972.

―――. *Thought into Speech: The Psychology of Language.* Englewood Cliffs, N.J.: Prentice-Hall, 1984.

DeFord, D. Young children and their writing. *Theory Into Practice*, 1980, *19*, 157–162.

deMause, L. Our forebears made childhood a nightmare, *Psychology Today*, April 1975, 24–27.

deMause, L., ed. *The History of Childhood.* New York: Harper & Row, 1974.

Demo, D. Sex differences in cognition: a review and critique of the longitudinal evidence. *Adolescence*, 1982, *17*(68), 779–788.

Demorest, A.; Silberstein, L.; and Gardner, H. From understatement to hyperbole: recognizing nonliteral language and its intent. Paper presented at the Society for Research in Child Development. Boston: 1981.

Dennis, W., and Najarian, P. Infant development under environmental handicap. *Psychology Monographs*, 1957, *71*.

Denny, D.; Denny, L.; and Rust, J. D. Preschool children's performance on two measures of emotional expressiveness compared to teacher's ratings. *Journal of Genetic Psychology*, 1982, *140*(1), 149–150.

Desmond, M. M.; Franklin, R. R.; Vallbona, C.; Hilt, R. H.; Plumb, R.; Arnold, H.; and Watts, J. The clinical behavior of the newly born: *Journal of Pediatrics*, 1967, *62*, 307–325.

Desor, J. A.; Maller, O.; and Andrews, K. Ingestive responses of human newborns to salty, sour, and bitter stimuli. *Journal of Comparative and Physiological Psychology*, 1975, *89*, 966–970.

DeSpelder, L. A., and Strickland, A. L. *The Last Dance: Encountering Death and Dying.* Palo Alto, Calif.: Mayfield, 1983.

Deutsch, M.; Deutsch, C. P.; Jordan, T. J.; and Grallo, R. The IDS program: an experiment in early and sustained enrichment. In *As the Twig is Bent: Lasting Effects of Preschool Programs.* Hillsdale, N.J.: Erlbaum, 1983.

Diaz, R. M., and Berndt, T. J. Children's knowledge of a best friend: fact or fancy? *Developmental Psychology*, 1982, *18*(6), 787–794.

Dickson, P. D. *Children's Oral Communication Skills.* New York: Academic Press, 1981.

Dileo, J. H. Graphic activity of young children: development and creativity. In *Art: Basic for Young Children*, ed. L. Lasky and R. Mukerji. Washington, D.C.: National Association for the Education for Young Children, 1980.

―――. *Interpreting Children's Drawings.* New York: Brunner/Mazel, 1983.

Dinkmeyer, D., and McKay, G. *Raising a Responsible Child: Practical Steps to Successful Family Relations.* New York: Simon & Schuster, 1982.

Dinnage, R. Understanding Loss: the Bowlby Canon. *Psychology Today,* May 1980, 56–60.

DiPietro, J. Rough and tumble play: a function of gender. *Developmental Psychology,* 1981, *17,* 50–58.

Dodd, D. H., and White, R. M., Jr., *Cognition: Mental Structures and Processes.* Boston: Allyn & Bacon, 1980.

Dodge, K. A.; Schlundt, D. C.; Schocken, I.; and Delugach, J. D. Social competence and children's sociometric status: the role of peer group entry strategies. *Merrill-Palmer Quarterly,* 1983, *29*(3), 309–336.

Doering, C. H. The endocrine system. In *Constancy and Change in Human Development,* ed. O. G. Brim, Jr. and J. Kagan. Cambridge: Harvard University Press, 1980.

Donaldson, M., and Wales, R. On the acquisition of some relational terms. In *Cognition and the Development of Language,* ed. J. Hayes. New York: Wiley, 1970.

Downs, A. C. Sex-role stereotyping on prime-time television. *Journal of Genetic Psychology,* 1981, *138,* 253–58.

Dreyer, P. H. Sexuality during adolescence. In *Handbook of Developmental Psychology,* ed. B. B. Wolman. Englewood Cliffs, N.J.: Prentice-Hall, 1982.

Dudek, S. Z. Creativity in young children-attitude or ability? *Journal of Creative Behavior,* 1974, *8,* 282–292.

———. Teachers stifle children's creativity: a charge too easily made. *Learning,* 1976, *5*(1), 98–104.

Dunlap, J. L.; Gerall, A. A.; and Carlton, S. F. Evaluation of prenatal androgen and ovarian secretions on receptivity in female and male rats. *Journal of Comparative and Physiological Psychology,* 1978, *92*(2), 280–288.

Dunn, J. Sibling relationships in early childhood. *Child Development,* 1983, *54*(4), 787–811.

Dunn, J., and Kendrick, C. *Siblings: Love, Envy and Understanding.* Cambridge: Harvard University Press, 1982.

Dunphy, D. C. The social structure of urban adolescence peer groups. *Sociometry,* 1963, *26,* 230–246.

Dupold, J., and Young, D. Empirical studies of adolescent sexual behavior: a critical review. *Adolescence,* 1979, *14,* 45–63.

Durkin, D. *Teaching Young Children to Read.* 3rd ed. Boston: Allyn & Bacon, 1980.

Duryea, E. J., and Glover, J. A. A review of the research on reflection and impulsivity in children. *Genetic Psychology Monographs,* 1982, *106*(2), 217–237.

Easterbrooks, M., and Lamb, M. The relationship between quality of infant-mother attachment and infant competence in initial encounters with peers. *Child Development,* 1979, *50,* 380–387.

Edwards, C. P. Moral development in comparative cultural perspective. In *Cultural Perspectives on Child Development,* ed. D. A. Wagner and H. W. Stevenson. San Francisco: W. H. Freeman, 1982.

Egoff, S. Precepts, pleasures, and portants: changing emphases in children's literature. In *Only Connect: Readings in Children's Literature,* ed. S. Egoff, G. T. Stubbs, and L. F. Ashley. New York: Oxford University Press, 1980.

Einstein, E. *The Stepfamily: Living, Loving, and Learning.* New York: Macmillan, 1982.

Eisenberg, N. Social development. In *The Child: Development in a Social Context,* ed. C. B. Kopp and J. B. Krakow. Reading, Mass.: Addison-Wesley, 1982.

Eisenberg, R. B. The organization of auditory behavior. *Journal of Speech and Hearing Research,* 1970, *13,* 461–464.

———. *Auditory Competence in Early Life.* Baltimore: University Park Press, 1975.

Eisenberg, R. B.; Griffin, E. I.; Coursin, D. B.; and Hunter, M. A. Auditory behavior in the neonate. *Journal of Speech Hearing Research,* 1964, *7,* 245–269.

Eisner, E. W. *Cognition and the Curriculum.* New York: Longman, 1982.

Elder, G. H. Parental power legitimization and its effects upon the adolescent. *Sociometry,* 1963, *26,* 50–65.

————. Democratic parent-youth relations in cross-national perspective. *Social Science Quarterly*, 1968, *49*, 216–228.

Elias, P. Beginning teacher induction programs. Paper presented at the American Educational Research Association, Boston, April 7–11, 1980.

Elkind, D. Egocentricism in adolescence. *Child Development*, 1967, *38*, 1025–1034.

————. *A Sympathetic Understanding of the Child: Six to Sixteen.* Boston: Allyn & Bacon, 1971.

————. *A Sympathetic Understanding of the Child: Birth to Sixteen.* 2nd ed. Boston: Allyn & Bacon, 1978.

————. Strategic interactions in early adolescence. In *Handbook of Adolescent Psychology*, ed. J. Adelson. New York: John Wiley, 1980.

————. *The Hurried Child: Growing Up Too Fast, Too Soon.* Reading, Mass.: Addison-Wesley, 1981(a).

————. *Children and Adolescents: Interpretive Essays on Jean Piaget.* 3rd ed. New York: Oxford University Press, 1981(b).

Elkind, D., and Bowen, R. Imaginary audience behavior in children and adolescents. *Developmental Psychology*, 1979, *15*, 38–44.

Elkind, D.; Koegler, R.; and Go, E. Studies in perceptual development: II. Part-whole perception. *Child Development*, 1964, *35*, 81–90.

Emde, R. N., and Harmon, R. J., eds. *The Development of Attachment and Affiliative Systems.* New York: Plenum, 1981.

Endres, J. B., and Rockwell, R. E. *Food, Nutrition, and the Young Child.* St. Louis: C. V. Mosby, 1980.

Endsley, R. C., and Bradbard, M. R. *Quality Day Care, A Handbook of Choices for Parents and Caregivers.* Englewood Cliffs, N.J.: Prentice-Hall, 1981.

Engel, R. Understanding the handicapped through literature. *Young Children*, 1980, *35*(3), 27–32.

Engen, T.; Lipsett, L. P.; and Peck, M. B. Ability of infants to discriminate sapid substances. *Developmental Psychology*, 1974, *10*, 741–744.

Enright, R. D.; Shukla, D. G.; and Lapsley, D. K. Adolescent egocentrism-sociocentrism and self-consciousness. *Journal of Youth and Adolescence*, 1980, *9*, 101–116.

Erikson, E. H. *Childhood and Society.* 2nd ed. New York: Norton, 1963.

————. *Identity: Youth and Crisis.* New York: Norton, 1968.

————. *Toys and Reason.* New York: Norton, 1977.

————. *Identity and the Life Cycle.* New York: Norton, 1980.

Eron, L. D. Prescription for reduction of aggression. *American Psychologist*, 1980, *35*, 244–252.

————. Parent-child interaction, televised violence, and aggression of children. *American Psychologist*, 1982, *37*, 197–211.

Eron, L. D.; Huesmann, L. R.; Brice, P.; Fischer, P.; and Mermelstein, P. Age trends in the development of aggression, sex-typing, and related television habits. *Developmental Psychology*, 1983, *19*, 71–77.

Escalona, S., and Heider, G. M. *Prediction and Outcome.* New York: Basic Books, 1959.

Estes, W. K. An experimental study of punishment. *Psychology Monographs*, 1944, *47*, 127–148.

Etaugh, C. Effects of nonmaternal care on children: research evidence and popular reviews. *American Psychologist*, 1980, *35*, 309–319.

Evoy, J. J. *The Rejected: Psychological Consequences of Parental Rejection.* University Park, Pa.: Pennsylvania State University Press, 1982.

Faber, A., and Mazlish, E. *How to Talk So Kids Will Listen and Listen So Kids Will Talk.* New York: Avon, 1980.

Fagot, B. I., and Kronsberg, S. J. Sex differences: biological and social factors influencing the behavior of young boys and girls. In *The Young Child: Reviews of Research*, ed. S. G. Moore and S. G. Cooper. Vol. 3. Washington, D.C.: National Association for the Education of Young Children, 1982.

Feagans, L., and Farran, D. C., eds. *The Language of Children Reared in Poverty: Implications for Evaluation and Intervention.* Papers from a conference, Chapel Hill, N.C., May, 1980. New York: Academic Press, 1982.

Federal Bureau of Investigation. Uniform crime reports for the United States. *Statistical Abstract of the United States.* Washington, D.C. Gov't Printing Office, 1980.

Fein, G. Pretend play: An integrative review. *Child Development,* 1981, *52,* 1095–1118.

———. Pretend play: new perspectives. In *Curriculum Planning for Young Children,* ed. J. F. Brown. Washington, D.C.: National Association for the Education of Young Children, 1982.

Fein, R. Research on fathering. In *The Family Transition,* ed. A. Skolnick and J. Skolnick. Boston: Little, Brown, 1980.

Feldman, D. H. *Beyond Universals in Cognitive Development.* Norwood, N.J.: Ablex, 1980.

———. *Developmental Approaches to Giftedness and Creativity.* San Francisco: Josey-Bass, 1982.

Feldstein, J. H., and Feldstein, S. Sex differences on televised toy commercials. *Sex Roles,* 1982, *8,* 581–593.

Fernald, A., and Simon, T. Expanded intonation contours in mothers' speech to newborns. *Developmental Psychology,* 1984, *20,* 104–113.

Ferriera, A. J. The pregnant woman's emotional attitude and its reflection on the newborn. *American Journal of Orthopsychiatry,* 1969, *30,* 553–561.

Feshbach, S., and Singer, R. D. *Television and Aggression.* San Francisco: Jossey-Bass, 1971.

Field, T.; DeStefano, L.; and Koewler, J. H. Fantasy play of toddlers and preschoolers. *Developmental Psychology,* 1982, *18,* 503–508.

Field, T. M.; Sostek, A. M.; Vietze, P.; and Leiderman, P.H., eds. *Culture and Early Interactions.* Hillsdale, N.J., 1981.

Fine, G. A. Friends, impression management, and pre-adolescent behavior. In *The Development of Children's Friendships,* ed. S. R. Asher and J. M. Gottman. New York: Cambridge University Press, 1981.

Finkelstein, N. W. Aggression: is it stimulated by day care? *Young Children,* 1982, *37*(6), 3–9.

Finkelstein, N. W., and Haskins, R. Kindergarten children prefer same-color peers. *Child Development,* 1983, *54*(2), 502–508.

Finley, K., and Finley, M. Nurturing your child's imagination. *Marriage and Family Living,* 1982, *64*(10), 18–21.

Fisher, C.; Berlinger, D.; Filby, N.; Mariave, R.; Cahen, D.; and Dishaw, M. Teaching behaviors, academic learning time, and student achievement: an overview. In *National Institute of Education,* ed. C. Denham and A. Lieberman. Washington, D.C., 1980.

Fisher, K. W. Illuminating the processes of moral development. *Monographs of the Society for Research in Child Development,* 1983, *48* (1–2, serial no. 200), 97–107.

Fisher, K. W., and Jennings, S. The emergence of representation in search: understanding the hider as an independent agent. *Quarterly Review of Development,* 1981, *1,* 18–30.

Fisher, W. A. Adolescent contraception: summary and recommendations. In *Adolescents, Sex, and Contraception,* ed. D. Byrne and W. A. Fisher. Hillsdale, N.J.: Erlbaum, 1983.

Fitzpatrick, E.; Eastman, N. J.; and Reeder, S. R. *Maternity Nursing.* 11th ed. Philadelphia: J. B. Lippincott, 1966.

Flavell, J. Cognitive monitoring. In *Children's Oral Communication Skills,* ed. W. P. Dickson. New York: Academic Press, 1981.

Flavell, J., and Ross, L., eds. *Social Cognitive Development.* New York: Cambridge University Press, 1981.

Flexer, B. K., and Roberge, J. J. I.Q., field dependence-independence, and the development of formal operational thought. *Journal of General Psychology,* 1980(a), *103,* 191–201.

———. Control of variables and propositional reasoning in early adolescence. *Journal of General Psychology,* 1980(b), *103,* 3–12.

Folb, E. A. *Runnin' Down Some Lines: The Language and Culture of Black Teenagers.* Cambridge: Harvard University Press, 1980.

Foreman, G. E., and Hill, F. *Constructive Play.* Monterey, Calif.: Brooks/Cole, 1980.

Formanek, R., and Gurian, A. *Why?: Children's Questions.* Boston: Houghton Mifflin, 1980.

Fowler, W. *Infant and Child Care: A Guide to Education in Group Settings.* Boston: Allyn & Bacon, 1980.

Francks, O. R. Scribbles? Yes, they are art! In *Curriculum Planning for Young Children*, ed. J. F. Brown. Washington, D.C.: National Association for the Education of Young Children, 1982.

Freeman, E. B. The Ann Arbor decision: the importance of teacher's attitudes toward language. *The Elementary School Journal*, 1982, *83*, 41–47.

Freeman, N. H. *Strategies of Representation in Young Children*. London: Academic Press, 1980.

French, P., and McClure, M. Teacher's questions, pupil's answers: an investigation of questions and answers in the infant classroom. *First Language*, 1981, *2*, 31–47.

Fried, P. A., and Oxorn, H. *Smoking for Two: Cigarettes and Pregnancy*. New York: Free Press, 1980.

Fu, V., and Leach, D. J. Sex-role preferences among elementary school children in rural America. *Psychological Reports*, 1980, *46*, 555–560.

Fuchs, F. Genetic amniocentesis. *Scientific American*, 1980, *242*(6), 47–53.

Fucigna, C.; Ives, K. C.; and Ives, W. Art for toddlers: a developmental approach. *Young Children*, 1982, *37*(3), 45–51.

Furman, E. Helping children cope with death. In *Curriculum Planning for Young Children*, ed. J. F. Brown. Washington, D.C.: National Association for the Education of Young Children, 1982.

Furman, W. Children's friendships. In *Review of Human Development*, ed. T. M. Field, A. Huston, H. C. Quay, L. Troll, and G. E. Finley. New York: John Wiley, 1982.

Furman, W., and Bierman, K. L. Developmental changes in young children's conceptions of friendship. *Child Development*, 1983, *54*(3), 549–556.

Furstenberg, F. K., and Nord, C. W. The life course *Journal of Family Issues*, 1980, *1*(4).

Furstenberg, F. F., and Nord, C. W. The life course of children of divorce: marital disruption and parental contact. *Family Planning Perspectives*, 1982, *14*, 211–212.

Furth, H. *Piaget and Knowledge: Theoretical Foundations*. Chicago: University of Chicago Press, 1981.

Gaines, R. Children's artistic abilities: fact or fancy? *Journal of Genetic Psychology*, 1983, *143*(1), 57–68.

Gaitskell, C. D. *Children and Their Art*. 4th ed. New York: Harcourt Brace Jovanovich, 1982.

Gallagher, J., and Reid, D. *The Learning Theory of Piaget and Inhelder*. Monterey, Calif.: Brooks/Cole, 1981.

Gallahue, D. L. *Developmental Movement Experiences for Children*. New York: John Wiley, 1982(a).

———. *Understanding Motor Development in Children*. New York: John Wiley, 1982(b).

Gallup, G. *Gallup Poll*. Princeton, N.J.: George Gallup Enterprises, Inc., 1981.

Garcia, E. E. Bilingualism in early childhood. *Young Children*, 1980, *35*(4), 52–66.

Gardner, H. *Artful Scribbles*. New York: Basic Books, 1980(a).

———. Children's art: the age of creativity. *Psychology Today*, 1980(b), *13*(12), 84–89.

Garn, S. M. Continuities and change in maturational timing. In *Constancy and Change In Human Development*, ed. O. G. Brim, Jr. and J. Kagan. Cambridge: Harvard University Press, 1981.

Geen, R. G. Behavioral and physiological reactions to observed violence: effects of prior exposure to aggressive stimuli. *Journal of Personality and Social Psychology*, 1981, *40*, 868–875.

Gelles, R. J. Violence in the family: a review of research in the seventies. *Journal of Marriage and the Family*, 1980, *42*, 873–885.

Gersoni, D. Sexism in children's books. In *Children and Books*, ed. Z. Sutherland and M. H. Arbuthnot. 5th ed. Glenview, Ill.: Scott, Foresman, 1977.

Gettys, L, D., and Cann, A. Children's perceptions of occupation sex stereotypes. *Sex Roles*, 1981, *7*, 301–308.

Getzels, J. W. Problem finding and inventiveness of solutions. *Journal of Creative Behavior*, 1975, *9*, 12–18.

Gibson, E., and Walk, R. D. The visual cliff. *Scientific American*, 1960, *202*, 64–71.

Giffin, M., and Felsenthal, C. *A Cry for Help*. New York: Doubleday, 1983.

Gilligan, C. *In a Different Voice.* Cambridge: Harvard University Press, 1982.

Gilstrap, R., ed. *Toward Self-Discipline: A Guide for Parents and Educators.* Washington, D.C.: Association for Childhood Education International, 1981.

Ginsburg, H. P. *Children's Arithmetic: How They Learn It and How You Teach It.* Austin, Tex.: PRO-ED, 1982.

Glassberg, S. The development of the beginning teacher. Paper presented at the American Educational Research Association, Boston, April 7–11, 1980.

Glazer, J. I. *Literature for Young Children.* Columbus, Ohio: Charles E. Merrill, 1981.

Glazer, S. M. *Getting Ready to Read: Creating Readers from Birth Through Six.* Englewood Cliffs, N.J.: Prentice-Hall, 1980.

Gleitman, L. R. Maturational determinants of language growth. *Cognition*, 1981, *10*, 103–114.

Glick, P. C. Marriage experiences of family life specialists. *Family Relations*, 1980(a), *29*(1), 111–118.

———. Remarriage: some recent changes and variations. *Journal of Family Issues*, 1980(b), *1*, 455–478.

Gold, M., and Petronio, R. J. Delinquent behavior in adolescence. In *Handbook of Adolescent Psychology*, ed. J. Adelson. New York: John Wiley, 1980.

Goldberg, S. Parent-infant bonding: another look. *Child Development*, 1983, *54*, 1355–1382.

Goldfarb, W. Infant rearing and problem behavior. *American Journal of Orthopsychiatry*, 1943, *13*, 249, 265.

Goldstein, E. B. *Sensation and Perception.* Belmont, Calif.: Wadsworth, 1980.

Gordon, T. *P.E.T. in Action.* New York: Bantam Books, 1978.

Gottesman, I. I. Personality and natural selection. In *Methods and Goals in Human Behavior Genetics*, ed. S. G. Vandenberg. New York: Academic Press, 1965.

Gottfried, A. E. Intrinsic motivation in young children. *Young Children*, 1983, *39*(1), 64–73.

Gottlieb, G. The psychobiological approach to developmental issues. In *Handbook of Child Psychology*, ed. P. H. Mussen. 4th ed. Vol. 2, *Infancy and Developmental Psychobiology.* New York: John Wiley, 1983.

Gottlieb, S. Modeling effects upon fantasy. In *The Child's World of Make-Believe*, ed. J. L. Singer. New York: Academic Press, 1973.

Gottman, J. M. How children become friends. *Monographs of the Society for Research in Child Development*, 1983, *48* (3, serial no. 201).

Gotwald, W. H., and Golden, G. H. *Sexuality: The Human Experience.* New York: Macmillan, 1981.

Greenberg, D. J., and Blue, S. Z. The visual-preference technique in infancy: effect of number of stimuli presented upon experimental outcome. *Child Development*, 1977, *48*(1), 131–137.

Greenfield, P. M., and Tronick, E. *Infant Curriculum.* Santa Monica, Calif.: Goodyear, 1980.

Grieve, R., and Dow, L. Bases of young children's judgment about more. *Journal of Experimental Child Psychology*, 1981, *32*(1), 36–37.

Griffing, P. Encouraging dramatic play in early childhood. In *Curriculum Planning for Young Children*, ed. J. F. Brown. Washington, D.C.: National Association for the Education of Young Children, 1982.

Groos, K. *The Play of Animals.* New York: Appleton, 1898.

Gross, R. T., and Duke, P. M. The effect of early vs. late maturation on adolescent behavior. *Pediatric Clinics of North America*, 1980, *27*, 71–77.

Grossman, A. Working mothers and their children. *Monthly Labor Review*, 1981, *104*(5), 49–54.

———. More than half of all children have working mothers. *Monthly Labor Review*, 1982, *105*(2), 41–43.

Grueling, J. W., and DeBlassie, R. R. Adolescent suicide. *Adolescence*, 1980, *15*, 589–601.

Grusec, J. E. Socialization processes in the development of altruism. In *Altruism and Helping Behavior*, ed. J. P. Rushton and R. M. Sorrentino. Hillsdale, N.J.: Erlbaum, 1981.

Grusec, J. E., and Arnason, L. Consideration for others: approaches to enhancing altruism. In *The Young Child: Reviews of Research*, ed. S. G. Moore and R. C. Cooper. Vol. 3. Washington, D.C.: National Association for the Education of Young Children, 1982.

Guilford, J. P. Creativity. *American Psychologist*, 1950, *5*, 444–454.

———. Three faces of intellect. *American Psychologist*, 1959, *14*, 469–479.

Gunderson, M. P., and McCary, J. L. Effects of sex education on sex information and sexual guilt, attitudes, and behaviors. *Family Relations*, 1980, *29*, 375–379.

Haaf, R. A. Visual response to complex facelike patterns by 15 and 20 week old infants. *Developmental Psychology*, 1977, *13*, 77–78.

Haber, R. N. Eidetic images. *Scientific American*, April 1969, 36–44.

Haber, R. N., and Haber, R. B. Eidectic imagery: I. Frequency. *Perceptual and Motor Skills*, 1964, *19*, 131–138.

Hale, J. Black children: their roots, culture, and learning styles. *Young Children*, 1981, *36*(2), 37–50.

Hall, G. S. *Adolescence: Its Psychology, and Its Relation to Physiology, Anthropology, Sociology, Sex, Crime, Religion and Education.* 2 vols. New York: Arno, 1970.

Halmi, K. A. Psychosomatic illness review: anorexia nervosa and bulimia. *Psychosomatics*, 1983, *24*, 111–132.

Hamid, P. N., and Wyllie, A. J. What generation gap? *Adolescence*, 1980, *15*, 385–391.

Hamilton, R. *The Herpes Book.* Boston: Houghton Mifflin, 1980.

Hansen, S. L., and Hicks, M. W. Sex role attitudes and perceived dating-mating choices of youth. *Adolescence*, 1980, *15*, 83–90.

Hardyck, C., and Petrinovich, L. F. Lefthandedness. *Psychological Bulletin*, 1977, *84*, 385–404.

Hardyck, C.; Petrinovich, L. F.; and Goldman, R. D. Lefthandedness and cognitive deficit. *Cortex*, 1976, *12*(3), 266–279.

Harlap, S., and Shiono, P. Alcohol, smoking, and incidence of spontaneous abortions in first and second trimester. *The Lancet*, July 26, 1980, 173–176.

Harlow, H. The nature of love. *American Psychologist*, 1958, *13*, 637–685.

———. The heterosexual affectional system in monkeys. *American Psychologist*, 1962, *16*, 1–9.

———. *Learning to Love.* San Francisco: Albion, 1971.

Harlow, H., and Zimmerman, R. R. Affectual responses in the infant monkey. *Science*, 1959, *130*, 421–432.

Harman, G., ed. *On Noam Chomsky: Critical Essays.* 2nd ed. Amherst, Mass.: University of Massachusetts Press, 1982.

Harner, L. Immediacy and certainty: factors in understanding future reference. *Journal of Child Language*, 1982, *9*(1), 115–124.

Harrell, R. F.; Woodyard, E.; and Gates, A. I. *The Effects of Mother's Diet on the Intelligence of the Offspring.* New York: Teachers College, 1955.

Harris, H. Development of moral attitudes in white and negro boys. *Developmental Psychology*, 1970, *2*, 376–383.

Harris, M. B., and Satter, B. J. Sex-role stereotypes of kindergarten children. *Journal of Genetic Psychology*, 1981, *138*(1), 49–61.

Harris, P. L.; Olthof, T.; Terwogt, M.; and Terwogt, M. M. Children's knowledge of emotion. *Journal of Child Psychology and Psychiatry and Allied Disciplines*, 1981, *22*(3), 247–261.

Harter, S. The perceived competence scale for children. *Child Development*, 1982, *53*, 87–97.

———. Developmental perspectives on the self-system. In *Handbook of Child Psychology*, ed. P. H. Mussen. 4th ed. Vol. 4, *Socialization, Personality, and Social Development.* New York: John Wiley, 1983.

Hartup, W. W. Peer interaction and social organization. In *Carmichael's Manual of Child Psychology*, ed. P. H. Mussen. Vol. 2. New York: John Wiley, 1970(a).

———. Peer relations. In *Perspectives in Child Psychology*, ed. T. D. Spencer and N. Kass. New York: McGraw-Hill, 1970(b).

———. Peer relations and family relations: two social worlds. In *Scientific Foundations of Developmental Psychiatry*, ed. M. Rutter. London: Heinemann Medical Books, 1980.

———. Peer relations. In *Handbook of Child Psychology*, ed. P. H. Mussen. 4th ed. Vol. 4, *Socialization, Personality, and Social Development.* New York: John Wiley, 1983.

Haskell, M. R., and Yablonsky, L. *Juvenile Delinquency.* 3rd ed. Boston: Houghton Mifflin, 1982.

Haswell, K. L.; Hock, E.; and Wenar, C. Techniques for dealing with oppositional behavior in preschool children. *Young Children*, 1982, *37*(3), 13–17.

Hawkins, R. Adolescent alcohol abuse: a review. *Journal of Developmental and Behavioral Pediatrics*, 1982, *3*(2), 83–87.

Hawkins, R.; Fremouw, W.; and Clement, P. *The Binge-Purge Syndrome.* New York: Springer, 1983.

Hayes, J. R. *The Complete Problem Solver.* Philadelphia: Franklin Institute, 1981.

Heater, S. H. *Teaching Preschool Reading.* Provo, Utah: Brigham Young University Press, 1980.

Helson, R. Childhood interest clusters related to creativity in women. *Journal of Consulting Psychology*, 1965, *29*, 353–361.

Hendren, R. L. Depression in anorexia nervosa. *Journal of the American Academy of Child Psychiatry*, 1983, *22*, 59–62.

Hendricks, G., and Hendricks, K. *The Moving Center: Exploring Movement Activities for the Classroom.* Englewood Cliffs, N.J.: Prentice-Hall, 1983.

Herbert, M.; Sluckin, W.; and Sluckin, A. Mother-to-infant bonding. *Journal of Child Psychology and Psychiatry and Allied Disciplines*, 1982, *23*(3), 205–221.

Hess, D. J., and Grant, G. W. Prime-time television and gender role behavior. *Teaching Sociology*, 1983, *10*(3), 371–388.

Hess, R. D., and Shipman, V. C. Early experiences and the socialization of cognitive modes in children. In *Exploring Early Childhood*, ed. M. Kaplan-Sanoff and R. Yablaus-Magid. New York: Macmillan, 1982.

Hetherington, E. M. Tracing children through the changing family. *APA Monitor*, 1981, *12*(5), 4–5.

Hicks, R. E., and Kinsbourne, M. Human handedness: a partial cross-fostering study. *Science*, 1976, *192*, 908–910.

Higgins, E. T.; Herman, C. P.; and Zanna, M. P., eds. *Social Cognition: The Ontario Symposium.* Hillsdale, N.J.: Erlbaum, 1981.

Higham, E. Variations in adolescent psychohormonal development. In *Handbook of Adolescent Psychology*, ed. J. Adelson. New York: John Wiley, 1980.

Hildebrand, V., and Hines, R. P. The pied pipers of poetry. *Young Children*, 1981, *36*(2), 12–17.

Hilliard, A. G., and Vaughn-Scott, M. The quest for the "minority" child. In *The Young Child: Reviews of Research*, ed. S. G. Moore and C. R. Cooper. Vol. 3. Washington, D.C.: National Association for the Education of Young Children, 1982.

Hindelang, M. J. Variations in sex-race-age-specific incidence rates of offending. *American Sociological Review*, 1981, *46*, 461–474.

Hindley, C. B.; Filliozat, A. M.; Klakenberg, G.; Nocolet-Meister, D.; and Sand, E. A. Differences in age of walking in five European longitudinal samples. *Human Biology*, 1966, *38*, 364–379.

Hirschman, C., and Butler, M. Trends and differentials in breast feeding: an update. *Demography*, 1981 *18*, 39–54.

Hobson, R. P. The question of egocentrism: The young child's competence in the coordination of perspectives. *Journal of Child Psychology and Psychiatry*, 1980, *21*, 325–331.

Hoff-Ginsberg, E., and Shatz, M. Linguistic input and the child's acquisition of language. *Psychological Bulletin*, 1982, *92*, 3–26.

Hoffman, M. L. Moral development in adolescence. In *Handbook of Adolescent Psychology*, ed. J. Adelson. New York: John Wiley, 1980.

Hogan, R. The gifted adolescent. In *Handbook of Adolescent Psychology*, ed. J. Adelson. New York: John Wiley, 1980.

Hojat, M. Loneliness as a function of parent-child and peer relations. *Journal of Psychology*, 1982, *112*, 129–133.

Holmberg, M. C. The development of social interchange patterns from 12 to 42 months. *Child Development*, 1980, *51*, 448–456.

Holt, K. S. Diets and development. *Child Care, Health and Development.* 1982, *8*(4), 183–201.

Holzman, M. *The Language of Children: Development in the Home and School.* Englewood Cliffs, N.J.: Prentice-Hall, 1983.

Hom, H. L., Jr., and Hom, S. L. Research and the child: the use of modeling, reinforcement/incentives, and punishment. In *Aspects of Early Childhood Education: Theory to Research to Practice,* ed. D. G. Range, J. R. Layton, and D. L. Roubinek. New York: Academic Press, 1980.

Honig, A. What are the needs of infants? *Young Children,* 1981, *37*(1), 3–10.

–––––. Research in review: prosocial development in children. *Young Children,* 1982(a), *37*(5), 51–62.

–––––. Language environments for young children. *Young Children,* 1982(b), *38*(1), 56–67.

–––––. Research in review: television and young children. *Young Children,* 1983(a), *38*(4), 63–76.

–––––. Research in review: sex role socialization in early childhood. *Young Children,* 1983(b), *38*(6), 57–70.

Honig, A., and Laly, R. *Infant Caregiving: A Design for Training.* 2nd ed. New York: Syracuse University Press, 1981.

Hopkins, L. B. Reading without words. *Day Care and Early Education,* 1973, *1*(2), 5–7.

Householder, J.; Hatcher, R. P.; Burns, W. J.; and Chasnott, I. Infants born to narcotic-addicted mothers. *Psychological Bulletin,* 1982, *92*(2), 453–468.

Houston, J. P. *Fundamentals of Learning and Motivation.* 2nd ed. New York: Academic Press, 1981.

Howard, D. V. *Cognitive Psychology: Memory, Language, and Thought.* New York: Macmillan, 1983.

Howard, J. A., and Barnett, M. A. Arousal of empathy and subsequent generosity in young children. *Journal of Genetic Psychology,* 1981, *138*(2), 307–308.

Howes, C. Patterns of friendship. *Child Development,* 1983, *54*, 1041–1053.

Hubert, H. B.; Fabsitz, R. R.; Feinleib, M.; and Brown, K. S. Olfactory sensitivity in humans: genetic versus environmental control. *Science,* 1980, *208*, 607–609.

Huck, C. S. *Children's Literature in the Elementary School.* 3rd ed. New York: Holt, Rinehart & Winston, 1976.

Hudson, L. M.; Guthrie, K. H.; and Santilli, N. R. The use of linguistic and nonlinguistic strategies in kindergartner's interpretations of "more" and "less". *Journal of Child Language,* 1982, *9*(1), 125–138.

Huesmann, L. R.; Eron, L. D.; Klein, R.; Brice, P.; and Fischer, P. Mitigating the imitation of aggressive behaviors by changing children's attitudes about media violence. *Journal of Personality and Social Psychology,* 1983, *44*, 889–910.

Hunt, D., and Sullivan, E. *Between Psychology and Education.* Hinsdale, Ill.: Dryden Press, 1974.

Hunter, F., and Youniss, J. Changes in functions of three relations during adolescence. *Developmental Psychology,* 1982, *18*(6), 806–811.

Hyde, J. S. *Understanding Human Sexuality.* 2nd ed. New York: McGraw-Hill, 1982.

Ilg, F. L.; Ames, L. B.; and Baker, S. M. *Child Behavior: Specific Advice on Problems of Child Behavior.* Rev. ed. New York: Harper & Row, 1981.

Illingworth, R. S. *The Development of the Infant and Young Child.* 2nd ed. Edinburgh and London: Livingstone, 1966.

Inazu, J. K., and Fox, G. L. Maternal influence on the sexual behavior of teenage daughters. *Journal of Family Issues,* March 1980, 81–102.

Inhelder, B., and Piaget, J. *The Growth of Logical Thinking from Childhood to Adolescence.* London: Routledge & Kegan Paul, 1958.

Irwin, D. M., and Bushnell, M. M. *Observational Strategies for Child Study.* New York: Holt, Rinehart & Winston, 1980.

Ives, W. Preschool children's ability to coordinate spatial perspectives through language and pictures. *Child Development,* 1980, *51*(4), 1303–1306.

Ives, W.; Wolf, D.; Furigna, G.; and Smith, N. The earliest two-dimensional symbols: properties, media, and strategies. Paper presented at the American Psychological Association, Los Angeles: September 1981.

Izard, C. E. The young infant's ability to produce discrete emotional expressions. *Developmental Psychology*, 1980, *16*, 132–140.

Izard, C. E., ed. *Measuring Emotions in Infants and Children.* Cambridge: Cambridge University Press, 1982.

Jackson, N. E.; Robinson, H. B.; and Dale, P. S. *Cognitive Development in Young Children.* Monterey, Calif.: Brooks/Cole, 1977.

Jacobson, D. S. Stepfamilies. *Children Today*, 1980, *9*, 2–6.

Jacobson, W. J., and Bergman, A. B. *Science for Children: A Book for Teachers.* Englewood Cliffs, N.J.: Prentice-Hall, 1980.

Jalongo, M. R. Using crisis-oriented books with young children. *Young Children*, 1983, *38*(5), 29–36.

Jarvie, G. J.; Lahey, B. B.; Graziano, W.; and Framer, E. Childhood obesity and social stigma: what we know and what we don't know. *Developmental Review*, 1983, *3*(3), 237–273.

Jeffree, D., and Skeffington, M. *Reading Is For Everyone.* Englewood Cliffs, N.J.: Prentice-Hall, 1984.

Jenkins, P. D. *Art for the Fun of it: A Guide for Teaching Young Children.* Englewood Cliffs, N.J.: Prentice-Hall, 1980.

Johnson, B. Single parent families. *Family Economics Review*, Summer-Fall 1980, 22–27.

Johnson, C. J.; Pick, H. L., Jr.; Siegel, G. M.; Cicciarelli, A. W.; and Garber, S. R. Effects of interpersonal distance on children's vocal intensity. *Child Development*, 1981, *52*, 721–723.

Johnson, H. C. Working with stepfamilies: principles of practice. *Social Work*, 1980, *25*, 304–308.

Johnson, R., and Carter, M. M. Flight of the young: why children run away from their homes. *Adolescence*, 1980, *15*, 483–489.

Johnston, L. D.; Bachman, J. G.; and O'Malley, P. M. *Highlights from Student Drug Use in American 1975–1981.* Rockville, Md.: National Institute on Drug Abuse, Division of Research, 1981.

Jones, S. *Good Things for Babies.* 2nd ed. Boston: Houghton Mifflin, 1980.

Jorgensen, S. R.; King, S. C.; and Torrey, B. A. Dyadic and social network influences on adolescent exposure to pregnancy risk. *Journal of Marriage and the Family*, 1980, *42*, 141–155.

Josselson, R. Ego development in adolescence. In *Handbook of Adolescent Psychology*, ed. J. Adelson. New York: John Wiley, 1980.

Julien, R. M. *A Primer of Drug Action.* 3rd ed. San Francisco: W. H. Freeman, 1981.

Jung, C. *Man and His Symbols.* New York: Doubleday, 1964.

Kagan, J. Impulsive and reflective children: significance of conceptual tempo. In *Learning and the Educational Process*, ed. J. Krumboltz. Chicago: Rand McNally, 1965.

———. Reflection-impulsivity: the generality and dynamics of conceptual tempo. *Journal of Abnormal Psychology*, 1966, *71*, 17–24.

———. *Change and Continuity in Infancy.* New York: John Wiley, 1971(a).

———. *Understanding Children, Behavior Motives and Thought.* New York: Harcourt, 1971(b).

———. *The Second Year: The Emergence of Self-Awareness.* Cambridge: Harvard University Press, 1981.

Kagan, J., and Kogan, N. Individual variations in cognitive processes. In *Carmichael's Manual of Child Psychology*, ed. P. H. Mussen. New York: John Wiley, 1970.

Kagan, J., and Lang, C. *Psychology and Education: An Introduction.* New York: Harcourt, 1978.

Kagan, J., and Madsen, M. C. Cooperation and competition of Mexican, Mexican-American, and Anglo-American children of two ages under four instructional sets. *Developmental Psychology*, 1971, *5*, 32–39.

Kagan, J.; Rosman, B.; Day, D.; Albert, J.; and Phillips, W. Information processing in the child. *Psychology Monographs*, 1964, *78*(1, Whole No. 578).

Kail, R. *The Development of Memory in Children.* 2nd ed. New York: W. H. Freeman, 1984.

Kail, R., and Hagen, J. W. Memory in childhood. In *Handbook of Developmental Psychology*, ed. B. B. Wolman. Englewood Cliffs, N.J.: Prentice-Hall, 1982.

Kamii, C. Application of Piaget's theory to education: the preoperational level. In *New Directions in Piagetian Theory and Practice*, ed. I. E. Siegel, D. M. Brodzinsky, and R. M. Golinkoff. Hillsdale, N.J.: Erlbaum, 1981(a).

————. Piaget, children and number. In *Exploring Early Childhood: Readings in Theory and Practice*, ed. M. Kaplan-Sanott and R. Yablans-Magid. New York: Macmillan, 1981(b).

————. *Number in Preschool and Kindergarten.* Washington, D.C.: National Association for the Education of Young Children, 1982.

Kandel, D. B. *Peer Influence In Adolescence.* Paper presented at the Society for Research in Child Development, Boston, April 1980.

Kantner, J. F., and Zelnik, M. Sexual and contraceptive experience of young unmarried women, 1979. *Family Planning Perspectives*, 1980, *16*, 17–24.

Kaplan, B. J. Malnutrition and mental deficiency. *Psychological Bulletin*, 1972, *70*, 321–334.

Kaplan-Sanoff, M. Motor Development: a broader context. In *Exploring Early Childhood: Readings in Theory and Practice*, ed. M. Kaplan-Sanoff and R. Yablans-Magid. New York: Macmillan, 1981.

Kastenbaum, R. J. *Death, Society, and Human Experience.* 2nd ed. St. Louis: C. V. Mosby, 1981.

Katchadourian, H. *The Biology of Adolescence.* San Francisco: W. H. Freeman, 1977.

Kaufman, E. Marital problems caused by marijuana use. *Medical Aspects of Human Sexuality*, 1982, *16*(12), 17–81.

Kay, D., and Anglin, J. M. Overextension and underextension in the child's expressive and receptive speech. *Journal of Child Language*, 1982, *9*(1), 83–98.

Kaye, C. Genetic counseling. *Medical Aspects of Human Sexuality*, 1981, *15*(3), 164–180.

Kaye, K. Why we don't talk "baby talk" to babies. *Journal of Child Language*, 1980, *7*, 489–507.

Kaye, K., and Fogel, A. The temporal structure of face-to-face communication between mothers and infants. *Developmental Psychology*, 1980, *16*(5), 454–464.

Keating, D. P. Thinking processes in adolescence. In *Handbook of Adolescent Psychology*, ed. J. Adelson. New York: John Wiley, 1980.

Keating, D. P., and Clark, L. V. Development of physical and social reasoning in adolescence. *Developmental Psychology*, 1980, *16*, 23–30.

Kelley, K. Adolescent sexuality: the first lessons. In *Adolescents, Sex, and Contraception*, ed. O. Byrne and W. A. Fisher. New York: McGraw-Hill, 1983.

Kelley, M. R. *A Parent's Guide to Television: Making the Most of It.* New York: John Wiley, 1983.

Kellogg, R. Understanding children's art. In *Readings in Educational Psychology Today*, ed. J. P. DeCecco. Del Mar, Calif.: CRM Books, 1970.

Kelly, C., and Goodwin, G. C. Adolescents' perception of three styles of parental control. *Adolescence*, 1983, *18*(71), 567–571.

Kendrick, C., and Dunn, J. Caring for a second baby: effects on interaction between mother and firstborn. *Developmental Psychology*, 1980, *16*, 303–311.

Keniston, K. Student activism, moral development and morality. *American Journal of Orthopsychiatry*, 1970, *40*, 580.

Kessen, W. *The Child.* New York: John Wiley, 1965.

————. Sucking and looking: two organized congenital patterns of behavior in the newborn. In *Early Behavior*, ed. H. W. Stevenson, E. H. Hess, and H. L. Rheingold. New York: John Wiley, 1967, 147–179.

————. Our disconnected child. *Harpers Magazine*, 1978, *35*, 16–24.

Kessner, D. M. *Infant Death: An Analysis by Maternal Risk and Health Care.* Washington, D.C.: National Academy of Sciences, 1973.

Kett, J. *Rites of Passage: Adolescence in America, 1790 to the Present.* New York: Basic Books, 1977.

Kidwell, J. S. Number of siblings, sibling spacing, sex, and birth order: their effects on perceived parent-adolescent relationships. *Journal of Marriage and Family*, May 1981, 330–335.

Kilbride, J. E.; Robbins, M. C.; and Kilbride, P. L. The comparative motor development of Baganda, American white and American black infants. *American Anthropologist,* 1970, 72, 1422–1428.

Kinard, E. M. Emotional development in physically abused children. *American Journal of Orthopsychiatry,* 1980, *50,* 686–696.

Kinsey, A. C.; Pomeroy, W. B.; and Martin, C. E. *Sexual Behavior in the Human Male.* Philadelphia: Saunders, 1948.

Kinsey, A. C.; Pomeroy, W. B.; Martin, C. E.; and Gebhard, P. H. *Sexual Behavior in the Human Female.* Philadelphia: Saunders, 1953.

Klatzky, R. L. *Human Memory.* 2nd ed. New York: W. H. Freeman, 1980.

Klaus, M. H., and Kennell, J. H. *Maternal Infant Bonding.* St. Louis: C. V. Mosby, 1976.

Kleiber, D. A., and Barnett, L. A. Leisure in childhood. *Young Children,* 1980, *35*(5), 47–53.

Klepsch, M., and Logic, L. *Children Draw and Tell: An Introduction to the Projective Uses of Children's Human Figure Drawings.* New York: Brunner/Mazel, 1982.

Kline, J. Drinking during pregnancy and spontaneous abortion. *The Lancet,* July 26, 1980, 176–180.

Knowles, D. W., and Reeves, N. *But Won't Granny Need Her Socks? Dealing Effectively with Children's Concerns About Death and Dying.* Dubuque, Iowa: Kendall/Hunt, 1983.

Knox, D., and Wilson, K. Dating behaviors of university students. *Family Relations,* April 1981, 255–258.

Kogan, N. Stylistic variation in childhood and adolescence: creativity, metaphor, and cognitive style. In *Handbook of Child Psychology,* ed. P. H. Mussen. Vol. 3, *Cognitive Development.* New York: John Wiley, 1983.

Kohlberg, L. *Stages in the Development of Moral Thought and Action.* New York: Holt, Rinehart & Winston, 1969.

———. Moral stages and moralization. In *Moral Development and Behavior,* ed. T. Lickona. New York: Holt, Rinehart & Winston, 1976.

———. *Philosophy of Moral Development.* New York: Harper & Row, 1981(a).

———. Moral education in the schools: a developmental view. In *Exploring Early Childhood: Readings in Theory and Practice,* ed. M. Kaplan-Sanoff and R. Yablans-Magid. New York: Macmillan, 1981(b).

Kohlberg, L., and Turiel, E. Continuities in childhood and adult moral development revisited. In *Life Span Developmental Psychology: Personality and Socialization,* ed. P. B. Baltes and K. W. Schaie. New York: Academic Press, 1973.

Kompara, D. R. Difficulties in the socialization process of stepparenting. *Family Relations,* 1980, 29, 69–73.

Konopka, G. Adolescent suicide. *Exceptional Children,* 1983, *49*(5), 390–394.

Koop, E. Teenagers and alcohol. *Public Health Reports,* 1983, *98*(1), 1.

Krannich, R. S. Abortion in the United States: past, present, and future trends. *Family Relations,* 1980, 29, 365–374.

Krebs, D., and Gillmore, J. The relationship among the first stages of cognitive development, role-taking abilities, and moral development. *Child Development,* 1982, *53,* 877–886.

Kress, G. *Learning to Write.* Boston: Routledge & Kegan Paul, 1982.

Kübler-Ross, E. *On Children and Death.* New York: Macmillan, 1983.

Kuczan, B. *Childhood Stress: Don't Let Your Child Be A Victim.* New York: Delacorte, 1982.

Kuhn, D. The role of self-directed activity in cognitive development. In *New Directions in Piagetian Theory and Practice,* ed. I. E. Siegel, D. M. Brodzinsky, and R. M. Golinkoff. Hillsdale, N.J.: Erlbaum, 1981.

Kupfersmid, J. H., and Wonderly, D. M. Moral maturity and behavior: failure to find a link. *Journal of Youth and Adolescence,* 1980, 9, 249–262.

Kurdek, L. A. An integrative perspective on children's divorce adjustment. *American Psychologist,* 1981, *36,* 856–866.

Labinowicz, E. *The Piaget Primer: Thinking, Learning, Teaching.* Menlo Park, Calif.: Addison-Wesley, 1980.

Labov, W. The logic of nonstandard English. In *20th Annual Round Table*, ed. J. E. Alatis. Washington, D.C.: Georgetown University Press, 1970.

———. *Language in the Inner City: Studies in the Black English Vernacular.* Philadelphia: University of Pennsylvania Press, 1973.

Labov, W., and Cohen, P. *Systematic Relations of Standard and Non-Standard Rules in the Grammars of Negro Speakers.* Project Literacy, Report No. 8. Ithaca, N.Y.: Cornell University Press, 1967.

Ladd, G. W. Effectiveness of a social learning model for enhancing children's social interaction and peer acceptance. *Child Development*, 1981, *52*, 171–178.

Lakin, M. Personality factors in mothers of excessively crying (colicky) infants. *Monographs of the Society for Research in Child Development*, 1957, *22*(whole no. 64).

Lamb, M. E., ed. *The Role of the Father in Child Development.* 2nd ed. New York: John Wiley, 1981.

———. Maternal attachment and mother-neonate bonding: a critical review. In *Advances in Developmental Psychology*, ed. M. E. Lamb and A. L. Brown. Vol. 2. Hillsdale, N.J.: Erlbaum, 1982(a).

———. Paternal influences on early socio-emotional development. *Journal of Child Psychology and Psychiatry and Allied Disciplines*, 1982(b), *23*(2), 185–190.

———. The Changing Role of the Father. Paper presented at the Greater New York Area Fatherhood Forum. Bank Street College of Education. June 17, 1983.

Lamb, M. E.; Easterbrooks, M. A.; and Holden, G. W. Reinforcement and punishment among preschoolers: characteristics, effects, and correlates. *Child Development*, 1980, *51*, 1230–1236.

Lamb, M. E.; Garn, S.; and Keating, M. T. Correlations between sociability and motor performance scores in 8-month-olds. *Infant Behavior and Development*, 1982, *5*(1), 97–101.

Lamb, M. E., and Hwang, C. P. Maternal attachment and mother-neonate bonding: a critical review. In *Advances in Developmental Psychology*, ed. M. E. Lamb and A. L. Brown. Vol. 2. Hillsdale, N.J.: Erlbaum, 1982.

Lamb, M. E., and Sherrod, L. R., eds. *Infant Social Cognition: Empirical and Theoretical Considerations.* Hillsdale, N.J.: Erlbaum, 1981.

Lamb, M. E., and Sutton-Smith, B. *Sibling Relationships: Their Nature and Significance Across the Lifespan.* Hillsdale, N.J.: Erlbaum, 1982.

Lambert, W. E. *Faces and Facets of Bilingualism.* Washington, D.C.: Center for Applied Linguistics, 1981.

Lamer, M. R., and Housker, S. L. Sexual permissiveness in younger and older adults. *Journal of Family Issues*, 1980, *1*, 103–124.

Landreth, C. *Preschool Learning and Teaching.* New York: Harper & Row, 1972.

Langer, J. *Theories of Development.* New York: Holt, Rinehart & Winston, 1969.

Langlois, J. H., and Down, A. C. Mothers, fathers, and peers as socialization agents of sex-typed play behaviors in young children. *Child Development*, 1980, *51*, 1217–1247.

LaRossa, R., and LaRossa, M. M. *Transition to Parenthood: How Infants Change Families.* Beverly Hills, Calif.: Sage, 1981.

Larson, L. E. The influence of parents and peers during adolescence: the situation hypothesis. In *Adolescent Behavior and Society*, ed. R. E. Muuss. 3rd ed. New York: Random House, 1980.

Lasky, L., and Mukerji, R. *Art: Basic For Young Children.* Washington, D.C.: National Association for the Education of Young Children, 1980.

Lasky, R. The effect of visual feedback of the hand on the reaching and retrieval behavior of young infants. *Child Development*, 1977, *48*, 112–117.

Lasky, R., and Klein, R. E. Fixation of the standard and novelty preference in six-month-old well and malnourished infants. *Merrill-Palmer Quarterly*, 1980, *26*, 171–178.

Lazar, I., and Darlington, R. B. Lasting effects of early education: a report from the Consortium for Longitudinal Studies. *Monographs of the Society for Research in Child Development,* 1982, *47*(2–3), 1–151.

Leach, P. *Babyhood.* 2nd ed. New York: Knopf, 1983.

Leadbeater, B. J., and Dionne, J. P. The adolescent's use of formal operational thinking in resolving problems related to identity resolution. *Adolescence,* 1981, *16*(61), 111–121.

Leavitt, F. *Drugs and Behavior.* 2nd ed. New York: John Wiley, 1982.

Leboyer, F. *Birth without Violence.* New York: Knopf, 1975.

LeMasters, E. E., and DeFrain, J. *Parents in Contemporary America.* 4th ed. Homewood, Ill.: Dorsey Press, 1983.

Lenneberg, E. H. Understanding language without the ability to speak. *Journal of Abnormal and Social Psychology,* 1962, *65,* 419–425.

————. *Biological Foundations of Language.* New York: John Wiley, 1967.

Lepper, M. R. Extrinsic reward and intrinsic motivation: implications for the classroom. In *Teacher and Student Perceptions: Implications for Learning,* ed. J. M. Levine and M. C. Wand. Hillsdale, N.J.: Erlbaum, 1983.

Lerner, R. M. *Concepts and Theories of Human Development.* Reading, Mass.: Addison-Wesley, 1976.

Lesser, G. S. Stop picking on Big Bird. *Psychology Today,* March 1979, 57–60.

Lester, B. M.; Kotelchuk, M.; Spelke, E.; Sellers, M. J.; and Klein, R. E. Separation protests in Guatemalan infants: cross-cultural and cognitive findings. *Developmental Psychology,* 1974, *10,* 79–85.

Levenkron, S. *Treating and Overcoming Anorexia Nervosa.* New York: Scribner's, 1982.

Leventhal, A. S., and Lipsitt, L. P. Adaptation, pitch discrimination and sound localization in the neonate. *Child Development,* 1964, *35,* 759–767.

Levin, D. Microcomputers: out of the toychest and into the classroom. In *Microcomputers in the Schools,* ed. J. L. Thomas. Phoenix, Ariz.: Oryx Press, 1981.

Levine, E. M. Middle class family decline. *Society,* 1981, *18,* 72–78.

Levine, S., and Carey, S. Up front: the acquisition of a concept and a word. *Journal of Child Language,* 1982, *9*(3), 645–657.

Lewin, K. *A Handbook of Child Psychology.* Worcester, Mass.: Clark University Press, 1933.

Lewis, M., and Coates, D. L. Mother-infant interaction and cognitive development in twelve-week-old infants. *Infant Behavior and Development,* 1980, *3,* 95–105.

Lewis, M., and Michaelson, L. *Children's Emotions and Moods: Developmental Theory and Measurement.* New York: Plenum, 1983.

Lickona, T. Research on Piaget's theory of moral development. In *Moral Development and Behavior,* ed. T. Lickona. New York: Holt, Rinehart & Winston, 1976.

Liebert, R. M.; Sprafkin, J. N.; and Davidson, E. S. *The Early Window: Effects of Television on Children and Youth.* 2nd ed. New York: Pergamon Press, 1982.

Lindberg, L., and Swedlow, R. *Early Childhood Education: A Guide for Observation and Participation.* 2nd ed. Boston: Allyn & Bacon, 1980.

Linderman, E. W., and Herberholz, D. W. *Developing Artistic and Perceptual Awareness: Art Practice in the Elementary Classroom.* 4th ed. Dubuque, Iowa: Wm. C. Brown, 1979.

Ling, D. Acoustic stimulus duration in relation to behavioral responses of newborn infants. *Journal of Speech Hearing Research,* 1972, *15,* 567–571.

Lipsitt, L. P. Taste, smell, and other pleasures of sensation. In *Neonatal Neurological Assessment and Outcome,* ed. A. W. Brann and J. J. Volpe. Report of the 77th Ross Conference on Pediatric Research. Columbus, Ohio: Ross Laboratories, 1980.

Lipsitt, L. P., ed. *Advances in Infancy Research.* Vol. 1. Norwood, N.J.: Ablex, 1981.

Lipsitt, L. P., and Levy, N. Electrotactual threshold in the neonate. *Child Development,* 1959, *30,* 547–552.

Livson, N., and Peskin, H. Perspectives on adolescence from longitudinal research. In *Handbook of Adolescent Psychology,* ed. J. Adelson. New York: John Wiley, 1980.

Loevinger, J. *Ego Development: Conceptions and Theories.* San Francisco: Jossey-Bass, 1976.

Logan, F. A. *Fundamentals of Learning and Motivation.* Dubuque, Iowa: Wm. C. Brown, 1970.

Logsdon, T. *How To Cope With Computers.* Hasbrouck Heights, N.J.: Hayden, 1982.

Londerville, S., and Main, M. Security of attachment, compliance, and maternal training methods in the second year of life. *Developmental Psychology,* 1981, *17,* 289–299.

Lonetto, R. *Children's Conceptions of Death.* New York: Springer, 1980.

Longstreth, L. E. Human handedness: more evidence for genetic involvement. *Journal of Genetic Psychology,* 1980, *137,* 275–283.

Lorenz, K. *King Solomon's Ring.* New York: Crowell, 1952.

Lounsbury, M. L., and Bates, J. E. The cries of infants of differing levels of perceived temperamental difficulties: acoustic properties and effects on listener. *Child Development,* 1982, *53,* 677–686.

Lowenfeld, V., and Brittain, W. L. *Creative and Mental Growth.* 7th ed. New York: Macmillan, 1982.

Maccoby, E. E. *Social Development.* New York: Harcourt Brace Jovanovich, 1980.

Maccoby, E. E., and Feldman, S. Mother-attachment and stranger-reactions in the third year of life. *Monographs of the Society for Research in Child Development,* 1972, *37*(1, Serial No. 146).

Maccoby, E. E., and Jacklin, C. N. *The Psychology of Sex Differences.* Stanford, Calif.: Stanford University Press, 1974.

———. Sex differences in aggression: a rejoinder and reprise. *Child Development,* 1980, *51,* 964–980.

MacKinnon, D. W. The nature and nurture of creative talent. *American Psychologist,* 1962, *17,* 484–495.

MacNeilage, P. F., ed. *The Production of Speech.* New York: Springer-Verlag, 1983.

Madsen, M. C. Developmental and cross-cultural differences in the cooperative and competitive behavior of young children. *Journal of Cross-Cultural Psychology,* 1971, *2,* 365–371.

Magarrell, J. Notes on computers. *The Chronicle of Higher Education,* 1982, *25*(8), 3.

Magg, P. B., and Ornstein, M. R. *Come With Us to the Playgroup: A Handbook for Parents and Teachers of Young Children.* Englewood Cliffs, N.J.: Prentice-Hall, 1981.

Mahoney, E. R. *Human Sexuality.* New York: McGraw-Hill, 1983.

Maier, H. W. *Three Theories of Child Development.* 3rd ed. New York: Harper & Row, 1978.

Malina, R. M. Motor development in the early years. In *The Young Child: Reviews of Research,* ed. S. G. Moore and C. R. Cooper. Vol. 3. Washington, D.C.: National Association for the Education of Young Children, 1982.

Maloney, M. J., and Klykylo, W. M. An overview of anorexia nervosa, bulimia, and obesity in children and adolescents. *Journal of the American Academy of Child Psychiatry,* 1983, *22,* 99–107.

Mansfield, R. S., and Busse, T. J. *The Psychology of Creativity and Discovery.* Chicago: Nelson-Hall, 1981.

Marano, H. E. Biology is one key to the bonding of mothers and babies. *Smithsonian,* February 1981, 60–69.

Marcia, J. E. Identity in adolescence. In *Handbook of Adolescent Psychology,* ed. J. A. Adelson. New York: John Wiley, 1980.

Marion, M. *Guidance of Young Children.* St. Louis: C. V. Mosby, 1981.

Markham, L. R. Assisting speakers of Black English as they begin to write. *Young Children,* 1984, *39*(4), 15–24.

Martin, G. B., and Clark, R. D. Distress crying in neonates: species and peer specificity. *Developmental Psychology,* 1982, *18,* 3–9.

Martin, J. A.; Maccoby, E. E.; and Jacklin, C. N. Mother's responsiveness to interactive bidding and nonbidding in boys and girls. *Child Development,* 1981, *52,* 1064–1067.

Martin, M. J., and Walters, J. Familiar correlates of selected types of child abuse and neglect. *Journal of Marriage and the Family,* 1982, *44,* 267–276.

Martindale, C. *Cognition and Consciousness.* Homewood, Ill.: Dorsey, 1981.

Maslow, A. H. *Toward a Psychology of Being.* 2nd ed. Princeton, N.J.: Van Nostrand, 1968.

———. *Motivation and Personality.* 2nd ed. New York: Harper & Row, 1970.

Masnick, G., and Bane, M. J. *The Nation's Families: 1960–1990.* Cambridge: Joint Center for Urban Studies of M.I.T. and Harvard University, 1980.

Masters, W. H.; Johnson, V. E.; and Kolodny, R. C. *Human Sexuality.* Boston: Little, Brown, 1982.

Masur, E. F. Mother's responses to infant's object-related gestures: influences on lexical development. *Journal of Child Language,* 1982, *9*(1), 23–30.

Matlin, M. *Human Experimental Psychology.* Monterey, Calif.: Brooks/Cole, 1980.

———. *Cognition.* New York: Holt, Rinehart & Winston, 1983.

Maurer, D. M., and Maurer, C. E. Newborn babies see better than you think. *Psychology Today,* October 1976, *10,* 85–88.

May, L. The focus of math: problem-solving. *Early Years,* 1982, *13*(2), 50–53.

McCabe, A. E.; Siegel, L.; Spence, I.; and Wilkinson, A. Class inclusion reasoning: patterns of performance from three to eight years. *Child Development,* 1982, *53*(3), 780–785.

McCauley, C.; Woods, K.; Coolidge, C.; and Kulick, W. More aggressive cartoons are funnier. *Journal of Personality and Social Psychology,* 1983, *44,* 817–823.

McClearn, G. E., and De Fries, J. C. *Introduction to Behavioral Genetics.* San Francisco: W. H. Freeman and Co., 1973.

McCoy, E. Childhood through the ages. In *Marriage and Family 83/84,* ed. O. Pocs and R. H. Walsh. Guilford, Conn.: Dushkin, 1983.

McCune-Nicolich, L. Toward symbolic functioning: structure of early pretend games and potential parallels with language. *Child Development,* 1981, *52*(3), 785–797.

McDonald, D. T., and Ramsey, J. H. Awakening the artist: music for young children. In *Curriculum Planning For Young Children,* ed. J. F. Brown. Washington, D.C.: National Association for the Education of Young Children, 1982.

McGhee, P. E. Development of the sense of humour in childhood: a longitudinal study. In *Children's Humour,* ed. P. E. McGhee and A. J. Chapman. New York: John Wiley, 1980.

McGhee, P. E., and Goldstein, J. H., eds. *Handbook of Humor Research, Vol. 1: Basic Issues.* New York: Springer-Verlag, 1983(a).

———. *Handbook of Humor Research, Vol. 2: Applied Studies.* New York: Springer-Verlag, 1983(b).

McGinnis, E., and Goldstein, A. P. *Skillstreaming the Elementary School Child: A Guide for Teaching Prosocial Skills.* Champaign, Ill.: Research Press, 1984.

McGuire, K. D., and Weisz, J. R. Social cognition and behavior correlates of preadolescent chumship. *Child Development,* 1982, *53*(6), 1478–1484.

McGurk, H.; Turnura, C.; and Creighton, S. J. Auditory-visual coordination in neonates. *Child Development,* 1977, *48*(1), 138–143.

McLaughlin, B.; White, D.; McDevitt, T.; and Raskin, R. Mother's and father's speech to their young children: similar or different? *Journal of Child Language,* 1983, *10*(1), 245–252.

McLoyd, V. C. Class, culture, and pretend play: a reply to Sutton-Smith and Smith. *Developmental Review,* 1983, *3*(1), 11–17.

McNamee, A. S. *Children and Stress: Helping Children Cope.* Washington, D.C.: Association for Childhood Education International, 1982.

McNeill, D. The development of language. In *Carmichael's Manual of Child Psychology,* ed. P. H. Mussen. 3rd ed. Vol. 1. New York: John Wiley, 1970.

McShane, J. *Learning to Talk.* Cambridge: Cambridge University Press, 1980.

McWilliams, P. A. *The Personal Computer Book.* 2nd ed. Los Angeles: Prelude Press, 1982.

Meredith, H. V. Relation between tobacco smoking of pregnant women and body size of their progeny: a compilation and synthesis of published studies. *Human Biology*, 1975, *47*, 451–472.

Michel, G. Right-handed: a consequence of infant supine head orientation preference? *Science*, 1981, *212*, 685–687.

Milavsky, J. R.; Kessler, R. C.; Stipp, H. H.; and Rubens, W. S. *Television and Aggression: A Panel Study.* New York: Academic Press, 1982.

Miller, B. C., and Sollie, D. Normal stresses during the transition to parenthood. *Family Relations*, 1980, *29*(4), 459–465.

Miller, G. A. *Language and Speech.* San Francisco: W. H. Freeman, 1981.

Miller, I. The micros are coming. In *Microcomputers in the Schools*, ed. J. L. Thomas. Phoenix, Ariz.: Oryx Press, 1981.

Miller, J. B. Psychological recovery in low-income single parents. *American Journal of Orthopsychiatry*, 1982, *52*(2), 346–352.

Miller, M. S. *Childstress! Understanding and Answering Stress Signals in Infants, Children and Teenagers.* Garden City, N.Y.: Doubleday, 1982.

Miller, N. E., and Dollard, J. *Social Learning and Imitation*, New Haven, Conn.: Yale University Press, 1941.

Miller, P. H. *Theories of Developmental Psychology.* San Francisco: W. H. Freeman, 1983.

Miller, P. H., and Weiss, M. G. Children's attention location, understanding attention, and performance on the incidental learning task. *Child Development*, 1981(a), *52*, 1183–1190.

———. Children's and adult's knowledge about what variables affect selective attention. *Child Development*, 1981(b), *53*, 543–549.

Miller, P. H., and Zalenski, R. Preschoolers' knowledge about attention. *Developmental Psychology*, 1982, *18*(6), 871–875.

Miller, S. A., and Brownell, C. A. Peers and persuasion: dyadic interaction between conservers and nonconservers. *Child Development*, 1975, *46*, 992–997.

Mischel, W., and Mischel, H. N. *Essentials of Psychology.* New York: Random House, 1977.

Mitchell, G. *A Very Practical Guide to Discipline with Young Children.* Mt. Ranier, Md.: Gryphon House, 1982.

Moerk, E. L. A behavioral analysis of controversial topics in first language acquisition: reinforcements, corrections, modeling, input frequencies, and the three-term contingency pattern. *Journal of Psycholinguistic Research*, 1983, *12*, 129–156.

Molfese, D.; Freeman, R. B., Jr.; and Palermo, D. S. The ontogeny of brain lateralization for speech and nonspeech stimuli. *Brain and Language*, 1975, *2*, 356–368.

Montgomery, T. A., and Leashore, B. R. Teenage parenthood. *Urban Research Review*, 1982, *8*(3), 1–13.

Moody, K. *Growing up on Television.* New York: Times Books, 1980.

Moore, K. L. *The Developing Human.* 3rd ed. Philadelphia: Saunders, 1981.

Moore, S. G. Prosocial behavior in the early years: parent and peer influences. In *Handbook of Research in Early Childhood Education*, ed. B. Spodek. New York: The Free Press, 1982.

Morell, P., and Norton, W. T. Myelin. *Scientific American*, 1980, *242*(5), 88–119.

Morris, N. M., and Udry, J. R. Validation of a self-administered instrument to assess stages of adolescent development. *Journal of Youth and Adolescence*, 1980, *9*, 271–280.

Morrison, E. S.; Starks, K.; Hyndman, C.; and Ronzio, N. *Growing Up Sexual.* New York: Van Nostrand, 1980.

Morrison, G. S. *Early Childhood Education Today.* 3rd ed. Columbus, Ohio: Charles E. Merrill, 1984.

Morton, J. P., and Acker, L. E. Television provoked aggression: effects of gentle, affection-like training prior to exposure. *Child Study Journal*, 1981, *12*, 27–43.

Moskowitz, B. A. The acquisition of language. *Scientific American*, 1978, *239*(5), 92–108.

Motulsky, A. G. Medical and human genetics 1977: trends and directions. *American Journal of Human Genetics*, 1978, *30*(2), 123–131.

Muller, R., and Goldberg, S. Why William doesn't want a doll: preschooler's expectations of adult behavior toward boys and girls. *Merrill-Palmer Quarterly*, 1980, *26*, 259–269.

Murphy, C. *Teaching Kids to Play.* New York: Leisure Press, 1983.

Murray, J. P. *Television and Youth: 25 Years of Research and Controversy.* Boys Town, Neb.: Boys Town Center for the Study of Youth Development, 1980.

Murstein, B. I. Mate selection in the 1970s. *Journal of Marriage and the Family,* 1980, *42*(4), 777–792.

Muuss, R. E. Social cognition: David Elkind's theory of adolescent egocentrism. *Adolescence,* 1982, *17*(66), 249–265.

Nadesan, A. Mother Goose: sexist? *Elementary English,* 1974, *51*(3), 375–378.

Naeye, R. L. Relationship of cigarette smoking to congenital anomalies and perinatal death. *American Journal of Pathology,* 1978, *90,* 289–293.

Nannarone, N. Career father. *Marriage and Family Living,* 1983, *65,* 8–11.

Nass, G. D., and McDonald, G. W. *Marriage and the Family.* 2nd ed. Reading, Mass.: Addison-Wesley, 1983.

National Academy of the Sciences. *Marijuana and Health.* Washington, D.C., 1982.

National Center for Health Statistics. Report. *Marriage and Divorce Today,* 1981, *7,* 3–4.
———. *Health, United States, 1982.* Washington, D.C.: Public Health Service, 1982.

National Commission on Youth. *The Transition of Youth to Adulthood: A Bridge Too Long.* Boulder, Col.: Westview Press, 1980.

National Institute of Health. *Cesarean childbirth.* Consensus Development Conference Summary, Vol. 3, no. 6. Washington, D.C.: U.S. Government Printing Office, 1981.

National Institute of Mental Health. *Television and Behavior: Ten Years of Scientific Progress and Implications for the Eighties.* Washington, D.C.: U.S. Government Printing Office, 1982.

National Institute on Drug Abuse. Special report on cocaine, March 9, 1981. Lang, J. S. Cocaine spreads its deadly net. *U.S. News and World Report,* March 22, 1982, 27–29.

Natriello, G., and Dornbusch, M. Providing direction and building commitment: a study of teacher standards and warmth. Paper presented at the American Education Research Association, Boston, April 7–11, 1980.

Nelson, K. Individual differences in language development: implications for development and language. *Developmental Psychology,* 1981, *17,* 170–187.

Nelson, K., ed. *Children's Language.* Vol. 4. Hillsdale, N.J.: Erlbaum, 1983.

Nelson, L. L., and Kagan, S. Competition: the star-spangled scramble. *Psychology Today,* 1972, *6,* 53–56, 90–91.

Nelson, N. M.; Enkin, M. W.; Saigal, S.; Bennett, K. J.; Milner, R.; and Sackett, D. L. A randomized clinical trial of the Leboyer approach to childbirth. *New England Journal of Medicine,* 1980, *302,* 655–660.

Neuman, P. A., and Halvorson, P. A. *Anorexia Nervosa and Bulimia: A Handbook for Counselors and Therapists.* New York: Van Nostrand Rheinhold, 1983.

Neuringer, C., and Lettieri, D. J. *Suicidal Women: Their Thinking and Feeling Patterns.* New York: Gardner Press, 1982.

Newcomb, A. F., and Brady, J. E. Mutuality in boys' friendship relations. *Child Development,* 1982, *53,* 392–395.

NIAID Study Group. *Sexually Transmitted Diseases: 1980 States Report.* NIH Publications No. 81-2213. Washington, D.C.: U.S. Government Printing Office, 1981.

Nicolich, L. M. Toward symbolic functioning: structure of early pretend games and potential parallels with language. *Child Development,* 1981, *52,* 785–797.

Nilles, J. M. *Exploring the World of the Personal Computer.* Englewood Cliffs, N.J.: Prentice-Hall, 1982.

Nimnicht, G.; McAfee, O.; and Meier, J. *The New Nursery School.* New York: General Learning Corporation, 1969.

Noble, E. *Having Twins: A Parent's Guide to Pregnancy, Birth and Early Childhood.* Boston: Houghton Mifflin, 1980.

Norman, D. A. *Learning and Memory.* New York: W. H. Freeman, 1982.

Norton, D. *Through The Eyes of a Child: An Introduction to Children's Literature.* Columbus, Ohio: Charles E. Merrill, 1983.

Nowlis, G. H., and Kessen, W. Human newborns differentiate differing concentrations of sucrose and glucose. *Science,* 1976, *191,* 865–866.

Nye, I. F. *Runaways: A Report for Parents.* Extension Bulletin No. 0743. Pullman: Washington State University, 1980.

Nye, I. F., and Lamberts, M. B. *School-Age Parenthood.* Pullman: Washington State University Cooperative Extension, 1980.

Olsho, L. Auditory frequency discrimination in infancy. *Developmental Psychology,* 1982, *18*(5), 721–726.

Orlick, T. D. Positive socialization via cooperative games. *Developmental Psychology,* 1981, *17*(4), 426–429.

Orthner, D. *Intimate Relationships.* Reading, Mass.: Addison-Wesley, 1981.

Osborn, D. K. *Early Childhood Education in Historical Perspective.* Athens, Ga.: Educational Associates, 1980.

Oskamp, S., and Mindick, B. Personality and attitudinal barriers to contraception. In *Adolescents, Sex, and Contraception,* ed. D. Byrne and W. A. Fisher. New York: McGraw-Hill, 1981.

Page, R. A. Longitudinal evidence for the sequentiality of Kohlberg's stages of moral judgment in adolescent males. *Journal of Genetic Psychology,* 1981, *139*(1), 3–9.

Papert, S. *Mindstorms.* New York: Basic Books, 1980.

Parikh, B. Development of moral judgment and its relation to family environmental factors in Indian and American families. *Child Development,* 1980, *51,* 1030–1039.

Paris, S. G., and Lindauer, B. K. The development of cognitive skills during childhood. In *Handbook of Developmental Psychology,* ed. B. Wolman. Englewood Cliffs, N.J.: Prentice-Hall, 1982.

Parke, R. D. *Fathers.* Cambridge: Harvard University Press, 1981.

Parke, R. D., and Slaby, R. G. The development of aggression. In *Handbook of Child Psychology,* ed. P. H. Mussen. 4th ed. Vol. 4, *Socialization, Personality, and Social Development.* New York: John Wiley, 1983.

Parr, S. R. *The Moral of the Story: Literature, Values and American Education.* New York: Columbia Teacher's College Press, 1982.

Parten, M. L. Social participation among preschool children. *Journal of Abnormal and Social Psychology,* 1932, *27,* 243–269.

Passman, R. H., and Halonen, J. S. A developmental survey of young children's attachment to inanimate objects. *Journal of Genetic Psychology,* 1979, *134,* 165–178.

Patterson, C. J., and Kister, M. C. The development of listener skills for referential communication. In *Children's Oral Communication Skills,* ed. W. P. Dickson. New York: Academic Press, 1981.

Payton, I. Single-parent households: an alternative approach. *Family Economics Review,* Winter 1982, 11–16.

Pederson, F. A., ed. *The Father-Infant Relationship: Observational Studies in the Family Setting.* New York: Praeger, 1980.

Peel, E. A. *The Pupil's Thinking.* London: Oldbourne Press, 1960.

Perry, D. G., and Bussey, K. *Social Development.* Englewood Cliffs, N.J.: Prentice-Hall, 1984.

Peters, A. M. *The Units of Language Acquisition.* New York: Cambridge University Press, 1982.

Peters, D. L.; Hodges, W. L.; and Nolan, M. E. Statewide evaluation of child care: problems and benefits. *Young Children,* 1980, *35*(3), 3–14.

Petersen, A., and Taylor, B. The biological approach to adolescence: biological change and psychological adaptation. In *Handbook of Adolescent Psychology,* ed. J. Adelson. New York: John Wiley, 1980.

Peterson, L. Influence of age, task competence, and responsibility focus on children's altruism. *Developmental Psychology,* 1983, *19,* 141–148.

Petrosko, J. M. Measuring creativity in elementary school: the current state of the art. *Journal of Creative Behavior,* 1978, *12*(2), 109–119.

Peyser, H. Stress and alcohol. In *Handbook of Stress: Theoretical and Clinical Aspects,* ed. L. Goldberger and S. Breznitz. New York: Free Press, 1982.

Pfouts, J. Birth order, age spacing, I.Q. differences, and family relations. *Journal of Marriage and Family,* August 1980, 519–525.

Piaget, J. *The Moral Judgment of the Child,* trans. M. Gabain. New York: Harcourt, 1932.

———. *Play, Dreams and Imitation in Children.* New York: Norton, 1951.

———. *The Origins of Intelligence in Children.* New York: Norton, 1952.

———. *The Psychology of Intelligence.* Paterson, N.J.: Littlefield, Adams, 1963.

———. Development and learning. In *Piaget Rediscovered,* ed. R. E. Ripple and V. N. Rockcastle. Ithaca, N.Y.: Cornell University Press, 1964.

———. *Six Psychological Studies.* New York: Vintage Books, 1967.

———. *Psychology of the Child.* New York: Basic Books, 1969.

Piaget, J., and Inhelder, B. *The Child's Conception of Space.* London: Routledge, 1956.

Pierce, L. H., and Pierce, R. L. The use of warmth, empathy, and genuineness in child care work. *Child Care Quarterly,* 1982, *11*(4), 257–266.

Piers, M. W., and Landau, G. M. *The Gift of Play: And Why Young Children Can't Live Without It.* New York: Walker, 1980.

Pierson, E. C., and D'Antonio, W. V. *Female and Male. Dimensions of Human Sexuality.* Philadelphia: Lippincott, 1974.

Pinard, A. *The Concept of Conservation.* Chicago: University of Chicago Press, 1981.

Pines, M. Invisible playmates. *Psychology Today,* 1978, *12*(4), 38–42.

Pipes, P. L. *Nutrition in Infancy and Childhood.* St. Louis: C. V. Mosby, 1981.

Pitcher, E. G., and Schultz, L. H. *Boys and Girls at Play: The Development of Sex Roles.* New York: Praeger, 1983.

Pittman, T. S.; Boggiano, A. K.; and Rubble, D. N. Intrinsic and extrinsic motivational orientations: limiting conditions on the undermining and enhancing effects of reward on intrinsic motivation. In *Teacher and Student Perceptions: Implications for Learning,* ed. J. M. Levine and M. C. Wang. Hillsdale, N.J.: Erlbaum, 1983.

Platt, C. B., and MacWhinney, B. Error assimilation as a mechanism in language learning. *Journal of Child Language,* 1983, *10,* 401–414.

Plomin, R., and Foch, T. T. Sex differences and individual differences. *Child Development,* 1981, *52,* 383–385.

Plumb, J. H. The great change in children. *Horizon,* Winter 1971, *13,* 4–13.

Plutchik, R. A general psychoevolutionary theory of emotion. In *Emotion: Theory, Research, and Experience,* ed. R. Plutchik and H. Kellerman. Vol. 1. New York: Academic Press, 1980.

Plutchik, R., and Kellerman, H., eds. *Emotion: Theory, Research, and Experience.* Vol. 2, Emotions in Early Development. New York: Academic Press, 1983.

Postman, N. *The Disappearance of Childhood.* New York: Delacorte, 1982.

Pressley, M. Elaboration and memory development. *Child Development,* 1982, *53,* 296–309.

Pribram, K. H. The biology of emotions and other feelings. In *Emotion: Theory, Research, and Experience,* ed. R. Plutchik and H. Kellerman. Vol. 1. New York: Academic Press, 1980.

Price, J. Who wants to have children? In *The Marriage and Family Reader,* ed. J. Rosenfeld. Glenview, Ill.: Scott, Foresman, 1982.

Pullis, M., and Cadwell, J. The relationship between children's temperament characteristics and teachers' classroom decisions. Paper presented at the American Educational Research Association, Boston, April 7–11, 1980.

Putallaz, M., and Gottman, J. M. Social skills and group acceptance. In *The Development of Children's Friendships,* ed. S. R. Asher and J. M. Gottman. Cambridge: Cambridge University Press, 1981.

Quay, L. C. Language dialect, age, and intelligence-test performance in disadvantaged black children. *Child Development*, 1974, *45*, 463–468.

Quisenberry, J., ed. *Changing Family Lifestyles.* Washington, D.C.: ACEI, 1982.

Rabin, A. I., and Beit-Hallahmi, B. *Twenty Years Later: Kibbutz Children Grown Up.* New York: Springer, 1982.

Radin, N. Childrearing fathers in intact families: some antecedents and consequences. *Merrill-Palmer Quarterly*, 1981, *27*(4), 489–514.

Ramey, C. T., and Haskins, R. The modification of intelligence through early experience. *Intelligence*, 1981, *5*, 5–19.

Read, K., and Patterson, J. *Nursery School and Kindergarten: Human Relations and Learning.* 7th ed. New York: Holt, Rinehart & Winston, 1980.

Reed, S. K. *Cognition: Theory and Application.* Monterey, Calif.: Brooks/Cole, 1982.

Reidy, T. J. The aggressive characteristics of abused and neglected children. In *Traumatic Abuse and Neglect of Children at Home*, ed. G. J. Williams and J. Money. Baltimore, Md.: Johns Hopkins University Press, 1980.

Reis, H. T., and Wright, S. Knowledge of sex-role stereotypes in children aged 3–5. *Sex Roles*, 1982, *8*, 10–49.

Reiss, I. L. *Premarital Sexual Standards in America.* New York: Free Press, 1960.

———. Some observations on ideology and sexuality in America. *Journal of Marriage and the Family*, 1981, *43*, 271–283.

Rest, J. R. The impact of higher education on moral judgment development. Paper presented at the Convention of the American Educational Research Association, Los Angeles, April 1981.

———. Morality. In *Handbook of Child Psychology*, ed. P. H. Mussen. 4th ed. Vol. 3, *Cognitive Development.* New York: John Wiley, 1983.

Rheingold, H. L., and Adams, J. L. The significance of speech to newborns. *Developmental Psychology*, 1980, *16*(5), 397–403.

Rice, M. The role of television in language acquisition. *Developmental Review*, 1983, *3*(2), 211–224.

Richards, F. A., and Commons, M. L. Systematic, metasystematic, and cross-paradigmatic reasoning: a case for stages of reasoning beyond formal operations. In *Beyond Formal Operations: Late Adolescent and Adult Cognitive Development*, ed. M. L. Commons, F. A. Richards, and S. Armon. New York: Praeger, 1982.

Richards, R. L. A comparison of selected Guilford and Wallach-Kogan creative thinking tests in conjunction with measures of intelligence. *Journal of Creative Behavior*, 1976, *10*(a), 151–164.

Richardson, T. F. Anorexia nervosa: an overview. *American Journal of Nursing*, 1980, *80*, 1470–1471.

Richarz, A. S. *Understanding Children through Observation.* St. Paul, Minn.: West, 1980.

Richey, M. H., and Richey, H. W. The significance of best-friend relationships in adolescence. *Psychology in the Schools*, 1980, *17*, 536–540.

Ridenour, M. V., ed. *Motor Development: Issues and Applications.* Princeton, N.J.: Princeton Book Company, 1980.

Riedesel, C. A., and Clements, D. H. *Coping With Computers In the Elementary and Middle Schools.* Englewood Cliffs, N.J.: Prentice-Hall, 1985.

Rierdan, J., and Koff, E. The psychological impact of menarche: integrative versus disruptive changes. *Journal of Youth and Adolescence*, 1980, *9*, 49–58.

Riggs, M. L. *Jump to Joy: Helping Children Grow Through Active Play.* Englewood Cliffs, N.J.: Prentice-Hall, 1980.

Ringler, N. M. The development of language and how adults talk to children. *Infant Mental Health Journal*, 1981, *2*, 71–83.

Roberts, R. J., Jr., and Patterson, C. Perspective taking and referential communication: the question of correspondence reconsidered. *Child Development*, 1983, *54*, 1005–1014.

Robertson, I. *Sociology.* 2nd ed. New York: Worth, 1981.

Robinson, I. E., and Jedlicka, D. Change in sexual attitudes and behavior of college students from 1965 to 1980: a research note. *Journal of Marriage and the Family*, February 1982, 237–240.

Robison, H. F. *Exploring Teaching in Early Childhood Education*. 2nd ed. Boston: Allyn & Bacon, 1983.

Roff, M. F. Childhood antecedents of adult neurosis, severe bad conduct, and psychological health. In *Life History Research in Psychopathology*, ed. D. F. Ricks, A. Thomas, and M. Roff. Vol. 3. Minneapolis: University of Minnesota Press, 1974.

Roffwarg, H. P.; Muzio, J. N.; and Dement, W. C. Ontogenetic development of the human sleep-dream cycle. *Science*, 1966, *152*, 604–619.

Rogers, C. R. *On Becoming a Person*. Boston: Houghton Mifflin, 1961.

Roman, M., and Raley, P. E. *The Indelible Family*. New York: Rawson, Wade, 1980.

Rosenberg, M., and Kaplan, H. B. *Social Psychology of the Self-Concept*. Arlington Heights, Ill.: Harlan Davidson, 1982.

Rowen, B. *Learning Through Movement: Activities for the Preschool and Elementary Grades*. 2nd ed. New York: Teachers College Press, 1982.

Royce, J. M.; Darlington, R. B.; and Murray, W. Pooled analysis: findings across studies. *As The Twig is Bent: Lasting Effects of Preschool Programs*. Hillsdale, N.J.: Erlbaum, 1983.

Rubin, K. H. Fantasy play: its role in the development of social skills and social cognition. In *Children's Play: New Directions for Child Development*, ed. K. H. Rubin. San Francisco: Jossey-Bass, 1980.

Rubin, K. H., and Everett, B. Social perspective-taking in young children. In *The Young Child: Reviews of Research*, ed. S. G. Moore and C. R. Cooper. Vol. 3. Washington, D.C.: National Association for the Education of Young Children, 1982.

Rubin, R. R.; Fisher, J. J.; and Doering, S. G. *Your Toddler*. New York: Macmillan, 1980.

Rubin, Z. *Children's Friendships*. Cambridge: Harvard University Press, 1980(a).

———. Self-disclosure in dating couples: sex roles and the ethic of openness. *Journal of Marriage and the Family*, 1980(b), *42*, 305–317.

Rushton, J. P. *Altruism, Socialization, and Society*. Englewood Cliffs, N.J.: Prentice-Hall, 1980.

Rutter, M. School effects on pupil progress: research findings and policy implications. *Child Development*, 1983, *54*, 1–29.

Saal, C. D. A historical and present-day view of the position of the child in family and society. *Journal of Comparative Family Studies*, 1982, *13*(2), 119–132.

Sadker, M. P., and Sadker, D. M. *Now upon a Time: A Contemporary View of Children's Literature*. New York: Harper & Row, 1977.

Safer, D. J. *School Programs for Disruptive Adolescents*. Baltimore, Md.: University Park Press, 1982.

Sagotsky, G.; Wood-Schneider, M.; and Konop, M. Learning to cooperate: effects of modeling and direct instruction. *Child Development*, 1981, *52*(3), 1037–1042.

Sahler, O. J. Z. Adolescent parenting: potential for child abuse and neglect. *Pediatric Annals*, 1980, *9*(3), 67–75.

Salapatek, P. Pattern perception in early infancy. In *Infant Perception: From Sensation to Cognition*, ed. L. B. Cohen and P. Salapatek. New York: Academic Press, 1975.

Salapatek, P., and Kessen, W. Visual scanning of triangles by the human newborn. *Journal of Experimental Child Psychology*, 1966, *3*, 113–122.

Salk, L. Mother's heartbeat as an imprinting stimulus. *Transactions of the New York Academy of Sciences*, 1962, 24, 753–763.

Saltzstein, H. D. Critical issues in Kohlberg's theory of moral reasoning. *Monographs of the Society for Research in Child Development*, 1983, *48*(1–2, Serial No. 200), 108–119.

Sandler, J.; Myerson, M.; and Kindler, B. L. *Human Sexuality: Current Perspectives*. Tampa, Fla.: Mariner Publications, 1980.

Sanoff, H. *Planning Outdoor Play: A Manual Organized to Provide Design Assistance to Community Groups.* Atlanta, Ga.: Humanics Limited, 1982.

Santrock, J.; Warshak, R.; Lindbergh, C.; and Meadows, L. Children's and parent's observed social behavior in stepfather families. *Child Development,* 1982, *53,* 472–480.

Saunders, R., and Bingham-Newman, A. M. *Piagetian Perspective for Preschoolers: A Thinking Book for Teachers.* Englewood Cliffs, N.J.: Prentice-Hall, 1984.

Saxe, G. B., and Sicilian, S. Children's interpretation of their counting accuracy: a developmental analysis. *Child Development,* 1981, *52,* 1330–1332.

Sayegh, Y., and Dennis, W. The effect of supplementary experiences upon the behavioral development of infants in institutions. *Child Development,* 1965, *36,* 81–90.

Scanzoni, J., and Fox, G. L. Sex roles, family, and society: the seventies and beyond. *Journal of Marriage and the Family,* 1980, *42,* 743–756.

Schacter, F. F., and Strage, A. A. Adult's talk and children's language development. In *The Young Child: Reviews of Research,* ed. S. G. Moore and C. R. Cooper. Vol. 3. Washington, D.C.: National Association for the Education of Young Children, 1982.

Schaefer, C. E. Imaginary companions and creative adolescents. *Developmental Psychology,* 1969, *1,* 747–749.

Schaefer, C. E., and Millman, H. L. *How to Help Children with Common Problems.* New York: Van Nostrand Rheinhold, 1981.

Schaffer, H. R., and Emerson, P. E. The development of social attachments in infancy. *Monographs of the Society for Research in Child Development,* 1964, *29*(Serial No. 94).

Schank, R. C. *Dynamic Memory.* New York: Cambridge University Press, 1982.

Schlaadt, R. G., and Shannon, P. T. *Drugs of Choice.* Englewood Cliffs, N.J.: Prentice-Hall, 1982.

Schleimer, K. Anorexia nervosa. *Nutrition Review,* 1981, *38,* 99–103.

Schmidt, C. R., and Paris, S. G. The development of children's communication skills. In *Advances in Child Development and Behavior,* ed. H. Reese and L. Lipsitt. New York: Academic Press, 1983.

Schmidt, R. *Motor Skills.* New York: Harper & Row, 1975.

———. *Motor Control and Learning: A Behavioral Emphasis.* Champaign, Ill.: Human Kinetics, 1982.

Schneider, S. Helping adolescents to deal with pregnancy: a psychiatric approach. *Adolescence,* 1982, *17*(66), 285–292.

Schofield, J. W. Complementary and conflicting identities: images and interaction in an interracial school. In *The Development of Children's Friendships,* ed. S. R. Asher and J. M. Gottman. Cambridge: Cambridge University Press, 1981.

Schofield, J. W., and Francis, W. D. An observational study of peer interaction in racially mixed "accelerated classrooms". *Journal of Educational Psychology,* 1982, *74,* 722–732.

Schofield, J. W., and Whitley, B. E., Jr. Peer nomination vs. rating scale measurement of children's peer preferences. *Social Psychology Quarterly,* 1983, *46,* 242–251.

Schuelle, D., and Kins, D. T. New technology in the classroom: computers and communication in the future. *Technological Horizons in Education,* April 1983, 16–24.

Schwartz, J. I. Children's experiments with language. *Young Children,* 1981, *36*(5), 16–26.

———. *Young Children Grow Up: The Effects of the Perry Preschool Program on Youth Through Age Fifteen.* Ypsilanti, Mich.: High/Scope, 1980.

Schweinhart, L., and Weikart, D. P. Can preschool education make a long lasting difference? *Bulletin of High/Scope Educational Research Foundation,* 1977, 4.

Searfoss, L. W., and Readence, J. E. *Helping Children Learn to Read.* Englewood Cliffs, N.J.: Prentice-Hall, 1984.

Sears, R. R.; Maccoby, E. E.; and Levin, H. *Patterns of Child Rearing.* New York: Harper & Row, 1957.

Sebald, H. Adolescent's concept of popularity and unpopularity, comparing 1960 with 1976. *Adolescence,* 1981, *16*(61), 187–193.

Segal, B.; Huba, G. J.; and Singer, J. L. Reasons for drug and alcohol use by college students. *The International Journal of the Addictions*, 1980, *15*, 489–498.

Segal, M., and Adcock, D. *Just Pretending: Ways to Help Children Grow Through Imaginative Play.* Englewood Cliffs, N.J.: Prentice-Hall, 1981.

Selman, R. The child as friendship philosopher. In *The Development of Children's Friendships*, ed. J. M. Gottman. Cambridge: Cambridge University Press, 1981.

Seymour, D. Z. Black children, black speech. In *Readings in Human Development*, 73–74. Guilford, Conn.: Duskin, 1973.

Shafer, R. E.; Staab, C.; and Smith, K. *Language Functions and School Success.* Glenview, Ill.: Scott, Foresman, 1983.

Shaffer, D. R. *Social and Personality Development.* Monterey, Calif.: Brooks/Cole, 1979.

Shallcross, D. J. *Teaching Creative Behavior: How to Teach Creativity to Children of All Ages.* Englewood Cliffs, N.J.: Prentice-Hall, 1981.

Shapira, A., and Madsen, M. C. Between and within group cooperation and competitive behavior among kibbutz and nonkibbutz children. *Developmental Psychology*, 1974, *10*, 140–145.

Sheldon, W. H. *The Varieties of Human Physique: An Introduction to Constitutional Psychology.* New York: Harper & Row, 1940.

———. Constitutional factors in personality. In *Personality and the Behavior Disorders*, ed. J. McV. Hunt. Vol. 1. New York: Ronald, 1944.

Shepard-Look, D. L. Sex differentiation and the development of sex roles. In *Handbook of Development Psychology*, ed. B. B. Wolman. Englewood Cliffs, N.J.: Prentice-Hall, 1982.

Shmukler, D. Mother-child interaction and its relationship to the predisposition of imaginative play. *Genetic Psychology Monographs*, 1981, *104*(2), 215–235.

Shneidman, E. S. *Death: Current Perspectives.* 3rd ed. Palo Alto, Calif.: Mayfield, 1985.

Shweder, R. A. What's there to negotiate? Some questions for Youniss. *Merrill-Palmer Quarterly*, 1981, *27*, 405–412.

Sideroff, S. I., and Jarvik, M. E. Conditional responses to a videotape showing of heroin-related stimuli. *The International Journal of the Addictions*, 1980, *15*, 529–536.

Siegler, R. S. *Developmental Sequences Within and Between Concepts.* Chicago: Chicago University Press, 1981.

———. Five generalizations about cognitive development. *American Psychologist*, 1983, *38*, 263–277.

Silber, T. Gonorrhea in adolescence: its impact and consequences. *Adolescence*, 1981, *16*(63), 537–541.

Silberman, M. L., and Wheelan, S. A. *How to Discipline Without Feeling Guilty.* Champaign, Ill.: Research Press, 1980.

Simner, M. L. Newborn's response to the cry of another infant. *Developmental Psychology*, 1971, *5*, 136–150.

Simon, J. A., and Martens, R. Youth sports: a challenge to parents. *PTA Today*, 1983, *8*(5), 14–17.

Singer, D. G. Piglet, Pooh and Piaget. *Psychology Today*, June 1972, 71–96.

———. A time to reexamine the role of television in our lives. *American Psychologist*, 1983, *38*, 815–816.

Singer, D. G., and Singer, J. L. *Make Believe: Games and Activities to Foster Imaginative Play in Young Children.* Oakland, N.J.: Scott, Foresman, 1985.

Singer, J. L. *The Child's World of Make-Believe.* New York: Academic Press, 1973.

———. *The Inner World of Daydreaming.* New York: Harper & Row, 1975.

Singer, J. L., and Singer, D. G. Come back, Mr. Rogers, come back. *Psychology Today*, March 1979, 56–60.

———. Television viewing and aggressive behavior in preschool children: a field study. *Forensic Psychology and Psychiatry*, 1980(a), *347*, 289–303.

———. Imaginative play in the preschooler: some research and theoretical implications. Paper presented at the American Psychological Association, Montreal, September 1980(b).

———. *Television, Imagination and Aggression: A Study of Preschoolers Play.* Hillsdale, N.J.: Erlbaum, 1981.

————. Psychologists look at television: cognitive, developmental, personality, and social policy implications. *American Psychologist*, 1983, *38*, 826–834.

Singer, J. L., and Switzer, E. *Mind Play: The Creative Uses of Fantasy.* Englewood Cliffs, N.J.: Prentice-Hall, 1980.

Singh, B. K. Trends in attitudes toward premarital sexual relations. *Journal of Marriage and the Family*, 1980, *42*, 387–393.

Skeels, H. M. A study of the effects of differential stimulation in mentally retarded children: a follow-up report. *American Journal of Mental Deficiency*, 1942, *46*, 340–350.

Skeen, P.; Robinson, B. E.; and Flake-Hobson, C. Blended-families: overcoming the Cinderella myth. *Young Children*, 1984, *3*(2), 64–74.

Skinner, B. F. How to teach animals. *Scientific American*, 1951, *185*, 26–29.

————. *Science and Human Behavior.* New York: Macmillan, 1953.

————. *Verbal Behavior.* New York: Appleton, 1957.

————. *Cumulative Record.* New York: Appleton, 1961.

Slobin, D. *Psycholinguistics.* Glenview, Ill.: Scott, Foresman, 1970.

Slobin, D., ed. *The Cross-Cultural Study of Language Acquisition.* Hillsdale, N.J.: Erlbaum, 1982.

Sluckin, A. *Growing Up in the Playground: The Social Development of Children.* London: Routledge & Kegan Paul, 1981.

Sluckin, W.; Herbert, M.; and Sluckin, A. *Maternal Bonding.* Oxford, England: Basil Blackwell, 1983.

Smilansky, S. Can adults facilitate play in children? Theoretical and practical considerations. In *Play: The Child Strives Toward Self-Realization*, ed. G. Engstrom. Washington, D.C.: National Association for the Education of Young Children, 1971.

Smith, C. H. *Promoting the Social Development of Young Children: Strategies and Activities.* Palo Alto, Calif.: Mayfield, 1982.

Smith, D. E. P. Dialectical dilemma: measuring black english. *Innovator*, September 1980, 1, 4–5.

Smith, E. E., and Medin, D. L. *Categories and Concepts.* Cambridge: Harvard University Press, 1981.

Smith, N. R. *Experience and Art: Teaching Children to Paint.* New York: Teachers College Press, 1983.

Smith, P. K.; Eaton, L.; and Hindmarch, A. How one-year-olds respond to strangers: a two-person situation. *Journal of Genetic Psychology*, 1982, *140*(1), 147–148.

Smith, R. E.; Zane, N. W.; Smoll, F. L.; and Coppel, D. B. Behavioral assessment in youth sports: coaching behaviors and children's attitudes. *Medicine and Science in Sports and Exercise*, 1983, *15*, 208–214.

Smith, R. F. Early childhood science education: a Piagetian perspective. *Young Children*, 1981, *36*(2), 3–10.

Smitherman, G., ed. *Black English and the Education of Black Children and Youth.* Detroit, Mich.: Wayne State University Center for Black Studies, 1981.

Solnit, A. J. Changing psychological perspectives about children and their families. *Children Today*, 1976, *5*(3), 5–9.

Sommerville, J. *The Rise and Fall of Childhood.* Beverly Hills, Calif.: Sage Publications, 1982.

Speer, J. R., and McCoy, J. S. Causes of young children's confusion of "same" and "different". *Journal of Experimental Child Psychology*, 1982, *34*(2), 291–300.

Spencer, H. *Principles of Psychology.* New York: Appleton, 1873.

Sperry, R. W. Some effects of disconnecting the cerebral hemispheres. *Science*, 1982, *217*, 1223–1226.

Spieler, S. Can fathers be nurturers? *Marriage and Divorce Today*, 1982, 7, 1.

Spitz, R. A. Hospitalism. In *Psychoanalytic Study of the Child*, ed. O. Fenichel et al. Vol I. New York: International Universities, 1945.

Spivak, H., and Varden, S. Classrooms make friends with computers. In *Microcomputers in the Schools*, ed. J. L. Thomas. Phoenix, Ariz.: Oryx Press, 1981.

Springer, S. P., and Deutsch, G. *Left Brain, Right Brain.* Rev. ed. San Francisco: W. H. Freeman, 1985.

Staffieri, J. R. A study of social stereotype of body image in children. *Journal of Personal and Social Psychology,* 1967, *7,* 101–104.

———. Body build and behavioral expectancies in young females. *Developmental Psychology,* 1972, *6*(1), 125–127.

Steele, B. F. Psychodynamic factors in child abuse. In *The Battered Child,* ed. C. H. Kempe and R. Helfer. Chicago: University of Chicago Press, 1980.

Steinberg, C. S. *TV Facts.* New York: Facts on File, 1980.

Steinhausen, H. C.; Nestler, V.; and Spohr, H. L. Development and psychopathology of children with the fetal alcohol syndrome. *Journal of Development and Behavioral Pediatrics,* 1982, *3*(2), 49–54.

Stevens, J. H., Jr. Everyday experience and intellectual development. *Young Children,* November 1981, 66–71.

Stevens, J. H., and Baxter, D. H. Research in review: malnutrition and children's development. *Young Children,* 1981, *36*(4), 60–71.

Stewart, I. S., and LeCompte, M. D. Children's beliefs about school socialization. Paper presented at the American Educational Research Association, Boston, April 7–11, 1980.

Stewart, R. B. Sibling attachment relationships: an observation of child-infant interaction in the stranger situation. Paper presented at the Society for Research in Child Development, Boston, April 1981.

Stillion, J., and Wass, H. Children and death. In *Death: Current Perspectives,* ed. E. S. Shneidman. 2nd ed. Palo Alto, Calif.: Mayfield, 1980.

Stipek, D. Work habits begin in preschool. *Young Children,* 1983, *38*(4), 25–32.

Stipek, D., and Weisz, J. Perceived personal control and academic achievement. *Review of Educational Research,* 1981, *51,* 101–137.

Stockard, J., and Johnson, M. The social origin of male dominance. *Sex Roles,* 1979, *5*(2), 199–218.

Stott, D. *Delinquents, Parents, and Maladjustment.* New York: SP Medical and Scientific Books, 1982.

Stott, J. C. *Children's Literature From A to Z.* New York: McGraw-Hill, 1984.

Strahle, W. M. A model of premarital coitus and contraceptive behavior among female adolescents. *Archives of Sexual Behavior,* 1983, *12,* 67–94.

Straker, G., and Jacobson, R. S. Aggression, emotional maladjustment, and empathy in the abused child. *Developmental Psychology,* 1981, *17*(6), 762–765.

Strauss, M. A.; Gelles, R. J.; and Steinmetz, S. K. *Behind Closed Doors: Violence In The American Family.* Garden City, N.Y.: Doubleday, 1980.

Streissguth, A. P.; Barr, H. M.; and Martin, D. C. Maternal alcohol use and neonatal habituation assessed with the Brazelton scale. *Child Development,* 1983, *54*(5), 1109–1118.

Strong, B.; Devault, C.; Suid, M.; and Reynolds, R. *The Marriage and Family Experience.* 2nd ed. St. Paul: West, 1983.

Sullivan, K., and Sullivan, A. Adolescent-parent separation. *Developmental Psychology,* 1980, *16,* 93–99.

Sullivan, M. *Feeling Strong, Feeling Free: Movement Exploration for Young Children.* Washington, D.C.: National Association for the Education of Young Children, 1982.

Suomi, S. J., and Harlow, H. F. Abnormal social behavior in young monkeys. In *Exceptional Infant: Studies in Abnormalities,* ed. J. Helmuth. Vol. 2. New York: Brunner/Mazel, 1971.

Super, C. M. Cognitive development: looking across at growing up. In *New Directions for Child Development,* ed. C. M. Super and S. Harkness. Anthropological Perspectives on Child Development No. 8. San Francisco: Jossey-Bass, 1980.

Suransky, V. P. *The Erosion of Childhood.* Chicago: University of Chicago Press, 1982.

Surber, C. F. Separable effects of motives, consequences, and presentation order on children's moral judgments. *Developmental Psychology,* 1982, *18,* 257–266.

Sutherland, Z.; Monson, D. L.; and Arbuthnot, M. H. *Children and Books.* 6th ed. Glenview, Ill.: Scott, Foresman, 1981.

Sutton-Smith, B. Commentary on social class differences in sociodramatic play in historical context: a reply to McLoyd. *Developmental Review*, 1983, *3*(1), 1–5.

Sutton-Smith, B., and Roberts, J. M. Play, toys, games, and sports. In *Handbook of Developmental Cross-Cultural Psychology*, ed. H. C. Triandis and A. Heron. Boston: Allyn & Bacon, 1981.

Swayze, M. C. Self-concept development in young children. In *The Self-concept of the Young Child*, ed. T. D. Yawkey. Provo, Utah: Brigham Young University Press, 1980.

Swigger, K. Computer-based materials for kids. *Educational Computer Magazine*, September/October 1982, 48–50.

Tanner, J. M. Earlier maturation in man. *Scientific American*, January 1968, 21–27.

———. *Fetus into Man: Physical Growth from Conception to Maturity*. Cambridge: Harvard University Press, 1978.

———. Growth and maturation during adolescence. *Nutrition Review*, 1981, *39*, 43–55.

Tavris, C., and Wade, C. *The Longest War: Sex Differences in Perspective*. 2nd ed. New York: Harcourt Brace Jovanovich, 1984.

Taylor, M., and Bacharach, V. R. The development of drawing rules: Metaknowledge about drawing influences performance on nondrawing tasks. *Child Development*, 1981, *52*, 373–375.

Terman, L. M. A symposium: intelligence and its measurement. *Journal of Educational Psychology*, 1921, *12*, 127–133.

Tesch, S. A. Review of friendship development across the life span. *Human Development*, 1983, *26*(5), 266–276.

Teyler, T. J. *A Primer of Psychobiology*. 2nd ed. New York: W. H. Freeman, 1984.

Thomas, A., and Chess, S. *Temperament and Development*. New York: Brunner/Mazel, 1977.

———. *The Dynamics of Psychological Development*. New York: Brunner/Mazel, 1980.

Thomas, M. H. Physiological arousal, exposure to a relatively lengthy aggressive film, and aggressive behavior. *Journal of Research in Personality*, 1982, *16*, 72–81.

Thomas R. M. *Comparing Theories of Child Development*. Belmont, Calif.: Wadsworth, 1984.

Thompson, C., and Rudolph, V. *Counseling Children*, Monterey, Calif.: Brooks/Cole, 1983.

Tietze, C. *Induced Abortion: A World Review*. New York: Population Council, 1981.

Titus, R. Local school support for micros is alive and growing. *InfoWorld*, 1982, *4*(46), 36.

Tizard, B. Language at home and at school. In *Language in Early Childhood Education*, ed. C. B. Cazden. Washington, D.C.: National Association for the Education of Young Children, 1981.

Tomaszewski, R. J.; Strickler, D. P.; and Maxwell, W. A. Influence of social setting and social drinking stimuli on drinking behavior. *Addictive Behaviors*, 1980, *5*, 235–240.

Tomikawa, S. A., and Dodd, D. H. Early word meaning: perceptually or functionally based? *Child Development*, 1980, *51*, 1103–1109.

Toner, I. J.; Holstein, R. B.; and Hetherington, E. M. Reflection-impulsivity and self control in preschool children. *Child Development*, 1977, *48*(1), 239–245.

Torbert, M. *Follow Me: A Handbook of Movement Activities for Children*. Englewood Cliffs, N.J.: Prentice-Hall, 1980.

Torrance, E. P. *Guiding Creative Talent*. Englewood Cliffs, N.J.: Prentice-Hall, 1962.

———. Current research on the nature of creative talent. In *Individual Differences*, ed. A. Anastasi. New York: John Wiley, 1965(a).

———. *Rewarding Creative Behavior*. Englewood Cliffs, N.J.: Prentice-Hall, 1965(b).

———. *Torrance Tests of Creative Thinking: Directions Manual*. Princeton, N.J.: Personnel Press, 1966.

———. Can we teach children to think creatively? *Journal of Creative Behavior*, 1972, *6*, 114–143.

———. Psychology of gifted children and youth. In *Psychology of Exceptional Children and Youth*, ed. W. W. Cruikshank. 4th ed. Englewood Cliffs, N.J.: Prentice-Hall, 1980.

Torrance, E. P., and Wu, T. A comparative longitudinal study of the adult creative achievements of elementary school children identified as highly intelligent and as highly creative. *Creative Child and Adult Quarterly*, 1981, *6*, 71–76.

Tronick, E.; Koslowski, B.; and Brazelton, T. B. Neonatal behavior among urban Zambians and Americans. Paper presented at the biennial meeting of the Society for research in Child Development, Minneapolis. April 4, 1971.

Trosborg, A. Children's comprehension of "before" and "after" reinvestigated. *Journal of Child Language*, 1982, *9*(2), 381–402.

Trotter, R. Born too soon. *Science News*, 1980, *118*, 234–235.

Tucker, N. *The Child and The Book*. New York: Cambridge University Press, 1982.

Turiel, E. *The Development of Social Knowledge: Morality and Convention*. New York: Cambridge University Press, 1983.

Turkington, C. Computers in class: who gets to learn? *The Monitor*, 1982, *13*(6), 1–30.

Turnbull, C. M. *The Forest People*. New York: Simon & Schuster, 1962.

Turner, J. S. Our battered American families. *Marriage and Family Living*, 1980, *62*(7).

————. My teenager is missing: the trauma of adolescent runaways. *Marriage and Family Living*, 1981(a), *63*(8).

————. Why kids cover up, cop out and tattle. *Elementary School Guidance and Counseling*, 1981(b), *16*(1), 7–14.

Tyler, B., and Dittmann, L. Meeting the toddlers more than halfway: The behavior of the toddler and their caregivers. *Young Children*, 1980, *35*(2), 39–46.

Tyler, L. E. *Thinking Creatively*. San Francisco: Jossey-Bass, 1983.

Ulbrich, P., and Huber, J. Observing parental violence: distribution and effects. *Journal of Marriage and the Family*, 1981, *43*, 623–631.

Ullian, D. Z. Why boys will be boys: a structural perspective. *Journal of Orthopsychiatry*, 1981, *51*(3), 493–501.

U.S. Bureau of the Census. *Current Population Reports*. Series p-20, nos. 326, 340, and 352. Washington, D.C.: U.S. Government Printing Office, December 1980.

U.S. Bureau of the Census. *Statistical Abstract of the U.S. 1982–83*. 103rd ed. Washington, D.C.: U.S. Government Printing Office, 1982.

U.S. Bureau of the Census. *Statistical Abstract of the United States: 1984*. 104th ed. Washington, D.C.: U.S. Government Printing Office, 1984.

U.S. Department of Health, Education, and Welfare. *Prevalence of Selected Impairments in the United States, 1971*. Vital and Health Statistics, Series 10, No. 99. Washington, D.C.: U.S. Government Printing Office, 1975.

Van Dyke, C. V., and Byck, R. Cocaine. *Scientific American*, March 1982, 128–141.

Vaughn, B. E., and Langlois, J. H. Physical attractiveness as a correlate of peer status and social competence in preschool children. *Developmental Psychology*, 1983, *19*, 561–567.

Vener, A. M., and Stewart, C. S. Adolescent sexual behavior in middle America revisited: 1970–1973. *Journal of Marriage and the Family*, 1974, *36*, 728–735.

Visher, E. B., and Visher, J. S. *How to Win As A Stepfamily*. New York: Dembner Books, 1982.

von Hofsten, C. Eye-hand coordination in the newborn. *Developmental Psychology*, 1982, *18*(3), 450–461.

Voydanoff, P., ed. *Work and Family: Changing Roles of Men and Women*. Palo Alto, Calif.: Mayfield, 1984.

Vukelich, C., and Golden, J. Early writing: development and teaching strategies. *Young Children*, 1984, *39*(2), 3–8.

Vygotsky, L. S. *Thought and Language*. Cambridge: MIT Press, 1962.

Wadeson, H. *Art Psychotherapy*. New York: Wiley-Interscience, 1980.

Wadsworth, B. J. *Piaget's Theory of Cognitive and Affective Development*. 3rd ed. New York: Longman, 1984.

Waldron, H., and Routh, D. K. The effect of the first child on the marital relationship. *Journal of Marriage and the Family*, 1981, *43*, 785–788.

Walk, R. D. Depth perception and experience. In *Modes of Perceiving and Processing Information*, ed. H. I. Pick and E. Saltzman. Hillsdale, N.J.: Erlbaum, 1978.

Walker, D. Reflections on the educational potential and limitations on microcomputers. *Phi Delta Kappan*, 1983, *65*(2), 103–107.

Walker, L. J. Cognitive and perspective-taking prerequisites for moral development. *Child Development*, 1980, *51*, 131–139.

———. The sequentiality of Kohlberg's stages of moral development. *Child Development*, 1982, *53*(5), 1330–1336.

Wallach, M. A., and Kogan, N. *Modes of Thinking in Young Children*. New York: Holt, Rinehart & Winston, 1965.

———. Creativity and intelligence in children's thinking. *Transaction*, 1967, *4*, 38–43.

———. A new look at the creativity-intelligence distinction. In *Readings in Adolescent Development and Behavior*, ed. J. P. Hill and J. Shelton. Englewood Cliffs, N.J.: Prentice-Hall, 1971.

Wallas, G. *The Art of Thought*. New York: Harcourt, Brace and World, 1926.

Wallerstein, J. S., and Kelley, J. B. *Surviving the Breakup: How Children Actually Cope with Divorce*. New York: Basic Books, 1980.

Walsh, H. M. *Introducing the Young Child to the Social World*. New York: Macmillan, 1980.

Walter, G. H., and Ashton, P. The relationship of teacher-offered empathy, genuineness, and respect to pupil classroom behavior. Paper presented at the American Educational Research Association, Boston, April 7–11, 1980.

Walters, J., and Walters, C. H. Trends affecting adolescent views of sexuality, employment, marriage, and child-rearing. *Family Relations*, 1980, *29*, 191–198.

Wass, H., and Corr, C. A., eds. *Helping Children Cope with Death: Guidelines and Resources*. Washington, D.C.: Hemisphere, 1982.

Watson, J. B. *Psychological Care of Infant and Child*. New York: W. W. Norton, 1928.

Watson, J. B., and Rayner, R. Conditioned emotional reactions. *Journal of Experimental Psychology*, 1920, *3*, 1–14.

Watson, J. D., and Crick, H. C. Molecular structure of nucleic acid—a structure for deoxyribose nucleic acid. *Nature*, 1953, *171*, 737–738.

Watts, D. H. Computer literacy: what should schools be doing about it? In *Microcomputers in the Schools*, ed. J. L. Thomas. Phoenix, Ariz.: Oryx Press, 1981.

Waxman, H. C., and Schiller, D. P. Teacher empathy and student achievement. Paper presented at the American Education Research Association. Boston, April 7–11, 1980.

Webster, R. L.; Steinhardt, M. H.; and Senter, M. G. Changes in infants' vocalizations as a function of differential acoustic stimulation. *Developmental Psychology*, 1972, *7*, 39–43.

Wehren, A., and DeLisi, R. The development of gender understanding: judgments and explanations. *Child Development*, 1983, *54*, 1568–1578.

Weikart, D. P. Preliminary results from a longitudinal study of disadvantaged preschool children. Paper presented at the 1967 convention of the Council for Exceptional Children. Mimeo.

———. A comparative study of three pre-school curricula. Paper presented at the biennial meeting for the Society for Research in Child Development, San Francisco, 1969.

Weikart, D. P.; Rogers, L.; and Adcock, C. *The Cognitively Oriented Curriculum*. ERIC-NAEYC publication in early childhood education. Urbana, Ill.: University of Illinois Press, 1971.

Weiner, I. B. Psychopathology in adolescence. In *Handbook of Adolescent Psychology*, ed. J. Adelson. New York: John Wiley, 1980.

Weingarten, H. Remarriage and well-being. *Journal of Family Issues*, 1980, *1*, 533–559.

Wellman, H. M. The foundation of knowledge: concept development in the young child. In *The Young Child: Reviews of Research*, ed. S. G. Moore and C. R. Cooper. Vol. 3. Washington, D.C.: National Association for the Education of Young Children, 1982.

Wenar, C. On negativism. *Human Development*, 1982, *25*(1), 1–23.

Wente, A. S., and Crockenberg, S. B. Transition to fatherhood: Lamaze preparation, adjustment difficulty and husband-wife relationship. *Family Coordinator*, 1976, *25*(4), 351–357.

Wessells, M. G. *Cognitive Psychology*. New York: Harper & Row, 1982.

Westlake, H. G. *Parenting and Children*. Lexington, Mass.: Ginn, 1981.

White, B. Viewpoint. Should you stay home with your baby? *Young Children*, 1981, *37*(1), 11–17.

White, J. *The Psychology of Blacks: An Afro-American Perspective*. Englewood Cliffs, N.J.: Prentice-Hall, 1984.

Whitehead, R. J. *A Guide to Selecting Books for Children*. Metuchen, N.J.: Scarecrow Press, 1984.

Wickstrom, R. L. *Fundamental Motor Patterns*. Philadelphia: Lea & Febiger, 1983.

Wiesenfeld, A.; Zander-Malatesta, C.; and DeLoach, L. Differential parental response to familiar and unfamiliar infant distress signals. *Infant Behavior and Development*, 1981, *4*(3), 281–295.

Wiggins, J. S., and Holzmuller, A. Further evidence on androgyny and interpersonal flexibility. *Journal of Research in Personality*, 1981, *15*, 67–80.

Wilcox, M. J., and Webster, E. J. Early discourse behavior: an analysis of children's responses to listener feedback. *Child Development*, 1980, *51*, 1120–1125.

Wilen, J. B., and Petersen, A. C. *Young Adolescents' Responses to the Timing of Pubertal Changes*. Paper presented at the conference "The Psychology of Adolescence", Michael Reese Hospital, Chicago, June 1980.

Wilkinson, A. C. Growth functions for rapid remembering. *Journal of Experimental Child Psychology*, 1981, *32*, 354–371.

Williams, F.; LaRose, R.; and Frost, F. *Children, Television, and Sex-Role Stereotyping*. New York: Praeger, 1981.

Williams, G. J. Management and treatment of parental abuse and neglect of children: an overview. In *Traumatic Abuse and Neglect of Children at Home*, ed. G. J. Williams and J. Money. Baltimore, Md.: Johns Hopkins University Press, 1980.

Williams, H. G. *Perceptual and Motor Development*. Englewood Cliffs, N.J.: Prentice-Hall, 1983.

Williams, J., and Stith, M. *Middle Childhood*. 2nd ed. New York: Macmillan, 1980.

Williams, T. M.; Zabrack, M. L.; and Joy, L. A. The portrayal of aggression on North American television. *Journal of Applied Social Psychology*, 1982, *12*, 360–380.

Williamson, P. M. Literature goals and activities for young children. In *Curriculum Planning for Young Children*, ed. J. F. Brown. Washington, D.C.: National Association for the Education of Young Children Publications, 1982.

Winchester, A. M. *Human Genetics*. 2nd ed. Columbus, Ohio: Charles E. Merrill, 1975.

Winer, G. A. Class-inclusion reasoning in children: a review of the empirical literature. *Child Development*, 1980, *51*, 309–328.

Winick, M. *Malnutrition and Brain Development*. New York: Oxford University Press, 1976.

———. The web of hunger: food and the fetus. *Natural History*, 1981, *90*(1), 76–81.

Winick, M.; Brasil, J.; and Valasco, E. G. Effects of prenatal nutrition upon pregnancy risk. *Clinical Obstetrics and Gynecology*, 1973, *16*, 104–198.

Winn, M. *Children Without Childhood*. New York: Pantheon Books, 1983.

Winner, E.; McCarthy, M.; and Gardener, H. The ontogenesis of metaphor. In *Cognitive and Figurative Language*, ed. A. P. Honeck and R. R. Hoffman. Hillsdale, N.J.: Erlbaum, 1980.

Wishart, J. G., and Bower, T. G. The development of spatial understanding in infancy. *Journal of Experimental Child Psychology*, 1982, *33*(3), 363–385.

Wishon, P. M.; Bower, R.; and Eller, B. Childhood obesity: prevention and treatment. *Young Children*, 1983, *39*(1), 21–28.

Wodarski, J. S., and Ammons, P. W. Comprehensive treatment of runaway children and their parents. *Family Therapy*, 1981, *8*(3), 229–240.

Wolf, F. M., and Larson, G. L. On why adolescent formal operators may not be creative thinkers. *Adolescence*, 1981, *16*, 345–348.

Wolfe, J. B. Effectiveness of token-rewards for chimpanzees. *Comparative Psychology Monographs*, 1936, *12*(60), 72.

Wolff, P. H. The causes, controls and organization of behavior in the neonate. *Psychological Issues*, 1966, 5(1).

Wolman, B. B. *Children's Fears*. New York: Grosset & Dunlap, 1978.

Wright, P. H., and Keple, T. W. Friends and parents of a sample of high school juniors: an exploration study of relationship intensity and interpersonal rewards. *Journal of Marriage and Family*, 1981, 43(3), 559–570.

Youngerman, J. K., and Canino, I. A. Violent kids, violent parents: family pharmacotherapy. *American Journal of Orthopsychiatry*, 1983, 53(1), 152–156.

Youniss, J. *Parents and Peers in Social Development*. Chicago: University of Chicago Press, 1980.

Zajonc, R. B. Family configurations and intelligence. *Science*, 1976, 192, 227–236.

Ziajka, A. *Prelinguistic Communication in Infancy*. New York: Praeger, 1981.

———. Microcomputers in early childhood education? *Young Children*, 1983, 38(5), 61–67.

Zigler, E., and Muenchow, S. Infant day care and infant care leaves. *American Psychologist*, 1983, 38, 91–94.

Zigler, E., and Turner, P. Parents and day care workers: a failed partnership? In *Day Care: Scientific and Social Policy Issues*, ed. E. F. Zigler and E. W. Gordon. Boston: Auburn House, 1982.

Zimbardo, P. G., and Radl, S. L. *The Shy Child*. Garden City, N.Y.: Doubleday, 1981.

Zion, L. L. Body concept as it relates to self concept. *Research Quarterly: American Association for Health, Physical Education and Recreation*, 1965, 36, 490–495.

Ziporyn, T. Taste and smell: the neglected senses. *Journal of the American Medical Association*, 1982, 247, 277–285.

Zuckerman, D. M., and Sayre, D. H. Cultural role expectations and children's sex role concepts. *Sex Roles*, 1982, 8, 453.

Name Index

Subject Index

Sources and Acknowledgments

This page constitutes a continuation of the copyright page.

Cover illustration: "Salon des Wohnhauses Moll" (1903) by Carl Moll, Historisches Museum der Stadt Wien (Vienna); p. 1 Sylvia Williams; p. 2 Hella Hammid/Photo Researchers, Inc.; p. 6 Robert T. Neisworth; p. 13 Eric Kroll/Taurus Photos; p. 17 Archives of the History of American Psychology, University of Akron, Ohio; p. 25 Elizabeth Crews; p. 29 courtesy of the APA *Monitor*; p. 33 compliments of Clark University, Worcester, Massachusetts; p. 37 UPI/Bettmann Newsphotos; p. 43 Archives of the History of American Psychology, University of Akron, Akron, Ohio; p. 45 Christopher S. Johnson, courtesy of B. F. Skinner; p. 48 courtesy of Albert Bandura; p. 52 UPI/Bettmann Newsphotos; p. 55 Archives of the History of American Psychology, University of Akron, Akron, Ohio; p. 59 Frank Siteman/Taurus Photos; p. 62 courtesy of the Western Pennsylvania School for the Deaf; pp. 69, 70, 71 The Bettmann Archive, Inc.; p. 79 Kirk Williams; p. 80 M. Rotker/Taurus Photos; p. 99 Dr. Landrum Shettles; p. 100 courtesy of Brooks/Cole Publishing Company; p. 113 Wayne Miller/Magnum Photos; p. 118 Eve Arnold/Magnum Photos; p. 123 courtesy of Wadsworth Health Sciences; p. 127 Nancy G. Turner; p. 128 Eve Arnold/Magnum Photos; p. 132 (left) Jean Shapiro; p. 132 (right) Elizabeth Crews; p. 138 Andrew Brilliant; pp. 144, 145, 150 Robert T. Neisworth; p. 147 Frank Keillor; p. 154 Clif Garboden/Stock, Boston; p. 156 Elizabeth Crews; p. 158 Jean Shapiro; p. 159 Robert T. Neisworth; p. 169 William Vandivert and *Scientific American*; p. 177 Phiz Mezey; p. 186 Bruce Roberts/Photo Researchers, Inc.; p. 189 Elizabeth Crews; p. 190 Frank Keillor; pp. 194, 195 Elizabeth Crews; p. 202 courtesy of Harry F. Harlow, University of Wisconsin Primate Laboratory; p. 206 Israel Government Tourist Office; p. 209 Robert T. Neisworth; p. 210 from the *New York Times* Magazine, September 22, 1968, reprinted with permission of John Huehnergarten; p. 215 Sylvia Williams; p. 216 from Conel, J. L., *The Postnatal Development of the Human Cerebral Cortex* (7 volumes), Cambridge, Mass., Harvard University Press, 1939–1963; p. 220 Elizabeth DeBeliso, courtesy of the Merrill-Palmer Institute; p. 221 Robert T. Neisworth; p. 222 Frank Keillor; p. 226 Robert T. Neisworth; p. 229 Carol Palmer; p. 231 Brian K. Williams; p. 233 courtesy of the Pittsburgh Child Development Center; p. 234 courtesy of the authors; p. 235 Robert T. Neisworth, courtesy of the University of Pittsburgh Child Development Center; p. 237 used by permission of Hank Ketcham & © by News America Syndicate; p. 241 Elizabeth Crews; p. 249 © 1984, Universal Press Syndicate, reprinted with permission, all rights reserved; p. 252 Elizabeth DeBeliso, courtesy of the Merrill-Palmer Institute; p. 254 Robert T. Neisworth; p. 260 Roberta Hershenson/Photo Researchers, Inc.; p. 262 Elizabeth Crews; p. 267 Barbara Rios/Photo Researchers, Inc.; p. 269 reprinted courtesy of Cowles Syndicate, Inc., all rights reserved; p. 272 Elizabeth Crews; p. 278 Suzanne Szasz/Photo Researchers, Inc.; p. 284 Elizabeth Crews; p. 287 Elizabeth DeBeliso, courtesy of the Merrill-Palmer Institute; p. 292 Elizabeth Crews; p. 300 Shirley Zerberg/Taurus Photos; p. 302 Suzanne Szasz/Photo Researchers, Inc.; p. 304 courtesy of Family Communications, Inc.; p. 308 Carol Palmer; p. 311 Erika Stone; p. 313 Carol Palmer; p. 314 © 1960 United Feature Syndicate, Inc.; p. 319 Carol Palmer; p. 326 reprinted courtesy of Cowles Syndicate, Inc., all rights reserved; p. 327 Kirk Williams; p. 328 Roberta Hershenson/Photo Researchers, Inc.; p. 333 reproduced from W. W. Greulich and S. I. Pyle, *Radiographic Atlas of the Hand and Wrist*, 2nd ed., Stanford, CA, Stanford University Press, 1959; p. 338 Robert T. Neisworth; p. 343 Karen R. Preuss/Taurus Photos; p. 349 Robert T. Neisworth, courtesy of the Presley Ridge Center for Young Children; p. 365 Robert T. Neisworth; p. 373 Erika Stone; p. 378 Elizabeth Crews; p. 386 Eric Kroll/Taurus Photos; p. 390 Roberta Hershenson/Photo Researchers, Inc.; p. 396 Erika Stone; p. 401 used by permission of Hank Ketcham & © by News America Syndicate; p. 409 (top and bottom) Robert T. Neisworth; p. 416 Shirley Zeiberg/Taurus Photos; pp. 419, 424 Elizabeth Crews; p. 429 reprinted courtesy of Cowles Syndicate, Inc., all rights reserved; p. 433 Jamie Breuer; p. 434 Robert T. Neisworth; p. 439 Elizabeth Crews; p. 444 Taurus Photos; p. 446 Andrew Brilliant; p. 449 Elizabeth Crews; pp. 453, 457 Robert T. Neisworth; p. 460 Elinor S. Beckwith/Taurus Photos; p. 463 Nancy Durrell McKenna/Photo Researchers, Inc.; pp. 465, 467 Robert T. Neisworth; p. 473 Frank Siteman/Taurus Photos; p. 478 Kelly Cameron; p. 481 Robert T. Neisworth; p. 486 John Veltri/Photo Researchers, Inc.; p. 492 Elizabeth Crews; p. 495 Frank Siteman/Taurus Photos; p. 499 Photo Researchers, Inc.; p. 502 Arthur Tress/Photo Researchers, Inc.; p. 514 Susan Rosenberg/Photo Researchers, Inc.; p. 518 Erika Stone; p. 521 Elizabeth Crews; p. 524 Bonnie Freer/Photo Researchers, Inc., pp. 525, 526 Robert T. Neisworth; p. 521 Elizabeth Crews.